Family, Religion, and Social Change in Diverse Societies

Edited by

Sharon K. Houseknecht
Jerry G. Pankhurst

New York • Oxford
OXFORD UNIVERSITY PRESS
2000

Oxford University Press

Oxford New York
Athens Auckland Bangkok Bogotá Buenos Aires Calcutta
Cape Town Chennai Dar es Salaam Delhi Florence Hong Kong Istanbul
Karachi Kuala Lumpur Madrid Melbourne Mexico City Mumbai
Nairobi Paris São Paulo Singapore Taipei Tokyo Toronto Warsaw

and associated companies in
Berlin Ibadan

Published by Oxford University Press, Inc.,
198 Madison Avenue, New York, New York, 10016
http://www.oup-usa.org

Library of Congress Cataloging-in-Publication Data

Family, religion, and social change in diverse societies / edited by
Sharon K. Houseknecht and Jerry G. Pankhurst.
p. cm.
Includes bibliographical references (p.).
ISBN 0-19-513117-7 (cloth : alk. paper). — ISBN 0-19-513118-5
(pbk. : alk. paper)
1. Family—Religious life. 2. Religion and culture.
I. Houseknecht, Sharon K., 1945- . II. Pankhurst, Jerry G.
BL625.6.F36 2000
306.6'911783585—DC21 98-49893
CIP

Printing (last digit): 9 8 7 6 5 4 3 2 1

Printed in the United States of America
on acid-free paper

Family, Religion, and Social Change in Diverse Societies

Contents

Acknowledgments

The editors of a collection of essays like this volume incur many debts as it is being produced. Above all, the contributors themselves must be acknowledged for their willingness to revise and revise their essays to our specifications and then to wait patiently during the preparation of the final manuscript.

We cannot name all those who gave us suggestions on topics for essays or advice on finding authors for entries, but many people talked with us about the book and gave valuable input of various sorts. We are grateful to all those who supported our project and shared insights and brainstorms with us.

Several of the essays included here appeared in their initial form as research conference papers. In particular, we appreciate the forum for research presentations and the meeting of minds that was provided by the conventions of the Association for the Sociology of Religion and the Society for the Scientific Study of Religion.

During manuscript preparation, the editors used the services of our home institutions, The Ohio State University and Wittenberg University, in numerous ways, and we gratefully acknowledge this support. While on sabbatical leave in 1997–98, Pankhurst was a visiting scholar at the Mershon Center at The Ohio State University, and he acknowledges the services and other assistance received in that setting. During the final phase, Pankhurst was a senior fellow at the Center for the Study of World Religions at Harvard University, where a congenial environment helped to bring the project to a successful conclusion.

Contributors

Mark Cammack is professor of law at Southwestern University School of Law. He received his J.D. from the University of Wisconsin, where he also did graduate work in Southeast Asian history. He was law clerk for Justice Roland Day of the Wisconsin Supreme Court, spent a year in Indonesia as a Fulbright fellow researching Islamic courts, and worked for three years as an assistant district attorney in New York City. His teaching and research focus on evidence and comparative law. His articles on those topics have appeared in Law Reviews and other publications.

Kevin J. Christiano is associate professor and former chair of the Department of Sociology at the Universiy of Notre Dame, where he has taught since 1983. In addition, he has been a visiting scholar at Princeton University (1986–87) and at Duke University (1994–95). He received his Ph.D. from Princeton, and his varied publications are found mostly in the sociology of religion and in the sociological study of Canadian politics. Christiano is the author of two books: *Religious Diversity and Social Change: American Cities, 1890–1906* (Cambridge and New York: Cambridge University Press, 1987) and *Pierre Elliott Trudeau: Reason Before Passion* (Toronto: ECW Press, 1994, 1995). He is currently writing a book on the policies of Canadian Prime Minister Jean Chrétien.

M. Herbert Danzger is professor of sociology at the Herbert M. Lehman College and the Graduate School and University Center of the City University of New York. He received his Ph.D. from Columbia University. He has held grants from the National Science Foundation and the National Institute of Mental Health for the study of social movements and has received numerous grants for research on the contemporary "return" to Judaism. He has served as senior lecturer at Bar-Ilan University in Israel and as Fulbright professor at the Hebrew University in Israel. His study of the "return" of American and Israeli Jews to traditional Judaism is described in his *Returning to Tradition* (New Haven, CT: Yale University Press, 1989) and in a series of articles and papers. He is presently engaged in a cross-cultural study of the "return" to Judaism of Jews of the former Soviet Union (FSU) who are now residing in Israel, the United States, and the FSU.

Susan Diduk is associate professor of sociology/anthropology at Denison University. With graduate degrees from University College London (Diploma) and Indiana University (Ph.D.), her major areas of specialization and past publications focus on issues of political economy, women's protest movements, twinship rituals, and the role of alcohol production in colonial and postindependence Cameroon. She has received numerous major grants for her research in Cameroon and has been a postdoctoral fellow at the Smithsonian Institution in Washington, DC, and a visiting scholar at the Institute of Social and Cultural Anthropology, University of Oxford.

Patricia Fortuny Loret de Mola is a researcher in the Center of Research and Advanced Studies in Social Anthropology (CIESAS/ OCCIDENTE) in Guadalajara, Mexico. She received her Ph.D. degree in social anthropology from the University College London. Since the 1980s, she has studied religious minorities, such as Pentecostals, Mormons, and Jehovah's Witnesses, in both rural and urban areas of Mexico. She has published a book, *Religión y Sociedad en el Sureste de México*, and numerous articles related to this topic. In 1995–97, she was the head of a Global Project, "Diversity of Religions in Guadalajara." During 1997–98, she was a Fulbright scholar at St. Mary's University, San Antonio, Texas.

Thomas Fricke is associate professor of anthropology, associate research scientist in the Institute for Social Research, and research associate in the Population Studies Center at the University of Michigan. He received his Ph.D. from the University of Wisconsin, Madison, and has research interests in the impact of social change on life course and family relationships, kinship and family theory, religion and life-course transition, culture and demography, and ethnographic and survey methods. He has conducted research in a variety of settings, including Nepal, Pakistan, Thailand, and Taiwan. His numerous publications include *Himalayan Households: Tamang Demography and Domestic Processes* (1994), and *Anthropological Demography: Toward a New Synthesis* (1997), coedited with David Kertzer. He is currently working on a book on the marriage practices among the Tamang people of Nepal.

Gillian Godsell is an independent researcher and lecturer in South Africa focusing on business networks, politics, education, and research methodology. She is currently doing research on microlending with the Centre for Policy Studies in Johannesburg and the Institute for the Study of Economic Culture in Boston. She formerly served as senior research consultant at the Centre for Developing Business at the University of Witwatersrand. She completed her undergraduate and M.A. studies in psychology and worked in South Africa's National Center for Personnel Research before pursuing her doctoral degree. She received her Ph.D. from Boston University through the University Professor's Program with a dissertation on "Social Networks of South African Entrepreneurs." She has published articles on entrepreneurs, work values, personnel aspects of management, and research methods.

Tim B. Heaton is professor of sociology and a research associate at the Center for Studies of the Family at Brigham Young University and was a visiting scholar at Cornell University in the summer of 1996. He received his Ph.D. from the University of Wisconsin. His research documents trends in family demographics and attitudes toward family issues in the United States and in the Third World. His current projects focus on marital dissolution in the United States and Indonesia, Palestinian families, and family interactions and children's well-being in Columbia and Bolivia. He recently coauthored two statistical handbooks on families and adolescents, a demographic profile of Utah, and a forthcoming book on interracial marriage in Hawaii.

Sharon K. Houseknecht, Ph.D., Pennsylvania State University, is associate professor of sociology, Ohio State University. From 1991 to 1995, she was a visiting senior research scientist at the Social Research Center, American University in Cairo. She has served as chair of the Family Section of the American Sociological Association and on the editorial boards of *Journal of Marriage and the Family* and *Journal of Family Issues*. Her current research focuses on the effects of primary ties and community embeddedness on children's social and physical well-being, cross-national studies of spousal income differentials and of the voluntary simplicity phenomenon, and the impact of race on family and career patterns. Recent articles include "Family 'Decline' and Child Well-Being: A Comparative Assessment" (with Jaya Sastry), "The Struggle for Power Between Family and Government: A Dimension of Political Modernization" (with Saad Z. Nagi), and "Status Profile and Fertility: A Conceptual Framework" (with Saad Z. Nagi).

John Jarvis is associate professor of communication and director of the International Study/Honors Programs at Robert Morris College. He earned his Ph.D. degree at Washington State University. His research focuses on the export of American culture and intercultural communication. He is currently the principal investigator for a five-year study of cultural change and institutional adaptation at Euro Disneyland Paris. This project examines the resolution of cultural conflict among representatives of some ninety-five national groups who work there. He is the coauthor of a multicultural reader-textbook, *Writing About the World* (1995).

Heidi Larson received her Ph.D. from the University of California at Berkeley with a dissertation on immigrant and minority children and the use of photography and videos as research tools. She is currently the social mobilization adviser to the World Health Organization Global Tuberculosis Programme in Geneva. She previously worked with the UNICEF Pacific Office in Suva, Fiji, investigating the social context of adolescent health and advising on policy and program development. She has published a number of articles on children and youth issues and has worked closely with the University of the South Pacific and the Australia Screen Directors' Association in producing a series of documentary films on Pacific youths and social change. She has also photographed and written a series of multicultural children's books. She has been awarded several fellowships for her research on children and is associate editor for both the *Journal of Visual Sociology* (USA) and the *Yearbook of Visual Anthropology* (Italy).

Kent Maynard is professor of sociology/anthropology at Denison University. He received his Ph.D. at Indiana University. His major research and publications have focused on religious identity among evangelical Protestants in Ecuador and a coauthored book on social change in the U.S. middle class. More recent collaborative research with Susan Diduk on the Kedjom societies of Cameroon, which received significant grant support, has examined the social history of indigenous and Western medicine in both the colonial and postindependence eras. In conjunction with this latter work, he has been a visiting scholar at London's Wellcome Institute for the History of Medicine.

Irving Palm is associate professor in the Department of Sociology of Uppsala University, Sweden, and he also earned his Ph.D. in sociology from Uppsala University. Focusing most of his research on religion and society issues, he has analyzed the relationship between the the working-class movement and the free-church movement. More recently, he has studied the ecumenical movement in Sweden. His newest project in this regard is "Local Ecumenicity in Sweden Before the Year 2000." He is also investigating organizational changes that result in dismissals within the public sector and their effects on governmental employees in Sweden.

Jerry G. Pankhurst, professor of sociology at Wittenberg University, received his Ph.D. from the University of Michigan. Starting with his dissertation research, which examined religious group adaptations to ideological atheism in the Soviet Union, he has specialized in the sociology of religion and political sociology, with special emphasis on communist societies. His publications include articles on family and ideology in the Soviet Union and the United States, the role of Soviet sociology, and various aspects of religion in Russia. Recent research has examined the role of religion under late communism and the consequences of Russian religious culture for adaptations of society, polity, and economy following the breakup of the Soviet Union. A recipient of numerous grants for research in the Soviet Union and the post-Soviet region, he has published (with Michael Paul Sacks) two volumes on the sociology of Soviet society. During 1997–98, he was visiting scholar at the Mershon Center, Ohio State University, and senior fellow of the Center for the Study of World Religions, Harvard University.

Maria José Fontelas Rosado Nunes is professor of sociology of religion at the Catholic University of São Paulo (PUC/SP), Brazil, and teaches feminist theory at the Methodist University of São Paulo (UMESP). She is also a senior research associate of the National Council of Scientific and Technological Development (CNPq). She received her Ph.D. degree in sociology from the École des Hautes Études en Sciences Sociales of Paris. She is currently investigating the situation of women in the Catholic Church in Brazil, especially the relationship between the gender-religion linkage and reproductive rights. She has published a book, *Vida Religiosa nos Meios Populares,* and numerous articles on this subject.

Stephen R. Smith, associate professor of anthropology at Wittenberg University, specializes in Japanese society and culture and the general field of medical anthropology. He is interested in the materialist perspective on cultural phenomena, including cultural aspects of the family. He received his Ph.D. and certificate of East Asian Studies from Columbia University. His recent research explores alcohol use and abuse, foodways, and alternative medical systems cross-culturally. He has received Fulbright grants to research drinking culture and alcoholism therapy in Japan and to teach anthropology in Korea. He has published articles and reviews in such journals as *Reviews in Anthropology* and *Monumenta Nipponica* and numerous edited volumes.

Arland Thornton is professor of sociology and research scientist at the Institute for Social Research, and research associate of the Population Studies Center at the University of Michigan. He received his Ph.D. from The University of Michigan. His research focuses on trends, causes, and consequences of marriage, cohabitation, divorce, fertility, gender roles, adolescent sexuality, and intergenerational relationships. He is particularly interested in the ways in which these dimensions of family life intersect with religious affiliation, commitment, and values. He conducts research on these topics in Taiwan, Nepal, and the United States. He is coauthor (with Hui-sheng Lin) of *Social Change and the Family in Taiwan* (Chicago: University of Chicago Press, 1994), which won the 1995 William J. Goode Book Award from the Family Section of the American Sociological Association, and the Otis Dudley Duncan Award from the Population Section of the American Sociological Association.

Jan Trost is professor in the Department of Sociology and director of the Family Research Center of Uppsala University, Sweden. He received his Ph.D. in sociology from Uppsala University. An internationally known scholar, he has published extensively on family and sexuality issues. He served for eight years as president of the Committee on Family Research of the International Sociological Association and has recently been named honorary president of this committee. Guided by the symbolic interactionist perspective, his current work centers on the meaning that the term, *family,* has for persons and groups in various situations and cultures.

Andrei Vardomatskii is director of the Laboratory of Axiometrical Research ("NOVAK"), a survey organization in Minsk, Belarus. He received his candidate of philosophy degree through the Belarusian State University, carried out postgraduate studies at the Institute of Sociology of the Soviet Academy of Sciences, and completed his doctorate in sociology through the Belarusian Academy of Sciences. He previously worked as a researcher at the Belarusian Institute of Cultural Studies and at the Institute of Sociology and the Institute of Philosophy and Law of the Academy of Sciences in Belarus. His research interests focus on ethics, morality, and values, and he has published two books and numerous articles on these topics in Belarusian and Russian. Recent publications have examined the methodology of studying values, especially in conditions of rapid social change like those occurring in Belarus and other previously Soviet societies.

Li-shou Yang is a research investigator at the Institute for Social Research at the University of Michigan. She received her Ph.D. in population studies and sociology from the University of Michigan. She coauthored seven chapters in the book, *Social Change and the Family in Taiwan*, by Arland Thornton and H. S. Lin, which won two awards from the American Sociological Association. She also received honorable mention in the 1995 Graduate Student Competition for Outstanding Paper in the Family Section of the American Sociological Association. Her research focuses on family life, the life course, and social change, and she has begun a project examining the Taiwanese family, concentrating on both parents and children.

Lawrence A. Young is associate professor of sociology at Brigham Young University. He received his Ph.D. from the University of Wisconsin, Madison, and his current research interests include the sociology of religion and the political economic transformation of the western United States. He is coauthor (with Richard A. Schoenherr) of *Full Pews and Empty Alters: Demographics of the Priest Shortage in the United States Catholic Dioceses* (Madison: University of Wisconsin Press, 1993), which received the 1996 Distinguished Book of the Year Award from the Society for the Scientific Study of Religion, and *Goodby Father: Power and Patriarchy in the Roman Catholic Church* (New York: Oxford University Press, forthcoming). He also coedited (with Marie Cornwall and Tim B. Heaton) *Contemporary Mormonism: Social Science Perspectives* (Urbana: University of Illinois Press, 1994) and edited *Rational Choice Theory and Religion: Summary and Assessment* (New York: Routledge, 1997).

Family, Religion,
and Social Change
in Diverse Societies

CHAPTER ONE

Introduction: The Religion–Family Linkage and Social Change— A Neglected Area of Study

JERRY G. PANKHURST
SHARON K. HOUSEKNECHT

Religion and family are two institutions that many social theorists have thought would be greatly weakened or eliminated in the course of rapid modernization. From this perspective, both institutions are viewed as archaic leftovers from the structures of premodern societies, filling needs that have been profoundly modified in the modern era. Consequently, their functional raison d'être is thought to have evaporated in the winds of time. This book challenges these orientations to religion and family and demonstrates that both institutions—however they may be undergoing significant transformations—are nevertheless well rooted in the modern age. Neither family nor religion is "withering away," as the Marxians had it (Engels [1884] 1973; Marx and Engels [1857] 1964; cf. Geiger 1968), nor are they "declining" (Popenoe 1988) or "secularizing" (cf. Beckford 1989) to the point of institutional irrelevance, as so many less-radical scholars have expected. Even social experiments that were designed to abolish the family or religion, such as utopian communism, have led to the creation of alternative structures that fulfill the essential functions of these two major institutions (Geiger 1968; Pankhurst 1988).

The social scientific notions of the disappearance or "vestigialization" of religion and family are deeply rooted in theoretical conceptions of the social processes that created the modern world and that are now transforming that modernity into postindustrial, postmodern society. Theories of modernization envision social change as entailing the rationalization of all spheres of existence. In a statement characterizing the classic modernization approach, Moore (1963:79) noted, "A major feature of the modern world . . . is that the rational orientation is pervasive and a major basis for deliberate change in virtually every aspect of man's concerns." There is little room for the seemingly irrational and unscientific impulses of religion, primary emotions, and familial concerns.

With this approach, the secularization of religion is a given. Moore (1963:80) stated: "Even with regard to the role of religion in human affairs, the 'rational spirit' takes the form of *secularization*, the substitution of nonreligious beliefs and practices for religious ones." Though religion survives, it addresses "personal misfortune and bereavement" above all else in modern society (Moore 1963:104).

Furthermore, "economic modernization" tends to have "negative consequences for extended kinship systems" and leads to "extensive 'family disorganization'" accompanying the "breakdown of traditional patterns and the incomplete establishment of new institutions" (Moore 1963:102). For modernization theorists, although families remain significant as consumption units, the "decline" of the family (Popenoe 1988) is, at a minimum, a metaphor for its consignment to a peripheral societal role. The analogue of the notion of the linear secularization of religion is the idea of the loss of family functions (Vago 1989).

Shaped in the eighteenth and nineteenth centuries, modernization theories have continued to dominate public opinion and much of social scientific discourse. In general, according to these views, both family and religion are relegated to the "private" sphere, are set apart from the broader social processes, and thus are less significant than those broader processes. This is not the place to engage in a full critique of modernization theorizing vis-à-vis religion and family; we can only touch on a few highpoints, acknowledging that there are many nuances of the theory that we cannot address here. Nevertheless, it must be understood that such theorizing has had a powerful—and, from our perspective, not always positive—impact on our understanding of the world.

Despite this widespread orientation, a revolution in the social sciences has been gaining momentum over the past twenty years or so. The message of this revolution is that the modernization perspective is no longer an adequate vision for understanding the dynamics of modernity or the potentials of postmodernity for religion and family. In the sociology of religion, the paradigm shift moves social science away from a focus on religion as a disconnected phenomenon to a much more complex view of the nature of religious interinstitutional relations. A spate of recent publications have examined religion as an influence on and an effect of numerous social, political, and economic variables (see Carter 1996; Cousineau 1998; Hammond 1985; Misztal and Shupe 1992; Roberts 1995; Rubenstein 1987; Shupe and Misztal 1998, Swatos 1992; and Witte 1993; to name a few). A market model of religion, based in rational-choice propositions, has become the most strongly debated version of the new way of looking at the religious institution (Hadden 1995; Warner 1993; Young 1997). We make use of this model later, together with more standard interinstitutional approaches, to develop propositions for further research on the relationship of religion and family to other institutions.

Similarly, there are many who now argue that in spite of its changing forms and functions, the family as an institution remains crucially central to social processes and to the patterns of change that determine the future of human societies (cf. Cherlin 1996). If not taken into consideration, family processes are liable to torpedo efforts to achieve planned social change and to deflect the vectors of unplanned change in unexpected directions (Settles 1996).

Attuned to the interinstitutional perspective, this volume examines the linkage between family and religion in diverse cultural settings and explores the public and private roles of these institutions in changing circumstances. We advocate an approach that views this linkage within the broader institutional context. After elaborating an integrative theme and establishing the value of comparative research, we discuss the special relationship between religion and family and consider why it has received so little scholarly attention. We then analyze social change processes, paying particular attention to institutional differentiation and institutional dominance, and highlight some of the important things learned from comparing the chapters in this volume. We make the point that the religion-family linkage is important today, not only in the burgeoning private sphere, but in the public realm. Finally, we generate several hypotheses that suggest directions for further research on the basis of the ideas presented in this book.

CLOSING THE GAP BETWEEN THE PRIVATE AND THE PUBLIC SPHERES: AN INTEGRATIVE THEME

This book focuses on what many analysts have seen as the institutions of the private sphere, a place where the problems of the world can be set aside. In the private sphere, one allegedly enjoys the rewards of closeness and intimacy in primary groups and pursues one's agenda without the usurpation of one's time and energy by the boss, the politician, or the bureaucrat. The private sphere, it is said, provides a haven of rest (cf. Lasch 1977) from the unpleasant and often painful demands emanating from the "public sphere" of economic pursuits and political demands.

We do not deny that this description of the private sphere has some validity, but we doubt that it is comprehensive. The family and primary relationships of most people evidence the deep imprint of the many stresses and strains of the workplace, the consumer marketplace, the economy in general, and the unjust power imbalances of the society. Although the realm of family and friends ideally should serve as a buffer from the problems of the modern technoindustrial revolution, as Mead ([1977] 1980) once said, we have found that it is not well insulated against these problems in many ways.

The private sphere is not an absorption chamber, taking in the troubles of the world and dissipating their effects with some kind of emotional balm. It also sends off all sorts of influences to the public sphere for good or ill. More and more sociologists are aware that little that happens in the public realm is without its private side. Attitudes toward work and spending and leisure and politics are all shaped and nurtured in the family and among friends and acquaintances. Furthermore, we have known for a long time that old-boy and, increasingly, old-girl networks supply the first candidates for open positions in business. Primary relationships are the source of the first list of eligibles, even for a president who is trying to pick administrative officeholders to fill important political and bureaucratic roles. And just as organizations exist in the context of primary, "private" relationships, these relationships are sometimes mobilized in extremely effective ways to foster or resist policies or plans. For example, the New Christian Right, dating from the late 1970s through the present, has effectively mobilized churches and religious people for political ends, that is, people from the supposedly private sphere of religion for significant public collective action. Consumer boycotts and public health and safety movements, like the ones against nuclear power, smoking, and driving under the influence of alcohol, to name just a few, are rooted in families and community social groups, such as churches.

This book demonstrates that what is normally conceived of as the public world, encompassing economy and politics, is intimately interdigitated with the private sphere of family and religion. To try to analyze the great dynamics of the modern world in totally secular and totally political economic terms is folly. We take as a central task of the book the destruction of this artificial barrier that has been constructed between the public and private spheres. Although the distinction between the spheres has some uses, it is taken for granted in the social sciences today. We can read reams of material on politics and economics and never see a word about family and religion. The fact is that the latter have clear and profound consequences for the public world that should not be ignored, and to ignore them is to be deceived about societal processes.[1]

Although only a few years ago, the weight of social scientific wisdom would have fallen on the side of the near-inevitable secularization of the modern world, the rise of fundamentalisms everywhere has put the lie to that assumption. Even short of extremist positions, there are signs of religious renewal across the mainstream of faiths that indicate the enduring nature of the religious impulse in social expression. Religion is not dying; unilinear secularization cannot be taken for granted. Instead, religion is a dynamic process with ups and downs in its prominence in society.

Similarly, sociologists have tended to see the family as a victim of the Industrial Revolution, characterized by breakdown and disorganization. But, in fact, the family persists and has creative impacts on the public life of individuals and groups. Families are not dying, although they are changing in form and function. They provide the soil in which public actors are rooted, and they often significantly influence the public actions of these actors.

Closing the gap between the private and the public spheres analytically is our primary goal in this volume. We use a comparative approach to examine the interrelationships between family and religion. These institutions intersect intensively in the private sphere, we argue, but they should not be consigned analytically to that sphere alone. They and their interrelationships have important effects broadly across the public sphere. From direct effects on the local community to extensive consequences for the whole society, these institutional relationships merit careful consideration.

IMPORTANCE OF THE COMPARATIVE STUDY OF RELIGION AND FAMILY

The study of the religion-family linkage and, beyond that, the comparative study of this linkage seem so clearly important that it is hard to understand why the topic has not been pursued systematically using this approach. Comparative research is a way of learning which theoretical generalizations or concepts have applicability beyond a single case study and thus allows for the development of more universal generalizations. Although each society has unique patterns and contexts, there are commonalities among societies. The comparative approach allows one to see what they are and how far they extend.

This book is comparative in several ways, each of which represents an important criterion for the inclusion of the particular studies. First, although no one chapter extensively compares the interrelations between family and religion in different countries, the volume as a whole does. Each chapter concentrates on a different country, and there is coverage of five of the world's seven continents (excluding Australia and Antarctica). Thus, it is possible to see some of the similarities and differences that occur.

For our purposes, one of the most important dimensions of variation is that of different religious traditions.[2] We expect that the dynamics of the private and public spheres would be influenced by type of religion. Our book includes studies that focus on East Asian institutional and folk religions (in Japan and Taiwan); Judaism (in Ukraine); Islam (in Egypt and Indonesia); Protestant, Catholic, and Eastern Orthodox Christianity (in Belarus, Brazil, Mexico, Sweden, and the United States); and African folk religion (in Cameroon).

It is important to evaluate variations in the structure of the religious sphere as well as type of religion, especially to assess the consequences of different religious markets. The societies covered in this volume range from those with relatively homogeneous religious spheres, such as Sweden, Egypt, and Brazil, to those like the United States and South Africa that are relatively pluralistic in religion. Several chapters focus on the dynamics of minority religious communities in pluralistic settings (Mormons in France; Punjabi Muslims, Hindus, and Sikhs in England; East Indian Muslims and Hindus and black Christians in South Africa; and Evangelical Protestants in Mexico). In addition, there are the special cases of Belarus and Ukraine. Under the Soviets, these countries were dominated by politically sponsored atheism overlaying what had been a historically majority Christian (Orthodox and Catholic) culture with a Jewish minority. These two cases represent state-controlled religious markets that have been recently opened.

Another important dimension of variation for our purposes is different family patterns. As in the case of religion, we anticipate that the dynamics of the private and public spheres would be affected by various aspects of family culture and social structure. To take one example, different types of family economies lead to different structures of interrelationship between the private and public spheres. The evolution of the historic Japanese household from a landed production-and-consumption unit to a unit focused on the support of urban wage labor illustrates a process of change in the public role of the family. A second example is Mormon families in France, who represent a criticism-in-practice of the French family situation and imply that the question of family well-being should be raised to the public level. These Mormon families pursue the general public function of caring for and rearing the young (cf. Cherlin 1996) more systematically than do others around them and thus represent a kind of revitalization of the public function for French families. The chapter on South Africa provides the final example; it shows that the public process of developing entrepreneurs is strongly related to types of family and kin networks.

As we stated earlier, theories of modernization contend that the public prominence of religion and family in societies declines with economic development. The countries discussed here were selected to represent wide variation on this variable and range, from those with less-developed economies (e.g., Cameroon and Egypt) to those with highly developed economies (e.g., Japan and the United States).

Another way in which this book is comparative is in a historical sense. Whether the analyses cover the ancient roots of a faith, as do those of Japan and Sweden, or concentrate on more recent history, as do those of South Africa and France, all encompass a social change component and so allow for comparisons over time.

THE RELIGION AND FAMILY LINKAGE

To understand the significance of religion and family for both the private and public spheres, one must see clearly their unique characteristics and how they interrelate. The interinstitutional relationships between family and religion are strong and qualitatively different from other institutional relationships. Berger (1967) noted that in premodern societies, kinship was permeated with religious meaning and in modern societies, religion remains closely connected to the family. In her systematization of the sociology of religion, Hargrove (1979) argued that religion and family have had a close relationship throughout history in both Western and non-Western societies. D'Antonio, Newman, and Wright (1982) also stressed the significance of the connections between these two institutions.

The uniqueness of the family-religion linkage is examined conceptually in Chapters 2 and 3. To summarize, both institutions are characterized by what MacIver (1970:45) called cultural, rather than secondary, interests. In other words, associations within the religious and familial spheres pursue interests for their own sake because they bring direct satisfaction, not because they are means to other interests, as in the case of economy and polity. Both family and religion are devoted to organizing primary-group relations. They stand out as the only two institutions that deal with the person as a whole, rather than just segmental aspects of individual lives. These various similarities between religion and family strengthen the interinstitutional ties between them.

The interrelationships between the institutions of religion and family are reciprocal (Thomas and Henry 1985; Thornton 1985). Religion provides the symbolic legitimation for family patterns (cf. Berger 1969), and the family is a requisite for a vigorous religious system because it produces members and instills them with religious values. In fact, numerous familial events (such as weddings and funerals) are marked in religious contexts, and many religious observances (for example, prayers at meals and bedtime) take place within the familial setting. Chapter 14, on Brazilian Catholicism, and Chapter 15, on Mexican Evangelical Protestant women, explore how religious factors have shaped family dynamics, specifically power. In contrast, the opposite causal direction is evidenced in Chapter 5, on Taiwan; Chapter 12, on Japan; and Chapter 13, on Cameroon. These chapters illustrate how family and kinship forces can affect phenomena in the religious sphere.

The special affinity of religion and family as institutions takes various forms. Almost everywhere, even in a highly secularized society like Sweden, religion provides ritual support for family and kinship structures, as Chapter 4 demonstrates. In some societies, this ritual support may be seen in ancestor rites or memorialization (for example, Cameroonian Kedjom rites, Japan's core religion, Taiwan's folk religion, and French Mormonism). Such practices support family life and, at the same time, fulfill a central function for religion.[3] In fact, in Chapter 9, familism, expressed both ritually and in church values, is viewed as the greatest asset of Mormonism in the eroding environment for traditional families in France. Moreover, utopian experiments and new religious movements often take the family as their essential focus. As is noted in Chapter 2, in the Unification Church ("Moonies"), "not only is the family the organizing metaphor for much that the group does, but it functions as a model for the Church's very conception of itself."

Although the focus of this book is primarily on the connections between family and religion, it must be understood that these two institutions relate to each other within the larger societal context that includes other institutions, such as polity and economy. Chapters 2, 3, 6, 7, and 14 evaluate interlinkages among family, religion, and polity in the United States, Egypt, Belarus, Indonesia, and Brazil, respectively, and stress the significance of political factors. More specifically, they provide examples of the struggle among these three institutions over the role of the state in religious and familial affairs—a struggle that is essentially over the dividing line between the public and private spheres.

The relevance of changing economic conditions is apparent in Chapter 3, on Egypt, and Chapter 13, on the Kedjom of Cameroon. Chapter 12, on Japan, views economic factors as the most basic structuring influences for both religion and family. Although reflecting an opposite causal order, an even stronger economic theme is sounded in Chapter 8, on South Africa, where, in an expanding economy, religion and familial patterns facilitate economic behavior among East Indians; this analysis turns Weber's ([1920] 1958) thesis on its head, given that it views South African Calvinism as anticapitalist. As with the polity, the interrelationships among economy, religion, and family that are depicted in these chapters reveal extensive efforts by the associations representing these institutions to influence each other.

All the chapters acknowledge that the interactions of the various institutions are dynamic, not static, and reflect ongoing processes of social change that affect even individual actions and attitudes. Although the collection has a macroanalytic perspective, some contributions emphasize microsocial processes along the paths of social change. For example, the devolution of the British Empire provides the essential context for the examination of the processes of adaptation and identity building in Chapter 11, on the religious imagery of children of Punjabi immigrants in England. Similarly, the changing sociocultural context of France, as it faces globalizing influences, creates stimuli for individuals to turn to Mormonism, according to Chapter 9. Another clear example is in Chapter 5, on Taiwan, which links declines in the values and practices reflecting ancestral authority mandated by folk religion to the post–World War II expansion of nonfamilial contexts for life-course experiences that took place as Taiwan industrialized and urbanized.

THE ACADEMIC NEGLECT OF RELIGION AND FAMILY

Neglect by Sociologists in General

This volume argues for the need to examine the religion-family linkage across societies as a way to bridge the gap between the private and public spheres. Before we pursue this linkage further, however, we must pause to take note of a characteristic of contemporary sociological scholarship: Sociologists in general tend to give little import to either family or religion, much less their linkage.

The contemporary academic and scholarly landscape in the social sciences contains only small edifices for religion and family. There are enormous monuments to economic relations and political affairs, for example, but religion, most significantly,[4] and the family, to a lesser extent, are not at the center of concern of any of the core social science disciplines in American educational and research circles. Research on religion and the family tends to be seen as topically suspicious. Too often, scholarly colleagues—not perceiving the importance of these institutions for the secular social, economic, and political issues that they study (cf. Casanova 1994, Cochran 1990, Wuthnow 1994b)—peripheralize investigations of them, viewing them as not central to their organizing theoretical ideas. Many are so captivated by the notion of secularization (the disappearance of religion), on the one hand, and notions of the decline or loss of function in the traditional family, on the other hand, that they tend to neglect both religion and the family when they think about major world issues. They are prone to imagine that these two institutions do not just bear a special relationship with each other in the private sphere, but are limited in their effects only to this sphere.

Why has the twentieth-century Western scholarly tradition so often omitted family and religion from analyses of core social processes? First, of course, one must recognize the consequences of intellectual atheism and agnosticism, which may make some think that what one does not accept philosophically is not worthy of attention (cf. Greeley 1989:3–4). In response, however, it must be noted that even from an atheistic or agnostic position, it is important to understand what motivates and energizes a large proportion of the world's population. After all, there are many who practice or believe in some religion.

Second, and probably more important, Western intellectuals have long been striving to break the bonds of religious doctrine and bureaucratic control that have stifled learning over and over again during the history of Judeo-Christian-Islamic civilization. Attempts to reimpose these bonds have been recently experienced in the form of the call to teach "religious sciences" of one or another sort, including "creation science." Social science scholars are tied to colleges and universities, for the most part, and the twentieth century has been punctuated by repeated battles over the restrictions on free speech and free thinking in religious institutions.[5] The secularization of the academy has been hard earned, and it continues to be challenged by religious activists, who, in the United States, come today mostly from the fundamentalist-evangelical Protestant population. This religious radicalism has made highly secularized academics hesitant to credit religion in any way in their research and study.[6]

The family, too, has seemed the arsenal of traditionalism and control over free thought. Symbolically tied to the religious right in America since the late 1970s by the public definition of the "pro-family" movement (Pankhurst and Houseknecht 1983), which has had its subsidiary cultural battles within academic circles, the family, seen in a traditional sense, seems to some scholars to be a retrograde phenomenon.

There may also be a sense in which the high mobility and family disruption-reorganization days of the post–World War II United States so destabilized the experience of the family—and, thus, thinking about the family—that intellectuals have been unable to assimilate fully its varied impact and centrality as a social institution. Settles (1996) noted that the family is too often thought of as the weak victim of social change, a sideshow to what is "really" going on. However, she asserted, "It is not the family that is fragile, it is the society," and that as other institutions have created social problems, families have become "the clean-up agents for all the inadequacies of other institutions" (p. 2). In short, the family's contributions resulting from the profound changes in all institutions have not been understood. Rather, it has been tacitly assumed that the family is adaptable in absorbing those impacts without any true social accounting.

Finally, it is clear that however important religion and family are in the modern world, they are not the dominant institutions. Subject to "fads and foibles," as Sorokin (1956) said, the social sciences often focus on the most prominent and financially lucrative interests, which today are those that are tied most directly to the economy and the polity.

In sum, we have argued that the scholarly study of family and religion has been neglected by sociologists in general, and we have reviewed the reasons for this neglect. We conclude that although the importance of religion and family is manifested in different ways in different contexts, these institutions are essential virtually everywhere in fundamental ways—in ways that cannot be extirpated from the general sociocultural field in which they exist—and in both the private and public spheres. To achieve a comprehensive understanding of any society, then, one must take the roles that religion and family play into account.

Neglect of the Linkage by Sociologists of Religion and Family

Despite the neglect of the study of religion and family by sociologists in general, there are, to be sure, significant scholarly literatures on these topics. Sociologists of family and religion have these topics as their primary concerns, but their work tends to focus on one of these institutions, not the linkage between the two. D'Antonio et al.'s (1982) analysis of the contents of texts on sociology of the family and sociology of religion and three major journals in sociology of religion from 1951 to 1980 supported this depiction of neglect. Similarly, Thomas and Cornwall (1990) assayed the contents of journals in the fields of family, religion, sociology, psychology, and therapy for studies in the 1980s on both religion and family. Although they found some growth in attention to the topic, they concluded that there is a "pressing need for more serious theoretical and conceptual work that incorporates multidimensional approaches and is specifically designed to illuminate the interrelationships between religion and family" (p. 983). The chapters in this volume address this need. The authors were guided by the interinstitutional perspective, and each used multiple research methods.

Our review of journal articles published since 1974 showed that there has been a tendency to restrict analyses of the connection between family and religion to bivariate relationships (cf. Thomas and Cornwall 1990). The work here calls for the broadening of this focus by viewing variables within their institutional contexts. We also found that there has been little comparative work on the family and religion linkage. Even the two major books devoted to this topic that were published in the 1980s (D'Antonio and Aldous 1983; Thomas 1988) were limited in this regard. A more recent book (Ammerman and Roof 1995) examined family and religion in relation to work issues, but it, too, did not include settings other than the United States. To assess the family and religion linkage in a comprehensive manner, it is necessary to study a wide array of settings. Only with a strategy of broad comparison can scholars see the limits of their generalizations.

SOCIAL CHANGE

The institutions of family and religion, in their interactions with each other and with the rest of society, evidence a full range of social change processes in both the private and public spheres. The various forms of dynamic interplay are represented in this book. All the chapters that make up this volume are complex analyses of changes occurring in particular societies, and are grouped into sections with different social change themes. Before we describe these themes, it is important to note that all the contributions are multidimensional and are not restricted to the theme of the section in which they have been placed.

Social change interactions can take different forms, including innovation, accommodation and conflict—regardless of whether religion and family are affecting or being affected. Innovation refers to the development or recognition of new elements or patterns in a culture. Accommodation is a type of social interaction that allows antagonistic entities to maintain their separate stances, with the exception of those that would lead to disruptive conflict. Conflict, of course, is a direct and conscious struggle between entities so that each may attain a particular goal. Defeat of the opponent is seen as essential for achieving the goal (Theodorson and Theodorson 1979).

Conflict is perhaps the most common cause of social change. In Chapter 2, on the United States, and Chapter 3, on Egypt, one sees conflict between the religious and familial institutions, on the one hand, and other societal institutions, on the other hand. In both societies, the directions of change in family and religion are topics of widespread and highly charged political debate and struggle. The locus of the struggle is the dividing line between the private and public spheres, with the state in each instance presuming a restricted private sphere for family and religion but familioreligious groups resisting this sequestration.

In sharp contrast to these two countries, Chapter 4 indicates that Sweden exemplifies accommodation to the major changes that have occurred in family and religion; rather than conflictual relations, this social democratic welfare state has adapted to pervasive secularism and a high degree of individualism in the family sphere. Similarly, Chapter 5 shows that despite the enormous socioeconomic change in Taiwan during this century, there is little evidence of widespread conflict in the realms of religion and family; instead, there is a pattern of accommodative adaptation. In both Sweden and Taiwan, the societies have accepted the relative privatization of religions and families, as least for the time being.

We argue that such conditions of accommodation or conflict are never permanent. And, in fact, we see accommodation and conflict as only relative positions on a continuum that permits infinite variation. Relatively conflictual circumstances can be made relatively accommodated by a variety of dynamics, and the pendulum can swing from relative accommodation to relative conflict, as well. The circumstances surrounding the 1979 Iranian Revolution provide a useful example. It appears that the shah's regime in

Iran had strayed from general religious and familial sensibilities and found itself in conflict with the population. The success of the Khomeini-led revolt reduced conflict between the state and the Islamic faith of the majority. However, almost twenty years later, we see signs of renewed conflict in Iran, now pitting the traditionalist Islamic state against a popular culture that has moved away from the esprit of the revolutionary period. The cultural conflict is animated by an assertion of familial autonomy by younger and more urban sectors of the population. Family relationships, gender, the degree of sanctions for "un-Islamic" behavior, and the like became major issues in the last presidential campaign, in which a comparative Islamic moderate won out over more conservative foes (Linzer 1997a, 1997b).

The conditions establishing relative conflict or relative accommodation are changed by a host of processes that occur in the interrelationships between religion, family, and other institutions. Accommodation sometimes disintegrates into conflict if for no other reason than that the market forces in the religious sphere are likely to lead some religious groups to mount family-values campaigns in the political arena as a means of increasing the number of their adherents (i.e., market share). Such a scenario seems to have happened in the United States in the 1970s and 1980s under the banner of the pro-family movement. As another example, the reduction of social welfare investment by a government facing fiscal constraints may arouse reactions from families and churches that battle for greater welfare resources in the policy venues. This scenario has been seen in the United States recently and may have even more salience for European societies, such as Germany and Sweden, as they contemplate significant welfare cutbacks. The main point is that conflict and accommodation must always be seen as dynamic qualities of any situation. Social change is endemic.

Chapters 2–5, on the United States, Egypt, Sweden, and Taiwan, make up Part I: "Societal Conflict and Accommodation."

Sometimes social change entails a relatively sudden, enormous upheaval in the structuring of social institutions, and families and religions cannot go untouched. The post–World War II era has witnessed a great number of such upheavals. Dramatic transformations of this sort characterized Belarus after the fall of the Soviet Union, Indonesia after the fall of the the Sukarno regime, and South Africa after the fall of the apartheid system. Chapter 6, on Belarus, examines changing religiofamilial practices and beliefs within the context of massive institutional realignment. Rapid economic development and political upheaval have reshaped Indonesian society over the past thirty years, as well. Chapter 7 discusses the conflict over the legal regulation of family matters in Indonesia that was part of the greater attempt by the Suharto-led state to control all aspects of the society. On the other hand, Chapter 8 focuses not on the total institutional realignment that is taking place in South Africa, but on the operation of ethnoreligious and familial networks in the development of entrepreneurship within the context of societal reconfiguration, thus making important linkages between macrosocial change and the processes of everyday life. These three chapters constitute Part II: "Dramatic Societal Transformations."

As is evident in Part III: "The Context of Innovation," the diffusion of innovation is undeniably one of the central processes of social change. This phenomenon is exemplified in Chapter 9, on French Mormonism, which assesses the growth of a uniquely American and familistic faith on foreign soil. The attractiveness of Mormonism for French converts stems from the desire to maintain traditional family patterns in the face of rapid social change. Also experiencing the diffusion of innovation are the Jews in Kiev, Ukraine, who had been deeply secularized by the long period of communist control and now face the reintroduction of lost cultural and religious traditions. According to Chapter 10, their identity as Jews and their communities are being reestablished with the support of foreign Jews, who are bringing back the customs and practices, now experienced as new cultural elements. Rather than portray the diffusion of innovation, Chapter 11 illustrates innovation itself, in this case, East Asian faiths that have taken root in England as a result of migrations within the British Commonwealth. It describes the means by which Punjabi Muslim, Hindu, and Sikh children in London maintain and adapt their religious identities in this new multicultural setting in which the influence of family remains strong. The French Mormons, the Kievan Jews, and the Asian immigrant children in Britain are trying to develop or recognize new ways to maintain, in some sense, old ways, identities, and traditions.

Innovation serves divergent purposes for the three populations described in Part III. It is important to note that innovation also affects the host society. Mormonism is influencing France in many ways by introducing new dynamism, particularly in the religious sphere. In a parallel, though different way, renewed Judaism in Ukraine may reinvigorate the historical cultural role of Jews in the arts and literature, for example. For the immigrant East Asian children in England, their play is part of the general pattern of adaptation to the local society in which they find themselves. In general, the imagery of God that the children have created bridges, to some extent, the cultural differences among the three immigrant groups, as well as between them and the host Christian society. This process is important for British society because it is part of the acculturation of these relatively new populations. According to Chapter 11, these children are not just reproducing the national identity of their grandparents or parents, but are inventing ethnic and national identities for the new generations of Sikhs, Muslims, and Hindus in Britain; in short, they are adapting to life in multicultural Britain. In the lands from which these children's families came, there is often violent confrontation among the groups. The creative play of the Punjabi children overcomes the old animosities that have pitted Hindus, Sikhs, and Muslims against each other and allows the three groups to live in a measure of accommodation not only with British society, but with each other.

In contrast to the general processes of social change that structure the first three parts of the book, Parts IV and V are devoted to the exploration of topical issues of change that have become ever more meaningful in the modern world. Chapters 12 and 13 in Part IV: "Economic Factors as a Force for Change" aptly illustrate the importance of the economy as a stimulus for change in the institutions of family and religion under conditions of development and modernization. Chapter 12 shows how the evolution of the Japanese economy, based on households that reflect the religious imagery of the family structure, has led to alterations in household structure and, subsequently, religious practice. Chapter 13 parses the interconnections between family ritual and economic shifts among the Kedjom people in postcolonial Cameroon. Here again, family structure is the basis for economic role structures, and both family and economic roles are sacralized in the folk religion. As the economy changes, so must the familial and religious roles that interconnect with it—especially the roles of women, as Chapter 13 demonstrates.

In Part V, "Gender and Social Change," Chapters 14 and 15 use different analytical approaches to examine the religious sources of changing conceptions of gender relations that serve to modify family patterns. Chapter 14 takes a long historical view and focuses on Catholicism in Brazil, whereas Chapter 15 assumes a more contemporary perspective to describe the effects of women's conversion to Evangelical Protestantism in Mexico, which, like Brazil, is dominated by Catholicism.

The social change processes that have been discussed here, including conflict, accommodation, and innovation, have implications for two broader patterns of social change: institutional differentiation and institutional dominance. Secularization can be seen as a special instance of institutional differentiation, and we discuss the concept and its use next, indicating the value of religious economy models over the conventional secularization approach. The processes of differentiation and institutional dominance have tended to make the private and public spheres distinct, but, we argue, have not consigned religion and family solely to the private sphere, as so many sociologists seem to think.

Institutional Differentiation

Underlying all the dimensions of social change indicated in the organization of the parts of this book is the notion of institutional differentiation. This phenomenon implies greater specialization, and all the social change processes discussed earlier can cause it to occur. Although the paths and extent of institutional differentiation vary across societies, when differentiation does proceed, we see fundamental changes in interinstitutional relations (cf. Alexander and Colomy 1990; Beckford 1989). Institutional differentiation affects all institutions, and the chapters of this book stress in various contexts the differentiation of politics and economy, in particular, in relation to family and religion. In this section, we examine the differentiation of religion and family conceptually.

Our previous description of the religion-family linkage as involving special affinity and being reciprocal was not to say that religion and the family always and everywhere are, or must be, equally intimately entangled. We can see a continuum in the level of differentiation of these institutions in the contributions to this volume. At one end of the continuum, Islam in Egypt, as Chapter 3 points out, evinces a lack of differentiation, an elaborate interweaving of the two institutions that makes each strongly dependent on the other. And the Cameroonian Kedjom pillow rite, discussed in Chapter 13, is an example of a religious practice that is hardly differentiated from the kinship context; it is precisely an affirmation of the kinship patterns of Kedjom society.

At the opposite end of the spectrum, Sweden, a country in which the Lutheran Church is officially established and a large majority of the population are nominal members, is highly secular. Developments in the family there have widely diverged from the traditional model that Protestant Christianity had advocated. In Sweden, the two institutions are intertwined only in limited ways, primarily in regard to life-cycle rites, as Chapter 4 demonstrates. The individualized faith of many Americans, described in Chapter 2, also accompanies a highly differentiated system of institutional relationships.

Theories of Secularization

Secularization is a special process of differentiation in which what was previously under the "sacred canopy" (Berger 1969) of religion is removed from that realm and placed in a nonreligious institutional context. Allegedly, education, the acceptance of science, urbanization, industrialized worklife, and the like take away the mystery of religion and strip it of its "plausibility" in many areas of concern. Thus, the cure of diseases, protection from misfortune, explanation of the universe, and so forth are made rational and not subject to religious intervention. In this approach, religion remains relevant only for personal spiritual questing and as solace in the private sphere, and most of its social institutional ramifications first become empty shells and eventually vanish.

The notion of a unilinear process of secularization has long troubled many sociologists (cf. Hadden 1987; Hadden and Shupe 1986; "Introduction" in Hammond 1985). Some have developed variants in which secularization is viewed as a cyclical process with long historical waves. Nisbet (1970), for example, discussed the rationality of the eras of classical Greece and of the Renaissance and Age of Reason and noted that from the time of first-century Rome to the Renaissance, Christianity had "virtually [eliminated] secular rationalism from the European continent for more than a thousand years" (p. 391). Though we are now in a rationalizing or secularizing age, "to argue permanence for this age would be, on the testimony of history, absurd" (p. 391). Recently, as we discuss later, sociologists of religion have focused on shorter waves of secularization and have viewed the process as self-limiting. The most prominent versions of this approach apply economic models to religious markets, putting aside the notion that religion must be irrational or otherwise antimodern. Some of these postsecularization theorists argue for a rational-choice approach to religion, an approach that is largely alien to the mode of thought underlying secularization theory.[7]

In the long debate about the validity of notions of secularization within the sociology of religion, it has become clear that secularization cannot be understood in a simplistic way if one wants to retain the concept at all. Although certain evidence of secularization seems apparent, there are countermovements that suggest that religion is truly vital in the modern world (Marty and Appleby 1995). The spread of Liberation Theology throughout Latin America in the 1970s and 1980s (Berryman 1987; Smith 1991), followed by the more recent explosion of Evangelical, Fundamentalist, and Pentecostal Protestantism in the same region (Martin 1990), indicates the power of the human concern for spiritual or nonempirical matters. Similarly, the tenacious attachment of Americans to the belief in God (Greeley 1989, 1992; cf. Wald 1986) and their high levels of religious activity indicate that religious sentiment of some sort is compatible even with a society that is highly developed socioeconomically. Going beyond the simple Marxist assertion that religion is illusion, even if religious claims are often masks for the interests of power or wealth, religion must be understood as a real and consequential part of sociocultural life.

Casanova (1994) conducted one of the most extensive recent cross-cultural analyses of religion, a close examination of the conditions of Evangelical Protestantism and Catholicism in the United States and of Catholicism in Brazil, Spain, and Poland. He argued that the social scientific literature depicts secularization as having three correlated dimensions, but his research challenged this idea by convincingly showing that the three dimensions are not always present together. First, Casanova accepted the validity of claims that secularization entails a structural differentiation of the religious institution from other institutions as societal modernization takes place. This differentiation means, in particular, the "emancipation of the secular spheres from religious institutions and norms" (Casanova 1994:6). However, the second dynamic that is often subsumed under secularization—the decline in religious beliefs and practices—cannot be taken for granted, and it does not necessarily follow from the first. The third dynamic, which is the core of the privatization thesis (discussed more fully later), is that religion will sequester itelf in the private sphere under modernity and, according to some analysts, will be marginalized there. However, this process, too, cannot be assumed to be associated with secularizing institutional differentiation. The second and third dynamics are unwarranted correlates of the first; while Casanova contended that the first is the true essence of secularization, he argued that the second and third are not supported by empirical evidence and should not be considered part of the secularization process.

While there is no question that institutional differentiation is a sort of master process of the modern era, one cannot assume that it has progressed equally far everywhere. As we already noted, the chapters in this volume show that although modern Egypt and Cameroon are both experiencing significant pressures toward greater differentiation, they evidence far less differentiation between family and religion and between these two and other institutions than does the United States, Sweden, or Belarus. Furthermore, even if there is great differentiation, one cannot presume that the influences of the religious and familial institutions end. As the debates on abortion policy illustrate, even in a highly differentiated society like the United States, there is plenty of room for religious assertions beyond the alleged parameters of secularized religion and into political life. This circumstance indicates that one cannot take for granted that religion is irrelevant for social policy, as secularist analysts are prone to do. We argue more broadly later that one cannot assume the interinstitutional isolation of religion and family in the private sphere, even in highly differentiated societies. The effects of these institutions are always felt across interinstitutional divisions in some measure.

In addition, it is possible for there to to be "dedifferentiation" in a highly differentiated society, as occurred in Belarus during the post-Soviet period (see Chapter 6). Better known by the U.S. public is the recent passage of laws in Russia favoring the Russian Orthodox Church (Pankhurst 1998) after many decades of antireligious, extremely secularist, communist control under the Soviets and a brief period of strict legal disestablishment of all religions between 1991 and 1997. Here are instances of seeming dedifferentiation, in which the gap between politics and religion is narrowed. Similarly, Chapter 7, on the debate in Indonesia over divorce law indicates efforts to reassert religious authority over a legal arena that had been under state control for several decades. This, too, is an example of dedifferentiation contrary to the expectations of secularization theory.

Although it is clear that the differentiation processes associated with secularization cannot be understood in a simple way, the whole theoretical apparatus of secularization approaches is challenged by the persistent religious interest and activity of the U.S. population, a society so economically developed that it should evidence advanced secularization in all its manifestations. Especially perplexing for secularization-oriented analysts has been the rise of Fundamentalist and Evangelical Protestants in the United States over the past three decades. The public voice and numerical growth of these groups does not fit the paradigm. Similarly incongruent with secularization reasoning has been the global increase in Fundamentalist movements in all major religious traditions (Hadden 1995; cf. Marty and Appleby 1995).

Religious and Familial Markets

The notion of unilinear secularization seems untenable, but there are certainly processes of decline and growth in religious phenomena that must be explained. The general interinstitutional perspective focuses attention on relationships that are important for these variations in the strength and character of religion. In addition, we have found market-model approaches useful within the general interinstitutional perspective for generating testable hypotheses about several aspects of religion and family in various societies.

Social differentiation approaches, including secularization theories, start from observations of society from the top down. An alternative approach is to look from the bottom up, moving from the level of individual social action to the institutional structures that the aggregation of such action creates. Such an approach is found in rational-choice theories, which begin by analyzing patterns of individual behavior according to the economic logic of consumer choice. In rational-choice approaches to religion, churches and other religious organizations are seen as firms that offer a variety of goods and services to consumer-believers and consumer-parishioners. When patterns of individual consumer choice are aggregated, market structures become apparent. Such markets provide the context within which patterns of supply and demand are worked out. They distribute goods and services to consumers, as well as a "market share" to religious firms. Seen from the market-model viewpoint, the issue of the strength of religion boils down to the likelihood that potential consumer-believers will buy into a given religious belief or practice or affiliate with a given religious firm, such as a temple or a missionary organization. Just as the level of economic purchases rises and falls over time, so does the level of various religious "products" like church membership or belief in God. What governs variations in purchases or adoptions (or church membership or belief in God) is the logic of rational choice among the options in the marketplace that are available to the consumer-believers or consumer-members. Religious organizational leaders, like business executives, proffer a variety of products to the consuming public and vary the price of such products to attract consumers (the faithful). The leaders seek market share in the religious market.

This emerging "new paradigm" for understanding religious change relies on economic models of the religious market to understand different levels of religious group affiliation and participation (Hadden 1995; Warner 1993; Young 1997). Stark and Bainbridge (1987) presented an elaborate deductive theory of religion based on rational-choice principles that provided the backdrop for a series of more recent studies by these authors and their collaborators (see Hadden 1996). Perhaps most prominent among the studies developed in connection with this theoretical approach is Finke and Stark's (1992) analysis of American religion, which showed that over the past three centuries, it has grown, rather than declined, in the number of participants and proportion of the U.S. population, contrary to what secularization theory would predict. The authors argued that the growth is the result of competition in a pluralistic market. Iannaccone (1995, 1997 and works cited in these sources), an economist, elaborated several propositions in line with the theory and expanded the application of economic modeling.

The approach seems to hold greater promise for explaining and predicting the dynamism of religious phenomena than do other approaches that are primarily based in traditional functionalist secularization theorizing. For the present purposes, its primary wisdom is that secularization processes are self-limiting. That is, when "the processes that erode commitments to a particular set of supernatural assumptions" (Stark and Bainbridge 1987:311) advance far enough, the religious market will be open to new options. These options, according to Stark and Bainbridge, take the form of cults, sects, or schisms from established groups.

Theoretically and conceptually, there are similarities and differences between the market approach and other approaches that merit notice here. First, since markets involve competition among firms for market share, they evidence a pattern of behavior that may be seen as conflictual. In fact, some forms of conflict theory (for example, Dahrendorf's [1959] interest-group notions) may be used to analyze these competitive processes. On the other hand, conflict theory, especially Marxian theory, assumes that there is a natural conflict among given parties or processes, such as social classes or ideological systems like capitalism and socialism. Market theory does not presuppose the nature of the competing forces; it presupposes only that the forces, organized as firms in some form, seek to win consumers, converts, or members. Competing firms are free to reorganize, reconstitute, or recreate themselves as times change in ways that serve their quest for a market share. There is no clear good or bad goal for this competition as there is in much of conflict theory.

In social movement theory, where conflict theory in a post-Marxian form can be seen to be developing vigorously today, the concept of moral entrepreneur has been borrowed from market models, indicating the closeness of this approach with the market approach. Moral entrepreneurs organize social movement organizations (SMOs), which are like economic firms, that, in turn, seek to attract adherents in a way that is fully analogous to attracting consumers or members in a market approach. An area for creative conceptual development is to link social movement theory and market-model approaches. However, we cannot envision all the variables we are interested in vis-à-vis family and religion fitting under the rubric of social movements.

A parallel set of considerations both link the market approach with Weberian approaches and distinguish it from them. First, Weber's conceptualization of the processes of rationalization that are entailed in modern social change support the market approach's construction on a foundation of rational choice (cf. Demerath 1995). As organizations and institutions rationalize, individuals are forced to act according to a "rational," means-end logic. Furthermore, in his sociology of religion, Weber acknowledged the competition among faiths for adherents and other assets like business connections and various forms of wealth. And the history of the market approach in the sociology of religion is intimately linked with the ongoing project to understand church-sect patterns, which include a series of issues suggested by Weber and highlighted strongly by his student and colleague,

Troeltsch (1931), in *The Social Teachings of the Christian Churches*. The market approach is deeply indebted to Weberian thought. Nevertheless, as they are presented by major advocates, rational choice theory and the market approach are open to a variety of applications that the early Weberians did not fully work out and focus attention on different processes more than different organizational structures. In addition, as we noted in regard to conflict theory, the construction of these approaches upon the base of individual rational choice keeps human agency in focus.

The economic model in which the market approach is rooted certainly has its own limitations. It is not the perfect approach, as are none of the others noted. Perhaps its biggest problem for many readers is the use of a language that has its own implications that do not and should not apply to religious and familial processes. To see churches as firms, for example, suggests not only that they are something other than places to worship God; this latter understanding is basic to all social scientific approaches to religion in some way. But such terminology also suggests that churches are only out to engage in competition, which ultimately amounts to striving to concentrate material assets in their own hands. According to the rational choice/market theory of religion, however, much more is at stake. In fact, the basic choices that people make are about access to eternal salvation, however it is defined (Stark and Bainbridge 1987). Investment in various religious organizations is precisely about religious motives but put in a rational-choice linguistic framework. There is only a peripheral theme of pecuniary advantage or maximization of monetary profits. Except in limited ways, money is only a metaphor for other desirable qualities in this theory. To be sure, some actors have political or economic motives as well, but these motives are pursued in connection with the general quest for religious salvation.

Beyond the problem of applying economic terms to religion, more substantive criticisms of the market approach have been developed recently in the sociology of religion. We briefly review a few of them here to indicate areas in which the approach must be developed.

From a strict theoretical perspective, perhaps the most daunting criticism of the theory argues that, by its nature, religious choice cannot be strictly rational (cf. Chaves 1995; Demerath 1995; Neitz and Mueser 1997). It is this point of view that has discredited the theory most strongly in the religious studies field, where its advocates are relatively few. In his review of Finke and Stark's (1992) revisionist study of American religious history, Martin Marty (1993:88) wrote that their "world contains no God or religion or spirituality, no issue of truth or beauty or goodness, no faith or hope or love, no justice or mercy; only winning and losing in the churching game matters." The work, Marty said, is reductionist, oversimplifying complex issues. Furthermore, Spickard (1998:110), though expressing considerable sympathy for the rational-choice model, has argued that "A rational-choice model can duplicate the overall structure of a religious marketplace, but it cannot demonstrate that individual people think in market terms."

In addition, some sociologists (Ammerman 1997; Ellison 1995; Sherkat 1997) have contended that the notion of rational choice does not adequately take into account the structuring of individual preferences by a host of contextual, cultural, or environmental variables. The approach also has been charged with being androcentric (Carroll 1996) and with ignoring gender as a variable (Neitz and Mueser 1997). Presumably, cross-cultural studies and studies in various settings that explore gender will help to clarify the adequacy of the rational-choice assumptions.

These are important criticisms, but none, we believe, is a fatal blow to the approach. Instead, as some critics have stated, they indicate an agenda for further research and conceptual development of the approach.

A final major criticism is that although the market approach is a useful way of looking at religion in the United States, with its open, pluralistic religious market, it does not easily work for other societies (cf., Warner 1997).[8] Chapter 6 attempts to apply the model to Belarus in its transition from the Soviet period. Other contributions suggest dimensions of variation across societies that may be viewed in light of religious markets. In particular, the current vitality of religion in various societies relates to its multivariate functions, rather than just to competition, which has been the primary focus of studies of religion in the United States. One could identify the economic analogues of religious functions, as Ellison (1995), Iannaccone (1995, 1997), and Sherkat (1997) have done in important conceptual studies. A goal for further analysis in the comparative study of religion and family will be to apply the market model explicitly to assess better its value in understanding non-U.S. settings.

It is interesting and important to note that the economic approach to religion relies on an understanding that religious choices are based in the household as much as in the individual. Religion is like recreation; households "'produc[e]' this commodity by combining purchased inputs (such as ski equipment, automobile services, or VCRs, televisions, and stereos) with their own skills and time" (Iannaccone 1997:29–30). Similarly, religious "goods" are "household commodities" that the household invests other goods, labor, and skills in producing, according to Iannaccone. This imagery of the *household* producing religion, then, again emphasizes the intimate connection between religion and family.

At this juncture, it should be noted that much of the logic that has just been applied in the discussion of religion could presumably be extended to families. Many social scientists overgeneralize from patterns of differentiation related to families in a way that is similar to the way Casanova described secularization thinking about religion (cf. Hargrove 1985). There is a widespread notion that changing patterns in the family (related to institutional differentiation) mean that the family is not central in the modern age. From this premise, one is led to focus on the "private" family to the neglect of the "public" functions that the family retains (Cherlin 1996). It is as if the many "problems" of families remove the family from useful consideration. Although scholars often take families for granted, there is clearly no more powerful socializer of the young and no other viable means for the reproduction of society through the birthing of new members than the family, whatever form it takes. If one assumes that the phenomenon can be identified by its function, that is, by what it does, rather than by its form, then one cannot imagine a society without families and without the effects that families have by definition.

Family sociologists and economists have long examined the economic side of families in its own right, investigating the effects of work on families, the division of labor in households, patterns of budgeting money and time, and the like. Significant studies have also used the market analogy to understand strictly familial phenomena, such as patterns of selecting mates and marriage (the "marriage market"). One could extend the economic logic of this approach to many additional functions of the family.[9] In an open "family market"—a notion that deserves much more elaboration and evaluation than we can give it here—the adoption of one family form over another (say, single parenting over dual parenting, the isolated nuclear household over interconnected extended kin networks, or formal marriage over nonmarital cohabitation) would relate to the participants' evaluation of the costs and rewards associated with the adoption of the given form. In assessing the costs and rewards, the individual would take into account the surrounding culture and relevant subcultures, which would presumably restrict options for "choice" in numerous ways.[10] In a sense, Chapter 4 outlines the conditions for a fairly open familial market system in Sweden.

As some work in the economic approaches to religion shows, one can include a consideration of contextual variables in developing criteria of "choice" in such matters (see, for example, Ellison 1995; Iannaccone 1997; Sherkat 1997). Among the significant influences on choice would be individual religious beliefs and the values of the religious affiliation a person may have, both of which are the products, to some degree, of the person's family socialization and experience in the community. We can extend this line of thought by including a range of cultural variables that allow the research to be fully comparative, potentially applicable to any society or subsocietal unit. In short, we believe that conceptually exploiting the analogy with economic markets has potential for the analysis not only of religion, but of family matters as well. In the end, such an approach would identify the conditions under which particular choices in the realm of families can be seen as signs of the strength of adaptive families, rather than of compromises of weak and ineffectual families. Thus, as with the economic modeling of religion cross-nationally, we advocate the cross-national application of economic modeling of families.

It should be reiterated that we see the market model as subsidiary to our overall interinstitutional perspective. All the chapters manifest the interinstitutional perspective, the major theoretical orientation of the book. Although not explicitly applied nor fully developed in most cases, many of the chapters also reflect certain aspects of the market approach.

Institutional Dominance in Modern Societies

Modern structures of institutional dominance—a concept first articulated by Williams in 1955 (1970) and discussed in Chapter 3—do not negate the importance of the religious and familial institutions. In many societies today, family and religion do not rank high in the relative dominance of major societal institutions. On the contrary, some other institution, most often the economy (as in Sweden and the United States), usually dominates the entire social system.[11] Although the economy is much more likely to be the instigator of social change in the less powerful institutions than vice versa, it does not follow that family and religion cannot initiate change as well. They can and they do, although such occurrences are much less frequent than in the case of the dominant institution or institutions.

We believe that it is inappropriate to ask, Do family and religion facilitate or hinder social change? This question is never asked about the economy or the polity. Perhaps it is raised in the case of religion and family because these two institutions are viewed as conservative—as part of the past that is dragging down forward motion. We reject this view, however. All societal institutions, including family, religion, polity, economy, education, health care, and welfare, both facilitate and hinder social change. The direction of their efforts depends on what best meshes with their interests at a particular time. Chapter 14, on Brazil, and Chapter 15, on Mexico, both illustrate the facilitating effects of religion for changes in gender roles. In fact, according to Chapter 14, Catholicism in Brazil did more than facilitate such changes, it orchestrated dramatic changes in women's roles, restricting women to a limited range of options within the household by the nineteenth century. Chapter 15 discusses how the mobilization of Protestantism in Mexico has provided for certain aspects of authority and legitimacy for women that the dominant Catholic culture did not support; that is, religion has fostered change in gender roles in a direction opposite to that of Brazilian Catholicism. Although these examples evidence the change-oriented qualities of religion and family, Chapter 3, on Egypt, provides a good contrasting example in that it describes the hindering influences that religion and family can have with regard to social change in other institutions. Finally, Chapter 8, on South Africa, presents examples of both the facilitation and hindrance of social change by the religious and familial institutions. Although the East Asian Hindu and Muslim networks promote entrepreneurship, the black African Christian ones tend to inhibit the development of entrepreneurial activities.

In the modern world, the intersection of institutions is largely in the realm of economic issues because of the dominance of the economic institution. This is true even in the interactions of noneconomic institutions, since the values and norms of the dominant institution "permeate a great many areas of life and enter into the operation of other institutions" (Gouldner and Gouldner 1963:496).

RELIGION AND FAMILY IN THE PRIVATE AND PUBLIC SPHERES

There is no question that religion and family are found in both the private and the public spheres and that these spheres are conceptually distinct. Our call to close the gap between them is essentially a demand for recognition of the public functions of religion and family alongside the more familiar private functions and for awareness of the connection between the private and public sides. In the following sections, we elaborate on the dynamics that are found within and between these spheres.

The Private Sphere

Some theorists have argued that "privatization" (Berger 1967; Luckmann 1967) characterizes religion in modern societies and that the private sphere is shared by the family (Berger 1969). With modernization, these two institutions tend to become more specialized and to take on new forms as they structure and give substance to the private sphere. A high degree of differentiation, though, does not put an end to the family and religion connection, even though it weakens the relationships that they have with each other and with other societal institutions. The private sphere may seem to be, in a macro sense, peripheral in the modern world, but it nevertheless is where a bedrock of mutually reinforcing relations between family and religion is found. As we noted earlier, both these institutions focus on primary relations, which, in the past, were much more encompassing of all interinstitutional relations, so that the points of intersection that these two institutions had with each other and with other societal institutions were many. In modernized societies, though, the relevance of primary relations is limited more to the private sphere than in the past. And it is in the private sphere in which one sees what is really unique about the family-religion linkage. It is in the private sphere that the connection is cut to the bare bones and one can see the affinity (although reduced) that persists despite differentiation.

With modernization and postmodernity, the private sphere has emerged as a unique social phenomenon. Although family and religion are dominated by other societal institutions in the modern setting, the private sphere that they constitute is of growing importance. It is a buffer zone in which individuals receive support that helps them absorb the stresses and strains brought on by their public activities in other institutional spheres. Because the public and private domains become less and less well integrated, the need for a retreat to privacy grows. Not only is the private sphere an essential retreat, but it is also a place in which people can devote more and more of the bounty of economic development—increased leisure time, less constant concern with mere survival, and greater financial and other material assets. In short, the private sphere is expanding in the modern world because of both the social psychological need for it and the availability of greater resources that can be devoted to it.

The growth of the private sphere signifies one way that the importance of family and religion is growing. Roof (1993) and Wuthnow (1994c) argued that a primary form of contemporary American religion is found in the self-help or support group (which is frequently located within the context of the church, though it need not be). Aimed at solving problems of individual adaptation, interpersonal relationships, and local community issues, such groups seem to represent a therapy technique for private troubles. As the private sphere grows, this function grows to match it. However, both Roof and Wuthnow also claimed that these groups are linking mechanisms that bring the private and public spheres into connection. They are means of overcoming one-dimensional individualism and of connecting the individual with the broader community.

The Public Sphere

The recognition that the private functions of religion and family are vital and even expanding in modern societies is not inconsistent with the fact that the public side of these two institutions retains significance (cf. Beyer 1994). Both family and religion provide important public functions that, in the end, demand attention. They are public functions that are in crisis in many ways in modern and globalizing societies, and understanding them clearly should aid those who seek to overcome the crises. Following the work of Cherlin (1996) on families and of Casanova (1994), Cochran (1990) and Wuthnow (1994a) on religion, we note that both these institutions provide a range of significant public goods. Such goods are general benefits for the society; they cannot be denied to those who did not participate in producing them, and they often are in short supply because of the tendency of nonproducers to "free-ride" on the efforts of those voluntary actors who take part in the production.

Families provide the public good of children—they give birth to them and raise them to be contributing members of society. These children, then, by being productive, paying taxes, and contributing to social security and other pension systems, help support all persons in the society, particularly those who have aged past the productive years. In addition to reproduction, Cherlin (1996) asserted that in bearing the burden of dependence created mostly by care for children and the frail elderly, families are providing public goods. These public functions are fewer than the public functions of families in the past (Demos 1970), but they are, nevertheless, extremely important in the modern world.

In a similar vein, religion provides important public goods. The first public good is moral values. In modern societies, many citizens do not nurture moral values through participation in and support of religious associations, yet the Ten Commandments are nearly universally honored as moral values. Although derived from religious sources and cultivated and regularly rehearsed in religious settings, the Ten Commandments are not perceived as sectarian or limited in applicability. They are the concrete form of broad societal values that are not in dispute, for the most part. Still, it is only the religious groups—aided by families, of course—who spend the time reminding the population of the importance of these fundamentals. Even atheists profit from the order and social stability that such an emphasis nurtures (cf. Cochran 1990). Although Durkheim (1973) thought that adequate progress would lead to the usurpation of this moral production role of religion by education, with schools sustaining the essential values for the modern society, this situation has not yet occurred. The difficulty in designing a moral program that can be taught in the schools seems only more and more dependent upon the interpretation of relevant faith traditions. The schools, rather than displacing the faiths in this task, seem to be calling on them for clarification and support (cf, Wuthnow 1994a).

Cochran (1990) stressed that religious settings are also important as a forum for public participation, that is, a places where people come together and discuss, evaluate, lobby, and generally keep informed about public issues and problems. In fact, while the private side of religion focuses on individual salvation, there is also the supremely public side of "prophetic" religion, to use Weber's ([1922] 1963) term for the kind of religion that challenges and calls for reform in society. As a forum for participation, the church, synagogue, mosque, or temple provides a venue in which individuals and families work out their positions vis-à-vis the politics and economics of their communities.

Casanova (1994) argued that more and more, religions are asserting their influence and enunciating their interest in secular affairs, mostly to prevent the state's and the market's incursion into religious matters. This is a new era, he asserted, of "public religion." The core of Casanova's argument is that instead religion retreating into a segregated and marginalized private sphere, it is "deprivatizing" throughout the world as one after another faith reasserts its claims to an active role in the broader society, especially in politics and economics. The mobilization of religious groups around the abortion debate in the United States is one such experience, with the well-known engagement of American Catholic and conservative Protestant groups in unexpected political contestation with the government. Another form of this deprivatization is the demand that the church not ally itself with the political and economic elites when the latter create and enforce policies or patterns of control that disenfranchise segments of the population, such as the poor or minorities. From within the faith, there has arisen the counterdemand that the poor should be given a chance to improve and to escape the bonds of poverty. This counterdemand was dramatically stated in the 1980s in the Liberation Theology movement in Latin America and is advocated by a variety of Christian groups in the United States (Hart 1996).

In the end, such processes indicate the reinvigoration of public religion around the world. For Casanova (1994), even Islamic movements can be seen in this light and should not be consigned to a peripheralized "fundamentalist reaction" to modernization. Whether progressive or conservative, public religions' calls for a new vision of politics and economic life are an essential characteristic of the present era. We cannot, think, then, of religion as circumscribed by the private sphere, Casanova argued, and must not neglect the public roles that religions play if we are to perceive the modern world clearly.

In sum, religion and family, both public and private, are essential components of modern life. If anything, their future roles seem to be growing, rather than shrinking. Biomedical advances promise to play out dramatically the questions of life and death, spirit and body, in the public church and the public family, which will have to adapt to longer life and, perhaps, longer periods of dependence for the elderly. The need to prepare children for appropriate careers in the new fields being created by technological advances will have to be addressed in the personal councils around the kitchen table that always strongly influence the occupational choices that young people make. Those occupational choices will rely, in some indirect but profound ways, on the economic ethic that is espoused in the religious community that a family adheres to. In the Third World, development hinges, to some degree, on the fertility decisions made in a family under the influence of the faith that defines appropriate sexual and reproductive behavior. In the process of economic and political change that many societies experience as disruption and disorganization, family and religion are important sources of stability and order, even as they adapt to the changing circumstances in which they find themselves. It is to family and religion that one should go to find the processes that are working out the morality for the new age and the lifestyles for the new era.

The examples could go on and on. The significance of family and religion for the future is undeniable. Let us add them to the center of our quest for understanding the modern world.

WHAT HAVE WE LEARNED?

Although the diversity of studies included in this volume does not allow us to assert conclusively relationships between specific concrete variables, we can draw several important conclusions when the various studies are considered together.

First—to reiterate a point that is basic to the whole book—the comparative approach used here shows that family and religion are important institutions in societies throughout the world. This point holds regardless of such things as level of economic development, whether the society is Western or non-Western, what historic religious traditions characterize the society, what family forms predominate in the society, and so on. One cannot calculate a general coefficient of importance for religion and family in a society, but even where they seem less important on the surface—where strong secularization or family "decline" has set in—significant dynamics of these institutions are always at work. These dynamics can be ignored only at the cost of a less comprehensive understanding of the processes of social change.

Second, the studies in this book affirm the special linkage between religion and family. One could argue, of course, that that is why we chose them to be included here, and thus to draw this conclusion is to affirm the consequent. However, we have not assembled a set of idiosyncratic analyses. Each, in its own way, addresses central issues of its setting, not inconsequential questions. And each demonstrates the unique interconnections between the institutions of religion and family. Religion and family may be primordial institutions, but they are also dynamic and "modern" institutions. The understanding of their special linkage will enrich analyses of social change in any sphere.

If the religion-family linkage is special and has an important role in social dynamics, then our third general conclusion is that they should not be seen as segmented into the private sphere alone. The previous section indicated the error of that predilection in many studies. The chapters in this book further undergird the notion that family and religion must be viewed in terms of their interactions with other institutions.

Fourth, though we have not directly tested the secularization thesis, the studies in this book cast further doubt on the general validity of this perspective. Religion, in league with family, shows signs of persistence and vitality that do not fit this paradigm well. Rationality in human affairs, if it is on the rise, does not vitiate the bases for religion. There seems to be no fully secularized society, and when faith ebbs, it always seems to be subject to the possibility of revival. Furthermore, the global dynamics[12] of migration and the diffusion of innovations often step in to reinvigorate religion where it has waned.

Our final general conclusion is that, apparently, one of the principle vehicles for the reinvigoration of weakened religion or its reformulation into a new variant is family processes. These processes include new socialization patterns for the young, new time-use allocations in the family that give religious ritual or ceremony a place, new values that articulate religious viewpoints, and the like.

The insights gained from comparing the studies in this book point the way to a wide range of research undertakings. The final section of this chapter suggests the richness of the options for future study.

DIRECTIONS FOR FUTURE RESEARCH

To stimulate the pursuit of scholarly work on the family-religion linkage within a comparative perspective, we set forth a preliminary comparative research agenda here. We begin by presenting a list of religion and family-related variables that could be used as a basis for formulating researchable propositions. All but two of the variables—the level of religioethnic conflict in society and the strength of family networks of religioethnic groups—

appear in the chapters in this book. The various studies indicate the complexity of investigation that can be involved in specific settings, although we do not consider every variable that is included in every study. The variables that follow are grouped into either family, religion, or combined family-religion categories. From this list of variables, we formulate a number of selected hypotheses about the interinstitutional interactions of religion and family with each other and with the rest of society. Underlying all the hypotheses is the notion of comparative social change. Given the dearth of comparative propositions about the connection between family and religion, these hypotheses may help guide future research efforts.

Selected Variables

Religion Variables

1. level of dominance/influence of religious institution in society
2. type of religion, e.g., folk, Buddhist, Christian (Eastern Orthodox, Mormon, Protestant, Roman Catholic), Hindu, Jewish, Muslim, Shinto
3. pluralistic versus monopolistic religious sphere
4. importance of economic interests for religious associations
5. level of religioethnic conflict in society
6. religious versus other associations with strong political motivations

Family Variables

1. level of dominance-influence of the family institution in society
2. strength of family networks of religioethnic groups
3. extent to which economic interests influence family functions
4. types and timing of family formation (e.g., timing of marriage and childbearing events, patterns of mate selection)
5. types of family authority structure
6. extent of family disruption

Combined Family and Religion Variables

1. relative dominance of the familial institution compared to the religious institution
2. degree of overlap between religious and familial networks
3. dissipating versus energizing religiofamilial networks
4. likelihood of religious associations to mount family-values campaigns
5. likelihood of religious associations compared to other types of associations to mount family-values campaigns

Selected Hypotheses

Hypothesis 1: When family and religion are dominant societal institutions and religion is centered outside the home, economic development will be thwarted.

Corollary 1A: With expanding dominance of the economic institution, increasing economic resources will increasingly become a major goal of religious associations.

The assumption is that religion cannot be dominant without a strong family system. Non-home-centered faiths have stronger organizational bureaucracies and so can oppose economic development more effectively. When a religious bureaucracy is established, it develops its own interests apart from the family-kinship system, and so is likely to obstruct change that is likely to realign the institutional dominance in the society in ways that are unfavorable to religion. Families, on the other hand, are more likely to perceive that the gains of economic development outweigh the costs associated with it. Thus, if the family is a dominant societal institution but religion is not, it is not expected that economic development would be so thwarted.

The rationale for Corollary 1 is that after economic dominance is established, religious associations, like all associations, find their interests increasingly centered on economic concerns. Under these conditions, economic values and norms infuse all areas of social life and thus shape the functioning of the various societal institutions.

Hypothesis 2: The greater the overlap of familial and religious networks, the lower the rate of deviance.

Both family and religion have well-known functions in the realm of social control. Other things being equal, the socialization processes of families and religious associations, when working consistently together, would guarantee fewer instances of deviant behavior and greater social control over potentially deviant individuals than would be the case if there were little or no network overlap.

Hypothesis 3: To the extent that religious associations in the societies of the former Soviet Union do not foster the strengthening of families and ally themselves with families, the ability of the religious institution to influence other societal institutions will be lessened.

In the countries of the former Soviet Union, religious associations have to be reconstituted and strengthened in substantial ways, and the primary means to do so is to get families on their side. Families are best equipped to carry out the massive, necessary job of resocializing the population in the whole range of religious knowledge and attitudes. The bigger and more committed the religious constituency, the more influence religious associations may wield in a society. In addition, because everyday life under communism was disrupted in many ways, family problems are prominent in these countries today. By effectively addressing these problems, religious associations would satisfy an important societal need, and so would even further raise their prestige and authority vis-à-vis other societal institutions.

> *Hypothesis 4:* When religioethnic groups are at odds, the conflict is more likely to be long term and internecine when the opposing groups have strong family networks.

Beisinger (1991) pointed out that violent protests require fewer organizational resources than do nonviolent ones. Family and kin networks provide relatively cheap resources that are accessible even to relatively resource-poor religioethnic groups. Intergenerational socialization continually reinforces conflict orientations and makes the conflict endemic.

> *Hypothesis 5:* Religious associations with strong political motivations will be more likely to mount campaigns emphasizing family values than will other associations with strong political aspirations.

Religious associations are likely to have political motivations when they perceive that the state is trying to take over prerogatives—usually in the area of the family—that they thought were theirs in the past. In the ensuing political struggle, religious associations, in contrast to political, economic, or other associations, are likely to emphasize family values for two reasons. First, the family is critical to the functional viability of religious associations, so these associations necessarily are concerned about any changes in the family. Second, religious authority as it applies to the definition of family relationships is being usurped by the state. Thus, contention over family values becomes the medium for the conflict between religion and the state.

Examples of state infringements on the religiofamilial domain include regulations related to abortion, official recognition of gay and lesbian couples, and parents' right to discipline their children physically as they see fit.

> *Hypothesis 6:* Religious associations in religiously pluralistic societies will be more likely to mount campaigns emphasizing family values than will religious associations in religiously monopolistic societies.

Because of religion's major role in defining relationships within the family, the family is a field of competition for the religious marketplace. Family-values campaigns can be considered advertising and merchandizing strategies that are carried out by religious firms-associations in their attempt to gain a market share in pluralistic societies. When the religious sphere is monopolized by a single association, there is little need to wage such a campaign, except when a religious monopoly is contending for authority with the state, as in several Muslim countries in the Middle East. The reasoning for the exception is found in the rationale for Hypothesis 5.

Hypothesis 7: The more rapid the rate of social change in societies, the more likely the religious institution will transform in response to changes in the family institution than that the family institution will transform in response to changes in the religious institution.

Under conditions of rapid social change, families are the first to experience the direct impact of transformations in the educational and economic spheres. Religious associations will respond to these changes in families and adapt to them (cf. Ammerman and Roof 1995), though not without some resistance. When the economic institution is dominant, there are few ways in which religious associations can affect changes in the family institution. The essential principle here is that religious associations need families more than families need religious associations. (The reasoning for this assertion was elaborated earlier in this chapter.)

Hypothesis 8: With increasing dominance of the economic institution, religion's role in shaping family relationships will decline.

The point of Hypothesis 7 is that religion changes in response to the family because religion needs the family. Despite the efforts of religion to accommodate, though, with increasing economic dominance, the family grows ever further apart from formal religious associations.

In significant measure, the family is an economic unit. It is a unit of consumption in modernized societies, and, historically, it was a unit of production. As the economy has grown in dominance, the consumption function has become more and more central to families and has profoundly transformed them. The transformation of the production role to an individualistic one has had an enormous impact on the family as well.

Although religious associations have made efforts to accommodate to these changes in the family, the accommodations have not kept stride with family needs. Religious values and norms have less and less to say about the everyday activities of families. Merely resorting to traditional religious formulas is out of sync with today's situation. In short, as economic influences have come to dominate family functions, the influence of religious values and norms in shaping family relationships has grown increasingly narrow.

Corollary 8A: As economic dominance increases and religion's role in shaping family relationships narrows, there will be an increase in family-values campaigns mounted by religious entrepreneurs.

This corollary reminds us that religion and family are closely intertwined, even when there is a fairly narrow range for intimate connections. This range is both important for religion and rich in its bounty for the entrepreneurs who choose to exploit it. Family-values campaigns tend to stimulate adherence by sincere and committed participants. Even highly differentiated societies provide the locale for exciting relations between the institutions of religion and family.

> *Hypothesis 9:* The more success religious entrepreneurs have in family-values campaigns, the more likely they will attempt to extend their power into nonreligious realms, especially economics and politics.

In the United States, we have become familiar with religious evangelists with political aspirations. Basing their activities first in family-values campaigns, they use the success of these campaigns to launch platforms for broader political careers. As the activities of Pat Robertson and his Christian Coalition, to name a well-known recent example, suggest, one may amass significant political power starting from a family-centered religious base and, in the process, amass wealth. In a similar way, as we previously suggested, the revolutionary leadership of the Ayatollah Khomeini—however many other aspects of his appeal one might highlight—had components of family-values campaigning that provided a strong base of commitment for the broader revolution in Iran. These two examples suggest the potency of the relationship between religion and family in the modern age. Even if the range for interrelating narrows, these two institutions will continue to give evidence of dynamism that will have broad societal consequences.

CONCLUSION

Whether religious and familial patterns are centered on the private sphere or more overtly integrated into sociopolitical and economic structures, the vectors of change in a society are built upon a lattice that includes elements of religion and family. It would be folly to ignore their roles, especially in a world so rapidly changing as ours. Whether we are interested in the determinants, the processes, or the directions and consequences of social change in societies (cf. Haferkamp and Smelser 1992), we must have comparative and historical analyses and consider a large array of possible institutional arrangements and interrelations. We hope that this chapter stimulates further research and critical thinking about the vital, but often neglected, family-religion linkage. Religious and familial patterns have had and continue to have great relevance for social change.

NOTES

1. Hart (1996) came to much the same conclusion about the politics of economic issues in the United States after a careful investigation of the economic ideas of members of religious groups.
2. Swatos (1977) argued that the sociology of religion has a particular need for comparative research approaches.

3. In this regard, Berger (1969:62) stated:

   > The individual finds his ancestors continuing mysteriously within himself, and in the same way he projects his own being into his children and later descendants. As a result, he acquires a (to him) quite concrete immortality, which drastically relativizes the mortality as well as the lesser misfortunes of his empirical biography.

4. The analysis of religious phenomena was central to classical sociology. However, as Hechter (1994:147) stated, "Considering its exalted and special position in classical sociological theory, the study of religion holds a surprisingly marginal status in present-day American sociology." We were given surprisingly vivid evidence of this fact recently when a colleague from a major research university recounted the findings of his informal review of the syllabi used in the introductory sociology course, often taught by graduate teaching assistants. Most instructors used regular introductory textbooks that have a fairly standardized outline that includes a series of chapters, each of which is devoted to a specific institution or realm of social behavior. The colleague found that the chapter on religion was the one that the instructors most often omitted from their syllabi. Apparently, either the instructors thought that this topic was the least important of the ones with chapters in the textbook, or they felt least competent to teach this subject because of lack of exposure to it in their own course work and study.
5. There is another side to this story, in which the church and religious institutions of learning were actually liberating in important ways. Indeed, the origin of modern learning in the West is deeply rooted in the theological and philosophical soil of religious culture—Catholic, Protestant, Jewish, or Islamic.
6. Wuthnow (1985) saw the roots of social science's neglect of religion in its own insecurities related to its immaturity as a scientific discipline.
7. Among the contributors to Young's (1997) compendium are the major articulators of this approach (who are discussed later in relation to the interests of this volume). In their articles, they provide a careful explication and defense of the rational-choice perspective on religion. Other articles in this extraordinary book develop a series of thoughtful criticisms of the perspective.
8. Warner (1993, 1997) was explicit about the fact that his initial enthusiasm for the "new paradigm" was related to its application to the United States. He warned that the applicability of this paradigm to other countries is not obvious and suggested that one must be cautious in trying to use it in analyses of other religious markets. Hadden (1995, 1996) advocated comparative studies using the paradigm to put it to the test. Although this book does not pursue that agenda systematically—it has a broader set of goals for examining the religion-family linkage comparatively—it makes some progress along the lines of that agenda.
9. Becker (1973, 1974, 1976, 1981; Becker, Landes, and Michael 1977), an economist, has been the most deliberate in applying analytical tools from economics to family matters. (His impact on the religious-economy approach was acknowledged by Iannoccone 1997.) Others who have used economic analytical tools in studies of aspects of families that are not formally economic include Grossbard (1978), Huber and Spitze (1980) and Johnson (1980).
10. In the religious economies approach, it is fairly obvious what the "firms" that are seeking market penetration and market share are. They are the churches, denominations, sects, cults, missionary societies, parachurch organizations, and the like, that populate the religious landscape. Prominent religious figures fill the role of entrepreneur in their respective religious movements. In imagining the nature of the familial economy, it is difficult to identify a direct analogue for firms, though one may posit that familial subcultures, which support particular

variants of family structure over others, are, in some sense, in this position. Perhaps kinship structures could fill this role, as well; as we already indicated, functionalist theorists considered extended kinship structures to be especially vulnerable to modernization and thus likely to lose their functions in modern societies. Acting as "firms," these kinship structures can be seen as devising various market strategies to preserve and enlarge their place (cf., Houseknecht and Nagi 1996). Nevertheless, there is a much weaker notion of what firms may be in the sociology of the family, and it is difficult to identify any component like the entrepreneur in this sphere without stretching the analogy too far. Even without clear firms and entrepreneurs, however, we can profitably use some of the concepts of the market approach to develop numerous insights.

(We would locate the leaders of the "pro-family" movement in the religious institution, though their primary religious focus is on family matters. They certainly can be seen as religious entrepreneurs, but one may entertain an argument that classifies them as family entrepreneurs, who lead movements to promote a given family form or pattern.)

11. Politics may dominate a contemporary society. For example, some analysts have argued that communist countries were dominated by the political institution of bureaucratic communism and thus did not remain adaptive to major changes in the economy of the world. This economic maladapation is seen as the root cause of the breakup of the Soviet Union and its loss of control over the countries of Eastern Europe. According to this view, successful reform, involving the freeing up of economic forces through privatization, is vital to the viability of post-Soviet nations. China's continuing vitality arises, it would be argued, from its freeing up of economic forces, even though it has not dropped the governmental control of communism. Seen this way, the Party in China has taken a lead in promoting the differentiation (at least, compared to the recent past) of the economy from the polity. In this volume, Chapter 3 argues that the military-bureaucratic regime and religion are in a profound struggle with each other for institutional dominance in Egypt today.
12. We have not been able to do justice to the theme of globalization in this chapter, but it has never been far beneath the surface of our thinking. Even in studies of discrete societies, as in the chapters in this book, there is no possibility of omitting a consideration of global influences and the consequences of globalization for identity. A quick review of the topics in the book indicates the relevance of globalization processes. Several chapters (especially Chapter 9, French Mormonism) provide insights based on globalization theory. For the present purposes, the key reference works in this area are those by Beyer (1994) and Robertson (1992).

References

Alexander, Jeffrey C., and Paul Colomy, eds. 1990. *Differentiation Theory and Social Change: Comparative and Historical Perspectives.* New York: Columbia University Press.

Ammerman, Nancy. 1997. "Religious Choice and Religious Vitality: The Market and Beyond." Pp. 119–32 in Rational Choice Theory and Religion: Summary and Assessment, edited by Lawrence A. Young. New York: Alfred A. Knopf.

Ammerman, Nancy Tatom, and Wade Clark Roof, eds. 1995. *Work, Family, and Religion in Contemporary Society.* New York: Routledge.

Becker, Gary S. 1973. "A Theory of Marriage: Part I." *Journal of Political Economy* 81:413–46.

———. 1974. "A Theory of Marriage: Part II." *Journal of Political Economy* 82: 511–26.

———. 1976. *The Economic Approach to Human Behavior*. Chicago: University of Chicago Press.

———. 1981. *A Treatise on the Family*. Cambridge, MA: Harvard University Press.

Becker, Gary S., Elisabeth M. Landes, and Robert T. Michael. 1977. "An Economic Analysis of Marital Instability." *Journal of Political Economy* 85:1141–87.

Beckford, James A. 1989. *Religion and Advanced Industrial Society*. London: Unwin Hyman.

Beisinger, Mark. 1991. "Protest and Mobilization Among Soviet Nationalities." Paper presented at the Annual Meeting of the American Sociological Association, Cincinnati.

Berger, Peter L. 1967. "Religious Institutions." Pp. 329–79 in *Sociology: An Introduction*, edited by Neil J. Smelser. New York: John Wiley & Sons.

———. 1969. *The Sacred Canopy: Elements of a Sociological Theory of Religion*. Garden City, NY: Doubleday Anchor Books.

Berryman, Phillip. 1987. *Liberation Theology: The Essential Facts About the Revolutionary Movement in Latin America*. New York: Pantheon Books.

Beyer, Peter. 1994. *Religion and Globalization*. London: Sage.

Carroll, Michael P. 1996. "Stark Realities and Androcentric/Eurocentric Bias in the the Sociology of Religion." *Sociology of Religion* 57:225–39.

Carter, Lewis F., ed. 1996. *The Issue of Authenticity in the Study of Religions* (Religion and the Social Order Series, Vol. 6). Greenwich, CT: JAI Press.

Casanova, José. 1994. *Public Religions in the Modern World*. Chicago: University of Chicago Press.

Chaves, Mark. 1995. "On the Rational Choice Approach to Religion." *Journal for the Scientific Study of Religion* 34:98–104.

Cherlin, Andrew. 1996. *Public and Private Families: An Introduction*. New York: McGraw-Hill.

Cochran, Clarke E. 1990. *Religion in Public and Private Life*. New York: Routledge.

Cousineau, Madeleine, ed. 1998. *Religion in a Changing World: Comparative Studies in Sociology*. Westport, CT: Praeger.

Dahrendorf, Ralf. 1959. *Class and Class Conflict in Industrial Society*. Stanford, CA: Stanford University Press.

D'Antonio, William V., and Joan Aldous, eds. 1983. *Families and Religions: Conflict and Change in Modern Society*. Beverly Hills, CA: Sage.

D'Antonio, William V., William A. Newman, and Stuart A. Wright. 1982. "Religion and Family Life: How Social Scientists View the Relationship." *Journal for the Scientific Study of Religion* 21:218–25.

Demerath, N. J., III. 1995. "Rational Paradigms, A-Rational Religion, and the Debate Over Secularization." *Journal for the Scientific Study of Religion* 34:105–12.

Demos, John. 1970. *A Little Commonwealth: Family Life in Plymouth Colony*. Oxford, England: Oxford University Press.

Durkheim, Emile. 1973. *Emile Durkheim: On Morality and Society*, edited by Robert Bellah. Chicago: University of Chicago Press.

Ellison, Christopher G. 1995. "Rational Choice Explanations of Individual Religious Behavior: Notes on the Problem of Social Embeddedness." *Journal for the Scientific Study of Religion* 34:89–97.

Engels, Frederick. [1884, 1891] 1973. *The Origin of the Family, Private Property and the State*. New York: International Publishers.

Finke, Roger, and Rodney Stark. 1992. *The Churching of America, 1776–1990: Winners and Losers in Our Religious Economy*. New Brunswick, NJ: Rutgers University Press.

Geiger, H. Kent. 1968. *The Family in Soviet Russia*. Cambridge: Harvard University Press.

Gouldner, Alvin W., and Helen P. Gouldner. 1963. *Modern Sociology: An Introduction to the Study of Human Interaction*. New York: Harcourt, Brace & World.

Greeley, Andrew M. 1989. *Religious Change in America*. Cambridge, MA: Harvard University Press.

———. 1992. "Religion in Britain, Ireland and the USA." Pp. 51–70 in *British Social Attitudes: The 9th Report*, edited by R. Jowell, L. Brook, G. Prior, and B. Taylor. Brookfield, VT: Dartmouth Publishing.

Grossbard, Amyra. 1978. "Towards a Marriage Between Economics and Anthropology and a General Theory of Marriage." *American Economic Review* 68:33–37.

Hadden, Jeffrey K. 1987. "Toward Desacralizing Secularization Theory." *Social Forces* 65:587–11.

———. 1995. "Religion and the Quest for Meaning and Order: Old Paradigms, New Realities." *Sociological Focus* 28:83–100.

———. 1996. "Foreword." Pp. 5–8 in the paperback edition of *A Theory of Religion* by Rodney Stark and William Sims Bainbridge. New Brunswick, NJ: Rutgers University Press.

Hadden, Jeffrey K., and Anson Shupe. 1986. "Introduction." Pp. xi–xxix in *Prophetic Religions and Politics: Religion and the Political Order* (Vol. 1), edited by Jeffrey K. Hadden and Anson Shupe. New York: Paragon House.

Haferkamp, Hans, and Neil J. Smelser, eds. 1992. *Social Change and Modernity*. Berkeley: University of California Press.

Hammond, Phillip E., ed. 1985. *The Sacred in a Secular Age: Toward Revision in the Scientific Study of Religion*. Berkeley: University of California Press.

Hargrove, Barbara. 1979. *The Sociology of Religion: Classical and Contemporary Approaches*. Arlington Heights, IL: AHM.

———. 1985. "Gender, the Family, and the Sacred." Pp. 204–14 in *The Sacred in a Secular Age: Toward Revision in the Scientific Study of Religion*, edited by Phillip E. Hammond. Berkeley: University of California Press.

Hart, Stephen. 1996. *What Does the Lord Require: How American Christians Think about Economic Justice*. (1st paperback ed.). New Brunswick, NJ: Rutgers University Press.

Hechter, Michael. 1997. "Religion and Rational Choice Theory." Pp. 147–159 in *Rational Choice Theory and Religion*, edited by Lawrence A. Young. New York: Routledge.

Houseknecht, Sharon K., and Saad Z. Nagi. 1996. "The Struggle for Power Between Family and Government: A Dimension of Political Modernization." *International Journal of Contemporary Sociology* 33:7–26.

Huber, Joan, and Glenna Spitze. 1980. "Considering Divorce: An Expansion of Becker's Theory of Marital Instability." *American Journal of Sociology* 86:75–89.

Iannaccone, Laurence R. 1995. "Voodoo Economics? Reviewing the Rational Choice Approach to Religion." *Journal for the Scientific Study of Religion* 34:76–89.

———. 1997. "Rational Choice: Framework for the Scientific Study of Religion." Pp. 25–45 in *Rational Choice Theory and Religion: Summary and Assessment*, edited by Lawrence A. Young. New York: Routledge.

Johnson, Robert Alan. 1980. *Religious Assortative Marriage in the United States*. New York: Academic Press.

Lasch, Christopher. 1977. *Haven in a Heartless World: The Family Beseiged*. New York: Basic Books.

Linzer, Stephen. 1997a. "A Cleric's Tolerant Orthodoxy Wins." *New York Times*, May 25, p. 10.

———. 1997b. "Many Iranians Hope Mandate Brings Change." *New York Times*, May 26, pp. A1, A4.

Luckmann, Thomas. 1967. *The Invisible Religion*. New York: Macmillan.

———. 1991. "The New and the Old in Religion." Pp. 167–82 in *Social Theory for a Changing Society* edited by Pierre Bourdieu and James S. Coleman. Boulder, CO/New York: Westview Press/Russell Sage Foundation.

MacIver, Robert M. 1970. *On Community, Society and Power*. Chicago: University of Chicago Press.

Martin, David. 1990. *Tongues of Fire: The Explosion of Protestantism in Latin America*. Oxford, England: Basil Blackwell.

Marty, Martin E. 1993. Review of *The Churching of America, 1776–1990: Winners and Losers in Our Religious Economy* (Rutgers University Press, 1992). *Christian Century*, January 27, p. 88.

Marty, Martin E., and R. Scott Appleby. 1995. *The Fundamentalism Project*. Chicago: University of Chicago Press.

Marx, Karl, and Friedrich Engels. 1964. *On Religion*. New York: Schocken Books.

Mead, Margaret. [1977]1980. "Can the American Family Survive?" Pp. 534–43 in *Marriage and Family in a Changing Society*, edited by James M. Henslin. New York: Free Press.

Misztal, Bronislaw, and Anson Shupe, eds. 1992. *Religion and Politics in Comparative Perspective: Revival of Religious Fundamentalism in East and West*. Westport, CT: Praeger.

Moore, Wilbert E. 1963. *Social Change*. Englewood Cliffs, NJ: Prentice-Hall.

Neitz, Mary Jo, and Peter R. Mueser. 1997. "Economic Man and the Sociology of Religion: A Critique of the Rational Choice Approach." Pp. 105–18 in *Rational Choice Theory and Religion: Summary and Assessment*, edited by Lawrence A. Young. New York: Routledge.

Nisbet, Robert A. 1970. *The Social Bond: An Introduction to the Study of Society*. New York: Alfred A. Knopf.

Pankhurst, Jerry G. 1988. "The Sacred and the Secular in the USSR." Pp. 167–92 in *Understanding Soviet Society*, edited by M. P. Sacks and J. G. Pankhurst. Boston: Unwin Hyman.

———. 1998. "Russia's Religious Market: Struggling with the Heritage of Russian Orthodox Monopoly." Pp. 129–37 in *Religion in a Changing World: Comparative Studies in Sociology*, edited by Madeleine Cousineau. Westport, CT: Praeger.

Pankhurst, Jerry G., and Sharon K. Houseknecht. 1983. "The Family, Politics and Religion in the 1980s: In Fear of the New Individualism." *Journal of Family Issues* 4:5–34.

Popenoe, David. 1988. *Disturbing the Nest: Family Change and Decline in Modern Societies*. New York: Aldine de Gruyter.

Roberts, Richard H., ed. 1995. *Religion and the Transformations of Capitalism: Comparative Approaches*. London: Routledge.

Robertson, Roland. 1992. *Globalization: Social Theory and Global Culture*. London: Sage.

Roof, Wade Clark. 1993. *A Generation of Seekers: The Spiritual Journey of the Baby Boom Generation*. New York: Harper SanFrancisco.

Rubenstein, Richard L., ed. 1987. *Spirit Matters: The Worldwide Impact of Religion on Contemporary Politics*. New York: Paragon House.

Settles, Barbara H. 1996. "The International Study of Families and Rapid Social Change: Issues for Family Sociologists and their Professional Organizations." Paper presented at the Annual Meeting of the American Sociological Association, August 16–20, New York.

Sherkat, Darren E. 1997. "Embedding Religious Choices: Integrating Preferences and Social Constraints into Rational Choice Theories of Religious Behavior." Pp. 65–86 in *Rational Choice Theory and Religion: Summary and Assessment*, edited by Lawrence A. Young. New York: Routledge.

Shupe, Anson, and Bronislaw Misztal, eds. 1998. *Religion, Mobilization, and Social Action*. Westport, CT: Praeger.

Smith, Christian. 1991. *The Emergence of Liberation Theology: Radical Religion and Social Movement Theory*. Chicago: University of Chicago Press.

Sorokin, Pitirim A. 1956. *Fads and Foibles in Modern Sociology and Related Social Sciences*. Chicago: Regnery.

Spickard, James V. 1998. "Rethinking Religious Social Action: What is 'Rational' About Rational Choice Theory?" *Sociology of Religion* 59:99–115.

Stark, Rodney, and William Sims Bainbridge. 1987. *A Theory of Religion*. New York: Peter Lang.

Swatos, William H. 1977. "The Comparative Method and the Special Vocation of the Sociology of Religion." *Sociological Analysis* 38:106–14.

———, ed. 1992. *Twentieth-Century World Religious Movements in Neo-Weberian Perspective*. Lewiston, NY: Edwin Mellen Press.

Theodorson, George A., and Achilles G. Theodorson. 1979. *A Modern Dictionary of Sociology*. New York: Barnes & Noble Books.

Thomas, Darwin L., ed. 1988. *The Religion and Family Connection: Social Science Perspectives*. Provo, UT: Religious Studies Center, Brigham Young University

Thomas, Darwin L., and Marie Cornwall. 1990. "Religion and Family in the 1980s: Discovery and Development." *Journal of Marriage and the Family* 52:983–92.

Thomas, Darwin L., and Gwendolyn C. Henry. 1985. "The Religion and Family Connection: Increasing Dialogue in the Social Sciences." *Journal of Marriage and the Family* 47:369–79.

Thornton, Arland. 1985. "Reciprocal Influences of Family and Religion in a Changing World." *Journal of Marriage and the Family* 47:381–94.

Troeltsch, Ernst. 1931. *The Social Teachings of the Christian Churches*. New York: Macmillan.

Vago, Steven. 1989. *Social Change* (2nd ed.). Englewood Cliffs, NJ: Prentice-Hall.

Wald, Kenneth. 1986. *Religion and Politics in the United States*. New York: St. Martin's Press.

Warner, Stephen R. 1993. "Work in Progress Toward a New Paradigm for the Sociological Study of Religion in the United States." *American Journal of Sociology* 98:1044–93.

———. 1997. "Convergence Toward the New Paradigm: A Case of Induction." Pp. 87–101 in *Rational Choice Theory and Religion: Summary and Assessment*, edited by Lawrence A. Young. New York: Routledge.

Weber, Max. [1920] 1958. *The Protestant Ethic and the Spirit of Capitalism*, translated by Talcott Parsons. New York: Charles Scribner's Sons.

Weber, Max. [1922] 1963. *The Sociology of Religion*. Boston: Beacon Press.

Williams, Robin M., Jr. [1955] 1970. *American Society: A Sociological Interpretation*. (3rd ed.). New York: Alfred A. Knopf.

Witte, John, Jr., ed. 1993. *Christianity and Democracy in Global Context*. Boulder, CO: Westview Press.

Wuthnow, Robert. 1985. "Science and the Sacred." Pp. 187–203 in *The Sacred in a Secular Age: Toward Revision in the Scientific Study of Religion*, edited by Phillip E. Hammond. Berkeley: University of California Press.

———. 1994a. *Producing the Sacred: An Essay on Public Religion*. Urbana: University of Illinois Press.

———. 1994b. "Religion and Economic Life." Pp. 620–46 in *The Handbook of Economic Sociology*, edited by Neil J. Smelser and Richard Swedberg. Princeton, NJ: Princeton University Press.

———. 1994c. *Sharing the Journey: Support Groups and America's New Quest for Community*. New York: Free Press.

Young, Lawrence A., ed. 1997. *Rational Choice Theory and Religion: Summary and Assessment*. New York: Routledge.

PART I

Societal Conflict and Accommodation

C H A P T E R   T W O

Religion and the Family in Modern American Culture

KEVIN J. CHRISTIANO

INTRODUCTION: A RELATIONSHIP OF RECIPROCITY

The standing of religion in American society is tied directly to the fate of certain forms and functions of the family. The reasons for this connection are not hard to specify. As Hart (1986:51–52) wrote, the "institutional roles" of families and religion have "many parallels":

> Both provide values; both provide a context where one is valued (more than elsewhere) as a whole person rather than on the basis of specific contributions; both provide companionship, support, and non-material pleasures; both help people who do not find much meaning in their work lives feel that their lives are meaningful; and both provide a framework for seeing oneself as a good person and one's life as basically good, independent of the success that one has in acquiring money, fame or power. Both are "private" spheres in contrast to work or politics and one's relation to the state, and as such are felt to be spheres of individual autonomy and dignity, free of the constraints one's job or government imposes.

Furthermore, the close relationship of religion and the family is of long duration. As Moran (1992:12) remarked modestly in an overview of historical writing on the Puritan family in early America, "the life of the family and the life of the spirit have intersected at numerous points" (cf. Thornton 1985). Families, after all, bring potential religious adherents into the world; give them their initial exposure to questions of faith; and, in most instances, dispatch young believers to more formal instruction and to services on the sabbath.

It is also true that families depend on religious institutions for the legitimation of customs, for the nurture and guidance of young people, for the regulation of sexual conduct and marriage, and for support—both emotional and material—in times of strain or crisis. Throughout the past, "families often behaved with religious strategies and goals in mind, while the church grew because of the initiatives of successive generations of pious householders," Moran (1992:45) asserted. "Moreover," he continued, "communal life was played out along networks that often centered in the church, and people dealt with dying in ways established and conditioned by religion" (p. 45).

Today, the effects of this record of reinforcement are obvious to any who care to notice. "Although the authority of churches over the decisions and behavior of individuals may have declined," Thornton (1985:386) observed, "religion still influences family behavior, as witnessed by the continuing differentials in family structure and behavior associated with different religious groups." From a more theoretical vantage, D'Antonio (1983:102) concurred, stating, "Religion, or more precisely religiosity, does predict differences in attitudes and behavior regarding such phenomena as interreligious marriage, fertility, abortion, premarital sex, and divorce."

The importance of the relationship between religion and the family for a proper understanding of both social institutions is underscored by a renewed professional interest in research on their mutual influences.[1] New inquiries have addressed numerous gaps in social scientific knowledge that are found at the intersections of subdisciplines (D'Antonio 1980; Thomas 1988; Thomas and Henry 1985).

Although the authors of studies that tracked the development of this hybrid field (see, for example, D'Antonio, Newman, and Wright 1982; Thomas and Cornwall 1990) conceded candidly that there are areas of enduring neglect (as well as ones in which academic emphasis is misplaced),[2] they also documented a rising level of published scholarship on the connection between religious beliefs and practices, on the one hand, and salient elements of family life, on the other hand. For example, the number of articles that treated religious and familial variables together in a flagship journal of family studies, the *Journal of Marriage and the Family*, increased by more than 50 percent from the first to the second half of the 1980s (Thomas and Cornwall 1990:984).

Such studies revealed that religious norms often influence the manner and timing of dating and marriage and, in some cases, dictate approaches to the bearing and rearing of children, as well as attitudes about the conditions under which marital bonds can and ought to be dissolved. Religions and families are related, then, as two institutions that occupy, and in some senses govern, the realm of personal intimacy for modern Americans. In addition, families are a usual locus for the process of socialization into a religious faith. Many families still attend worship services as a unit, while the home is another setting for ritual devotion, and events that occur there are principal occasions for the moral training of children.

Churches recognize this reliance and so lend strong support to a continuing search for stability in family patterns. Formal religious practice is replete with references to symbols of divine favor for familial harmony. Moreover, this campaign has taken on broader political tones as a movement for the reintroduction of "traditional family values" in the United States. The state of the American family has thus become a fulcrum for efforts to pry from the national establishment further power for what has been termed the "new Christian Right."

This chapter examines these and other developments in the relationship between religions and families in the United States. To begin, the examination assumes a historical perspective, returning the reader to the much-depicted world of the New England Puritans. Then it follows the link between the religious and the familial that the early Americans forged well into the nineteenth century, when a distinctive "domestic Christianity" was created in the middle-class American home. Next, the narrative describes the role of religion in entrenching familism as a dominant ideology of the twentieth century.

In the contemporary period, the chapter surveys the means by which the faiths of individuals influence their marital attachments. It assesses the degree to which married couples follow traditional religious expectations for fertility or its limitation. It then discusses research on the effectiveness of attempts to use the family as the main agent for religious indoctrination of the young. It also offers a brief look at the centrality of the family (albeit in various shapes) to ideologies framed by new religious movements that have operated in the United States for decades. Finally, it traces the course of debates that have propelled "family values" out of the domestic sphere and into the political arena.

PIETY AND DOMESTICITY: A BRIEF HISTORY

In American society, the family and religion have been joined from the earliest stages of European contact. Historians of the colonial era in the New World have recounted how the first English settlers of North America used their religious convictions to arrange both the major themes and the minute details of their domestic lives. From the seventeenth-century pulpit, interpersonal commitments were likened to episodes of religious conversion, and betrothal to another was compared to a believer's fidelity to the Lord. (Taking these appeals to heart, some early Americans even came to regard marital love and love for God as competing impulses.)

Such similes worked in both causal directions to strengthen the natural nexus between the institutions of religion and the family. Morgan (1966:166), the eminent historian, summarized the relationship concisely with his comment that the metaphor of church as family "seems to have dominated Puritan thought so completely as to suggest that the Puritans' religious experiences in some way duplicated their domestic experiences." Moreover, the attachment to which Morgan referred was as symmetrical a one as social structures predictably yield. The Puritans, added Moran (1992:13; see also Greven 1977), "not only clothed piety with ideas taken from household experience but also invested family life with religious values. Each sphere supplied codes for interpreting acts played out in the other sphere."

This pattern of fluid reciprocity between religion and the family continued well after the founding of the United States (Booth, Johnson, Branaman, and Sica 1995). Indeed, among both Protestants and Catholics in the new nation, it flourished later in a somewhat different form: the fusion of the heavenly and the homespun in a carefully constructed cult of domestic Christianity.[3] This movement endeavored to make the home, according to the words of one of its advocates, "a bright temple filled with the light of God's presence, blessed and protected by God's visiting angels, and fragrant with the odor of paradise." A prominent theologian of the nineteenth century, Horace Bushnell, insisted that a Christian household "should become the church of childhood, the table and hearth of a holy rite" (quoted in McDannell 1986:xiii and 48).

Thus, under this conception of religion, every abode would be established as an unconsecrated house of worship, and every family would be transformed into an unofficial congregation. The family, faithful Protestants were taught, "is as strictly a religious institution as the Church"; Catholics, for their part, were told to emulate the Holy Family of Jesus Christ and change their homes into "a second Nazareth" (quoted in McDannell 1986:77 and 122). Therefore, "like the church," McDannell (p. xiii), argued, in nineteenth-century American culture, "the home (as both a physical space and a kinship structure) promoted a religious perspective" (see also Browning, Miller-McLemore, Couture, Lyon, and Franklin 1997:84–92).

FAITH OF AND FAITH IN OUR FATHERS AND MOTHERS: FAMILISM IN TWENTIETH-CENTURY AMERICAN RELIGION

The logical product of an orientation in which the mundane activity of the domestic world was merged with the reverence that is customarily reserved for religion is the ideology called familism. This belief holds that throughout human history, the family has been the fundamental component of a civilized society. Right individual behavior and sound collective organization, in this view, depend alike on the family for the very possibility of their existence.

In the service of familism, religious promoters of domestic life have gone as far as to preach that the traditional family is a design ordained by God for the spiritual discipline of human beings and the accomplishment of divine will on earth. A clerical booster (quoted in McDannell 1986:1), for example, counted the family as one of the "two institutions that have come down to us from Eden to perpetuate some of its purity and peace." (The other, incidentally, was Protestant-style observance of the sabbath.)

In its subsidiary formulations, familism encourages premarital sexual restraint, dedication to one's partner in a lifelong marital covenant, procreation, and the vigorous raising of children who are subject absolutely to parental (especially paternal) authority (D'Antonio 1983). All these values suggest, in addition, that, over time, religion and the family have come to occupy contiguous spaces on the private side of social experience. That is, the abundant attention that churches bestow, through their rhetoric and programs, on the condition of the family in society is not a coincidence, for reasons that Berger (1967a:373) explained:

> As we might expect from the similar fate undergone by the institutions of religion and family in industrial society, religion has found itself in a state of social "proximity" to the family in the private sphere. The family is the institutional area in which traditional religious symbols continue to have the most relevance in actual everyday living. In turn, the family has become for the religious institutions the main "target area" for their social strategy. This affinity between the two institutions—both "victims" of the process of privatization—has expressed itself clearly in the emergent ideological configuration common to both: the ideology of familism. Broadly speaking, this is a set of both cognitive and normative assertions that interpret the family as *the* crucial social institution, both for the individual and for society as a whole. (emphasis in the original)

Whether from strategic intention or functional necessity, organized religion in the United States more and more is staking its claims to significance squarely in the middle of the most personal affairs of individuals.

In the United States, evidence from sample surveys and observational studies of modern communities appears to confirm the persistence of ties between religious commitment and family life that one would expect in a culture in which familism has remained a plainly operative ideology. A prime example of this viability can be discovered in data that were collected for the Middletown III project (see Caplow, Bahr, Chadwick, Hill, and Williamson 1982; Caplow, Bahr, Chadwick, and Hoover 1983). Middletown III was a return visit to a bellwether American town (Muncie, Indiana) a half-century after it was twice probed by the pioneering husband-and-wife team of Lynd and Lynd (1929, 1937) around the time of the Great Depression.

In the 1920s and 1930s, residents of Middletown (as Muncie was dubbed for the original studies) believed the family to be the institutional bedrock of a God-fearing community. Ideally, for them, the family took a conventional shape: It was "monogamous, fertile, permanent, and child valuing" (Caplow et al. 1982:249).

By the 1970s, when a new group of researchers canvassed family sentiment in Middletown, little in this portrait of preferences had shifted. Yet some slippage in social pressures toward conformity had occurred. For one thing, compared to the original findings, fewer of the adolescents to whom the third wave of interviewers spoke professed a conviction that "being an active church member" was one of the most desirable traits to distinguish a parent. And fewer of them reported friction with their own parents over expectations of attendance at church services (Caplow et al. 1982).

Nevertheless, the latest study also revealed strong signs of continuity in how Middletown families approached religious practice. Numerous married women in both 1924 and 1978 confessed that they participated in worship out of habit and because they saw some gain in their actions for their children. Indeed, references to a presumed benefit to children were actually *more* common at the later date. The same respondents were, in turn, less inclined than earlier ones to stress purely social or business-related motives for church attendance (Caplow et al. 1982).

Survey data from the Middletown replication also testify to the tenacity of traditional familism and the lasting quality of its relation to religious affiliation and action. Fifty years after their first dissection by the Lynds, Middletowners still associated family norms and religious commitment. Persons in Middletown who were married and whose marriages persisted were more likely to have a clear religious preference than were those who never married or who had divorced or separated from their first spouses. Among currently married respondents, identifying with a church and attending its services also correlated with higher levels of satisfaction in the marital relationship. Finally, couples who were church adherents had more children, on average, than did those with no preference in religion (Bahr and Chadwick 1985; cf. Christiano 1986; Heaton and Goodman 1985; Heaton, Jacobson, and Fu 1992; Marler 1995; Sherkat and Wilson 1995; Stolzenberg, Blair-Loy, and Waite 1995; J. Wilson and Sandomirsky 1991; J. Wilson and Sherkat 1994).

As these results demonstrate, faiths and families in the United States maintain their historically close connection through the ideology of familism. Two of the Middletown III investigators freely conveyed their impression, drawn from more evidence than this, "that the vitality of these two institutions is related." After lengthy discussions with the typical townspeople of Muncie, they reported that "people often reaffirmed their religious faith and devotion to their families in the same conversation, many times explicitly linking the two" (Bahr and Chadwick 1985:413).

RELIGION AND THE FAMILY: INFLUENCES IN THE PRIVATE SPHERE

According to Berger (1967b), familism thrives in modern societies not *in spite of* but *because of* the segregation of religion and its relegation to the private sphere of life. In the management of intimate relations, he observed that "religion continues to have considerable 'reality' potential, that is, continues to be relevant in terms of the motives and self-interpretations of people in this sphere of everyday social activity" (p. 133). The accuracy of Berger's claim is proved in the results of sociological inquiry into three areas of private life: the conduct of modern marriages, the mediation of joint decisions about parenthood, and patterns in the socialization of children. In each domain, research confirms that religion still holds powerful sway.

Man and Woman Together: Religion's Role in Marital Relationships

Religious affiliation is a social factor that exerts measurable control over a range of thoughts and actions in marriage, from the initial choice of a nuptial partner and satisfaction in the marital relationship to the regulation of the common household and the execution of parental duties (for a summary, see Lehrer 1996).

Couples in the United States exhibit high degrees of religious homogamy, or concordance with respect to religious preference (Alston, McIntosh, and Wright 1976; Greeley 1970; Johnson 1980). Homogamy is the highest for Protestants, although a statistical artifact is partly responsible for this state. (It would be impossible for *all* Protestants, as members of the religious majority, to choose mates from outside their group.) By the late 1970s, 93 percent of married Protestant Americans had Protestants as spouses. More impressive are the findings that 88 percent of married Jews in the United States were joined to other Jews, and 82 percent of Catholics who were married shared that relationship with coreligionists. However, survey data that were collected between 1957 and 1978 suggest that religiously mixed matches were becoming more common for all categories of married persons (Glenn 1982; see also Bumpass 1970; Kalmijn 1991; McCutcheon 1988).

The smaller the religious minority and the greater the openness of the society, the more probable is a match to a partner who does not share the same affiliation—and the more potentially threatening a subsequent intermarriage would be to the survival of the group's identity. Of special concern, for this reason, is the trend toward religious exogamy among Jews in the United States. "The subject of intermarriage evokes considerable passion among Jews," one team of researchers (Medding, Tobin, Fishman, and Rimor 1992:3) wrote, "because it arouses fears about elemental issues of group survival." Indeed, "concern about intermarriage," Heilman (1995:129) reflected, "has overshadowed almost all the older outstanding Jewish concerns about political anti-Semitism and economic discrimination."

Estimates of the frequency of this practice, based on studies of Jewish communities in U.S. metropolitan areas, ranged from 11 percent in New York in 1983, through 30 percent in Denver in 1981, to about 58 percent in Kansas City in 1985 (Judd 1990:251, 261, 264; cf. Heilman 1995; Medding et al. 1992). The 1990 National Jewish Population Survey fixed the overall incidence of intermarriage at 31 percent of all persons who were born Jewish, up from 7 percent in 1971 (Goldstein 1992:126; Heilman 1995:130; Lazerwitz 1981:32–33; 1995:434, 441). But in the case of first marriages contracted by Jews since 1985, the majority (52 percent) have been to members of other religious groups (Heilman 1995:129–30; cf. DellaPergola 1991; Lazerwitz 1995).

On one level, widespread religious homogamy is the consequence of a habit of some marriageable persons to select potential mates from a pool of prospects that is defined by recognized denominational boundaries. Still, religious inmarriage is just one way to create homogamous unions.

Another way is the increasingly apparent process whereby one party to a religiously discrepant match changes his or her affiliation at or around the time of marriage to render the couple homogamous (Musick and Wilson 1995; Newport 1979). The change thus endows the partners with a joint identity that was not originally present. In remarking on the volume of religious conversions in the United States that transpire after childhood, Glenn (1982:561) insisted that "it is almost certain that much if not most of that switching, which resulted in homogamy in current denominational preference, occurred for the express purpose of achieving that homogamy." In particular, converts to Judaism, Catholicism, and Lutheranism are more likely to have made the switch to attain homogamy than for other reasons (Lazerwitz 1995; Musick and Wilson 1995).

One can probably envision why achieving religious homogamy would be an important goal for soon-to-be-married or just-married couples. "Marital companionship is enhanced when individual spirituality can be shared and is inhibited when the partners must look outside the marriage for religious intimacy," Lehrer and Chiswick (1993:386) hypothesized. They continued:

> Similarity in religious beliefs and practices of husband and wife implies that the spouses can participate jointly in religious observances both at home and in church. Religion also influences many activities beyond the purely religious sphere, including the education and upbringing of children, the allocation of time and money, the cultivation of social relationships, the development of business and professional networks, and even the choice of place of residence. Clearly, households in which the partners differ in their preferences and objectives in this area would be characterized by reduced efficiency and potentially more conflict. (p. 386)

Indeed, were shifts toward homogamy not to be made, early research predicted severe interpersonal strain, followed by a likely detriment to the couple's religious practice. Conflicts within the marriage over issues of religious identification were believed to discourage especially wives' involvement in church (Babchuk, Crockett, and Ballweg 1967; Crockett, Babchuk, and Ballweg 1969; cf. Alston et al. 1976).

Much sociological research supports these predictions. On the issue of happiness, for instance, Glenn (1982) found that the percentage of spouses who professed to be "very happy" with their marriages was the greatest in religiously homogamous unions (cf. Alston et al. 1976; Greeley 1991b; Heaton and Pratt 1990). The least happy were self-proclaimed Protestants, Catholics, or Jews who had married persons with no religious preferences.

A study of religious practices among Roman Catholic couples who resided in the Diocese of Memphis, Tennessee, further tested these predictions. L. R. Petersen (1986) first uncovered little indication that being the child of a religious outmarriage of a Catholic (when no switch reinstated homogamy) did anything to diminish religious commitment in the second generation (cf. Myers 1996). Where a religiously mixed marriage did appear to have an impact was in the conduct of the Catholic spouses themselves, but only in two areas: attendance at Mass and the receipt of Holy Communion (L. R. Petersen 1986). More specifically, Catholics who were wedded to conservative Protestants performed each behavior less frequently; marriage to a liberal Protestant, in contrast, was much less crucial to the Catholic spouse's devotional practice.

Moreover, research has shown that prayer and other manifestations of religious devotion are closely linked to happiness. "Whether they pray often together or not," Greeley (1991b:189) noted of couples he surveyed for *Psychology Today*, "is a very powerful correlate of marital happiness, the most powerful we have yet discovered." Furthermore, a statistical control for fundamentalism does not obliterate this relationship.

Ritual devotion, too, holds a position of prominence in inducing marital happiness, in that Heaton (1984) determined that attendance at services is the vehicle through which the more abundant satisfaction of a religiously homogamous marriage is actually imparted (see Call and Heaton 1997; Greeley 1991b; Shehan, Bock, and Lee 1990). "Homogamous marriages are characterized by a higher level of church attendance which, in turn, is associated with greater likelihood of high marital satisfaction," Heaton (1984:732) reported, "but the partial association between homogamy and satisfaction is nil. . . . Patterns of religious involvement apparently underlie the higher level of satisfaction expressed in religiously homogamous marriages."

Similarly, Hunt and King (1978) found that happiness in marriage was related to greater religious motivation and to higher levels of participation in organized church activities. Consistent with this finding, a separate body of research has established that participation in church services and religious rituals of various sorts enhances the commitment to and adjustment in marriage (see, for example, Larson and Goltz 1989; M. R. Wilson and Filsinger 1986; but cf. Booth et al. 1995).

Religious homogamy has also been related, in a number of investigations, to greater stability of marriages (see Bumpass and Sweet 1972; Heaton and Pratt 1990; Landis 1949). That is, spouses who claimed the same denominational identification were less likely to divorce than were those who maintained different affiliations or none. Data from vital statistics on marriages in Iowa between 1953 and 1959 indicated a higher rate of survival for homogamous marriages, especially when both partners were Catholic (Burchinal and Chancellor 1963).

More recent research has done nothing to upset this pattern. Using data from the National Survey of Families and Households (1987–88), Lehrer and Chiswick (1993:398) found that "with the exception of age at marriage, changes in none of the other variables" they considered "produce such a large variation in the probability of marital dissolution" as religious intermarriage. And couples in which one spouse converted to match the professed faith of the other, they discovered, reached an even higher level of stability than originally homogamous marriages (cf. Lazerwitz 1995).

Although members of different denominations appear to embrace various ideas about gender roles, the obligations of spouses and parents, and other aspects of life in the marital context, the most easily detected splits in attitudes about "family values," research has shown, prevail between persons who express a religious preference and those who do not. The results from a random sample of households in Utah (Bahr 1982), for example, indicated almost universal agreement among the respondents with the assertions that families should generate their own income and counsel and care for preschool children without outside assistance. Members of the Church of Jesus Christ of Latter-day Saints (Mormons) also preferred, more than adherents of other denominations, to confine their leisure-time pursuits and solicitations for help with problems to the family circle.

But the participants with no religious identification were the least family centered, compared to believers of various traditions. In addition, they were the most likely to approve of a husband and wife sharing equally in the burden of providing materially for the family. About 2 in 5 of the unaffiliated supported this view, compared to 1 in 5 Protestants and Catholics and only 1 in 9 Mormons. In answer to a series of questions, the respondents with no religious preference were consistently readier to accept "alternative" or "nontraditional" definitions of roles in the family. However, on questions dealing with the actual *behavior* of family members, fewer differences among groups were evident (Bahr 1982:208).

Analyses by Alwin (1986) likewise revealed that denominational distinctions may no longer dictate orientations to child rearing nearly as much as generic measures of religious commitment like church attendance. Since the late 1950s, differences between white Protestants and Catholics in the United States over what values children ought to manifest have largely disappeared, to be survived by differences stemming from ethnicity and social class. The remaining religious division is behavioral, Alwin stated, not nominal:

> Parents who participate in church activities more frequently, regardless of denomination, are significantly more likely to value obedience in their children relative to other qualities . . . the evidence for a relationship is apparent, and the magnitude of the relationship is considerably stronger than the relationships of parental values and the religioethnic categories. (pp. 435–36)

An exception to the fading of denominational differences in parenting styles is the persistent preference of theologically conservative Protestants for the corporal punishment of children. However, a detailed study of attitudinal data by Ellison and Sherkat (1993a; see also Ellison, Bartkowski, and Segal 1996) demonstrated clearly that the popularity of physical discipline among religious conservatives is connected to their tendency to assume literal interpretations of scriptural admonitions. Biblical literalism, in turn, is related to the belief that humans are naturally sinful and must, out of obedience to God and for their own good, be corrected in a decisive manner. "Individuals who feel that human nature is sinful and corrupt and that sinful behavior should be punished express strong support for the principle of corporal punishment" (Ellison and Sherkat 1993a:139; see also Lienesch 1991).

Ellison and Sherkat observed a similar relationship between the distinctive theological commitments of conservative Protestants and a preference for obedience in their children. (This finding was confirmed in the survey by Danso, Hunsberger, and Pratt [1997]). Catholics were also found to value obedience more than other Americans and to be slightly less inclined to encourage autonomy, but these attitudes were not the consequence of the same string of theological views that motivated the results for Protestants (Ellison and Sherkat 1993b).

Conceptions of family roles that arise from religious teachings on gender do affect the degree of socioeconomic disadvantage that women experience. An analysis of data from the 1971 and 1981 Canadian censuses by Heaton and Cornwall (1989) discovered that smaller religious bodies with more conservative convictions about the role of women (such as the Jehovah's Witnesses, some Reformed churches, Anabaptists, and Mormons) were marked by the greatest inequality between men and women. In particular, the more a group believed that the energies of women should be concentrated at home as wives and mothers, the higher were the levels of difference in educational attainment, labor-force participation, and income between its male and female members. (A comparable analysis with census data for the United States is not possible because the federal government does not compile information on religious affiliations.)

Religion and Reproduction: Fertility and Its Normative Regulation

For about four decades, large-scale surveys of American couples have permitted accurate estimation of fertility rates for the nation's principal religious divisions. Less certain, however, are the exact processes whereby religious preference is presumed to influence family planning, the measurable extent of that influence, and whether the impact of religion has declined to insignificance in recent years. A brief summary of the results of one of the earliest studies (Westoff, Potter, and Sagi 1964:133), for example, maintained that "religious preference . . . is the strongest of all major social influences on fertility" (cf. Goldscheider 1967). Yet shortly thereafter, the author of a popular textbook on demography (W. Petersen 1969:538) claimed, to the contrary, that "the effect of religion *per se* on the reproductive behavior of most persons in the West is now probably close to nil."

What *has* been obvious since at least the mid-1950s is that members of the country's diverse array of religious denominations approached their fertility in distinctive ways. In the words of a team of contemporary demographers (Mosher, Johnson, and Horn 1986:367), "religious affiliation has been one of the most important social characteristics affecting fertility and contraceptive use in the United States." Regardless of whether the counts involved the *actual* number of children ever born, the *desired* number of births, or the number of children that women *expected* to have, studies repeatedly showed that Roman Catholics as a group intended to have and produced the largest families, followed, in descending order, by Protestants and then by Jews, who had the lowest fertility (Goldscheider 1967; Mosher and Hendershot 1984a, 1984b; W. Petersen 1969; Poston and Kramer 1986; Thornton 1985; Westoff et al. 1964).

In 1955, to be more precise, Catholic wives expected to have an average of 0.56 more children than their Protestant counterparts and 1.03 more than Jewish wives (Mosher and Goldscheider 1984:103). So common, in particular, was the finding of relatively high fertility among American Catholic women that it has been termed "traditionally one of the indisputable generalizations in demography" (Williams and Zimmer 1990:475).

During the years of the so-called baby boom, Catholic fertility departed widely from benchmarks set by the rest of the national population. But since that time, the difference in childbearing between Catholic wives and others has narrowed. For example, between 1955 and 1975, national surveys of women in their reproductive years reflected a falling rate of total marital fertility for Catholics, from a high of 4.25 as recently as 1961–65 to a low of 2.27 in 1971–75. (The relevant statistics for non-Catholics at each point were 3.14 and 2.17, respectively.) Thus, although fertility for both categories dropped sharply, what had been a substantial difference between Catholics and others of 1.11 children declined in a decade or so to just 0.10. By 1982, white Catholic women aged 15 to 44 expected approximately 2.6 children; the corresponding figure for Protestant women was 2.3 (Goldscheider and Mosher 1988:48–49).

Impressed by the seeming thoroughness of this process of convergence, leading demographers were moved in the late 1970s to announce "the end" of unique fertility patterns for Catholics (Westoff and Jones 1979) and the seamless "blending" of all types of Catholic reproductive behavior into a broader cultural mainstream (Westoff 1979). Two observers of fertility trends (Westoff and Jones 1979:213; see also Westoff 1979) insisted, in a controversial article, that "the distinctiveness of traditionally higher 'Catholic' fertility appears to have all but disappeared." At the same time, they attempted to finish off the topic for good: "The rapid blurring of distinctive identities" for Catholics in the United States, they predicted, "makes future divergence seem unlikely" (Westoff and Jones 1979:217).

A concomitant development that has fostered change in Catholic fertility is what was described as nothing less than a "revolution" in contraceptive practices among Catholic couples (Westoff and Bumpass 1973). In spite of an unambiguous prohibition against "artificial" birth control, a ban reiterated in the 1968 encyclical *Humanae vitae,* the proportion of white, married Catholic women aged 18 to 39 who used a contraceptive method other than periodic continence (the "rhythm" method) increased from 51 to 68 percent between 1965 and 1970 (Westoff and Bumpass 1973:42). "It seems clear," Westoff and Bumpass (p. 41) observed, "that the papal encyclical has not retarded the increasing defection of Catholic women from this teaching." Instead, the data suggested that Catholic women were "just ignoring Church teaching on birth control" (p. 42). The nearly inevitable consequence of such a habit, Westoff and Bumpass thought, would be, in short order, to render Catholics "virtually indistinguishable in their birth control practices" from other Americans (p. 44; see also Westoff 1979:234).

A later analysis, incorporating returns from 1975, confirmed this preliminary projection. "The continued trend away from conformity is dramatically evident," Westoff and Jones (1977:204) wrote. "Rarely do social science data provide such an orderly pattern." Emboldened by the newest results, Westoff and Jones further predicted that by 1980, the sole family planning regimen approved by the Catholic Church, the rhythm method, "is destined to be of historical interest only" (p. 207). Indeed, except for a slightly greater aversion to surgical sterilization (see Eckhardt and Hendershot 1984), the survey data showed that Catholics adopted a range of contraceptive techniques at about the same rates as did other Americans (Westoff 1979; cf. Goldscheider and Mosher 1988; Mosher and Goldscheider 1984).

Although competing studies did not dispute the basic theme of the argument, they nevertheless contended that the forecast of the demise of "Catholic" fertility and of a general convergence of patterns across religious groups in the United States was decidedly premature. Even after the usual statistical controls for age, education, and residence, Catholic couples still reported higher fertility as of 1976 (Mosher and Hendershot 1984a, 1984b; Williams and Zimmer 1990).

In addition, and contrary to previous findings, the most religiously dedicated Catholic wives (as measured by the frequency of their attending Mass and receiving Holy Communion) retained a profile of higher fertility, as others accommodated to new norms (Mosher and Hendershot 1984a; Williams and Zimmer 1990). Similar differences by religious commitment surfaced in the attitudes of Catholic adolescents toward the prospect of parenthood (Blake 1984). Furthermore, these studies could not attribute the total responsibility for Catholic fertility rates to official values governing the use of contraceptives. In fact, black Catholics exhibited much *lower* fertility than did black Protestants (Mosher and Hendershot 1984b).[4] A more tempered conclusion, then, labeled religious affiliation "an indispensable datum" for demographic studies like these (Mosher and Goldscheider 1984:101, 110; Mosher and Hendershot 1984b:671, 676).

The latest round of research, however, has brought demographers into greater consensus on religious differences or similarities in fertility. Mosher et al. (1986) calculated that from 1977 to 1981, rates of total marital fertility among Catholic and non-Catholic white women still showed Catholic women's preference for larger families. Catholic wives whose first marriages were intact averaged 2.54 children, compared to 2.28 for their non-Catholic counterparts. "The meaning of the differential was changing, however," Mosher et al. (1986:370) noted, "because of changes in the composition of the population—specifically, the growing number of Hispanics in the United States."

Hispanics in this country are overwhelmingly Catholic, and Hispanic women's levels of fertility are about 40 percent higher than those of other Americans. The result of this conjunction of traits is that by the 1980s, the difference in fertility between Catholics and non-Catholics "was becoming less a religious differential and more an ethnic/immigrant differential" (Mosher et al. 1986:370). Indeed, from 1977 to 1981, the total marital fertility rate for non-Hispanic Catholic women was 2.27, negligibly lower than the 2.29 calculated for white first-time wives who were neither Hispanic nor Catholic. In the same period, Hispanic Catholic women had 3.56 children, compared to only 1.97 for non-Catholic Hispanic wives.[5] "The absence of a religious difference for non-Hispanics and the large religious differential among Hispanics indicates that the Catholic–non-Catholic differential in the TMFR [total marital fertility rate] in recent years was due entirely to the high fertility of Hispanic Catholics" (Mosher et al. 1986:370).

Nevertheless, a religious fertility gap remained if one examined total fertility rates (rates for *all women* of childbearing age, regardless of marital status) for whites between 15 and 39. But in this case, the fertility of Catholics was *already slightly lower* than that of non-Catholics. The reason for this difference is the propensity among Catholics never to have married and thus not to be currently married. Forty percent of Catholic women in the National Surveys of Family Growth had never married, as opposed to only 27 percent of Protestant women (Mosher et al. 1986:371).[6]

As a result of this pattern of nonmarriage, delayed marriage, and less frequent marriage among Catholics, the lower total fertility rate for Catholic women lasted through the 1980s. "Among white women," Mosher, Williams, and Johnson (1992:204) estimated, "Catholics, Jews, and those with no religious affiliation all have significantly *fewer* children than Protestants" (emphasis in the original). Non-Hispanic white Catholics had 1.08 children ever born (almost indistinguishable from the Jewish rate of 1.07), while Protestant women reported an average of 1.31. "In the United States," Mosher et al. (1992:199) concluded, "the baby boom-era pattern of high Catholic and low Protestant fertility has ended." Although Catholic women predicted larger families for themselves, their relatively later age at first marriage would probably preclude the fulfillment of their wishes.

American Jews have consistently reported rates of fertility that are considerably lower than those of other religious groups. The difference between the fertility of Jewish couples and others has been, in the words of one analyst (DellaPergola 1980:261), "remarkably persistent." Not only does this fact apply to the contemporary United States, but historical and cross-national research have revealed that the same pattern was evident more than a century ago in this country and marks most other modernized societies as well—with the possible exception of Israel (DellaPergola 1980; Goldscheider 1967).

The Jewish population of the United States, though small, is heavily concentrated in a few metropolitan areas (Heilman 1995). Compared to their fellow citizens of different religious backgrounds, Jewish partners typically marry at somewhat later ages—often after advanced education—and, once married, use chemical and mechanical means of contraception sooner and with great effectiveness (Fishman 1996; Goldscheider 1967; Heilman 1995; Schmelz and DellaPergola 1982).

The combination of population characteristics that most Jewish Americans share would incline any group toward small families. As Goldstein (1992:78) observed, "Jews have reached new heights in educational achievement, and occupational choice, as well as greater freedom in selection of place of residence, memberships, friends, and spouses. Together, these changes help explain associated demographic features such as later age at marriage, low fertility, more intermarriage and divorce, and high mobility." But the historical rates of Jewish fertility in the United States have been lower than even the levels that these surrounding social conditions would dictate.

In other words, after controls for urban residence, social class, educational attainment, and related factors, Jewish fertility is still beneath the standards set by other religious communities (see, for example, Mosher and Hendershot 1984b; Mosher et al. 1992). Of course, one cause of lower fertility among Jewish couples has been their ready resort to, and practiced facility in using, the most efficient methods of birth control, such as barriers. By the 1970s, indeed, the contraceptive methods that were chosen disproportionately by Jewish couples included condoms and diaphragms, as well as intrauterine devices (Mosher and Goldscheider 1984).

The social consequences of a distinctive pattern of lower fertility for Jewish couples are now clearly evident. In the words of two demographers of American Jews (Schmelz and DellaPergola 1982:180), "For U.S. Jewry, in the long run, to achieve growth or even maintain its size ('zero population growth'), it would be necessary to either raise fertility, curb assimilatory losses, attract immigration, or attain a combination of these positive influences, and moreover do so very substantially."

Other religious groups that are relatively small also exhibit differences in fertility and related family behaviors that seem to resist explanation by reference to the social statuses of their adherents. Two outstanding cases, fundamentalist Christians and Mormons, tend to have large families and traditional domestic arrangements (Mosher et al. 1992; J. Wilson, Parnell, and Pagnini 1997). The groups in question offer both a strongly "pronatalist" ideology and a tightly knit system of social bonds that make acting on that belief less burdensome for married couples than it might otherwise be.

Studies of religion and fertility seldom isolate individual Protestant denominations, or homogeneous "families" in the Protestant tradition, for special scrutiny. But an important analysis by Marcum (1981) of data from the 1965 National Fertility Survey suggested that followers of conservative

Protestant churches may pursue more seriously than liberal believers the directive of Genesis 1:28 (KJV) to "be fruitful, and multiply, and replenish the earth, and subdue it" (cf. Falwell 1981:105). Controlling for socioeconomic status, place and region of residence, age, and age at marriage, Marcum discovered a higher rate of fertility for wives in conservative Protestant churches who engaged in religious activities in the home.

Pronatalism in Mormon religious culture far surpasses the stress on solid and happy families that is discernible in many competing denominations (Smith 1985). According to an authoritative text on Mormon theology, "Among the saints the *family* is the basic unit of the Church and of society, and its needs and preservation in righteousness take precedence over all other things" (McConkie 1966:273; emphasis in the original). Proper Latter-day Saint (LDS) families begin in what is called a "celestial marriage," and, Mormons are advised,

> *The most important things that any member of The Church of Jesus Christ of Latter-day Saints ever does in this world are: 1. To marry the right person, in the right place, by the right authority; and 2. To keep the covenant made in connection with this holy and perfect order of matrimony—thus assuring the obedient persons of an inheritance of exaltation in the celestial kingdom.* (McConkie 1966:118; emphasis in the original)

The theology of the Saints holds that childbearing cooperates in a pair of holy purposes: crafting a mortal existence for the "spiritual offspring" of the deity and placing these children of God in earthly homes. Parents and progeny together, the family's members constitute a unit that, according to Mormon theology, will survive into eternity:

> If the family unit continues, then by virtue of that fact the members of the family have gained eternal life (exaltation), the greatest of all the gifts of God, for by definition exaltation consists in the continuation of the family unit in eternity. Those so inheriting are the sons and daughters of God, the members of his family, those who have made their callings and elections sure. They are joint-heirs with Christ to all that the Father hath, and they receive the fulness of the glory of the Father, becoming gods in their own right. (McConkie 1966:117–18; see also Bushman with Bushman 1996; Heaton 1986; 1989; Heaton and Goodman 1985; Smith 1985; Thornton 1979)

But in Mormonism, such a religious elevation of family life is not confined solely to the dry pages of official theology. Consider, for example, this candid description of LDS belief from one of Mormonism's former leaders:

> The Church itself exists to exalt the family, and the family concept is one of the major and most important of the whole theological doctrine. In fact, our very concept of heaven itself is the projection of the home into eternity. Salvation, then, is essentially a family affair, and full participation in the

> plan of salvation can be had only in family units. (quoted in Holman and Harding 1996:52)

From the outside, Foster (1981:239), a historian, ratified this view succinctly:

> Mormons saw family life and the relationship between family and larger kinship networks as the ultimate basis for all progression, not only on earth but throughout all eternity. To an almost unparalleled extent, the Mormon religion really was *about* the family; earthly and heavenly family ideals were seen as identical. (emphasis in the original)

"Pronatalism developed as part of the Mormon experience in the United States," Heaton (1989:407) elaborated, "and it is here that the most consistent patterns are found."

These patterns pertain to a strikingly high level of fertility, a trait of LDS populations that predates statehood for Utah, the Mormon Zion (Smith 1985; Thornton 1979). Currently, Mormon wives average approximately 3.3 children each, a figure higher than those for Catholics and conservative or liberal Protestants (Heaton 1986:248). Although the LDS Church at one time took a formal stance in opposition to birth control, this restriction has loosened considerably (Thornton 1979). Accordingly, higher levels of fertility for Mormons appear to be associated more with the greater value that they attach to additional children than with any lingering disapproval for the limitation of family size (Heaton 1986; Heaton and Calkins 1983; Smith 1985).

Indeed, the evidence amassed from demographic research indicates that committed Mormons establish larger families than church members who were not married in a Mormon temple, who do not attend services weekly, and whose own parents were not active Saints (Heaton 1986). But this advantage is not entirely the contribution of theology. Rather, "an institutional setting designed to aid in child rearing and a reference group with similar life situations" (Heaton 1986:257) help to sustain the distinctiveness of Mormon culture (see also Cornwall and Thomas 1990).

Thus, whether mediated or not, religion has a profound impact on reproductive behavior among American Mormons; one need not confine the influence of doctrine to residuals that are deposited after the effects of prior variables are separated. Furthermore, as Thornton (1979:136) declared, "there is no reason to expect a quick removal of the relatively high level of Mormon childbearing." In fact, by his calculation, were Mormon fertility behavior to resume convergence toward societal norms, at historical rates the trend could take as long as 150 years.

Righteous Raising: The Efficacy of Religious Socialization

Each new addition to a family needs to undergo a process of training in the meanings embedded in his or her religious culture if that family is to continue as part of the larger constituency for religion in the United States. This process of apprehending religious symbols, learning their proper use, and appreciating their full significance is known as religious socialization. According to two psychologists of religion (Visscher and Stern 1990:105):

> The family is the arena where subjective needs are met; emotional communication is at the core of family expectations, identity and face-to-face rapport is a continuous event. The religious "doing" of families is expressed in what they do together; it is this doing that will reveal what they believe and what they find important in those beliefs.

In most situations, religious socialization is accomplished by either or both of two means. The first is through deliberate efforts at religious education (see, for example, Himmelfarb 1979) that occur normally within and outside the strict confines of the family. The second is by undirected exposure to religious thinking and the informal modeling of the religious behaviors of selected others, primarily within the family. Social scientists have studied both dynamics closely. Yet, as varied and even haphazard as are the concrete forms that attempts at socialization assume, several notable regularities emerge from this research.

In the simplest terms, the religious values of preadolescent, adolescent, and college-age children usually resemble those that their parents have endorsed (Kelley and De Graaf 1997; Myers 1996; but cf. Ploch and Hastings 1998)—although some intergenerational differences are likely to remain. To be specific, a frequent finding in analyses of religious socialization is the salient influence of *mothers* in the process of shaping the religious orientations of their children, especially if these offspring are male. Particularly in the area of traditional religious beliefs (as opposed to actual devotional practices), the impact of a mother's guidance and example repeatedly suggests itself (Acock and Bengston 1978; Dudley and Dudley 1986; Myers 1996; but cf. Clark, Worthington, and Danser 1988).

This recurrent result achieves a special importance in that by virtually every standard measure of religious commitment, women are markedly more religious than men (see de Vaus 1982; Francis 1997). Research from Australia (de Vaus and McAllister 1987) attributed the persistence of the difference in religiosity by gender to the lower rate at which women are engaged as full-time workers in the paid labor force. Although this finding has received partial support in studies of specific denominations (on Mormons, see Chadwick and Garrett 1995) and of other societies (on Canada, see Gee 1991), it does not seem to apply with equal force to national samples from the United States (de Vaus 1984; Ulbrich and Wallace 1984; but cf. Hertel 1995).

In short, with respect to religious socialization, it is mothers who matter most. For instance, in a study of more than 250 two-parent/one-child triads, Hoge, Petrillo, and Smith (1982) contended that, in general, sons derive their politics from their fathers but acquire a religious sensibility from their mothers (see also Nelsen 1980). Across their analyses (which incorporated data from Baptist, Methodist, and Roman Catholic churches), Hoge et al. found clear connections between parents' religiosity and children's religious values. These empirical relationships, moreover, outstripped in strength most evidences of socialization from one generation to the next that were unrelated to religion.

More directly, Hunsberger and Brown (1984:250) reported that 1 out of 4 respondents to their survey of psychology students (in Australia) named his or her mother as having "had the greatest influence on religious development." Finally, Nelsen's (1981:635) inquiry among elementary school students in southern Minnesota concluded that "the best predictor of preadolescent religiosity is maternal religiosity."

If any practical lesson can be drawn from this research, it is that families in which the intimate bond between mothers and their growing children is preserved intact will function optimally as environments for the transmission of religious beliefs and values to succeeding generations.

IDEAL FAMILIES: UTOPIAN AND MINORITY VISIONS

If, as Berger (1967a; 1967b) maintained, religion and the family occupy similar positions in the structure of any modern society, the two institutions should share some important connections. And, as the research reviewed to this point demonstrates, they do. But in the United States, several groups have gone much further, fusing the family with religion in a righteous drive to fabricate the social foundation for an approaching heaven-on-earth.

They have thus succeeded in carrying the logic of religiously supported familism to its feasible extreme. Yet, as aberrant as these groups may appear to the casual observer or the hostile outsider, a closer inspection reveals that they have grasped—though arguably in a stranglehold—some of the most normal expectations of American family life (Cartwright and Kent 1992). Their deviance resides not in a radical departure from prevailing social norms about the family but, rather, in the single-mindedness with which they adhere to a cultural ideal that is more widely diffused, if less thoroughly honored, in other strata of society.

Indeed, utopian efforts to reconstruct and reinvigorate the traditional family are a veritable fixture throughout the history of the United States. Whether it was polygamy among the nineteenth-century Mormons, "complex marriage" in the Oneida community, or the biblically inspired patriarchy of the Old Order Amish, the American experience overflows with instances of sects or cults that redefined sexual behavior, gender roles, and communal structures to give new meanings to old, and even time-honored, forms of the family (Foster 1981).[7] In this section, attention is confined primarily to a single new religious movement, the Unification Church, which has sought to turn familistic imagery into theology and family life into the vital link between God and humanity.

Of the numerous new religions to arise in, or to be transplanted to, the United States in the post–World War II period, probably none allocates as much weight to the symbolism of the family as the Holy Spirit Association for the Unification of World Christianity—the Unification Church, for short. (In this country and elsewhere around the world, members of the Unification Church are also known popularly by the sometimes derisive designation of Moonies, after the surname of the movement's founder, the Korean evangelist Sun Myung Moon.)

Three sociologists who have studied the Moonies closely (Bromley, Shupe, and Oliver 1982:120) judged that, of the many new religions that are deemed "cults" by their opponents, the Unification Church "has developed and legitimated an alternative family structure most fully." In Unification theology, as explicated by the Reverend Moon himself, the family plays a crucial role; it is "one of the most important, if not the central concept" for the Church (Bromley et al. 1982:121). Not only is family the organizing metaphor for much that the group does, but it functions as a model for the Church's very conception of itself.

Persons who are affiliated with the Unification Church refer to themselves as brothers and sisters in the "United Family" of the Reverend Moon. In this figurative family, Moon and his wife are honored as "True Parents," and all members, in turn, are counted as the couple's "spiritual children." The Church's sacred scripture, the *Divine Principle*, teaches that holy action in the world mirrors this structure through a premise that is termed "the Four-Position Foundation"—a symbolic configuration consisting of God, a husband and a wife, and their children (Barker 1983; Bromley et al. 1982; Fichter 1983, 1985; Grace 1985; Heinz 1983).

From this tenet proceeds the conviction that, for committed Moonies, "the fundamental unit of society is the family—neither man nor woman being complete in him[-] or herself until being blessed in a God-centered marriage" that also brings forth children (Barker 1983:37). No less a spokesperson than the Reverend Moon has said as much: "the family will always be the basic unit of happiness and cornerstone of the kingdom of God on earth and thereafter in heaven" (quoted in Sontag 1977:155). By relating religion to the family, Unificationists accomplish two aims simultaneously: First, the Church "deliberately models itself on a family system and focuses its worship on God, the father of all creation," and second, its followers establish that "religion is for them the most important ingredient in marital and familial love" (Fichter 1983:291 and 289).

In Moon's retelling of the Christian story, the saving mission of the Lord was thwarted when an unprepared and uncomprehending world crucified Jesus before He had the occasion to fulfill His true purpose on earth, which, according to Moon, was to marry and to father children, leading ultimately to the onset of a familistic Kingdom of God. Hence, the death of Jesus was not, as other Christians believe, the opening moment of a pivotal stage in salvation history, but instead a missed opportunity. Its premature timing instituted the need for a "Second Advent," wherein a later messiah would visit the earth to spawn spiritual fellowship through the form of the perfect family (Barker 1980; Bromley et al. 1982; Fichter 1983; Heinz 1983). For years, the belief supposedly was not an authoritative element of Unification theology, but many current members of the Church hold that the Reverend Moon is "the Lord of the Second Advent," this new messianic emissary from God (see Bainbridge 1997).

With this reasoning as a basis, it is easy to see how, for Moonies, in the words of Fichter (1983:293), a sympathetic outsider to the movement,

> the establishment of God-centered families is not merely for the salvation of the individual involved, nor is it simply a foundation upon which the larger community, nation, and world can be built. It is the essential salvific link between the sinful past and the prophetic millennium.

In emulation of this connection, every member of the Unification Church, without exception, has a vocation to marriage and parenthood (Fichter 1983). A survey of unmarried Moonies revealed that typical Church members look forward to eventual marriage after three years of mandatory celibacy, although about three-quarters of those questioned envisioned a longer wait than that. They expected, furthermore, that conservative values would govern their marital relationships and that these relationships would yield large families. Not one respondent intended to remain childless, and 32 percent indicated a desire for *seven or more* children! Almost two-thirds (63 percent) said that they would use no birth control (Bromley et al. 1982:123–26).

With personal plans as traditional as these, Moonies may seem unlikely to be cast as ominous threats to the American way of family life. Yet their critics perceive them to be a force that splinters existing families by isolating adult children from their parents, exerting a domineering control over choices of spouses and the scheduling of weddings, and so monopolizing the time and energies of members as effectively to estrange them from nonmember parents, siblings, and other relatives.

Because the Unification Church appears to duplicate authentically—if in darker and somewhat more intense hues—the picture of a happy extended family, some researchers have hypothesized that this highly visible aspect of the group's structure may be its chief appeal to potential recruits. In a wider society in which marital discord, separation, divorce, single parenthood, and the abuse of children are growing ever more commonplace, what could be more attractive than the promise of a loving and all-encompassing "surrogate" for the ideal family that one never really managed to attain on one's own? In this view, as conditions that support stable families in the external society progressively deteriorate, the secure inner confines of a familistic new religion will beckon. Those who are especially drawn to groups like the Unification Church, then, should be young people whose family ties collapsed well shy of the idealized cultural standard (Barker 1980, 1983; Fichter 1983; Wright and D'Antonio 1993).

However, neither impressionistic evidence (Fichter 1983), nor participant observation (Barker 1980), nor more rigorous empirical data (Wright and Piper 1986) have confirmed this hypothesis. Persons who join new religions (including the Unification Church) appear to have been relatively satisfied with their families of origin. On the whole, they report pleasant feelings toward their families; uneventful passages through adolescence; and, in some cases, outright admiration for their parents. It is not deprivation of familial closeness and warmth that appears to propel young people into new religions but, rather, the idealistic urge to guarantee their continuation beyond the point of individual autonomy that is reached early in adulthood (cf. Wright and D'Antonio 1993). As Barker (1980:396–97) wrote reassuringly in a magazine for English Catholic clergymen:

> It is, furthermore, a strange twist of fate that many of the children have been susceptible to the Unification Church not in spite of, but because of, their parents' attempts to inculcate such ideals as love, duty, service, loyalty, devotion and truth.

THE POLITICS OF FAMILY ISSUES: THE NEW CHRISTIAN RIGHT AND BEYOND

In his theoretical writing on religion, Berger (1967b:134) is careful to note that, although an institutionalized faith reinforces what he calls "private virtue," religion also "manifests itself as public rhetoric." No follower of politics needs to be reminded that churches today play an active part in responding to changes in social conditions and in formulating ideas for their improvement.

But the range of issues on which religious organizations may appropriately comment is not infinite. Indeed, the political will of the churches to the contrary notwithstanding, that spectrum probably is shrinking. Nevertheless, because religion and the family share social proximity, it should come as no shock that in this age, persons who are unsettled by the moral condition of American culture should concentrate their proposals for reform on the family. This strategy is both practical and theoretical.

On the practical side, a loose coalition of social and religious conservatives whom writers classify as the "New Christian Right" has emerged to fight the decisive battles in what principal actors in both the traditionalist and progressive camps have billed as the next "culture war" (see Hunter 1991, 1994; Pankhurst and Houseknecht 1983). "The New Christian Right has embraced the family as one of its dominant issues," Heinz (1983:68) asserted, because "the family presented itself as the kind of issue on which a new social movement could ride to visibility and political power."

Few social movements in American history can rival the New Christian Right in the stress that its theory places on reordering family life by restricting intimate relationships to traditional models. This is an estimation about which operatives in the movement *and* their academic adversaries can agree. On one side, there is the Reverend Jerry Falwell: evangelist, pastor, church planter, university chancellor, founder of the now-defunct Moral Majority, and host of the *Old Time Gospel Hour* on radio and television. Each week, Falwell preaches chastity, heterosexuality, nuptiality, monogamy, and marital fidelity—and the virtue of patriotism—to his flock of supporters who are situated literally from sea to shining sea. "The family," Falwell (1981:104) has instructed:

> is the God-ordained institution of the marriage of one man and one woman together for a lifetime with their biological or adopted children. The family is the fundamental building block and the basic unit of our society, and its continued health is a prerequisite for a healthy and prosperous nation. No nation has ever been stronger than the families within her. America's families are her strength and they symbolize the miracle of America.

A successor to Falwell in the leadership of the Christian Right, Ralph Reed, former executive director of the Christian Coalition, reiterated Falwell's message about the importance of the family. "We must never retreat," he wrote in an excerpt from *Active Faith* (1996b), his call to arms for religious conservatives in the 1990s, "from our principled defense of the traditional marriage-based family as the foundation of our society" (Reed 1996a:29).

On the opposite side, Corbett (1990:285), an observer who is sharply critical of the television programming that is produced by conservative Protestant clergy, summarized if not endorsed this sentiment: "The family is a central, if not *the* central unit of the 'religious right's' agenda" (emphasis in the original). Hadden, a more balanced analyst of televangelism, said much the same thing several years earlier. Of the four basic social issues that he described the New Christian Right as having defined for its political crusades through the 1980s ("family, life, morality, and country"), "the family," Hadden (1983:252) contended, "is fast emerging as the *master* issue" (emphasis in the original). Moreover, it is an issue with a manifest and particular rhetorical resonance for conservatives.

One crude index of the rhetorical importance of the family is the degree to which the very word is invoked by combatants in the skirmishes over tradition that now commonly punctuate cultural debate. Of the thirty-five conservative special-interest groups covered in a "resource guide" prepared for the working press by consultants for the *Columbia Journalism Review* (Political Research Associates 1993), for example, six feature the word *family* in their corporate names.[8] In blunt contrast, none of the twenty-nine liberal organizations listed as "key contacts and resources" referred to the family in its title.

Conservative Christians look to the family not simply to serve as a cherished repository of the earthly purpose and spiritual peace that humans, with God's help, strive to obtain for themselves, but to perform a function of social control (see Hadden 1983; Lienesch 1991; 1993). The Christian family, lifted to a posture of vigilance by strict adherence to God's commandments, is always on the lookout for any sign of virtue's erosion against the encroaching tides of licentiousness. Such threats to order may come from within: from personal forces of lust and greed that have been insufficiently subdued, and from without: from agencies of government (the Internal Revenue Service, the Department of Education, and the National Endowment for the Arts are particularly suspect) and from high-level conspiracies in the elite media. As one commentator (Corbett 1990:290) noted: Christian evangelicals ordinarily "believe that the family is the principal force for order in society. Strong traditional families are the main check on the passions of a sinful human race."

One might reasonably conclude from such forceful expressions of resolve that the Christian Right family is little more than a seat of harsh judgment—not a haven tucked away from a heartless world, but an intrusion of heartlessness into precisely those domains of personality in which an understanding mind and a healing spirit are called for most. Yet interviews with evangelicals and fundamentalists themselves, as well as observations of family dynamics behind the domestic scenes, do not ratify this impression. Instead, a growing body of research (see, for example, Ammerman 1987; Demmitt 1992; Hall 1995; McNamara 1985a, 1985b; Rose 1987; cf. Corbett 1990) testifies to the fact that flexibility, negotiation, and a vibrant give-and-take among members of the household are not alien to everyday life in the godly homes of conservative Christians.

Imperatives of political organization aside, careful study of New Christian Right symbolism pertaining to the family suggests that the movement is much more than a reactionary attempt to reintroduce the strictures of misogyny and sexual repression in a society that has outlived those patterns. To be sure, Hadden (1983:250) admitted, "anger and moral indignation run deep" in the conservative movement, "and resentment about what is happening in and to America has been growing for a long time." Certainly, too, the movement labors with its peculiar burden of ulterior motives. "The family can also serve as a code word for a return to patriarchy, a recovery of male dominance, a containment of the women's movement, a restriction on female sexual freedom," Heinz conceded (1983:68; see also Heinz 1985; Pankhurst and Houseknecht 1983). But the groups making up the New Christian Right also possess a theoretical (as opposed to an exclusively tactical) rationale for what they do.

Although as Heinz (1985:154) pointed out, "there is no little truth" in a portrait of the New Christian Right as a movement animated by impulses to denounce and prohibit, there is an affirmative thrust to many of its positions. In brief, he argued, the New Christian Right is "engaged in a contest over the meaning of America's story" (p. 155). And in a society that has long prided itself on the permeability of its social boundaries, on the power ceded by the state to the common individual, and on the consequently contentious quality of its public life, what could be more genuinely American?

"The New Christian Right," Heinz (1985:166) continued, "finds in the family a means to recover a lost meaning, a lost past." In its eyes, the family is more than a besieged social institution; it is the paramount symbol in the "countermythology" of American life that the Right offers. As such, the New Right version of the family has a dual function: It permits participants in the movement to reconstitute the experience of what has been lost to the wider world, and it wages this struggle "as an ideological weapon by which a system which ignores or threatens family values can be subjected to coercive reform" (Heinz 1983:69).

Correctly recognized or not, this latter function was the essence of the often-misunderstood initiative by candidates of the Republican Party to provoke a discussion of "family values" in the 1992 campaign (Bush 1994; Lawton 1992). Although their prompts degenerated rapidly into partisan name-calling—not to mention the near-farcical parsing of the critique framed by an uninformed vice president of the "lifestyle choices" made by a fictional character in a television situation comedy (Quayle 1994)—activists on the Christian Right, unlike other Americans, needed no reminder of the deadly serious implications of the questions they raised (see, for example, Whitehead 1993).

To them, the fight for the family is a fight for America itself, and by theological extension, it is a mission to ensure God's blessings on the United States well into the future (Hadden 1983; Heinz 1983). That these activists are anchored in local churches means, in addition, that they have access to pools of funds, to audiences that assemble regularly to hear their message, to lines of communication beyond the lone congregation, and to repertoires of leadership skills that make the New Christian Right a formidable political force at the grassroots level (Pankhurst and Houseknecht 1983).

Nevertheless, for all the continued strength of Christian conservatives, keen monitors have chronicled substantial changes since their movement began to take form in the late 1970s. Moen (1992b) argued that a "transformation" of the Christian Right over the previous two decades can be seen in a pair of trends: the increasing sophistication of its activists in the mechanics of politics and a drift away from purely moral appeals toward the secular symbols of grievance. Concretely, such grievances take the form of complaints about exclusion (of religious viewpoints) from open debate, injustice (toward religious persons) in state processes, and inequality (of religion as opposed to secularism) before the law. The substance of the claims may be new, but their *form* is derived directly from the history of political liberalism in twentieth-century America.

The former development is one for which even the Right's adversaries are willing to give it credit. As an official of Americans United for the Separation of Church and State, a group that opposed many of the initiatives in public morality of the 1980s, commented:

> The Christian Right went through a rather inarticulate phase of existence in its early days. . . . Over time [though], the old guard of the movement

> has mostly disappeared from the scene. Those early people were strongly motivated by fundamentalist religion, but were not particularly sophisticated in politics. . . . They gradually dropped out or were moved to the sidelines, leaving the political arena to the somewhat less narrowly sectarian, but more sophisticated people. (quoted in Moen 1992b:3; 1992a:75–76)

This change can be witnessed in microcosm in the fate of the most famous organizational arm of the Christian Right, Falwell's Moral Majority, during the 1980s. The Moral Majority opened the decade as a presumably potent electoral force, with Republican candidates making their way to Lynchburg, Virginia, to beg Falwell's blessing on their aspirations. But throughout the administration of President Ronald Reagan, the group's narrow issues were co-opted by Washington, and its leaders were pressured to "broaden" their political involvement into areas, like foreign policy (the Middle East, Central America, and South Africa), where they could claim no expertise. At the same time, the Moral Majority's so-called negatives mounted in response to a series of stunning miscues.

By 1986, Falwell folded the Moral Majority into a new group, the Liberty Federation, and in 1989, with little fanfare or media attention, he declared his "mission accomplished," shuttered both organizations, and withdrew quietly to Lynchburg to tend his church and university (Moen 1992b). He had left the field of battle not to his fundamentalist coreligionists, but to young secular conservatives who had arrived in the capital as political appointees in two successive Reagan administrations.

These right-wing operatives spoke a language that relied less on allusions to a shared moral tradition than on a common commitment in American society to fairness in official treatment. Thus, their appeals resonated with "the rhetoric of liberalism, with its emphases on freedom, liberty, rights, and choice" (Moen 1992a:93). As Michael Schwartz of the conservative Free Congress Foundation remarked,

> The Christian Right has fewer "Bible toters" today. There is less attention to the rhetoric of morality as a result. Today, Christian-Right activists speak of the need for citizens to work for the public good, rather than speak of a need for Christians to clean up a morally decadent country. (quoted in Moen 1992b:132; cf. Moen 1992a:89–92; 1994:352)

"Set against the nature of the movement in its early days," Moen (1992a:95) contended, "the secularization of the Christian Right by the end of the 1980s was considerable."

Still, it would be a mistake to think that the moral agenda of the Christian Right no longer carries any weight with the electorate. After an analysis of voting data from the 1992 presidential campaign, Hammond, Shibley, and Solow (1994: 289; see also Hertel and Hughes 1987) concluded that the "family" dimension of values is "the likeliest candidate" to perpetuate the liberal-versus-conservative split in national politics.

CONCLUDING REFLECTIONS

Whether the analysis concentrates on the level of personal choices or examines public initiatives, it is clear from this overview that religion remains a potent force for families in modern American culture. It is clear as well that family forms and functions affect patterns of religious practice in the United States. So far withstanding—though not deflecting—assaults on the tie that binds them, families and religions doubtlessly will persist as fields of contention over cultural incursions into the private sphere of life. Just the same, at least a portion of this seemingly general and reciprocal influence may be illusory because this survey has probed specific sectors of institutional life but, for the most part, has neglected the question of how these areas are integrated.

Berger (1967a, 1967b), whose theories have served to organize much of this presentation, was himself doubtful that religion could sustain the weight in society that it once did because it is no longer a common basis for action and reflection *except* in the private sphere, where its low degree of commonality is relatively unimportant. In public affairs, the effective "reality" of a religious orientation breaks down amid the modern situation of pluralism, in which essential experience is separated into "enclaves of social life," "sub-worlds," or "fragmented universes of meaning" (Berger 1967b:134). Such venues may exist entirely apart from, if not in direct opposition to, the sense-making activity that occurs within the family.

The potential impact of religion in the life-worlds of believers is therefore inevitably limited, according to Berger (1967b:134), for "insofar as religion is common it lacks 'reality,' and insofar as it is 'real' it lacks commonality." The consequence is, in Berger's (1967b:134) words, "very curious."

Ironically, the robust character of the bond between religion and the family to date may reduce the impacts of each in a broader world that sorely needs their moderating influences. A small-scale but suggestive survey by Tamney and Johnson (1985) pointed out how religion's strongest institutional attachment is to the realm of family life. Fifty-nine percent of their respondents reported that "religious beliefs and values" had greatly affected how they treated their families. In contrast, only 37 percent claimed that religion was similarly instrumental to their job performance, while a mere 10 percent said that it dictated the political candidates for whom they voted (p. 366).

What Berger's descriptions of modernity portend for the family is still to be seen. But the outlook from his theory is not positive. The modern family, in Berger's (1967b: 134) eyes, is "notoriously fragile," and its prospects for success are not enhanced by being yoked to a religious institution with ever-shortening horizons. The "tenuousness" of the family-religion relationship *must* eventually be remedied, Berger stated, but to accomplish that goal, the relationship must first be better understood. This chapter is a hopeful step toward that end.

Notes

1. J. Wilson (1978) reviewed the earlier literature on this topic; Jenkins (1991) provided a more comprehensive and up-to-date summary.
2. But the experts themselves do not invariably agree. D'Antonio et al. (1982:222) concluded from an extensive survey of specialized textbooks that "there appears to be a substantial need for the development of more social psychological research focusing especially on the cognitive links between family life and religious institutions." However, Thomas and Cornwall (1990:988) drew the opposite lesson from a review of the accumulating periodical literature: "Unfortunately, it is the macrosociological approach that is most lacking."
3. For a broad introduction to the religious climate of American society in the late nineteenth century, see Christiano (1987). To supplement the discussion of ideology here, this work contains a great deal of data on the institutional and structural correlates of religion in that period.
4. In terms of social status, black Catholics are an atypical population in their own community. They have lower rates of fertility than do black Protestants because they are generally more highly educated and upwardly mobile (see Feigelman, Gorman, and Varacalli 1991)—traits that are associated in almost every racial or ethnic group with smaller families. In this one respect, black Catholics are socially more similar to their white coreligionists than to blacks in other denominations.
5. Non-Catholic Hispanics are like black Catholics in that they are a minority within a minority. Their religious affiliation usually results from conversion in the process of attaining educational advancement or higher-status occupations (see Greeley 1990, 1991a). Thus, Hispanics who are not Catholic also have fewer children.
6. These figures are *not* a measure of the proportion of respondents who will not wed at any point in their lives. Bear in mind that any sample such as this contains a substantial number of younger women (teenagers) who presumably will marry in later years.
7. An interesting counterpart (and contrast) to the study of new religious movements is the analysis of venerable world religions when the latter are transferred to a new cultural environment. For a case in point, see Waugh's (1991) account of how Muslims have adapted their traditions to life in North America.
8. The six traditionalist organizations were the American Family Association (Tupelo, Mississippi), Colorado for Family Values (Colorado Springs, Colorado), Family Life Ministries (Washington, DC), the Family Research Council (Washington, DC), Focus on the Family (Colorado Springs), and the Family Research Institute of the Institute for the Scientific Investigation of Sexuality (Washington, DC) (Political Research Associates 1993:38–39).

References

Acock, Alan C., and Vern L. Bengston. 1978. "On the Relative Influence of Mothers and Fathers: A Covariance Analysis of Political and Religious Socialization." *Journal of Marriage and the Family* 40:519–30.

Alston, Jon P., William A. McIntosh, and Louise M. Wright. 1976. "Extent of Interfaith Marriages Among White Americans." *Sociological Analysis* 37:261–64.

Alwin, Duane F. 1986. "Religion and Parental Child-Rearing Orientations: Evidence of a Catholic-Protestant Convergence." *American Journal of Sociology* 92:412–40.

Ammerman, Nancy Tatom. 1987. *Bible Believers: Fundamentalists in the Modern World.* New Brunswick, NJ: Rutgers University Press.

Babchuk, Nicholas, Harry J. Crockett, Jr., and John A. Ballweg. 1967. "Change in Religious Affiliation and Family Stability." *Social Forces* 45:551–55.

Bahr, Howard M. 1982. "Religious Contrasts in Family Role Definitions and Performance: Utah Mormons, Catholics, Protestants, and Others." *Journal for the Scientific Study of Religion* 21:200–17.

Bahr, Howard M., and Bruce A. Chadwick. 1985. "Religion and Family in Middletown, USA." *Journal of Marriage and the Family* 47:407–14.

Bainbridge, William Sims. 1997. *The Sociology of Religious Movements.* New York: Routledge.

Barker, Eileen. 1980. "Free to Choose? Some Thoughts on the Unification Church and Other Religious Movements, II." *Clergy Review* [London] 65:392–98.

———. 1983. "Doing Love: Tensions in the Ideal Family." Pp. 35–52 in *The Family and the Unification Church,* edited by Gene G. James (Conference Series No. 15). Barrytown, NY: Unification Theological Seminary.

Berger, Peter L. 1967a. "Religious Institutions." Pp. 329–79 in *Sociology: An Introduction,* edited by Neil J. Smelser. New York: John Wiley & Sons.

———. 1967b. *The Sacred Canopy: Elements of a Sociological Theory of Religion.* Garden City, NY: Doubleday.

Blake, Judith. 1984. "Catholicism and Fertility: On Attitudes of Young Americans." *Population and Development Review* 10:329–40.

Booth, Alan, David R. Johnson, Ann Branaman, and Alan Sica. 1995. "Belief and Behavior: Does Religion Matter in Today's Marriage?" *Journal of Marriage and the Family* 57:661–71.

Bromley, David G., Anson D. Shupe, Jr., and Donna L. Oliver. 1982. "Perfect Families: Visions of the Future in a New Religious Movement." Pp. 119–29 in *Cults and the Family,* edited by Florence Kaslow and Marvin B. Sussman (*Marriage and Family Review* Series). New York: Haworth Press.

Browning, Don S., Bonnie J. Miller-McLemore, Pamela D. Couture, K. Brynolf Lyon, and Robert M. Franklin. 1997. *From Culture Wars to Common Ground: Religion and the American Family Debate* (The Family, Religion, and Culture Series). Louisville, KY: Westminster/John Knox Press.

Bumpass, Larry L. 1970. "The Trend of Interfaith Marriage in the United States." *Social Biology* 17:253–59.

Bumpass, Larry L., and James A. Sweet. 1972. "Differentials in Marital Instability: 1970." *American Sociological Review* 37:754–66.

Burchinal, Lee B., and Loren E. Chancellor. 1963. "Survival Rates Among Religiously Homogamous and Interreligious Marriages." *Social Forces* 41:353–62.

Bush, Barbara. 1994. *A Memoir.* New York: Charles Scribner's Sons.

Bushman, Claudia L., with Richard L. Bushman. 1996. "Latter- day Saints: Home Can Be a Heaven on Earth." Pp. 22–37 in *Faith Traditions and the Family,* edited by Phyllis D. Airhart and Margaret Lamberts Bendroth (The Family, Religion, and Culture Series). Louisville, KY: Westminster/John Knox Press.

Call, Vaughn R. A., and Tim B. Heaton. 1997. "Religious Influence on Marital Stability." *Journal for the Scientific Study of Religion* 36:382–92.

Caplow, Theodore, with Howard M. Bahr, Bruce A. Chadwick, Reuben Hill, and Margaret Holmes Williamson. 1982. *Middletown Families: Fifty Years of Change and Continuity.* Minneapolis: University of Minnesota Press.

Caplow, Theodore, Howard M. Bahr, Bruce A. Chadwick, and Dwight W. Hoover.

1983. *All Faithful People: Change and Continuity in Middletown's Religion*. Minneapolis: University of Minnesota Press.

Cartwright, Robert H., and Stephen A. Kent. 1992. "Social Control in Alternative Religions: A Familial Perspective." *Sociological Analysis* 53:345–61.

Chadwick, Bruce A., and H. Dean Garrett. 1995. "Women's Religiosity and Employment: The LDS Experience." *Review of Religious Research* 36:277–93.

Christiano, Kevin J. 1986. "Church as a Family Surrogate: Another Look at Family Ties, Anomie, and Church Involvement." *Journal for the Scientific Study of Religion* 25:339–54.

———. 1987. *Religious Diversity and Social Change: American Cities, 1890–1906*. Cambridge, England: Cambridge University Press.

Clark, Cynthia A., Everett L. Worthington, Jr., and Donald B. Danser. 1988. "The Transmission of Religious Beliefs and Practices from Parents to Firstborn Early Adolescent Sons." *Journal of Marriage and the Family* 50:463–72.

Corbett, Julia Mitchell. 1990. "The Family as Seen through the Eyes of the New Religious-Political Right." Pp. 285–94 in *Religious Television: Controversies and Conclusions*, edited by Robert Abelman and Stewart M. Hoover (Communication and Information Science Series). Norwood, NJ: Ablex.

Cornwall, Marie, and Darwin L. Thomas. 1990. "Family, Religion, and Personal Communities: Examples from Mormonism." *Marriage and Family Review* 15:229–52.

Crockett, Harry J., Jr., Nicholas Babchuk, and John A. Ballweg. 1969. "Change in Religious Affiliation and Family Solidarity: A Second Study." *Journal of Marriage and the Family* 31:464–68.

Danso, Henry, Bruce Hunsberger, and Michael Pratt. 1997. "The Role of Parental Religious Fundamentalism and Right-Wing Authoritarianism in Child-Rearing Goals and Practices." *Journal for the Scientific Study of Religion* 36:496–511.

D'Antonio, William V. 1980. "The Family and Religion: Exploring a Changing Relationship." *Journal for the Scientific Study of Religion* 19:89–104.

———. 1983. "Family Life, Religion, and Societal Values and Structures." Pp. 81–108 in *Families and Religions: Conflict and Change in Modern Society*, edited by William V. D'Antonio and Joan Aldous. Beverly Hills, CA: Sage.

D'Antonio, William V., William M. Newman, and Stuart A. Wright. 1982. "Religion and Family Life: How Social Scientists View the Relationship." *Journal for the Scientific Study of Religion* 21:218–25.

DellaPergola, Sergio. 1980. "Patterns of American Jewish Fertility." *Demography* 17:261–73.

———. 1991. "New Data on Demography and Identification Among Jews in the U.S.: Trends, Inconsistencies, and Disagreements." *Contemporary Jewry* 12:67–97.

Demmitt, Kevin P. 1992. "Loosening the Ties That Bind: The Accommodation of Dual-Earner Families in a Conservative Protestant Church." *Review of Religious Research* 34:3–19.

de Vaus, David A. 1982. "The Impact of Children on Sex Related Differences in Church Attendance." *Sociological Analysis* 43:145–54.

———. 1984. "Workforce Participation and Sex Differences in Church Attendance." *Review of Religious Research* 25: 247–56.

de Vaus, David, and Ian McAllister. 1987. "Gender Differences in Religion: A Test of the Structural Location Theory." *American Sociological Review* 52:472–81.

Dudley, Roger L., and Margaret G. Dudley. 1986. "Transmission of Religious Values from Parents to Adolescents." *Review of Religious Research* 28:3–15.

Eckhardt, Kenneth W., and Gerry E. Hendershot. 1984. "Religious Preference, Religious Participation, and Sterilization Decisions: Findings from the National Survey of Family Growth, Cycle II." *Review of Religious Research* 25:232–46.

Ellison, Christopher G., John P. Bartkowski, and Michelle L. Segal. 1996. "Conservative Protestantism and the Parental Use of Corporal Punishment." *Social Forces* 74:1003–28.

Ellison, Christopher G., and Darren E. Sherkat. 1993a. "Conservative Protestantism and Support for Corporal Punishment." *American Sociological Review* 58:131–44.

———. 1993b. "Obedience and Autonomy: Religion and Parental Values Reconsidered." *Journal for the Scientific Study of Religion* 32:313–29.

Falwell, Jerry. 1981. *Listen, America!* New York: Bantam Books.

Feigelman, William, Bernard S. Gorman, and Joseph A. Varacalli. 1991. "The Social Characteristics of Black Catholics." *Sociology and Social Research* 75:133–43.

Fichter, Joseph H., S.J. 1983. "Family and Religion Among the Moonies: A Descriptive Analysis." Pp. 289–304 in *Families and Religions: Conflict and Change in Modern Society*, edited by William V. D'Antonio and Joan Aldous. Beverly Hills, CA: Sage.

———. 1985. *The Holy Family of Father Moon*. Kansas City, MO: Leaven Press.

Fishman, Sylvia Barack. 1996. "American Jewry: Families of Tradition in American Culture." Pp. 100–13 in *Faith Traditions and the Family*, edited by Phyllis D. Airhart and Margaret Lamberts Bendroth (The Family, Religion, and Culture Series). Louisville, KY: Westminster/John Knox Press.

Foster, Lawrence. 1981. *Religion and Sexuality: Three American Communal Experiments of the Nineteenth Century*. New York: Oxford University Press.

Francis, Leslie J. 1997. "The Psychology of Gender Differences in Religion: A Review of Empirical Research." *Religion* 27:81–96.

Gee, Ellen M. 1991. "Gender Differences in Church Attendance in Canada: The Role of Labor Force Participation." *Review of Religious Research* 32:267–73.

Glenn, Norval D. 1982. "Interreligious Marriage in the United States: Patterns and Recent Trends." *Journal of Marriage and the Family* 44:555–66.

Goldscheider, Calvin. 1967. "Fertility of the Jews." *Demography* 4:196–209.

Goldscheider, Calvin, and William D. Mosher. 1988. "Religious Affiliation and Contraceptive Usage: Changing American Patterns, 1955–82." *Studies in Family Planning* 19:48–57.

Goldstein, Sidney. 1992. "Profile of American Jewry: Insights from the 1990 National Jewish Population Survey." Pp. 77–173 in *The American Jewish Year Book 1992*, edited by David Singer and Ruth R. Seldin. New York: American Jewish Committee; Philadelphia: Jewish Publication Society.

Grace, James H. 1985. *Sex and Marriage in the Unification Movement: A Sociological Study* (Studies in Religion and Society, Vol. 13). New York: Edwin Mellen Press.

Greeley, Andrew M. 1970. "Religious Intermarriage in a Denominational Society." *American Journal of Sociology* 75:949–52.

———. 1990. *The Catholic Myth: The Behavior and Beliefs of American Catholics*. New York: Macmillan.

———. 1991a. "The Demography of American Catholics: 1965–1990." Pp. 37–56 in *Religion and the Social Order*, Vol. 2: *Vatican II and U.S. Catholicism*, edited by Helen Rose Ebaugh. Greenwich, CT: JAI Press.

———. 1991b. *Faithful Attraction: Discovering Intimacy, Love, and Fidelity in American Marriage*. New York: Tor Books.

Greven, Philip J., Jr. 1977. *The Protestant Temperament: Patterns of Child-Rearing, Religious Experience, and the Self in Early America.* New York: Alfred A. Knopf.

Hadden, Jeffrey K. 1983. "Televangelism and the Mobilization of a New Christian Right Family Policy." Pp. 247–66 in *Families and Religions: Conflict and Change in Modern Society,* edited by William V. D'Antonio and Joan Aldous. Beverly Hills, CA: Sage.

Hall, Charles. 1995. "Entering the Labor Force: Ideals and Realities Among Evangelical Women." Pp. 137–54 in *Work, Family, and Religion in Contemporary Society,* edited by Nancy Tatom Ammerman and Wade Clark Roof. New York: Routledge.

Hammond, Phillip E., Mark A. Shibley, and Peter M. Solow. 1994. "Religion and Family Values in Presidential Voting." *Sociology of Religion* 55:277–90.

Hart, Stephen. 1986. "Religion and Changes in Family Patterns." *Review of Religious Research* 28:51–70.

Heaton, Tim B. 1984. "Religious Homogamy and Marital Satisfaction Reconsidered." *Journal of Marriage and the Family* 46:729–33.

———. 1986. "How Does Religion Influence Fertility? The Case of Mormons." *Journal for the Scientific Study of Religion* 25:248–58.

———. 1989. "Religious Influences on Mormon Fertility: Cross-National Comparisons." *Review of Religious Research* 30:401–11.

Heaton, Tim B., and Sandra Calkins. 1983. "Family Size and Contraceptive Use Among Mormons: 1965–75." *Review of Religious Research* 25:102–13.

Heaton, Tim B., and Marie Cornwall. 1989. "Religious Group Variation in the Socioeconomic Status and Family Behavior of Women." *Journal for the Scientific Study of Religion* 28:283–299.

Heaton, Tim B., and Kristen L. Goodman. 1985. "Religion and Family Formation." *Review of Religious Research* 26:343–59.

Heaton, Tim B., Cardell K. Jacobson, and Xuan Ning Fu. 1992. "Religiosity of Married Couples and Childlessness." *Review of Religious Research* 33:244–55.

Heaton, Tim B., and Edith L. Pratt. 1990. "The Effects of Religious Homogamy on Marital Satisfaction and Stability." *Journal of Family Issues* 11:191–207.

Heilman, Samuel C. 1995. *Portrait of American Jews: The Last Half of the 20th Century* (Samuel and Althea Stroum Lectures in Jewish Studies). Seattle: University of Washington Press.

Heinz, Donald. 1983. "The Family: The New Christian Right's Symbol for a Lost Past, the Unification Movement's Hope for a Second Advent." Pp. 67–85 in *The Family and the Unification Church,* edited by Gene G. James (Conference Series No. 15). Barrytown, NY: Unification Theological Seminary.

———. 1985. "Clashing Symbols: The New Christian Right as Countermythology." *Archives de sciences sociales des religions* 59:153–73.

Hertel, Bradley R. 1995. "Work, Family, and Faith: Recent Trends." Pp. 81–121 in *Work, Family, and Religion in Contemporary Society,* edited by Nancy Tatom Ammerman and Wade Clark Roof. New York: Routledge.

Hertel, Bradley R., and Michael Hughes. 1987. "Religious Affiliation, Attendance, and Support for 'Pro-Family' Issues in the United States." *Social Forces* 65:858–82.

Himmelfarb, Harold S. 1979. "Agents of Religious Socialization Among American Jews." *Sociological Quarterly* 20:477–94.

Hoge, Dean R., Gregory H. Petrillo, and Ella I. Smith. 1982. "Transmission of Religious and Social Values from Parents to Teenage Children." *Journal of Marriage and the Family* 44:569–80.

Holman, Thomas B., and John R. Harding. 1996. "The Teaching of Nonmarital Sexual Abstinence and Members' Sexual Attitudes and Behaviors: The Case of Latter-day Saints." *Review of Religious Research* 38:51–60.

Hunsberger, Bruce, and L. B. Brown. 1984. "Religious Socialization, Apostasy, and the Impact of Family Background." *Journal for the Scientific Study of Religion* 23:239–51.

Hunt, Richard A., and Morton B. King. 1978. "Religiosity and Marriage." *Journal for the Scientific Study of Religion* 17:399–406.

Hunter, James Davison. 1991. *Culture Wars: The Struggle to Define America*. New York: Basic Books.

———. 1994. *Before the Shooting Begins: Searching for Democracy in America's Culture War*. New York: Free Press.

Jenkins, Kip W. 1991. "Religion and Families." Pp. 235–88 in *Family Research: A Sixty-Year Review, 1930–1990, Volume 1*, edited by Stephen J. Bahr. Lexington, MA: Lexington Books.

Johnson, Robert Alan. 1980. *Religious Assortive Marriage in the United States* (Studies in Population). New York: Academic Press.

Judd, Eleanore Parelman. 1990. "Intermarriage and the Maintenance of Religio-Ethnic Identity—A Case Study: The Denver Jewish Community." *Journal of Comparative Family Studies* 21:251–65.

Kalmijn, Matthijs. 1991. "Shifting Boundaries: Trends in Religious and Educational Homogamy." *American Sociological Review* 56:786–800.

Kelley, Jonathan, and Nan Dirk De Graaf. 1997. "National Context, Parental Socialization, and Religious Belief: Results from 15 Nations." *American Sociological Review* 62:639–59.

Landis, Judson T. 1949. "Marriages of Mixed and Non-Mixed Religious Faith." *American Sociological Review* 14:401–07.

Larson, Lyle E., and J. Walter Goltz. 1989. "Religious Participation and Marital Commitment." *Review of Religious Research* 30:387–400.

Lawton, Kim. 1992. "Bush: Start with Revival." *Christianity Today* 36 (October 26):64–65.

Lazerwitz, Bernard. 1981. "Jewish-Christian Marriages and Conversions." *Jewish Social Studies* 43:31–46.

———. 1995. "Jewish-Christian Marriages and Conversions, 1971 and 1990." *Sociology of Religion* 56:433–43.

Lehrer, Evelyn L. 1996. "The Role of the Husband's Religious Affiliation in the Economic and Demographic Behavior of Families." *Journal for the Scientific Study of Religion* 35:145–55.

Lehrer, Evelyn L., and Carmel U. Chiswick. 1993. "Religion as a Determinant of Marital Stability." *Demography* 30:385–404.

Lienesch, Michael. 1991. "'Train Up a Child': Conceptions of Child-Rearing in Christian Conservative Social Thought." *Comparative Social Research* 13:203–24.

———. 1993. *Redeeming America: Piety and Politics in the New Christian Right*. Chapel Hill: University of North Carolina Press.

Lynd, Robert S., and Helen Merrell Lynd. 1929. *Middletown: A Study in American Culture*. New York: Harcourt, Brace.

———. 1937. *Middletown in Transition: A Study in Cultural Conflicts*. New York: Harcourt, Brace.

Marcum, John P. 1981. "Explaining Fertility Differences Among U.S. Protestants." *Social Forces* 60:532–43.

Marler, Penny Long. 1995. "Lost in the Fifties: The Changing Family and the Nostalgic Church." Pp. 23–60 in *Work, Family, and Religion in Contemporary Society*, edited by Nancy Tatom Ammerman and Wade Clark Roof. New York: Routledge.

McConkie, Bruce R. 1966. *Mormon Doctrine* (2nd ed.). Salt Lake City, UT: Bookcraft.

McCutcheon, Allan L. 1988. "Denominations and Religious Intermarriage: Trends Among White Americans in the Twentieth Century." *Review of Religious Research* 29:213–27.

McDannell, Colleen. 1986. *The Christian Home in Victorian America, 1840–1900* (Religion in North America). Bloomington: Indiana University Press.

McNamara, Patrick H. 1985a. "Conservative Christian Families and Their Moral World: Some Reflections for Sociologists." *Sociological Analysis* 46:93–99.

———. 1985b. "The New Christian Right's View of the Family and Its Social Science Critics: A Study in Differing Presuppositions." *Journal of Marriage and the Family* 47:449–58.

Medding, Peter Y., Gary A. Tobin, Sylvia Barack Fishman, and Mordechai Rimor. 1992. "Jewish Identity in Conversionary and Mixed Marriages." Pp. 3–76 in *The American Jewish Year Book 1992*, edited by David Singer and Ruth R. Seldin. New York: American Jewish Committee; Philadelphia: Jewish Publication Society.

Moen, Matthew C. 1992a. "The Christian Right in the United States." Pp. 75–101 in *The Religious Challenge to the State*, edited by Matthew C. Moen and Lowell S. Gustafson. Philadelphia: Temple University Press.

———. 1992b. *The Transformation of the Christian Right*. Tuscaloosa: University of Alabama Press.

———. 1994. "From Revolution to Evolution: The Changing Nature of the Christian Right." *Sociology of Religion* 55:345–57.

Moran, Gerald F. 1992. "The Puritan Family and Religion: A Critical Reappraisal." Pp. 11–58 in *Religion, Family, and the Life Course: Explorations in the Social History of Early America*, by Gerald F. Moran and Maris A. Vinovskis. Ann Arbor: University of Michigan Press.

Morgan, Edmund S. 1966. *The Puritan Family: Religion and Domestic Relations in Seventeenth-Century New England* (rev. ed. enlarged). New York: Harper & Row.

Mosher, William D., and Calvin Goldscheider. 1984. "Contraceptive Patterns of Religious and Racial Groups in the United States, 1955–76: Convergence and Distinctiveness." *Studies in Family Planning* 15:101–11.

Mosher, William D., and Gerry E. Hendershot. 1984a. "Religion and Fertility: A Replication." *Demography* 21:185–91.

———. 1984b. "Religious Affiliation and the Fertility of Married Couples." *Journal of Marriage and the Family* 46:671–77.

Mosher, William D., David P. Johnson, and Marjorie C. Horn. 1986. "Religion and Fertility in the United States: The Importance of Marriage Patterns and Hispanic Origin." *Demography* 23:367–79.

Mosher, William D., Linda B. Williams, and David P. Johnson. 1992. "Religion and Fertility in the United States: New Patterns." *Demography* 29:199–214.

Musick, Marc, and John Wilson. 1995. "Religious Switching for Marriage Reasons." *Sociology of Religion* 56:257–70.

Myers, Scott M. 1996. "An Interactive Model of Religiosity Inheritance: The Importance of Family Context." *American Sociological Review* 61:858–66.

Nelsen, Hart M. 1980. "Religious Transmission Versus Religious Formation: Preadolescent-Parent Interaction." *Sociological Quarterly* 21:207–18.

———. 1981. "Religious Conformity in an Age of Disbelief: Contextual Effects of

Time, Denomination, and Family Processes Upon Church Decline and Apostasy." *American Sociological Review* 46:632–40.

Newport, Frank. 1979. "The Religious Switcher in the United States." *American Sociological Review* 44:528–52.

Pankhurst, Jerry G., and Sharon K. Houseknecht. 1983. "The Family, Politics, and Religion in the 1980s: In Fear of the New Individualism." *Journal of Family Issues* 4:5–34.

Petersen, Larry R. 1986. "Interfaith Marriage and Religious Commitment Among Catholics." *Journal of Marriage and the Family* 48:725–35.

Petersen, William. 1969. *Population* (2nd ed.). New York: Macmillan.

Ploch, Donald R., and Donald W. Hastings. 1998. "Effects of Parental Church Attendance, Current Family Status, and Religious Salience on Church Attendance." *Review of Religious Research* 39:309–20.

Political Research Associates. 1993. "Covering the Culture War: A Resource Guide." *Columbia Journalism Review* (July–August):37–40.

Poston, Dudley L., Jr., and Kathryn B. Kramer. 1986. "Patterns of Childlessness Among Catholic and Non-Catholic Women in the U.S.: A Log-Linear Analysis." *Sociological Inquiry* 56:507–22.

Quayle, Dan [J. Danforth Quayle]. 1994. *Standing Firm: A Vice-Presidential Memoir.* New York: HarperCollins.

Reed, Ralph. 1996a. "'We Stand at a Crossroads': The Religious Right Must Give Ground—or Risk Irrelevance." *Newsweek* 127 (May 13):28–29.

———. 1996b. *Active Faith: How Christians Are Changing the Soul of American Politics.* New York: Free Press.

Rose, Susan D. 1987. "Women Warriors: The Negotiation of Gender in a Charismatic Community." *Sociological Analysis* 48:245–58.

Schmelz, U. O., and Sergio DellaPergola. 1982. "The Demographic Consequences of U.S. Jewish Population Trends." Pp. 141–87 in *The American Jewish Year Book 1983*, edited by Milton Himmelfarb and David Singer. New York: American Jewish Committee; Philadelphia: Jewish Publication Society of America.

Shehan, Constance L., E. Wilbur Bock, and Gary R. Lee. 1990. "Religious Heterogamy, Religiosity, and Marital Happiness: The Case of Catholics." *Journal of Marriage and the Family* 52:73–79.

Sherkat, Darren E., and John Wilson. 1995. "Preferences, Constraints, and Choices in Religious Markets: An Examination of Religious Switching and Apostasy." *Social Forces* 73:993–1026.

Smith, James E. 1985. "A Familistic Religion in a Modern Society." Pp. 273–98 in *Contemporary Marriage: Comparative Perspectives on a Changing Institution*, edited by Kingsley Davis, with Amyra Grossbard-Shechtman. New York: Russell Sage Foundation.

Sontag, Frederick. 1977. *Sun Myung Moon and the Unification Church.* Nashville, TN: Abingdon Press.

Stolzenberg, Ross M., Mary Blair-Loy, and Linda J. Waite. 1995. "Religious Participation in Early Adulthood: Age and Family Life Cycle Effects on Church Membership." *American Sociological Review* 60:84–103.

Tamney, Joseph B., and Stephen D. Johnson. 1985. "Consequential Religiosity in Modern Society." *Review of Religious Research* 26:360–78.

Thomas, Darwin L., ed. 1988. *The Religion and Family Connection: Social Science Perspectives* (Specialized Monograph Series, No. 3). Provo, UT: Religious Studies Center, Brigham Young University.

Thomas, Darwin L., and Marie Cornwall. 1990. "Religion and Family in the 1980s: Discovery and Development." *Journal of Marriage and the Family* 52:983–92.

Thomas, Darwin L., and Gwendolyn C. Henry. 1985. "The Religion and Family Connection: Increasing Dialogue in the Social Sciences." *Journal of Marriage and the Family* 47:369–79.

Thornton, Arland. 1979. "Religion and Fertility: The Case of Mormonism." *Journal of Marriage and the Family* 41:131–42.

———. 1985. "Reciprocal Influences of Family and Religion in a Changing World." *Journal of Marriage and the Family* 47:381–94.

Ulbrich, Holley, and Myles Wallace. 1984. "Women's Work Force Status and Church Attendance." *Journal for the Scientific Study of Religion* 23:341–50.

Visscher, Adrian M., and Merle J. Stern. 1990. "Family Rituals as Medium in Christian Faith Transmission." Pp. 103–18 in *Current Studies on Rituals: Perspectives for the Psychology of Religion*, edited by Hans-Günter Heimbrock and H. Barbara Boudewijnse (International Series in the Psychology of Religion 2). Amsterdam: Rodopi.

Waugh, Earle H. 1991. "North America and the Adaptation of the Muslim Tradition: Religion, Ethnicity, and the Family." Pp. 68–95 in *Muslim Families in North America*, edited by Earle H. Waugh, Sharon McIrvin Abu-Laban, and Regula Burckhardt Qureshi. Edmonton: University of Alberta Press.

Westoff, Charles F. 1979. "The Blending of Catholic Reproductive Behavior." Pp. 231–40 in *The Religious Dimension: New Directions in Quantitative Research*, edited by Robert Wuthnow. New York: Academic Press.

Westoff, Charles F., and Larry Bumpass. 1973. "The Revolution in Birth Control Practices of U.S. Roman Catholics." *Science* 179 (January 5):41–44.

Westoff, Charles F., and Elise F. Jones. 1977. "The Secularization of U.S. Catholic Birth Control Practices." *Family Planning Perspectives* 9:203–07.

———. 1979. "The End of 'Catholic' Fertility." *Demography* 16:209–17.

Westoff, Charles F., Robert G. Potter, and Philip C. Sagi. 1964. "Some Selected Findings of the Princeton Fertility Study: 1963." *Demography* 1:130–35.

Whitehead, Barbara Dafoe. 1993. "Dan Quayle Was Right." *Atlantic Monthly* 271 (April):47–50, 52, 55, 58, 60–62, 64–66, 70–72, 74, 77, 80, 82, 84.

Williams, Linda B., and Basil G. Zimmer. 1990. "The Changing Influence of Religion on U.S. Fertility: Evidence from Rhode Island." *Demography* 27:475–81.

Wilson, John. 1978. *Religion in American Society: The Effective Presence*. Englewood Cliffs, NJ: Prentice-Hall.

Wilson, John, Allan M. Parnell, and Deanna L. Pagnini. 1997. "Religious Fundamentalism and Family Behavior." *Research in the Social Scientific Study of Religion* 8:163–91.

Wilson, John, and Sharon Sandomirsky. 1991. "Religious Affiliation and the Family." *Sociological Forum* 6:289–309.

Wilson, John, and Darren E. Sherkat. 1994. "Returning to the Fold." *Journal for the Scientific Study of Religion* 33:148–61.

Wilson, Margaret R., and Erik E. Filsinger. 1986. "Religiosity and Marital Adjustment: Multidimensional Interrelationships." *Journal of Marriage and the Family* 48:147–51.

Wright, Stuart A., and William V. D'Antonio. 1993. "Families and New Religions." Pp. 219–38 in *Religion and the Social Order*, Vol. 3 (Part A): *The Handbook on Cults and Sects in America*, edited by David G. Bromley and Jeffrey K. Hadden. Greenwich, CT: JAI Press.

Wright, Stuart A., and Elizabeth S. Piper. 1986. "Families and Cults: Familial Factors Related to Youth Leaving or Remaining in Deviant Religious Groups." *Journal of Marriage and the Family* 48:15–25.

CHAPTER THREE

Social Change in Egypt: The Roles of Religion and Family

SHARON K. HOUSEKNECHT

INTRODUCTION

Egypt is an Islamic society. From the seventh century until the early nineteenth century, it was ruled by a state sanctified by this religious ideology. The reign of Muhamed Ali (1805–49) marked the beginning of secularization of the government. Ali's goals were to increase the functions and autonomy of the government and to build a strong modern army. Although Ali did not attempt to secularize society in general, he curbed the political influence of religious leaders (Farah 1986).

The move toward institutional secularization has continued since the time of Ali. At first, governmental expansion did not cause great disruption in the traditional economic, educational, and legal institutions that were mainly under the purview of religious leaders. But over time, the evolving state bureaucracy began to seek extensive societal control by performing functions normally left to religious groups (cf. Crecelius 1980). Despite many efforts, though, no regime to date has managed to free either itself or the other institutions completely from religious influence.

Today, numerous religious associations and the government are locked in a battle for the control of major societal institutions, including the economy, education, law, and polity. The goals for the government are to hold on to its power and to move forward with modernity and developmental efforts. The goal for the religious groups (Islamists) is desecularization. The Islamists want to overturn the present regime and establish a more pure version of Islamic society. An important fact to understand is that Islam is more than just a religion; it represents an entire way of life. Islamic law, which is central to the Islamic tradition, constitutes a blueprint for the ideal society. It is believed to be relevant and integral to all other institutions (cf. Esposito 1991).

The struggle between the religious associations and the government may be thought of as a struggle over structural differentiation (Parsons 1961, 1971), with opposition mainly from the religious sphere. That all institutions have not structurally differentiated from religion to the same degree does not mean that there is less conflict over some than others. All are considered important because all are thought to fit into an organic whole. The family, in comparison with the economy, education, law, and polity, is the least differentiated from religion. It has been much less transformed by modernity than these other institutions. It is noteworthy in this regard that the only part of Islamic law that is still applied today is that which pertains to the family. Religion and family are the most traditional of the various institutions so they are also the most threatened by the government's modernity efforts. And because there is a strong mutually reinforcing link between religion and the family in Egypt, a significant part of the conflict over politics, the economy, education, and law that is taking place between the religious associations and the government can be traced to the concern of the religious associations with the *cultural invasion* that they believe is modernizing family life (see, for example, El Ghazaly 1991a).

The focus of this chapter is social change in contemporary Egypt and the roles of religion and family in that change. The chapter examines the reinforcing relations between religion and family and the conflict between religious associations and the government over politics, the economy, education, and law. It considers whether the decline in religious influence on education, the economy, law, and polity has been accompanied by changes in the family that are contrary to Islamic doctrine. Finally, it describes how even without inconsistencies with Islamic doctrine, the family could serve as an impetus for social change efforts by religious associations.

This is not the first work to assess the interactions of institutions in Egypt. However, although a number of scholars (see, for example, Crecelius 1980; Farah 1986; Hopwood 1991; McDermott 1988) have examined the course of secularization in modern Egypt and have provided an excellent account of some institutional relationships, they did not mention the influential role of the family in all that was happening.

CONCEPTUAL FRAMEWORK

This analysis is guided by the interinstitutional perspective. For a long time, the bulk of the research in sociology of religion and in family sociology has been either social psychological or intrainstitutional or has looked at the interactions of either family or religion with other institutions (cf. Houseknecht 1988; National Research Council 1988; Spitzer 1988). Although there is no question but that these approaches provide essential insights, it is also worthwhile to consider both religion and family in relation to other institutional contexts to attain a more comprehensive understanding. Family and religion share a special affinity, a point that is elaborated to some extent later in this chapter, as well as in Chapter 1, the Introduction to this book. Thus, it is relevant to take the interactions between them into account. Family and religion also relate to each other within the larger societal context, a context that is especially important to consider, given that socially patterned values, norms, and behaviors in a particular institutional sphere are interdependent with those in all other institutional spheres (c.f. Merton 1970; Weber 1930; Williams [1955] 1970).

The emphasis here, then, is on interinstitutional relations. Of utmost concern are the reinforcing and conflicting connections between social structures, cultural structures (normative and value systems), and the functions of different institutions and how they influence social change. A reinforcing connection can be seen in the interrelations of religion and family in Egypt. The religious socialization and social control functions are carried out by both religious associations and families. Although the educational and legal institutions contribute in this regard, their roles are not always thought to be satisfactorily reinforcing because of efforts both within and outside these institutions to secularize them. And, of course, the kinds of changes that have occurred in connection with economic development are considered to have made it all the more difficult to carry out these functions. This situation leads to the notion of interinstitutional conflict. Most social change that ensues from interinstitutional relations is the result of conflict.

The most intense interinstitutional conflict in Egypt in recent times has been between religious associations and the government. But the incompatible interests of the religious and political institutions are closely connected to happenings in all other institutions in Egypt, since the interactions of institutions do not take place in a vacuum. The issue of institutional dominance, first articulated by Williams ([1955] 1970) in 1955, is relevant here. According to Gouldner and Gouldner (1963:496):

> In many societies one institution dominates the total social system. Its values and norms permeate a great many areas of life and enter into the operation of other institutions. So pervasive might be the domination of one institution that other institutions inculcate the values of the dominant one.

Williams ([1955] 1970:549) proposed two criteria for determining the relative dominance of institutions:

> A first approach to the problem is the controlled observation of *change*. If we find that changes in institution A are invariably followed by important changes in institution B . . . n but that changes in institution B . . . n are followed by few or insignificant changes in institution A, then A is presumably a "prime mover" or dominant vector in the social system. . . . A second and more specific procedure for appraising dominance consists of systematic observation of what occurs when *various sets of institutional norms conflict* in particular situations. If particular norms, conceived of as part of institution A, always or in some preponderant proportion take precedence over the *other* norms, this is a test of the extent to which one institutional complex is more predictive of behavior than others.

The issue of institutional dominance is explored in this chapter because of its relevance to social change. First, however, it is useful to take a more in-depth look at the reinforcing relations between religion and the family in

Egypt. But before I do so, I want to stress that the relations between family and religion are not always mutually reinforcing. Sometimes these two institutions are in conflict, a point illustrated by Goody (1983) in his analysis of the family-religion linkage in Europe during the Middle Ages. Regardless of whether the relations are reinforcing or conflicting, though, they always reflect the uniqueness of the family-religion connection.

REINFORCING RELATIONS BETWEEN RELIGION AND FAMILY IN EGYPT

Religion and family are qualitatively different from the other major institutions. According to MacIver (1970:45), the social structural component of institutions is made up of associations that "come into being as means or modes of attaining interests." MacIver distinguished between secondary interests, which, by their very nature, are means to other interests, and cultural interests, which are pursued for their own sake because they bring direct satisfaction. Economics and politics exemplify the former, since they seem to be instruments for attaining other interests. Religion and family, on the other hand, exemplify cultural interests. In general, their utilitarian service is incidental to the fact that they tend to be pursued for their own sakes because they bring direct satisfaction. MacIver viewed education as intermediate between cultural and secondary interests because it is pursued both for its own sake and as a means to an end.

It is relevant to look at points of intersection between the institutions of religion and the family. One is the efforts of both to define the nature of social relationships in the family. Most religions take strong stands on many different aspects of family life. The influence, though, is not one way, since the values that shape the nature of relationships in the family find expression in the beliefs and practices of religious groups (D'Antonio 1980, 1983). Of course, one of these institutions may exert greater influence over the other at times. When religion holds a prominent position in society, the family receives a lot of attention.

The connection between a strong religious institution and family focus is apparent in Egypt. 'Abd al 'Ati (1977:21), referring to Egypt, said:

> Family rights and obligations are not private family affairs of no concern to the rest of society. It is true that these are assigned to the family members who are enjoined to administer them privately. But, if the situation becomes unmanageable, religion commands society, represented by designated authorities as well as conscientious individuals, to take whatever action is necessary to implement the law, in order to maintain equity and harmony (see, for example, the *Koran*, 2:225–237; 3:140; 4:127–130, 135, 176; 5:47–50). This is a natural result of the fact that the mutual expectations of the family members are not established only by familial relationships, but also by the membership in a larger social system which derives from a com-

> mon religious brotherhood. This brotherhood has its own implications. It is so conceived as to reinforce the family ties, complement them, or prevent their abuse (see, for example, the *Koran*, 2:177–182; 3:103–104; 4:34–37; 9:23–24; 17:23–24; 33:4–6; 49:10; 64:14–16).

In Egypt, families promote the values of the religious institution through their socialization and social control practices. Muslim parents, for example, are enjoined to "show the child in words as well as in deeds the Islamic way of life, hoping that this early socialization will be effective in later years" ('Abd al 'Ati 1977:199). Because religion is dependent upon the family to fulfill these functions, its considerable concern for the family is understandable. Contrast this situation to one in which the economy is dominant, as in the United States. As the economy grows in influence, it gradually frees itself of control by families; no longer is the family the center of production. In an expanding wage-based economy, the individual can be the economic unit. In fact, the economy thrives more on individuals than on families. For example, employees who have a primary commitment to their work and are willing to be geographically mobile are especially desirable (Hunt and Hunt 1982). And advertising appeals are increasingly directed to different members of the family who represent separate categories of consumers (cf. Frenzen, Hirsch, and Zerrillo 1994).

It cannot be assumed that either religion or family is a conservative force, maintaining tradition and stabilizing long-term social and cultural arrangements. Strauss (1972), for example, observed that it is not the number of functions performed by kin groups that has a modernity inhibiting effect, but the ability of the kin group to adapt, to devise new responses to situations for which no behavioral pattern is available. To the extent that the kin groups are *modern*, then the culture that they transmit and enforce will also tend to be modern. With regard to religion, Latin American liberation theology illustrates the point. The movement's efforts to change internal societal oppression and the structure of the world economic system are markedly different from the concern with spirituality that is unconnected to political, social, and economic issues that have historically characterized the mainstream Catholic Church in Latin America (Robertson 1984).

In the case of Egypt, though, both religion and family represent conservative forces. Furthermore, religion has been resilient throughout the century. As Crecelius (1980:70) noted, "Egypt remains an Islamic state in form and essence, just as its society remains faithful to traditional beliefs and practices despite more than a century of evolution towards secularism." Marshall (1984:513) concurred: "In Muslim North Africa, Islam tends to be the most salient symbol of cultural identity." And, of course, Islam has fostered particular family values throughout this time. In Islam, religion and law are indivisible. According to Esposito (1991:75), "Law is essentially religious, the concrete expression of God's guidance . . . for humanity." From 639 C.E., when Egypt became an Islamic country, until now, Egypt's family law (governing marriage, divorce, inheritance, and the like), in contrast to its civil law, has resisted all but relatively minor reform and remains the province of the traditional *Shari'a* (Islamic law) (Najjar 1988).

> The *Shari'a* draws primarily from the *Koran* (the word of God as revealed to Mohammed), as well as from the *Sunna* and *Hadith* (the collection of traditions and sayings of Mohammed), the *Qiyas* (the body of reasoning developed by religious jurists over time), and the *Ijma* (consensus of a group of judges representing a Moslem community). (Weeks 1988:6)

Since 1955, when religious courts were abolished (Crecelius 1980), the state system of courts has administered *Shari'a* family law, applying it only to Muslims; Christians are permitted to have their own laws regarding family matters. There is no question, then, but that both religion and family in Egypt serve to maintain tradition and stabilize long-term social and cultural arrangements, especially given the interrelated dominance of these two institutions in the society.

CONFLICT BETWEEN RELIGION AND GOVERNMENT

Interconnections among religion, family, and law have just been mentioned, and the list can be expanded to include yet other institutional linkages that help one comprehend the processes of social change in contemporary Egypt. The intense interinstitutional conflict that has characterized this country in recent years is, in some ways, not so different from what has been going on for centuries. From early Islam until now, the two major antagonists have been religion and the government. Crecelius (1980:50–51) pointed out:

> [I]n early Islam . . . it became the function of the *Ulama* [a conclave of religious scholars at Al-Azhar University] to preserve, study, interpret and propagate the sacred law and religious principles through their teachings, and it fell upon the state to defend and apply the sacred law . . . the *Ulama* did not attempt to wield political power so much as to manipulate it, hoping to influence state and society through their teachings and pious conduct . . . [And] this traditional self-view the *Ulama* held of themselves as advisers, not rulers, has characterized the Sunni concept of the relationship between religion and the state to the present.

Islamic doctrine does not support the idea of an institutionally differentiated society. This applies across the board to politics, law, education, economics, and family. Obedience to God is of utmost importance, and God's will is set forth in Islamic law, which covers all these institutional spheres. This arrangement, though, represents the ideal, not the real situation that has existed since the early days. Rulers generally recognized the superiority of the *Shari'a* and sought the approval of the *Ulama* for their actions; the *Ulama*, on the other hand, were often forced to compromise in the face of power exerted by their rulers. Nevertheless, the *Ulama* held a traditional "veto" power, whose preservation is one of the demands of many religious enthusiasts today (cf. Crecelius 1980).

The organic unity between the religious and political institutions that existed in the past, despite the conflict between the two, is breaking down. Recent governments, including Nasser's (1952–70), Sadat's (1970–81), and Mubarak's (1981 to the present), have altered what Gouldner and Gouldner (1963) called *multiplicity in functions* for the religious institution. Although religion has remained an important force in the religious life and culture of many Muslims (91 percent of the population in Egypt is Muslim; see Weeks 1988:8), its political role has been progressively circumscribed (c.f. Esposito 1991). Religious leaders are being denied meaningful participation in the political realm. This kind of action is related to the government's commitment to modernity and its awareness of the power of religious conservatives and Islamist associations (Gaffney 1991; Najjar 1988).

In 1993, one of the Arab world's most listened-to radio stations, Cairo's *Mahatta el Koran el Karim* (Holy Koran Station), was issued a gag order from the government because of its "inflammatory" religious commentary. The station's director was involuntarily replaced with one known to be more secular, and only pro-government religious figures could speak thereafter (Warg 1993). The strong reaction of some religious groups to the curtailed political role of religion has entailed efforts to topple the current secular government, headed by Mubarak, and to replace it with a theocracy (Al-Sayyid 1993; "Egypt," 1992). It is interesting that both religion and polity are seeking structural *dedifferention* (cf. Parsons 1961, 1971). Rather than have either separate or shared spheres of activity, each wants to keep its own functions and, at the same time, take primary responsibility for the functions of the other. For example, Al-Sayyid (1993:241) averred, "the government's efforts to outbid Islamist groups in the claim to conformity to religious, particularly Islamic, values." It was also reported (Hubbell 1992:324) that

> many liberal Egyptians feel that the government is going too far in brandishing its Islamic credentials, by increasing religious television programming and making frequent references to Islamic law in drafting of new legislation [and that] . . . successive governments, fearful for their own legitimacy, have sought to control what goes on in mosques by hiring and dismissing religious leaders at will and by exerting control over the sheiks at al-Azhar University in Cairo—one of the most prestigious seats of learning in Islam.

On the other hand, as part of its the effort to take over the government, religious associations are assuming a diverse array of governmental functions. In addition to sermons in mosques, the Islamists are spreading their message through a network of schools, clinics, and Islamic charities (Hedges 1993). One 58-year-old shop owner was quoted as saying:

> When we have trouble the Muslims come quickly to help. If someone treats you unfairly, you can go to the Muslims and they will speak to him or beat him. If he tries to flirt with your daughter, they threaten him. If you are in debt, they tell the money lender to be patient (quoted in Hedges 1992a:A7).

Private religious associations, then, are providing services—education, job training, health care, and day care—in the face of the government's unwillingness or inability to make those services available as promised (Gaffney 1991; Hubbell 1992; Sullivan 1990). Noteworthy, too, is the fact that in many Cairo neighborhoods, hard hit by the October 12, 1992, earthquake, the Islamists were the only groups dispensing food and blankets for the first few days (Hedges 1992a).

So-called Islamist extremists have been waging a guerilla war against Egypt's secular government for years in the hopes of setting up an Islamic state. The rise of these militant Islamic groups dates back to the founding of the Muslim Brotherhood in 1928, although the brotherhood did not use violence until the late 1940s. One of the avowed principles was the creation of an Islamic society through the application of *Shari'a* (S. Ibrahim 1980). The timing of the formation of the brotherhood followed what Crecelius (1980:57) called "the key period of secular gestation" in Egyptian society, the latter half of the 1800's.

Although Islamic militancy has had a long history in Egypt, in late 1991 there was a major escalation of the campaign for an Islamic state (cf. "Egyptian Terrorists" 1994). It is relevant to ask, What precipitated escalation at that time? Although this is a difficult question to answer, it is possible to point to some of the societal events and conditions that existed then. Two things, of course, that fit the timing precisely were the Persian Gulf crisis of 1990–91 and the simultaneous introduction of CNN, the latter having a great deal of symbolic import as far as the spread of Western ways is concerned. In fact, CNN was also a major source of information on the Gulf War. In addition, the government's attempt in 1986 virtually to take over private mosques in an effort to prevent independent *Imams* (primary prayer leaders at all mosques) and Islamic workers from exercising their influence (cf. Gaffney 1991) helped set the stage for the strong reactions to the later events.

Many of the conflictual dynamics between religious associations and the government have been elaborated here. But where does the family fit in? As was mentioned earlier, the religious associations want to maintain and strengthen not just religious traditions, but family traditions as well. In Egypt, where only limited structural differentiation has occurred between religion and family, the family is a critical element in the vitality of the religious institution. Because the *cultural invasion* is viewed as having both direct and indirect (via the family) effects on religion, the religious opposition actually is reacting to what it perceives as secular change in both spheres (cf. El Ghazaly 1991a; Y. Ibrahim 1994) Concern for what is happening to the family is apparent in some of the topics dealt with in regular editorials in the Socialist Labor Party's newspaper, *El Sha'ab*, the party having been taken over by Islamists in March 1989 (cf. Singer 1993). These topics include the decline in parental discipline, premarital sex, adultery, the conservativeness of women's clothing, and women's use of makeup (see, for example, El Din 1993; El Ghazaly 1991a, 1991b, 1991c; El Hoda Saad 1994).

Feminist strivings are at issue here, too. The mobilization of women in Egypt is stymied by a political system that limits the role of pressure groups: demonstrations and unauthorized group meetings are banned, for example. Nevertheless, there is a weak feminist movement comprised of elite women. One of the movement's concerns is polygamy, which the feminists believe is acceptable but only under certain conditions and with the first wife's consent. Other concerns are that divorce should be the right of both men and women, compensation should be based on need, and clear legislation should be passed on women's right to work. That there is strong opposition to such strivings by some religious associations is apparent in the government's expressed fear that any public action by women would stir up Islamic extremists (Friedman 1985).

Economy as a Stress Factor

In addition to the Persian Gulf crisis and CNN, there are problems associated with the Egyptian economy:

> The country has a huge, inefficient and still largely state controlled industrial sector, an overvalued currency, a near penniless central bank and a crippling $46 billion foreign debt. Unemployment is rising, inflation is running at 25 percent, and the population of 55 million grows by a million every nine months. (Chesnoff and Robison 1990:34)

Furthermore, many perceive official corruption to be rampant ("Egypt" 1993; Man 1993). We see here some of the ways in which the economic institution is related to social change processes in Egypt. But, there are others, too. Crecelius (1980:59–60), for example, said this about economic development:

> [S]ocioeconomic change began the inexorable transformation of Egyptian society . . . destroying the intricate pattern of relationships upon which [the *Ulama's*] . . . influence, functions, and concepts were dependent. . . . Entirely new social groups emerged to perform a vast range of skills not found within traditional society. The lawyers, doctors, journalists, novelists, professional politicians, engineers, and others, themselves both the product of socioeconomic change and the chief motive force for further development, now challenged the political, intellectual, and social leadership [of] the Ulama. . . . Socioeconomic change also gave impetus to secularism in the changing attitudes, values, beliefs, habits, even in the dress and style of the modernizing urban social groups.

Secular ideas and attitudes found their way into literature, formed the basis of new fields of study, were popularized in the burgeoning native press, and were taught in modern schools and courts.

In short, there is no question but that the economic institution played a major role in the rift between the religious and political institutions. It is interesting, though, that the Islamist associations mainly blame the government, not the economy, for the various problems that abound. Although the recent attacks on banks would seem to indicate that the Islamist extremists are targeting the economy, they are viewed as a means to get at the government, not as an end in themselves. El-Sayed Yasseen, director of Al Ahram Stategic Studies Center, made this point clear:

> All these groups [Islamists], not withstanding their diversity, have only one aim from which they will not be diverted, namely, to bring about the collapse of the present secularist state in Egypt, replacing it with a religious authority based on religious texts and under slogans that only God, not men, will rule (quoted in Y. Ibrahim 1994:Al, A10).

The deteriorating economic conditions have created a great deal of dissatisfaction within the population at large, the result being an increase in the number of sympathizers with the Islamist extremists' efforts to bring about change. And, in fact, the extremist groups would like to provoke widespread reaction to the present regime, one indicator being their efforts in recent years to topple Egypt's large tourism industry (Hedges 1992a; Y. Ibrahim 1994), a principal foreign-exchange earner (Sullivan 1990).

Competition for Control of Education and Law

Religion and the government are locked in a struggle for control of the educational and legal institutions. One indication of this struggle with regard to education was the death threats against the minister of education, Hussein Baha'eddin, for trying to change the school curriculum. Baha'eddin said:

> The real debate is my campaign to combat infiltration inside the schools. For the fundamentalists [Islamists], the real target is to seize control of the schools. If they do, they will seize power (quoted in Lief 1993, p. 43).

The increase in modern secular schools has relegated religious schooling to a secondary status and has contributed to this reaction in the religious sphere (cf. Crecelius 1980). In 1989–90, for example, there were three times as many modern schools as religious schools at the primary level, eight times as many at the preparatory level, and four times as many at the secondary level (*Statistical Year Book* 1991:160–64). As Y. Ibrahim (1994:A1) indicated, the Islamists have had some success in their efforts to take control of the schools: "In most public schools, particularly in the south of Egypt, teachers have imposed the veil on girls as young as six and altered school books to emphasize Islamic teachings."

At the university level, Islamists have been growing in influence, and they now control the elected student and faculty associations at many of the institutions. They have been described as preventing certain cultural activities that might have been held on the campuses, pressuring female students to wear head scarves, stipulating that male and female students must ride in separate buses on university trips, advocating that women and men sit on opposite sides of the classroom, and influencing the curriculum. Their basic demand is for an altered intellectual climate that is more consistent with traditional attitudes. In response, the government has reassigned hundreds of teachers to nonclassroom jobs, ousted suspected radicals from university dormitories, begun to appoint top university officials, and started screening candidates for student leadership posts (Bollag 1991, 1994).

The same kind of competition is taking place over matters related to the legal sphere. The Parliament, for example, which contains both conservatives and secularists, has been studying ways in which specific *Shari'a* laws, including Koranic punishments, may be revived (Crecelius 1980:69). An editorial by El Ghazaly (1993), the editor of the Islamist-controlled *El Sha'ab* newspaper, stated:

> I feel that the laws made by man that control many parts of the Islamic world are very old, and we should replace them with God's laws that were applied in the pure centuries. These new laws have poisoned Islamic beliefs and created new traditions. Now we are still losing by using these laws without end.

And in the early 1990s, there was "court testimony from a noted Islamic scholar that appeared to sanction the killing of 'apostates' by individuals if the state did not do its Islamic duty and punish them" (Murphy 1993:1).

It is noteworthy that the Egyptian Bar Association, known as a trade union, now reflects an Islamic orientation. An example particular to the family was the resistance to changing Egypt's family law. According to Najjar (1988:319):

> The relatively limited changes introduced in 1979 by Law 44 were short-lived: the law was struck down as unconstitutional on May 1985. [Decreed] by President Anwar Sadat, while the People's Assembly was in recess, two years before his assassination, the invalidated law had provided welcome relief for Egyptian women by seeking to break the grip of male dominance. The High Courts ruling sparked considerable debate between reformists, who advocated the liberalization of marriage and divorce laws, and conservatives, who held that [marriage and divorce] are regulated by the *Shari'a* and are not susceptible to modification by human legislation.

The law that was repealed had given a wife the right to know if her husband was going to take a second wife, to divorce if her husband was going to take a second wife, and to keep the couple's apartment (Friedman 1985).

The reason that control of the educational and legal institutions is so desirable, of course, is that they are the two institutions, other than the family, that are most responsible for inculcating societal norms and values. Growing secularization in these two spheres, in addition to having a direct negative effect on religion, also has the potential to weaken traditional family patterns. The direct negative effects, together with the fact that primary responsibility for religious socialization and social control lies with the family (and traditional families are more likely than nontraditional ones to uphold traditional religious patterns), explains why there is strong resistance by some religious associations to secularization in the realms of education and law.

The Complexity of Institutional Dominance

All the major social institutions in Egypt are experiencing a lot of strain and conflict. What is occurring is what Janowitz (1978) referred to as the "disarticulation of institutions." "Institutions are thought to be disarticulated when their interrelations contribute to the weakening of self-regulation and control" (p. 365). Exactly how the situation will play out is difficult to know. With regard to the two major institutional adversaries, Crecelius (1980) noted the historical dominance of the polity over religion in Egypt. One must ask, though, what exactly does dominance mean in this regard?

Since power is basic to the notion of institutional dominance, Wrong's ([1979] 1988) distinction between coercive and legitimate authority is useful in answering this question. Obtaining compliance through threats and the selective use of force (coercion), is very effective, at least in the short run. This type of power, however, is resource intensive, since the means and instruments of force must be kept in constant readiness. In contrast, legitimate authority, which induces willing compliance, does not depend on force or threats of force. Rather, it is based on the internalization of norms that prescribe obedience to the source, not the content, of a command. Legitimate authority presupposes shared values and entails disapproval if one does not fulfill the obligation to obey. Although it is not resource intensive, it ensures more reliable conformity than does coercion.

With regard to capability and the willingness to use force, there is little question that the government has had the upper hand in Egypt. The government's use of resources and force in an effort to control religiously based political opposition has been impressive. For example, on December 8, 1992, the government sent more than ten thousand security police into a Cairo suburb that was reputed to be a stronghold of one of the militant Islamic groups, and a similar operation was mounted against Islamist leaders in Upper Egypt ("Egypt" 1992). The government's frustration is apparent in the following statement:

> [T]he Egyptian government has unleashed its security forces in a bloodletting and a wave of detentions not seen in Egypt since the assassination

> of President Anwar Sadat in 1981. . . . The confrontation signals the administration's resolve to curtail or shut down any Muslim group that appears to be politically inclined (Hedges 1993:A1).

On the other hand, considering the cultural sphere, there is little question but that religion is and has been the dominant force in Egypt. According to S. Ibrahim (1980:425) the militant islamic groups "represent the small hard core of a broad but amorphous mass of religiosity in the society as a whole." The importance of religion in Egypt is further confirmed in the following statement by Tuma (1988:1188–89):

> Religion, as practiced, is the most relevant institution . . . because it encompasses the society and reaches to all aspects of Egyptian life . . . religion is considered a way of life and not simply a relationship between the worshipper and the deity. Egyptians resort to a high degree of religious symbolism and overt practices in their daily behavior. They invoke the name of God to seek help and to offer thanks for both their successes and failures, and they invoke it to wish others well or to pile up curses on them. The call to prayer five times a day, from minarets, on loudspeakers, and on T.V. and radio is a constant reminder of the place of religion in this society. Regardless of what program is in progress on the media, it will be interrupted by the call to prayer. Similarly, the call to prayer is brought into the home, the shop, the classroom, and elsewhere.

The complexity of the issue of institutional dominance in Egypt is apparent. Recognition of this fact leads me to question Crecelius's (1980) conclusion about the dominance of polity over religion. Earlier it was noted that both religion and polity are seeking structural dedifferentiation. In other words, each institution wants to continue to carry out its own primary functions as well as to take major responsibility for the functions of the other institution. There is an important qualitative difference in these aspirations, though. Some religious associations would definitely like to take the leading role in the political realm; for them, the goal to attain power is an end in itself. In contrast, the government's greater and greater involvement in the religious sphere does not reflect a true desire to take on the functions of the religious institution; rather, such actions are a means to an end. The expanding religious role of the government is mainly for the purpose of attaining legitimacy (cf. Esposito 1991:157).

According to Wrong ([1979] 1988:121), those who rule by coercive means "strive, usually with at least partial success, to convert might into right by establishing a claim to legitimacy in the eyes of their subjects." It is interesting that the most effective way to achieve legitimacy is thought to be through the institution with which the government has had the most conflict. This is because the Islamic orientation of the society is much broader than those extremist groups who seek a pure Islamic society and with which the government is in open confrontation. There are also those who wish to preserve Islamic culture but who would like to steer clear of the political arena. And there are those who are willing to have a society that utilizes the best elements in the Islamic and Western traditions (Haynes 1994). Regardless of the (uncountable) category, though, there is no lack of Islamic piety. Esposito (1991:171) reported that "concern about leading a more Islamically informed way of life can be found among the middle and upper classes, educated and uneducated, peasants and professionals, young and old, women and men." It is clear that the dominance of the religious institution is an important force that must be reckoned with.

ISLAMIC DOCTRINE AND FAMILY PATTERNS: HOW MUCH CONSISTENCY?

Given the centrality of the family in Islamic social organization (cf. Marshall 1984) and the efforts of militants to reassert Islam in Egypt, it is instructive to inquire what social change has occurred in the family institution. It was noted earlier that Islam promotes particular family values and norms and enforces the latter via *Shari'a*, family law. Was it the case, though, that, as Egyptian society modernized and religion tended to loose some of its force, the family changed, too, so that now there are efforts to change it back to achieve greater consistency with Islam? The dependence of religion on family socialization practices for inculcating children with religious values makes it conceivable that there would be a strong reaction within the religious institution if there were signs that family patterns had shifted away from those promoted by Islamic doctrine.

The following sections examine five Islamic prescriptions regarding the family to determine whether family life in Egypt in recent times has reflected the religious doctrine. These principles include marriage as both a religious duty and a social necessity, the prohibition of sex outside marriage, the husband's obligation to provide for his wife, the wife's obligation to obey her husband, and the obligation to be kind to one's relatives of whatever degree and to have concern for their well-being. Islamic principles must be distinguished from Islamic practice, since the latter is influenced by different national cultures. Nonetheless, in Egypt, these particular principles have been strongly upheld in the past, and the question is whether they have continued to be upheld in recent times.

Marriage as Both a Religious Duty and a Social Necessity

The first Islamic principle that will be examined is the admonition to marry unless one cannot afford to do so or is physically unfit ('Abd al 'Ati 1977; Ashraf 1971; Esposito 1991; Weeks 1988). "Prophet Mohammed referred to marriage as 'half the religion' and said, 'Marriage is my tradition. He who rejects my tradition is not of me'" (Weeks 1988:7). Table 3.1 presents the percentages of ever-married Muslim women and men in 1976 and 1986. It shows that during that decade, there was virtually no change in the percentage of

Table 3.1
PERCENTAGES OF EVER-MARRIED MUSLIM MALE AND FEMALE ADULT POPULATIONS, BY AGE: 1976 AND 1986

	1976		*1986*	
Age	Men	Women	Men	Women
20–24	20.1	62.1	19.3	63.8
25–29	57.5	86.6	56.9	86.7
30–34	83.6	93.2	85.2	93.1
35–39	93.1	95.4	94.3	95.2
40–44	94.8	95.3	96.3	95.5
45 and over	96.0	95.6	96.9	95.9
Total	75.5	88.1	74.5	88.3

Sources: Percentages for 1976 were calculated using data from Arab Republic of Egypt Census, *Census of Population, Housing and Establishments 1986* (Vol. 2, Table 13). Cairo Egypt: Central Agency for Public Mobilization and Statistics. Percentages for 1986 were calculated using data from Arab Republic of Egypt Census, *Census of Population, Housing and Establishments 1986* (Vol. 2, Table 33). Cairo, Egypt: Central Agency for Public Mobilization and Statistics.

men and women in any age category who were married. It is rare that women and men do not marry. Women marry earlier than men—87 percent of all Muslim women aged 25 to 29 were ever married, compared to only 57 percent of all Muslim men in both years. But of those aged 45 and older, almost all the Muslim men (96 percent in 1976 and 97 percent in 1986) and women (96 percent in 1976 and 1986) were ever married.

Further evidence for the continuing universality of marriage among women comes from El-Zanaty, Husein, Hassan, and Way (1993), cited in Nawar, Lloyd, and Ibrahim 1994:3): "There has been virtually no change in the prevalence of marriage among women of reproductive age in the last decade. During the peak child childbearing years between ages 25–34, 90 percent of Egyptian women are currently married." And with regard to socialization, the majority (79 percent) of women in Egypt in 1988 expected their daughters to marry by age 20 (Nawar et al. 1994). In sum, there is no evidence yet of a decline in the propensity to marry.

Prohibition of Sex Outside Marriage

That the universality of marriage does not seem to be changing does not mean that age of marriage is also holding steady. In fact, it is not. Demographic reports have indicated a systematic rise in age at first marriage for both sexes (El-Tawila and Fraser 1994). In 1986, the mean age at first marriage was 31.0 for men and 22.7 for women—up from 25.5 for men and 19.8 for women in 1966 (El-Tawila 1993:62).

Age at first marriage is not an irrevelant issue when considered in light of the Islamic prohibition against sex outside marriage (Koran 23:5–7,

70:29–31; see also 'Abd al 'Ati 1977; Willis 1984). An older age at first marriage enhances the possibility of nonmarital sex, although there has been no systematic evidence of such an increase. There is great concern for family honor in Egypt, and it stems, to a large degree, from this religious principle, especially when women's sexual behavior is at issue (cf. Omran and Roudi 1993). Religious adherence and the importance attributed to family honor, then, could lead to heightened anxiety in the face of a rising age at first marriage.

The Husband's Obligation to Provide for the Wife

Another Islamic principle is the husband's responsibility to provide for the wife:

> The wife's maintenance entails her incontestable right to lodging, clothing, food, and general care . . . [a right that is] established by authority of the *Koran,* the *Sunnah,* the unanimous agreement of jurists ('Abd al 'Ati 1977:148–49).

The provision of such overall support would necessitate, in most cases, the husband to be employed and would suggest that the wife would not be employed for pay outside the home.

Table 3.2 presents the percentages of men and women in different marital-status categories who were in the labor force in 1986. It appears that married men tended to provide financial support for their wives in that a much higher proportion of married men (88 percent) than married women (7.1 percent) were employed for pay. In addition, lower percentages of divorced men and never-married men than married men were employed. Among women, the smallest percentage employed were widowed (3.2 percent), followed by married women (7.1 percent). These findings suggest that

Table 3.2
PERCENTAGES OF MEN AND WOMEN IN THE PAID LABOR FORCE, BY MARITAL STATUS, 1986

Marital Status	Men in Paid Labor Force	Women in Paid Labor Force
Ever married*	88.0	7.1
Contractually married†	78.8	18.5
Divorced	75.5	12.8
Widowed	37.6	3.2
Never married*	49.5	8.9
Total	72.3	7.1

*Ever married includes persons ever married at any age; never married includes females aged 16 and older and males aged 18 and older.

†Persons who are legally married although their marriages have not been consummated.

Source: Percentages were calculated using data from Arab Republic of Egypt Census, *Census of Population, Housing and Establishments 1986* (Vol. 2, Tables 10 and 19). Cairo, Egypt: Central Agency for Public Mobilization and Statistics.

the situation in Egypt as regarding the maintenance of wives is consistent with the Islamic principle on this matter.

Although women with higher levels of education are more likely than women with lower levels of education to be working for wages (Nawar et al. 1994), the fact is that the majority of women in Egypt do not have high levels of education. In 1990, the proportions of persons who were illiterate among 15–24 year olds were 46 percent for women and 27 percent for men, and among those aged 25 and over, the proportions were 78 percent for women and 50 percent for men (United Nations 1995:100). Furthermore, the deteriorating economic situation in Egypt has meant that more pressure is placed on women to seek outside employment and less pressure is exerted by their families to keep them from seeking it (Mohsen 1985). Nonetheless, the figures in Table 3.2 make it clear that in 1986, most women, regardless of their marital status, were not working for wages. And more recent data from the United Nations (1995:142) confirmed the low economic activity rate of women in Egypt.

It is interesting that although the great majority of women are not working for wages,

> almost all women who work (95 percent) do so to support their families . . . and more than half of the working women in urban areas [56 percent] report that they are responsible for all household expenses (but only 16 percent in rural areas) (Nawar et al. 1994:16).

Rugh (1985) noted that a family that permits its women to work risks appearing needy, and a husband in such a family is viewed as a poor provider. She also noted that lower-class men often have difficulty supporting rapidly increasing families. Further research is needed to determine if women who are responsible for all the household expenses are predominately in lower-class families.

The Wife's Obligation to Obey the Husband

The wife's obligation to obey the husband

> is taken by most writers to be based almost entirely on two statements in the *Koran*. The *Koran* (2:228) states that women have rights even as they have duties in an equitable manner, but men have a degree above women. Again, it states (4:34) that men are the guardians, protectors, or custodians of women because God has made some of them excel others and because men expend of their means to maintain women. ('Abd al 'Ati 1977:173)

Moghadam (1993:1) cited yet another Koranic verse (4:38) that pertains to this principle:

> Men are the managers of the affairs of women for that God has preferred in bounty one of them over another. . . . And those you fear may be rebellious admonish; banish them to their couches, and beat them.

In examining the issue of a wife's obedience, it is important to consider the attitudes and behavior of both men and women. Looking first at men's attitudes, 1991–92 national-level survey data revealed that 60 percent of the married men believed that they alone decided about visits to family members and friends, 64 percent thought that they alone made decisions on household budget matters, and 78 percent believed that they were the sole deciders about their wives' employment. Related to this last point is the finding that 70 percent of the husbands in Cairo disapproved of wives working (Population Reference Bureau 1994:22–23). It is likely that this latter figure would be even higher in rural areas, since traditional attitudes are typically more pervasive there. An additional bit of insight on men's attitudes toward wives' obedience comes from an account of an exchange that took place between male psychologists and social workers and their female colleagues regarding the acceptability of polygamy. "The men argued that women voluntarily went into marriages with men who were already married. They said that marriage is comfortable for women because they are taken care of and, therefore, a woman must obey her husband" (Friedman 1985:14).

A 1995 study by Abdel Aziz at Zagazig University (reported by Abdel Kader 1995:5) that combined male and female students' attitudes found that although 89 percent emphasized the right of women to education and 83 percent supported women's right not to wear a *hijab* (head scarf), 82 percent saw women as needing men's advice and guidance.

A focus on women's attitudes toward wives' obedience reveals that these attitudes are similar to men's. A comprehensive investigation of women's autonomy (Nawar et al. 1994), based on a complete enumeration of all households and their members in three areas, was reasonably representative of the three major areas of Egypt—urban governorates, other urban areas, and rural areas. This study found that

> Overall, Egyptian women are remarkably consistent in expressing dependence on their spouses with respect to family decision-making. . . . The mean level of autonomy for all married women in the 1991 sample is 1.8 out of a maximum score of 5—a fairly low score (p. 20).

One question asked married women whether it was important for a woman to seek her husband's permission on every matter or decision. On the whole, only 10 percent said that it was not always important to do so (Nawar et al. 1994:8).

Despite the relatively low level of women's autonomy in general, it is important to note that in this study, certain other variables made a difference. Age, education, employment status, residence and standard of living all had an impact. Women who were younger, had higher levels of education, were employed, lived in urban areas, and ranked higher on the standard of living index had higher levels of autonomy. Education seemed to have the greatest effect, with the autonomy index ranging from 1.4 for illiterate women to 3.2 for those with at least a high school education. Nonetheless, Nawar et al. (1994:8) reported that regardless of how the women fell on each of these variables, "the overwhelming majority . . . felt the need to seek their husbands' permission."

Turning to specific behavioral examples of wives' obedience, Nawar et al. (1994:13) stated:

> Within contemporary Egyptian families, as has been traditionally the case, the majority of married women report that their husbands decide important family matters [although] joint decisions of husbands and wives are more likely to occur when wives are working or highly educated, reside in urban areas, live in nuclear families, and also in cases where the age-gap for spouses is not too wide. . . . In cases where differences of opinion arise between husband and wife, the majority of wives say they finally agree or choose to accept their husbands' opinion. However, working women [and] more educated women . . . are much less willing to accept their husbands' opinions in cases of disagreement and are more likely to try to convince husbands of their opinion. On the other hand, it is rare for wives to insist on their own opinion, at least in their reports to survey takers.

The information that has been presented here suggests that autonomous opinion and behavior among Egyptian wives is fairly low in relation to their husbands'. This situation, generally speaking, is in keeping with the Islamic principle that wives should obey their husbands.

Obligation to Be Kind to One's Relatives of Whatever Degree and to Have Concern for Their Well-Being

Each Muslim is commanded by Islamic doctrine to be kind to his or her relatives of whatever degree of relationship and to have concern for their well-being ('Abd al 'Ati 1977:214). And some scholars (Barakat 1985; Rugh 1984) claim that family bonds are both strong and extensive in Egypt. In this section, several patterns that would seem to reflect the close integration and interdependence of family members are explored to see how common they are. These patterns include extended-type households, the family's involvement in the decision to marry, marriage between relatives, patrilocal residence patterns at the time of first marriage, and family care for children whose parents cannot or do not care for them.

Extended-Type Households. Some researchers have noted the reduced prevalence of extended households in Egypt (Barakat 1985; Nawar et al. 1994). My comparison of Egyptian census data for 1976 and 1986 confirms this point (see Table 3.3). The type of extended households containing a married couple with children (all or some of whom were married) or with or without unmarried children but including other relatives declined from 41 percent of all households in 1976 to 27 percent of all households in 1986. Nuclear households containing a married couple with unmarried children increased by 13 percentage points during this same period. With the excep-

Table 3.3
HOUSEHOLD COMPOSITION IN EGYPT, 1976 AND 1986 (PERCENTAGE)

Household Composition*	1976	1986
1. Extended-type household	41.0	27.2
a. Married couple with some married children and/or relatives other than own children	23.4	13.0
b. Husband or wife with some married children and/or relatives other than own children	13.0	11.2
c. Group of relatives not related by marriage	4.2	3.1
2. Married couple with unmarried children	45.3	58.2
3. Married couple without children	6.6	7.8
4. Persons living alone	6.0	6.4
5. Group of unrelated individuals	1.08	.3

*There is no specific category in either the 1976 or 1986 Egyptian census for single parents living apart from other relatives. It is not clear which of the other categories contains this family form. Using data from a different nationally representative survey (the Egyptian Demographic and Health Survey), El-Tawila (1993:65) reported that 7.1 percent of all households in Egypt in 1988 were single-parent households.

Sources: Percentages for 1976 are from Fahad Al-Thakeb, 1981, "Size and Composition of the Arab Family: Census and Survey Data," *International Journal of Sociology of the Family* 11:171–78 (Table 1). Percentages for 1986 were calculated using data from Arab Republic of Egypt Census, *Census of Population, Housing and Establishments 1986* (Vol. 2, Table 12). Cairo, Egypt: Central Agency for Public Mobilization and Statistics.

tion of these two categories, there was relatively little change in household composition. The dramatic shift in these two categories, though, could cause some to be concerned that the family is becoming less traditional and so less aligned with the Islamic principle regarding kindness and concern for relatives.

Family Involvement in the Decision to Marry. According to Nawar et al. (1994), a majority of married women in 1991 were not primarily responsible for selecting the men they married. These researchers reported that regardless of educational level, age at marriage, or household type, most Egyptian women marry men chosen by relatives, rather than make a fully independent decision. This does not mean that age and education do not have any effect on women's input into these decisions. The study revealed that, for the the 21 percent of the women who married before they were age 16, the likelihood was 1 in 10 that they chose their husband. For the women who married after they were age 25, 40 percent had selected their own husbands. The women who were the most likely to have chosen their husbands were those with educational levels of high school or beyond (46 percent).

Marriage Between Relatives. Muslims in Egypt have adopted preferential cousin marriage. Although Islam does not "require" or perpetuate the appeal of this marital form ('Abdal al 'Ati 1977:135), such endogamous marriages provide yet another indication of the concern that people have for the kin group. Among the advantages of endogamy are the convenience of a lower bride-price and the retention of wealth and property within the kin group (Barakat 1985).

In 1991, marriage to a relative (often a first cousin) was common in Egypt. Twenty-nine percent of the currently married women were married to relatives. And it is likely that this figure would be higher if it were not for the limited availability of marriageable cousins that is always a factor. The women's ages did not make much difference in whether they were in relative or nonrelative marriages. However, age at first marriage did in that women who married in the youngest age categories were more than twice as likely to be married to relatives (35 percent and 33 percent) than were those married after age 25 (15 percent). Education also made a difference, with more than twice as many illiterate women (33 percent) married to relatives than women with a high school or higher education (15 percent) (Nawar et al. 1994).

Patrilocal Residence Patterns. Living arrangements at the time of first marriage are yet another indicator of the strength of commitment and concern among relatives in Egypt. Traditionally, Egypt was characterized by a patrilocal residence pattern. A study by El-Tawila and Fraser (1994) sheds some light on the commonality of this pattern in present times. Using national probability data, these researchers found that in 1991 46 percent of ever-married women had their own homes at the time of marriage (with 15 percent of them providing accommodations for relatives at that time and not exclusively living on their own), while 54 percent lived in someone else's home—mainly the husbands' parents (both parents or only one parent). They noted, though, that the higher the education of the women, the higher their chances of establishing independent homes at the time of marriage.

Attending to Abandoned Children. In Islam, adoption is not legal under any condition ('Abd al 'Ati 1977:191). The religious rationale for this stance is that adoption has the potential for generating at least covert hostility and estrangement among the kin. Family members may be upset if the adopted person takes on the God-ordained duties of blood relatives, receives an inheritance, or gets a cousin in marriage that someone else in the family or kin group wants to marry ('Abd al 'Ati 1977). Nevertheless,

> it is the consensus of [Islamic] jurists that whoever finds an abandoned child must attend to it immediately. . . . if no man claims the child, it remains the

> trust of the finder, who will be responsible for its upbringing and socialization. The Public Treasury [is to] supply the funds necessary to raise the child unless the trustee volunteers to undertake it at his expense and privately. . . . in case the Treasury can provide no adequate funds, it becomes the generalized duty of the Muslim community to raise the money required to meet the [child's] needs." ('Abd al 'Ati 1977:197)

This religious prescription may account for the fact that street children are far less prominent in Egypt than in other parts of the world.

In my discussion with Dr. Adel Azer (on March 10, 1994), a researcher with the United Nations Children's Fund in Cairo, he noted that the topic of street children in Egypt has not been studied in depth and that there are no estimates of the size of the problem. Azer said that the issue had been brought to the fore only in the previous three or four years. If street children are defined as those with no family care, then Azer believes that the incidence is relatively low in Egypt, especially compared to places like Brazil, Columbia, and Russia (cf. Agnelli 1986). Other professionals in Egypt with research interests in families and children (Dr. Saad Nagi, director of the Social Research Center at the American University in Cairo, for example) have also indicated that street children are not numerous in Egypt.

The interpretation of the jurists regarding abandoned children meshes well with the popular notion of the pervasiveness of Egyptian family group responsibility. Given the endogamous nature of the kinship unit in Egypt, relatives are the most likely to identify an abandoned child. Rugh (1981:205, 231-232) concluded from her 1980–81 study of Egyptian orphanages:

> Families . . . do not appear to willingly abrogate their responsibilities; they are usually forced by poverty, limited space, distance, social sanctions, the conflict of allegiance to a spouse, inability to provide appropriate care, and other reasons to abandon their obligations. . . . Most Egyptians will say that when a child is orphaned by the death of one or both the parents, some relative will step in to take care of and support the child through childhood to maturity.

Needy children, then, are typically cared for within the larger kinship system. The exceptions are instances in which the well-being of the family is viewed as incongruent with the well-being of the child. One example is children who are the products of illegitimate alliances and are abandoned by the natural parents to avoid public knowledge of the relationship (Rugh 1981). It should be noted here that, although

> Islam itself seems to not impose constraints on the use of contraception . . . that does not prevent rural peasants, urban villagers and even clergymen themselves from raising objections to fertility control for a variety of reasons that may be labeled as "tradition" rather than "religion" (Weeks 1988:19).

In sum, there is little evidence that the family in Egypt has been increasingly rejecting its obligation to care for children. There are some factors other than family breakdown, though, that may be expected to lead to a rise in the incidence of street children. One is the current economic crisis. That there has not been a noticeable upsurge in the incidence of street children, despite widespread economic difficulties, further corroborates the strength of Egyptian family group responsibility.

THE FAMILY: AN IMPETUS FOR SOCIAL CHANGE

The foregoing discussion made clear that Islamic doctrine is widely reflected in family life. Almost all Muslim women and men marry, the large majority of married men seem to provide financial support for their wives, women's and men's attitudes and behavior reflect the fact that wives obey their husbands, and there are several indications of kindness to and concern for relatives. Widespread family involvement in marital decisions, the commonality of marriage to a relative, and a patrilocal residence pattern at the time of marriage provide support for this latter point. The two major exceptions that may create concern for the consistency between Islamic doctrine and family patterns is the increase in age at marriage among men and women, which enhances the possibility of nonmarital sex and the dramatic decline in the prevalence of extended-type households that is related to the Islamic principle specifying kindness to and concern for relatives.

The situation, however, is even more complicated than the summary presented here would suggest. One confounding factor is women's educational levels. Women with higher levels of education are more likely to be employed, and their employment, in turn, has implications for the extent of support that their husbands provide. Higher levels of education are associated with higher levels of autonomy among women and so have some impact, although limited, on women's obedience to their husbands. Women with high school or higher educational levels were more likely to select their own husbands. Women's education was inversely associated with marriage to relatives and independent residences at the time of marriage.

In sum, there is no question that Islamic doctrine is widely reflected in Egyptian family life, but, at the same time, some changes are occurring that could be worrisome to those with a strong religious orientation. In addition to the increase in age at marriage and the decrease in extended families, the impact of women's education on various family patterns must be obvious to many. Although the proportion of women who attain higher levels of education is still small, women's educational levels have been increasing (World Bank 1996:200). This assessment would suggest that the Islamist movement is reacting to some actual changes in family patterns, as well as to the fear of what could happen to the family in the future as a result of women's rising levels of education and the growing awareness of alternative family patterns stemming from the so-called cultural invasion by the media, tourists, and others.

With regard to the cultural invasion, it was reported that Islamists in Egypt are

> determined to rid the screen of love affairs, scanty costumes, drugs, and discussion of topics like homosexuality and divorce [and that they] have burned video shops, attacked movies as "degenerate," and threatened the lives of people in the industry. (cf. Hedges 1992b; Malkmus 1988).

This state of affairs is due, in part, to the fact that government censorship eased markedly under Mubarak (Hedges 1992c), allowing for more diverse and less narrowly restrained media and entertainment. Then, too, there has been the large tourism industry, one of Egypt's principle foreign-exchange earners (Man 1993; Sullivan 1990). Before the decline in tourism that occurred in the first half of this decade as a result of Islamist terrorist activities, it was reported that 4 million Egyptians were employed in this business (Man 1993). These people, along with many others who were not directly involved in tourism, had a great deal of exposure to Western ways.

The family institution, then, has not experienced a great deal of change, but it nevertheless provides an important impetus for social change. Because of its close alliance with religion, which was discussed earlier, it is concern for what could happen to the family system, more than what has happened, that serves as the most significant stimulus for conflict between the religious and political institutions.

CONCLUSION

In conclusion, Egypt is one of the relatively few countries in the world today in which religion holds such a high place in the institutional structure. It is difficult for many Westerners even to contemplate a society with this sort of institutional dominance. From a social change point of view, Egypt represents a particularly interesting case because the strong influence of the religious institution is perhaps more threatened than at any time in the past. Forces within the country, as well as powerful interests outside, are creating a lot of instability in all of the major social institutions. The fear of a decline in traditional family patterns is heightening concerns. The decline in these patterns would result in a weakened religious institution because of the integral connection between religion and family in Egypt.

The outcome is difficult to predict. It is known, of course, that the weakening of traditional religion and the corresponding secularization of society is only a presumed uniformity in the modernity process (cf. Gusfield 1967; National Research Council 1988). It is theoretically possible for modernity to proceed even when religion is a strong, but perhaps not the dominant, institution in a society. And this outcome is possible only when the interests of religion are not strongly conservative.

In Egypt, because of the adamant antimodernity stance of the Islamist movement, it is not likely that a powerful religious institution would be compatible with many aspects of advancing modernity. At this point, though, only time will tell the victor in the institutional struggle for dominance that is taking place in Egypt. What can be said is that the numerous governmental accommodations to the Islamists over the past few years (Y. Ibrahim 1994), despite the generally coercive tactics used by the government in the ongoing conflict, are an indication of the strength of these religious associations.

At the same time, there are some who say that as of 1995, the surge of Islamic militancy in Egypt began to abate. But accompanying this point of view is an acknowledgment that the salience of Islam as a motivating source of ideology has not diminished (Lancaster 1996). And a comment by a senior European diplomat is interesting: "The Egyptians tell us that, if they hold free elections, the Islamic militants will win" (Hedges 1995:A4).

REFERENCES

'Abd al 'Ati, Hammudah. 1977. *The Family Structure in Islam.* New York: American Trust Publications.

Abdel Kader, Said. 1995. "Egypt Youth Support Democracy and Economic Liberalization." *Al Nidaa Al Gadid* 9:5.

Agnelli, Susanna. 1986. *Street Children: A Growing Urban Tragedy: Report for the Independent Commission on Humanitarian Issues.* London: Weidenfeld & Nicolson.

Al-Sayyid, Mustapha K. 1993. "A Civil Society in Egypt?" *Middle East Journal* 47:228–42.

Al-Thakeb, Fahad. 1981. "Size and Composition of the Arab Family: Census and Survey Data." *International Journal of Sociology of the Family* 11:171–78.

Arab Republic of Egypt Census. 1976. *Census of Population, Housing and Establishments* (Vol. 2). Cairo, Egypt: Central Agency for Public Mobilization and Statisitics.

Arab Republic of Egypt Census. 1986. *Census of Population, Housing and Establishments* (Vol. 2). Cairo, Egypt: Central Agency for Public Mobilization and Statistics.

Ashraf, SH. Muhammad. 1971. *The Fifth Book of Islam: Marriage, Divorce and Sex* (rev. ed.). Lahore, Pakistan: Ashraf Press.

Barakat, Halim. 1985. "The Arab Family and the Challenge of Social Transformation." Pp. 27–48 in *Women and the Family in the Middle East: New Voices of Change,* edited by Elizabeth Warnok Fernea. Austin: University of Texas Press.

Bollag, Burton. 1991. "Enrollment Boom, Rise of Fundamentalism Put Egypt's Universities Under Pressure." *Chronicle of Higher Education,* June 12, pp. A31, A32.

———. 1994. "Battling Fundamentalism: Crackdown on 'Islamists' at Egypt's Universities Brings a Storm of Protests." *Chronicle of Higher Education,* February 2, pp. A42–A44.

Chesnoff, Richard Z., and Gordon R. Robinson. 1990. "Egypt's Uncertain Way Forward: Some Progress, But Host of Big Problems." *U.S. News and World Report,* April 16, pp. 34–35.

Crecelius, Daniel. 1980. "The Course of Secularization in Modern Egypt." Pp. 49–70 in *Islam and Development,* edited by John L. Esposito. Syracuse, NY: Syracuse University Press.

D'Antonio, William V. 1980. "The Family and Religion: Exploring a Changing Relationship." *Journal for the Scientific Study of Religion* 19:89–104.

———. 1983. "Family Life, Religion, and Societal Values and Structure." Pp. 81–108 in *Families and Religions: Conflict and Change in Modern Society,* edited by William V. D'Antonio and Joan Aldous. Beverly Hills, CA: Sage.

"Egypt: When Taming Is Inflaming." 1992. *The Economist,* December 19, p. 41.

"Egypt: The Insurgency That Will Not Stop." 1993. *The Economist,* May 15, p. 44.

"Egyptian Terrorists Kill Five in Highway Ambush." 1994. *Columbus Dispatch,* September 18, p. 11A.

El Din, Saad. 1993. "Voice of Women: When Honor Becomes Disgraceful." *El Sha'ab,* April 9.

El Ghazaly, Mohamed. 1991a. "This Is Our Religion" (Editorial). *El Sha'ab,* December 31.

———. 1991b. "This Is Our Religion" (Editorial). *El Sha'ab,* January 8.

———. 1991c. "This Is Our Religion" (Editorial). *El Sha'ab,* June 18.

———. 1993. "This Is Our Religion." *El Sha'ab,* May 11.

El Hoda Saad, Nour. 1994. "The Past and the Present." *El Sha'ab,* January 14.

El-Tawila, Sahar I. 1993. "Population." Pp. 29–96 in *The Governorates of Aswan and Ouena: Development Profiles* by Mohamed H. Abdel Aal, Sahar I. El-Tawila, Tarek Hatem, Nicholas S. Hopkins, N. Gordon Knox, Sohair Mehanna, and Saad Z. Nagi. Cairo, Egypt: Social Research Center, American University in Cairo.

El-Tawila, Sahar, and Elvis E. Fraser. 1994. "The Impact of Socioeconomic Change on the Transition to First Marriage in Egypt: A Hazard Model Approach" (Working paper). Cairo, Egypt: Social Research Center, American University in Cairo.

El-Zanaty, Fatima H., A. A. Sayad Husein, H. M. Zaky Hassan, and Ann Way. 1993. *Egypt Demographic and Health Survey, 1992.* Cairo, Egypt, and Calvern, MD: National Population Council and Macro International.

Esposito, John L. 1991. *Islam: The Straight Path.* (expanded ed.). New York: Oxford University Press.

Farah, Nadia Ramsis. 1986. *Religious Strife in Egypt: Crisis and Ideological Conflict in the Seventies.* New York: Gordon & Breach.

Frenzen, Jonathan, Paul M. Hirsch, and Phillip C. Zerrillo. 1994. "Consumption, Preferences, and Changing Lifestyles." Pp. 403–25 in *The Handbook of Economic Sociology,* edited by Neil J. Smelser and Richard Swedberg. Princeton, NJ: Princeton University Press.

Friedman, Jane. 1985. "Women in Egypt Mobilize to Protect Their Marital Rights." *Christian Science Monitor,* June 28, p. 14.

Gaffney, Patrick D. 1991. "The Changing Voices of Islam: The Emergence of Professional Preachers in Contemporary Egypt." *The Muslim World* 81:27–47.

Goody, Jack. 1983. *The Development of the Family and Marriage in Europe.* New York: Cambridge University Press.

Gouldner, Alvin W., and Helen P. Gouldner. 1963. *Modern Sociology: An Introduction to the Study of Human Interaction.* New York: Harcourt, Brace & World.

Gusfield, Joseph R. 1967. "Tradition and Modernity: Misplaced Polarities in the Study of Social Change." *American Journal of Sociology* 72:351–362.

Haynes, Jeff. 1994. Religion in Third World Politics. Boulder, CO: Lynne Rienner.

Hedges, Chris. 1992a. "As Islamic Militants Thunder, Egypt Grows More Nervous." *New York Times* November 12, Pp. A1 and A7.

———. 1992b. "That's Entertainment. But Is It Blasphemy, Too?" *New York Times International* November 18, P. A4.
———. 1993. "Egypt's War with Militants: Both Sides Harden Positions." *New York Times,* April 1, pp. A1, A6.
———. 1995. "Mubarak's Challenge." *New York Times International,* April 3, p. A4.
Hopwood, Derek. 1991. *Egypt: Politics and Society 1945-1990.* New York: Harper Collins.
Houseknecht, Sharon K. 1988. "The Inter-Institutional Perspective in Family Research." Paper presented at the annual meeting of the American Sociological Association, Atlanta, GA, August.
Hubbell, Stephen. 1992. "Rebellion in Upper Egypt: True Belief's Grim Patience." *The Nation,* September 28, pp. 320–24.
Hunt, Janet G., and Larry L. Hunt. 1982. The Dualities of Careers and Families: New Integrations or New Polarizations?" *Social Problems* 29:499–510.
Ibrahim, Saad Eddin. 1980. "Anatomy of Egypt's Militant Islamic Groups: Methodological Note and Preliminary Findings." *International Journal of Middle East Studies* 12:423–53.
Ibrahim, Youssef M. 1994. "Fundamentalists Impose Culture on Egypt." *New York Times,* February 3, pp. A1, A10.
Janowitz, Morris. 1978. *The Last Half-Century: Societal Change and Politics in America.* Chicago: University of Chicago Press.
Lancaster, John. 1996. "A Fundamental Cooling Down: The Threat of Islamic Extremism Is Lessening in Egypt as Some of Its Tactics Backfire." *Washington Post National Weekly,* April 1–7, p. 16.
Lief, Louise. 1993. "The Battle for Egypt: Terror in New York Is Part of a Larger War." *U.S. News and World Report,* July 19, pp. 42–44.
MacIver, Robert M. 1970. *On Community, Society and Power.* Chicago: University of Chicago Press.
Malkmus, Lizbeth. 1988. "The 'New' Egyptian Cinema: Adapting Genre Conventions to a Changing Society." *Cineaste* 16:30–33.
Man, Igor, 1993. "The Rifts in Egypt's 'Village'." *World Press Review,* July, p. 32.
Marshall, Susan E. 1984. "Politics and Female Status in North Africa: A Reconsideration of Development Theory." *Economic Development and Cultural Change* 32:499–524.
McDermott, Anthony. 1988. *Egypt from Nasser to Mubarak: A Flawed Revolution.* New York: Croom Helm.
Merton, Robert K. 1970. "1970 Preface." Pp. vii–xxix in *Science, Technology and Society in Seventeenth Century England.* New York: Harper & Row.
Moghadam, Valentine M. 1993. *Modernizing Women: Gender and Social Change in the Middle East.* Boulder, CO: Lynne Rienner.
Mohsen, Safia K. 1979. "New Images, Old Reflections: Working and Middle-Class Women in Egypt." Pp. 56–71 in *Women and the Family in the Middle East: New Voices of Change,* edited by Elizabeth Warnock Fernea. Austin: University of Texas Press.
Murphy, Caryle. 1993. "A Cairo Divorce Case Tests the Limits of Fundamentalist Intolerance." *International Herald Tribune,* July 23, p. 1
Najjar, Fauzi M. 1988. "Egypt's Laws of Personal Status." *Arab Studies Quarterly* 10:319–44.
National Research Council, Committee on Basic Research in Behavioral and Social Sciences. 1988. "Modernization: Family and Religion." Pp. 140–44 in *The Behavioral and Social Sciences: Achievements and Opportunities,* edited by Dean R. Gerstein, R. Duncan Luce, Neil J. Smelser, and Sonja Sperlich. Washington, DC: National Academy Press.

Nawar, Laila, Cynthia B. Lloyd, and Barbara Ibrahim. 1994. "Women's Autonomy and Gender Roles in Egyptian Families." Paper presented at the Population Council Symposium on Family, Gender, and Population Policy: International Debates and Middle Eastern Realities, Cairo, Egypt, February.

Omran, Abdel R., and Farzaneh Roudi. 1993. "The Middle East Population Puzzle." *Population Bulletin* 48:1–40.

Parsons, Talcott. 1961. "Some Considerations on the Theory of Social Change." *Rural Sociology* 26:219–39.

———. 1971. *The System of Modern Societies.* Englewood Cliffs, NJ: Prentice-Hall.

Population Reference Bureau, International Programs). 1994. *Chartbook: Paths to Demographic Change in the Near East and North Africa.* Washington, DC: Author.

Robertson, Roland. 1984. "Liberation Theology in Latin America: Sociological Problems of Interpretation and Explanation." Paper presented at the conference on Prophetic Religions and Politics, Martinique, Novemeber.

Rugh, Andrea B. 1981. "Orphanages and Homes for the Aged in Egypt: Contradiction or Affirmation in a Family Oriented Society." *International Journal of Sociology of the Family* 11:203–33.

———. 1984. *Family in Contemporary Egypt.* Syracuse, NY: Syracuse University Press.

———. 1985. "Women and Work: Strategies and Choices in a Lower-Class Quarter of Cairo." Pp.273–288 in *Women and the Family in the Middle East: New Voices of Change,* edited by Elizabeth Warnock Fernea. Austin: University of Texas Press.

Singer, Hanaa Fikry. 1993. *The Socialist Labor Party: A Case Study of a Contemporary Egyptian Party.* Vol. 16, Monograph 1, *Cairo Papers in Social Science.* Cairo, Egypt: The American University in Cairo Press.

Spitzer, Robert J. 1988. "Review of *Religion and Politics in the United States* by Kenneth D. Wald." *Journal for the Scientific Study of Religion* 27:302–04.

Statistical Year Book, Arab Republic of Egypt. 1991. Cairo, Egypt: Central Agency for Public Mobilization and Statistics.

Strauss, Murray A. 1972. "Family Organization and Problem Solving Ability in Relation to Societal Modernization," *Journal of Comparative Family Studies* 3:70–83.

Sullivan, Dennis J. 1990. "The Political Economy of Reform in Egypt." *International Journal of Middle East Studies* 22:317–34.

Tuma, Elias H. 1988. "Institutuionalized Obstacles to Development: The Case of Egypt." *World Development* 16:1185–98.

United Nations. 1995. *The World's Women 1995: Trends and Statistics.* New York: Author.

Warg, Peter. 1993. "Egypt Gags Preachin' Station." *Variety,* April 5, p. 59.

Weber, Max. 1930. *The Protestant Ethic and the Spirit of Capitalism,* translated by Talcott Parsons. London: Allen & Unwin.

Weeks, John R. 1988. "The Demography of Islamic Nations." *Population Bulletin* 43(4):1–55.

Williams, Robin M., Jr. [1955] 1970. *American Society: A Sociological Interpretation* (3rd ed.). New York: Alfred A. Knopf.

Willis, David K. 1984. "The Practice of Islam: How Differing Cultural Traditions Color Muslim Life Around the World." *Christian Science Monitor,* July 24, p. 17.

World Bank. 1996. *From Plan to Market: World Development Report 1996.* Oxford, England: Oxford University Press.

Wrong, Dennis H. [1979] 1988. *Power: Its Forms, Bases, and Uses.* Chicago: University of Chicago Press.

CHAPTER FOUR

Family and Religion in Sweden

IRVING PALM
JAN TROST

INTRODUCTION

During the past 150 years, Sweden, like so many other countries, has experienced many important changes. Modernization and industrialization started in the mid-nineteenth century. From an almost totally agrarian society, Sweden rapidly became, first, an industrial and then a postindustrial society with increasing pluralism. After World War II, the process of modernization moved in a new direction. Sweden became a social welfare society, and the government's influence at the local, regional, and national levels became strong. The process of urbanization, which had begun with industrialization, intensified. From the beginning of the 1960s, the role of housewife that had emerged under industrialization changed rapidly to a renewal of the previous system, so that almost all women, as well as men, were economically productive, that is, in the labor force.

The changes from an agrarian to a postindustrial society with its social welfare have also had effects on the social institutions of the family and religion. The importance and influence of the churches and the denominations on overall social life have decreased. Although a few Evangelical and Fundamentalist movements exert a significant impact in certain spheres, as is discussed later, in general, society has become secularized. The traditional influence that religion had on families has almost disappeared. Family life and religious life have both changed radically and are becoming increasingly individualized and privatized.

Legal and religious marriage as a social institution has become less important, and nonmarital cohabitation has been institutionalized alongside marriage (Trost 1981); consequently, the marriage rate has decreased. In addition, the divorce and separation rates have increased rapidly. Same-sex couples have become more accepted, and same-sex unions can be registered officially and are recognized as almost equivalent to marriages.

In the religious arena, the influence of the churches and the denominations on social and family life has decreased. For example, the numbers of active members of both the Swedish Lutheran Church and of non-Lutheran denominations have declined radically. Comparative studies (see, for example, Gustafsson 1988) have found that Sweden is one of the most secularized countries in the world. Religion and family have both become highly individualized.

In this chapter, we briefly summarize some of the history of religion in Sweden and deal with rites of passage, such as christening, confirmation, marriage, and burials. Since the Lutheran Church is still a state church with a large majority of the population as members, much of the discussion focuses on it. We also discuss the role of minority religious movements in Sweden, which may have direct relevance not only for their followers, but some influence on the practices and beliefs of the majority church adherents, as well. Finally, we deal with socialization and family patterns as they relate to religion.

HISTORY OF RELIGION AND FAMILY IN SWEDEN

What is now known as Sweden has not always been just one country. Some 1,500 years ago, there were a number of kingdoms, and the population was very limited compared to what is now the case. In what are currently Denmark, Iceland, Norway, and Sweden, the main population was Vikings, who were farmers, hunters, fishermen, and international traders. During their travel for trade, they also fought with people who were not "friendly enough," according to the Vikings' definition. Their religion was based on what is today called the Asa-belief, and their gods were collectively known as Asa-Gods. As far as can now be understood, these gods were presumed to behave and think as humans do. They seem to have been just wiser and stronger than humans, but they were not supernatural. After people died, they went to Valhalla where the Asa-Gods lived, where they would eat the meat from a pig named Särimner and drink a lot of Mjöd (mead), a special beer. Every morning Särimner woke up, and every evening it was slaughtered. When Christian missionaries first arrived, around 800 CE, they were looked upon with suspicion. Some were soon killed by the Vikings, and some returned to where they had come from. When traveling, however, some of the Vikings found that if they pretended to be Christians, trade was easier. Thus, they decided that the Christian religion might not be so bad. Subsequently, from around 1000 CE, more and more of the kings converted to Christianity and forced their people to do the same. The most famous example is from what is now Norway, where, in 1000 CE, King Olav, resorting to the use of the sword, made people convert or die. King Olav was later made Saint Olav.

It seems evident that people did not care much about religion during the time of the Asa-belief or even later during the first centuries of Christianity. An important indicator of the relative lack of religious influence is connected to the marriage ritual. By tradition, the marriage ritual was separated into three steps. The first step was the betrothal (*fästningen*), or the formal announcement of the engagement. The second step was the marriage ceremony (*giftermålet*), which was the handing over of the bride to the bridegroom by the bride's father or eldest brother. The third and final step was the "bedding" (*sängledningen*), when the bride and bridegroom went to bed together in front of witnesses (some of the influential participants in the ceremonies and the wedding party) (cf. Carlsson 1972; Trost 1979).

This tradition was mentioned over the centuries, and there is clear evidence that the pope sent bulls to his bishops ordering them to make people marry according to Christian rules, rather than in their pagan and, according to the pope, nonlegal way. Eventually, it seems that most people came to follow the Christian rules. However, there is evidence that quite a few couples never married but just lived together. Sundt ([1855] 1975) found this to be the case during the nineteenth century in Norway and Sweden, and Björnsson (1971) noted that a large number of people in Iceland still followed the old tradition and disregarded Christian marriage rituals.

In 1527, the Swedish King Gustavus Vasa decided that Sweden should adopt Luther's ideas and reject the old Christianity. This decision had no reference among the people, nor was it based on the king's religious beliefs. Rather, Sweden was at war with the Danes, and to afford the war, the king borrowed money from the Hanseats, which he needed to pay back. Therefore, he stripped the churches of their copper bells, which he had melted down to make weapons and took the churches' considerable wealth to pay off the war debts. However, the king's decision was not codified into law until it was supported by the Uppsala-meeting in 1593. It was then that Sweden really became Lutheran. The Lutheran Church became a state church, and all other churches or denominations were forbidden—a situation that prevailed for a long time. When Sweden imported one of the marshals of Napoleon's army, who became King Karl XIV Johan in 1818, the new king had to abandon Catholicism and become a member of the state Lutheran church. His wife, Desiré, refused to abandon her Catholicism and was given the exclusive right to remain in it, although as queen she should have belonged to the state church.

In 1741, the rules of the solemnity of the Lutheran state church were changed to the effect that immigrants who were members of a Reformed Christian church were allowed to remain in it. Starting in 1781, immigrants of any Christian church were allowed to remain in their churches, and, in 1782, Jews were permitted to live in Sweden, albeit only in some of the cities. Much later, in 1860, Swedes were allowed to convert to another church or denomination. It was not until 1952, however, that Swedes were permitted not to belong to any church or religion at all, and since that year Swedes have had the official right to be atheists.

Sweden started its process of modernization fairly late, in the middle of the nineteenth century. Connected to this process, which altered all parts of Swedish society, were such subprocesses as industrialization, urbanization, and liberalization. In response to these processes, Swedish society changed from a mainly rural character to a mixture of rural and urban, and the traditional values became more liberal and permissive. As was mentioned, the traditional monopoly of the Swedish Lutheran Church was questioned, and several Christian denominations were established apart from the state church (cf. Palm 1982, 1993).

During and after World War II, immigration from Catholic and other Christian countries, as well as from Muslim countries, increased. Swedes and others commonly think of Sweden as a homogeneous Christian society built upon its Lutheran state church. A hundred years ago this perspective was reasonable, but, with the immigration since World War II, Sweden has become a more pluralistic and multicultural society.

Other important components of the modernization of Swedish society during the two past centuries are rationalization and secularization. In this connection, we stress the increased specialization and differentiation that has followed, as evidenced by the changes in the relationship between religion and other social institutions (Gustafsson 1988; Luckmann 1974).

By tradition, the Lutheran state church has had a special interest in education and child care. From 1910 to 1955, its influence on the compulsory school system decreased at all levels, including the high school level. The official connection between the church and the universities disappeared. Sweden got a fully confessionless educational system.

Consequently, the influence and power of the church has diminished or disappeared. The relation to the family as a social institution has also changed. Fewer and fewer members of the church ask for the services of various sorts that the church offers. Fifty years ago, all but a few percent married with a religious ceremony; now less than two-thirds do. Nonmarital cohabitation precedes marriage, if couples ever marry. Fewer have their children christened (Trost 1993). Even in lawmaking, the church has almost no influence. For example, the liberal abortion law of 1974 was passed despite protests from the church. Similarly, in 1994, Parliament passed a law giving same-sex couples the right to register their partnerships despite protests from the church.

The decline of the power of religion in society through specialization and the decreased interest in the activities of traditional churches and other denominations, however, does not mean that people are not interested in questions of an existential nature or of the supernatural. What has happened is that the organized activities of religious nature have become marginalized. Religion has turned from a common urgency to be a private activity. In the following sections, we present concrete examples of changes in the areas of family and religion that further highlight the tendencies toward secularization and privatization.

RITES OF PASSAGE AND OTHER ACTIVITIES

For many Swedes, religion as a belief and an activity has little everyday relevance, although almost all Swedes belong to one of the churches or denominations. In 1992, 88 percent were at least passive members; that is, they went to church only a few times a year or never, although they were registered as members of the Swedish state church. Of the Swedes in Sweden, 92 percent were members of the Swedish state church, and of the half million non-Swedes living in Sweden, only 21 percent were (*Statistical Yearbook* 1993).

Church membership is connected to various rituals. The first church ritual in a person's life is the christening ceremony; about 77 percent of the children born in Sweden are christened. However, quite a few newborns automatically become members of the state church without being christened; it is enough that their parents (or their mothers) are members. Thus, it is possible to find youngsters who, although members of the church, have to be christened before they are confirmed; in 1992, 2,500, or 3 percent of all those who were confirmed were christened during their studies for confirmation (Alwall 1993).

For parents with strong beliefs, the christening ceremony is not only a ritual, it is a rite of passage; that is, the babies are transformed from being pagans to being Christians and members of the church. However, for most parents whose babies are christened, the religious aspect is of minor importance, and the church ceremony is just a part of the ritual. They use the christening ceremony as an excuse to have a party to introduce their babies to their relatives and friends. In this respect, one could say that the ceremony is a rite of passage, not for the baby but for the parents—to show the people who are close to them that the family has enlarged from just the two spouses or cohabitants or from a small family to a larger one. Customarily, the baby receives gifts from all who are invited to the party (invitations are usually sent for the party and the religious ceremony). Furthermore, many parents also name their babies' godparents at this time. For the most part, the parents do not know or care about the original function of godparents, namely, to take care of a child in case the parents cannot. Rather, they see the naming of godparents just as a tradition, what is to be done, and recognize that such a practice could be good later, since godparents are supposed to give the children gifts on birthdays and other important occasions.

The second church ritual is the confirmation ceremony, for which young teenagers prepare by taking confirmation lessons. One could say that the christening gives the child an ascribed status as a Christian and that the confirmation gives the child an achieved status. Traditionally, confirmation was regarded as a rite of passage from childhood to adulthood, but since today no one would look upon a 14- or 15 year old as an adult, the ceremony is no longer considered to be a rite of passage.[1] The ceremony is more of a tradition, what should be done unless the child actively rejects the ideas of Christianity. Social pressure is exerted on both the parents and the children to get them to participate in the lessons and the ceremony. Furthermore, the parents usually organize a party for relatives and friends after this religious ceremony, as in the case of the christening, and both they and the guests are supposed to give gifts to the newly confirmed child. Many children think of the confirmation as an event for which they receive gifts. Somewhat more than half the children who are christened are eventually officially confirmed.

The third church ritual for many Swedes is the wedding ceremony. In 1992, out of a total of 34,812 marriages, 21,555 (or 62 percent) were within the Swedish church; the remaining marriages were mainly civil, and some were within other churches or denominations (*Statistical Yearbook* 1993). In this connection, it is important to discuss the changes that have occurred in the past thirty-five years. Nonmarital cohabitation "under marriagelike conditions" emerged in the mid-1960s and after just a decade became a social institution alongside marriage (cf. Trost 1979). Traditionally, marriage was connected to four normative elements that were closely connected in time: the wedding ceremony, shared living quarters, sexual intimacy, and child-bearing within about a year. The normative structure was such that almost no couples lived together before they married. But the norms against premarital sex were only ideal norms and never behavioral norms. Everyone knew that almost all couples who were engaged to be married had sex together, but people did not talk about it. One indication is that during the 1960s, about 33 percent of the brides were pregnant when they married, and quite a few had children prior to their marriages (Befolkningsrörelsen 1962).

In the mid-1960s, the previously high marriage rate started to decrease rapidly, and from 1966 to 1975, the rate decreased by more than 40 percent. Nonmarital cohabitation increased rapidly and became an important social institution alongside marital cohabitation. Since the mid-1970s, almost no couples marry without first cohabiting "under marriage-like conditions" (cf. Trost 1979). The marriage rate is now less than half of what it would have been had no changes occurred.

The four normative elements that were previously closely connected in time are now fully separated in Sweden as they are in some other countries, including Denmark. In most Western countries, the tendency has been the same. More and more couples start cohabiting long before they eventually marry, and some separate or experience death before they manage to marry. In many countries, however, there is still a connection between marriage and having children. For example, in Belgium and the Netherlands, few children are born to unmarried mothers. In Sweden, in contrast, more than half the children who are born are born to unmarried mothers, and for first-born children, the figure is two-thirds (Trost 1993). Most of the mothers, however, are cohabiting with the children's fathers.

The fourth religious ceremony is usually the funeral. Since about 90 percent of the population belongs to the Swedish state church, most of those who die are elderly, and most elderly people are members of the church, the majority of funerals (91 percent of the total of 94,710) are within the Swedish church. Of the remaining 9 percent of funerals, most are within other churches or denominations, and a few are civil ceremonies. Few Swedes attend other religious events. For example, in 1992, only 8,210,072 persons went to Sunday mass (a mean of 1.1 visits per member per year) and 8,747,992 went to other worship services (a mean of 1.2 visits per member per year, excluding musical services). In addition, only 2,329,279 took Holy Communion within the Swedish church, which amounts to 0.3 communions per member per year (*Statistical Yearbook* 1993).

NON-LUTHERAN FAITHS

The social and structural changes during the late nineteenth- and early twentieth centuries and the process of modernization also affected non-Lutheran religious movements. During that period, the church and religious communities in the villages lost their previous central position and no longer had control over the population. Newly founded free religious movements gained increasing numbers of supporters and members in most parts of the country. These newly established denominations attracted mainly new social classes in the society, such as the new lower class in rural areas and the growing working- and middle classes in small urban areas.

Among these new religious movements, three main streams can be observed (Palm 1982):

1. *The new evangelical movement.*[2] The general movement resulted in the organization within the Swedish church of the *Evangeliska fosterlandsstiftelsen* (the Swedish Evangelical Mission). Outside the Swedish church two other groups were formed: *Svenska Missionsförbundet* (the Swedish Covenant Church) and *Svenska Alliansmissionen* (the Swedish Alliance Mission).

2. *The Baptist movement.* For some decades, those who joined this movement were heavily attacked by the leaders of the Swedish church, who considered the theology and practice of adult christening to be too deviant and separatist to be accepted or even tolerated. The oldest Baptist movement is *Svenska Baptistsamfundet* (the Baptist Union of Sweden). Other major denominations are *Örebromissionen* (the Örebro Mission) and *Pingströrelsen* (the Pentecostal movement). The latter now has the largest number of members of all the traditional free movements (Palm 1993).

3. *The Methodist movement. Metodistkyrkan* (the Methodist Church) and *Frälsningsarmén* (the Salvation Army) both belong to this stream. These two denominations were strongly influenced by religious developments in the United States and Great Britain. From the Salvation Army, with its international connections, a fraction broke off and established a domestic variant—the Swedish Salvation Army—which has never attracted many followers.

Membership in most of these denominations has declined since the 1960s because of increasing urbanization and the development of the Swedish welfare state. The older denominations (the Methodist Church, the Swedish Covenant Church, and the Baptist Union of Sweden) lost most of their members during this period (Gustafsson 1991). These movements or denominations, except the Salvation Army, which has one-third of its members in the three major cities in Sweden, have had problems gaining access to members in the major urban areas. Thus, they are represented mainly in towns, villages, and rural areas. Furthermore, women and older persons are heavily over represented among the members within most of the denominations. During the past 10 to 15 years, these movements have lost their lower-class character and now are based more in the middle class, as indicated by the increasing number of members who are public servants, have higher educational levels, and live in houses rather than apartments (Palm 1993).

Although only 5 percent of the Swedish adult population is involved with the traditional free movements (Gustafsson 1991), these movements have had an important influence in Swedish politics and everyday life. This influence is partly connected to their activities for and with children, adolescents, and elderly in the community, as well as study courses of various sorts, in which many nonmembers participate.

Many members of the free movements are also engaged in various sectors of social and organizational life. In party politics, many members are active on both the municipal and national levels. There is an overrepresentation of members of free movements in the Swedish Parliament and, over the decades, several of the governmental ministers have been members. In 1991, a coalition government, including the Christ Democratic Party, was formed. This party's leader, Alf Svensson, belongs to the Pentecostal movement, and he and two other members of the Pentecostal movement were ministers in the Swedish government from 1991 to 1994.

Hamberg and Pettersson (1994) demonstrated that in Swedish municipalities in which the free churches were the most numerous, there was higher religious activity by the population as a whole. This finding confirmed their theoretical expectation—derived from rational-choice theory (cf. Hadden 1995; Warner 1993; Young 1997)—that increased market diversity and, thus, competition, would stimulate churches to develop "products" that satisfy the seeming needs of the population. Providing a diverse array of religious "products," in turn, would increase the demand for the products that churches supply. Since Hamberg and Pettersson used municipalities as their units of analysis, they could hypothesize these dynamics without challenging the notion of the overall high secularity of the population.

Hamberg and Pettersson (1994) argued that the free churches that are growing represent the opening up of the religious market in Sweden after its many-century monopolization by the Lutheran Church. Monopoly conditions tend to lead to the decline of religious practices, consistent with the arguments we presented earlier. Rational-choice theory suggests that the consequences of monopoly are long lasting in depressing the "demand" for religious products. According to this view, the relatively slow growth of the Swedish free churches, until now may be the result of the inertia of the old monopolistic situation, but the accelerating growth of a few of them may indicate that this inertia is eroding. If the religious market becomes truly pluralistic and open, over the long run Hamberg and Pettersson expect some recovery of the religious practice and beliefs in the population led by these groups, in spite of the rationalistic tendencies of the Swedes today. The competition that these groups engender would, theoretically, stimulate an increased demand for religious "products" in a free religious market.

The extremely high secularity of the Swedes, compared to that in other countries, can be explained in an intriguing way by this approach. It also permits one to see some sources of dynamism in this otherwise seemingly static situation. However, one can only speculate on the possibilities for the future.

Besides the three major types of free religious movements, the religious sphere of Sweden has also become more diverse because of increased immigration. During the past few decades, almost all immigrants have been refugees, many from countries with much different religious and cultural backgrounds. As a result, what are sometimes called immigrant churches are playing a more prominent role in the religious life of Sweden. For example, membership in the Catholic Church and the Greek Orthodox and other Eastern churches increased from 18,000 and 7,000, respectively, in 1950; to 52,500 and 40,000, respectively, in 1970; and to 142,000 and 97,100, respectively, in 1990. In addition, the number of refugees from non-Christian religious backgrounds has increased. The largest group of these refugees is Muslim; at the end of the 1980s, there were about 70,000 members of Islamic denominations in Sweden (Gustafsson 1991).

Sweden also has religious sects and new spiritual movements, most of which are small as far as their membership and influence are concerned. One of the bigger sects is *Jehovas Vittnen* (Jehovah's Witnesses), which, through an active recruitment program, increased from 8,100 members in 1960 to 21,900 in 1990. During the 1980s, a new religious movement often labeled the belief movement, started in Sweden. The denomination *Livets ord* (the Word of Life) has its main site in Uppsala, and its leader, Ulf Ekman, is a charismatic pastor. The movement, which is based on charisma and a Fundamentalist view of the Bible, has a membership of about 8,000 members (Skog 1993).

Parallel to the increased variety within the religious sphere has been the development of the ecumenical movement during this century. A crucial event for this movement was the World Church meeting in Stockholm in 1925, organized by the Swedish archbishop, Nathan Söderblom. As a result of this meeting, the ecumenical organization, Life and Work, was established. This organization later became a part of the World Council of Churches when it was established in 1948.[3]

BELIEFS AND SOCIALIZATION

Sweden has been labeled a Christian society and considers itself as such. As was discussed earlier, a large majority of the population—even about 70 percent of the members of the free movements—are members of the Swedish Lutheran Church (Palm 1993).[4] However, overt and active participation in religious activities is infrequent. Thus, two questions arise: Has the Swedish

Lutheran Church transformed into a sort of bureaucracy, mainly taking care of certain rites, like christenings, confirmations, weddings and funerals? Do people, as reported earlier, go to church only on these occasions?

In opinion polls, probability samples of Swedes have been asked, "Do you believe that there is a God?" In 1947, 83 percent said yes, 8 percent said no, and 9 percent said they did not know. In contrast, in 1990, only 38 percent said they believed there is a God, 46 percent said they did not, and 16 percent were uncertain (Gustafsson 1991). Other studies from the late 1980s found that more Swedes believe there is a God, believe that a supernatural power is controlling us, or say they are "Christian in my own personal way" than those who answered yes to the simple and diffuse question just mentioned. However, the number of Swedes who say that they profess Christianity is low, about 10 percent (Gustafsson 1991). Christian belief seems to have diminished, and beliefs seem to be more privatized.

Some indices of Christian beliefs are participating in services, reading the Bible, and saying prayers. Many studies have shown that parallel to the decreased commitment to Christian beliefs, religious engagement has diminished. Only a small fraction of the members of the Swedish Lutheran Church participate in worship services, and few read the Bible regularly or say prayers. Within the traditional free movements, however, the majority of the members are active—participating in services, studying the Bible, and saying their prayers regularly. As could be presumed, more women than men participate in religious activities, especially in the frequency of saying prayers, and are believers. Studies have also found that older people are more religious than are younger people (Gustafsson 1991; Palm 1993).

One of the important tasks of Christianity is to transfer the Christian belief system and the Christian tradition to new generations and to support parents in socializing their children to be good Christians. Although most primary socialization occurs in the home, the atmosphere in preschool day care is also important. Subsequently, other social institutions gain prominence in the socialization of belief systems. By tradition, the Christian denominations in Sweden have provided many activities for children and adolescents, Sunday schools were influential, as evidenced by the large number of children who attended. In recent years, these activities have decreased and have been replaced by more activities throughout the week. Indicative of this trend is the number of participants in the Sunday preschools of the Swedish Lutheran Church, which decreased from 96,359 in 1970 to 8,521 in 1990. On the other hand, there has been an increase in participation in the Swedish Lutheran Church's "children's hours," during which adults read from the Bible or other relevant texts to preschool children. The number of preschool children who attended these children's hours rose from 38,584 in 1970 to 102,810 in 1990 (Alwall 1993).

Comparative European studies have shown Sweden to be one of the most secularized countries in the Western world with respect to religiosity and religious engagement. Furthermore, these studies have indicated that both Christian belief and the Swedish Lutheran Church have lost a great deal of ground since World War II (Pettersson 1992). In a study of 739 students aged 20–23 at Uppsala University in 1993, only 10 percent said that religion was very important to them, 40 percent of the men and 23 percent of the women had not been to church during the previous twelve months, and only about 10 percent had been to church once a month or more often.[5] A conclusion that could be drawn from the foregoing discussion is that there is little primary and secondary socialization of children and adults into religious beliefs and activities.

RELIGIOUS GROUPS' PERSPECTIVES ON THE FAMILY

All the various religious groups seem to be positive toward the nuclear family, and some hesitantly accept other forms as well. The official view is not always followed in social reality; there is a clear difference between the ideal norms set in the doctrine and behavioral norms. For example, the Catholic Church in Sweden follows in the ideal norms of the pope and his restricted view on the use of contraceptives, but it is realistic enough to realize that, if the behavioral norms were the same, the church would not have many members.

Many religious groups do not take an official stand on controversial issues. The Swedish Lutheran Church, for instance, keeps a low profile on the issue of homosexual couples living together, though it is openly against the idea of registering partnerships for same-sex couples. And although some officials openly declare their dislike and condemnation of same-sex couples and homosexual behavior, it is well known that quite a few clergy, both male and female, live as de facto same-sex couples.

The issue of legal abortion is also complicated. Most of the religious groups are against abortion, but some probably realize that since more than half the Swedish women will have had abortions before they reach menopause, many of their members have or will have had abortions. Politically, some groups realize that strong opposition to abortion may have negative consequences for them. An example is the Christ Democratic Party, which is represented in the Parliament (*Riksdagen*); this party has decided officially to keep a low profile on this issue and not to work either for or against legal abortion. Since the beginning of the 1970s, Sweden has had no or almost no illegal abortions; some of the policy makers realize that a restrictive abortion law would increase the number of illegal abortions and would not lower the total abortion rate.

Another issue is nonmarital cohabitation. As far as is known, all religious institutions are pro marriage and thus not pro-nonmarital cohabitation. However, they keep a low profile on this issue as well. If they were officially and openly to condemn nonmarital cohabitation, they would act against their members' social reality and behavior. Sweden was the first Western country in which cohabitation rapidly became socially institutionalized alongside legal marriage (Trost 1981).

CONCLUDING REMARKS

Since the Reformation in the sixteenth century, when Sweden converted to the Lutheran doctrine, the Swedish Church has been closely associated with the Swedish state. During preindustrial times, the church had special responsibility, for example, for education and care of the poor, and its traditions influenced daily family life. At the beginning of the twentieth century, almost all children were still being christened and confirmed, and children were taught Luther's shorter catechism at school.

When the process of modernization began, the Swedish church's position started to weaken, and religious life became differentiated. New denominations were established, and the civil society took over several tasks from the church. The school became confessionless. The church is still a state church, but a process of separation has started. From 2000, the church will be almost fully disassociated from the state.

During the decades after World War II, Sweden was transformed into a welfare state. The population became less and less interested in Christian beliefs, and the church's activities decreased. Comparative international studies have shown that Sweden now is one of the most secularized societies in the world. The Swedish church has lost its normative effect in many societal and individual moral areas, and its members attend services only on special occasions. However, many of the religious Christian traditions are still alive, albeit without any evident connection to their religious background; for example, Whitsuntide is celebrated with three days off from work, but almost no one knows its religious origin.

Although Sweden is supposed to be one of the most secularized countries in the world, almost all Swedes are members of the state Lutheran Church or of other churches or denominations even though they are not active members. At the same time, Sweden is one of the oldest democracies in the world and has lived in peace for two hundred years, with no foreign troops fighting or occupying any part of the country. The freedom given by democracy, by the welfare society, and the absence of war may be connected to the degree of secularization. People who live under severe circumstances are often in need of the salvation that religious faith can give. Although Swedes still experience the limitations posed by gender and other dimensions of social inequality, in many ways thay have been free of the stressful circumstances that support religion.

If the need for religious services seems to have declined in Sweden owing to the welfare state conditions and general security, it also can be argued that the religious needs of the population have been depressed by the limited market conditions in the religious sphere. The religious market is still structured by the legacy of the historical Lutheran monopoly. As this legacy fades, the development of competition among religious groups may lead to a new type of interpretation of the "need" for religion that would stimulate the growth of churches. We cannot identify the signs of a major market change of this type now, but it may be possible to do so in the future.

As this chapter has indicated, many factors have been working toward the privatization of family and religion in Sweden. The official religion no longer attracts people to the same degree as previously, the influence and power of the churches have decreased, and the societal institutions have become more and more specialized.

NOTES

1. In Norway, there is also a civil confirmation, in which children participate in a ceremony, usually at a town hall, under the auspices of the Human Association. Sweden has no civil confirmation.
2. The movement stressed the importance of personal Christian conversion.
3. During the ongoing ecumenical process in Sweden various free religious movements and members have been important actors (Palm 1992; 1993).
4. Some members of the free movements, especially Baptists, chose to leave the Swedish Lutheran Church when the possibility arose in the early 1950s. Others, a clear majority, chose to remain and to be members of the Swedish Lutheran Church, as well as of the free movement. A common argument for remaining was, and still is, that the Swedish Lutheran Church serves as a basis for the national unification of Christian values and counterbalances the tendency toward secularization.
5. Data collected by the second author.

REFERENCES

Alwall, Jonas. 1993. "Svenska kyrkans statistik 1992—kontinuitet och förändring." Pp. 7–30 in *Perspektiv på Svenska kyrkans statistik 1992*, edited by Jonas Alwall. *Tro och Tanke* 3(9). Uppsala, Sweden: Svenska kyrkans forskningsråd.

Befolkningsrörelsen. 1962. *Befolkningsrörelsen år 1960*. Stockholm: Statistiska Centralbyrån.

Björnsson, Björn. 1971. *The Lutheran Doctrine of Marriage in Modern Icelandic Society*. Oslo: Universitetsforlaget.

Carlsson, Lizzie. 1972. *Jag giver Dig min dotter*. Lund, Sweden: Nordiska Bokhandeln.

Gustafsson, Göran. 1991. *Tro, samfund och samhälle*. Örebro, Sweden: Libris.

———. 1988. "Religiös struktur och vardaglig religiositet." Pp. 461–88 in *Sverige—vardag och struktur*, edited by U. Himmelstrand and G. Svensson. Stockholm: Norstedts.

Hadden, Jeffrey K. 1995. "Religion and the Quest for Meaning and Order: Old Paradigms, New Realities." *Sociological Focus* 28:83–100.

Hamberg, Eva A., and Thorleif Pettersson. 1994. "The Religious Market: Denominational Competition and Religious Participation in Contemporary Sweden." *Journal for the Scientific Study of Religion* 33:205–16.

Luckmann, Thomas. 1974. *The Invisible Religion*. New York: Macmillan.

Palm, Irving. 1982. *Frikyrkorna, arbetarfrågan och klasskampen*. Uppsala, Sweden: Acta Universitatis Upsaliensis.

———. 1993. "Frikyrkofolket och ekumeniken." *Tro och Tanke* 3(5):37–88. Uppsala, Sweden: Svenska kyrkans forskningsråd.

Pettersson, Thorleif. 1992. "Kyrkan, folket och framtiden." Pp. 19–28 in Religionsfrihet och folkkyrka, edited by Jörgen Straarup. *Tro och Tanke* 2(3). (Uppsala, Sweden: Svenska kyrkans forskningsråd.

Skog, Margareta. 1993. "Trosrörelsen i Sverige." *Tro och Tanke* 3(5):89–139. Uppsala, Sweden: Svenska kyrkans forskningsråd.

Statistical Yearbook. 1993. Stockholm: Liber.

Sundt, Eilert. [1855] 1975. *Om giftermål i Norge*. Oslo: Gyldendal Norsk Forlag.

Trost, Jan. 1979. *Unmarried cohabitation*. Västerås: International Library.

———. 1981. "Cohabitation in the Nordic Countries: From Deviant Phenomenon to Social Institution." *Alternative Lifestyles* 4:401–27.

———. 1993. *Familjen i Sverige*. Stockholm: Liber Utbildning.

Warner, Stephen R. 1993. "Work in Progress Toward a New Paradigm for the Sociological Study of Religion in the United States." *American Journal of Sociology* 98:1044–93.

Young, Laurence A., ed. 1997. *Rational Choice Theory and Religion*. Boston: Routledge.

CHAPTER FIVE

Religion and Family Formation in Taiwan: The Decline of Ancestral Authority

LI-SHOU YANG
ARLAND THORNTON
THOMAS FRICKE

INTRODUCTION: POPULAR RELIGION AND FAMILY IN TAIWAN

Religion is usually viewed as systematic beliefs, ritualistic practices, and organizational relationships. The religion prevailing in Taiwan,[1] which has no specific name, is a form of popular or folk religion. It is characterized by beliefs, rituals, and organizations that deeply permeate the secular life of the individual and the society. It has theology, rituals, and organizational relations that are interrelated with other social organizations, among which the family is particularly important. The family is an important source of inspiration for religious ideas and an important organization for the transmission of religious beliefs. It is also an important locus in which many religious rituals are performed.

In the historical Chinese context, the family dominated individual life to such an extent that people experienced a great part of their activities, associations, information, means of subsistence, authority, and cosmology within its framework (Thornton and Fricke 1987; Thornton, Fricke, Yang, and Chang 1994). The family has evoked some important cosmological ideas and, in turn, the cosmological view has shaped people's definition of family and interpersonal relationships. Some of the ideas on the family and people's views of religion are intertwined, so it is virtually impossible to separate religious notions from familial concepts. One of the most significant examples is the place of ancestors in both the cosmos and individual lives.

An important idea in Chinese culture is the continuity of generational relationships and obligations unbroken by death. Just as in earthly intergenerational relationships, the living and their dead ancestors are believed to be bound within a complex web of reciprocal obligations, support, and exchange. Thus, familial relations are perceived to be extended from life to death and from death to life. This belief links the limited life span of each generation to form a family line with the potential of continuing through all eternity. Through the ritual of ancestral ceremony, the individual spirit is thought to be able to cross the boundary between life and death and to integrate with the immortality of the family. The important value of an individual life is thus to maintain the continuity of the family line.

The linkage of generations across death helps the living person to deal with ultimate matters of human life, such as the tragedy of death and a finite life span. It also provides an explanation for the meaning, purpose, and value of individual existence. This idea thus has both religious connotations and familial ramifications. Because of the belief in the unbroken continuity of the family, the concept of family is extended from the living family members to include the unborn future generations and the deceased past generations. It is also manifest in many important aspects of family life. The integration of family and religion is the most distinguishing feature of the family system and folk religion in the Chinese cultural context. In the following section, we focus on the implications of these beliefs for folk religion in Taiwan and in a later section turn to its implications for the family. Finally, we summarize the findings from a previous study (Thornton, Fricke et al. 1994) to show the impact of social change on the ancestor-related beliefs and rituals during the second half of the twentieth century when the Taiwanese mode of social organization changed from a familial toward a less familial one.

IMPORTANT FEATURES OF POPULAR RELIGION IN TAIWAN

Unlike highly institutionalized religions, such as Roman Catholicism, the popular Taiwanese religion has neither missionaries nor a priesthood specifically developed for religious education and discipline.[2] In addition, it has nothing comparable to a Bible as a canonical basis for its creeds and no congregation taking part in regular religious services. Without a centralized authority to establish, define, and elaborate orthodoxy, it allows the worshipers to have more freedom and latitude in constructing their own beliefs and practices (DeGlopper 1974; Harrell 1974).

There is ample evidence in the anthropological literature of variations in beliefs, rituals, and institutions in the Taiwanese popular religion (DeGlopper 1974; Harrell, 1974; Smith 1974; S-C Wang 1974; Weller 1986; A. Wolf 1974). Following the mainstream Chinese folk religion, the popular religion in Taiwan is made up mainly of Confucian, Buddhist, and Taoist elements. In this system, people neither practice all three elements together nor each separately. It is common to find temples in Taiwan mixing deities associated with different sources. Buddhas, the immortals of Taoism, and the deified emperors, empresses, scholars, and heroes of Confucianism could all be accepted as gods in a temple; the important consideration for worshipers is probably the power of a deity to fulfill their petitions, rather than the origin of a deity. Adherents are highly diversified in the pantheon they believe in (Harrell 1974). Taiwanese informants, including both ordinary believers and religious specialists, do not agree on religious assumptions (Weller 1986). In addition, the practice of religious rituals and the calendar of religious festivals are different from one place to another (DeGlopper 1974).

Variation, however, is not to be taken for chaos; Freedman (1974) posited that the popular religion of the Chinese was not an outcome of randomly assembled elements, and one may expect an order of some sort behind the superficial diversity. Thus, an important issue is to find the basic themes underlying popular religion in Taiwan, so it can be considered as a religious system, rather than a term summing up the multitude of observed practices, cults, and customs. In addition, an understanding of central religious themes can illuminate Taiwanese views on the ultimate meaning and purpose of life, which have many implications for the ways people organize their lives.

Underlying the diversity of Taiwanese popular religion is a systematic cosmological view of the afterlife as an extension of the earthly world. Adherents of popular religion believe that the world of the afterlife is where a person's spirit goes after death. The spirits in that world are subject to the same needs they had while living in the terrestrial world—food, clothing, shelter, and money. They also retain feeling, emotion, and temper from their state as human beings. In this belief system, a person's merits in this world become important determinants of the person's position in the supernatural hierarchy and of the quality of life in the afterlife. The worldly merits transmitted through familial ties are particularly important to virtually all. The extension from the living world to the afterlife is also reflected in the conceptualization of the structures and orders of the afterlife.

People in Taiwan tend to view the configuration of the afterlife world as similar to that of the living world, particularly the social landscape of imperial China (Feuchtwang 1974; Harrell 1974; A. Wolf 1974). From a Chinese layperson's perspective, the family and feudal bureaucracy are important in this social landscape. People use the principles and concepts from these two earthly organizations to visualize the outline of the afterlife and interpret the general states of harmony or discord in the cosmos.

Ancestors

The broadly accepted concept of unbroken generational ties across the mortal and immortal domains makes ancestors and ancestral ceremonies an important part of popular religion in Taiwan. From the viewpoint of a living person, the family context in which one is embedded is the creation of previous generations. The life, property, and social status one currently has are one's inheritance from the ancestors. Since the individual is the beneficiary of the ancestors' merits accumulated in this world, he or she is indebted to the ancestors and obligated to show reverence and support for them. From this perspective, the dead who are ritually worshiped as ancestors and given offerings of food, wine, and money by their descendants are better off than the dead who do not receive such respect and support (Feuchtwang 1974; Jordan 1972). With such assistance from the living, the ancestors can live a fairly content afterlife, but without it—because of the lack of descendants or for the failure of descendants to provide them with offerings—the dead live in the afterlife as miserable and starving entities (Ahern 1971; Hsu 1971; Jordan 1972). Taiwanese also believe that the ancestors' spirits are with them and are continuously keeping watchful eyes on them. Therefore, the good or bad fortune of the family in this world can be related to the actions of the deceased ancestors (Ahern 1971; M. C. Yang 1945). The ancestors and the living descendants thus are linked in their ability to affect each other's fate.

People believe that being treated appropriately—frequently worshipped and provided with offerings—makes the ancestors benevolent and benign.[3] Hence, daily worship of ancestors at the family altar is one of the most widespread ritual acts in Taiwan (Weller 1987). The family altar is a publicly visible long, high, and narrow table placed against the wall of the main room of the household. Ancestral tablets (wooden tablets inscribed to the dead forebears) are placed on the left segment of the altar, and the statues of the gods that the household chooses to worship are placed on the right side (Freedman 1970; Jordan 1972). Separate incense pots for the ancestors and gods are also set on the altar. A representative of the family, usually the head of the household or his wife, burns sticks of incense at the altar to show filial respect for the ancestors. In addition to daily incense burning, there are particular occasions for commemorating the more immediate ancestors. People hold ancestral ceremonies on the death days or birthdays of their closest ancestors, whom they treat as though they were still living kinsmen (Fricke, Chang, and Yang 1994). On these occasions, other than burning incense, the descendants serve the ancestors full meals with their favorite foods. Remote ancestors, whose birthdays or death days are no longer in living memory, are worshiped as a group on the ninth day of the ninth lunar month. Ancestors, both close and remote, also receive offerings on numerous other occasions during the year[4] and whenever a family member has an important life event, such as marriage. These frequent activities continuously integrate the living and the dead.

The ceremonies for ancestors imply that the ancestors are not entirely dead, that their spirits continue to live, watch over, and participate in the lives of their descendants. In addition to the daily ancestral worship at home, extra-domestic rituals for ancestors are held in the ancestral hall and in the graveyard. The ceremonies in the ancestral hall are mainly for common ancestors of larger kin groups; this practice is not universal, since the ancestral hall is available only when the lineage organization is strong (Freedman 1970). On the other hand, graveyard worship is widespread; on the day of the *Ching-ming* festival in early April, people visit and care for the tombs of their ancestors.

Looking after the graveyard again shows the descendants' care of their ancestors. But the ancestral graveyard ritual has another significant meaning. For most Taiwanese, the buried ancestor has two sides: a disembodied spirit, *hun*, and a mystified set of bones. As a spirit form, the ancestor is attached to a tablet and hovers above the grave; as a set of bones, he or she is permanently buried in the earth. It is believed that the relationship of the ancestor's bones to the surroundings has a direct influence on the fate of the descendants (Freedman 1966). This belief in the geomancy of graves, *feng-shui* (which means "winds and water"), leads Taiwanese to seek a site for their ancestral tombs where the winds and water are most favorable as a means of establishing or maintaining wealth, prestige, and progeny (Freedman 1970). Geomantic arranging and grave offerings ensure the comfort of the ancestor as a set of bones and benefit the good fortune of the descendants.

Gods

Political bureaucracy is an important social organization in the imperial Chinese society that goes beyond the family. Although the influence of the bureaucratic system on a person's life is not as immediate as the family's influence, people recognize the authority of bureaucrats in forming legislative regulations and maintaining social order. Correspondingly, people conceive of the afterlife world as bureaucratic in structure, in which gods are the supernatural counterparts of the bureaucrats in the earthly world (A. Wolf 1974). Like human bureaucrats, gods are hierarchically ranked. Generally everyone agrees that at the top of this hierarchy is the Jade Emperor (Jordan 1972); below him are local deities, such as *Tu Di Gong* (the Earth Gods); household deities, such as the Kitchen God; and other deities associated with Buddhism, Confucianism, and Taoism, including *Guan Yin*, *Guan Gong*, and *Ma Tsu*. Gods in different positions have different judicial or administrative responsibilities. Some control people's lifespans and destinies in this world and the afterlife, some keep the peace and security of a community district, and some keep records of the life of each individual (Feuchtwang 1974; Jordan 1972; A. Wolf 1974). Because of the large number of gods and the lack of a central authority to interpret the order of the afterlife, the hierarchy is unclear; people usually cannot sort out a consistent ranking for different gods (A. Wolf 1974).

In their association with the administrative hierarchy, the gods are viewed as bureaucrats who rule communities, states, and the cosmos. In contrast to the explanation for the ancestral ceremony, which is based mainly on generational responsibilities and mutual dependence, people see the worship of deities in terms of the metaphor for politics (Weller 1987). According to A. Wolf (1974), Taiwanese men and women usually worship the gods under whose jurisdiction they live because the worship is often a community activity and it is especially prudent to maintain good relations with these gods. But unlike the worship of the ancestors, it is clear that people do not feel morally obligated to make offerings to any god. People worship gods to gain their assistance in having a desirable number of children—particularly sons—a reasonable income, good fortune, a peaceful life, and so on (Harrell 1974; Stafford 1992). If a god lacks authority over them, people turn to another god who is more powerful (A. Wolf 1974). These gods can be bribed; when people appeal to a god, they make a small sacrifice and promise a larger one if the god will grant the petition (Harrell 1974; A. Wolf 1974). The relationships of the practitioners of the popular religion with the gods are literally "contractual, with payment on delivery of requested goods or events" (Stafford 1992:365). Although people worship gods on regular holidays and on the gods' birthdays, it is unnecessary to worship gods at other times unless one encounters problems and needs special help (A. Wolf 1974).

Most of the gods were human beings who, for various reasons, were promoted to some important function or office in the afterlife (Harrell 1974). One popular theory is that to be promoted to godhood in the afterlife, individuals should have done exceptional deeds, accumulated merits, or devoted themselves to the salvation of others in this world (Jordan 1972). Considering the numerous competitors throughout history, the number of positions available in the celestial government is relatively limited, so the opportunity for an individual to be classified as a god in the afterlife is extremely slim (Jordan 1972). Thus, with only few exceptions, all the dead fall into a nonbureaucratic category in the afterlife.

Ghosts

The nonbureaucratic spirits are an unstructured mass and inhabit an intermediate realm, in contrast to the gods who are hierarchically structured and inhabit heaven (Feuchtwang 1974; Jordan 1972). Conceptually, they are judged by the gods and are punished for their earthly transgressions (Jordan 1972). Nevertheless, because of the continuity of generational ties, it is believed that the well-being of the dead without bureaucratic status is not equal. As was mentioned previously, those who have been identified and worshiped by the living as ancestors can receive worldly support. In addition to providing them with subsistence and money, the living descendants can save the ancestors by hiring priests who know how to obtain the services of the afterlife officials who can help them avoid the harshness of punishment in purgatory (Weller 1987). Thus, only those who are not ritually worshiped by any living descendant will suffer in the afterlife.

The dead who have no bureaucratic standing as gods and no kinship standing as ancestors fall into the category of ghosts. They include those who have no descendants to provide them with offerings, those who have unfilial descendants who do not worship them, and those who die violently—through accidents, murder, suicide, or wars and seek to avenge themselves on the living (Harrell 1974). A. Wolf (1974) argued that ghosts are metaphors for people who do not occupy proper positions in the social structure, such as bandits, beggars, and gangsters. Ghosts are thus socially marginal beings in the afterlife (Weller 1987).

Although everyone agrees that people who die inappropriately—either without filial descendants or by violence—become ghosts in the afterlife, the term *ghost* (*kuei*) sometimes is used more broadly. Some people refer to everyone else's ancestors as ghosts (A. Wolf 1974; Weller 1987). For these people, all the dead except those promoted to godhood are essentially alike—they are all ghosts—and the key to the distinction between ghosts and ancestors is the presence or absence of a familial tie. From this perspective, the relations between ancestors and descendants are private; the ancestors are important only to men and women with kinship relations (Harrell 1974). Whereas one's ancestors are the dead senior generations of the family, the ancestors of other people are dead strangers and are considered ghosts. Although the ghosts who are other people's ancestors are perceived as harmless, those who are not anyone's ancestors are thought of as malicious, since they have no connection with the living world and suffer in the underworld. The latter ghosts are desperate and thus dangerous, and people usually think of them as primary explanations for disaster. This group is the core of the ghost category for whom people perform ghost rites.

It is said that people do not worship ghosts, but work to keep them from doing harm (Harrell 1974). Holding a ceremony for ghosts will buy them off. Offerings are given to ghosts on regular occasions to forestall their random malevolence and at times of crisis to persuade them to stop the harm they are causing (A. Wolf 1974). For some people, the ritual for ghosts is more like charity; the reports of village people in northern Taiwan show that the major reason for observing rites for ghosts is to act generously to those in this pitiful state (Weller 1987).

Adherents of Folk Religion

A systematic theology may not be clear to all the adherents of Taiwanese popular religion, but they consistently classify the supernatural spirits into gods, ancestors, and ghosts (Feuchtwang 1974; Harrell 1974; Jordan 1972; S-C Wang 1974; Weller 1987; A. Wolf 1974). This three-way distinction reflects the social structure of bureaucrats, family and lineage, and heterogeneous outsiders in imperial China (Wolf 1974). For most people, the gods are strangers with power and ghosts are strangers with no position in the supernatural structure; only ancestors are close relations of whom they have intimate knowledge. The rites for gods, ghosts, and ancestors reflect the way people perceive their relations to these three types of supernatural spirits.

Although people often group the supernatural beings into three types, the positions of these beings are not static. As in the earthly world, there is mobility in the supernatural world. Anthropological reports have documented that amoral ghosts may gradually become gods if they successfully grant all requests (Weller 1987) and may become ancestors if they successfully discipline the unfilial descendants regarding the observance of ancestral ceremonies or force an unrelated living person who has no obligation to worship them as ancestors.[5] Gods may be demoted or vanish if they do not perform like gods (A. Wolf 1974). An extinct god may be an ancestor or a ghost, depending on whether there is someone observing the ancestral ceremonies for him or her. The status of ancestors is also not invariable. Ancestors may become gods if the merits they accumulated in the living world become widely recognized, but they may turn into ghosts if their descendants forget to worship them.

Ancestors can be easily transformed into ghosts as time passes if they are not remembered ritually by being worshiped in ancestral ceremonies. While the dead are still known, it is ritually possible to worship them as ancestors; as records and memories fade, however, they become less known and less defined. Then it is not easy to differentiate masses of ghosts and masses of cursory ancestors whose death days are unobserved and who are worshipped only on occasions in the ritual calendar when ancestors are statutorily worshipped collectively and not by name (Feuchtwang 1974). In other words, as the life images and stories of dead people gradually become unclear in the memories of the living descendants, the concrete attachment of the living to these dead ancestors gradually disappears and there is a convergence of the ancestors and ghosts.

The permeability of categorical boundaries among gods, ghosts, and ancestors again reveals that the adherents of Taiwanese popular religion visualize the world of the afterlife as similar to the social world of mortality in which people can cross the categories of relatives, bureaucrats, and strangers. For example, remote relatives are close to strangers, and relatives can be bureaucrats. Although it is not sensible to conclude that the Taiwanese conception of spiritual beings is nothing more than a reflection of their perspective on society, it is likely that the social world is an important source of inspiration for many religious ideas. Therefore, the religious world becomes a metaphor for the social world.

The adherents of Taiwanese folk religion are not merely passive receivers or followers; they are also active designers who are involved in forming and shaping the religion. People can create gods on the basis of historical legends and produce ghosts according to community beliefs.[6] They also can make gods and ghosts move across the supernatural hierarchical categories by either identifying the ancestors and upholding their status in the afterlife or neglecting the ancestors and downgrading them to ghosts. The active involvement of ordinary people in forming the religion is one explanation for the diversity in dogmas and rituals found in Taiwanese folk religion.

The notions of ancestors are the most unified aspect of the system of popular religion in Taiwan (Weller 1987). Hsu (1985) commented that the folk religion is a collection of gods and spirits without any clear distinction between their adherents, except for the care of ancestors' graves, the observance of ancestors' death anniversaries, and the Lunar New Year festival. In other words, the ancestral element is a relatively consistent and unclouded part of folk religion in Taiwan. In addition, although the ancestors may not be the most powerful among the three categories of supernatural beings, they are the most relevant to individual life, as will be discussed later.

The centrality and extensiveness of ancestral worship are probably related to the adherents' close relations with the ancestors. The domestic ancestral ceremonies conceptually and ritually incorporate ancestors into a model of kinship. As was indicated earlier, the ancestors are the deceased family members; the descendants worship them to preserve their memory, serve their needs, and satisfy the demands of their authority. It often is mentioned that the reason for observing the ancestral ceremony is to fulfill filial piety, to keep good relations with the ancestors so they will protect the descendants in the earthly world. Another important reason for ancestral worship may be the descendants' hope that they can design a better future for themselves in the afterlife. This is an intention with significant implications for Taiwanese folk religion that has been overlooked.

The adherents of popular religion are close to the ancestors not only because the ancestors are their dead relatives, but also because they identify themselves as the future dead ancestors or the current living ancestors of their offspring. The identification with ancestors may lead people to put more emphasis on the ancestral element in both religion and the family. Almost all the people anticipate their future in the afterlife as ancestors because turning into a ghost after death is a misfortune and becoming a god is extremely unlikely. Being someone's ancestor elevates one's well-being in the afterlife and is a rational hope for all the adherents of popular religion. Nevertheless, to retain one's ancestral status, one's descendants must diligently observe the ancestral ceremony to demonstrate the intensive ties between them and the dead ancestors. In doing so, people intentionally cultivate a social environment in which their children are socialized to the idea of unbroken generational ties. Through these rituals, the children become strong supporters of the ancestors, and the continuation of the family line becomes the most important life value and ancestral worship the most important ritual. Thus, one can ensure his or her future welfare as an ancestor in the afterlife. Therefore, advocating for the ancestors' well-being can be viewed as promoting one's future well-being in the afterlife, as well as taking care of the current ancestors' welfare.

In other words, the adherents of popular religion have their own private reasons for consistently emphasizing the ancestors and ancestral ceremonies. Their strong identification with ancestors probably contributes to making the ancestral element a significant part of the folk religion and an influential force in individual lives. Taiwanese men and women work together to strengthen the institution of the ancestral ceremony and to enhance their own ancestral status. The family is the locus of their efforts and serves these purposes well. In the following section, we review the anthropological and historical literature with reference to the intercorrelation of the ancestral complex and family formation in early Taiwanese society.

ANCESTORS AND FAMILY FORMATION IN HISTORICAL TAIWAN

As was mentioned previously, the historical concept of the family is of an ideally endless family line or chain that includes the numerous dead ancestors at one end and the numerous unborn descendants at the other, with the living familial members in between. The ideas that the living are instrumental in maintaining the continuation of the familial chain and that being an ancestor ensures one's eternal well-being are important orientations that shape individual values and behaviors, structure family relationships, and help maintain kinship ties (Ahern 1971; Freedman 1970; Hsu 1971; Thornton, Yang, and Fricke 1994; M. C. Yang 1945). As historical and ethnographic reports have indicated, a great part of individual and family activities was regulated by the power of the invisible ancestors. The ideas associated with ancestors were manifest in the ways in which the family was established. The many different ways of organizing the currently living familial unit, *chia*, that are found in Taiwanese history involved the ultimate goals of continuing the family line and obtaining a niche in the family line for an individual to become an ancestor. Here, we summarize the significant influence of ancestors and ancestral connotations in the process of family formation in Taiwan on the basis of historical and ethnographic reports.

Ancestors and Chia

For Taiwanese, *chia* is only a momentary expression of the immortal family line. The ideal model of *chia* held by the historical Taiwanese was an organization in which the parents, their married sons, and the sons' conjugal families (which could be extended several generations in depth) lived together, sharing production and consumption and retaining the rights and obligations of descent and inheritance. In reality, given demographic, economic, and other constraints, the actual historical Taiwanese families were not always large or complex in structure. A family could be organized in the extended form at a particular time, but with the death, birth, or migration of its members, the form might not remain extended and complex, or it could again be transformed into the extended model at a later time. Thus, *chia* existed in many different forms in early Taiwanese history (Cohen 1970; Hsieh 1981; S-H. Wang 1985; A. Wolf 1985).

Chia varied with respect to residential arrangement and economic activities. *Chia* members could live within the same household or in different households and could perform as an economic unit or as economically independent individuals (Cohen 1970). At its basic level, *chia* is a kin group with a series of claims of one sort or another on the *chia* estate (Cohen 1970, 1976)—an important element that ties the group together. The *chia* estate could vary in size and value; at one extreme, it could consist of a humble farmhouse, a few agricultural tools, and tenants' rights to a small lot; at the other extreme, it could consist of many plots of owned land (Cohen 1970).

Viewing the familial estate as a key element of a *chia* is consistent with the idea of the family line. The *chia* in historical Taiwan was primarily an inclusive economic unit, in which the family members pooled their incomes from different sources. Families in Taiwan usually managed their human and natural resources to create a collective, but often diversified, economy (Cohen 1976). Historically, one of the major resources of most Taiwanese families was the farmland they owned or rented. After the frontier era in Taiwan, inheritance was the major way either to own or obtain tenants' rights to farmland. Almost all the families in Taiwan owned estates that were inherited from the ancestors because all male descendants had the right to equal inheritance. Any secondary sources of income, such as those gained by adult children working as merchants or craftsmen, were combined with income from the land. Since land was a major economic resource, most of the families would purchase farmland if they had excess money and land was available. The family estate was thus a combination of the inheritance from the ancestors and the pooled economic resources of the living members. The existence of the familial estate symbolized the economic unity of the deceased ancestors and the living familial members. Therefore, seeing the familial estate as a key component of *chia* organization is compatible with the concept of the family line. The inherited familial estate reminded the living about the prominence of ancestors in familial organization. Thus, the inheritance of property was itself an important reason for observing the ancestral ceremony.[7]

Normally, the historical Taiwanese family followed patrilineal principles. The core of this family system was men tied by descent and the right to inherit property.[8] Ultimate authority in each *chia* resided with the oldest man. The paternal authority did not originate from the father alone, but also stemmed from the father's numerous forebears (Hsu 1971). For example, a father had the authority to organize, distribute, and divide the familial estate. While he was alive, he acted as the ancestors' agent; after death, he would become one of the ancestors who had a strong influence on the lives of his sons and the younger generations.

Ideally, the father's authority could endure throughout his life and be a major ingredient of family solidarity (Freedman 1966). Therefore, in most cases, the division of the family occurred after the father's death. Sometimes the separation of family, *fen chia,* would occur when the father was still alive because the generational relationships might alter as both the father and children moved along their own life courses. As the father aged and his sons became more mature, he was less likely to exercise his power over them. Marriage was probably a turning point for the father-son relationship. To help a married son establish authority over his own conjugal family (*fang*), a father usually treated him more like a household partner than a subordinate (M. C. Yang 1945). A family might choose to divide the family estate among the brothers before the father's death because of tension among the family members, particularly the daughters-in-law; limited familial space; and the economic conditions of the family and the surrounding community (Cohen 1976; Freedman 1966; M. Wolf 1972).

The division of the familial estate, including the ancestral estate and the property accumulated by the living family members, could take place gradually or quickly (Hsieh 1985; S-H Wang 1985). Separation of the pooled economic resources might occur first, in which case the new families might begin to cook at separate stoves, signifying that their households were independent economic entities. It was not unusual to find that, after brothers separated from the family economy, they still kept the ancestral altar intact, so they could go back to the household where the familial altar was located during important festivals, their separate households remaining joined as a religious unit. This type of arrangement was sometimes referred to as a religion family (Kulp 1925). Since the ancestral altar was the ultimate symbol of the family's solidarity, the ancestral tablets were preserved within a family until the last stage of division (Weller 1987). Sometimes, many decades might pass before independent ancestral tablets were established in the new households. In communities where ancestral halls were common, the families in the newly formed households might take or copy the tablets of their most immediate ancestors and install them in the new households but move the tablets of the remote ancestors to an ancestral hall to symbolize the strong lineage tie (Ahern 1973; Freedman 1958).

Chia units were tightly integrated, and many important activities were performed centrally or organized by familial groups as a whole. Of particular relevance to this chapter is that *chia* were organizations for both socialization and ritual. Almost all the children completed their socialization within the *chia* environment. The most important task of socialization was training children in filial piety (Hsu 1971), which was considered the foundation of all kinds of virtue. Filial piety meant that the children had to please, obey, and support their parents, particularly their fathers, while their parents were alive and mourn and ritually serve their parents after their death, and they had to reproduce and continue the family line. Since filial piety was an important means of upholding ancestral authority and the worship of ancestors, Chinese parents usually mentioned their obedience to their own parents while persuading their children to be obedient (Lang 1950). Through the process of socialization, the family prepared the children to live according to the wishes of the ancestors and the parents, to learn to respect the authority of elders as the primary organizers of family activities, and to formulate the value of maintaining and glorifying the family line.

Marriage

Unlike most current marriages in Western societies, which symbolize adult children's independence from the parents' household, most of the marriages in historical Taiwan marked the start of a new generation in the family continuum. From the historical Chinese perspective, marriage formed a conjugal unit for legal childbearing that provided a socially accepted opportunity to extend the family line into the future. In the early history of Taiwan, marriage was an indicator of a person's transition to adulthood; from then on the young man or woman assumed the responsibility of continuing the family line, which was also an important step toward achieving ancestral status. Given the cultural emphasis on the possession of a niche in and continuing the family line, marriage was one of the most important events for an individual and a family.

Marriage was particularly important for women. In the historical Taiwanese family, daughters were considered transitory members. It was only through marriage, that women were accepted as permanent members of their husbands' families, that they were integrated into a family line that ensured acceptance and care both in this life and in the afterlife (Ahern 1971; Freedman 1979; Hsu 1971; A. Wolf and Huang 1980; M. Wolf 1972). When daughters married, they were expected to identify themselves with and worship the ancestors of their husbands' families. In contrast, the sons' membership in their families of origin lasted throughout their lives.

Viewing marriage as an important mechanism for obtaining ancestral status and extending the family line made marriages of children a central concern of Taiwanese parents. Parents tended to see the arrangement of their sons' marriages as fulfilling the responsibilities to the ancestors as well as to the sons. From the time of the marriage, the succession responsibility of the family line rested upon the son, which meant that the parents were no longer responsible for continuing the family line. In addition, through the marriage of a son, both the parents and the son were elevated one step in the long process of becoming ancestors. Unlike a son's marriage, normally the marriage of a daughter was a contribution to the line of her husband's family. Thus, from a parental perspective, arranging a daughter's marriage was done solely to fulfill the parents' responsibility to place their daughter in a setting in which she would be accepted as a permanent member of a *chia* during her lifetime and as an ancestor of that family after her death. Parents who did not arrange marriages for their sons considered themselves unfilial to their ancestors and irresponsible to their sons, and those who failed to arrange marriages for their daughters considered themselves irresponsible to their daughters. As a result, marriage was nearly universal historically for the men and women in Taiwanese society.

Taiwanese parents usually arranged early marriages for their children, so they could be released from their responsibilities early. To ensure that the sons could have wives when they were old enough to marry, many Taiwanese parents brought their future daughters-in-law into the family when the sons were young children (M. Wolf 1972). One motivation for this practice was the scarcity of women in early Taiwan, combined with the cultural emphasis on the family line. As a frontier society, the ratio of males to females in the early Taiwanese population was extremely high; for example, in 1905 the ratio of men to women aged 10 to 40 was more than 1.20 to 1 (Barclay, 1954:212). With such a predominance of males, the parents were well advised to secure daughters-in-law as early as possible.

Since ancestors were perceived as being able to foresee the future and were a major reason for arranging marriages, they were explicitly involved in the process of selecting mates. The process began with the parents' search for available prospects. After the parents found a potential candidate, a formal meeting would be arranged. If the two parties both had good impressions of each other, then the two families would exchange the eight characters of the two young people (the year, month, day, and hour of both births, which could be used for divination) as a sign of preliminary consent. These eight characters would be placed on the ancestral altar of each family for three days. During this three-day observation, any misfortune that occurred in the family (which could be as small as breaking a bowl or a cup) would be interpreted as a negative response from the ancestors, and the marriage negotiations would be terminated. If there were no sign of ancestral objection, then the negotiations would begin in earnest (Fricke et al. 1994).

The ancestors were also important witnesses to the marriage process. Historically, the engagement and wedding ceremonies were performed in front of the ancestral altars so that ancestors could be part of them. The engagement ceremony was performed in front of the ancestral altar of the bride's family. The wedding ritual consisted of two ceremonies: one performed in the bride's parental home to inform the ancestors about her departure, and another performed in the groom's home to introduce her to his ancestors as a new member of the family. The ceremony in the groom's family was often referred to as *pai-tang-chen-hun,* which literally means undergoing the kneeling rituals in the ceremonial hall and becoming a married couple. The couple performed the kneeling rituals in front of the groom's ancestral altar to pay respect to heaven and earth, to the dead ancestors, to the groom's parents, and to each other. Although heaven and earth were involved in the wedding rituals, the focal point of the wedding was the ceremonial, often simultaneous, introduction of the bride to her husband's ancestors, parents, and other relatives in front of the ancestral altar (Hsu 1985).

This description shows the ancestors' involvement in a normal pattern of marriage. The power of the ancestral complex was even more apparent in nonnormative marriages whose forms were modified so the family line could be perpetuated and/or the individual could obtain a position in a family line after death. One such modified form was the uxorilocal marriage, undertaken when a family had no son to continue the family line. In such a case, Taiwanese parents historically would arrange an uxorilocal marriage for one of their daughters, in which a son-in-law was brought into the wife's family to live with her kin. Ideally, the husband of the uxorilocal marriage changed his surname to that of the wife's father and renounced a claim on his children as descendants of his own patriline.[9] But in practice, uxorilocal marriage conflicted with the social emphasis on the continuation of the family line through the male descendants. To resolve the conflict of continuing the family lines of both the husband and wife, a common feature of the contract of an uxorilocal marriage was that the uxorilocal son-in-law kept his own family name and assigned the wife's family name either to alternating children or only to the first son. In this way, the wife's family line would continue through the children who bore the maternal surname, while the husband's family line would be perpetuated through the children who bore the paternal surname.

Another modified form, the ghost marriage, also demonstrates the powerful influence of the concept of family line in the Taiwanese marriage pattern. This type of marriage was designed to deal with the problematic souls of unmarried girls who had no affiliation to any family line.[10] According to the rule of the patrilineal system, a girl who died before marriage would become a ghost with no position in the afterlife. Because a woman's position in the family line was acquired through marriage, a daughter could never be adopted to the altar of her parental home.[11] To help the dead unmarried daughter obtain a position in a family line, so she could have someone to worship her and provide her with offerings, the parents might arrange a posthumous marriage for her.[12] The posthumous marriage symbolized the transference of the ghost bride's status from the parental home to the marital home, as if she were alive. Then, the ghost bride retained a standing in the family into which she married. The groom in this type of marriage was allowed to have a worldly wife to reproduce offspring, who were obligated to worship the soul of the ghost bride as a mother.

Reproduction

The primary purpose of the historical Taiwanese marriage was to produce offspring, particularly sons to carry on the family line. This purpose was reflected in the common toast of the wedding festival, which was either "bear a son soon" or "have lots of sons." Given the high mortality rate in early Taiwan, people preferred to have numerous sons to ensure that at least one would survive long enough to produce the next generation and to have someone to assume the responsibilities of continuing the family line (L-S Yang 1995). The birth of the first child, particularly a boy, was a joyful event for the whole family. Even if the first birth was a girl, it signified the fecundibility of the daughter-in-law, which implied that the birth of a boy could be anticipated.

According to an old Taiwanese custom, the thirtieth day after a baby's birth was referred to as "full month." The family usually had a full-month feast for both baby boys and girls, but the feast for a boy was more elaborate than that for a girl. For a boy's full-month celebration, the family either invited neighbors and clan members to the feast or distributed food to them so they might share the family's joy in the newborn generation. In addition, this celebration had its ritual aspects; the family took this occasion to observe ancestral ceremonies to express gratitude, to report the arrival of the new member, and to pray for the safety of the new life (Hsu 1971). The first birthday of a male child was also celebrated ceremonially. Again, an offering to the ancestors was an essential part of this occasion (M. C. Yang 1945). The son's maternal relatives came to the celebration with presents, including jewelry made of silver and gold, clothes, and other luxuries. Similar to the full month celebration, the celebration of the first birthday for a girl was less elaborate than that for a boy.

Childbearing was tremendously important to a married woman, whose major responsibility was to produce a male descendant to continue the husband's descent line. It was through childbearing and the contribution to the husband's patriline that a woman's position in the marital family was secured. According to the ancient legal code, a man could divorce his infertile wife or take a concubine, which could threaten the wife's status in the family. A son's birth, therefore, enhanced a woman's status in the husband's family.

Although a married woman without a child was at risk of being divorced or deserted, an unmarried woman who conceived a child was often considered a member of the man's family by the parents of both sides, and a marriage contract would usually result within a short time (Hu 1984). Even without an accountable man to marry the single pregnant woman, the pregnancy was not considered completely negative, since the woman's family might obtain a male descendant through the pregnancy, particularly if the family had no son to assume responsibility for continuing the family line.

Other Approaches to Perpetuate the Ancestral Line

Although marriage and childbearing were the normal paths to forming a new generation, there were other ways to maintain the family line. One way was for couples who could not have children or whose children died to adopt children (M. Wolf 1972). An adoption could also be applicable to a childless widow to ensure that her dead husband could be worshipped as an ancestor (Hsu 1971). It was preferable to adopt children from closely related agnates of the husband. It was not always possible to adopt a son because families were reluctant to release their own sons and adopting sons was expensive. An alternative strategy was to adopt a daughter and extend the family line through her uxorilocal marriage (M. Wolf 1972).

The position of sons in the family was assured, except for those who died as infants.[13] The sons who did not survive until marriage could be accepted as ancestors in the family line through two approaches. First, a son who died in childhood could achieve security as an ancestor by "returning" to the ancestral line a generation or two after his death. Usually the scenario of returning to the ancestral line began with some misfortune in the family, which a shaman might suggest was due to the anger of a neglected forebear who died as a child in the previous generation. To solve the problem, the family would set up a tablet and make regular offerings for the deceased ancestor who died in childhood (A. Wolf 1974). Thus, a boy who died young could obtain a place on the family altar and be worshiped as an ancestor by the offspring of his brother. Second, the great majority of men who died after early childhood but before marriage could be worshiped by their surviving brothers and their descendants. According to the age principle, younger brothers should defer to their older brothers. But according to a common belief in Taiwan, "the child who died first is the eldest," and those who survived were considered junior regardless of their birth order. Therefore, an older brother could appropriately worship a younger brother who had no descendant of his own (A. Wolf 1974).

THE DECLINE OF ANCESTRAL AUTHORITY IN TRANSITIONAL TAIWAN

As was discussed in the previous sections, the ancestral component of the Taiwanese popular religion is closely integrated with the concepts of family and the rules of family formation. Thus, if family organization changed under the influence of other large-scale social and economic changes, then the ancestors' domination of the lives of living individuals might be weakened and would signify an important change in Taiwanese popular religion, as well as in family life. In the remainder of this chapter, we focus on change and continuity in ancestor-related attitudes and ritual behaviors in post–World War II Taiwanese society.

Taiwanese Society in Transition

Historically, Taiwanese men, women, and their children experienced socialization, production, residence, and social connections mostly within the family or within organizations intertwined with intensive kin relations. Therefore, ancestors—the founders of this family system—and parents—the representatives of ancestors in the earthly world—had tremendous influence over their lives.

Since the early decades of this century, Taiwanese society has undergone many important social transformations (Fricke et al. 1994; Hermalin, Freedman, and Liu 1994). The construction of the islandwide transportation network, the public school system, and food manufacturing began during the period of Japanese occupation (1895–1945). The end of World War II saw the return of Taiwan to the administration of the Chinese Nationalists. During the postwar era, education expanded, there was a movement from agricultural to industrial production, and there was a growth of big cities. Exposure to ideas and messages from other cultures, particularly Western culture, increased through newspapers, magazines, television, and movies. These social changes created many opportunities for young men and women to experience socialization, employment, residence, recreation, and social participation through nonfamilial organizations and thus can be characterized as the emergence of a more nonfamilial mode of social organization (Thornton and Fricke 1987; Thornton, Fricke et al. 1994).

The movement toward a more nonfamilial mode of organization resulted in new elements and institutions in the macro environment, which, in turn, altered the opportunities and constraints encountered by the Taiwanese and could have encouraged individuals and their families to change historically Chinese ways of thinking, acting, and organizing interpersonal relationships. The shift to a nonfamilial mode could also have had important implications for the ideas of perpetuating the family line. Industrialization provides alternative sources of economic well-being, which could have reduced individuals' reliance on the ancestral farms as the means of production. It increased people's dependence on their own educational achievement, which could have dramatically changed the nature of intergenerational ties (Thornton, Yang, and Fricke 1994). In addition, schools as new sources of ideas, authority, and means of interactions with peers have shifted the nature of children's relationships with their parents (Thornton, Fricke et al. 1994). Although schools still stress filial piety, their emphasis on scientific and experiential knowledge challenges some fundamental beliefs in the folk religion, such as the material needs in the afterlife. Taiwan has also experienced substantial exposure to Western ideas and values, which strongly emphasize immediate familial relationships, rather than ties between ancestors and future descendants. As a result of these changes, the core cultural emphasis on the family chain may have been weakened and ancestral authority in individual and familial lives may have declined.

In our previous study (Thornton, Yang, and Fricke 1994), we used survey data to investigate the attitudes and behaviors of people from different marriage cohorts and to explore possible changes in important ancestral ideas and ritual behaviors. We also examined whether large-scale social changes, such as the expansion of education and the emergence of nonfamilial employment, could account for the cohort trends regarding ancestral ideas and ritual behaviors. In the following section, we summarize the important results of that study.

Continuation of the Family Line as a Life Value

During the quarter century after the end of World War II, Taiwan was heading toward a more nonfamilial mode of organization. The 1976 Value of Children Survey, which documented the important life values of Taiwanese men and women in the childbearing ages at that time, asked men and women to express their perceptions about the level of importance and relative ranking of nine life values. One life value was linking ancestors, the living, and descendants. The other eight life values were being financially secure, not being disliked by people, having fun and enjoyment in life, being close to a spouse, not being lonely, having a sense of accomplishment or doing things well, being remembered and cherished after death, and having a happy family. Being financially secure, having a happy family, and maintaining the family chain were the three highest-rated values by those in the earliest marriage cohorts. Furthermore, these cohorts ranked the family chain as much more important than having a happy family and being financially secure.[14]

In the more recent marriage cohorts, we found a modest decline in the percentages who listed the continuation of the family line as among the most important of the nine values. However, there was a more dramatic decline in the choice of the continuation of the family line as the most highly ranked value. Thus, although 42 percent of the women who married in the early 1950s ranked maintaining the family line as the most important value, this proportion declined steadily across the marriage cohorts, so that only 22 percent of the women who married in the early 1970s reported it as their most important value. We found similar downward trends across marriage cohorts in men's reports of the importance of this value.

In contrast, there were upward trends across the marriage cohorts in the choice of a happy family as the most important value by both the men and the women. The proportion of women who said that having a happy family was the most important thing in life rose from 26 percent of those who married in the early 1950s to 42% of those who married in the early 1970s. Furthermore, the ranking of financial security was relatively stable across different marriage cohorts. Given that the more recently married men and women may represent a more contemporary cultural view, the historical cultural emphasis on continuing the family line seems to be weakening, and there has been a relative shift in the importance of values from family continuity to family happiness. This shift may imply that people have transferred their central value from multigenerational relationships to relationships with their immediate families.

Value of Children in Continuing the Family Line

In examining people's reports on the value of children, we found a decline in the perpetuation of the familial line as a motivation for reproduction (Thornton, Yang, and Fricke 1994). The data on people's motivation for bearing children in the 1976 Value of Children Survey clearly confirmed the historical role of children in continuing the family line. For the women who married in the early 1950s, linking the ancestors, the living, and descendants was the most highly endorsed of all the reasons for having children. However, across marriage cohorts, there was a decline in women's views of the importance of this motivation for reproduction: from 93 percent of women who married in the early 1950s to 82% of those who married in the early 1970s.

Data from three repeated cross-sectional surveys also confirmed the decline in women's belief in the importance of having sons to continue the family line (Thornton, Yang, and Fricke 1994). While about 90 percent of the married women in a 1973 survey said that having a boy to continue the family line was important or very important, 76 percent in a 1980 survey and 69 percent in a 1986 survey expressed the same viewpoint. In addition to this decline across survey years, within each survey, the importance of having a boy to maintain the family line shifted across different cohorts. Generally, women in the more recent marriage cohorts tended to place less emphasis on the importance of having a boy to continue the family line.

Ancestors' Influence on the Family's Future

An important underlying reason for ancestral rituals was the belief that taking care of the deceased ancestors would enhance the reciprocal relations between the dead and living generations and thus promote the well-being of the family. Using data from the 1973, 1980, and 1986 Taiwan surveys of married women, we also examined women's beliefs in the geomantic arrangement of graves (Thornton, Yang, and Fricke 1994). In 1973, 3 out of 4 married women aged 20 to 39 thought that the positioning of ancestors' graves had important implications for their immediate family's well-being. This proportion dropped to just under two-thirds in 1980 but increased to 70 percent in 1986. In spite of the nonmonotonic decline in this belief across the surveys, when we controlled for the survey year, the percentage who said that ancestral graves were important for the fortune of the family consistently declined across marriage cohorts.

When women were asked in the 1986 survey to express their beliefs in the importance of observing ancestral ceremonies for the family's future, over half said that doing so was somewhat important or very important. Here, too, the percentage of women who said that the ancestral ceremony was important for the family's future declined across marriage cohorts.

Observing Ancestral Ceremonies

Although there was a decline in acknowledging the influence of ancestral rituals on the family's future, we did not find evidence that Taiwanese women had become less diligent in observing domestic ancestral ceremonies in the 1973, 1980, and 1986 surveys. Unlike the other trends examined earlier, in this case there was an unexpected increase over the survey years. Nevertheless, within each survey year, the percentage who observed ancestral ceremonies declined across marriage cohorts. Thus, while the proportion of women who observed ancestral ceremonies increased from 81 percent in 1973 to 90 percent in 1986, when the survey year was controlled, women in the more recent marriage cohorts were less likely to observe the ancestral ceremonies. The exact reason for this upward trend in ancestral worship across survey years is not clear. One explanation may be that as the standard of living in Taiwan improved, people had more resources to observe ancestral ceremonies. Another explanation may be that there was a shift across the survey years from the sacred relationship with ancestors to a more secular view of the world and family relationships (Thornton, Yang, and Fricke 1994). It is also possible that, in the early years, people tended to divide their families economically but to continue to observe ancestral ceremonies as extended families. In more recent years, however, they may have simultaneously formed economically and religiously independent households, and each new household independently observed its ancestral obligations. This kind of change in the division of the family would lead to an increase in the reported household observance of ancestral ceremonies.

The 1980 Taiwan survey specifically asked whether the household had an ancestral tablet and there was monthly worship in front of the familial altar. The data indicated that in 1980, two-thirds of the women both reported the presence of household ancestral tablets and performed worship in front of the ancestral altar each month. However women from the more recent marriage cohorts were less likely than those in the earlier marriage cohorts to have ancestral tablets in their households and to perform monthly familial worship. The 1980 data suggest that the ownership of ancestral tablets and the observance of ancestral ceremonies may be highly correlated. Nevertheless, the lack of data on the ownership of ancestral tablets at multiple points in time prevented us from examining whether the more common observance of ancestral ceremonies in the more recent surveys was due to an increase in the ownership of ancestral tablets over the surveyed years.

The Influence of Life Experience

Our observation of cohort trends in the importance of linking past and future generations, the importance of sons to continue the family line, beliefs of ancestral influence, observance of ancestral ceremonies, and household possession of ancestral tablets are all consistent with the general reorientation of family cosmology in Taiwan society. We also found that these attitudes and behaviors were closely related to women's educational attainment. Since women from the more recent marriage cohorts tended to have higher levels of educational attainment, we explored the hypothesis that a higher level of education is a major component of the explanation for changes in attitudes and behaviors associated with family cosmology.

Multivariate analyses demonstrated that women's increased educational attainments indeed contributed to these trends. In addition to education, we explored the influence of other life experiences that are associated with different domains of social change. Our analyses suggested that women's educational attainment, premarital employment, and fathers' education and occupation and the fertility of the women's mothers-in-law accounted for a significant part of the cohort trends in attitudes and behaviors toward ancestors. These ancestor-related attitudes and behaviors included the value of sons for continuing the family line, the observance of ancestral ceremonies, the belief in the influence of ancestral ceremonies, and ancestral graves. In other words, social change away from familial organization of life-course experiences was linked to a decline in the attitudes and behaviors associated with the integration of family relationships beyond the earthly realm.

CONCLUDING REMARKS

In this chapter, we began with a description of the beliefs, rituals, and organization of folk religion in early Taiwanese history. An important feature of Taiwanese folk religion was the strong parallel between people's perceptions of the earthly world and the world of the afterlife. Since the family was the central organizational principle in the historical Taiwanese context, it was not surprising to find that the afterlife counterpart of the worldly familial network was a significant part of Taiwanese folk religion and that the observance of ancestral ceremonies was an essential religious activity.

The spirits of ancestors were believed to live on and had power to bless or curse their descendants, depending on whether they were appropriately worshiped. The belief in the active engagement of ancestors in worldly events connected the living and dead in a single stream. The living were expected to uphold the family line, bring honor to their ancestors, and prepare to become ancestors themselves. Men and women practiced ancestral ceremonies and produced descendants to fulfill their responsibilities to their ancestors, on the one hand, and to prepare to become ancestors themselves, on the other hand.

It seems that the ancestral connection served to buttress family solidarity and filial piety, which simultaneously enhanced the living parents' authority and ensured the ancestors well-being in the afterlife. Consequently, conceptions of ancestors and the practice of ancestral ceremonies became a consistent part of the popular religion and a core of the family system in Taiwan. In the second part of the chapter, we reviewed historical and ethnographic reports on the influence of ancestors on the normative and nonnormative approaches of family building in Taiwan, paying specific attention to the formation of marriages and the production of sons to continue the family line.

During the second half of this century, Taiwan has undergone dramatic social changes. As never before, Taiwanese have been exposed to the emergence of a nonfamilial mode of social organization. Outside the home, there are nonfamilial educational, occupational, and other new social resources, and within the home, Taiwanese experience the culture of other societies through television and radio programs. Like many societies around the world, Taiwan has been undergoing a process of secularization in which the religious interpretations of the relationship between people and the cosmos have been undermined. Limited by the information available, our exploration of the impact of social change on folk religion concentrated on the part related to ancestors. We reviewed the findings of our previous study and found that the influence of ancestors on individuals and on the motivation for having children has weakened and beliefs in the influence of ancestral ceremonies and the importance of ancestral graves have declined. It seems that the observance of ancestral ceremonies have been more persistent than the values and attitudes toward ancestors. It is possible that while the ancestral rituals continue, their original meanings and centrality have changed. It is important to determine whether the ancestral ceremony has been divested of much of its specifically religious content and taken on a nonreligious meaning. If people put less faith in ancestors' mysterious influence but retain a strong memorial sentiment toward their ancestors, the observance of ancestral ceremony could be sustained but have less of a religious connotation.

With the decline of faith in ancestors, ancestral ceremonies could turn into a simple lineage ritual, rather than an observance that blends both religious and familial purposes. A shift in the motivation for childbearing away from continuing the family line also means a reduction of the religious element from people's reproductive attitudes and behaviors. More important, the less emphasis on the life value of linking the living, the dead, and future generations may create a break in the eternal family line—a shared central theme of Taiwanese family and folk religion. All these changes seem to suggest that folk religion and family in Taiwan could gradually lose their important common ground. If they do, does it imply an increasing independence of the family and folk religion in Taiwan? And to what extent will these changes affect Taiwanese familial and religious lives? We leave the task of answering these questions to further studies.

NOTES

1. It was estimated that over 90 percent of Taiwan's rural residents were practitioners of Taiwanese popular religion in the 1980s (Chu 1985).
2. In general, priests of the popular religion in Taiwan are hired to perform rituals, rather than to provide people with religious education (DeGlopper 1974).
3. Whether the ancestors are always benign is debatable (Lee 1985). Although many believe that ancestors are benevolent and protective (Freedman 1979; Hsu 1971; A. Wolf 1974), some reports have suggested that ancestors are occasionally capricious and malevolent (Ahern 1973).
4. These occasions include the important feasts, such as the New Year; the Dragon-Boat Festival (on the fifth day of the fifth lunar month); the Ghost Festival, also referred to as the Universal Salvation Festival (on the fifteenth day of the seventh lunar month); and the Mid-Autumn Festival (on the fifteenth day of the eighth lunar month).
5. The ghost bride is an example of a ghost who turns into an ancestor. A woman who dies before marriage is considered a ghost who wanders around the world of the afterlife. If a posthumous marriage is arranged for her, she gains ancestral status.
6. Therefore, A. Wolf (1974) suggested that to study folk religion in Taiwan, one should consider the social and economic history of a particular community.
7. In fact, inheriting an estate and the responsibility for taking care of the dead are highly correlated (see Ahern 1971).
8. In addition to gender, generation and age were important attributes by which family members were stratified (Greenhalgh 1985). Because the gender hierarchy outweighed the generation hierarchy, a woman was expected to defer to her sons after her husband's death. Within the generation hierarchy, age was an important principle of deference.
9. Usually, the men of uxorilocal marriages were from poor families with limited resources. They entered this type of marriage to obtain a means of living.
10. The dead unmarried men had other ways to obtain ancestral status that are mentioned later. Therefore, they did not need posthumous marriage to do so.

11. Therefore, when a young daughter-in-law died before she entered into the conjugal relationship, she still had a place in the altar of the family in which she had arranged to marry. But, a daughter did not have the right to be placed in the familial altar. Since a position in the family was so important, it could have been another reason why parents took young daughters-in-law into their homes.
12. In the early days, Taiwanese parents would trap a husband for their deceased daughter by placing her eight characters with an attractive bait beside the road. The man who picked up the girl's eight characters was considered to be fated to marry her (A. Wolf 1974).
13. People considered those who died as infants or toddlers as evil spirits or as creditors from a previous life who would come back to ask parents to pay their debts. Thus, parents would assume that those children did not belong to the family (A. Wolf 1974).
14. For example, 4 out of 10 women who married in the early 1950s ranked continuing the family line as the most important value. The next most frequently endorsed value was having a happy family, selected by 26 percent of these women, followed by financial security, which was the first choice of approximately 21 percent of these women. In other words, almost 90 percent of the women who married in the early 1950s chose one of these three values as the most important value in their lives.

References

Ahern, Emily M. 1971. "The Cult of the Dead in Ch'inan, Taiwan: A Study of Ancestor Worship in a Four-Lineage Community." Ann Arbor, MI: University Microfilms.

———. 1973. *The Cult of the Dead in a Chinese Village*. Stanford, CA: Stanford University Press.

Barclay, George W. 1954. *Colonial Development and Population in Taiwan*. Princeton, NJ: Princeton University Press.

Chu, Hai-yuan. 1985. "The Impact of Different Religions on the Chinese Family in Taiwan." Pp. 221–31 in *The Chinese Family and Its Ritual Behavior* (Monograph Series B, No. 15), edited by J. C. Hsieh and Y. C. Chuang. Taipei, Taiwan: Institute of Ethnology, Academia Sinica.

Cohen, Myron. 1970. "Development Process in the Chinese Domestic Group." Pp. 21–36 in *Family and Kinship in Chinese Society*, edited by M. Freedman. Stanford, CA: Stanford University Press.

———. 1976. *House United, House Divided: The Chinese Family in Taiwan*. New York: Columbia University Press.

DeGlopper, Donald R. 1974. "Religion and Ritual in Lukang." Pp. 43–70 in *Religion and Ritual in Chinese Society*, edited by A. P. Wolf. Stanford, CA: Stanford University Press.

Feuchtwang, Stephan. 1974. "Domestic and Communal Worship in Taiwan." Pp. 105–30 in *Religion and Ritual in Chinese Society*, edited by A. P. Wolf. Stanford, CA: Stanford University Press.

Freedman, Maurice. 1958. *Lineage Organization in Southeastern China*. London: University of London.

———. 1966. *Chinese Lineage and Society: Fukien and Kwangtung*. New York: Humanities Press.

———. 1970. "Ritual Aspects of Chinese Kinship and Marriage." Pp. 163–87 in *Family and Kinship in Chinese Society*, edited by M. Freedman. Stanford, CA: Stanford University Press.

———. 1974. "On the Sociological Study of Chinese Religion." Pp. 19–42 in *Religion and Ritual in Chinese Society*, edited by A. P. Wolf. Stanford, CA: Stanford University Press.

———. 1979. *The Study of Chinese Society*. Stanford, CA: Stanford University Press.

Fricke, Thomas, Jui-shan Chang, and Li-shou Yang. 1994. "Historical and Ethnographic Perspectives on the Chinese Family." In *Social Change and the Family in Taiwan*, edited by A. Thornton and H. S. Lin. Chicago: University of Chicago Press.

Greenhalgh, Susan. 1985. "Sexual Stratification: The Other Side of 'Growth with Equity' in East Asia." *Population and Development Review*, 11:265–314.

Harrell, Stevan. 1974. "When a Ghost Becomes a God." Pp.191–206 in *Religion and Ritual in Chinese Society*, edited by A. P. Wolf. Stanford, CA: Stanford University Press.

Hermalin, Albert, Deborah Freedman, and Liu Paul K. C. 1994. "The Social Economic Transformation of Taiwan." Pp. 49–87 in *Social Change and the Family in Taiwan*, edited by A. Thornton and H. S. Lin. Chicago: University of Chicago Press.

Hsieh, Jih-chang. 1985. "Meal Rotation." Pp. 70–83 in *The Chinese Family and Its Ritual Behavior* (Monograph Series B, No. 15), edited by J. C. Hsieh and Y. C. Chuang. Taipei, Taiwan: Institute of Ethnology, Academia Sinica.

Hsu, Francis L. K. 1971. *Under the Ancestors' Shadow: Kinship, Personality and Social Mobility in China*. Stanford, CA: Stanford University Press.

———. 1985. "Field Work, Cultural Differences and Interpretation." Pp. 19–29 in *The Chinese Family and Its Ritual Behavior* (Monograph Series B, No. 15), edited by J. C. Hsieh and Y. C. Chuang. Taipei, Taiwan: Institute of Ethnology, Academia Sinica.

Hu, Tai-li. 1984. *My Mother-in-Law's Village: Rural Industrialization and Change in Taiwan*. Taipei, Taiwan: Institute of Ethnology, Academia Sinica.

Jordan, David K. 1972. *Gods, Ghost, and Ancestors*. Berkeley: University of California Press.

Kulp, Daniel Harrison. 1925. *Country Life in South China*. New York: Bureau of Publications, Teachers College, Columbia University.

Lang, Olga. 1950. *Chinese Family and Society*. New Haven, CT: Yale University Press.

Lee, Yih-yuan. 1985. "On Conflicting Interpretations of Chinese Family Rituals." Pp. 263–81 in *The Chinese Family and Its Ritual Behavior*, (Monograph Series B, No. 15), edited by J. C. Hsieh and Y. C. Chuang. Taipei, Taiwan: Institute of Ethnology, Academia Sinica.

Smith, Robert. 1974. "Afterword." Pp. 335–48 in *Religion and Ritual in Chinese Society*, edited by A. P. Wolf. Stanford, CA: Stanford University Press.

Stafford, Charles. 1992. "Good Sons and Virtuous Mothers: Kinship and Chinese Nationalism in Taiwan." *Man* 27:363–78.

Thornton, Arland, Jui-shan Chang, and Li-shou Yang. 1994. "Determinants of Historical Changes in Marital Arrangements, Dating, and Premarital Sexual Intimacy and Pregnancy." Pp. 178–201 in *Social Change and the Family in Taiwan*, edited by A. Thornton and H. S. Lin, Chicago: University of Chicago Press.

Thornton, Arland, and Thomas Fricke. 1987. "Social Change and the Family, Comparative Perspectives from the West, China, and South Asia." *Sociological Forum*, 2:746–72.

Thornton, Arland, Thomas Fricke, Li-shou Yang, and Jui-shan Chang. 1994. "Theoretical Mechanisms of Family Change." Pp. 88–115 in *Social Change and the Family in Taiwan*, edited by A. Thornton and H. S. Lin. Chicago: University of Chicago Press.

Thornton, Arland, Li-shou Yang, and Thomas Fricke. 1994. "Weakening the Linkage Between the Ancestors, the Living, and Future Generations." Pp. 359–95 in *Social Change and the Family in Taiwan*, edited by A. Thornton and H. S. Lin. Chicago: University of Chicago Press.

Wang, Shih-Ch'ing. 1974. "Religion Organization in the History of a Chinese Town." Pp. 183–92 in *Religion and Ritual in Chinese Society*, edited by A. P. Wolf. Stanford, CA: Stanford University Press.

Wang, Sung-hsing. 1985. "On the Household and Family in Chinese Society." Pp. 50–60 in *The Chinese Family and Its Ritual Behavior* (Monograph Series B, No. 15), edited by J. C. Hsieh and Y. C. Chuang. Taipei, Taiwan: Institute of Ethnology, Academia Sinica.

Weller, Robert P. 1987. *Unities and Diversities in Chinese Religion*. Seattle: University of Washington Press.

Wolf, Arthur. 1974. "Gods, Ghosts, and Ancestors." Pp 131–82 in *Religion and Ritual in Chinese Society*, edited by A. P. Wolf. Stanford, CA: Stanford University Press.

———. 1985. "Chinese Family Size: A Myth Revitalized." Pp. 30–49 in *The Chinese Family and Its Ritual Behavior* (Monograph Series B, No. 15), edited by J. C. Hsieh and Y. C. Chuang. Taipei, Taiwan: Institute of Ethnology, Academia Sinica.

Wolf, Arthur, and Chieh-Shan Huang. 1980. *Marriage and Adoption in China, 1845–1945*. Stanford, CA: Stanford University Press.

Wolf, Margery. 1972. *Women and the Family in Rural Taiwan*. Stanford, CA: Stanford University Press.

Yang, Li-shou. 1995. "Social Change and Preferences for Gender of Children among Women in Taiwan." Ph.D. dissertation, Department of Sociology, University of Michigan, Ann Arbor.

Yang, Martin C. 1945. *A Chinese Village: Taitou, Shantung Province*. New York: Columbia University Press.

PART II

Dramatic Societal Transformation

CHAPTER SIX

Belarus on the Cusp of Change: The Relationship Between Religion and Family in a Newly Open Religious Market

ANDREI VARDOMATSKII
JERRY G. PANKHURST

Since the end of World War II, no events have compared in magnitude to the demise of the Soviet Union. With the breakup of the Soviet Union, the balancing structure of global superpower relations that had existed for over four decades ended and the ideological center of communism disintegrated. Although one need not accept the exaggerated assertion that this event marked the "end of history" (Fukuyama 1992), it profoundly changed the essentials needed for understanding the world order. It also changed in innumerable ways the lives of millions of people who lived in the Soviet Union and the East-Central European communist states. One challenge for scholars is to understand the connection between the global changes related to the collapse of the Soviet Union and the adaptations of the people in their social and cultural lives under these circumstances.[1]

This chapter examines the relationship between religion and family at the height of the change, namely, at the end of the period of perestroika in 1990, just before the breakup of the Soviet Union, which was formalized at the end of 1991. During the approximately five years before the fifteen former Soviet republics gained independence, perestroika, or "restructuring," especially in the economic sphere (and the concomitant policy of glasnost, or "openness"), brought significantly greater freedom for religion and family relationships, as well as broadly significant measures of freedom of speech and association.

RELIGIOUS ECONOMY THEORY AND BELARUSIAN REALITY

In 1990, Belarus was just emerging from the period of Soviet communist ideological domination that entailed both a policy of state-sponsored atheism, including the repression of religion, and a family policy that subordinated personal life to centralized economic management. In this chapter, we examine the impact of these policies and conditions on this society as it embarked on a more open religious market and a changing family sphere that was beginning to experience new forms of demands from the state and the economy. In particular, we assess the state of religious belief in Belarus and the relationship between religion and the family during the transition.

Given the dearth of data on religion and family in Belarus in earlier periods, we cannot make strong conclusions about change, but we can see the context of change at a particularly critical time in the 1990 data. In this context, we examine propositions from the approach to religion that go under the rubric of "religious economy" or, in social psychology terms, the rational-choice approach.[2] On the basis of this theory, we argue that in 1990, Belarus was *characterized by a relatively weak national moral community (or communities) of religion* that was due, in large measure, to two primary factors. The first factor was that Belarus had an extremely unstable national history during which its national identity was not crystallized very strongly (Urban and Zaprudnik 1993; Zaprudnik 1993). The subordination of Belarus to Soviet power (including its ideological antireligious program) was just the most recent assault on the autonomy of this would-be national community. Since religion is often an intrinsic part of a national identity—neighboring Poland and Lithuania, for example, have strongly integrated Catholicism into their national identities—a strong national identity could be interlinked with a strong faith. That is, the forces that nurture a national identity may nurture a national religion. However, in Belarus, whose national identity was undernurtured, there was little associated support for a national faith around which a moral community could be established.

The second factor was the would-be monopolization of the religious sphere by two churches: the Orthodox and Roman Catholic. According to the theory of religious economy, monopolization practices would reduce the "demand" for religion in Belarus. That is, because monopolies lack significant competition from alternative groups, they do not work hard to attract "customers" and to cultivate customers' interests adequately, so the attractiveness of their "product," religious faith, gradually fades. Indeed, there is little evidence that the Orthodox and Catholic churches in Belarus have mounted significant campaigns to increase adherence or commitment. Naturally, under Soviet control, it was nearly impossible to do so. At the end of the perestroika period, the "religious market" was beginning to open up. However, the churches devoted their efforts to reestablishing their parish and clerical infrastructures and to providing normal religious services to traditional constituencies, rather than to pursuing broad evangelization or missionary work. In this sense, each church took care of its own flock but did not interfere with the other's flock. This is a form of a dual-monopoly structure or, at least, a highly differentiated oligopoly.

Moreover, each of the major churches was cross-pressured vis-à-vis the Belarusian national identity, a factor that, other things being equal, might have supported the attractiveness of the religious choice. Theoretically, especially when the national identity is under stress, religious faiths may be called on to help define and direct identity building. However, despite the indigenizing movements within both Belarusian churches, the dominant orientation of the leadership of the churches was toward external national origins. Note that the Orthodox Church in Belarus was (and remains) a branch—an exarchate—of the Russian Orthodox Church under the Moscow Patriarchate (though its formal name is now the Belarusian Orthodox Church); it was (and is) headed by an ethnic Russian, Metropolitan Filaret; and it has not cultivated a clear Belarusian identity (Rich 1997; Zaprudnik 1993). Similarly, the Catholic Church in Belarus was (and is) lead largely by ethnic Poles, and its popular strength was found (and remains) in regions that are contiguous to Poland and populated by ethic Poles (most of whom have been permanent residents of Belarus at least since its borders were settled at the end of World War II).

Although both the Orthodox and the Catholic churches have recently signified their support for some forms of Belarusization, they have not promoted the national identity without major qualifications. And in 1990, the time of our study, the externalizing tendencies were distinctly dominant over the indigenizing patterns that have become relatively more prominent recently. In the meantime, the churches served as vehicles of Russianization, on the one hand, and Polonization, on the other. Neither church, then, could unequivocably profit from the search by Belarusians for a national identity in the late Soviet period, although either or both may assume more of the role of a national church in the future.

At present, two uniquely Belarusian religious options are in place, but they are new arrivals—or, more properly, rearrivals, since both had existed previously but had been banned in Soviet Belarus. They are the Belarusian Eastern-Rite Catholic Church ("Uniates") (Flynn 1993) and the Belarusian Autocephalous Orthodox Church (Broun 1997; Rich 1997).[3] These churches were too small at the time of our study to merit significant attention here. However, any thoughtful evaluation of the post-Soviet period and the future must take them into account as possible means for Belarusian believers to opt out of the ethnonationalist dilemmas posed by the established Orthodox and Catholic Churches.[4]

Under these circumstances, hypothetically, we should expect that (1) *religion would be rather weak in Belarus* and that (2) *the tie between religion and family would also be weak*. Soviet antireligious policy and the monopolistic aspirations and practices of these churches mediated against a strong pursuit of religious "goods" by Belarusians in the late Soviet period. By 1990, some upswing in religious interest might have occurred, however, because of the signs of religious freedom, which had been apparent starting in 1988, the one thousandth anniversary of the Christianization of the Eastern Slavs (Ukrainians, Russians, and Belarusians). However, the antipathy of the Soviet state to religion and the monopolistic tendencies of the major faiths in Belarus should have reduced belief and practice to comparatively low levels and the traditional linkage between religion and family to a minimum. Not even a vigorous nationalistic independence movement could rapidly stimulate religious interest, or the demand for religious goods, to use the economic term, given the ambivalent positions of the two major churches in Belarus.

After we examine these propositions using 1990 data, we explore some evidence of change after the collapse of the Soviet Union in 1991 in the conclusion of the chapter to seek indicators of the sociocultural trajectory in the future. Most important, unless the forces that are working to restrict the religious sphere to only the Russian Orthodox and Catholic Churches are successful in creating legal monopolies (Corley 1998; Rich 1997), the theory of religious economy would lead us to expect a growth of religion consistent with the growth in diversity in the religious market as new religions appear on the national scene.

FAMILIES IN CRISIS?

We have suggested that the Belarusian religious situation in 1990 was fraught with many problems and anomalies. According to religious economy theory, there are strong institutional connections between family and religion, so an important means of addressing problems in religion, presumably, would be to address them through the family. Families have the primary responsibility for engendering what Iannaccone (1997) called "religious human capital."

The term *human capital* refers to the attitudes and skills that people gain from socialization and, perhaps, formal education, that support their success in the job market and other economic pursuits. *Religious human capital*, then, refers to people's orientations and understandings that underlie their ability to make religious choices. Seen as a rational-choice issue, religious human capital needs to be developed for individuals to make appropriate and satisfying religious decisions about where and when to worship or pray; which religious group to affiliate with; how much time, energy, and money to devote to religious activities and associations; where and when to apply religiously based moral precepts; and so forth. Ultimately, the aggregation of such choices gives the religious institution a structure and defines its role in the overall social system of the society.

Given the importance of religious human capital in general, it seems even more consequential when the task of reconstructing a society's entire religious sphere is at issue, as was the case with Belarus in 1990. Thus, not only is the family-religion connection interesting, but it is extremely significant in regard to large-scale social change. Although we cannot fully evaluate the condition of the Belarusian family here, it is clear that the family was under extreme strain from several quarters. Most well known are the economic difficulties that all Soviet families faced (and continue to face) under the conditions of profound economic disruption. While family life under the Soviets was generally not affluent, basic life requirements were largely guaranteed. Under marketization, however, many families fell to poverty; only an elite few did not suffer the privations of the period (Joint Economic Committee 1993).

In addition to economic difficulties, there were other indications of trouble in the Belarusian family. Demographic measures underscore the crisis (Haub 1994). Like the other European societies that gained independence from the Soviet Union, Belarus was experiencing a decline in the birth rate—from a total fertility rate of 2.1 in 1985 to 1.6 in 1993. The use of contraceptives was low, but abortions—with a rate of 78 legal abortions for every 100 births in the early 1990s—and other means of birth control (such as the rhythm method and withdrawal) kept the birth rate low. There also was a drop in life expectancy, especially for men. In 1993, the life expectancy rates at birth were 63.8 years for males and 74.4 years for females. In the same year, the republic actually registered an excess of deaths over births ("natural decrease") in the population for a rate of natural increase of −0.1, though a small in-migration kept the population from actually declining. Population projections suggest a nearly unchanging population size in the foreseeable future. Although a comparatively high mortality rate and a low fertility rate point to a problem, they also represent a kind of "opportunity cost" that is being lost in Belarus. For example, the society cannot experience an economic stimulus from demographic growth itself, which, when it occurs, entails an increase in the size of the aggregate of consumers of economic goods. Furthermore, in the religious sphere, low fertility may keep the society from focusing on the development of religious human capital among the young. As in the post–World War II baby boom in the United States, large cohorts of children are sometimes accompanied by pro-family movements centered in churches that seem to mobilize their resources to inculcate the faith.

Data on marriage and divorce also demonstrate some of the stresses in the family in Belarus. First, like other parts of the former Soviet Union,

> There has been a sharp drop in the number of marriages since the USSR's breakup. . . . This may reflect a temporary loss of confidence in the future, but it could also mark a new direction in marriage patterns—perhaps toward the Western European model. (Haub 1994:16)

In addition, for every 100 marriages, there were 50 divorces in Belarus during the years just after the collapse of the Soviet Union.

With the family in crisis, stable socialization and the creation of human capital in all spheres was undermined. In the findings and conclusion sections of this chapter, we assess the impact that the family patterns have had vis-à-vis religious human capital.

BELARUS AS AN OBJECT OF STUDY

Before we turn to the analysis, several points need to be made about Belarus as an object of study. First, in 1990, the time we examine, Belarus was officially the Belorussian Soviet Socialist Republic (BSSR), one of the fifteen constituent republics of the Soviet Union. When the Soviet Union finally collapsed in 1991, Belarus won its independence, along with all the other republics. Consequently, the data we examine refer to the end of the Soviet period and reflect the conditions of Soviet power and Soviet history.

Selecting Belarus, rather than the entire Soviet Union or a large republic like Russia, to study reduces the variables that must be taken into account. In 1990, Belarus was (and still is) a relatively small and compact region, encompassing 80,154 square miles, with a 1989 population of 10,128,000 (Zaprudnik 1993:xix).[5] Both the biconfessional religious structure and the ethnic group structure in Belarus were relatively simple. In 1989, the population of Belarus was comprised of the following nationalities: 77.8 percent Belarusians, 13.2 percent Russians, 4.1 percent Poles, 2.9 percent Ukrainians, 1.1 percent Jews, and 0.9 percent "others" (Urban and Zaprudnik 1993).

Our primary empirical data come from the 1990 World Values Study survey in the BSSR, which was conducted by the Institute of Sociology of the Belarus Academy of Sciences under the direction of the first author. The BSSR sample was part of the ongoing World Values Study, and its questionnaire and procedures conform to those of the larger project.

BELARUSIAN STATE AND SOCIETY

The Republic of Belarus (its official name following independence) is located geographically in the center of Europe. To the east, it borders on Russia, to the south on Ukraine, to the west on Poland, and to the north on Lithuania and Latvia. Historically, Belarus has often been under the control of one or more of its neighbors, and although there were a few periods when the culture flourished, its language and culture had been undermined for centuries by Polish, Lithuanian, and Russian rulers. In this century, much of Belarus was occupied by Poland between World War I and World War II. Belarus emerged from World War II a profoundly wounded nation; it had been laid waste by the Nazi invasion, first, and then by its reconquest by Soviet troops as they marched victoriously toward Berlin (cf. Tumarkin 1994). With its cities demolished, the republic faced the great task of rebuilding its physical infrastructure and, along the way, overcoming its spiritual devastation. It needed to develop a sense of national identity suited to the new circumstances of Soviet rule. The job of building that national identity was never completed under the Soviets, and establishing it in a form suited to the circumstances after the demise of the Soviet Union and at the end of the twentieth century remains a great unmet challenge (Grichtchenko and Gritsanov 1995; Urban and Zaprudnik 1993; Zaprudnik 1993).

After World War II, Belarus experienced an enormous economic revival. Much of the population, made up largely of peasants, moved to the cities and took up urban lifestyles during the period of reconstruction following the war. By the 1980s, Belarus had one of the highest standards of living and levels of economic development of any of the constituent Soviet republics (Schroeder 1993). Although it had a strong agricultural base, it was an industrial republic, a kind of national assembly shop in which trucks, tractors, refrigerators, televisions, computers, machine tools, and many other products were produced (Zaprudnik 1994). Thus, Belarus depended heavily on its ability to import raw materials and components and to export finished goods. In 1990, with the impending breakup of the Soviet Union, the elimination or severe disruption of cross-border trade with the other constituent republics greatly strained its economy. The continued tenuousness of trade relations in the region has presented a major obstacle to the economic recovery and expansion of Belarus.[6]

The recent fate of Belarus is inextricably associated with the consequences of the Chernobyl catastrophe of 1986. For the people of Belarus, these consequences are comparable to the tragedy that Belarus experienced during World War II. Although the Chernobyl power plant lies just within Ukraine, 70 percent of the radiation that was released by the Chernobyl explosion fell on neighboring Belarus, directly affecting more than 2 million people through fallout and contaminating approximately one-third of the land (Batalden and Batalden 1993; Urban and Zaprudnik 1993; Zaprudnik 1993). In the context of the material presented here, the Chernobyl disaster is especially important in that the affected zone is a place of "limit situations" (O'Dea 1966), that is, where religious processes and feelings attain their most highly developed forms. The Chernobyl phenomenon is unique from the viewpoint of the theory of religious processes and the social psychology of religion. In this case, parents save their children by taking them away, and old people save their memories and try to save their roots in the land. A special atmosphere of risk and fear surrounds young people who are preparing to become parents (Haub 1994).

Under these circumstances, we can envision contradictory forces in the spheres of religion and the family. The national culture has been buffetted hard over both the long historical span and more recently, and one might expect a problem with integration. This weak national identity must also deal with the strain produced by the Chernobyl catastrophe. Both national identification and the catastrophe would, hypothetically, have consequences for religion and the family. Although it will be difficult to disentangle evidence of these consequences, they must be borne in mind as we proceed.

THE GREAT SOVIET EXPERIMENT

Conditions in Belarus, still the BSSR in 1990, can be understood only in relation to Soviet domination that set the parameters of social life in myriad ways. The Soviet state was created following the Bolshevik Revolution of 1917, and by the end of World War II, it encompassed virtually all the territory of the former tsarist Russian Empire.[7] After the initial period of consolidation following the revolution, Soviet society became a grand experiment in reconfiguring all social institutions. Guided by Marxist ideology, the communist leadership sought to create a new society that would put the values of state socialism into practice. The political and ideological pressure for change varied in the different social institutions, and the special conditions of World War II particularly affected the drive for change in many ways. However, the thrust of central planning—for political, economic, and social goals—was always present throughout the existence of the Soviet Union.

The massive Soviet experiment was carried out on all levels. However, given the centrality of economic factors in the Marxian theory and ideology that guided the Bolshevik Revolution, the need to structure the socialist economy always provided the leaders with the overall guidelines for devising policies and programs for the changes they envisioned. Economic reorganization directly affected Soviet families in many ways, and the families were the object of extensive manipulation for this and other ideological reasons during the pre–World War II period (Geiger 1968; Liegle 1975; Pankhurst 1982). By the end of the war, the Soviet family had been transformed from a peasant one to an industrial and urban one. And Belarusian families were rapidly influenced by the same processes as Belarus was reintegrated into the Soviet Union to constitute one of the Soviet republics. Some significant changes in family policy were introduced later under Nikita Khrushchev and Leonid Brezhnev; notably, abortion was permanently relegalized in 1955 (after a twenty-year period when it was forbidden) and divorce procedures were streamlined in the late 1950s and 1960s. However, the Soviet Belarusian family was never to return to its prerevolutionary form or functions (Juviler 1977; Lapidus 1978; Pankhurst 1982).

In the 1980s, Soviet marriage and family were fraught with contradictions (Shlapentokh 1984). Although the old ideological prescriptions oriented citizens outward toward the economy and society, not inward toward the family, the Soviet people considered marriage and family to be primary values, at least from the 1960s. Shlapentokh (1984:82) argued that this "drift to domesticity" was the direct result of the erosion of the official ideology and represented a way to resist the state. Nevertheless, his review of Soviet research showed that many men were only weakly bonded with their wives, and many marriages were based on practical rationality, rather than affective ties. Despite the value placed on love and romance together with marriage, friendships outside the family often outweighed spousal relationships in the security and depth of emotion they evidenced. The family sphere in general, Shlapentokh found, was in a state of anomie by the 1980s.

Religion was also disrupted by governmental leaders for narrow economic reasons; for example, in the early years the leaders expropriated much of the gold and many of the art treasures owned by the Russian Orthodox Church. More broadly, however, the primary motivation for the repression of religion seems to have been the Communist Party's general need for control over the population (Pankhurst 1988). Marxist theory viewed the essence of religion as nothing more than an illusion but one that could not be tolerated because its primary function was to serve the oppression of the working class. Thus, it was natural for the Communist Party elite to take away much of the privilege and legitimacy of the churches. As Bociurkiw (1973) noted about the pre–World War II period, the repression of the churches also served to promote the party's control of the peasants and other groups whom the elite could not easily discipline to follow the directives of their plans, which were aimed at developing an urban, secular proletariat.

In a symbolic way, the repression of religion in the Soviet Union signified the victory of communism—which was a political party, economic organization, and ideology all at once—over the tsarist system that the Russian Orthodox Church had served so unquestioningly. Perhaps the importance of that symbolism explains why the antireligious program was one of the last systematic forms of Soviet repression to fall during the program of reconstruction launched by Mikhail Gorbachev, the General Secretary of the Communist Party of the Soviet Union, in 1986–87. Religious liberty began to grow from 1988 and was legally formalized by statutes passed in 1990 (Pankhurst and Welch 1993; Powell 1994).

In 1986–87, under Gorbachev's leadership the Soviets entered a new stage of guided social change with the slogan of perestroika. The leadership sought to refit the economy to include market mechanisms and to remake the society to include freedom of expression.[8] Although perestroika was initiated by the Communist Party leaders, whose grip on power had been legendary, the leaders lost control of the central direction such that their own authority was eventually undermined. Internationally, the loss of authority was symbolized by the fall of the Berlin Wall in 1989, when the "satellite" states of Eastern and Central Europe went their own ways. And the Soviet empire itself was soon to fall.

Although ideological fervor for communism had waned during the last few decades of the Soviet Union, the legacy of the communist vision remains in almost every sphere of social life (Millar and Wolchik 1994), including the family (Dobson 1994; Kligman 1994) and religion (Powell 1994). Now, social institutions face new challenges as the societies attempt to denationalize their economies, democratize politics, and generally loosen control.

Given this dramatic social and political history, it should be apparent that the conditions experienced by Belarusians in 1990 were pivotal. The Belarusians were living on the very cusp of historical change. Behind them was the closed, authoritarian phase. Would the future repeat the past, or would it hold new opportunities for the integration of their national identity and the development of a vigorous and free religious market?

WORLD VALUES SURVEY DATA

Data derived from the World Values Survey, conducted in 1990, permitted us to get a picture of religious and familial relations in this critical period. The World Values Survey is a global longitudinal research project, which, in the beginning, conducted surveys in a series of Western countries in the 1970s.[9] By 1990, forty-three countries of the world were represented in the project, and that diversity has given researchers the opportunity to carry out broad cross-cultural comparisons, such as those reported by Abramson and Inglehart (1995) and Inglehart (1997). Although we make some brief comparisons with the United States and Western Europe to illustrate points, we do not make broader comparisons here.

A sample of 1,015 respondents, representing the adult population of Belarus, was surveyed. The respondents were selected using a randomized quota-sampling procedure based on the address tables of urban areas and the residence lists of the village soviets (councils) in the countryside. The questionnaire included questions on practically all value spheres of human life, and a significant amount of attention was given to questions about both religious and family values.

These data are particularly valuable because they refer to a period of exceptionally rapid change in the society. Collected during the year before the dissolution of the Soviet Union, the data need to be evaluated carefully for their context. The problem of surveying a population that was still under a communist government was not totally solved with this survey. The responses reflect, in part, the people's experience with their Soviet domination. In addition, relatively few surveys had been conducted on general values in the Soviet Union, and many of those that were carried out were of dubious methodological quality.[10] Unfortunately, this situation means that we cannot make comparisons with earlier surveys. We hope that future research will develop a longitudinal time frame for analysis using the 1990 data as a baseline for comparison.

RELIGION IN BELARUS

Religion in any society is made up of individual beliefs and actions, on the one hand, and institutional and organizational structures, on the other. It is instructive to compare these two sides of religion, for doing so can elucidate important dynamics in the religious sphere. As we indicate, the problematic connection of individual faith with group attachments is a consequential issue in Belarus.

Following the many years of Soviet communist domination and the rapid urbanization and industrialization of the republic after World War II, it is not surprising that the level of individual faith in Belarus was lower than in Western Europe or the United States. In our sample, 35.7 percent of the respondents identified themselves as "believers," 37.9 percent called themselves "nonbelievers," 7.7 percent considered themselves "convinced atheists," and 18.9 percent did not know where they fit in these three categories.[11] The relatively large size of the atheist, nonbeliever, and "don't know" categories is the result, in large measure, of the communist regime's patterns of socialization and social control. Even though the population would have been secularized to some degree without communism, the figures for atheism, which the communist regime particularly nurtured, were surely larger than one would find in similar countries that did not experience communism.

Of the nineteen economically developed countries that Inglehart (1997:372) used as indicators of his "culture shift" toward "postmaterialist" values, none had a level of belief in God as low as Belarus's. For Belarusians, only some 36.4 percent said they believed in God. Even in Sweden, by nearly all accounts the most irreligious society in Europe, the level of belief in God exceeded 40 percent. The figure for the United States was over 90 percent.

The biconfessional structure of religion in Belarus reflects its location on the boundary between the Eastern and Southern Slavs, who traditionally practiced Eastern Orthodoxy, and the Western Slavs, who had a historical allegiance to Roman Catholicism. Traditionally, the majority of believers have been Orthodox and the minority, Catholics, but the exact proportions are difficult to ascertain. There is a small but significant number of Evangelical Christian Baptists in Belarus; other confessions (for example, Judaism) comprise small minorities.

Although respondents were asked their denominational or confessional attachments, many did not identify with a specific church or faith, even if they claimed to believe in God. Specifically, 68.3 percent of those who identified themselves as believers in God were attached to some traditional faith. That about one-third of the believers in God did not identify a denominational attachment is a point that we will return to.

Turning the question around, 30.1 percent claimed a denominational affiliation. The largest denominational category of respondents was Orthodox (23.1 percent), and the next largest category was Catholic (6.5 percent). The other confessions (such as Islam, Judaism, Old Believers, and Greek Catholicism) were not named by more than 0.1 percent of the respondents, with the exception of the Evangelical Christian Baptists, at 0.4 percent.

Of the respondents who named a denominational affiliation, 89.8 percent said they believed in God. In contrast, although self-identified Catholics and Protestants in Western Europe total 85 percent of the population—that is, 85 percent claim adherence to the two traditional West European faiths—the figure for self-identified believers is only 65 percent (Harding, Phillips, and Fogarty 1986). Thus, many West Europeans have a traditional attachment to the major faiths but do not consider themselves believers. In Belarus, this differentiation between traditional adherent and subjective believer does not exist in any significant measure. Perhaps this is the case because the church organizations were so clearly targeted for persecution under the Soviet regime (Pankhurst 1988) that few people retained a casual or sentimental attachment to them. The Soviet national identity, of course, called for absolute religious nonaffiliation and atheistic beliefs. Only those who were clearly sincere, faithful believers retained a denominational identification.

The confessional structure of the United States also presents a diametrically opposite picture of variety as contrasted with Belarus. In the 1990 World Values Survey of the United States (*N* = 1,839),[12] denominational distribution took the following form:

Protestants	49.6 %
Catholics	35.5 %
Jews	2.3 %
Hindus	0.5 %
Buddhists	0.3 %
Muslims	0.1 %
Other	9.4 %
Affiliation not given	2.2 %

In these data, two important features differentiate the Belarusian structure from the American. First, the latter is much more diverse than the Belarusian. Note the category "other"; in the Belarusian sample it is 0.1 percent, but in the U.S. sample it is 9.4 percent. In the Belarusian case, two major confessions coexist; in the United States case, more than ten statistically large socioconfessional groups can be counted, and this number does not take into account the wide diversity of Protestant churches included within the Protestant category.

A positive quality of the Belarusian variant of biconfessionality is the peaceful neighborliness of the two basic creeds. Although there have been many episodes of political strife between the Polish powers to the west and the Russians to the east, they have never led to overt religious clashes between the Catholics and Orthodox in Belarus that each power, respectively, supports. The future of independent Belarus may contain some seeds for interconfessional strife, though these seeds are not obvious at present. However, social scientists should seek to determine whether an interconfessional line of social tension, like the one that exists in Northern Ireland between Catholics and Protestants, could arise in Belarus. Both Belarus and Northern Ireland have been divided between stronger neighbors, and the two major confessions have experienced tensions (though not so severe as Protestant-Catholic strife in Ireland) elsewhere, most notably in nearby Ukraine. What is the difference between the Irish conditions, which gave rise to many years of tragedy, and the conditions in the Belarusian variant of biconfessionalism that permit representatives of the distinct creeds to live harmoniously and peacefully next to each other? For such occasions, the wise folk saying goes, "don't crow." Future analysis should try to discern the sources of the benign interrelationship so as to continue to nurture them in an independent Belarus.

The 1990 World Values Survey data must be viewed as being derived from a specific context of change in Soviet and Belarusian society. In particular, at the end of the 1980s and the early 1990s, religion was newly legitimated. In these posttotalitarian circumstances, the number of respondents who called themselves believers increased. However, religion and religious faith were, to a certain extent, a matter of fashion, especially among urban youths. To some degree, this fashionableness raised the number who placed themselves in the category of believer in the survey. That is, there was not so much a factual increase in the number of believers as an increase in the number of people whom we might call, for lack of a better term, "verbal believers."

A second relevant point is that in the Soviet period, it was difficult to answer social survey questions on religious issues. It was simply dangerous from the viewpoint of one's career; to be a believer and to pursue a social or professional career was practically impossible. In the current situation of openness, absent totalitarian fear, "hidden believers" have suddenly appeared, claiming that they were always believers, even in the Soviet period, but simply feared to reveal themselves openly.

Whether because of cultural fashion or reasons related to the lifting of ideological controls and the new ability to express oneself freely in independent Belarus, the number of church adherents appears to have grown since the 1990 survey. According to data collected by the first author, in 1993 62.4 percent of the Belarusians were Orthodox and 4 percent were Catholics, and in 1994 the proportions were 79.6 and 6.3 percent, respectively. In addition, the expressed public confidence in the institution of "the church" in Belarus was, by the mid-1990s, relatively high. A survey by the Open Media Research Institute in the spring of 1995 found that some 67 percent of the Belarusian sample expressed confidence in the church—a figure that considerably outstripped confidence in the military (59 percent) and the presidency (50 percent) (Gibson 1996).

Given this ambiguous dynamic among "verbal believers" and emerging "hidden believers," the interpretation of the empirical data on religion must proceed cautiously. The situation can be misinterpreted if the special circumstances of religion in the late period of communist rule are not taken into account.

That being said, we can venture a preliminary conclusion about the nature of the newly open religious market in Belarus in 1990. Namely, it was ripe for activity of religious entrepreneurs seeking to find a "market share" for their religious products. As we noted earlier, a significant proportion of the population asserted a belief in God but did not identify a denominational affiliation. The later data suggest that both the Catholic and Orthodox churches, as well as other groups, have begun to reach this underserved population. Monitoring the situation over the next several years and decades should provide a good picture of the dynamics of a newly opened religious market.

FAMILY, RELIGION, AND LIFE VALUES

This section places the family and religion in the broader system of life values. The tables that follow summarize responses to questions on the 1990 World Values Survey in Belarus. One basic issue is the importance various interests in life have to the respondents. Table 6.1 indicates the hierarchical ranking of six life values in order of decreasing importance.

As the table shows, family and religion occupy directly opposite locations in the hierarchy: Family is at the top and religion is at the bottom. Note that it is not important how the hierarchy was formed—by simply choosing the percentage who answered "very important" or by summing the percentages for "very important" and "quite important." The order in both cases is almost the same. The exception is the last two positions—for religion and politics—which evince a significant difference between ranks in the summed index while the difference using only the "very important" responses is insignificant.

It may be significant to note that among the Belarusian sample, 6 percent could not indicate a level of importance for religion, the highest level of "don't know" response among the value choices. Religion was fashionable in some sectors and newly out of the closet in others, but it was also a puzzle for many who had not been exposed to it over the years of communist control.

Before concluding too much from these data, we must ask how unique such a structure of values is in the world. Is it an especially Belarusian (or Slavic or posttotalitarian) phenomenon, or is it some type of global value hi-

Table 6.1
THE IMPORTANCE OF SIX SPHERES OF LIFE FOR BELARUSIANS: 1990 (PERCENTAGE; $N = 1{,}015$)

Sphere of Life	Very Plus Quite Important	Very Important	Quite Important	Not Very Important	Not at All Important	Don't Know
Family	94.9	74.8	20.1	3.0	0.6	0.6
Work	80.2	53.6	26.6	13.9	2.5	1.8
Friends and acquaintances	78.5	34.9	43.6	17.8	1.1	1.5
Leisure time	70.1	34.5	35.6	22.0	2.7	3.5
Politics	37.2	14.0	23.2	46.9	12.2	2.2
Religion	29.9	14.1	15.8	39.2	22.8	6.0

Table 6.2
THE IMPORTANCE OF SIX SPHERES OF LIFE FOR AMERICANS: 1990 (PERCENTAGE; N = 1,839)

Sphere of Life	Very Plus Quite Important	Very Important	Quite Important	Not Very Important	Not at All Important	Don't Know
Family	98.6	92.5	6.1	1.0	0.3	0
Work	86.5	62.3	24.2	7.3	6.2	0
Friends and acquaintances	93.4	53.4	40.0	6.4	0.2	0
Leisure time	85.1	42.6	42.5	14.0	0.8	0
Politics	50.4	15.9	34.5	37.8	11.7	0
Religion	78.9	52.8	26.1	16.5	4.7	0

erarchy? Though a complete answer to this question must be deferred to further analyses, for the sake of comparison, Table 6.2 presents the data for the same questions for the United States.

As the table indicates, the family is in the same strong first position in value choices in the United States as in Belarus. On the other hand, the religious sphere is much higher in importance in the American value system. Note that the percentage of the combined "very important" plus "quite important" responses for religion is over 2½ times greater for the United States than for Belarus (78.9 percent versus 29.9 percent). Furthermore, the gap between the combined "very" and "quite important" responses for religion as compared to family is a mere 20 percentage points for the United States, but 65 points for Belarus. How can this difference be interpreted? With the family retaining the highest value position in both societies, the answer lies in the realm of religion. Although we must acknowledge the unusual strength of religion in the United States, the most obvious explanation for the enormity of the difference with Belarus may be the shadow of atheist totalitarianism that lay in the consciousness of the Belarusian people.

In this sense, Belarus, perhaps along with some of the other states of the former Soviet Union, has an atypical pattern in regard to family and religion. On the basis of data from the forty-three countries included in the 1990 wave of the World Values Surveys, Inglehart (1997) found that the high importance of the family usually goes along with the high importance of religion. Both, he argued, represent a more traditional authority structure in society. Given this broad cross-national pattern, we need to be especially attentive to the aberrant relationship shown in the Belarusian data. The overarching explanation for the separation of religion from family concerns seems to be that the cultural and political experience under the Soviets made religious values problematic and weakened the expression of individually articulated values in general.

In the latter regard, and from the viewpoint of the measurement of values, a special quality of these comparative data must be stressed. That is, there is a significant difference in the character of the "saturation" of the positions of the value hierarchy. In the American hierarchy of values, all the positions are more saturated, that is, they have higher percentages of strong positive support. For example, as Table 6.3 shows, the first value position, importance of the family, was selected by 92.5 percent as "very important" in the United States, but by only 74.8 percent in Belarus. Similarly, the second position was chosen by 62.3 percent and 53.6 percent, respectively, and so on through the other positions. Thus, the U.S. and Belarusian hierarchies are fundamentally different on axiometrical and system parameters of saturation; any percentage in the right-hand American column in Table 6.3 is greater than the percentage in the lefthand Belarusian column.

The pattern demonstrated in Table 6.3 provides evidence of a fundamental culturological difference in the social psychology of the two peoples. Setting American particularism aside,[13] how much of the value pattern for Belarusians is a result of their long cultural history or of the shorter and more recent experience of the communist order is an important question for further analysis.

VALUES FOR MARRIAGE

Naturally, we would expect Belarusians to evaluate family matters within the context of their broader value commitments. Here, we briefly examine values related to marriage and, in the next section, to child rearing, to assess the level of consistency of values in the family with the other contextual values. Consonant with the previous findings, a lesser weight for religion appears in various patterns of values elicited from the responses to questions on these two family topics.

Table 6.3

RANK-ORDERED PERCENTAGES OF RESPONDENTS DESIGNATING SIX VALUE SPHERES AS "VERY IMPORTANT" IN BELARUS AND THE UNITED STATES: 1990 (N = 1,015 FOR BELARUS AND 1,839 FOR THE UNITED STATES)

Rank	Belarus Very Important	United States Very Important
1	74.8 (family)	92.5 (family)
2	53.6 (work)	62.3 (work)
3	34.9 (friends)	53.4 (friends)
4	34.5 (leisure)	52.8 (religion)
5	14.1 (religion)	42.6 (leisure)
6	14.0 (politics)	15.9 (politics)

Table 6.4
RANK-ORDERED QUALITIES VALUED FOR A SUCCESSFUL MARRIAGE IN BELARUS: 1990 (PERCENTAGE; N = 1,015)

Rank	Quality	Very Important	Rather Important	Not Very Important
1	Faithfulness	80.7	14.9	4.2
2	Children	80.6	16.1	2.0
3	Mutual respect and appreciation	71.3	11.0	1.6
4	Understanding and tolerance	68.0	27.8	2.9
5	Good housing	59.8	31.8	6.5
6	An adequate income	57.3	24.0	4.3
7	Happy sexual relationship	55.6	35.6	8.0
8	Living apart from your in-laws	47.5	31.5	19.3
9	Tastes and interests in common	45.0	41.5	11.1
10	Sharing household chores	29.4	37.0	32.3
11	Being of the same social background	16.9	17.5	63.7
12	Shared religious beliefs	15.7	16.8	65.2
13	Agreement on politics	9.4	15.4	72.1

The respondents were asked about the parameters of a successful marriage. Their responses, summarized in Table 6.4, defined a system of values in the marital sphere that was parallel to that for the general totality of life values on an extremely broad scale (see Table 6.1).

The data in Table 6.4 show the low rating of the need for shared religious beliefs for marital success. There seem to be four possible explanations for this finding. First, one might argue that the lack of emphasis on shared religious beliefs in marriage is an outcome of the historic interconfessional tolerance in Belarus that already has been mentioned. However, given high ethnic consciousness (a tendency facilitated by the Soviet system in a variety of ways), one might expect such tolerance to be based in an orientation by which one would demand shared beliefs with a mate while respecting the rights of other couples or families to hold different beliefs. To evaluate the validity of this argument fully, we would need to have data on religious intermarriage that are not available. However, on the face of it, tolerance alone seems inadequate to explain the large disconnect between family and religion that the data in Table 6.4 indicate.

Second, one might argue that if the population is not made up of many believers in the first place, then shared religion will not be important for those who are not interested in religion. There is a consistency between the 29.9 percent of the sample who said that religion was "very" or "quite important" in their lives (Table 6.1) and the 32.5 percent who said that "shared religious beliefs" were either "very" or "rather important" for a successful marriage (Table 6.4). However, "shared religious beliefs" can include shared atheism or religious indifference, as well as convicted faith, and in this case, there is some ambiguity as to how the respondents interpreted this answer. Clearly, some respondents who did not consider religion important nevertheless thought that shared religious beliefs were important for marriage. Thus, a further explanation is needed, it seems. Even so, one could argue that the low importance of shared religious beliefs simply mirrors the low levels of religious self-identification in Belarus.

Third, one might conclude that high secularity had led Belarusians to segregate their family sphere from their religious sphere. However, even though this is a relatively irreligious population, the relative recency of the urban migration of the majority of the population and their nearness to their peasant roots would provide conditions that should militate against the exclusion of religious issues from salience in marriage. Since they are so close to their rural and agricultural roots, this outcome would not support most theories of secularization, which see the impetus for the reduction of religiousness in urbanization and education, unless we could posit that an extremely rapid—perhaps unrealistically rapid (cf. Wilson 1985)—process of secularization took place.

On the other hand, perhaps in 1990 Belarusians still thought that this sphere of concern should be eliminated from consideration in marital affairs because it was so dangerous, given the antireligious ideological context that they had been used to. The impact of the late-Soviet sociopolitical milieu seems apparent. Note that the system's impact seems similarly apparent in the responses that social background differences are not "very important" for marital success. The Soviet system promoted an egalitarian ideology, and many qualities of social leveling characterized it. Social background differences were not *supposed to* make a difference in interpersonal relations, and they had few enduring means of external expression (such as conspicuous consumption for the wealthy) under the communist regime. Thus, it is not surprising that they were not assessed as critical for success in marriage. In the end, it appears that the consequences of the Soviet sociopolitical system were being expressed in these responses on the marital importance of social background, as well as of religion.

CHILD-REARING VALUES AND RELIGIOUS SOCIALIZATION

A second question that indicated the "insignificance" of the religious sphere referred to the qualities of personality that parents would like to include in their children's upbringing (see Table 6.5).

The tenth position for religious faith in the range of qualities that the respondents wanted for their children speaks strongly of the Sovietized orientation to upbringing in Belarus, in which little weight was placed on personal religious values. It is striking that even with almost 30 percent of the

Table 6.5
RANK-ORDERED QUALITIES SEEN AS IMPORTANT FOR CHILD REARING IN BELARUS: 1990 (*N* = 1,015)

Rank	Quality	Percentage
1	Feeling of responsibility	82.3
2	Hard work	81.4
3	Tolerance and respect for other people	80.0
4	Good manners	70.9
5	Thrift, saving money and things	55.3
6	Determination, perseverance	40.0
7	Independence	29.7
8	Unselfishness	26.4
9	Obedience	22.7
10	Religious faith	7.6
11	Imagination	6.7

respondents saying (in Table 6.1) that religion was "very" or "quite important" in their lives, only 7.6 percent saw it as a quality that children should learn in the home. Here, perhaps, one can see not only the inhibition about teaching religion to children in any form, which was characteristic of the communist system, but the effects of the long-term lack of religious education for the parents. That is, the parents had not been much exposed to religious teachings themselves and had not learned much about their religious faith. Thus, they may have thought that they could not teach their children about their faith even though they were religious.[14]

In spite of the responses to the questions on marital success and child rearing that seem to indicate very little importance for religion in family life, it would be incorrect to evaluate the significance of the religious sphere in the family only by the results of projective questions such as these. A somewhat different representation of the role of this part of family life is given by the distribution of responses concerning the respondents' own religious upbringing.

When the respondents were asked, "Were you brought up religiously at home?" 22.5 percent said that they were. Thus, while only 7.6 percent of the current parents and potential child rearers wanted to instill religious convictions and qualities in their children, about three times as many had received a religious upbringing at home. In light of these data, it may be appropriate to speak of the secularization of the upbringing of children in the home, that is, a reduction in the likelihood of families providing religious socialization to children. Time will tell whether this type of secularization will lead to a reduction in the number of religious believers in the population. However, as our discussion so far has suggested, there are frequently alternative explanations for the responses than to see them as direct measures of the level of interest or behavior in the area of the question. Since the responses refer to the period still under Soviet rule, they may reflect the old antireligious ideology, so that the respondents may have given socially and politically expected answers more than accurate statements of their attitudes or behavior.

In any case, the family is usually an important channel for the religious socialization of children. If the churches of Belarus expect to grow, they clearly will need to stimulate greater religious training of children in the home or provide significant new resources for religious education in the parishes and congregations. Either way, they will need to reshape the socialization context for religion in a manner that assists and exploits families' resources. More broadly, how the family, as a vehicle for socialization, will adapt to a more open religious sphere in the post-Soviet era needs to be explored further.

FAMILY RITUALS

In addition to personal beliefs, denominational attachments, and socialization practices, it is instructive to examine the ritual sphere as it relates to the family. Examples like Sweden (see Chapter 5) suggest that even when there is widespread secularization, ritual accompaniments to family life may be popular. The responses summarized in Table 6.6 clarify the role of religious ceremonies for the most important events in family life.

As the table indicates, the birth of a child is the family event for which it is most important to hold a religious service, in that three-quarters of the respondents advocated such a service even in this seemingly secular environment. Furthermore, the fact that over two-thirds of the respondents saw the need for a religious service to mark death and a majority thought it was necessary for marriage also demands further explanation. How can these figures be so much higher than the value choices assessed earlier? The answer may lie in the dramatic social change taking place in Belarus.

In an extensive oral history project conducted between 1990 and 1994, Ransel (1996) collected accounts by women in Russian villages of their child-

Table 6.6
THE IMPORTANCE OF FAMILY RITUALS IN BELARUS: 1990 (PERCENTAGE; $N = 1{,}015$)

	Religious Service		
Family Event	Yes	No	Don't Know
Birth	75.6	16.3	6.7
Death	67.9	21.7	9.2
Marriage	56.5	31.2	10.4

rearing and ritual practices during the various phases of the Soviet period. He found that children were baptized throughout the Soviet era in spite of the regime's antireligious policies. The women he interviewed thought that baptism safeguarded the children's spiritual and physical health. Ransel concluded that baptism provided a particularly important arena for expressing the imperatives of family life beyond the control of the Communist Party and the state. For the women whom he interviewed, baptism was the "basic ritual of incorporation" of children into their communities and families—an act apart from the larger national identity. As both an expression of the special expertise of women, who understood its power and implemented its requirements, and a symbolic locale outside the political realm, baptism was especially potent. Ransel (1996:76) stated that the women's "insistence that baptism be performed, no matter the risks, and their ability in most cases to achieve this, strengthened both the families and the women themselves by according them the power to act effectively, beneficially, and in defiance of the ideological state."

The data we reviewed for Belarus suggest that the ritual realm, especially that of baptism, is the most powerful symbolic sphere for expressing familial autonomy through the spiritual incorporation of new members. Although religious values and beliefs have been eroded over the decades of Soviet rule (Pankhurst 1988) and all forms of religious expression are still hindered by the legacy of communism, the most basic acts that unite faith and family have survived much more fully. The mutual support that family rituals provide for both the family and religion make their sustenance and development the first requirement for the establishment of a modern religious institutional sphere in Belarus as the country tries to remake itself in a new image that respects and honors its history and culture.

CONCLUSION

In a period of rapid social change as deep as that experienced in Belarus over the past decade, there is bound to be much evidence of ambiguity and ambivalence among the population. The religious situation in Belarus seems to be clearly unsettled, as our data suggest. The presence of a large number of "verbal" believers who are following a social script without significant personal background and the emergence of many previously "hidden" believers as the persecution of faith has waned suggest some of the complications in the religious institution that are being worked out over time. The social value of the family to Belarusians and the seemingly significant collectivity of underserved believers, those without a church affiliation in Belarus, suggest that families may be mobilized more fully in the future (and the process may have already started) to develop a greater store of religious human capital for the society.

We have hardly mentioned the general consequences of the opening of a new "free market" for religion, in which the traditional faiths are challenged by internal and external rivals, such as foreign evangelists, schismatics, and new religious movements. The competitive conditions are proving to be the source of considerable controversy and division in the historic religions of Belarus (Corley 1998; Rich 1997), and are a fascinating subject that is in need of further analysis. Preliminarily, however, we can assert that the Belarusian population would be much better prepared to relate to this competition—above all, not to be victimized by it—if families cultivated greater religious human capital. Such a process would not only serve to enrich the religious sphere of Belarus, but would contribute to the solution of the problem of a national identity by clarifying the nature of the connection between religious affiliation and ethnonational ideals. Only with a clearer national identity can Belarus develop a civil society in support of democratic governance.

Although our research finds that the commitment to family is stronger than the commitment to religion, Belarusian families, like the religious groups, have been challenged by several generations of struggle against the intrusion of politics and difficult economic conditions. Our data indicate that Belarusians are not as strong in family and other values as are other societies, and there are hints of ongoing difficulties. The improvement in these conditions, it would seem, requires a balanced approach, involving families and religious groups together with other institutional spheres in the society.

In the context of the disorienting change going on, the chicken-and-egg question comes to mind. Can Belarus begin to mend its social fabric by enhancing its familial and religious institutions, or must its economy and politics be made more equitable and stable for the family and religion to mend? Many economic and social planners would assume the latter approach without question. However, after the many years of communist control, there are signs of movement on both sides of this question. We believe that the values and practices surrounding the family and religion are at the heart of the change, and their role in healing the society cannot be ignored.

NOTES

The second author received support for parts of this research from the Faculty Research Fund of Wittenberg University and from the International Research and Exchanges Board. This support is gratefully acknowledged. None of the analysis or the views expressed is the responsibility of Wittenberg University or IREX.

1. This is one example of the problem of the micro-macro linkage, which has become an important interest of sociologists in recent decades (Alexander, Giesen, Münch, and Smelser 1987).
2. During the past decade, an increasing number of studies in the sociology of religion took a religious-economy or rational-choice approach (Warner 1993). The major components of the general theory that link all levels of analysis were mapped out by Stark and Bainbridge (1996). The theory's most extensive empirical application is found in Finke and Stark's (1992) reinterpretation of the his-

tory of religion in the United States. An up-to-date and clear-eyed evaluation of the approach is found in Young (1997).

3. Of course, they, too, have external constituencies, the support of which tarnishes their "purity" in the eyes of some Belarusians, who have been conditioned by the poorly crystallized national identity to see threats from anything foreign. The Eastern-Rite Catholics are thought to be too liable to Ukrainian influence, since this church is strong in western Ukraine. The Autonomous Orthodox Church is thought by some to be a means for the Belarusian diaspora, with its entanglements with Western European and North American powers, to infiltrate the Belarusian culture and society. Besides these problems, neither church has been able to develop a clear social base in Belarus.
4. Post-Soviet contentiousness about these issues was demonstrated in interviews the authors conducted in Minsk in August 1993. Orthodox Metropolitan Filaret of Minsk complained that the Catholic Church was becoming more and more Polonized, a process that "is a danger for Belarus and for national consciousness." He also rejected the authenticity of Uniate efforts to claim the status of being the genuine Belarusian church. Among the Uniates in Belarus, he said, were nationalists who were fulfilling a long historical strategy of the Vatican to enter into conflict in Belarus for its own benefits. In an interview just three days later, a Belarusian-speaking Roman Catholic priest portrayed the importation of Polish priests as a pragmatic move to rejuvenate the Catholic Church in Belarus, especially among Polish-speaking citizens in the western areas. However, the priest described the Belarusian Catholic Church as an authentic domestic voice for Belarusian identity, even though external financial support for its development was being neglected by all relevant parties, ranging from the diaspora to the Vatican. He saw the Uniates as a missionary effort from the Ukraine that was legitimate, given the long history of Uniatism in Belarus, but thought that the Orthodox Church was far too tied to Russian interests and that Metropolitan Filaret had no claim to a role as protector of the Belarusian identity. The Belarusian Autocephalous Orthodox Church did not come up in these interviews, although by spring 1996, fifteen Orthodox parishes had switched to its jurisdiction in apparent protest against "Russified leadership under Metropolitan Filaret of Minsk and sermons in Russian" (Broun 1997).
5. Batalden and Batalden (1993:44–45) gave slightly different figures. They indicated a territory of 80,134 square miles and a population of 10,152,000.
6. This economic cul-de-sac may explain, in large measure, the attempts by some Belarusian leaders to reunite Belarus in some fashion with the Russian Federation (cf. Prazauskas 1994; Zaprudnik 1994).
7. In the agreements settling World War I, Poland, which had been under Russian control, was made an independent state. Between 1919 and 1939, much of present Belarus was within the territory of Poland, although Belarus had formerly been part of the Russian Empire. The location of the borders of the Russian Empire and the Soviet Union at various points in time can be seen in the maps prepared by Gilbert (1993). Batalden and Batalden (1993) presented a useful overview of these and related matters for each republic of the former Soviet Union.
8. Twinned with perestroika and actually created before it in the reform process was the slogan of glasnost, which referred directly to open discussion and, at least secondarily, to free speech.

9. *Culture Shift in Advanced Industrial Society*, by Inglehart (1990), is the primary description of the general project of the World Values Survey, which Inglehart initiated and directs. Inglehart's (1997) book, *Modernization and Post-Modernization*, presents details and analyses through the 1990 wave, of which the data from Belarus used here were a part. This latter volume contains all the questionnaire items and protocols of the World Value Surveys for this wave. It should be noted that this chapter is not directly concerned with the "culture-shift" thesis, although the general orientation affects what has been written here.
10. Shlapentokh (1982) reviewed the best of the studies of values in the Soviet Union. Unfortunately, the studies that have relevant data provide litte specific information on Belarus (then the BSSR).
11. The perentages sum to 100.2 due to rounding error.
12. The 1990 World Values Survey in the United States was carried out by the Gallop Organization. Further details on its methodology and that of all the World Values Surveys can be found in Inglehart (1997), as well as in the codebook, which is available from the Inter-University Consortium for Political and Social Research.
13. When data from all the 43 countries participating in the World Values Survey in 1990 are combined, the order of importance of the value spheres is as follows: family, work, friends, leisure, religion, politics (Inglehart 1997:209). Thus, using the order alone, Belarus is more characteristic of other countries than the United States. However, 28 percent of the world's 1990 respondents said religion was very important, compared to Belarus's 14.1 percent and the United States' 52.8 percent. Thus, contrasting Belarus and the United States emphasizes extremely high and low values of religion.
14. The Harvard Project, which studied Soviets who were displaced as a result of World War II, found a similar pattern among its respondents (Inkeles and Bauer 1961).

References

Abramson, Paul R., and Ronald Inglehart. 1995. *Value Change in Global Perspective*. Ann Arbor: University of Michigan Press.

Alexander, Jeffrey C., Bernhard Giesen, Richard Münch, and Neil J. Smelser, eds. 1987. *The Micro-Macro Link*. Berkeley: University of California Press.

Batalden, Stephen K., and Sandra L. Batalden. 1993. *The Newly Independent States of Eurasia: Handbook of Former Soviet Republics*. Phoenix, AZ: Oryx.

Bociurkiw, Bohdan R. 1973. "The Shaping of Soviet Religious Policy." *Problems of Communism* 32(2):37–51.

Broun, Janice. 1997. "Divisions in Eastern Orthodoxy Today." *East-West Church and Ministry Report* 5(2), Part I. Unpaginated Internet publication from the Center for East-West Christian Studies, Wheaton College, Wheaton, IL.

Corley, Felix. 1998. "Differing Views of New Draft Law on Religion in Belarus." *Keston News Service*. Unpaginated internet publication of the Keston Institute, Great Britain, May 26.

Dobson, Richard B. 1994. "Communism's Legacy and Russian Youth." Pp. 229–51 in *The Social Legacy of Communism*, edited by James R. Millar and Sharon L. Wolchik. Washington, DC: Woodrow Wilson Center Press.

Finke, Roger, and Rodney Stark. 1992. *The Churching of America: 1776–1990*. New Brunswick, NJ: Rutgers University Press.

Flynn, James T. 1993. "The Uniate Church in Belorussia: A Case of Nation-Building?" Pp. 27–46 in *Religious Compromise, Political Salvation: The Greek Catholic Church and Nation- Building in Eastern Europe* (Carl Beck Papers, No. 1003), edited by James Niessen. Pittsburgh, PA: Center for Russian and East European Studies, University of Pittsburgh.

Fukuyama, Francis. 1992. *The End of History and the Last Man*. New York: Avon Books.

Geiger, H. Kent. 1968. *The Family in Soviet Russia*. Cambridge, MA: Harvard University Press.

Gibson, David G. 1996. "High Public Confidence in the Church." *Transition* 2(April 5):29.

Gilbert, Martin. 1993. *Atlas of Russian History* (2nd ed.). New York: Oxford University Press.

Grichtchenko, Jane M., and A. A. Gritsanov. 1995. "The Local Political Elite in the Democratic Transformation of Belarus." *Annals of the American Academy of Political and Social Sciences* 540(July):118–25.

Harding, Stephen, David Phillips, and Michael Fogarty. 1986. *Contrasting Values in Western Europe: Unity, Diversity and Change*. Basingstoke, England: Macmillan.

Haub, Carl. 1994. "Population Change in the Former Soviet Republics." *Population Bulletin* 49(4). Washington, DC: Population Reference Bureau.

Iannaccone, Laurence R. 1997. "Rational Choice: Framework for the Scientific Study of Religion." Pp. 25–45 in *Rational Choice Theory and Religion: Summary and Assessment*, edited by Lawrence A. Young. New York: Routledge.

Inglehart, Ronald. 1990. *Culture Shift in Advanced Industrial Society*. Princeton, NJ: Princeton University Press.

———. 1997. *Modernization and Post-Modernization: Cultural, Economic and Political Change in 43 Societies*. Princeton, NJ: Princeton University Press.

Inkeles, Alex, and Raymond A. Bauer. 1961. *The Soviet Citizen: Daily Life in a Totalitarian Society*. Cambridge, MA: Harvard University Press.

Joint Economic Committee, Congress of the United States. 1993. *The Former Soviet Union in Transition*, edited by Richard F. Kaufman and John P. Hardt. Armonk, NY: M. E. Sharpe.

Juviler, Peter H. 1977. "Women and Sex in Soviet Law." Pp. 244–65 in *Women in Russia*, edited by Dorothy Atkinson, Alexander Dallin, and Gail W. Lapidus. Stanford, CA: Stanford University Press.

Kligman, Gail. 1994. "The Social Legacy of Communism: Women, Children, and the Feminization of Poverty." Pp. 252–70 in *The Social Legacy of Communism*, edited by James R. Millar and Sharon L. Wolchik. Washington, DC: Woodrow Wilson Center Press.

Lapidus, Gail W. 1978. *Women in Soviet Society: Equality, Development, and Social Change*. Berkeley: University of California Press.

Liegle, Ludwig. 1975. *The Family's Role in Soviet Education*. New York: Springer.

Millar, James R., and Sharon L. Wolchik, eds. 1994. *The Social Legacy of Communism*. Washington, DC: Woodrow Wilson Center Press.

O'Dea, Thomas F. 1966. *The Sociology of Religion*. Englewood Cliffs, NJ: Prentice-Hall.

Pankhurst, Jerry G. 1982. "The Ideology of 'Sex-Love' in Post-Revolutionary Russia: Lenin, Kollontai and the Politics of Lifestyle Liberation." *Alternative Lifestyles* 5:78–100.

———. 1988. "The Sacred and the Secular in the USSR." Pp. 167–92 in *Understanding Soviet Society*, edited by Michael Paul Sacks and Jerry G. Pankhurst. Boston: Unwin Hyman.

Pankhurst, Jerry G., and Carolyn Welch. 1993. "Religion under Gorbachev." Pp. 322–36 in *The Gorbachev Encyclopedia*, edited by Joseph L. Wieczynski. Salt Lake City, UT: Charles Schlacks, Jr.

Powell, David E. 1994. "The Religious Renaissance in the Soviet Union and Its Successor States." Pp. 271–305 in *The Social Legacy of Communism*, edited by James R. Millar and Sharon L. Wolchik. Washington, DC: Woodrow Wilson Center Press.

Prazauskas, Algimantas. 1994. "The Influence of Ethnicity on the Foreign Policies of the Western Littoral States." Pp. 150–84 in *National Identity and Ethnicity in Russia and the New States of Eurasia*, edited by Roman Szporluk. Armonk, NY: M. E. Sharpe.

Ransel, David L. 1996. "Baptism in Rural Russia: Village Women Speak of Their Children and Their Way of Life." *History of the Family* 1(1):63–80.

Rich, Vera. 1997. "Belarus: Soviet Stance on Religion Returns." *Frontier* 4:4–5.

Schroeder, Gertrude E. 1993. "Regional Economic Disparities, Gorbachev's Policies, and the Disintegration of the Soviet Union." Pp. 121–45 in *The Former Soviet Union in Transition*, edited by Richard F. Kaufman and John P. Hardt for the Joint Economic Committee, Congress of the United States. Armonk, NY: M. E. Sharpe.

Shlapentokh, Vladimir. 1982. "The Study of Values as a Social Phenomenon: The Soviet Case." *Social Forces* 61:403–17.

———. 1984. *Love, Marriage, and Friendship in the Soviet Union: Ideals and Practices*. New York: Praeger.

Stark, Rodney, and William Sims Bainbridge. 1996. *A Theory of Religion*. (1st paperback ed.). New Brunswick, NJ: Rutgers University Press.

Tumarkin, Nina. 1994. *The Living and the Dead: The Rise and Fall of the Cult of World War II in Russia*. New York: Basic Books.

Urban, Michael, and Jan Zaprudnik. 1993. "Belarus: A Long Road to Nationhood." Pp. 99–120 in *Nation and Politics in the Soviet Successor States*, edited by Ian Bremmer and Ray Taras. Cambridge, England: Cambridge University Press.

Warner, R. Stephen. 1993. "Work in Progress toward a New Paradigm for the Sociological Study of Religion in the United States." *American Journal of Sociology* 98:1044–93.

Wilson, Bryan. 1985. "Secularization: The Inherited Model." Pp. 9–20 in *The Sacred in a Secular Age: Toward Revision in the Scientific Study of Religion*, edited by Phillip E. Hammond. Berkeley: University of California Press.

Young, Lawrence, ed. 1997. *Rational Choice Theory and Religion: Summary and Assessment*. New York: Routledge.

Zaprudnik, Jan. 1993. *Belarus: At a Crossroads in History*. Boulder, CO: Westview Press.

———. 1994. "Development of Belarusian National Identity and Its Influence on Belarus's Foreign Policy Orientation." Pp. 129–49 in *National Identity and Ethnicity in Russia and the New States of Eurasia*, edited by Roman Szporluk. Armonk, NY: M. E. Sharpe

CHAPTER SEVEN

The State, Religion, and the Family in Indonesia: The Case of Divorce Reform

MARK CAMMACK
LAWRENCE A. YOUNG
TIM B. HEATON

Until comparatively recently, the rate of marital dissolution through divorce among the Muslim populations of Southeast Asia was one of the highest in the world. In the 1950s, the divorce rate for the Muslims of Indonesia and Malaysia was several times higher than the highest rates ever achieved in the United States or any other developed nation. It was also much higher than the divorce rate found in any other Islamic country.

As divorce rates in most of the developed world have risen over the past half century, the rate of marital dissolution in Islamic Southeast Asia has declined dramatically. The upward trend line for "Western" divorce rates crossed the downward trend line for Southeast Asia sometime in the 1970s or 1980s; today, the divorce rates of most Southeast Asian Muslim groups are less than half as high as the highest rates in the industrialized West.

The extraordinarily high rates of divorce that characterized Southeast Asia in the past and the marked decline in the frequency of divorce in recent decades have intrigued and, to some extent, confounded scholars and policy makers alike. In this chapter, we examine one aspect of the divorce phenomenon—the effect of legal restrictions on divorce in reducing its frequency in Indonesia. It has long been assumed that one explanation for the frequency of divorce among Southeast Asian Muslims was the ease with which divorces could be obtained. Under Indonesian law until the mid-1970s, a Muslim husband could divorce his wife at any time for any reason by simply uttering the repudiation formula or *talak*[1]—"I divorce you." In 1974, the Indonesian legislature passed a law restricting the use of the *talak*. Under the statute, which was not actually implemented until mid-1975, a Muslim husband is obliged to obtain judicial approval to divorce, and the repudiation itself must be pronounced in the presence of the court.

The Indonesian government's efforts to curb divorce through law reform raise important questions about the relation between Islam and the state in Indonesia, the world's largest Islamic country. The imposition of restrictions on the Muslim husband's power of unilateral repudiation is, for many Muslims, a matter of utmost significance. The sacred law, or *shariah*, is believed to embody an objective interpretation of the divine revelation as contained in the Koran and the inspired example of the Prophet. Adherence to the law, primarily the rules of ritual practice but also the family law provisions, is regarded as the measure of religious piety. Interference with the terms of the law is seen as threatening religion itself.

Because of the intimate association of law with religious belief and practice in Islam, the Indonesian government's efforts to reduce divorce through legislative restrictions on the *talak* raise profound questions about the boundaries of state and religious authority. One avenue for exploring the tensions inherent in the Indonesian government's attempt to legislate Islamic family law is to investigate how far legislative norms are influencing Muslim behavior. A number of commentators have claimed that the restrictions on divorce in the 1974 legislation have been effective in reducing the rate of divorce. In this chapter, we use the results of a large marriage and family survey conducted in 1993 to evaluate that claim. Our results confirmed the conclusions of other researchers that the frequency of divorce in Indonesia has been declining since the early 1950s. They also showed, however, that the imposition of legal restrictions on divorce in the mid-1970s had no effect on that long-term decline. We conclude that the reason the statute failed to affect divorce behavior is that many Indonesian Muslims continue to regulate their family life on the basis of Islamic legal doctrines, notwithstanding the existence of conflicting state rules. This situation suggests that control over family law continues to be an arena of genuine struggle between Islam and the Indonesian state. Some reasons for the long-term decline in divorce are discussed briefly but are not empirically investigated.

THE PRE-1970S DIVORCE PROBLEM

Southeast Asia's Historically High Divorce Rates

For much of the twentieth century and probably longer, the Muslims of Southeast Asia had the highest recorded rate of marital dissolution through divorce of any major group in the world (Guest 1991:Table 1). In the 1950s, the ratio of divorces to marriages in the same year for Indonesian Muslims ranged around 50 percent (Jones 1994b:Figure 5.1). The general divorce rate—the number of divorces per 1,000 persons aged 15 and over—was 15.1. In contrast, the general divorce rate in the United States in 1950 was 3.5, and the divorce rate in Egypt, the highest among Islamic countries in the Middle East, was 4.8 (Jones 1994b:Table 5.8).

The frequency of divorce among some subgroups was higher still. In the Indonesian province of West Java, the general divorce rate in the mid-1950s was nearly 25 per 1,000 population (Jones 1994b:Table 5.8). Among all Malays in peninsular Malaysia, the general divorce rate for 1950 was 20.3, while the northeast coast state of Kelantan had an astonishing general divorce rate of 43.1 in 1950 (Jones 1994b:Table 5.8) and maintained a ratio of divorces to marriages of 70 percent between 1948 and 1957 (Raybeck 1974:228). By comparison, by 1990, the general divorce rate in the United States, the highest among developed nations, had reached "only" 6.0, less than half the rate among Indonesian Muslims in the 1950s (Jones 1994b:Table 5.8).

Although divorce data for the region before the 1950s are not as precise or comprehensive, all the available information points to the conclusion that high rates of divorce had been prevalent in the region for some time.[2] Census data for Java and the adjacent island of Madura for 1929 through 1931 show a ratio of divorces to marriages of over 50 percent (Prins 1951:290; Vreede-de Stuers 1960:129). On the basis of data from locations in Central Java, Jones (1994b:187) estimated that the ratio of divorces to marriages ranged from 40 percent to 55 percent between 1830 and 1880. More impressionistic information suggests that divorce was common throughout Southeast Asia in earlier periods as well (Reid 1988:152–53).

Explaining Southeast Asian Divorce Rates

Identifying the causes of the high rates of divorce in Southeast Asia has proved difficult, in part because the marriage and family practices in this vast and diverse region largely defy generalization. The variety of kinship structures,[3] patterns of marriage and domestic relations,[4] religious outlooks,[5] and conceptions of gender and gender roles[6] is such that there is little the region has in common that might explain its high divorce rate. Although some analysts have linked frequent divorce with the kinship structure (Tsubouchi 1975) or patterns of family relations (Siegel 1969), these explanations are plainly inadequate, since all three types of kinship organization (bilateral, matrilineal, and patrilineal) and a variety of family patterns are found in the region and a high incidence of divorce is not identified with any one of them. West Sumatra, which has a matrilineal kinship structure, has one of the highest divorce rates in the area. The other regions with similarly high rates—parts of Java and the northeast coast of Malaysia—reckon descent bilaterally and have nuclear households. Specifying the role of religion has proved especially problematic. On the one hand, Christian populations and Hindu Bali have generally lower rates of divorce than do Muslim groups. On the other hand, regional variations in rates of divorce are not correlated with religiosity or the perceived strength of Islam. The northeast coast of Malaysia, which is regarded as the most devoutly Islamic area on the peninsula, also has the highest rates of divorce. In contrast, parts of central and east Java, which are not regarded as deeply Islamicized, also have high divorce rates, whereas other parts of Indonesia, in which the influence of Islam is believed to be strong—Aceh, for example—have comparatively low incidences of divorce. Finally, there are significant and enduring regional differences in rates of divorce that largely defy explanation. For instance, one of the highest divorce regions—

an area on the northwest coast of Java—is abutted on two sides by regions with comparatively low rates.

The number, diversity, and complexity of Southeast Asian cultures cautions against attempts to specify any single regionwide explanation for divorce. Certainly, it seems doubtful that the causes of the high rate of divorce among all Muslim populations of Southeast Asia could be spelled out with a high degree of specificity. On the other hand, the prevalence of frequent divorce across diverse cultures and, even what is more significant, the universal trend toward lower rates of divorce in recent years strongly suggest the existence of some regionwide general attitudes or practices that operate to promote or facilitate divorce.

One factor that is clearly important, but just as clearly not sufficient, as an explanation for the high incidence of divorce is the absence of any legal restraint on husbands' divorcing their wives. Under the rules of Islamic law as practiced in Indonesia, a husband could terminate his marriage by simply reciting the *talak*—"I divorce you."[7] A first or second *talak* exercised against the same wife was revokable for three months, after which it became final. A third *talak* was irrevokable.[8] State law required that the husband's repudiation be registered with the local religious affairs office, but failure to register did not affect the validity of the divorce (Lev 1972).

Although the right of repudiation belonged exclusively to husbands, evidence from various sources suggests that the decision to divorce was, by no means, invariably made by men (Jones 1994b). The grossly unequal legal standing of husbands and wives in Islamic doctrine was not mirrored in actual control over exit from marriage. Approximately one quarter to one third of all *talak* divorces were instigated by wives. Another quarter to one third were based on the desire of both spouses. At most, half the *talak* divorces were on the initiative of the husband alone (H. Geertz 1961:72; Jones, Asari, and Djuartika 1995:402; Lev 1972:147; Nakamura 1983:Table V-2; Siegel 1969:174–75).

A wife who wished to divorce but could not persuade or coerce her husband to repudiate her (or, as was more often the case, who did not know her husband's whereabouts) faced considerably greater expense and inconvenience, but was not without options. The Syafi'i school of Islamic law that was practiced in Indonesia recognized a number of grounds on which a court would dissolve a marriage that basically failed in its essential purpose (Lev 1972).[9] Under standard Syafi'i doctrine, a wife could also buy a divorce from her husband if he agreed to the separation (Lev 1972). In addition to these standard avenues for divorce, Indonesian practice had expanded the divorce options for women beyond what is recognized in the Syafi'i tradition in a number of ways. The most significant development in the divorce law was the use of a suspended repudiation or *taklik talak*—the husband's declaration at the time of the marriage ceremony that a *talak* would automatically ensue upon the occurrence of certain specified events (Lev 1972). In the 1950s, the Department of Religion began printing a standard set of conditions on the back of official marriage certificates, including desertion for more than six months, failure to provide obligatory support for three months, physical maltreatment, or neglect for six months (Lev 1972). Because the terms of the conditional repudiation were subject to the agreement of the spouses, other conditions, such as a promise not to take a second wife, were sometimes included.[10]

The absence of any legal restrictions on husbands divorcing their wives was clearly an important factor in the high incidence of divorce. It was manifestly not the only factor, however, since Muslim men in many other countries had equivalent divorce powers but did not use them with anything like the frequency of Southeast Asians. Also commonly cited as an explanation for the high incidence of divorce is the social and economic position of women. Although its manifestations differed somewhat from culture to culture, a relatively strong and autonomous role for women in the economy and society seems to be a consistent and long-standing feature of Southeast Asian life (Reid 1988:146). Women play an active part in wet-rice agriculture, which is practiced through large parts of the region,[11] and are involved in all types of trade. Women also own and manage property. A common marital property scheme distinguishes between separate property owned prior to marriage or acquired by gift or inheritance and marital property that results from the joint efforts of the husband and wife (ter Haar 1948). Neither spouse has any claim to the separate property of the other in the event of death or divorce; marital property is divided evenly or according to a formula favoring the husband (ter Haar 1948).[12]

The predominant kinship and inheritance schemes also reflect a comparatively strong social and legal position for women. The most common method of tracing descent and inheritance is bilaterally—through both parents. The region is also home to the largest matrilineal group in the world. The most common form of household organization is nuclear or conjugal. There is a preference, much stronger among some groups than others, for married couples to live with or near the wives' families, especially in the early years of marriage. Women participate in, and in some areas dominate, household management and decision making. The domestic pattern in parts of Sumatra and areas of the Malay peninsula is one of male absence and female dominance (Peacock 1973; Siegel 1969). Among several of the region's cultures, women manage their husbands' incomes (Brenner 1995; Hatley 1990; V. Hull 1996; Keeler 1987; Papanek and Schwede 1988; Peletz 1988; Rabeck 1974), although it should be emphasized that control over money is not necessarily associated with social power or prestige.[13]

Another circumstance that evidently contributed to the high rate of divorce, at least in some areas, is the preference for early, parentally arranged marriage. Although the marriage age for girls was relatively young throughout the region, early marriage, often at or before puberty, was particularly common among the Javanese (H. Geertz 1961),[14] who occupy the eastern two thirds of the island of Java; the Sundanese, who occupy the western third of Java (McDonald and Abdurahman 1974); and the Malay population of the state of Kalanten on the northeast coast of Malaysia (Firth 1966).[15]

These groups also had some of the highest divorce rates in the region (Jones 1994b). An analysis of survey data confirmed a strong correlation between age at marriage and the probability of divorce (Guest 1991).

Early marriage is often associated with parental arrangement of marriage, a practice that is widespread in the region. An analysis of survey data identified a link between the arrangement of marriages and the probability of divorce when age at marriage was controlled (Jones 1994b).

Thus, although generalization about the causes of divorce in Southeast Asia invariably obscures a great deal of diversity and complexity, the high rates of divorce that characterized many Southeast Asian Muslim populations appear to have resulted from a variable mix of structural and normative factors. The comparatively strong social and economic standing of women, more pronounced in some regions than others, and the ready availability of divorce through the use of the *talak* were clearly important factors. In addition, popular attitudes about marriage and divorce contributed to the high rate of marital disruption among some groups. Malay marriages were, as one observer put it, "normatively unstable" (Wilder 1982:70). It was more or less taken for granted that "a couple of false starts followed by a permanent choice" was nothing out of the ordinary (Firth 1966:44). Similar attitudes prevailed in much of Java. Throughout much of Muslim Southeast Asia, divorce was not associated with deviance or moral failure, despite the condemnation of divorce in Islamic morals as sinful. Indeed, among some elements of the matrilineal Minangkabau of West Sumatra, who by some accounts had the highest divorce rate of any group in Indonesia, a man who had only one wife was ridiculed as having been "used up by one woman" (Al Hadar 1977:26). A record of frequent marriages and divorces for a woman in West Java was regarded as proof of her sexual attractiveness (Grijns 1987).

LEGISLATING MARITAL STABILITY

The Southeast Asian case illustrates that judgments about whether divorce is socially good or bad or how much divorce is "too much" are problematic. On the one hand, for many young Southeast Asian girls, easy divorce was a welcome antidote to the practice of nonconsensual child marriage. Many of the divorces in the region occurred in marriages of relatively short duration, some that were not even marriages in any but a technical legal sense. According to various studies, as many as 50 percent of the divorces were to marriages that did not produce children (Jones 1994b:235). Women initiated or acquiesced in a large percentage of divorces. On the other hand, frequent divorces undoubtedly took a toll on many women and children. Although most occupations were open to women and divorced wives could usually find a way to support themselves, the lot of a single mother in a country of widespread poverty was certainly not easy (Jones 1994b).

Early Efforts to Reform the Marriage Law

The high rate of divorce in Southeast Asia has long been regarded as a serious social problem, especially as it affects women (Prins 1951). Concern about divorce, child marriage, and polygamy, voiced most consistently by an energetic and well-organized women's movement (Vreede-de Stuers 1960), produced a more or less steady stream of marriage-reform initiatives that continued for nearly half a century. All the efforts to tackle Indonesia's high rate of divorce through law reform, including, we argue, the 1974 Marriage Act, have foundered on Muslim opposition to any legislative interference with the content of Islamic divorce rules.

The first serious effort to introduce legislative reforms of Indonesian family law was a Dutch initiative put forward as part of a broader reorganization of Islamic legal institutions in the 1930s (Benda 1958; Prins 1951; Vreede-de Stuers 1960). Both the aims and the fate of this early proposal were largely typical of later Indonesian efforts as well. The draft would have established a voluntary registration procedure granting protection against arbitrary divorce and polygamy to wives whose marriages had been registered. It provided that a marriage that had been registered could not be dissolved through the husband's unilateral repudiation, but was terminable only by means of judicial decree based on specified legal grounds. The proposal also included provisions regulating the consequences of divorce (Prins 1951; Vreede-de Stuers 1960).

For reasons that are not entirely clear, the Dutch submitted their marriage reform proposal to various Indonesian organizations for comment and received a heavily negative reaction. Some women's groups supported the measure, but Muslim organizations, both traditionalist and reformist, opposed it as an improper interference with the sacred religious law. The measure was also opposed by the major nationalist parties, who regarded it as an illegitimate intrusion by the Dutch into native affairs (Benda 1958; Prins 1951; Vreede-de Stuers 1960). In the face of such seemingly broad opposition, the proposal was abandoned.

Attempts to reform the law of marriage and divorce in independent Indonesia—independence came in 1945—faced the same problem of Muslim opposition that had doomed the Dutch efforts.[16] Moreover, in addition to the widespread popular opposition to governmental interference with Islamic rules, the government itself was divided, if not on the broad question of the desirability of marriage law reform, certainly over the form that any marriage legislation should take. One critical point of division was between the Ministries (later "Departments") of Religion and Justice (Lev 1972). The Ministry of Religion, which assumed primary responsibility for the day-to-day administration of Muslim marriages and the Islamic courts, was controlled by religious leaders who were sensitive to Muslim objections to changing the substance of Islamic rules.[17] The Ministry of Justice, which administered the civil courts and presumed broad authority over the course of legal change in general, was dominated by lawyers who were trained in the civil law tradition and favored more fundamental change based on civil law models. This difference in outlook impeded efforts to change the marriage law throughout the course of Indonesian history.

The first attempt to change the marriage law, undertaken early in the life of the new state, reflected the cautious approach of the Ministry of Religion. Law No. 22 of 1946 required that all Muslim marriages and divorces be registered with local religious affairs offices (Lev 1972). The failure to register was punishable with a small civil fine, but did not affect the validity of the marriage or divorce (Lev 1972). A Ministerial Instruction promulgated the following year advised marriage registrars to counsel men against repudiating their wives and to urge them to reconcile if they had already done so (Vreede-de Stuers 1960). Neither the statute nor the Ministerial Instruction addressed the substance of Indonesian marriage law, which was simply assumed to be governed by Islamic rules.

Over the ensuing two decades, reform of the marriage law was more or less constantly on the agenda but never actually acted on (Soewondo 1977). At the instance of women's organizations, a commission was established in 1950 to study the issue of matrimonial law and make recommendations for legislation (Vreede- de Stuers 1960). A number of drafts were produced, but none received serious legislative consideration. The ostensible reason for the failure to act was disagreement over whether there should be one set of marriage law rules applicable to all Indonesians, the approach favored by women's groups and Christian interests, or separate regulations for different groups, as the Muslims demanded (Soewondo 1977). This disagreement was rooted in the more fundamental difference between the Muslims' insistence that the divine law could not be reworked by mundane legislators and the view of women's organizations and others that the terms of Muslim law were precisely what needed changing.

Some effort was made to reduce the frequency of divorce and enhance the legal position of women without changing the law. In the mid-1950s, marriage counseling boards were established first in Jakarta and Bandung and then gradually throughout much of the country (Lev 1972; Vreede-de Stuers 1960).[18] The Department of Religion instructed marriage registrars to refer couples who were contemplating divorce to the local boards for counseling (Lev 1972). The boards, consisting of prominent men and women from the community, would attempt to identify each couple's problem and bring about a reconciliation. On a different front, the Department of Religion acted to make divorce more readily available to wives who had been deserted, neglected, or mistreated by printing a standardized version of the conditional repudiation formula on the back of official marriage certificates (Lev 1972; Vreede-de Stuers 1960).

Marriage Law Reform in the New Order

In the mid-1960s, President Sukarno, who had led Indonesia since independence, was replaced as head of state by General Suharto.[19] Suharto ruled Indonesia for more than thirty years until student-led social unrest in May 1998 forced him to cede power to his Vice President, B. J. Habibie.

Once it had consolidated control in the early 1970s, Suharto's self-styled "New Order" government established a dramatically different leadership style and inaugurated a different set of priorities from what had preceded it. The revolutionary ethos that had characterized the Sukarno era gave way to a more low-key bureaucratic mentality that was committed to establishing order, stability, and control. The earlier emphasis on nation building was replaced by a dedication to consolidating the power of the state (Anderson 1983). Although the vaguely defined objective of achieving modernity had been a shared ideal of all Indonesian political leaders, that goal acquired a new emphasis and meaning after 1965 (McVey 1996). Under Sukarno, the accent had shifted from elite conceptions of Indonesian nationalism to more popular versions emphasizing revolutionary as opposed to bureaucratic values. In the New Order, the emphasis on modernization as the essence of Indonesian nationalism was revived (McVey 1996). Development, primarily economic but also social,[20] became the paramount goal and the asserted justification for rule.

In line with its emphasis on development, the New Order assigned a higher priority to family policy than had the Old. This change was manifest most clearly in an aggressive and successful family planning program begun in 1968[21] and a commitment to reforming family law that was adequate to ensure its passage (Vreede-de Stuers 1974). Along with more action, family policy was also given a new direction (Blackwood 1995; Guinness 1994; Hatley 1990; Lev 1996). The Indonesian political leadership, during the first two decades after independence, was committed, if not to gender equality, at least to some degree of gender equalization (Lev 1996). The New Order leaders espoused, at least in their official rhetoric, a gender ideology that relegates women to the private, "noneconomic" domestic realm (Blackwood 1995). The Suharto regime's vision of a modern society was built on an image of stable nuclear households in which men function as providers and wives manage domestic affairs.[22]

A desire to restructure society in line with its conception of the conditions for economic and social development was part of the impetus for the government's aggressive support for reforming the family law in the early 1970s. An equally if not more prominent purpose was political (Cammack 1997). Although Muslim interests provided critical support in the anticommunist purges that brought the government to power, once in control, the regime set about to neutralize Islam as a basis for political mobilization (McVey 1983).[23] And while Islamic courts and family law doctrine hardly posed a political threat, they were symbolic of Muslim strength among the populace. Replacing Islamic family law rules with positive state legislation would serve as a potent symbolic vindication of the state's authority over Indonesian society.

The first initiative to change the marriage law in the post-1965 era was essentially a replay of earlier unsuccessful efforts. Legislation was introduced in 1967 and 1968 that would have recognized distinct marital regimes for different religious groups, but the effort foundered on objections from Catholic interests (*Tempo* 1973a, 1973d). A much more serious effort was mounted in 1973, after the government had scored a decisive electoral victory in 1971. The 1973 proposal was sponsored in the legislature by the Minister of Justice (*Tempo* 1973b). Islamic leaders were not consulted on the terms of the proposal, and the Department of Religion played only a minor role in its preparation (Suryadinata 1989; *Tempo* 1973c). Both the impetus for the proposal and the terms of the draft were apparently the work of an inner circle of informal but powerful presidential advisers who were bent on neutralizing political Islam (Crouch 1978; Suryadinata 1989).

The 1974 National Marriage Act

The draft national marriage law that was introduced in 1973 reflected both the government's agenda for social change and its political purpose of expressing the subordination of Islam to state authority.[24] It described marriage as "a spiritual and physical union between a man and a woman with the objective of creating a happy and everlasting family (household) based on the one God,"[25] and stated that husbands and wives bear the responsibility of building homes to become the foundation of society (Article 32). The rights and standing of wives were declared to be "equivalent" (*seimbang*) to the rights and standing of husbands, both within the home and in the larger society (Article 33[1]). The respective duties of husbands and wives were defined differently. Husbands were obliged to protect their wives and provide for all the needs of the home according to their ability (Article 36[1]); wives were obliged to manage well the affairs of the home (Article 36[3]).

The draft would have made civil registration a requirement for a valid marriage (Article 2[1]). It stated that marriage must be based on the consent of the parties (Article 6[1]) and prescribed minimum marriage ages of 21 for men and 18 for women (Article 7[1]). Although marriage was declared to be monogamous "in principle," the statute authorized husbands to marry multiple wives with the permission of a civil court upon satisfaction of statutory criteria (Article 4). The bill stated that a marriage was dissolved as a result of death, divorce, or the unexplained absence of either spouse for two years (Article 40[1]). It clearly intended that a divorce could be effected only by a judicial order of divorce; the draft required that a request for divorce had to be filed in court and contained an exhaustive list of legal grounds for divorce (Article 41).

Islamic organizations, both traditionalist and reformist, and a wide spectrum of Islamic leaders expressed angry opposition to the proposal.[26] They complained that they had been excluded from the preparation of the bill, denounced various provisions as contrary to Islamic law, and accused the government of being party to a strategy of covert Christianization (*Tempo* 1973c). They specifically objected to the requirement of registration for marriage, provisions recognizing adoption, a provision stating that differences in religion are not an impediment to marriage, and several others (Hassan 1980; *Tempo* 1973e). Except for an article granting the court the power to require divorced husbands to support their former wives, the divorce provisions of the draft were not specifically objected to, though the substantial changes made to the divorce rules in the revised bill that was eventually enacted suggest that the decision not to take public issue with the divorce provisions was largely tactical.

The vehemence of Muslim opposition to the proposal persuaded the government of the necessity for compromise. Military officers initiated negotiations over the proposal with Islamic leaders outside the formal legislative process (Crouch 1978; Suryadinata 1989; *Tempo* 1973g), and the outlines for a compromise statute were agreed upon (Katz and Katz 1975; *Tempo* 1973h).[27] The terms of the agreement were incorporated into a revised version of the bill, which was then rushed through the legislature to be ready for enactment on Indonesian mothers' day (*Tempo* 1973i).[28]

The treatment of divorce was a principal focus of concern in the negotiations over the government's proposal. One of the conditions demanded by the government and agreed to by the representatives of Muslim interests was the need for "regulations to prevent arbitrary divorce." For its part, the military agreed that Islamic marriage law would not be diminished or changed and that all matters contrary to Islamic law would be removed from the draft (*Tempo* 1973h). On its face, it is not apparent how these two conditions could both be accommodated. How, that is, could the statute restrict arbitrary divorce, which Islamic law permits, and not infringe on Islamic law?

The answer is not apparent in the terms of the statute. Under the heading "Dissolution of Marriage and its Consequences," the statute states that "marriage can be dissolved because of a) death; b) divorce or c) on the decision of the court."[29] The next article provides that "divorce can only be carried out in the presence of the Court" (Article 39[1]); that "to carry out divorce there must be adequate reason why the husband and wife can no longer live together in harmony" (Article 39[2]); and that procedures for divorce carried out in the presence of the court would be spelled out in separate implementing regulations (Article 39[3]). The next article states that "divorce complaints shall be filed with the Court" and that the procedures for such complaints would be included in separate regulations (Article 40).

The meaning of these vague provisions became apparent only after the implementing regulations were promulgated—more than a year and a half after the statute was passed.[30] It seems likely, however, that the terms of the implementing regulations were understood and agreed upon by the principals at the time the statute was enacted. Furthermore, the divorce scheme contained in the implementing regulations is similar to the provisions of the Muslim-backed proposal that failed to win approval in 1968, which suggests that Muslim interests gave up little in their negotiations with the government.

The regulations, as interpreted by the courts, establish two separate divorce procedures, one that is available only to men who were married according to Islamic law and a second for the use of all others. Under the first procedure, which we call a "petition divorce," a Muslim husband "who is going to divorce his wife, must file a petition with the court where he resides, containing a statement of his intention to divorce his wife, accompanied by his reasons, together with a request that the court convene for such purpose" (Article 14). The court is instructed to examine the petition and to convene to witness the divorce only if it finds that one of six grounds for divorce are satisfied and it is of the opinion that the couple can no longer live in harmony as husband and wife (Articles 15, 16). The divorce is deemed valid from the date it is "expressed" in court (Article 18) and is evidenced by a "Certificate Concerning the Occurrence of Divorce" (Article 17). Although the word appears only once—in the official elucidation to the regulation—it is apparent that the procedure contemplated by the statute and the regulation is a court-supervised *talak*.

The second procedure establishes a contentious divorce action, including provisions for notice and opportunity to be heard (Articles 20–34). Divorce is available under this "complaint" procedure on the basis of the same six grounds required for a petition divorce. The regulations provide that the court's "decision regarding the divorce complaint is to be pronounced in open court" (Article 34[1]) and state that the divorce is deemed effective upon the issuance of the court's decision (Article 34[2]).

DECLINING DIVORCE RATES

Law Reform and Divorce Behavior

The frequency of divorce began to decline in Indonesia well before the legal restrictions on divorce in the 1974 marriage law were implemented. Although the onset of the decline cannot be specified with precision and the trend doubtless began at different times in different parts of the country, the rate of divorce for the Muslim population as a whole was clearly declining by the early or mid-1950s. Using official records of the number of divorces registered annually, Jones (1994b: Table 5.8) showed that the general divorce rate for all Indonesian Muslims fell from 16.7 in 1955 to 1.1 in 1990. The ratio of divorces to marriages also declined precipitously—from around 50 percent in the early 1950s to less than 10 percent in the 1990s (Jones 1994b: Figure 5.1). Our analysis of survey data from *The 1993 Indonesian Family Life Survey* (IFLS)[31] revealed comparable changes. We used event-history methodology (Heaton and Call 1995) to convert the reported beginning and ending of marriages into a year-by-year record of the number of people who were married and divorced in any given year, from which we could calculate the probability of marital disruption in any given year. Between 1950 and 1990, the probability of divorce fell from about 5 percent to about .5 percent, a tenfold decrease, which is roughly comparable to the decrease in the general divorce rate.

It is apparent from the timing of the onset of the trend in declining divorce rates that the marriage law could not be the sole or precipitating factor in the change in divorce behavior. On any measure of divorce and regardless of the data source used, by 1975, when the new restrictions on the *talak* went into effect, dramatic reductions in the rate of divorce had already taken place. According to Jones's (1994b:Table 5.8) calculations based on governmental records, the divorce rate had declined to 4.6 per 1,000 by 1975, less than one third its 1950s level. Our analysis of the IFLS survey data revealed a probability of divorce slightly above 1 percent, also less than a third of the probability in 1950. All agree that the enactment of legal restrictions on the availability of divorce at most accelerated a trend that was already well under way.

Although it is clear that factors other than the marriage law contributed to the changes in divorce behavior, a number of analysts claim to have identified a link between the enactment of legal restrictions on divorce and declining rates of marital disruption. On the basis of an analysis of official court records, Jones (1994b:259) has concluded that legal restrictions on divorce "played an important role in strengthening a trend that was clearly already established."[32] Another less systematic analysis that was based on national statistics cross checked with local records claimed to have identified a 70 percent reduction in the divorce rate following the implementation of the statute (Katz and Katz 1978:310). The most in-depth evaluation of the effect of the marriage law on divorce behavior was a study by Jones et al. (1995) that focused on West Java. On the basis of registered marriages and divorces, the authors found a sharp drop in the frequency of divorce in 1976, the first year after the law went into effect. The decline in 1976 was preceded and followed by much smaller increases in divorce, presumably short-term effects of the law. On this basis, Jones et al. cautiously concluded that the law affected the rate of divorce to some extent. In addition to these systematic studies, it has been widely assumed that the Marriage Act has successfully inhibited divorce (Goode 1993; Hugo, Hull, Hull, and Jones 1987; McNicoll and Singarimbun 1986).

Newly available data call into question the conclusion that the Marriage Act has reduced the divorce rate. To evaluate the impact of the law on the long-term trend toward lower divorce rates, we plotted the probability of divorce since 1948 using data from the IFLS (Frankenberg and Karoly 1995). The IFLS was based on interviews with a probability sample of 7,224 households spread across thirteen provinces on the islands of Java, Sumatra, Bali, Kalimantan, Sulawesi, and West Nusa Tenggara. The sample covered approximately 83 percent of the Indonesian population. The survey included information on fertility, marriage, health, education, migration, and employment. Marital disruption was determined by reported years when marriages began and ended and the reasons for termination. Marriages that ended because of the death of either spouse were not considered because of our focus on divorce.

Figure 7.1 shows the trend in marital disruption since 1948. The probabilities were averaged over three-year periods to eliminate some of the random fluctuation caused by sampling error, although some of the variation is still likely caused by sampling error. Despite this variation, there was a clear and persistent decline in marital disruption throughout this period. The decline appears somewhat steeper before the mid-1960s, but the trend does not appear to differ before and after the implementation of the marriage law.

Table 7.1 reports the results of various logistic regression models predicting the marital disruption rate. The first model fits a linear trend. The coefficient for year indicates that the rate has declined by nearly 7 percent per year. The two subsequent models fit a quadratic trend (a term for year squared is added) and a logistic trend (the natural logarithm of year is used). Although either of these two models would account for the nonlinear trend in theory, the statistical fit, as judged by the χ^2 statistic, is not better in these two alternative models. In the second set of estimates, an additional variable is included that is coded 0 before the implementation of the law (1975 or earlier) and 1 after 1975. The coefficient for this variable (law) shows the average difference in divorce before and after the law passed after the long-term trend has been taken into account and indicates that disruption rates were actually higher after the implementation of the law in the linear model. This could be an artifact of the nonlinear trend, however. In the quadratic

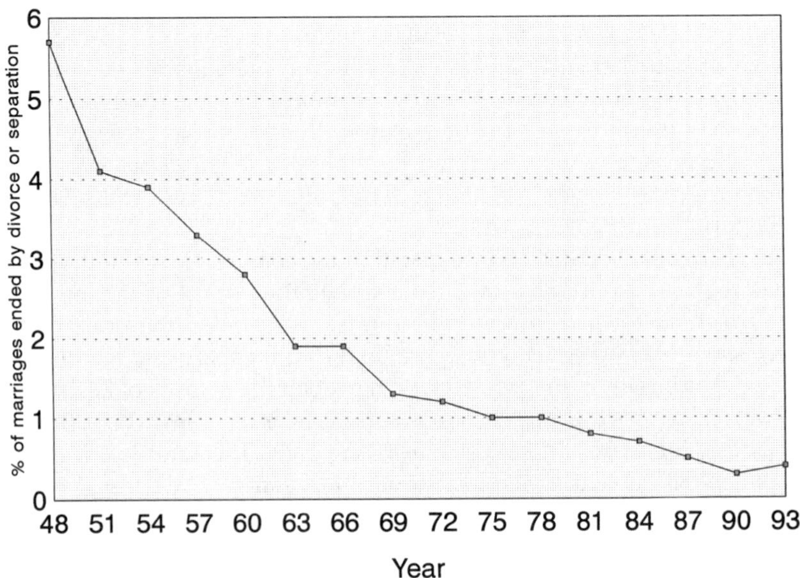

Figure 7.1. Trend in Martial Disruption. *Source:* 1993 Indonesia Family Life Survey.

Table 7.1
LOGISTIC REGRESSION MODELS SHOWING THE TREND IN MARITAL DISRUPTION AND THE IMPACT OF THE 1974 MARRIAGE LAW

	Functional Form of Trend		
Trend	Linear	Quadratic	Logistic
1. Yearly trend			
Year	−.067*	−.071*	−4.715*
Year squared	—	.00003	—
Model χ^2	1278.5	1278.6	1272.6
2. Yearly trend and law			
Year	−.071*	−.063*	−4.733*
Year squared	—	−.00006	—
Law	.119	.128	.007
Model χ^2	1280.9	1281.0	1272.7
3. Yearly trend, law, and change in trend after the law			
Year	−.070*	−.084	−4.421*
Year squared	—	.0001	—
Law	.389	.835	1.664*
Law x year	−.004	−.010	−.021*
Model χ^2	1281.1	1281.2	1281.5

* Statistically significant at the .05 level.

model, the coefficient for law is also positive, but in the logistic model, the effect is virtually zero. In no model is the coefficient for law statistically significant. In other words, the change after the law could easily be an artifact of fluctuation that is due to sampling. In any event, there is no indication that implementation of the law reduced the divorce rate.

The third set of models tests whether the trajectory of the divorce rate shifted after the implementation of the law. For example, if implementation took several years, such that the effect became more obvious in subsequent years, then we would observe a change in the slope of the line after 1975. The interaction term modeling this change in trajectory (the product of law and year) is not large or statistically significant in two of the three models. In the third model, the interaction is statistically significant but very small relative to the secular decline (−.021 compared to −4.421), indicating that the slope did not change appreciably after the law was passed.

To determine whether the statute may have had an effect in some regions but not in others and possible differences between urban and rural areas, we estimated the simple form of the model with linear decline and a possible shift after the implementation of the law for major regions and for rural and urban areas (see Table 7.2). The decline appears to have been somewhat steeper in Sumatra, West Java, and Central Java than in East Java and outlying islands. The decline was nearly equivalent in rural and urban areas. In some regions the coefficient for law is positive, and in other regions

Table 7.2
LOGISTIC REGRESSION MODELS SHOWING THE TREND IN MARITAL DISRUPTION BY REGION AND URBANIZATION

Region and Urbanization	Yearly Trend	Before and After Implementation of the Law
Region		
Sumatra	−.084*	.401
Jakarta	−.075*	.095
West Java	−.073*	.144
Central Java	−.083*	.096
East Java	−.058*	−.034
Other islands	−.054*	−.133
Urbanization		
Urban	−.067*	.008
Rural	−.073*	.164

* Statistically significant at the .05 level.

it is negative, *but in no case is the effect of the law statistically significant*. In other words, chance variations that were due to sampling most likely produced the results. The analysis of the IFLS data indicated that the implementation of the law had no statistically measurable impact on divorce trends, which calls into question the conclusions of most scholars who previously commented on the law's impact.

Why the Law Did Not Affect Divorce Behavior

In explaining the discrepancy between our findings and the results of earlier research, we note that the most conspicuous difference was our use of a different data source. We relied on self-reports of marital history, whereas the studies that concluded that the divorce rate declined following the implementation of the law relied on records of officially recognized divorces. The fact that the two measures of the divorce rate do not coincide indicates that some people divorced (or, more precisely, regarded themselves as having divorced) without having complied with state-prescribed procedures. For that to be the case, some of those who considered themselves divorced must have accepted criteria for "divorce" other than those specified by state marriage rules.

Although the matter cannot be demonstrated conclusively, it appears that the enactment of legal restrictions on divorce did not affect the rate of marital disruption because Islamic legal definitions of divorce continued to govern the marriage behavior of a significant part of the population after the law was passed. In other words, a portion of the Muslim community continued to regard the Islamic *talak* as efficacious after the 1974 Marriage Act was enacted and used the *talak* to dissolve their marriages without first obtaining judicial approval.[33] One indication that they did so is that the Marriage Act itself supports the view that unauthorized *talak* are nonetheless legally valid. As we explained earlier, the divorce provisions of the statute applicable to Muslim men established a procedure for a court-sanctioned *talak* divorce. The statute's implementing regulations require a court's authorization based on a finding of legal grounds before a husband may repudiate his wife. The divorce itself, however, is effected not by the court's action, but by the husband's pronouncement of the Islamic repudiation formula. Neither the statute nor the more detailed regulations state that a *talak* pronounced outside a court and without judicial approval is invalid.

The view that the statute requires court approval to divorce but does not affect the validity of *talak* pronounced extra-judicially is consistent with the understanding of the drafters of the law that it did not change Islamic doctrine. It also conforms with widely held views about the immutability of Islamic rules and the proper role of the state in the administration of Islamic law. Islamic jurisprudence regards the terms of the law as an expression of God's will and therefore sacrosanct.[34] Legal theory, however, has long recognized the power of governments to institute procedures for the enforcement of the divine law (Coulson 1964). From the perspective of Islamic legal theory, an attempt to invalidate the *talak* legislatively would be wholly ineffectual, but it is entirely within the state's power to institute procedures that are designed to discourage men from making use of their power to repudiate their wives, a goal that is also consonant with Islam's negative moral evaluation of divorce.[35] On this view, the divorce provisions of the Marriage Act do not address the validity of the *talak*, but are designed to regulate its use (Cammack 1989). A *talak* pronounced in violation of the statute is therefore unauthorized and illegal but nonetheless effective.

There is no direct evidence that the belief in the continued validity of extra-judicial *talak* is widespread. However, the discrepancy between official and self-reported rates of divorce is, of course, telling indirect evidence of such a view. In addition, the media periodically report the activities of religious leaders who preside over unauthorized marriages and divorces,[36] women's advice columns in magazines periodically offer advice to women who have been divorced extra-judicially (Woodcroft-Lee 1983), and we encountered state marriage registrars who insisted that court action was not necessary for divorce. Moreover, Islamic courts, the institutions charged with enforcing the Marriage Act for Muslims, routinely ratified *talak* divorces performed outside the courtroom,[37] although that practice may be changing in the face of an aggressive campaign by the Department of Religion and Supreme Court to treat unauthorized *talak* as nonbinding (Cammack 1997). The most definitive evidence of the continued belief in the validity of extra-judicial *talak* is the fact that the Nahdlatul Ulama (NU), the country's largest Islamic organization with some 30 million members, issued an opinion in 1989 upholding the efficacy of noncomplying divorces (Masyuri 1997). The NU has a broad influence over Muslim education and Islamic doctrine. Furthermore, popular opinion among NU members is likely to be more conservative than the formally stated position of the leadership. Thus, the organization's official declaration that a *talak* pronounced outside a court shall nonetheless be counted as valid is convincing confirmation that local religious leaders and ordinary Muslims do not regard official divorce processes as necessary to terminate their marriages.

DISCUSSION

Our analysis of marital history survey data demonstrates that the imposition of legal restrictions on the availability of divorce did not affect the rate of marital disruption among Indonesian Muslims. A comparison of the survey results with official divorce records shows that the statute did not affect behavior because Indonesian Muslims elevate religious criteria for marriage and divorce over legal definitions that have their source in the state. Indonesian Muslims continue to regard themselves as "divorced" as long as Islamic formalities have been satisfied, regardless of whether they are divorced in the eyes of the state.

The fact that the statute failed to reduce the divorce rate and, more particularly, the *reason* for that failure, provide convincing confirmation of our argument in an earlier article on child marriage rules (Cammack, Young, and Heaton 1996) that marriage legislation has not affected behavior because Indonesian Muslims attach more significance to Islamic criteria for the existence of family relationships than to state-based legal rules. It has been a central assumption of all of Indonesia's leaders that the state has a monopoly over the exercise of public power. In this view, law comes exclusively from the legislative machinery of the government. Part of the government's project in pushing for national matrimonial legislation was to "Indonesianize" the law and vindicate the state's monopoly over lawmaking. Although the state is gradually succeeding in its efforts to impose new conceptions of the family that are consistent with its vision of social and economic development, the fact that many Indonesian Muslims continue to regard themselves as divorced because they have complied with Islamic doctrine as it is conventionally understood, shows that the state has not yet succeeded in establishing its authority as the source of social and legal meanings. Many Muslims continue to regard the regulation of family life as a matter of religious faith that is not subject to temporal intervention. The sacred law comes into force by virtue of its divine ordination and is not dependent on the state's recognition for its validity.

In previous articles (Cammack 1997; Cammack et al. 1996), we described the process by which the Indonesian state is seeking to overcome resistance to its marriage-reform initiatives by attempting to establish its authority over family law. The details of that discussion need not be repeated here. Essentially, the government is attempting to transcend the conflict between state and Islamic lawmaking by arrogating for itself the power to declare Islamic law. Under a revisionist interpretation of the National Marriage Act promoted by the Supreme Court and the Department of Religion, an extra-judicial *talak* that does not comply with state-ordained procedures is ineffective not because it violates state rules, but because compliance with statutory procedures mandating judicial supervision and court approval to divorce is a requirement of Islam. A noncomplying *talak*, therefore, is ineffective under Islamic law.

The prospects for asserting that state's authority over divorce are, in one respect, more favorable than the prospects for imposing effective regulation over marriage. It seems likely that the Islamic courts will acquire greater control over divorce as Indonesians increasingly turn to the courts to resolve disputes that arise as a result of the dissolution of their marriages. The drafters of the 1974 National Marriage Act were concerned almost exclusively with preventing divorce, not with regulating it.[38] Little attention was given to arranging the consequences of divorce: assignment of rights and responsibilities over children, disposition of property claimed by both spouses, and continuing financial obligations between the spouses after a divorce. In most of the developed world, in contrast, the emphasis is reversed. Partly out of recognition of the futility of legislating intimate relationships,[39] the trend in the developed world over the past century has been to shift attention away from prescribing when a couple may dissolve their marriage and to focus governmental efforts on regulating divorce when it occurs.[40] In the past in Indonesia, issues of child custody, the division of property, and spousal support were generally resolved without formal state intervention. As the country becomes more prosperous, property disputes at the time of divorce will doubtless become more common. At the same time, informal mechanisms for arranging the consequences of divorce are likely to become less effective and formal legal rules and procedures more salient. As divorce becomes increasingly judicialized and the courts come to be seen as the forums for sorting out issues arising from the termination of marriage, the courts and the state under which they operate will also presumably become identified as the authority capable of dissolving marriage.

An analysis of the factors that are actually driving the long-term trend toward more stable marriages in Indonesia is beyond the scope of this chapter but will be taken up in a separate study. In connection with the present argument, we note only that the survey data do not support the theory most often used to explain changing marriage and divorce behavior—that the changes in family life result from the social and ideational transformations associated with the impersonal forces of industrialization and urbanization (Jones 1997). A comparison of the trend in divorce with the timing of economic change does not support a conclusion that the forces of economic transformation are driving the move toward lower divorce rates. Although Indonesia has experienced dramatic social and economic transformations in recent years, most of the decline in divorce occurred well *before* real economic change had set in. The divorce rate declined sharply from the late 1940s through the late 1960s. During that period, the probability of marital disruption fell from nearly 6 percent to just over 1 percent. After the late 1960s, the rate of divorce continued to decline, but much more slowly. Between 1969 and 1990, the probability of divorce declined by an additional 1 percent. Significant economic change, in contrast, began to occur only in the late 1960s and early 1970s with the reforms inaugurated by the Suharto government.[41] Indeed, based on the timing of the two trends alone, it appears that economic changes are generating pressure for more, rather than less, divorce, since the period of greatest economic change is associated with a leveling off of the long-term decline in divorce rates.[42]

Although economic change does not appear to be driving the trend toward more stable marriages, the possibility remains that economic developments have contributed to the trend by undermining the arrangements that supported the practice of frequent divorce (Goode 1993). Expanding education has no doubt also played a role in inculcating new ideas about marriage and the family.[43] However, the explanation for changing divorce patterns that accords best with the timing of the trends in marital disruption focuses not on social or economic changes but on developments in the political realm. It has been suggested that nationalist and revolutionary ideals and the general sense of social and cultural upheaval that accompanied independence affected personal life as well (T. Hull and Singarimbun 1989; McDonald and Abdurahman 1974). The timing of the onset of declining divorce rates supports the conclusion that the "cognitive restructuring" (Glendon 1989:194) that has occurred around Indonesian family life over the past half century is, to a significant extent, an adjunct of the larger project of Indonesian nationalism, which has always been understood as a rejection of the "feudal" past in favor of a "modern" future (McVey 1996). Thus, although the enactment of legal reforms that were designed to make the dissolution of marriage more difficult did not affect the rate of divorce, we suspect that both an official rhetoric idealizing stable families as the foundation of a prosperous society and conscious state policies to discourage divorce are helping anchor Indonesian marriages in an emergent Indonesian family ideology.

CONCLUSION

Our finding that legal restrictions on the Islamic *talak* did not affect the rate of marital disruption through divorce is consistent with the results of our previous research on minimum marriage-age legislation, in which we found that the implementation of statutory minimum marriage ages of 19 for boys and 16 for girls had no direct effect on the rate of underage marriage by girls (Cammack et al. 1996). Research on the impact of legal change on divorce rates in other settings has yielded somewhat more positive assessments, although the results have not always been clear. Contrary to early research (see Jacobs 1988 citing studies) concluding that the liberalization of divorce laws in the United States did *not* affect the divorce rate, recent empirical studies (Marvell 1989; Nakonezny, Shull, and Rodgers 1995) concluded that legal restrictions on divorce did inhibit divorce to some extent in some states.

Likewise, a study of the effect of stricter divorce laws in Germany (Glass, Tiao, and Maguire 1971) found a decline in the frequency of divorce associated with the implementation of the law. Our analysis of the reasons for the failure of the Indonesian statute suggests that the critical variable in the Indonesian case is the relative strength of religion in relation to the state. It is not simply that religious commitments influence divorce behavior. The failure of the statute to affect the divorce rate is rooted in the fact that many Indonesians elevate Islamic definitions of divorce over criteria whose source is in state law.

Although we conclude that the Indonesian Marriage Act was ineffective as a coercive mechanism for controlling divorce behavior, our analysis generally affirms the power of the state to shape intimate aspects of everyday life. Divorce rates have declined dramatically over the past half century. Although their decline may be attributable partly to the deterministic forces of social and economic change that resulted from the integration of Indonesia into the capitalist world economy, we suspect that the "divorce revolution" in Southeast Asia is also partly the result of conscious state policies and ideologies that idealize stable families and a gender-based division of the social world into a male-dominated public sphere and a female-dominated private realm. To be sure, state policies succeeded because they were aligned with the forces of social and economic change and because they built on family and gender ideologies that were present in the culture. Moreover, the role of legislation in transforming gender and family ideologies was probably minor compared to other influences. The insight that law is not simply regulatory but constitutive of social relations is now widely accepted (C. Geertz 1983). However, the content of national legal norms is far removed from the day-to-day experiences of most Indonesians; the ideological message of law codes never reaches most people and does not much interest most of those it does reach. Education, through which the state is able to impinge on the awareness of its citizenry much more directly and profoundly, is clearly a much more effective way of shaping the national consciousness than is legislation. All these issues will be explained in greater detail in a companion piece to this chapter.

Finally, an important question raised but not resolved by our research is whether the reform of the Indonesian family law has worked to the benefit or detriment of women. Much of the impetus for changes in the law came from women's groups who were anxious to ameliorate the grossly unequal treatment of men and women under Islamic doctrine. On a symbolic level at least, the 1974 Marriage Act represents a clear advance for women. The revocation of Muslim husbands' legal authority arbitrarily to divorce their wives is a significant statement in favor of more equal treatment of men and women. At the same time that the government has pressed for greater legal equality, it has been working to inculcate unequal gender roles that are prejudicial to women. How far those ideas have taken hold and whether improvements in women's formal legal status have affected their position in marriage, divorce, and the society at large are important questions for further research.

NOTES

1. Arabic-derived legal terms are spelled according to standard Indonesian transliteration.
2. The pre-1950s divorce rates for the highest divorce regions could hardly have been higher. Jones (1994b) noted that to maintain the 1950s ratios of divorces to marriages, some people must have been marrying, divorcing, remarrying, and divorcing all in the same year.
3. Unlike most of East and South Asia, the predominant method for reckoning descent and inheritance in Southeast Asia is bilateral. The region is also home to the largest matrilineal population in the world, the Minangkabau of west Sumatra, and has several large patrilineal groups.
4. For example, although parental arrangement of marriage is common, in Bali and parts of West Nusa Tenggara, a form of elopement marriage is practiced.
5. Although we are concerned here only with divorce among Indonesian Muslims, there is significant religious diversity among those who identify themselves as Muslim (C. Geertz 1960).
6. In a rare attempt to generalize about gender ideas throughout Southeast Asia, Errington (1990) correlated ideas about gender with broader cosmological outlooks. What she called the "centrist archipelago" is composed of societies that are "preoccupied with unity" and "regard men and women as very much the same sort of people." Power and prestige differences between the sexes in centrist societies are more often the result of built-up patterns of advantaging males than of categorical rules involving the differential allocation of opportunities. The "exchange archipelago," which includes Sumatra, the Lesser Sundas, and the islands in far eastern Indonesia, represent both the cosmos and gender in oppositional terms. "[G]ender ideologies of the exchange archipelago stress complementary difference rather than unity or sameness" (pp. 54–56).
7. The law of marriage and divorce for Indonesian Muslims as it existed before the 1974 reform is summarized in Lev (1972). The substantially similar practice in Singapore is described in Djamour (1966). Commonly cited English-language treatments of Islamic marriage law include those by Abu Zahra (1955), Esposito (1982), Fyzee (1964), and Schacht (1964).
8. Although men had the power to divorce their wives without invoking the help of officials, popular awareness of the formalities of divorce was not necessarily high among some Southeast Asian groups. As a result, laypeople relied on religious leaders for information on the technical requirements for divorce (H. Geertz 1961).
9. The most commonly recognized grounds for such a divorce, which is known as *fasach*, were insanity, leprosy, elephantiasis, impotence, poverty, and failure to provide proper support (Lev 1972).
10. A collection of *taklik talak* formulas used or proposed at various times and places is contained in Vreede-de Stuers (1960).
11. Traditionally, certain aspects of the cultivation of paddy and other crops were performed exclusively by women, while other tasks were reserved for men.

12. A common rule for dividing marital property on divorce is to grant two parts to the husband to one part to the wife. This rule is expressed in the metaphor still commonly heard in Java comparing the male method of carrying loads—two baskets on a shoulder pole—to the technique used by women—one basket on the back.
13. Among the Javanese, economic activity and the personal qualities associated with financial success are decidedly undervalued. Ironically, the ideological association of women with economics and material pursuits serves to reinforce male dominance, since social power and prestige within Javanese culture is derived from mystical, rather than material, accomplishment (Brenner 1995; Keeler 1987; Wolf 1992). Brenner (1995) argued that there is also an alternative, counterhegemonic construction of gender according to which men find it more difficult than women to control their passions.
14. A survey of marriage practices in a village near the central Javanese city of Yogyakarta conducted in the early 1970s found that 23 percent of the women in the sample reported having been married before their first menstruation (Singarimbun and Manning 1974).
15. For a thorough discussion of trends in marriage age throughout the region, see Jones (1994b:Chap. 3).
16. Although Indonesian support for changing the marriage law was certainly not broad based and any effort to alter the substance of Islamic marriage rules was certain to be resisted by Islamic leaders as an interference with divinely ordained religious precepts, the reform of the marriage law was not an exclusively Dutch idea or initiative. The Indonesian women's movement, which grew up with and was essentially an adjunct to the nationalist movement, made such reform a central priority (Vreede-de Stuers 1960). Reforming Islamic marriage practices—child marriage, polygamy, and arbitrary divorce—was also a natural corollary of Indonesian nationalism, which was understood as much in terms of achieving a modern society as independence from the Dutch (McVey 1996).
17. From its establishment in 1946 until the appointment of Mukti Ali as minister of religion in 1971, the Ministry of Religion was dominated by the members of the Nahdlatul Ulama, the most important organization of traditionalist Islam, which takes a very conservative attitude toward any kind of legal change (Noer 1978).
18. Lev (1972) pointed out that in addition to their purpose of inhibiting divorce, the marriage counseling boards were, to some extent, an effort by Muslim interests to prove their bona fide concern over the high incidence of divorce but to avoid changes in Islamic divorce rules.
19. Suharto came to power on the heels of a botched coup by a group of middle-ranking army and air force officers on September 30, 1965. Six senior army officers were killed. Major General Suharto, head of the strategic reserve command, assumed control over the army and restored order in Jakarta. The military blamed the Communist Party for the attempted coup, and hundreds of thousands of suspected communist sympathizers were massacred in the latter part of 1965 and 1966. Sukarno formally ceded authority to Suharto in March 1966. For a thorough discussion of the attempted coup, including an assessment of the various theories regarding who was behind the action, see Crouch (1978).
20. Though clearly not political.
21. For summaries of the New Order's achievements in fertility control, see Hugo et al. (1987); T. Hull (1994).

22. The government's gender policy has not been altogether consistent, and its actions have not always coincided with its pronouncements. Although the Suharto government promoted what has been aptly called a "discourse of domesticity" in its official rhetoric, it did not exclude women from participation in public life. Suharto's oldest daughter, for example, was a Deputy Chair of the state political organization. And the military announced in 1996 that it would accept women into its training academy (Antara 1996). Perhaps what is most significant for the role of women in society is that the gender gap in educational attainment narrowed dramatically under Suharto's rule (Jones 1994a).
23. Beginning in the mid-1980s, the Suharto government's policy toward Islam appeared to change course, though it is uncertain how far those developments reflect a change in policy or simply a recognition of changed political realities. For assessments of Islam and the New Order state by leading scholars of Indonesian Islam, see Hefner (1993) and Liddle (1996).
24. The text of the proposal is on file with the first author. Discussions of the terms of the proposal can be found in Cammack (1989), Hassan (1980), and Katz and Katz (1975).
25. Draft Marriage Law, Article 1 (1973) (Indon.). Citations in this paragraph and the next refer to the provisions of this draft law.
26. For an account of the controversy provoked by the proposal, see Emmerson (1976). At one point, several hundred Muslim youths occupied the floor of the legislature and had to be forcibly removed by the army (*Tempo* 1973f).
27. The five points agreed to were that (1) the Islamic marriage law would not be diminished or changed; (2) the role of the Islamic courts would not be decreased; (3) matters contrary to Islamic law would be removed from the draft; (4) a marriage would be valid if it was carried out according to the religious law of the parties, and registration would not be necessary for a valid marriage; and (5) measures were needed to prevent arbitrary divorce and polygamy.
28. In revising the draft to meet Muslim objections, the government made significant changes. The most important change was in the provision on the requirements for a valid marriage: The statute provides that a marriage is valid when it is carried out according to the religious law of the parties. Like the draft, the statute includes provisions that require the consent of the parties and the minimum marriage age, but the force of those requirements is cast in doubt by the stipulation that compliance with religious formalities is all that is needed to contract a marriage and the addition of a new provision stating that the consent requirement is effective only insofar as the religious law of the parties does not specify otherwise. The didactic provisions related to the definition of marriage and the obligations of the spouses were not changed. A complete English translation of the Marriage Act is contained in Hering (1976). For summaries, see Hanifa (1983), Katz and Katz (1975), and Soewondo (1977).
29. National Marriage Act, Law No. 1, Article 38 (1974) (Indon.). Citations in this paragraph refer to the provisions of this act.
30. The implementing regulations were issued on April 1, 1975, and went into effect on October 1, 1975. They are contained in Gov. Reg. No. 9 (1975) (Indon.). A government regulation requires the approval of the entire cabinet. Citations in the following two paragraphs refer to the provisions of this regulation.
31. For a description of the IFLS data set, see the later discussion.
32. Jones (1994b) noted that enforcement of the law is sometimes slack and ac-

knowledged that not all marriages and divorces are registered. He concluded, however, that these practices are probably not widespread.

33. Simple ignorance of the law is undoubtedly responsible for some degree of noncompliance with statutory procedures. Localized studies of the extent of popular knowledge of the requirements of the Marriage Act have found consistently low levels of awareness. However, ignorance is plainly not the explanation for the discrepancy between our findings and those of other researchers, since the evidence for a decrease in divorce following the implementation of the Marriage Act is based on a decline in the number of *registered* divorces. The evidence of the widespread lack of awareness of the law suggests that official records have understated the rate of divorce, both now and in the past.
34. The attitude of Islamic legal theory toward legal change is actually complex. The view that the corpus of Islamic law is closed is based on the belief that by the turn of the tenth century, there was a decisive consensus among legal scholars concerning the correct interpretation of the primary sources of law—the Koran and the inspired example of the Prophet (Coulson 1964). In fact, prominent Muslim jurists have claimed the privilege of interpreting the divine sources, or *ijtihad*, throughout history (Voll 1983). Since the advent of Islamic modernism in the eighteenth century, the possibility of legal change through reinterpretation of the divine revelation in light of contemporary circumstances has been widely, though by no means universally, acknowledged (Rahman 1979). Although Islamic modernism is well established in Indonesia, until recently the Islamic bureaucracy and Islamic courts were strongholds of "traditionalism," insisting that the proper attitude of jurists was "imitation" (*taklid*) of the interpretive efforts of the classical-era scholars (Lev 1972).
35. Although Islamic law allows men great freedom to dissolve their marriages by simply reciting the repudiation formula, Islam regards groundless or arbitrary divorce as morally blameworthy and punishable by God (Rasjid 1954).
36. Such marriages and divorces are referred to in a variety of ways that implicitly recognize their unofficial status: "preacher marriages" (*kawin kiyai*), "secret" marriages or divorces (*kawin/talak sirri*), "village" marriages or divorces (*kawin/talak kampung*), and illicit marriages or divorces (*kawin/talak liar*). Jones (1994b) mentioned the practice of unauthorized marriage and divorce, but dismissed the possibility that it is sufficiently common to explain the decline in reported divorces.
37. Examples of first-instance Islamic court decisions ratifying extra-judicial *talak* include *Syafnil bin Ahmad v. Yaneta Hakam binti Hakam*, Pengadilan Agama Padang No. 387 (1980), decided by the Islamic court for Padang, West Sumatra, and *M. Teguh bin H.A. Rohman v. H.A. Rohman bin Husin dan Nurmah binti Rohasan*, Pengadilan Agama Kayu Agung No. 26 (1982), decided by the Islamic court for Kayu Agung, South Sumatra. Because decisions of Islamic courts are not routinely published, it is not possible to determine with certainty the position of Islamic judges toward extra-judicial *talak*. The cited cases were included in a compilation of decisions from Islamic courts published by the Supreme Court. We have reviewed enough cases and spoken with enough judges to feel confident that most judges, at least in the past, regarded extra-judicial *talak* as effective.
38. The official elucidation to the Marriage Act states that one purpose of the act is to make divorce more difficult. National Marriage Act, Law No. 1, General Elucidation, Article 4(e) (1974) (Indon.). No mention is made of the need to regulate the consequences of divorce.

39. As was stated in a Swedish law reform commission report in 1913, (quoted in Glendon 1989:183), "Ordinarily, it is not desirable, either from the point of view of the community or with regard to the spouses, that in such situations [of breakdown] a marriage can be held together by force. The State can enforce the external bond alone; but a community of life which carries into effect the moral content of a marriage cannot be enforced by external pressure."
40. Glendon (1987:63–64) referred to this transformation as the "dejuridification of marriage." For a fuller treatment of the shift in state emphasis from controlling the formation and termination of marriage to an almost exclusive emphasis on regulating the consequences of divorce, see Glendon (1989).
41. Between 1965 and 1990, the proportion of Indonesians who engaged in agriculture fell from 71 percent to 55 percent, and the proportion who were employed in industry rose from 9 to 14 percent (World Bank 1987:Table 32, 1996:Table 4). The proportion of the population who were living in urban areas grew from 16 percent in 1965 to 31 percent in 1991 (World Bank 1987:Table 33, 1993:Table 31). During the same period, the per capita gross domestic product more than tripled, from $190 in 1965 to $570 in 1990 (Hill 1994:Table 2.1).

    Among the most dramatic changes in recent years have been those related to mobility and access to information. Improved roads, huge increases in the number of motor vehicles (Hill 1994), and the ubiquitous "colts"—small commercial passenger vans—have made the cities accessible to an increasing number of people, while satellites; rural electrification; and access to radios, televisions, and other mass media have brought the outside world into the villages (Drake 1989). As Drake (1989:236) wrote, "whereas [in the mid-1970s] there was still some substance in the stereotype of villagers who had never visited their neighboring town, now in many villages most people under forty have spent at least some time working in the city and have brought back with them a much more dynamic outlook to the village when they returned."
42. The lack of fit between economic trends and trends in divorce behavior does not necessarily mean that the two phenomena are unrelated. It is possible that the ideology of industrialism and urban life have spread more quickly than the underlying changes that spawned them.
43. One way in which education has influenced the frequency of divorce is indirectly through its effect on the age at marriage and the selection of spouses. It has also been suggested that education is inhibiting divorce by inculcating in a broader cross section of society negative attitudes toward divorce that were once limited to the upper classes (V. Hull 1996). We will explore these issues in more detail in a forthcoming article on the reasons for the declining divorce rates.

References

Abu Zahra, Muhammad. 1955. "Family Law." Pp. 132–78 in *Law in the Middle East, Volume I: Origin and Development of Islamic Law*, edited by M. Khadduri and H. J. Liebesny. Washington, D.C.: Middle East Institute.

Al Hadar, Yasmine S. 1977. *Perkawinan dan Perceraiain di Indonesia: Sebuah Studi antar Kebudayaan* (Fertility and Mortality Survey Monograph No. 4). Jakarta: Demographic Institute of the Faculty of Economics, University of Indonesia.

Anderson, Benedict. 1983. "Old State, New Society: Indonesia's New Order in Comparative Perspective." *Journal of Asian Studies* 42:477–96.

Antara. 1996. "Panjab: Wanita Abri Lulusan Akabri Bisa Jadi Jenderal." November 12 (on-line edition).

Benda, Harry J. 1958. *The Crescent and the Rising Sun: Indonesian Islam under the Japanese Occupation 1942–1945*. The Hague, the Netherlands: W. van Hoeve.

Blackwood, Evelyn. 1995. "Senior Women, Model Mothers, and Dutiful Wives: Managing Gender Contradictions in a Minangkabau Village." Pp. 124–58 in *Bewitching Women, Pious Men: Gender and Body Politics in Southeast Asia*, edited by A. Ong and M. G. Peletz. Berkeley: University of California Press.

Brenner, Suzanne A. 1995. "Why Women Rule the Roost: Rethinking Javanese Ideologies of Gender and Self-Control." Pp. 19–50 in *Bewitching Women, Pious Men: Gender and Body Politics in Southeast Asia*, edited by A. Ong and M. G. Peletz. Berkeley: University of California Press.

Cammack, Mark. 1989. "Islamic Law in Indonesia's New Order." *International and Comparative Law Quarterly* 38: 53–73.

———. 1997. "Indonesia's 1989 Religious Judicature Act: Islamization of Indonesia or Indonesianization of Islam?" *Indonesia* 63:143–68.

Cammack, Mark, Lawrence A. Young, and Tim Heaton. 1996. "Legislating Social Change in an Islamic Society: Indonesia's Marriage Law." *American Journal of Comparative Law* 44:45–73.

Coulson, Noel J. 1964. *A History of Islamic Law*. Edinburgh: Edinburgh University Press.

Crouch, Harold. 1978. *The Army and Politics in Indonesia*. Ithaca: Cornell University Press.

Djamour, Judith. 1966. *The Muslim Matrimonial Court in Singapore*. London: Athlone.

Drake, Christine. 1989. *National Integration in Indonesia: Patterns and Policies*. Honolulu: University of Hawaii Press.

Emmerson, Donald K. 1976. *Indonesia's Elite: Political Culture and Cultural Politics*. Ithaca: Cornell University Press.

Errington, Shelly. 1990. "Recasting Sex, Gender, and Power: A Theoretical and Regional Overview." Pp. 1–58 in *Power and Difference: Gender in Island Southeast Asia*, edited by J. M. Atkinson and S. Errington. Stanford, CA: Stanford University Press.

Esposito, John L. 1982. *Women in Muslim Family Law*. Syracuse, NY: Syracuse University Press.

Firth, Rosemary. 1966. *Housekeeping among Malay Peasants* (2d ed.). London: Athlone.

Frankenberg, Elizabeth, and Lynn A. Karoly. 1995. "The 1993 Indonesian Family Life Survey: Overview and Field Report" (Labor and Population Program). Santa Monica, CA: RAND Corp.

Fyzee, Asaf A. A. 1964. *Outlines of Muhammadan Law* (4th ed.). Delhi, India: Oxford University Press.

Geertz, Clifford. 1960. *The Religion of Java*. Chicago: University of Chicago Press.

———. 1983. *Local Knowledge: Further Essays in Interpretive Anthropology*. New York: Basic Books.

Geertz, Hildred. 1961. *The Javanese Family: A Study of Kinship and Socialization*. Glencoe, IL: Free Press.

Glass, Gene V., George C. Tiao, and Thomas O. Maguire. 1971. "The 1900 Revision of German Divorce Laws: Analysis of Data as a Time-Series Quasi-Experiment." *Law and Society Review* 5:539–62.

Glendon, Mary Ann. 1987. *Abortion and Divorce in Western Law: American Failures, European Challenges*. Cambridge, MA: Harvard University Press.

———. 1989. *The Transformation of Family Law: State, Law, and the Family in the United States and Western Europe*. Chicago: University of Chicago Press.

Goode, William J. 1993. *World Changes in Divorce Patterns*. New Haven, CT: Yale University Press.

Grijns, Mies. 1987. "Tea-Pickers in West Java as Mothers and Workers: Female Work and Women's Jobs." Pp. 104–19 in *Indonesian Women in Focus: Past and Present Notions*, edited by E. Locher-Scholten and A. Niehof. Dordrecht, the Netherlands: Foris.

Guest, Phillip. 1991. "Marital Dissolution and Development in Indonesia." *Journal of Comparative Family Studies* 23:96–113.

Guinness, Patrick. 1994. "Local Society and Culture." Pp. 267–304 in *Indonesia's New Order: The Dynamics of Socio-Economic Transformation*, edited by H. Hill. Honolulu: University of Hawaii Press.

Hanifa, S. 1983. "The Law of Marriage and Divorce in Indonesia." *Islamic and Comparative Law Quarterly* 3:14–26.

Hassan, Muhammad Kamal. 1980. *Muslim Intellectual Responses to "New Order" Modernization in Indonesia*. Kuala Lumpur, Malaysia: Department of Education, Council on Language and Literature.

Hatley, Barbara. 1990. "Theatrical Imagery and Gender Ideology in Java." Pp. 177–207 in *Power and Difference: Gender in Island Southeast Asia*, edited by J. M. Atkinson and S. Errington. Stanford, CA: Stanford University Press.

Heaton, Tim B., and Vaughn Call. 1995. "Modeling Family Demographics with Event History Techniques." *Journal of Marriage and the Family* 57:1078–90.

Hefner, Robert W. 1993. "Islam, State, and Civil Society: ICMI and the Struggle for the Indonesian Middle Class." *Indonesia* 56:1–35.

Hering, B. B. 1976. "A Translation of the Indonesian Marriage Law." Pp. 91–114 in *Indonesian Women: Some Past and Current Perspectives*, edited by B. B. Hering. Brussels: Center for the Study of Southeast Asia and the Far East.

Hill, Hal. 1994. "The Economy." Pp. 54–122 in *Indonesia's New Order: The Dynamics of Socio-Economic Transformation*, edited by H. Hill. Honolulu: University of Hawaii Press.

Hugo, Graeme J., Terence H. Hull, Valerie J. Hull, and Gavin W. Jones. 1987. *The Demographic Dimension in Indonesian Development*. Singapore: Oxford University Press.

Hull, Terence H. 1994. "Demographic Perspectives: Fertility Decline in the New Order Period: The Evolution of Population Policy, 1965–90." Pp. 123–45 in *Indonesia's New Order: The Dynamics of Socio-Economic Transformation*, edited by H. Hill. Honolulu: University of Hawaii Press.

Hull, Terence H., and Masri Singarimbun. 1989. "The Sociocultural Determinants of Fertility Decline in Indonesia 1965–1976" (Working Paper Series No. 31). Yogyakarta, Indonesia: Population Studies Center, Gajah Mada University.

Hull, Valerie J. 1996. "Women in Java's Rural Middle Class: Progress or Regress?" Pp.78–95 in *Women of Southeast Asia* (2nd ed.), edited by P. van Estrick. DeKalb, IL: Center for Southeast Asian Studies, Northern Illinois University.

Jacob, Herbert. 1988. *Silent Revolution: The Transformation of Divorce Law in the United States*. Chicago: University of Chicago Press.

Jones, Gavin W. 1994a. "Demographic Perspectives: Labour Force and Education." Pp. 145–78 in *Indonesia's New Order: The Dynamics of Socio-Economic Transformation*, edited by H. Hill. Honolulu: University of Hawaii Press.

———. 1994b. *Marriage and Divorce in Islamic South-East Asia*. New York: Oxford University Press.

———. 1997. "Modernization and Divorce: Contrasting Trends in Islamic Southeast Asia and the West." *Population and Development Review* 23:95–114.

Jones, Gavin W., Yahya Asari, and Tuti Djuartika. 1995. "Divorce in West Java." *Journal of Comparative Family Studies* 25:395–416.

Katz, June S., and Ronald S. Katz. 1975. "The New Indonesian Marriage Law: A Mirror of Indonesia's Political, Cultural, and Legal Systems." *American Journal of Comparative Law* 23:653–81.

———. 1978. "Legislating Social Change in a Developing Country: The New Indonesian Marriage Law Revisited." *American Journal of Comparative Law* 26:309–20.

Keeler, Ward. 1987. *Javanese Shadow Plays, Javanese Selves*. Princeton, NJ: Princeton University Press.

Lev, Daniel S. 1972. *Islamic Courts in Indonesia: A Study in the Political Bases of Legal Institutions*. Berkeley: University of California Press.

———. 1996. "On the Other Hand?" Pp. 191–202 in *Fantasizing the Feminine in Indonesia*, edited by L. J. Sears. Durham, NC: Duke University Press.

Liddle, R. William. 1996. "The Islamic Turn in Indonesia: A Political Explanation." *Journal of Asian Studies* 55:613–34.

Marvell, Thomas B. 1989. "Divorce Rates and the Fault Requirement." *Law and Society Review* 23:543–67.

Masyuri, K. H. A. Aziz. 1997. *Masalah Keagamaan Nahdlatul Ulama: Hasil Muktamar dan Munas Ulama Kesatu-1926 sampai dengan Kedua Puluh Sembilan—1994*. Surabaya, Indonesia: Dinamika Press.

McDonald, Peter, and Edeng H. Abdurahman. 1974. "Marriage and Divorce in West Java: An Example of the Effective Use of Marital Histories" (Working Paper). Jakarta, Indonesia: Demographic Institute of the Faculty of Economics, University of Indonesia.

McNicoll, Geoffrey, and Masri Singarimbun. 1986. *Fertility Decline in Indonesia: Analysis and Interpretation*. Yogyakarta, Indonesia: Gajah Mada University.

McVey, Ruth. 1983. "Faith as an Outsider: Islam in Indonesian Politics." Pp. 199–225 in *Islam in the Political Process*, edited by J. P. Piscatori. Cambridge, England: Cambridge University Press.

———. 1996. "Building Behemoth: Indonesian Constructions of the Nation State." Pp. 11–25 in *Making Indonesia: Essays on Modern Indonesia in Honor of George McT. Kahin*, edited by D. S. Lev and R. McVey. Ithaca, NY: Cornell Southeast Asia Program.

Nakamura, Misako. 1983. *Divorce in Java: A Study of the Dissolution of Marriage among Javanese Muslims*. Yogyakarta, Indonesia: Gajah Mada University.

Nakonezny, Paul A., Robert D. Shull, and Joseph Lee Rodgers. 1995. "The Effect of No-Fault Divorce Law on the Divorce Rate Across the 50 States and Its Relation to Income, Education, and Religiosity." *Journal of Marriage and the Family* 57:477–88.

Noer, Deliar. 1978. *Administration of Islam in Indonesia* (Publication No. 58). Ithaca, NY: Cornell Modern Indonesia Project.

Papanek, Hanna, and Laurel Schwede. 1988. "Women Are Good with Money: Earning and Managing in an Indonesian City." Pp. 71–98 in *A Home Divided: Women and Income in the Third World*, edited by D. Dwyer and J. Bruce. Stanford, CA: Stanford University Press.

Peacock, James L. 1973. *Indonesia: An Anthropological Perspective*. Pacific Palisades, CA: Goodyear.

Peletz, Michael Gates. 1988. *A Share of the Harvest: Kinship, Property, and Social History Among the Malays of Rembau*. Berkeley: University of California Press.

Prins, Jan. 1951. "Adatlaw and Muslim Religious Law in Modern Indonesia." *Welt des Islams* 1:283–300.

Rahman, Fazlur. 1979. *Islam* (2d ed.). Chicago: London: University of Chicago Press.

Rasjid, H. Sulaiman. 1954. *Fiqh Islam*. Bandung, Indonesia: Sinar Baru.

Raybeck, Douglas A. 1974. "Social Stress and Social Structure in Kelantan Village Life." Pp. 225–42 in *Kelantan: Religion, Society and Politics in a Malay State*, edited by W. Roff. Kuala Lumpur, Malaysia: Oxford University Press.

Reid, Anthony. 1988. *Southeast Asia in the Age of Commerce, 1450–1680: Volume 1. The Land Below the Winds*. New Haven, CT: Yale University Press.

Schacht, Joseph. 1964. *An Introduction to Islamic Law*. London: Oxford University Press.

Siegel, James T. 1969. *The Rope of God*. Berkeley: University of California Press.

Singarimbun, Masri, and Chris Manning. 1974. "Marriage and Divorce in Mojolama." *Indonesia* 17:67–82.

Soewondo, Nani. 1977. "The Indonesian Marriage Law and its Implementing Regulations." *Archipel* 13:283–94.

Suryadinata, Leo. 1989. *Military Ascendancy and Political Culture: A Study of Indonesia's GOLKAR*. Athens: Ohio University Center for International Studies.

Tempo. 1973a. "Sambil Menanti Undang-Undang Hawa." June 30:48–50.

Tempo. 1973b. "RUU 9 Titik Api." August 18:6.

Tempo. 1973c. "RUU Perkawinan, Aksi dan Reaksi." September 8:6–8.

Tempo. 1973d. "Terlepas Dari Soal 'Islam' dan 'Non- Islam.'" September8:8–9.

Tempo. 1973e. "Beberapa Pasal Masalah." September 8:9–10.

Tempo. 1973f. "Ada 'Allahu Akbar' dari Luar." October 6:6–7.

Tempo. 1973g. "Yang Didrop dan Diubah." December 15:6–7.

Tempo. 1973h. "Masih Pasal 1." December 22:9–10.

Tempo. 1973i. "Dan Lahirlah UU Itu—Dengan Afdruk Kilat." December 29:5–8.

ter Haar, B. 1948. *Adat Law in Indonesia*. Edited with an Introduction by E. A. Hoebel and A. A. Schiller. New York: Institute of Pacific Relations.

Tsubouchi, Yoshihiro. 1975. "Marriage and Divorce among Malay Peasants in Kelantan." *Journal of Southeast Asian Studies* 6:135–50.

Voll, John. 1983. "Renewal and Reform in Islamic History: *Tajdid* and *Islah*." Pp. 32–47 in *Voices of Resurgent Islam*, edited by J. L. Esposito. New York: Oxford University Press.

Vreede-de Stuers, Cora. 1960. *The Indonesian Woman: Struggles and Achievements*. The Hague: Mouton.

———. 1974. "A Propos du 'R.U.U.,' Histoire d'une Legislation Matrimoniale." *Archipel* 8:21–30.

Wilder, William D. 1982. *Communication, Social Structure and Development in Rural Malaysia*. London: Athlone.

Wolf, Diane Lauren. 1992. *Factory Daughters: Gender, Household Dynamics, and Rural Industrialization in Java*. Berkeley: University of California Press.

Woodcroft-Lee, Carlien Patricia. 1983. "Separate but Equal: Indonesian Muslim Perceptions of the Roles of Women." Pp. 173–92 in *Women's Work and Women's Roles: Economics and Everyday Life in Indonesia, Malaysia and Singapore*, edited by L. Manderson. Canberra: Australian National University Development Studies Centre.

World Bank. 1987. *World Development Report 1987*. Washington DC: Author.

———. 1993. *World Development Report 1993*. Washington DC: Author.

———. 1996. *World Development Report 1996*. Washington DC: Author.

C H A P T E R   E I G H T

Religious and Familial Networks as Entrepreneurial Resources in South Africa

GILLIAN GODSELL

INTRODUCTION

South African society is not inherently entrepreneurial; societal attitudes toward entrepreneurship have ranged from apathy to antipathy. Yet some groups and some individuals have defied the odds and produced remarkable entrepreneurial successes. In the absence of political or ideological support for individual entrepreneurial endeavors and a flourishing entrepreneurial system or set of helpful rules or role models, what resources have successful entrepreneurs been able to draw on? This chapter explores the role that familial and religious networks have played in the successes of some of the disadvantaged groups in South Africa. Throughout, it distinguishes between groups that have succeeded because of these networks and groups in which individuals have succeeded despite the surprising absence of networks.

This examination of religion and family vis-à-vis entrepreneurship is made especially dramatic because of the rapid social changes that have redefined capitalism in South Africa. Under apartheid, severe restrictions constrained the economic activity of all South Africans who were not white. Blacks were barred from many occupations, and the limited trading they were allowed was restricted to specific areas. Indians were allowed into more occupations, but many flourishing Indian businesses were shut down or shifted, and a plethora of laws restricted the establishment of new businesses. It has been only since the mid-1980s that these laws have been first ignored and then repealed. Although the economic policy espoused by the previous (Nationalist) government was, in theory, capitalist, the capitalism that was practiced was a grossly distorted form (O'Dowd 1991). It offered protected employment in the civil service to the dominant Afrikaner group, rather than rewards and approval for individual entrepreneurial efforts. Entrepreneurship was not supported by the groups opposed to apartheid either, since their protest was often couched in socialist terms. Hence, both those who supported apartheid and a large number of its opponents functioned in an anticapitalist mode. Significant factors that encouraged or facilitated entrepreneurship, in the face of this negative context, could be found in the religious and familial spheres.

The findings reported here were drawn from a study of entrepreneurial networks in South Africa (Godsell 1990) that was part of a larger research project conducted under the auspices of the Institute for the Study of Economic Culture at Boston University. In this project, the impact of cultural factors on the development of entrepreneurship was studied in a number of different countries (B. Berger 1991).

This chapter compares two groups of South Africans—urban blacks and Indians—who are similar in that they both were in disadvantaged positions under apartheid. Among other constraints, the Group Areas Act of 1950, which was abolished in 1991, strongly affected entrepreneurship. This legislation allowed racially exclusive zones, both residential and economic, to be defined, and no one was allowed to live or locate his or her business in a zone allocated to a different racial group. At least 600,000 people (Beinart 1994:147) were removed from land they owned or occupied to comply with laws created in accordance with the Group Areas Act. The laws operated chiefly to the advantage of whites and the detriment of other groups, and the areas for blacks and Indians were often far removed from important industrial or commercial centers. A major difference between the blacks and Indians was the familial and religious resources they were able to mobilize to overcome the disadvantages related to these laws and similar constraints in the economic sphere.

ROLE OF RELIGIOUS AND FAMILIAL NETWORKS IN ENTREPRENEURIAL ACTIVITY: A CONCEPTUAL FRAMEWORK

Economists have tended to emphasize the role of macroeconomic systems and policies in achieving or hindering economic progress. However, all individual economic actors are embedded in cultural contexts and may be expected to respond in different ways to the same macroeconomic stimuli. As P. Berger (1994:110) put it, "the manifold forms of capitalist activity are intimately connected with the distinctive economic cultures which surround and animate them." Religion, family, ethnicity, and social status are all cultural factors that may affect economic behavior. One of the first descriptions of the influence of religious belief on economic behavior was made in Weber's ([1904] 1958) study of the Puritans, which linked the Protestant Ethic to the rise of capitalism.

Increasingly, the entrepreneurial literature is focusing on the importance of networks to entrepreneurial success (Birley 1985). For example, it has been noted that groups whose occupational mobility is blocked in professional and corporate directions may move into small businesses, developing their own networks to compensate for other resources denied to them. Kim (1985) suggested this as a reason for the preponderance of Korean immigrant entrepreneurs in the United States.

In a discussion of entrepreneurial ethnic enclaves in the United States, Model (1985) proposed that political and social exclusion may be expected to influence economic activity among blacks. The role of ethnicity has been well explored in the literature (Boissevain and Grotenberg 1987; Min 1987; Model 1985; Sowell 1981; Ward 1987; Ward and Jenkins 1985). There appear to be two main fields in which ethnicity may contribute to the development of small businesses—in providing resources (e.g., markets, suppliers, physical assistance, and group financing) and in creating a specific demand for cultural artifacts, such as clothing, food, or religious items.

However, the most significant role of a network may be not in the provision of tangible assets, such as markets and shop assistants, but in the intangible area of the *status* of the undertaking. Hagen (1971a, 1971b) suggested that groups who suffer from discrimination often seek to achieve the status denied them in social and other spheres through economic achievements. However, economic success does not bestow status on all groups. For this means of status enhancement to succeed, there must be a prior valuing of economic activity and economic success. Religion can provide one source of this valuing.

Redding (1990:8) summarized Weber's ([1904] 1958) discussion of the relationship between the Protestant ethic and the rise of capitalism as follows: "no capitalist development without an entrepreneurial class; no entrepreneurial class without a moral charter; no moral charter without religious premises." For the Puritans, Protestantism provided the moral charter and the religious premises. Redding argued cogently that Protestantism was not the only religion that was able to provide this moral charter for business; Confucianism was also able to do so for Overseas Chinese at the end of the twentieth century.

None of the South African black respondents in this study listed religion as a helpful factor: Coreligionists did not provide practical help, and religious beliefs did not uphold them in their economic endeavors. In contrast, for the South African Indian respondents, religious and community approval for success in business and the pursuit of wealth, backed by family practice, clearly provided both charter and premises. Somehow, this group managed to create an enterprise-friendly microclimate in an environment that was not friendly to entrepreneurs in general, not friendly to Indians in general, and pointedly and specifically hostile to successful Indian entrepreneurs.

To understand how South African Indians were able to create such a climate, one must distinguish between two kinds of networks: strategic and organic (Godsell 1990). *Organic networks* develop naturally in communities that are full of rich linkages, such as bonds of family, religion, and culture. Reciprocity is neither intentional nor immediate: The young girl who helps to care for other women's children does so because it is expected of girls of her age in her community; she is not necessarily aware that she will benefit from the system in time. Because many networks exist in a community, individual effort may be put into one network, and benefits may be derived from a completely different network. The community insider will not always recognize the existence of a network, taking both the benefits and the obligations for granted. Organic networks will develop around activities that are accorded a high status within a particular community, so different communities will harbor organic networks that are dedicated to different functions. Discovering the nature and scope of networks may therefore provide an outsider with a guide to which activities are important in a particular community.

The South African Indian community appears to provide the best examples of business-oriented organic networks. In this community, both the extended family and the religious community are involved, and language and caste play roles as well. Vather (1991) reported, for example, that a celebration, such as a wedding, involves many hundreds of people—the entire Gujerati-speaking Hindu community in a town, as well as community members who have traveled from far away. Thus, such a celebration is "a very important meeting place for the community, where old alliances, friendships and associations are revisited. It also provides an opportunity for businessmen to discuss common problems, opportunities, and threats" (Vather 1991:38). The celebration of a festival like Diwali would provide opportunities for such discussion, as would attendance at meetings of Gujerati-Hindu sociocultural clubs. Attached to a Hindu community temple there is usually a community hall, "where vernacular classes and society functions are held, for example, engagement ceremonies, weddings, 'gharba' dancing [a Hindu folk dance], Diwali celebrations, social club meetings, etc." (Vather 1991:38). Frequent religious and family gatherings provide the context within which networks develop. Within this context, reciprocal obligations stretch back across generations; the respondents related how their grandfathers had come from the same village in India or traveled to South Africa on the same boat and that help given then required responses from grandchildren and great-grandchildren. The community or family seem to be involved in all aspects of businesses: extending credit, supplying stock, helping in the shop, providing national and international contacts, and giving business advice and hands-on training.

Individuals who need support, but have not been fortunate enough to be born into an automatically functioning organic network, must construct *strategic networks* of their own. Strategic networks are consciously developed, whereas organic networks are inherited. Reciprocity in a strategic network is intentional: An individual puts effort into a specific network to derive benefits from it. Reciprocity is usually immediate; the levels of trust required to sustain extended reciprocity are more likely to be found in organic networks. Like organic networks, strategic networks may serve different purposes: business, child rearing, or consumption. Unlike the participants in organic networks, however, those in strategic networks are never unaware of their functioning.

Many resources may be used in developing a strategic network: school friends, neighbors, colleagues, and church members. The first step in developing a strategic network is to identify people with the same needs. Merely having survival needs in common, however, does not guarantee that a network will function. There must be a degree of compatibility—which exists automatically in an organic network—at various levels. The first level is simply behavioral. The next level is the level of belief or value. It is difficult, for example, to include within a child care network people who do not share beliefs on corporal punishment, cleanliness, or courtesy. It is the sharing of values that makes religious links a particularly suitable basis for a strategic network. Women's cooperatives are the most frequently cited strategic networks in Southern Africa (Godsell and Van Dijk 1988); they range from Afrikaner women expanding traditional domestic skills into cooperative home-produce shops to Swazi women knitting bedspreads.

Networks may vary in level of trust and in complexity of reciprocal obligations. The most complex reciprocities probably occur in the organic networks, where grandparents' favors and obligations may be an essential determinant of current behavior. Whatever the level at which these reciprocities operate, it is crucial that all the participants understand and adhere to them. Whether a network is inherited or constructed, its maintenance requires high levels of effort and skill.

Not all entrepreneurial research has considered networks. One strong tradition in entrepreneurial research situates all generative entrepreneurial factors in the individual. This may be called the entrepreneur-as-Lone-Ranger tradition, which sees the entrepreneur as an individual who succeeds against all odds and provides explanations in terms of individual psychology (De Vries 1977; McClelland 1961). However, there is another tradition, which situates the individual entrepreneur within a larger social context, whether the family, economic group, or ethnic minority (Benedict 1968; Greenfield, Strickon, Aubey, and Rothstein 1979; Leff 1978). Most of the first type of research applies to North American and, to a lesser extent, European, entrepreneurs, while the second type applies to entrepreneurs in Third World countries. This variation may be due as much to researchers' bias as to differences in functioning in different countries. Exceptions to this pattern of analysis include Blicksilver's (1979) study of kinship and friendship in Georgia and Rothstein's (1979) examination of social networks and investment among the slaveholding elites in the South in the early nineteenth century. It is the location of the enterprising individual within a helpful or harmful communal context that provides both tension and interest in this study.

EFFECTS OF ECONOMIC AND POLITICAL BACKGROUND ON ENTREPRENEURS IN SOUTH AFRICA

This section provides a larger context for the primary focus of this chapter. It examines the economic and political background of entrepreneurship in South Africa and sets the stage for a discussion of the specific roles of family and religion by presenting a historical account of the economic and political barriers to entrepreneurship that the urban black and Indian communities faced.

Economic Development in the Urban Black Community

Historically, economic power in South Africa has been in the hands of the English-speaking section of the community (De Kiewiet ([1941] 1978). This section has not traditionally been entrepreneurial, but has relied on the large mining houses and merchant banks. Virtually from the days of the Huguenots, who pioneered the first vineyards, and the freed Malay slaves, who were independent artisans in the Cape, many small immigrant ethnic groups have been significant entrepreneurs.

In attempting to counter the biased stereotype of blacks as inherently unsuited to business, recent historians have been at pains to stress the long history of black entrepreneurship in South Africa. Bundy (1979) was the first to do so, pointing out that some black farmers adapted so well to new systems of agriculture and land allocations that were different from those administered by the tribal chiefs that they were able to compete with white commercial farmers and even outdo them. Bundy saw a significant role for the missionaries, intent on "civilizing" as well as evangelizing their flock, in creating a new attitude toward the accumulation of individual wealth. That the accumulation of individual wealth was in conflict with tribal values is shown by Bundy's remark that the change in social attitudes was often accompanied by a physical relocation to the mission station "to avoid traditional sanctions against the accumulation of wealth" (p. 42).

This missionary attitude is confirmed by a list of graduates of the famous Lovedale Mission (*Lovedale, Past and Present* 1887), apparently to counter criticism that training for trade was wasted on black students. Lovedale's graduates were cataloged according to their occupations and included a goodly number who were self-employed transport riders, farmers, and traders. One category was simply labeled "returned to heathenism"; no further details were given about the heathen. Clearly, the compilers of the catalog believed that the practice of gainful employment was compatible only with Christianity.

Other, more recent, writers have followed suit and documented the existence of thriving black entrepreneurial communities (Louw and Kendall 1986), usually prior to the enactment of the various laws that impeded the operation of businesses by blacks. The Group Areas Act of 1950 prevented black (and Indian) traders from operating in areas other than their own and, in particular, prevented access to the lucrative white market. Additional restrictions were imposed on trading in black townships. Traders, for example, were not allowed to establish enterprises within three kilometers of one another; trade in alcohol was prohibited for blacks; and beerhalls, which generated much of the revenue for running the black townships, were to be operated by the local authority. In addition, blacks were not allowed to own their own homes in urban areas; thus mortgage bonds or houses used as collateral were not available to aspirant black businessmen as a means of raising money for their businesses. This legislation was repealed, and all forms of racial discrimination have been outlawed in the Interim Constitution of South Africa, which passed into law in 1994. Intangible entrepreneurial assets are not so easily legislated into or out of existence.

Economic Development in the South African Indian Community

It is not only in South Africa that family and/or religion play a significant role in the lives of Indian immigrant entrepreneurs. King (1977:25) described Kenyan businesses as including

> a good deal of the Indian skilled class with long family traditions of working in tin, glass, wood, iron, and other more specialised occupations. These families were responsible for introducing to Kenya a technology intermediate between that of the large colonial corporations and the traditional crafts of the various African communities.

In Kenya, as in South Africa, the Indian traders came predominantly from Gujerat and established "a commercial network that stretched from the wholesaler in Mombasa to the remotest country store" (Marris and Somerset 1971:3). In South Africa, too, Kharsany (1971) reported that the Indians who were then in the Transvaal (the most economically powerful of the four provinces into which South Africa was divided until 1994) were mainly Muslims from the Gujerat province of Surat, who have a reputation for being remarkably astute and competent businessmen.

The history and subsequent economic development of the South African Indians is probably better documented than that of any other South African group. The Indian community is small, still just over 1 million (South African Institute of Race Relations 1998); they form a homogeneous and distinctive group, and their substantial economic progress has clearly warranted further exploration. By the second half of the nineteenth century, Indians in South Africa comprised three groups: indentured laborers under contract to the sugar cane farmers in Natal; free Indians, who had completed their period of indenture and chose to stay in South Africa, rather than return to India; and passenger Indians, who traveled to South Africa at their own cost and were traders (Bagwandeen 1989). The indentured laborers were predominantly Hindus, particularly Tamilians (Kharsany 1971), while the passengers were a trading class comprised mainly of Gujerati-speaking Hindus and Muslims (Pillay, Naidoo, and Dangor 1989). The Gujerati-speaking groups have been particularly successful in maintaining a separate cultural identity (Reddy 1989).

Soon after the Indians arrived in South Africa, trade and agriculture became their two major occupations, with the free Indians, as market gardeners, achieving a monopoly on supplying markets in the Durban and Pietermaritzburg areas (Kharsany 1971). Although discriminatory legislation against Indians was introduced as early as 1906 (Beinart 1994), the major blow to Indian trade came with the Group Areas Act of 1950. Hundreds of Indian traders were moved from central shopping areas to their own, inevitably peripheral, districts. One respondent in the current study described the consequences for his family: "It breaks my heart to go through the center of Standerton [a thriving town] now. My people used to run that." In 1975 alone, 5078 Indian traders were barred from occupying their existing premises in terms of the Group Areas Act. Only 1277 were resettled in business centers subsidized by the government (South African Institute of Race Relations 1977).

Some Indian businesspeople were quick to take the necessary evasive action, and response to the first discriminatory legislation was fast and practical. A respondent explained: "When the first Group Areas Act was passed, the D—— family in Krugersdorp formed a company using a white nominee. In black areas, black nominees were used."[1] Thus, the gray clouds of harassment often appeared to produce silver linings of profit. "It boomeranged to us," explained a businessman with satisfaction, recounting how city council pressure forced him to abandon his existing premises and to move his retail business from an industrial site in Laudium (an Indian township). He now occupies boomingly successful premises in central Pretoria.

METHODOLOGY

Data were gathered on South African entrepreneurs using an essentially qualitative methodology, partly because of the exploratory nature of the study. Not knowing in advance exactly what sort of networks were likely to exist or what areas of business life might be supported by networks, it was necessary first to obtain simple descriptions of the respondents' business lives: how they started, their current positions, what they hoped for in the future. The respondents were not necessarily aware of their own networks *as networks*. Careful questioning, differing from respondent to respondent, was necessary to elicit the exact relationships (or lack of relationships) that together made up their networks.

When researchers use this methodological approach, some safeguards must be built in. One safeguard is the use of more than one interviewer and/or analyst to guard against the unconscious eliciting of views that are favorable to the central hypothesis. Another safeguard, although an extremely tedious and time-consuming one, is to use full transcripts to ensure that inconvenient views do not get lost in compiling a synopsis. In this study, some interviews were carried out by the researcher, and others were conducted by contracted interviewers from different racial and language groups. Contracted interviewers were used to minimize researcher bias and because it was thought that the respondents might talk more freely with interviewers of their own language group. Interviews carried out in the vernacular were audiotaped in the original language, and written translations into English were made from the tapes. The existence of the original tapes made it possible to check the accuracy of the translations.

Two research tools were used: an in-depth interview, based on an open-ended questionnaire, and a group discussion, or focus-group, technique (Morgan 1988). The use of individual interviews in qualitative work is self-explanatory, but the other technique requires some elaboration. An advantage of group discussion is that the respondents appear to give one another confidence and seem freer to introduce new ideas, so ideas or values that the researcher is unaware of may surface more easily. Researchers cannot probe for such ideas in one-to-one interviews if they are unaware of them. In a country such as South Africa, where there may be hostility, suspicion, or simply social distance among groups, the presence of peers seems to give group members confidence. Of course, the presence of peers may have an inhibiting effect, which is why this method is used in combination with individual interviews. When members of a group know one another, they may corroborate details; remind one another of illustrative episodes; and, of course, collude to avoid issues or present a particular image.

The samples interviewed for this study are not representative. The unavailability of reliable statistics on small businesses made the composition of either random or sectorally representative samples impossible. This was not a major drawback in this qualitative study in which the objective was to produce insights. Nevertheless, the customary caution against generalization from nonrepresentative data must be sounded.

All the respondents conducted their businesses in the Pretoria-Witwatersrand-Vereeniging (PWV) area. The PWV, one of the nine new provinces created after the 1994 election in South Africa and renamed Gauteng, is the economic heartland of the country. Although it is the smallest province, it has the highest population density and the highest per capita income and contributes almost 40 percent of the country's gross domestic product (South African Institute for Race Relations 1994). It also has the highest urbanization rate, and, although one may well expect family and tribal links, with their obvious network potential, to be stronger in the rural areas, the more interesting issue is how these links have survived and adapted to urbanization.

Because of the unfavorable political and economic conditions in which the respondents had been forced to operate, an open definition of entrepreneurship was adopted. All the respondents had been operating businesses for at least two years and employed at least two other people. The data are drawn from interviews and discussions with 35 black respondents and 40 Indian respondents (21 Muslim and 19 Hindu). Initially the Hindu and Muslim responses were analyzed separately, but the data were combined because the patterns of behavior were so similar to each other and so different from the other groups in the study. An analysis of the origins of these patterns found that the strength of family influence was the same for both groups, as was religious support for strong family structures.

The direct religious influence on business practices differed for the two groups. The Muslims constantly quoted from the Koran to justify specific practices. This behavior reflects the nature of the Koran: "Islam spells out the way of life it proposes; it pinpoints it, nailing it down through explicit injunctions" (H. Smith 1958:235). As Cavendish (1980:220) noted, "Frequent quotation [from the Koran] is a Muslim habit." Hinduism, by contrast, "does not have any formal treatises on ethics" (J. Smith 1995:449). Acquiring wealth, though not the highest aim of Hinduism, is an initial life goal (Cavendish 1980). Although only the Muslims quoted from the Koran to justify specific business practices, both groups clearly benefited from religious approval for their business undertakings. In terms of offering and receiving business help, the first source for both groups was family members, the second was friends or coreligionists, the third was other Indians.

In addition to interviews with business proprietors, interviews were conducted with people from both the private and public sectors who were engaged in the support and development of small business to obtain background information and test ideas.

FINDINGS: ENTREPRENEURIAL NETWORKS

Three major areas of difference between black and Indian business proprietors emerged in the study: status of the proprietor, reciprocity of networks, and trust in the family.

Status of the Black Business Proprietor

Before I discuss the findings for South Africa, it is worth noting the position of business proprietors in some nearby African countries. In Mashiga (Kenya), independence did not bring with it the boost to business that the successful traders had expected; instead, the old trade dwindled away and, as Marris and Somerset (1971:42) stated,

> the true heirs to the Masai traders of the nineteenth century were not Mashiga's businessmen, but the leaders of its drive for schools . . . education supplanted trade as the ruling passion.

And in Ghana, business enterprise was a relatively low-status occupation, and local businessmen were often treated with ridicule and contempt by the media and governmental officials (Kennedy 1980).

Lloyd (1966) found that in Africa as a whole, an entrepreneurial elite was absent because industrial and commercial activity was shunned by the most highly educated groups in favor of politics and the professions. Lloyd thought that the principal exception to this pattern was South Africa. Although the number of entrepreneurs may be greater in South Africa than elsewhere, the present study found that in South Africa, the *status* of black entrepreneurs, far from being high, was, at best, undecided.

Different factors, both political and behavioral, combined to shape a black aversion to small businesses. Liberation movements espoused a Marxist or socialist economic doctrine, and liberation rhetoric equated capitalism with apartheid oppression. Indian businessmen did not see themselves as siding with the oppressor by generating personal wealth (although their black customers might well have regarded them as exploiters), but the attitude toward the creation of personal wealth in the black community was ambivalent (De Bruin 1991).

In the Indian community, as is discussed later, both family practices and religious beliefs actively enhanced the status of businesses. In the black community, neither family nor religion were able to act as a buffer against the political definition of the creation of personal wealth as undesirable.

To understand this attitude, it is important to recognize that one of the consequences of apartheid was an interruption of the natural process of urbanization for black people, particularly black families. The apartheid ideal was a country in which cities were white (or at least "white-at-night"), and all blacks lived in rural areas. This ideal led to a brutal assault on family life, since men with jobs could get permission to live in cities as "temporary sojourners," but their families either lived illegally in the cities or remained in the rural areas. Forced removals under apartheid legislation compounded the assault on families as entire communities were uprooted, shifted, and split. Although respect for elders and senior family members remained a strong tribal value in extended rural families, urban, nuclear families had little opportunity to retain it.

On the one hand, apartheid attacked patterns of family authority by demeaning and humiliating black adults. The liberation movement eroded these patterns further by supporting youth militancy. One of the clearest examples of the erosion of this value was the 1976 "riots" or "uprising" (depending on one's political inclination) in the black schools. The schoolchildren were hailed as the liberators who had succeeded where their cowardly, incompetent, inadequate parents had failed, and traditional family relationships were overturned.

It may also be argued that the same family and religious structures that provided the Indians with a bulwark against the economic effects of apartheid protected them against the destructive onslaughts of the liberation movement. The family was supported by and, in turn, supported, religious and community beliefs and institutions. Within these supportive structures, individual self-respect and competence were nurtured. No such support existed for black individuals and families. Thus, one sees a strange, and surely unintended, pattern whereby both apartheid and its antithesis managed to work together to undermine the family. This pattern is repeated in the lack of status accorded to businesses in the black community. Indian family and community structures are still largely intact, postapartheid and postliberation, but black family and community structures have not survived well (Sono 1994). This chapter describes the role of family and religion in assisting the survival of Indian businesses under these assaults and the absence of similar supports for black businesses.

Often the attacks on the business proprietors who took part in this study appeared to be spearheaded by children, as the following comments by the black respondents show: "We help each other with many things: change, keep stock if it is delivered and they are not there, chase children who bully customers or hassle them when they come to our store." "My children do not play any role in this shop because I myself do not want them to come and help me, because I am suspecting that they might pinch some of my money." "Workers are the biggest problem, especially because we cannot hire the local children; they are naughty and troublesome." One respondent, when asked about the disadvantages of being self-employed, answered that it was a disadvantage "when the schoolchildren burn your shop."

If the shattered urban black family can provide no protective bulwark for the development of business skills and success, what of religion? No help appears to be forthcoming from religion either. The definition of the rich capitalist as oppressor is echoed in many of the tenets of Christian-based South African Liberation Theology. The structural position of the poor and oppressed is regarded as privileged (Leatt, Kneifel, and Nurnberger 1986). The poor are righteous simply because they are poor (Durand 1989); who would want to risk this righteousness by generating personal wealth?

Religious beliefs, whether among adherents of the "mainstream" Christian churches or the syncretistic African Independent Churches (Bekker, Cross, Evans, and Oosthuizen 1992), have not only provided no moral charter for entrepreneurial activities, but have invested individually rewarding economic activity with, at best, a moral ambiguity. What is striking about black entrepreneurs is not their embeddedness in networks, but their aloneness and independence and the limited resources on which they are able to draw for success.

Black entrepreneurs are always alone and vulnerable. The general anticapitalist ideology, initially espoused by liberation movements, seemed to turn small businesses into legitimate targets. In addition to ideological condemnation, small businesses were accessible and vulnerable to small-scale lootings and burnings, which the large corporations were not.

The 1989 strike by workers at South African Breweries illustrates the process well. In solidarity with the strike, a beer boycott was called for. Shebeen operators, running township taverns that were formerly illegal, were the obvious vehicle for this boycott. Soon, however, the Soweto Taverners' association was complaining that "About 100 shebeen operators had their stocks damaged and were assaulted and robbed by youth enforcing the boycott of South African Breweries products" (Rawana November 8, 1989). The *Star* newspaper ("Youth Gangs . . ." November 25, 1989) described "coldly efficient teenage hit teams . . . raiding shebeens and smashing stocks of beer" in Natal. Lucky Michaels, the president of the National Taverners Association, summed up the shopkeepers' dilemma: "We have kept out for two weeks with the hope that [the union] . . . and the SAB would solve their problems, but now we are dying in the process" (Molefe November 10, 1989).

Solidarity—black solidarity, the solidarity of the oppressed, the solidarity of the struggle—requires that the needs of individual entrepreneurs become secondary to the needs of the people. However, nowhere do the entrepreneurs benefit from this solidarity. Pilfering is as rife in the townships as it is anywhere else. It is not necessarily that township people steal more from black shops; it is simply that they do not seem to steal any less. Black entrepreneurs are regarded as fair game, the same as white entrepreneurs (Mkhize 1980). They are on the wrong side of the divide between the haves and have-nots. When it comes to boycotts or demands for "contributions" to pay for funerals and other political activities, they are once again on the wrong side, only this time in the opposite direction, because their entrepreneurial identity must take second place to a racial identity. They are defined as entrepreneurs when this definition makes them legitimate targets, but never as black entrepreneurs when this definition would entitle them to help or, at least, exemption. Since the inception of the new government in 1994, explicit attempts have been made to provide benefits for black or "emergent" businesses. It is too early to say how these attempts will influence community attitudes.

The status of business has also been influenced by the behavior of black traders. Until 1991, black trading rights were extremely circumscribed, even in the black townships (Rudman 1988). As happens with any limited commodity that is controlled by a bureaucracy, corruption was a problem. Perhaps even more than economic corruption, political corruption occurred because the provision of licenses and sites was the province of state officials. Traders who received licenses or sites were regarded as collaborating with the government; those who did not, by definition, did not trade.

Because the market was captive, shopkeepers did not need to attract customers, and, indeed, customers were often badly treated and denigrated. Mokoatle (1979) wrote that the status of black entrepreneurs was low in his community and that the ambivalent attitude toward black entrepreneurs resulted from a conflict between traditional and business values. In the eyes of black customers, the denigrating attitude in the dealer-client relationship to which blacks had been subjected by the dominant white group seemed to be adopted as a preferred business value by black traders as well. Mokoatle commented that it was odd that whereas good human relations was an esteemed value in the background culture, it was abandoned in the business context. Whereas family teaching and religious precepts shaped the business behavior of Indian traders, no such modifying factors operated in the black townships. Perhaps because being in business was regarded as being beyond the pale, beyond-the-pale behaviors were adopted, too.

None of this helped the status of black traders or, by extension, trading as an occupation. Furthermore, stores in black townships were prohibited by law from expanding, so natural innovators sought other occupations. The stereotype of the township trader—with obvious exceptions in real life, but firmly entrenched in the townships' consciousness—was of a rude and uneducated individual, often corrupt, and in cahoots with the white governing structure.

The conflict between economic and political interests is painfully illustrated by the plight of one respondent, who told of his impossible situation vis-à-vis the Soweto rent boycott (enforced, at least partially, by intimidation). The stock he carried was perishable, so he relied on several large refrigerators to keep his goods from spoiling. To avoid having his electricity cut off, he paid his electricity bill and rent for his shop, but not for his house. Because he did so, he was labeled a collaborator, and his home, car, and shop were petrolbombed.

Mokoatle's (1979) observation that black businessmen are denigrated by other blacks was borne out by the respondents' accounts of their families' opposition to their setting up businesses: "There was no help from the family. My husband said it was going to be a loser." "Family members were disconsolate about my leaving my so-important job, my job that was paying me enough, am I mad and so forth . . . they were totally against [me] for the next three years."

Mokoatle (1979) suggested further that black business proprietors may have had low status because the blacks' experience was that success required some professional qualifications, which the traders and businesspeople did not have. It is interesting to note that a business does not provide its own legitimacy; the legitimacy must come from what the business does for the community. A specific working goal may be to "employ my people." So respondents said things like, "If I can open up 100 jobs for my people, I'll be the most happiest person." One respondent noted that he enjoyed being in business because "you are the one who feeds the nation."

Status of the Indian Business Proprietor

Among both the Muslims and Hindus in the Gauteng province of South Africa, Gujeratis predominate. "Although each functions as a separate ethnic group, they nevertheless have close economic ties, as there are private and public business companies, members of which belong to both groups" (Vather 1991:36). Indian businesses in Africa have commonly been run by Muslims who had "individuals disposed to trading and a system of values that encouraged the quest for material prosperity" within their communities (Nanji 1994:52). It may be argued that in South Africa, the strength of the cultural ties of the Gujerati-speaking community led to a sharing of economic values, with the Muslim economic patterns transplanting easily to the Hindu worldview in which the acquisition of wealth is an initial aim in life (J. Smith 1995). This sharing of economic values may have been strengthened by forced geographic proximity and shared oppression. The Gujerati-speaking groups have a strong cultural identity, separate from other Indian groups, that is actively maintained through both religious and cultural practices (Reddy 1989; Vather 1991).

The passenger Indians who traveled from Gujerat brought with them three things: long experience with trading, strong family and community ties, and an enduring system of religious beliefs. These three sets of traditions interacted to ensure that the status of business was maintained in the community. Both family and religious traditions supported a patriarchy that was conducive to the maintenance of family businesses (Jithoo 1978, 1985). Religious practices helped promote family stability, and vice versa; one element without the other would have been much less powerful. It has already been noted that the existence of community networks indicates that a particular activity has high status in that community. Clearly, the status of business involvement is high in the Indian community. The onus is on the individual to achieve success, and the wherewithal for this success is provided.

For the Muslim Indians, it must be emphasized that it is the particular interpretation of the Koran in South Africa that is conducive to business success (Ali 1986). Islam is not in all instances a business-friendly religion. In a study of entrepreneurship in the Soviet economy, Connor (1991) found a much lower level of entrepreneurial activity in the predominantly Muslim republics, such as Tadzhikistan. In the South African study, however, one thing that struck the author most forcibly was the open mention of religion in discussions of Indian business practices. The following quotes show two interesting things: that the Koran is a source of practical business information—something far more specific than a generalized approval—and that the family is the transmitter of religious beliefs and particular religious interpretations. "My dad trusted in God. He had a firm determination to succeed and strongly believed that one's luck was in God. God provided it that one should see to the increment of one's fortunes for the sake of the children." "Islam shows you how to run your business." "We buy cheap and sell cheap—a ruling that has its foundations in the Islamic way of thinking—that is why we are successful." "You've got to have faith in God. Ultimately, our belief is that if you have good intentions, if you're honest and straightforward and you do hard work, you must see success."

The role of both family and religion in a second-generation business start-up is well illustrated in the following case: "My nephew starts a business. I give him a sum of R786.19. This is a magic figure. In Arabic 786 stands for In the Name of God. The amount I gave him was a wedding present, and most fortunately it came in handy. . . . His dad gave him a store, you can sell whatever you want, and he decides to sell dress fabrics. . . . His dad gave him R40,000 [U.S. $20,000] and said he must pay it back in a year."

Although the family is the most common resource for the construction of the business network, friends and coreligionists also play an important role, as one respondent noted. As stated in my research notes,

> His friend assisted him because of their Muslim commitments to one another and because they try to put into practice what they are taught. So the friend supplied goods which could be sold at cost price to generate funds for buying other lines. They had been friends through the Islamic movement for a long time. The friend continued supplying, and now some profit has been made on some of the other lines.

Another respondent told a similar story: "I started work at 16 in Pretoria North, in a big shop called Solomon Stores. It was a school in itself, so I learned by myself." Asked how he got this particular job, he said: "Just friends I met at the mosque one day. I worked for them for 15 years." The origin of this friendship may have been geographic: "My father borrowed money from friends who came from the same village in India." Religion may also be a source of friendship. Certainly, whatever the origin of friendship, the role played by friends is a testimony to the Indian entrepreneurs' ability to maintain and manage business-related networks emanating from a variety of sources. This ability to manage networks may be as important a factor in their success as the help provided by actual networks.

Family members play a direct role in business teaching, particularly in transmitting business values: "Mother was the keypin to the whole family unity; she kept us united, gave us courage, pushed us, promoted us, showed us how to behave as businesspeople and be enterprising." "On the general ethics or a general business point of view, I would go to my dad and I would thank him for his influence on me in life, in teaching me right from wrong, and not for business tricks as such." The moral teaching role ascribed to mothers and fathers neatly encapsulates the role of the family as the carrier of religious beliefs and business practices, and the interaction between the two.

Even the Prophet's wife is a role model. As this respondent noted: "The Prophet's wife, Khadija, she was a business lady; she was a very dynamic businessman, really she was one of the top business ladies of all time. She proposed marriage to the Prophet and already at that time you find a dynamic business lady, independent in her own right, standing on her own two feet, getting married to the Prophet."

FINDINGS: RECIPROCITY, ETHNICITY, AND FAMILY TRUST

Reciprocity and Trust in Black African Businesses

According to the literature (Benedict 1968, B. Berger 1988; Kassem and Timmons 1988), the extended family may be an economic help or hindrance, an unsurpassed business resource or a constant drain, leaching away the profits of the small business, preventing the accumulation of capital and expansion, or even the mere survival of the business.

For the successful urban black entrepreneurs in South Africa, there is no doubt that the extended family has been a hindrance more than a help. Help is to be found within the nuclear family, but not from all its components. In writing about neighboring Botswana, Mushonga (1981;86) made the following point that is important in evaluating the role of the extended family: "[T]he African believes that if he uses his money to help his unfortunate relatives he will have achieved more value than what thousands of dollars tucked away in the bank can give him."

Therefore, the researcher needs to bear in mind that what may seem to be a drain on funds from one point of view is providing a sort of moral capital from the viewpoint of a different value system. It also is worth noting the apparent mutual exclusiveness of dollars in the bank and helping family. It is not a question of all the family members helping one another and growing rich together, of helping out a retailer so he can provide a market for a manufacturer's goods, a pragmatic view expressed often by the South African Indian sample. This is philanthropic, top-down help. The relatives are poor, and the entrepreneur helps them out of the goodness of his heart and to gain prestige in the community. Helping networks are in place, but economically reciprocal networks are not. Such economic linkages as are to be found are hierarchical, not reciprocal, and the roles of donor and recipient are not interchangeable.

The lack of reciprocal economic networks is supported by the findings of Keirn (1970), who studied voluntary associations among urban South African women. Keirn described eight types of voluntary associations she encountered in Kwa-Mashu, near Durban, in 1969, but they included no economically oriented voluntary associations. The point is not that black networks do not exist. Groups, such as burial societies and revolving credit associations in various forms, are an integral part of township life. Credit is granted for consumption, not the creation of wealth, and business networks are absent.

One of the possible reasons for the lack of reciprocal economic networks may be found in Mushonga's (1981) comment that mistrust of others is a serious handicap for African entrepreneurs. The fear of being cheated may lead to the avoidance of partnerships, of starting companies with others, or of allowing other people to handle the cash in one's business. It is, of course, dangerous to generalize about "African businessmen," but this theme of mistrust was also expressed by the South African sample. Clearly, it is not an inescapable characteristic, but it is an important theme.

Marris and Somerset (1971) also found evidence of this sort of mistrust. They painted a rather bleak picture of the African entrepreneur in Kenya, hampered by mistrust and suspicion and somehow unable to convert family ties into business resources, as his Asian counterpart has been able to do:

> [The] lack of confidence in partners and workers forces an entrepreneur to rely on direct personal control, constricting the scale of his organization; family ties cannot compensate for their mistrust and link business rela-

> tionships to long-standing loyalties. This same lack of confidence also troubles the external dealings of the business. It is caught between the mistrust of its suppliers and its own mistrust of its customers. (p. 151)

A clearly demarcated group of black respondents in the South African study not only did not employ family members, but were explicitly opposed to this practice. Relatives, they complained, do not accept the authority of the business owner. A successful chemical manufacturer from Soweto was forthright on the topic of family businesses:

> I don't believe in family businesses; it has not worked many times in our cases. I have seen it working with Indians and other nations, but with us it does not work. What it actually does is it deprives us of having the right people. The kind of industry I am in is very sophisticated, and it needs specialized people who are hard to find; most of these people have been usurped by big companies. I am only looking for the right people, any nation, I would not even mind taking a white person.

When family members do work together, they are likely to be selected members of the immediate family, rather than members of any extended network. It is noteworthy that, in some cases, the reasoning is not "I employ X or Y because they are family (and, therefore, trustworthy)" but "I employ them because they are trustworthy (despite being family)." Often a particular family member is employed, with reference to his or her reliability or responsibility, while a general disapproval of the practice of employing family members is expressed. As one respondent put it: "The seventh employee is my mother. . . . She handles money and solves complaints and disputes. . . . She is the only person I can confide in, and I trust her very much." Another respondent was clear about the roles in which she would and would not employ family members: "I would also help members of the family by employing them to get them involved in the business. But I would never make them responsible for money or tills."

A degree of ambivalence between immediate and extended family members was expressed by another respondent, who was unusual in that he not only wanted to see his children take over the business, but was already involving the children, aged 5 and 2, in small tasks in his shop. He said: "Maybe, when they grow up, their uncles will tell them a different story . . . because at times you get irresponsible family members who are careless, who mislead your children."

Aspirations to create a family business were certainly present: "I would be glad if my family would join me and we could work together." "Everyone's wish is to have their children take over the business. Most unfortunately, it's not in the children; they always have other ideas." However, the aspirations often seem to outstrip the reality, so that the pattern set in Hart's survey (1972), in which in only five cases, out of a potential seventeen, children were working in the businesses, continues.

Sadly, the low status of business in the black community makes family succession extremely unlikely. The Indian pattern, in which a senior businessman thinks nothing of rolling up his shirtsleeves and serving behind a shop counter, simply does not apply here. The general attitude of many of the children, that the shops are legitimate targets for anything from petty pilfering to arson, is only one expression of communitywide contempt and suspicion.

The individual township business proprietor, unsupported by reciprocal systems, is also free of reciprocal obligations. A particularly sharp picture of the heady aloneness that may accompany modernity was portrayed by a 50-year-old coal merchant, a widower. He clearly knew many details about his relatives' lives, but their working lives were separated by the peculiarly modern bugbear, the lack of time. As he noted:

> I have got many relatives. Some are staying nearer my place. Some are far from my place. Most of them are educated. Few of them are not. They work as teachers some of them, some work as nurses, some are working in factories, some in shops as salesladies. They do not play any role in this business of mine, since they are people who are busy working.

The man had one friend who was in the same business: "I had a friend who has the same type of this business, but he was selling and using animals, that is, donkeys for moving from one place to another." The respondent used a truck, not donkeys, so his friend was also left behind in the roar of the internal combustion engine. And the respondent stated, with a mixture of pride and trepidation: "I will help myself when I am in trouble."

No social system of obligation, sanction, or reciprocity could be determined: "This thing depends largely on individuals. . . . If he thinks, man I was helped, he can do the same to other people. . . . It's not a real commitment. It doesn't work today." A pragmatic reciprocity tended to be viewed with suspicion; people seemed to feel that a moral basis was required. One respondent stated: "The white Chamber of Commerce were very interested to help us. But they were interested for their own interest. They were mainly interested in you as their customer." For this reason, the help proffered by this Chamber of Commerce was rejected. Some respondents reported helping other businessmen to get started. This help seemed to amount to a sort of patronage, rather than help as part of a reciprocal network. There was no mention of either sanction or reciprocal benefits.

Reciprocity and Trust in the Indian Group

In Indian business, credit often seems to be extended or withheld, depending on the credit worthiness of the family name. Reputation and family name play a role that seems to be unique in the Indian community. As one respondent said: "They would just listen to the name Garda and then give you an unlimited line of credit as long as you never default payments." It seemed that a credit-worthy family name could be developed, over generations, in South Africa or inherited from India. The reverse also seemed to be true—that without the name, it was harder to get help. "If you are Mr. Somebody they will help you, but not if you are down and out."

The hardships experienced by the Indian community in South Africa clearly played a role in forging the strong bonds in this community. Hardship does not automatically have this effect; it is the response to the hardship that is crucial. It seems that the religious tenets and the family support in this community ensured that the external social definitions of the Indians as inferior were never internalized. The Indians' definition of themselves as actors with the potential to influence their environment was never in question. Their social and political marginalization never succeeded in severing the link between cause and effect. Devout religious practice remained a source of the status that they were denied externally. Economic success was also a source of status. The effort required by the individual for religious piety and economic and professional success was well understood, and, therefore, community respect was forthcoming for the fruits of this effort. "Participation in social, religious, educational and cultural organizations can enhance one's business reputation and extend contacts and communication" (Vather 1991:30).

In Johannesburg, many successful Indian businessmen talked nostalgically of the poor conditions in which they grew up in Vrededorp. Ironically, or perhaps not ironically, Vrededorp is an Afrikaans name that means "Town of Peace." "In Vrededorp", one respondent remembered, "you never had to worry about your children. If you were hungry, you would pop into the nearest house and there would be a plate of food for you. That kind of social harmony you won't find anywhere in the world. In Vrededorp, there was genuine love although there was no comfort." The harshness of their circumstances forged the bonds that fed the networks that stand them in good stead to this day. Of course, it would be absurd to suggest that the Indians have been successful only because of apartheid. Up and down Africa, Indians have succeeded as entrepreneurs without any such odious goad. What is remarkable about the Indian entrepreneurs in South Africa is that they have not merely survived the limitations and harassment of apartheid legislation, they have transcended them and turned their deprivations into an unparalleled resource.

The ability to use networks, the understanding of reciprocity, clearly indicates the relationship of other people to the business. There is a clear distinction between credit to consumers, which is frowned on, and credit to clients, which will ultimately build the business. On this point, one respondent noted:

> He says, OK, I'm a little better off than you, I'll give you 60 days; then you go off and give someone else 60 days. Because you can give 60 days, you can sell more goods, he's going to sell more goods. We know in our minds that you are helping a person, but while you're helping him, you are building yourself.

This arrangement is in clear contrast to the helping relationships of the black entrepreneurs to others in business, which are philanthropic and paternalist, but not often reciprocal.

To the outside observer, the networks that function around Indian businesses are the most complex and sophisticated that were encountered in this study. However, the respondents did not perceive of them this way. When asked specifically whether Indians made use of networks, one respondent answered: "No. Unfortunately [for us], I think that happens a lot in other communities around the country. Certain other communities in the country . . . such as the Jewish community . . . they have that type of . . . schoolboy network."

The Indian businessman, in contrast to his black colleague, is never alone. The most extraordinary range of people play a role in Indian businesses: grandparents, spouses, fellow worshippers met casually at the mosque, and someone who might be described as "the brother of the man who used to work next door to the factory." Even Abdul, the greengrocer, who was not doing well, received no help from his wealthy family, and bewailed the loss of the old-fashioned spirit of helping among Indians, got help from a friend who gave him fixtures and fittings and was able to borrow another friend's truck to fetch fresh produce from the market. Clearly, this is a formidable network.

Indian Ethnicity

Family and religion both play an important part in Indian networks. However, they are not sufficient, in themselves, to explain all aspects of the networks. A broader, more nebulous concept, that of "Indianness," must be invoked. This is the only group to whom it makes sense to ask, "Did you get help from other members of your broader community?" The concept of "Indian" is one that makes sense in a business context. Whether it was the first member of a clan to immigrate to Southern Africa, getting work as a cleaner with "Asians in Maputo" over 100 years ago, or is the present generation investing with the Hindu bank or the Islamic Corporation, the Indianness or otherwise makes a difference to business behavior.

Initially, the question asked about starting up a business was, "How did you acquire the capital to start your business?" Again, this question proved too simple to encompass Indians' responses. Help with an undertaking took many forms. It might be, "all the shop fittings were done by my brother and his friends," or it might be credit and technical expertise, as in the following case:

> I went to a wholesaler who later became my father-in-law who is now my ex-father-in-law with this sample (for a uniform for a black school). He had about 4,000 meters of Trevira material in stock. He gave me six months to pay—no interest with six months to pay. The word, *interest*, never entered the mind altogether. . . . Then a small factory owner [who] was my dad's closest friend for forty years and whose son is to marry my niece, promised

> to make the garments for me. I provided the pattern and material. They said I should pay back whenever I could.

Like the black participants, the Indians agreed that the spirit of helpfulness is no longer as strong as it was in the old days. "In the old days, Muslims did help other Muslims to get started. . . . today people are scared to lend as, often, the money isn't repaid." Another respondent thought that the modern Indian family is not as close knit as its predecessors and that the academic aspirations are higher. "The only time you find a lot of [business] involvement is where people do not have a very strong interest in acquiring an education, and they feel that it's more convenient to get involved in the business. Or financial—they can't afford." Some respondents believed that help is no longer as forthcoming as it once was: "Today you've got to help yourself."

Black Ethnicity

Theoretically, the black entrepreneurs should have provided the richest lode of data on networks in the study. Many of the factors that have elsewhere been seen to promote the development of networks were present here: both the need factors, a result of being barred from other avenues of survival and status, and the resource factors, which draw on ethnicity, family, and a history of communality.

The existence of communalism in black tribal history is not really the subject of debate. Its role in a modern context is, however, the subject of much rhetoric and, unfortunately, less research. The rise of Black Consciousness brought with it an emphasis on the positive attributes of the black historical and cultural legacy and placed black communalism in a positive light over white or Western individualism, which is seen as cold, uncaring, and exploitative. This positive group orientation is embodied in the isiZulu word, *ubuntu*, or its seSotho equivalent, *botho*[2] (Godsell 1986). It is not easy to distinguish the *ubuntu*-induced respect for individuals from what is enjoined (although, of course, not always followed) in the Western Judeo-Christian ethic. Sherwood (1980) suggested that it has been the physical separation of the races, rather than any ideological difference, that has led to a black perception of whites in South Africa as cold and uncaring. The research question here is, of course, whether this perception imparts a particular way of doing communal business.

What was revealed during the interviews was something different. The black respondents came across as sturdy, independent individualists in almost all aspects of running a business. For example, their own savings provided start-up capital for the largest group. In this regard, they were no different from the South African black population in general. In a table of spending patterns by population group for 1975 (Committee for Economic Affairs 1984), the percentage of the blacks' income that went to savings was 3.17 percent, higher than that of the Asians (1.4 percent) and the coloreds

(1.8 percent) (the figure for whites was not given). These figures confirm trends elsewhere in Africa. After surveying several studies of small businesses in Africa, Berry (1978) concluded that the most important source of initial capital for small enterprises is the entrepreneurs' own savings.

Several black respondents ran another small business, usually part time, to provide start-up finance; they reported no start-up help from friends or other blacks. How does their experience compare with those found in other studies? The proportions seem roughly similar to other South African groups. Mokoatle (1979) reported that personal savings and loans from relatives accounted for 75 percent of the start-up capital, though, unfortunately, he did not separate the two sources. In a study of the manufacturing sector in Soweto, Jagoe (1984) found that 69 percent of the initial finance came from personal savings, 16 percent from business partners, 6.5 percent from family loans, 4.5 percent from *Mashonisa* (loan sharks), and 1.2 percent from friends. Hart (1972) also noted that the most important single source of start-up capital was personal savings (43 percent) and part-time business activities (10 percent). It is worth noting that out of a total of seventy-eight subjects, Hart reported only four family partnerships and two nonfamily partnerships.

Personal savings and other forms of individual effort are mobilized by black entrepreneurs. Self-employment remains a minority occupation. Such data as are available indicate that under apartheid, 8.6 percent of the economically active Indian population were entrepreneurs, compared to 10.8 percent of the white population and 1.8 percent of the economically active black population (Committee for Economic Affairs 1984). These statistics must be treated with great caution, however, since it was in the interests of the black respondents to keep illegal economic activities hidden from officialdom. Nevertheless, the pattern is clear: Independent Indian economic activity has thrived despite apartheid, and independent black economic activity has not.

CONCLUSIONS

Although the Indian entrepreneurial networks described in this study are clearly successful, it is also apparent that successful entrepreneurs may operate outside networks. Networks themselves are not all helpful, and as this study found, there is a distinction between *energizing* and *dissipating* networks. An energizing network constantly replenishes the resources of all the participants. The most important source of this replenishment appears to be not so much the physical resources contributed to the network (such as time, physical labor, or financial credit in the case of a business). Rather, it is the intangible resources that matter, particularly the valuing of the activity to which the network is devoted and the affirmation of the competence of the network's members.

All members of an energizing network must be regarded by the other members as competent contributors to the network; their competence is constantly elicited by the expectations of other members and affirmed by the other members' approval. There is no place in an energizing network for a passive victim: All the members must be effective actors. Within the extended trading families of the Indian community, a process of business socialization takes place, starting at a young age. Business competence and confidence are taught and expected. It is the family networks that produce the competent actors who are essential to energizing networks. The valuing aspect of the energizing business network has its roots in religious valuing of business activity. And it is the interaction between family-taught behaviors and religion-derived values that ensures the success of these networks.

A dissipating network, on the other hand, includes members who contribute no resources and eventually consume the resources of the active members. All the members of a dissipating network are not competent actors and contributors. Since all do not equally value the central activity (such as the generation of profits), they feel no obligation to contribute to it and no shame in consuming the resources of those who do contribute. So it is clear that the two aspects are mutually dependent: the valuing of the central activity and the need and ability to contribute to it.

The Indian and black entrepreneurs were both victims of apartheid legislation that removed them from profitable locations, limited their trading rights, and denied them access to credit via home ownership. The Indian entrepreneurs had a sort of spiritual capital to draw on. They were able to harness their families' resources and religious approval to fight back and to establish successful undertakings, ranging from corner shops to manufacturing empires. No campaigns had to be launched to legitimate trading and commerce in the Indian community—the religious and social approval was there already. It was only the practical problems that needed to be overcome, although these problems were huge. The energizing networks of family members, friends, and fellow worshippers were the ideal tools for doing so. A business philosophy of low prices, low profit margins, and low overheads was facilitated by the employment of family members for minimal financial rewards.

In other African countries, the price the Indian community has paid for economic success has been political isolation and vulnerability, most extremely illustrated in Uganda, where 50,000 Asians were expelled by dictator Idi Amin in 1972. Marris and Somerset (1971) noted that the commercial structure pioneered by the Indians in Kenya depended on caste and kinship and that the opportunities that were generated were jealously guarded for family members and friends. The combination of political insecurity and social self-enclosure prevented the Kenyan Indians from exploiting the opportunities of an African state. Although the actual businesses owned by Indians in Kenya may not have been the same as those owned by their counterparts in South Africa, the two groups' style of functioning is clearly comparable. However, the South African Indians do not share the vulnerable isolation of their East African counterparts. Their active political involvement has ensured them significant political representation in all spheres, from trade union leadership to Speaker of the House of Assembly. Their economic future and positive contributions to South African development seem assured.

No equivalent process to that which aided the Indians came to the aid of the black entrepreneur. The extended family appears to function as a dissipating, rather than an energizing, network perhaps because business is not a valued undertaking or because of the incapacity of the family itself. Malao (1994:14) wrote of the "degree of disrepair that has visited our family institutions" and the "moral disintegration and social fragmentation especially in the African society." She pointed out that "the basic unit in African society is the family, but the concept of family in African society is more extensive than that of the Western world. If the centre—which is the family—collapses, then the rest of the concentric circles which are clearly related to the inner concentric circle equally become degraded."

Not only did black entrepreneurs lack family support, but they often had no religious approval for their undertakings. In the study, the black respondents hardly mentioned religion. The one reference to religion came from a black organizer in the informal sector, who stated categorically that, as a Christian, he disapproved of profit. The origins of the particular intepretation of Christian doctrine that gave rise to this view are not clear; perhaps it came via the Afrikaner missionaries.

In the years when South Africa was still a British colony, the Afrikaner leadership explicitly equated capitalism with oppression and condemned individual profit seeking as an alien and immoral ideology (O'Meara 1983). This view was similar to what the black liberation leaders advocated half a century later. In the 1930s the Afrikaner leadership, including leading *dominees* (ministers of religion), began to refashion Afrikaner Nationalist ideology to incorporate an approval of individual wealth creation, articulated as a sort of Christian National Capitalism. Particular efforts were made to persuade young Afrikaners to regard business as a legitimate occupation (Du Plessis 1964).

Perhaps the missionaries passed on their idea of tainted money without communicating the recanting of the 1930s? Certainly, neither Calvinism nor any of the other mainstream religions has provided the black entrepreneur with a moral charter equivalent to that provided for the Indians. Nor has politics provided a justification, as it came to do for the Afrikaners. Politically, capitalism has been the bogeyman, identified with oppression. Proprietors of township businesses have been regarded as a source of "voluntary contributions" for funerals and other occasions and as allies, willing or otherwise, in various boycott campaigns. They have not been the recipients or beneficiaries of political organization or rhetoric but, rather, the contributors of resources in a dissipating network.

What of the future of black entrepreneurs? The tenacity with which the businesspeople in this study have survived is remarkable. In the face of an extremely hostile macroenvironment, the Indian community has created for itself an enterprise-friendly microclimate, within which individual businesses have flourished. In the face of hostile macro- and microenvironments, black entrepreneurs have survived. Perhaps this individual tenacity will be a major factor in reshaping the balance between individual and group, creating more space and respect for the individual in the current South African society in transition.

Right now, there is a conflict of views about the proper role of business in the new South Africa. One view considers business a proper channel for redress and restitution, with ethnicity providing an entitlement to business ownership. Another view (Shubane 1995) sees business as the natural preserve of energetic black individualists, who have done well against heavy odds and are likely to forge ahead with these barriers removed. Although it is clear that the black middle class will grow rapidly, it is not clear whether this growth will result in the development of "a dependent bureaucratic bourgeoisie . . . more interested in parasitism than the enlargement of their freedoms . . . [or] . . . a surge of black professionals and entrepreneurs" (Welsh 1994:43). Both process and outcome of this debate will be crucial for the shaping of South African society.

In April 1995 one of the first black-owned companies was listed on the Johannesburg Stock Exchange. The capital for this company was provided by a clear strategic network of trade unions, independent churches, and other black institutions. Whether this network is energizing or dissipating remains to be seen. Time will also tell whether, in this instance, other institutions can carry out the valuing and competence-providing functions of familial and religious networks.

Notes

1. Using a nominee from a different racial group provided access for members of the prohibited group, but the real owner was vulnerable to the nominee's breach of faith or dishonesty.
2. *Ubuntu*, derived from the root *ntu* = person, is best translated as humanism. African humanism is a familiar theme from the first generation of post-*Uhuru* African leaders, such as Kenneth Kaunda.

References

Ali, Rachid. 1986. *The Social and Economic Outlook in the Islamic State (from the Holy Quran and the Works of Dr. Fazlul Rahman Ansari)* (Unpublished pamphlet) Johannesburg: Small Business Advisory Service.

Bagwandeen, D. 1989. "Historical Perspectives." Pp. 1–22 in *The Indian South Africans*, edited by A. J. Arkin, K. P. Magyar, and G. J. Pillay. Durban, South Africa: Owen Burgess.

Beinart, William. 1994. *Twentieth-Century South Africa*. Cape Town: Oxford University Press.

Bekker, S. B., C. R. Cross, J. P. Evans, and G. C. Oosthuizen. 1992. *Rise Up and Walk: Development and the African Independent Churches in Durban*. Durban, South Africa:

Centre for Social and Development Studies, University of Natal; Research Unit for New Religious Movements and Independent Churches, University of Zululand.

Benedict, Burton. 1968. "Family Firms and Economic Development." *Southwestern Journal of Anthropology* 24:1–19.

Berger, Brigitte. 1988. "The Urban Poor and the Formation of a Viable Industrial Culture." Pp. 16–24 in *The Social Context of Small-Scale Business Development*, edited by Gillian Godsell and Hanlie van Dijk. Johannesburg: Centre for Policy Studies, University of the Witwatersrand.

———. ed. 1991. *The Culture of Entrepreneurship*. San Francisco: Institute for Contemporary Studies.

Berger, Peter. 1994. "The Gross National Product and the Gods." *MacKinsey Quarterly* 1:97–110.

Berry, Sara S. 1978. *Custom, Class and the "Informal Sector": Why Marginality Is Not Likely to Pay* (Working Paper No. 1). Boston: African Studies Center, Boston University.

Birley, Sue. 1985. "The Role of Networks in the Entrepreneurial Process." Pp. 325–27 in *Frontiers of Entrepreneurship Research: Proceedings of the Fifth Annual Entrepreneurship Research Conference*. Wellesley, MA: Babson College.

Blicksilver, Jack. 1979. "Kinship and Friendship in the Emergence of a Family-Controlled Southern Enterprise." Pp. 89–122 in *Entrepreneurs in Cultural Context*, edited by Sidney M. Greenfield, Arnold Strickon, and Robert T. Aubey. Albuquerque: University of New Mexico Press.

Boissevain, Jeremy, and Hanneke Grotenberg. 1987. "Ethnic Enterprise in The Netherlands." Pp. 105–31 in *Entrepreneurship in Europe: The Social Processes*, edited by R. Goffee and R. Scase. London: Croom Helm.

Bundy, Colin. 1979. *The Rise and Fall of the South African Peasantry*. London: Heineman.

Cavendish, Richard. 1980. *The Great Religions*. London: Contact.

Committee for Economic Affairs of the President's Council. 1984. *Report on Measures Which Restrict the Functioning of a Free Market Oriented System in South Africa* (PC1/1984). Pretoria, South Africa: Government Printer.

Connor, Walter D. 1991. "The Rocky Road: Entrepreneurship in the Soviet Economy 1986–1989." Pp.189–209 in *The Culture of Entrepreneurship*, edited by Brigitte Berger. San Francisco: Institute for Contemporary Studies.

De Bruin, Carol. 1991. "The Relationships Between Spaza Shops and Their Communities." Unpublished master of management thesis, University of the Witwatersrand, Johannesburg.

De Kiewiet, C. W. [1941] 1978. *A History of South Africa: Social and Economic*. Oxford, England: Oxford University Press.

De Vries, Kets. 1977. "The Entrepreneurial Personality." *Journal of Management Studies* 14(February):34–57.

Du Plessis, E. P. 1964. *'n Volk Staan Op: Die Ekonomiese Volkskongres en Daarna*. Cape Town: Human & Rousseau.

Durand, Jaap. 1989. "Engelssprekende Kerke: Gevangenes Van Apartheid." *Die Suid-Afrikaan* 23(October):30–31.

Godsell, Gillian. 1986. "Work Values in Organizations." Pp. 101–24 in *Behavior in Organisations: South African Perspectives* (2nd ed.), edited by Julian Barling, Clive Fullagar, and Stephen Bluen. Johannesburg: McGraw-Hill.

———. 1990. "The Social Networks of South African Entrepreneurs." Unpublished Ph.D. dissertation, Boston University.

Godsell, Gillian, and Hanlie van Dijk, eds. 1988. *The Social Context of Small-Scale Business Development*. Johannesburg: Centre for Policy Studies, University of the Witwatersrand.

Greenfield, Sidney M., Arnold Strickon, Robert T. Aubey, and Morton Rothstein. 1979. "Studies in Entrepreneurial Behavior: A Review and Introduction." Pp. 3–20 in *Entrepreneurs in Cultural Context*, edited by Sidney M. Greenfield, Arnold Strickon, Robert T. Aubey, and Morton Rothstein. Albuquerque: University of New Mexico Press.

Hagen, Everett E. 1971a. "How Economic Growth Begins: A Theory of Social Change." Pp. 123–38 in *Entrepreneurship and Economic Development*, edited by Peter Kilby. New York: Free Press.

———. 1971b. "The Transition in Colombia." Pp. 191–224 in *Entrepreneurship and Economic Development*, edited by Peter Kilby. New York: Free Press.

Hart, Gillian. 1972. *Some Socio-Economic Aspects of African Entrepreneurship* (Occasional paper 16) Grahamstown: Institute of Social and Economic Research, Rhodes University.

Jagoe, H. M. 1984. "A Study of the Operating Features and Problems Relating to the Formal Manufacturing Sector in Soweto." Unpublished MBA thesis, University of the Witwatersrand, Johannesburg.

Jithoo, Sabita. 1978. "Complex Households and Joint Families Amongst Indians in Durban." Pp. 86–100 in *Social System and Tradition in Southern Africa*, edited by J. Argyle and E. Preston-Whyte. Cape Town: Oxford University Press.

———. 1985. "Indian Family Businesses in Durban South Africa." *International Journal of Comparative Family Studies* 16:365–76.

Kassem, M. Sami, and Sherman A. Timmons. 1988. "Family Business East and West: An Initial Comparison." Pp. 178–84 in *The Proceedings of the 33rd World Conference of the International Council for Small Business*, edited by G. Roberts, H. Lasher, and E. Malicke. Marietta, GA: School of Business, Kennesaw College.

Kennedy, Paul T. 1980. *Ghanaian Businessmen: From Artisan to Capitalist Entrepreneur in a Dependent Economy*. Munich: Weltforumverlag.

Keirn, Susan. 1970. Voluntary Associations Among Urban African Women. *Communications from the African Studies Center* (University of Florida) 1:25–40.

Kharsany, Ebrahim E. 1971. "A Profile of the South African Indian Business Community—Reasons for Success and Failure." Unpublished MBA thesis, Graduate School of Business Administration, University of the Witwatersrand, Johannesburg.

Kim, Kwang Chung. 1985. "Ethnic Resources Utilization of Korean Immigrant Entrepreneurs in the Chicago Minority Area." *International Migration Review* 19:82–111.

King, Kenneth. 1977. *The African Artisan*. London: Heinemann Educational.

Leatt, James, Theo Kneifel, and Klaus Nurnberger. 1986. *Contending Ideologies in South Africa*. Cape Town: David Philip.

Leff, Nathaniel H. 1978. "Industrial Organization and Entrepreneurship in the Developing Countries: The Economic Groups." *Economic Development and Cultural Change* 26:661–75.

Lloyd, P. C. 1966. *The New Elites of Tropical Africa*. Oxford, England: Oxford University Press.

Louw, Leon, and Frances Kendall. 1986. *South Africa: The Solution*. Johannesburg: Amagi Press.

Lovedale, Past and Present: A Register of Two Thousand Names. 1887. Lovedale, South Africa: Lovedale Press.

Malao, Neo. 1994. "Keynote Address." Pp. 11–16 in *African Family and Marriage under Stress*, edited by Thembe Sono. Pretoria, South Africa: Centre for Development Analysis.

Marris, P., and A. Somerset. 1971. *African Businessmen: A Study of Entrepreneurship and Development in Kenya*. London: Routledge & Kegan Paul.

McClelland, D. C. 1961. *The Achieving Society*. Princeton, NJ: Van Nostrand.

Min, Pyong Gap. 1987. "Factors Contributing to Ethnic Business: A Comprehensive Synthesis." *International Journal of Comparative Sociology* 28:173–93.

Mkhize, Khaba. 1980. "The Stick that Beats the Baas." *Frontline* 1(February):31–32.

Model, Suzanne. 1985. "A Comparative Perspective on the Ethnic Enclave: Blacks, Italians, and Jews in New York City." *International Migration Review* 19:64–81.

Mokoatle, B. N. 1979. "The Black Entrepreneur in South Africa: A Product of Social Change." Pp. 217–41 in *South Africa's Urban Blacks: Problems and Challenges*, edited by G. Marais and R. Van der Kooy. Pretoria, South Africa: Centre for Management Studies, University of South Africa.

Molefe, Phil. 1989. "Call from the Shebeens: Settle the Beer Boycott." *Weekly Mail* November 10.

Morgan, David L. 1988. *Focus Groups as Qualitative Research*. London: Sage.

Mushonga, B. L. B. 1981. *African Small-Scale Entrepreneurship with Special Reference to Botswana* (Working Paper No. 34). Gaborone: National Institute of Development and Cultural Research, University College of Botswana.

Nanji, Azim. 1994. "Beginnings and Encounters: Islam in East African Contexts." Pp. 47–55 in *Religion in Africa*, edited by Thomas Blakely, W. van Beek, and D. Thomson. London: James Currey.

O'Dowd, Michael. 1991. *The Growth Imperative*. Johannesburg: Jonathan Ball.

O'Meara, Dan. 1983. *Volkskapitalisme: Class, Capital, and Ideology in the Development of Afrikaner Nationalism*, 1934–1948. Johannesburg: Raven Press.

Pillay, Gerald J., Tillayvel Naidoo, and Suliman Dangor. 1989. "Religious Profile." Pp. 145–70 in *The Indian South Africans*, edited by A. J. Arkin, K. P. Magyar, and G. J. Pillay. Durban, South Africa: Owen Burgess.

Rawana, Theo. 1989. "Violence Prompts Tavern Owners to End Beer Boycott. *Business Day* November 8.

Redding, Gordon. 1990. *The Spirit of Chinese Capitalism*. New York: Walter de Gruyter.

Reddy, Y. G. 1989. "Cultural Perspective: Literature." Pp. 195–213 in *The Indian South Africans*, edited by A. J. Arkin, K. P. Magyar, and G. J. Pillay. Durban, South Africa: Owen Burgess.

Rothstein, Morton. 1979. "The Changing Social Networks and Investment Behavior of a Slaveholding Elite in the Ante-Bellum South." Pp. 65–88 in *Entrepreneurs in Cultural Context*, edited by Sidney M. Greenfield, Arnold Strickon, and Robert T. Aubey. Albuquerque: University of New Mexico Press.

Rudman, Theo. 1988. *The Third World: South Africa's Hidden Wealth*. Cape Town: Business Dynamics.

Sherwood, Rae. 1980. *The Psychodynamics of Race: Vicious and Benign Spirals*. Sussex, England: Harvester Press.

Shubane, Kehla. 1995. *The Wrong Cure: Affirmative Action and South Africa's Search for Racial Equality* (Development Policy Series No. 8:4). Johannesburg: Centre for Policy Studies.

Smith, Huston. 1958. *The Religions of Man*. New York: Harper & Row.

Smith, Jonathan, ed. 1995. *The HarperCollins Dictionary of Religion*. San Francisco: HarperCollins.

Sono, Themba, ed. 1994. *African Family and Marriage under Stress*. Pretoria, South Africa: Centre for Development Analysis.

South African Institute of Race Relations. 1977. *A Survey of Race Relations in South Africa, 1976*. Johannesburg, South Africa: South African Institute of Race Relations.

South African Institute of Race Relations. 1994. "Provinces in Profile." *Fast Facts* 7.

South African Institute of Race Relations. 1998. *South African Survey 1997–1998*. Johannesburg, South Africa: South African Institute of Race Relations.

Sowell, Thomas. 1981. *Markets and Minorities*. New York: Basic Books.

Vather, Sunil. 1991. "The Contribution of Informal Networks to Entrepreneurial Behaviour in the Gujerati-Speaking Hindu Community." Unpublished MBA research report, University of the Witwatersrand, Johannesburg.

Ward, Robin. 1987. "Ethnic Entrepreneurs in Britain and Europe." Pp. 83–104 in *Entrepreneurship in Europe: The Social Processes*, edited by Robert Goffee and Richard Scase. London: Croom Helm.

Ward, Robin, and Richard Jenkins, eds. 1985. *Ethnic Communities in Business*. Cambridge, England: Cambridge University Press.

Weber, M. [1904] 1958. *The Protestant Ethic and the Spirit of Capitalism*. New York: Charles Scribner's Sons.

Welsh, David. 1994. "Liberals and the Future of the New Democracy in South Africa." *Optima* 40(2):39–44.

"Youth Gangs Spill Beer to Bolster Strike and Boycott." 1989. *Star* November 25.

PART III

The Context of Innovation

CHAPTER NINE

Mormonism in France: The Family as a Universal Value in a Globalizing Religion

JOHN JARVIS

INTRODUCTION

The French are a troubled people these days. Like other peoples in Europe, the United States, and elsewhere in the world, they are experiencing the painful social upheavals brought on by the diminishing importance of national borders and the globalization of extended social, economic, and political networks. The internationalization of goods, services, communication networks, and travel is creating a new world that is as foreign to the French today as the "New" World was to Columbus and others who journeyed across the Atlantic five centuries ago.

In Columbus's time, people had to adapt to the expansion of their individual conceptual worlds into "new places" that often deeply contradicted their established notions of what the world was all about. Today, people around the world face an opposite process. Now the forces of globalization are rapidly bringing about what Robertson (1992:6) succinctly termed "the compression of the world into a single space." Cultural differences and contradictory practices no longer exist in the relative security of exotic, far-off places. It is all "here," happening "right now." In France, as elsewhere, people are struggling to adapt to the loss of the familiar amid the flood of the unfamiliar in every aspect of their lives.

But if globalization brings unique new challenges to individuals in various cultures around the world, it also brings new options for responding to the challenges. The purpose of the study presented in this chapter was to push beyond a preoccupation with the problems of global change to examine the solutions that a growing number of people around the world are finding to make sense of the world as it comes to occupy a "single place."

The study specifically targeted a religious response to globalization because despite a rich archaeological and historical record detailing religion's fundamental role in the human experience since time immemorial, religion is currently receiving relatively little attention in scholars' explorations of the most recent trends in global identity building and the development of transnational social structures. Although religion may have ceased to matter to the scholars who study global events, I argue here that it still matters a great deal to the everyday individuals who wake up each morning to face the chaos and uncertainty that global changes are bringing into their lives.

Beyer (1994) reinforced this functional argument for including religion in the study of global processes, pointing out that functional systems like politics, economics, and science, which have received much more attention in social scientific attempts to explain globalization, "leave vast areas of social life underdetermined and create serious problems that they do not solve" (p. 105). These problems range from challenges to individual and community identities, to threats to the environment, to increasing gulfs between the rich and the poor and between social groups. Beyer suggested that this area is where we should look for religion to assume an important role in globalization. As he put it: "The question for religion and its carriers is, how to take advantage of this situation" (p. 105).

This study turns to the French branch of the Church of Jesus Christ of Latter-Day Saints (the LDS Church, or the Mormons) to illustrate how one specific and rapidly growing religious movement is "solving the problems" of globalization for its membership. The Mormon Church numbers about 24,000 adherents in France. In modern times, it has moved beyond its base in the United States, where, by 1980, it had become the fifth largest church (Stark 1984). It has now established itself in 138 nations and territories around the globe where 47 percent of its nearly 10 million members reside (*Deseret News* 1994:12). It is the Church's success beyond U.S. borders that makes it a particularly promising site for a study of religion and globalization.

The underlying purpose of this chapter is to demonstrate how French Mormons, themselves a direct result of a globalizing institution, turn to religion to repair certain stresses and tears in the social fabric of their lives brought about by a rapidly changing world. I will focus on the "stresses and tears" that seem to concern people in France the most these days, the decline of family culture and the disintegration of kinship and community ties. My findings from fifteen years of contact with French Mormonism, culminating in an intensive, three-month ethnographic and sociological field study of French LDS communities in 1990, suggest that French Mormons are finding new ways of making sense of their lives through a religion that reestablishes family, kinship, and community as ultimate values in a new and uniquely Mormon worldview.

Theoretical work on religious mobilization by Stark and Iannacone (1994) suggested that as a religious economy becomes more pluralistic, one can expect individual movements to "specialize," which Stark and Iannacone defined as catering "to the special needs and tastes of specific market segments." French Mormonism supports this proposition through its unique theological and organizational focus on the family and in its extension of family culture to the Church community. Although most French clergy preach the brotherhood of man in abstract terms to highly homogeneous congregations, Mormon missionaries are in the streets of every major French city inviting prospective recruits to join their dynamic young communities where the brotherhood of man is practiced daily through a great variety of Church meetings and programs.

As a result of this "hands-on," "in-the-street" approach to religious recruitment, Mormonism positions itself to make a direct and successful appeal to two major segments of the French population—native-born citizens and the growing number of immigrants. My work in France indicated that the Church's primary focus on building healthy families and extending immediate family culture through genealogical research and temple rituals to include deceased ancestors has great appeal to French families who are feeling threatened by the growing divorce rate and familial instability.

But this is only one part of the French LDS recruitment story. My field research has shown that only two-thirds of French Mormons are actually French. Another third of the Church (32 percent) is made up of a great diversity of immigrants from over twenty nations across four continents around the world (Jarvis 1991). Mormonism's literal interpretation of the human race as "children" of the same God and the Church's active commitment to bringing this "divine family" together encourage native French converts to open their doors and their lives to a great diversity of immigrant peoples who would otherwise remain marginalized by mainstream French society.

In short, Mormonism's key to success in France seems to be its ability to appeal both to established and uprooted segments of the population in a manner that is satisfying and meaningful to both. At the heart of this appeal is an extended and religiously charged notion of the family that provides common ground for bridging local and global cultures. My findings suggest that rather than succeeding in France *despite* the stresses of globalization, Mormonism's success there is *due to* these stresses and to the reassuring answers the Church provides to them.

RESEARCH METHODS

My research on French Mormonism grew out of a long history of personal connections to the LDS community in that country. In the 1970s and early 1980s, I spent four years living and teaching in France. During that time, I established lasting contacts within the French branch of the Church and was an active participant in a number of congregations. My experiences among the French Mormons afforded me a unique "insider-outsider" relationship that I was able to draw upon more recently for a focused study of the cultural impact of Mormonism in France.

The information and core data for this chapter came from a three-month field study conducted in northern, central, and southern France in 1990. Fieldwork for the project combined sociological and ethnographic methods that included distributing to and collecting an extended survey questionnaire from 190 French LDS family groups, examining the membership rosters of six congregations, conducting three dozen interviews, and integrating myself into three French LDS households as a participant observer in their daily routines (Jarvis 1991). These data and follow-up information gathered during a subsequent visit to France in August 1994, provide the chapter's factual core. I spread the three dozen interviews across as representative a sample of the LDS population as possible, meeting with leaders and general members in numbers corresponding to the gender, race-ethnicity, family size, and age of the overall sample.

Ethnographic Research

To enhance the interview data, I selected three families—one with young children, one with teenage children, and one with adult children—and lived with them for a week to ten days each. The family with young children was made of up of a native-born Frenchman, aged 29, who had married an Algerian immigrant woman two years older. The man drove trucks and served as an all-around "handyman" for a seafood distribution company in Avignon. His wife stayed at home and cared for their four children, aged 3, 5, 8, and 10. Theirs was a working-class family of lower-than-average income.

The family with teenage children also resided in Avignon. It consisted of a husband and wife who were native-born French; a 19- year-old daughter; and two sons, aged 15 and 16. The husband, aged 49, had recently left a sales position in an international beverage company (Schweppes) to start his own restaurant-supply company. His 38-year-old wife worked with him in this new undertaking, often putting off household duties to travel with him when he visited clients throughout France and Switzerland. Though previously a lower-middle-class family in income, the family was experiencing a time of economic uncertainty because of the father's career change.

The third family resided in Lyon, the heartland of France, where the 50-year-old father worked as an administrator in the city fire department and his wife, aged 46, stayed at home to care for their 12-year-old daughter. The couple also had a married son, aged 26, who lived separately with his wife and infant daughter, and another son, aged 25, who had recently returned from serving a two-year LDS mission in the Carribean and who was living separately. The family members were all native-born French. This family was the most economically stable of the three families I spent time with and was of upper-middle-class income. I stayed ten days with them, dividing my time between the parents' home and the apartment of the 25-year-old son, observing familial adjustments as the two older sons were pushing out on their own to begin new families.

Homestays permitted me to observe firsthand and to participate in the families' daily routines at home, at play, and at church meetings and gatherings. Each stay was with a family who I had known for no less than eight and up to fifteen years, which allowed me deeper access into ongoing conversations about their beliefs, struggles, and the meanings they were making of their lives.

Survey Research

To contextualize and test ethnographic insights into the transplantation of Mormon religion in France, I relied on a twelve-page questionnaire. I distributed the questionnaires among members of six congregations that were representative of the Church's French membership in terms of length of existence, geographic location, and size. Two congregations were long established in the older parts of Paris and Lyon, two were younger congregations that had been recently organized in the suburbs of each city, and two were communities in Avignon and Lemans that were still directly dependent upon missionary support and without official administrative status as full-fledged congregations. The six congregations combined provided a broadly representative sample of 1,300 members, or 6.5 percent of the total French LDS population of 20,000 at the end of the 1980s (*Deseret News Church Almanac* 1989).

To conduct the survey, I began field research in each congregation by meeting with the equivalent of its priest or pastor, who provided detailed membership rosters that included the names, sex, ages, marital status, and family sizes of all 1,300 persons in my study. With the assistance of leaders in five of the six congregations,[1] I was also able to establish member-retention rates, levels of participation, and general ethnic and racial origins of 1,178 persons. In addition, the local leaders helped me set up formal introductions for distributing the questionnaires to families in each congregation. Of the 620 families represented on the membership rosters, 413 were selected for inclusion in the study. The 46 percent response rate resulted in 190 completed questionnaires. Of the 190, 20 were dropped from consideration because they were American missionaries; this left a sample of 170 for the purposes of analysis. The introductions by the congregational leaders were usually held during a part of the Sunday meeting set aside for announcements. In the presence of full congregations, I would give a brief overview of my scholarly interest in the Church and then invite members to participate in a sociological survey of French Mormon beliefs, values, and practices.

In most instances, I followed this invitation to participate by immediately distributing questionnaires to one predetermined individual in each family that was selected to participate—either the father, the mother, or the family's only adult church member in the case of single parents and individuals who had joined independently. The sample was not a strict probability sample because although every household in the small congregations was included, only alternate households in the large congregations were included in the sample solicitation. However, on most dimensions, the sample seemed representative of the congregations, and the membership rosters made exact preselection possible. The participants were encouraged to fill out the questionnaires at home and to return them in the attached, stamped and addressed envelopes. The questionnaires were distributed alternately to male and to female household members to obtain a representative sampling by sex—male respondents made up 51.9 percent of the sample, female respondents accounted for 48.1 percent—with only one questionnaire per family to ensure as broad a sampling as possible. Addresses on membership rosters also made it possible to mail questionnaires to active members who were not present to receive them directly and to members who had ceased to participate.

PRELIMINARY FINDINGS: INSTITUTIONAL DYNAMISM AND DIVERSITY

A Rapidly Growing Church

One important early finding of my research was that the LDS Church is doing well in France. Growth statistics offer the most obvious indications of the institution's dynamic nature. The Church s growth in France has been fairly consistent over the past two decades, expanding from 9,800 members in 1974 to 24,000 in 1991, a healthy increase of around 8 percent per year. This rate compares to an annual growth rate of between 3 percent and 4 percent for the U.S. branch of the Church over the same period (Jarvis 1991:183; *Deseret News* 1994:219, 395).

My observations in 1990 confirmed the dynamic condition of the Church in France. On-site visits and interactions with members and local, regional, and national leaders brought me repeatedly into contact with signs of institutional growth. I found the establishment of new congregations and the construction of new church buildings to be common. In Lyon and Avignon, where I have had regular contact with LDS congregations for over eighteen years, active LDS populations have tripled and quadrupled since the mid-1970s. Lyon went from 70 active members in 1976 to 220 in 1990; Avignon increased from 15 to 55 active members and was preparing for the construction of a chapel (Jarvis 1991).

French Mormonism: A Community of Migrants and Immigrants

From a demographic point of view, the most startling characteristic of French Mormonism I encountered during my 1990 study was the diversity of its members. Through an analysis of membership rosters, responses to 170 extended survey questionnaires, and more than 30 personal interviews, I found that over 400 persons, a full 32 percent of my overall sample of 1,300 French LDS members were not French at all. They were foreign nationals or immigrants representing 20 different racial and ethnic groups from four continents and the Caribbean and Pacific islands. Table 9.1 sums up these findings.

As might be expected, the largest non-French group was made up of North Americans (8 percent), the source of a majority of the missionaries laboring in France. Less expected was that Sub-Saharan Africans (blacks) were

Table 9.1
GEOGRAPHIC ORIGINS OF THE FRENCH LDS RESPONDENTS COMPARED TO THE FRENCH POPULATION

Place of Birth	French LDS Sample (N = 170)	French Population*
France	68%	93%
Africa	13	3
Sub-Saharan Africa	7	†
North Africa	6	3
America	12	†
North America	8	†
South or Central America	4	†
Europe	7	3
Other (Middle East, India, Asia)	1	1

*From George (1986:18, 36).

†Figures less than .5 percent were omitted; all other percentages were rounded to the nearest whole number.

the second largest group of nonnative members (7 percent), and their number was increasing far more quickly than any other group in the sample. Africans overall (blacks and Arabs from North Africa combined = 13 percent) had already outgrown the total number of Americans (North, South, and Central Americans combined = 12 percent), with Europeans and "others" (Indians, Asians, Middle Easterners) making up the final 7 percent to 8 percent of my sample.

In sum, one third of the French LDS sample I studied was of non-French origin. This finding is especially significant since only 7 percent of the total population of France is foreign born (George 1986). Comparatively, the LDS Church seems to be a gathering place for participants from a wide diversity of cultural backgrounds.

THE CULTURAL CONTEXTS OF AN "AMERICAN-MORMON-FRENCH" STUDY

It is important to underscore that the field research supporting this chapter was not conducted in a vacuum, nor were the people I encountered in France cut off from the larger world around them. Transformations in their beliefs, practices, and ways of seeing the world are only part of a much larger, ongoing historical and cultural narrative. This section presents some of the major themes in this narrative as a context for the analysis of how the French Mormons are using religion as a way of coping with the destabilizing effects of globalization.

Mormonism as an American Religion

Although Mormonism's early social experimentation with polygamy and its resistance to democratic pluralism throughout the nineteenth century caused many critics to condemn the young movement as un-American, there is much to recommend Mormonism as a patently American religion. First, there is the obvious. The Church was organized with six members, all New Englanders, in upstate New York in 1830. Furthermore, its founder and first prophet, Joseph Smith, Jr., descended from five generations of Congregationalists in Topsfield, Massachusetts.

Smith based his claim to prophetic status upon a new book of scripture, the *Book of Mormon*, that he added to the sacred canon. In what is perhaps Mormonism's most symbolic connection to American roots, Smith claimed to have taken the golden tablets containing the *Book of Mormon* record directly from the American earth. According to his personal account, the tablets had been hidden in a hillside in upstate New York for over a thousand years before he was chosen by God to reveal them to the modern world (Bushman 1984; Roberts 1902). Smith's subsequent "translation" of the *Book of Mormon* grafted a 500-page panorama of American history, theology, and prophecy into the biblical epic contained in the Old and New Testaments.

With roots sunk deep into a revealed version of the American past, the young LDS Church absorbed an eclectic blend of community-centered American beliefs, practices, and values between 1830 and 1900 as it grew into an established American religious movement. Mormonism is perhaps best understood as one of the more clearly structured and most enduring expressions of nineteenth-century American religious and material utopianism that exists today. Generally, the Mormons have remained in opposition to the self-centered materialism, social indifference, and loss of a sense of community that geographic expansion and economic opportunity engendered in the industrial revolution of the past century. People who join the LDS Church tend to have little interest in the supremacy of the individual and the democratic free-for-all that has been endemic since the Jacksonian era. Rather, they value a sense of community that is both spiritual and material. At the heart of this community, they place individual families, not individual persons. Mormons consider the family, the Church, and society as best governed by a patriarchal authority emanating from God that overrides the democratic autonomy of any one individual.

As the Mormon movement has taken on the trappings of an institutionalized religion, its identity has increasingly become characterized by a unique paradox. At the same time that it presents itself as a prophetic movement that looks to the future, its institutional beliefs, values, and behaviors frame a church that looks to the American past more than any other major American church. For example, today, the LDS Church requires its members to abstain from alcoholic consumption as completely as members of the American Christian Temperance Society did a century ago. The use of tobacco and caffeinated drinks remain as much a cause for concern and condemnation in the Church as they were during the Popular Health Reform Movement of the nineteenth century, led by Samuel Thomson, Sylvester Graham (inventor of the Graham cracker), and other proponents of herbalist medicinal practices (Bush 1979, 1981; Smith 1979; Starr 1982).

The American past is uniquely expressed in virtually all aspects of Mormon life. A Victorian sense of modesty and proper sexual behavior are maintained by the Church's requirements of chastity before marriage and conjugal faithfulness after marriage. Members who go to the Mormon temples (a necessity for achieving the full benefits of good standing in the faith) participate in a set of rituals that draw liberally from nineteenth-century Masonic rites and Christian theology. After their initiation into temple rituals, the members are required to wear symbolic underclothing issued by the Church that is a modernized version of the long-handled underwear common in the American West at the turn of the century.

In its first years, the LDS Church required its members to turn all their earthly goods and wealth over to the Church leadership to be shared communally. This was a standard practice among other utopian and communitarian movements of the nineteenth century like the Shakers, the Oneida Colony, and the followers of Charles Fourier. Today, to sustain the leadership and a wide variety of Church programs, believers are asked to give 10 percent of their annual incomes to the Church. Payment of these "tithes" is required for good standing in the faith.

Mormonism and the Influence of the American Frontier

A lot has been written and a lot can be said about the American nature of Mormonism. Yet none of the discussion and study of the LDS Movement to date has done much to explain why this "American" religion is having high levels of success outside the United States. As a scholar of French culture, for example, I would think that asking the French to give up their wine, coffee, and cigarettes; to abstain from extramarital sex; and to hand over 10 percent of their incomes to a foreign church would be the best way to ensure the speedy failure of a religious movement in France. And yet my research indicates that Mormonism is doing well on French soil.

The key to understanding Mormonism's success abroad has a great deal to do with the movement's American past, but it is a part of that past that most scholarship has heretofore overlooked. Mormonism is a frontier religion. It was born amid the great religious experimentation and social upheaval of the New York wilderness in the early 1800s. The circumstances of this genesis and subsequent relocations farther and farther into the American West have tremendous implications for the family focus that Mormonism's institutional identity and message have taken on over time. It is this family focus, a veritable "theology of the family," that must be understood before one can understand the appeal of Mormonism beyond American borders at this time.

As Cross's (1950) seminal work on religious innovation in upstate New York pointed out, Mormonism began as a migrant religion. In the early nineteenth century, New York was literally overrun by the children of New England Puritans, who were forced by raw economic realities to leave their families, churches, and communities to seek new opportunities and new lives on the frontier. Not only was the first LDS community organized by these westward migrants, but the entire community pulled up stakes and relocated farther West *seven* times in its first fourteen years of existence (Davis 1953; Hansen 1967, 1981). These relocations were necessitated by the high tensions that the close-knit Mormon community developed with its neighbors in New York, Ohio, Missouri, and Illinois. Finally, in 1845, the major portion of the Mormons in Nauvoo, Illinois, followed Brigham Young to the far West, where they established the Church headquarters that still exists in Salt Lake City, Utah.

Once it was established in Salt Lake City, the LDS Church undertook an ambitious foreign mission program that met with tremendous success in the British Isles and Scandinavia. The most attractive feature of this missionary effort was the Church's financial support for relocating converts to the American West. This crucial era of growth in the Church's history is referred to as the "gathering to Zion," and it brought upward of 100,000 immigrants into Mormon communities in the West between 1845 and 1900 (Arrington 1958; Arrington and Bitton 1979; Leone 1979).

From its beginnings, Mormonism has been a religion of the dispossessed, the uprooted, the migrant, and the immigrant. In this sense, it embodies a central feature of the American story as completely as any other social or cultural institution in U.S. history. The Mormon faith was molded by uprooted people who had suffered the anguish and uncertainties of leaving families, loved ones, and community networks behind before they encountered the LDS Church. The founders of Mormonism were ambitious and hardworking young New Englanders who made the difficult choice to sacrifice family ties for new lives on the frontier. As the Church grew on American soil, its growth was fueled by converts from abroad who made similar choices to leave their families and communities behind in the old countries to start fresh amid the promising expanses of a new land.

Knowing something about the frontier history of Mormonism makes it much easier to understand what these uprooted immigrants did with their religious visions and aspirations in the rough isolation of the American West. Among other things, they created an extension of Christian theology that pushes beyond more traditional notions of the divine family to a cosmological view that promises the reunion of entire extended human family networks in the life after death. Mormonism's "theology of the family" is part of a larger religious tradition that historian Shipps (1986) convincingly described as being to the rest of Christianity as Christianity is to Judaism. Religious scholars like Shipps are increasingly coming to see Mormonism as a unique new religious tradition in its own right, rather than as another branch of Christianity (Stark 1984). LDS teachings on the family provide one of the best illustrations of theological and ritualistic innovation that distinguishes Mormonism as something new in the Christian landscape.

Mormon theology replaces individual salvation with what members of the Church see as a greater good—the salvation of entire extended family networks. The Mormons have even added a new word—*exaltation*—to their religious vocabulary to describe the joy and fulfillment of family salvation in God's presence. Genealogical research has become a cornerstone of the faith in the past generation, permitting baptism and "eternal marriage" by proxy for deceased relatives and distant ancestors to ensure the "exaltation" of extended family units in the afterlife (*Eglise de Jésus Christ* 1986).

Ultimately, it is this family-centered expression of immigrant longing for connectedness and community that is among the most American features of Mormonism. Furthermore, the family-centered, community-building solutions that the Mormons found as they established their world in the American West helps explain the ongoing success of the movement among other groups around the world today. There are a great number of dispossessed and alienated people out there these days, and the Mormon message has been uniquely shaped by time, place, and human events to have an especially strong appeal to them.

THE CONTEMPORARY CRISIS OF FRENCH RELIGION AND THE FRENCH FAMILY

To understand Mormonism's appeal to a diversity of people in France, it is valuable to place the processes of recruitment in context with other important cultural upheavals and transformations in contemporary French society. Mainstream church attendance figures below 10 percent are only part of the much larger pattern of social change in modern France and throughout Europe (Hervieu-Léger 1990). In 1977, a group of European scholars formed the European Value System Study Group in an ambitious effort to discover the degree to which the countries of Europe shared a common, coherent base of fundamental values. From 1977 to 1981, they carried out a sociological survey among 12,463 persons in nine countries. More than anything else, the survey revealed a troubled and tension-ridden era of great change and diverse values in Europe, in general, and France, in particular (Stoetzel 1983).

In the survey, France scored the highest of all nine countries on scales of permissiveness (based on attitudes toward the excusability of twenty-two various behaviors, such as cheating on taxes, premarital sex, homosexuality, drug use, abortion, euthanasia, divorce, and killing in self-defense). Only Denmark had lower levels of religious practice. At the same time, over 70 percent of the French joined 85 percent of all Europeans in calling for a renewed emphasis on traditional family life, one area where the general spirit of permissiveness was causing grave concerns (Stoetzel 1983:122).

The impact of permissiveness on the family was only one area in which conflicting traditional and modern values were at the root of social tension.

Because of the large proportion of respondents who identified themselves as not "religious" persons (31 percent) or as "convinced atheists" (10 percent), France lost its historical identification as a Catholic-Christian nation, joining Belgium and Holland in a new category of "lay" countries for value comparisons with Catholic and Protestant majorities in other nations (Stoetzel 1982:90; Center for Applied Research 1982b:11).

It is not surprising that the redefinition of national values that is apparent in contemporary French society is accompanied by a significant degree of social and political tension as various groups vie for control of the directions the changes will take. As was just indicated, one area in which the liberalization of traditional values is causing the greatest tension and the loudest public outcry is in the family domain. As Monneron and Rowley (1986:305) noted in a detailed study of the historical changes in France over the past twenty-five years: "If the decline of patriotism and religion seem irreversible and mobilize only a weak portion of the French, the family crisis is a subject of scandal for all." At the heart of the scandal is a divorce rate that has tripled in 2½ decades and a startling 30 percent decrease in total marriages in the twelve years from 1972 to 1984 as couples increasingly chose to cohabit without official legal ties. Linked to changes in the nature of the couple was a drop in the birth rate to 1.7 children per couple (well below the 2.1 needed for population replacement) that prompted heated national debate, as well as remedial legislation providing direct economic incentives to encourage larger families.

Amid the social tensions surrounding these changes in France, scholars in the European Value Study identified two largely incompatible camps, characterized by "those attempting to keep ongoing contact with their 'roots'" and "others [determined] to obtain emancipation and the new possibilities that it offers" (Stoetzel 1983:9). Monneron and Rowley (1986:305) interpreted France's response to the particular crisis of the family as evidence of a "much greater difficulty for individuals to give up family ideals than other traditional attachments." They phrased their overall view of the impact of the changes in the family unit in similar language to that of the European Value System Study Group: "The crisis has brought about a weakening of consensus which encourages an increase of feelings of exclusion and marginalization and an overall impression of insecurity and vulnerability" (p. 309).

THE APPEAL OF FRENCH MORMONISM IN A TIME OF SOCIAL CRISIS

A Unique Message: Family Salvation

The studies reviewed earlier suggested that the French are troubled about the directions in which they are going, that many of them are attempting to remain in contact with their roots, and that the family is the "root" that matters most to them. As unsettling as such feelings of rootlessness may be, they provide an important sense of common ground between the native-born French and France's immigrant population. Some 4 million immigrants have left families and communities behind, usually in former French colonies scattered across Africa, the Carribean, the Pacific Islands, and Southeast Asia, to come to France to look for better lives. This mixture of migrant and immigrant provides, in effect, an ideal social environment in which the Mormon message is most likely to have great appeal. Of the tens of thousands of young LDS missionaries who are currently carrying a message of "family salvation" to peoples around the world, nearly eight hundred are laboring in France.

The first lesson that the Mormon missionaries share with prospective converts introduces The Plan of Our Father in Heaven, more commonly referred to by Church members as the Plan of Salvation (*Eglise de Jésus Christ* 1986). The Plan of Salvation is the cosmological system that gives clearest expression to the LDS worldview. It explains human existence as an intermediate, developmental stage between a preexistence as spirit-children of God and a postmortal reunion with God and a divine, eternal family.

The role of the LDS Church is to teach believers the nature of their identities as children of God and to set them on a clearly defined path of moral decisions and appropriate behaviors that will lead to the fulfillment of their divine potential. This divine potential is inseparably intertwined with the ultimate source of meaning in the Mormon cosmological system: reunion with one's eternal family. When Mormons use the word *family* in the eternal context, they do not mean it in a vague, generic sense as in the "family of man." They teach that each individual may continue current family relationships in the afterlife and may even link such immediate family networks to those of ancestors, as well as to those of the generations that follow. Such a family-centered cosmology allows Mormons to emphasize from the outset that the most important success human beings can achieve in mortal life is to build strong and loving families on Earth that are based on the divine model.

The ultimate, otherworldly message of the Plan of Salvation is that earthly families can be reunited after death in God's presence and can inherit eternal life as interconnected family networks. This reunion is dependent, however, on the observance of certain rituals and codes of conduct by faithful believers here on Earth (*Eglise de Jésus Christ* 1986; McConkie 1966). In a comparative context, Mormonism differs from other world religions in a significant way. Whereas other religions offer potential converts salvation or enlightenment on a personal level, Mormonism presents salvation ("exaltation") as a group-centered process that can transport entire extended family units into God's presence in the afterlife.

Impact of the Mormon Message in France

My 1990 field research confirmed two things: The Mormon message is having a significant impact on a diversity of converts in France and the family-centeredness of the message is why it is succeeding (Jarvis 1991). These findings became especially clear when I asked the respondents to list the Mormon teachings that most influenced them to join the Church. I explored their open-ended answers in more depth during three dozen interviews and through personal observations in various Church meetings at the same time that I was circulating the questionnaires. The ten most compelling reasons that the native French and nonnative members gave for joining the Church are listed in Table 9.2.

Far and away the primary teaching that was cited most often as leading to the decision to join the Mormon Church was the Plan of Salvation. More than half the native-French and nonnative respondents alike chose this core of instruction that links all Mormons to God's eternal family. The second-most-cited reason the respondents gave was also related to Mormonism's family-centered message; 1 out of 3 persons in each group listed their desire to gain "eternal life with their families."

Perhaps the most significant finding of the analysis of the respondents' reasons for conversion was the degree to which teachings on the family provided a common ground between the native French and nonnative members. After prioritizing family-centered teachings, each group found a unique

Table 9.2
RANKING OF THE TOP FIVE LDS TEACHINGS THAT LED TO THE SUCCESSFUL RECRUITMENT OF NATIVE AND NONNATIVE RESPONDENTS*

Native French Respondents (N = 88)	Nonnative Respondents (N = 36)
1. The Plan of Salvation (53 percent)†	1. The Plan of Salvation (61 percent)
2. Eternal life with family (33 percent)	2. Eternal life with family (33 percent)
3. Joseph Smith's prophetic mission (27 percent)	3. *The Book of Mormon* (25 percent)
4. Divinely inspired authority/leadership of LDS Church (22 percent)	4. Joseph Smith's prophetic mission (19 percent)
5. Baptism of adults; for remission of sins; by proper authority; for the dead (15 percent)	5. The nature and mission of Jesus Christ (17 percent)

*The open-ended survey question read: "What teachings from the missionary discussions had the most influence on your decision to join the Church?" Since only the five most frequently mentioned teachings are listed in the table, the N's are reduced because some respondents did not provide answers in the top five.

†The percentages show the proportions of each group who mentioned a given teaching in response to the open-ended survey question. The percentages do not total 100 because most converts listed multiple teachings that influenced their conversions.

profile of other reasons for adopting their new faith (items 3–5 in Table 9.2). The importance accorded the Plan of Salvation and gaining eternal life with one's family suggests, however, that the Church is able to establish a core of shared values on which to build a sense of community that can accommodate what the converts themselves see as less important differences.

One would expect that people who joined a religious movement for its teachings about the family probably placed a disproportionately high value on the family unit *before* they encountered the new religion. This logic would suggest that people who join the LDS Church in France do so because it allows them to operationalize values they already hold dear. Indeed, I found this to be the case when I looked at pre- and postconversion value profiles of my French Mormon sample—but there was an important twist. As it brought new members into the fold, the LDS Church seemed to be able to attach the preexisting, "this-worldly" family values of the converts to a new core of "other-worldly" Mormon values as part of the conversion process. Table 9.3 presents an overview of this link. It is important to note that premembership responses reflect retrospective claims by individuals who were already recruited and should be understood only as approximations of previous values. However, the primacy of the family-centered value attachments claimed by the French LDS sample before recruitment accords well with the findings of the European Values Study and other national surveys conducted in France over the past two decades (Monneron and Rowley 1986; Stoetzel 1983).

Prior to membership, according to their retrospective claims, native French converts already attached the highest value to such family-oriented things as faithfulness in marriage (item 1), being a devoted parent (item 2), and spending time with family (item 4). They also ranked a number of common secular values in their top ten preconversion priorities, including a good education (item 3), obeying the law (item 5), being a good neighbor (item 6), good health (item 7), and career success (item 8). Of the top ten values the French members held before conversion, otherworldly notions of having eternal life with one's family (item 9) and concern for life after death (item 10) were already present among things that seemed to matter. However, these values were not given top priority.

The bottom half of Table 9.3 shows a similar pattern of values for the nonnative converts in France. Even more than their native counterparts, the immigrant members of the Church seemed to attach the highest importance to family-oriented values before they converted. Being a devoted parent (item 1) and faithfulness in marriage (item 2) ranked among their two top values, as was the case for the native French converts. However, spending time with family (item 3) replaced the importance the French accorded education. Another notable shift was the importance that the nonnative respondents gave the concept of having eternal life with one's family (item 5), which was ranked ninth by the French.

At the same time that the prerecruitment values suggested that the two segments of the French LDS Church had a great deal in common, an

Table 9.3
PRE-LDS MEMBERSHIP RANKING OF THE TEN MOST IMPORTANT VALUES

NATIVE FRENCH RESPONDENTS (N = 115)	
This-Worldly Values	Other-Worldly Values
1. Faithfulness in marriage (1.16)*	
2. Being a devoted parent (1.19)	
3. A good education (1.49)	
4. Spending time with family (1.57)	
5. Obeying the laws of one's country (1.76)	
6. Being a good neighbor (1.83)	
7. Taking an interest in personal health (1.88)	
8. Career success (1.92)	
	9. Eternal life with family (1.81)
	10. Concern for life after death (2.16)
NON-NATIVE RESPONDENTS (N = 55)	
This-Worldly Values	Other-Worldly Values
1. Being a devoted parent (1.22)	
2. Faithfulness in marriage (1.29)	
3. Spending time with family (1.49)	
4. A good education (1.58)	
	5. Eternal life with family (1.72)
6. Being a good neighbor (1.83)	
7. Career success (1.92)	
8. Obeying the laws of one's country (2.05)	
9. Taking interest in personal health (2.19)	
	10. Interest in spiritual Life (2.27)

*Figures in parentheses represent the mean for each value. The respondents were asked to rank each value on a scale of 1 (very important) to 5 (not important).

overview of the postrecruitment values indicated that the value attachments of each group underwent similar shifts during the conversion process (see Table 9.4).

The postconversion ranking by native French members in Table 9.4 reveals two key shifts in the converts' values. First, the converts replaced a number of secular values with patently Mormon values (see items 4 and 6–10). Second, their values indicated a greater emphasis on the primacy of the family. Of the top five values, four reflected a preoccupation with family culture compared to three before conversion. Faithfulness in marriage (item 1) and being a good parent (item 2) remained the top two French LDS values. Attaining eternal life with fellow family members (item 3), ranked ninth in the preconversion French profile, shifted to become part of the top

Table 9.4
POST-LDS MEMBERSHIP RANKING OF THE TEN MOST IMPORTANT VALUES

NATIVE FRENCH RESPONDENTS (N = 115)	
This-Worldly Values	Other-Worldly Values
1. Faithfulness in marriage(1.04)*	
2. Being a devoted parent (1.08)	
	3. Eternal life with family (1.14)
	4. The saving sacrifice of Jesus Christ (1.17)
5. Spending time with family (1.18)	
	6. Keeping the body clean and pure as a temple of God (1.20)
	7. Eternal progression (1.21)
	8. The proper authority for doing God's work on Earth (1.30)
	9. A final judgment with just rewards for all (1.277)
	10. Following the counsels of a living prophet (1.34)
NONNATIVE RESPONDENTS (N = 55)	
This-Worldly Values	Other-Worldly Values
	1. Eternal life with family (1.0192)
2. Faithfulness in marriage and being a devoted parent (both = 1.0196)	
	3. The saving sacrifice of Jesus Christ (1.03)
4. Spending time with family (1.08)	
	5. Reading the *Book of Mormon* (1.11)
	6. The proper authority for doing God's work on Earth (1.13)
	7. Eternal progression (1.15)
	8. A final judgment with just rewards for all and avoiding premarital sex (both = 1.17)
	9. Following the counsels of a living prophet (1.21)
	10. Keeping the body clean and pure as a temple of God (1.23)

*Figures in parentheses represent the mean for each value. Respondents were asked to rank each value on a scale of 1 (very important) to 5 (not important).

five postconversion values. Another addition to the cluster of family-centered values was the saving sacrifice of Jesus Christ (item 4). It is important to note that in the LDS Plan of Salvation, the personal acceptance of Jesus' saving sacrifice is presented as the key to starting out on the divinely ordained path leading to eternal life with family. Thus, when spending time with family (item 5) is added to the top five postrecruitment values, each of the five has significant links to family ideology for a typical Mormon.

Table 9.4 also shows that the value shifts for the nonnative LDS converts in France were similar to those of the French converts. As was the case with French postconversion values, the values of the Church's nonnative converts likewise moved from the secular realm toward a greater emphasis on family culture. The final result is a cluster of the same top five values held by the native French members, headed by eternal life with family (item 1), faithfulness in marriage and being a good parent (both ranked 2), the saving sacrifice of Jesus Christ (item 3), and spending time with family (item 4). These values were followed by a list of "otherworldly" LDS values that was compatible with the list given by the native French members (see items 5–10).

With the exception of reading the *Book of Mormon* (item 5) and avoiding premarital sex (tied in item 8 with a final judgment with just rewards for all), the native French and nonnative respondents ranked the same value concepts among the top ten rank-levels of things that they cared about most after they became members of the LDS Church. Only the relative rankings of these values shifted somewhat between the groups (for example, item 6 for the native French became item 10 for nonnatives, and item 8 for the French became item 6 for the nonFrench). The nature of the LDS message and the way it is presented helps explain this high degree of conformity. In the missionary lessons, all the Church's teachings are presented as integated parts of one whole worldview. Converts are not encouraged to pick and choose what they will believe. Rather, the missionaries present family salvation as the core of a larger body of religious teachings that must be believed or disbelieved in its entirety.

In a study of how utopian institutions recruit and retain committed members, Kanter (1972:73) argued convincingly that the successful development of a religious community depends upon the "extent to which group life can offer identity, personal meaning, and the opportunity to grow in terms of standards and guiding principles that the member feels are expressive of his own inner being." Examination of the value changes encouraged by Mormonism in France suggests that the LDS movement is applying Kanter's insights in an explicit and effective manner. By offering a group life rich in identity concepts and personal meaning that enhance the significance of the family, the church reinforces and builds on existing familial values that are likely to be expressive of important aspects of the recruit's "inner being." This sacralization of the family is then attached to an ordered set of standards and principles that promise to guide the recruit in a path of personal and group development toward the attainment-fulfillment of what appear to be long-held, family-centered values.

What Converts Say About Family and Religion in France Today

Although I spent a lot of time surveying French LDS values and people's reasons for joining the Church, my most important insights did not come from responses to the questionnaires and statistical analyses. The deepest insights came from talking to the people involved. I spent weeks living with individual member families from a variety of backgrounds. I attended church meetings, social gatherings, prayer sessions, meals, recreational activities, and family discussions. I faced family crises as well as moments of family rejoicing. I spent a good deal of time talking to young people, to their parents, and even to their parents' parents. The following is some of what I learned.

A longtime member of the French Mormon Church and a mother of three summed up the current crisis of the family in France in critical terms when I visited her at home in a low-income housing project in the suburbs of Paris. She placed the blame for the breakdown of the family, and the resulting loss of social values and proper comportment among the younger generation, on women's increasing absence from the home. She saw the great increase in two-career families as improving the material aspect of life, while the spiritual side suffered. As she put it, "Like dogs and cats, parents kick their children out the door every day," trading their responsibilities as parents for the benefits of an extra income. What parents generally failed to recognize, she thought, was that placing their children in public institutions for twelve hours a day from age 2 onward left an emotional void that was catastrophic for the children.

When I asked this woman why she thought the Mormon Church was succeeding in France, she returned to the topic of the family: "It gives hope of returning to the presence of God, of having a family and stability in our lives. By applying the gospel, we can overcome the problems of this world." This woman had consistently "applied the gospel" in her life for some twenty-four years, staying home and devoting herself to her children and then to her first grandchild who had recently been born. A sign that perhaps even devoted parenting and strict adherence to LDS teachings cannot stem the advancing tide of social change, this "sister" of the church was caring for her granddaughter while her own daughter, an active church member, worked full time.

Everywhere I went, I found similar attitudes among the French LDS members toward the seeming disintegration of the family and social changes more generally. In the heartland near Lyon, I spent a weekend at the country home of a family who had been deeply impressed by the first lesson the missionaries presented them in 1975. It was what the Mormons call a Family Home Evening. Family relationships and the value of time spent together was the topic of the lesson, not religion. The father, orphaned as a boy and determined to give his family a life he never had, was deeply touched by the family centeredness of the message. Formerly, the father had been in the navy and regularly spent long periods away from his family while at sea.

After he joined the LDS Church, he found work as a firefighter, stayed close to home, and devoted himself to building a magnificent house in the country where they still reside. During the many years of their marriage, his wife has stayed at home to raise their children and counts it a blessing from God to have been able to do so. Although her husband had no choice but to run between what they called "the two worlds" of the gospel and of society, she had been able to remain at home, "closer to God, sheltered from so many bad influences."

At a birthday party for a 12 year old in southern France, I ate lemon cake and ice cream with the parents of four children. Two LDS women missionaries were there to share the celebration, one an American, the other a 23-year-old French woman. When I asked them why Mormonism seemed to be doing so well these days in France, I quickly found myself in a lively round-table discussion. Everyone agreed that the French generally feel let down (*déçu*) by traditional churches. They further agreed that many people were feeling a great deal of uncertainty about their personal values. As the French missionary put it: "[People] are seeking principles for living, family stability; there is no dividing line between good and evil. People are not at ease like that. There is a malaise of values . . . divorce, disequilibrium at the family level. This leads to a quest for integrity. Some seek this integrity in belief; others seek it by other means."

THE PARADOX OF FRENCH MORMON CONVERSION

During interviews, conversations, and attendance at LDS Church meetings throughout France, I found evidence that French Mormons were as aware of and as involved in the public debate on the demise of the family and the crisis of social values as their fellow citizens who responded to the European Values Study. Such a finding corroborated the high levels of my survey respondents who listed family-oriented teachings as having been the most influential in their conversions and supported the family-centered values profiles they provided.

Yet, at this point, I was left with a serious contradiction in my study. At the same time that the French converts were identifying attachment to family values as key to their conversions, joining the LDS Church in France represented one of the most divisive and destabilizing actions they could take within a familial context. A constant component of the conversion stories I encountered was the disfavor and alienation from fellow family members that came with the decision to adopt their new faith.

My research on American Mormonism suggested an answer to this conversion paradox. In the American case, as overviewed earlier, the people most likely to become associated with the Church during its first century of existence were the migrants and immigrants who already felt a deep sense of separation from the families and communities that they had left behind in their quest for better lives in America. The large immigrant population among Mormons in France suggests that a similar phenomenon is occurring as the Church establishes itself there. For the immigrants, their families are simply no longer immediately present to contest their conversions. Indeed, it is the very absence of family and community that the immigrants are attempting to replace by joining a profoundly family-oriented church.

To account for the native French conversions (representing two-thirds of the Church population), I conducted further demographic probings to find just how "settled" the French converts were in terms of family and community networks. The first thing I learned was that only a third of the French members had resided in their current communities for more than twenty years (Jarvis 1991). The other two-thirds of them shared with the large immigrant population the common experience of having left homes and families in rural areas and small villages to relocate to Paris, Lyon, Avignon, and other large urban areas where jobs were more plentiful. When I applied the findings about length of residence to the total sample of 1,300 persons, I determined that fewer than 300 individuals (about 23 percent) represented a fixed population that had resided in their current cities for twenty years or more.

These findings help explain the conversion paradox among Mormons in France. Some 75 percent of the LDS Church population is made up of migrants and immigrants for whom concern about the disintegration of family and community networks is real and immediate. For them, the Church represents a way of reclaiming their families and renewing family ties, both in this life and in the hereafter.

As much as my demographic probings helped me gain a better understanding of the forces that bring together a great diversity of peoples in a common cause in the French Mormon Church, they also suggested that the greatest challenge for the French LDS institution is to find effective ways of dealing with tremendous human diversity as it attempts to mend fractured family and community networks. This challenge warrants particular attention, if only because it is the very challenge faced by individuals and organizations in every region and nation of the planet.

BUILDING UNITY AMID DIVERSITY: CHURCH PROGRAMS, MEMBER RETENTION, AND COMMON NOTIONS OF RIGHT AND WRONG

All indications suggest that Mormonism in France is doing well in its efforts to build a sense of unity within a highly diverse and mobile population. Raw growth rates of nearly 8 percent per year provide initial evidence of a healthy organization. Another indicator of success is the retention rate of new converts. An analysis of membership records during my 1990 study (Jarvis 1991) showed that between 40 percent and 50 percent of new members continue to participate actively for at least four years (as far back as I was able to determine from the available records). This figure is much higher that the regular participation rates of under 10 percent for mainstream Catholics in France (Baubérot 1988; Hervieu-Léger 1990).

The Familial Nature of Life in the Church

My analysis of all available information suggests that the family, as both a metaphorical symbol and a social institution, serves as the fundamental construct for pulling together the diverse strands of the French LDS population. One of the most immediately obvious indicators of this family-oriented unity is that potential new members are encouraged to call each other "Brother" and "Sister" on their first visits to the Church. Members who are already in the community make it a standard practice to affix these identifiers to each others' last names.

The familial nature of the Church goes well beyond naming practices, however. In addition to typical religious services on Sunday morning, the organization offers members of all ages a great variety of activities throughout the week that are geared toward preparing them to fulfill better their roles as members of their families and of the Church. Children, aged 6–12, participate in Primary, a one-hour-per-week gathering for religious instruction similar to catechism that also teaches lessons about respect for parents, obedience, service to others, proper behavior at home and in church, and so forth. At age 12, boys are encouraged to become involved in the Church's scouting program, while girls learn homemaking skills in a parallel young women's organization. Men attend a weekly Priesthood Meeting in which they participate in some Church decision making and receive religious and practical instruction on their roles as husbands and fathers in the Church. Women attend Relief Society, the counterpart to Priesthood Meeting, in which they are taught how better to carry out their spiritual and physical roles as wives and mothers in the Church.

All the members are also asked to participate in the Church's ambitious home-visit program. Divided up into teams of two (men with men and women with women), they are assigned several families to visit each month. Home visitors bring monthly spiritual messages into the homes of the "brothers" and "sisters" they visit. They also become involved in the physical well-being of individual families, helping fellow members with job searches, painting houses, yard work, baby-sitting, baking, sharing meals, and the like. Home visits are one of the most focused community-building activities that the Church offers all members.

In addition to the weekly meetings and monthly home visits, a variety of occasional gatherings fill up the year. These activities include congregational picnics; barbecues; evening dances; athletic team practices and games; talent shows; genealogical outings for gathering information about ancestors; and various holiday observances, such as a Christmas party, a Valentine's Day dance, and an Easter picnic. Also on an occasional basis throughout the year, there are organized trips to Mormon temples. French members typically set aside several weekends per year to make a three-day pilgrimage to temples in Switzerland and Germany, where they carry out sacred temple rites to offer salvation and exaltation to deceased ancestors.

From social activities for the youngest participants to genealogical research and temple work for the oldest, French Mormonism is a family-centered organization. People who join the Church tend either to have a family or to be interested in building one. When I compared French LDS fertility rates with French national norms, I was not surprised to see significant differences. As Table 9.5 indicates, 40 percent of the native-born French Mormon households and 51 percent of the nonnative French LDS families had three children at home versus the national norm just short of 19 percent (Verdié 1989). The average size of a French LDS household ranged from 3.77 persons (native born) to 3.94 (nonnative), whereas a typical French household contained 3.06 family members (Stoetzel 1983).

The fertility rate in France has risen to 1.84 children per woman in recent years, which is still not enough for the society to reproduce itself and has come only after great effort by the government to encourage larger families through ambitious social programs and outright cash payments at the birth of each child (Monneron and Rowley 1986; Verdié 1989). French Mormons do not seem to share their fellow citizens low interest in reproductivity. As Table 9.5 shows, the fertility rate of native-born French LDS women is 2.13 children and that of nonnative LDS women is 2.62. Mormonism's family-centered religious message and the family nature of Church programs and activities seem to be successfully recruiting members of the group for which they are designed. However, recruiting members does not automatically ensure the organization's success. There is the serious problem of keeping those who join.

Table 9.5
COMPARISONS OF LDS AND NON-LDS FERTILITY LEVELS IN FRANCE

	French LDS*		
	French Born (N = 101)	Born Elsewhere (N = 31)	French Population
Percentage of households with a third child present	41	51	18.7†
Fertility rate‡	2.13	2.62	1.84†
Average household size	3.77	3.94	3.06§

*Unmarried persons living alone and couples without children were not included.
†Data from Verdié (1989:44, 71).
‡Averages based on the number of children born per couple.
§Data from Stoetzel (1983:285).

Retention: Who Stays and Who Goes

The rich family-centered life that the LDS Church offers its members on a day-to-day basis brings with it certain dangers. One danger is, of course, that the Church will lose its appeal to persons who are not immediately involved or interested in the family. Indeed, Table 9.6, reveals striking differences in the participation patterns of individuals and larger family units in the LDS Church.

On the basis of a sample of 1,178 persons distributed among 620 family groups[2], I found a direct correlation between family size and regular Church participation (Jarvis 1991). Whereas only 24 percent of the families with one or two members continued to be "active" in the Church, 90 percent to 100 percent of the largest families (seven or more members) did so. In addition, well over half the families with three to four members (54 percent) and five to six members (69 percent) were being retained. Clearly, just as the family seemed to exert a major influence on conversion, it also seemed to play a pivotal role in whether members remained active.

Such patterns of retention further illustrate the power of the family as a conceptual and organizational tool for quickly building a large community of believers. The French LDS organization attracts and holds those persons who are the most likely to bring the greatest number of other persons with them into the Church in the short and the long terms. Furthermore, it stands to benefit from established familial ties as it struggles to build the larger family community of the Church. By targeting family units with its spiritual message and offering a great variety of family-centered activities and programs to keep families in the fold, the Church is able to establish its larger sense of community upon the smaller community building blocks that are already available.

Table 9.6
SIZE OF FRENCH LDS HOUSEHOLDS, BY LEVEL OF CHURCH PARTICIPATION (PERCENTAGES)*

Level of Participation	*HOUSEHOLD SIZE* 1–2	3–4	5–6	7–8	9–10
Active†	24%	54%	69%	90%	100%
Inactive†	76	47	31	10	0
Total sample	48	25	21	5	2
	(*N* = 563)	(*N* = 292)	(*N* = 245)	(*N* = 56)	(*N* = 22)

*The calculations were based on 1,178 persons distributed among 620 family groups. The percentages were rounded to the nearest whole number. For more details on the methods used here, see Jarvis (1991).

†Active is defined as attending Sunday Church meetings at least twice per month. Inactive is defined as attendance less than twice per month.

Common Beliefs and Behaviors: Making Mormons out of "Frenchmen"

People with whom I share my work often express surprise and a certain disinclination to believe that such a thing as a "French Mormon Community" even exists. Indeed, for those who know the French, especially French men, it is a most unlikely cultural marriage to consider. Furthermore, a great body of social science research has affirmed the impression that the French are the most "un-American" and the Americans are the most "un-French" among modern, Western societies. On virtually every sociological and cultural measure, the two are in direct opposition to each other, with even greater differences between the French in general and the American Mormons. For example, the French have led the Western world in per capita alcohol consumption since researchers began keeping records nearly a century ago (Zeldin 1979). Americans have led other Western nations in abstinence during the same period (Evron, Keller, and Gurioli 1974). And Mormons have led Americans in strict abstinence, making a complete ban on alcohol a prerequisite to good standing in the Church.

Pronounced contrasts among the French, American, and American Mormon cultures appear on virtually every other measure of attitudes, beliefs, and social practice as well. Among the peoples of Western, industrialized nations, Americans are the most likely (95 percent) and the French are the least likely to express a belief in God. (62 percent). Americans are the most likely to consider themselves "religious" (81 percent), while the French are the least likely (51 percent) (Center for Applied Research 1982a). With regard to sexual mores, the French Court of Cassation (equivalent to the U.S. Supreme Court) declared in 1970 that unmarried couples living together was no longer "contrary to today's morals." In 1972, the Court accorded children born out of wedlock the same rights as children of married parents and, in 1978, concubines received the same status as wives for social security benefits (Zeldin 1982:113, 118).

Mormons offer fierce resistance to such liberalization of sexual codes. As the current president and "Prophet" of the Church put it: "For your own sakes, for your happiness now and in all the years to come, and for the happiness of the generations who come after you, avoid sexual transgression as you would a plague" (Hinckley 1987:47–48). Furthermore, the Church actively enforces its codes of sexual conduct, systematically disfellowshipping and excommunicating wayward members who practice premarital or extramarital sex or who cohabitate before marriage.

In sum, at least three things can be said about the cultural differences between the French and the Mormons: There are a lot of them; they run deep; and they involve things that tend to matter, such as concepts of God, religious belief, proper moral behavior, and attitudes toward sexuality and marriage. Such differences are what one could expect between a profoundly Anglo-Saxon, Protestant, American cultural institution like Mormonism, born in the ashes of Puritanism and raised on a healthy diet of rigid Victorianism, and the *Gaulois*, Catholic, Mediterranean heritage of the French, whose only links to Puritanism and Victorianism were systematic rejection and outright war (intellectual, artistic, religious, and military) on most everything these two traditions stood for.

Which brings me back to the question: Is it *really* possible to make good Mormons out of the French? My findings suggest that it is, indeed, possible. One indicator of such a cultural transformation came when I asked Mormons in France what they thought of key LDS teachings from the United States that were the most likely to conflict with their traditional attitudes and values. On the survey questionnaire, I asked the respondents to tell me how serious they considered certain behaviors ("sins") that are overtly discouraged by the Church. Table 9.7 sums up their responses.

Table 9.7 shows the degree to which it is possible to "make Mormons" not only from immigrants living in France, but from the French themselves. It is not surprising to find a nearly complete consensus among the French LDS members about the seriousness of adultery (native French = 97.3 percent; nonnatives = 96.4). These are people who considered faithfulness in marriage their highest value both before and after they joined the Church. However, it *is* surprising that Mormon attitudes toward drinking hard liquor, engaging in sex before marriage, paying tithes to the Church, and consuming other proscribed beverages are now a part of what the nonnative and native recruits in France have come to consider serious "sinful" be-

Table 9.7
ATTITUDES TOWARD PRACTICES DISCOURAGED BY THE CHURCH* (PERCENTAGES)

	NATIVE FRENCH (N = 113)		*NONNATIVE MEMBERS (N = 56)*	
Practices	Serious	Not Serious†	Serious	Not Serious†
1. Committing adultery	97.3	2.7	96.4	3.6
2. Consuming hard liquor	92.9	7.1	88.9	11.1
3. Engaging in sex before marriage	90.9	9.1	96.4	3.6
4. Not paying tithes to the Church	88.8	11.2	92.7	7.3
5. Smoking	86.6	13.4	83.3	16.7
6. Consuming wine	84.9	15.1	85.2	14.8
7. Consuming beer	83.9	16.1	81.5	18.5
8. Consuming coffee	75.9	24.1	75.9	24.1

*The survey question asked the respondents to indicate how serious they considered it to be to engage in a variety of activities discouraged by the Church.

†"Serious" includes all answers the respondents coded as "very serious" or "pretty serious." "Not serious" includes all answers coded as "not very serious" or "of no importance."

haviors (all of which received ratings of "serious" from more than 75 percent of the respondents).

Of course, there is not always a direct correlation between what people believe and what they do. So I asked the respondents to indicate how often they actually engaged in activities discouraged by the Church. Ninety percent or more of all the respondents said that they "seldom or never" drink strong liquor (94 percent abstinence) or smoke (91 percent abstinence). Significant majorities likewise indicated that they "seldom or never" consume wine (89 percent abstinence), drink beer (88 percent abstinence), or drink coffee (83 percent abstinence).

These findings confirm the personal observations I made during three months of living among Mormons in France and participating in their lives. In general, I found them to be a devout people who stake their integrity on making their actions a reflection of their new beliefs. A constant theme that surfaced in my conversations with LDS members throughout France was the hypocrisy they had encountered in other churches. They criticized Catholics, Protestants, the Jehovah's Witnesses, and others for preaching messages of love, benevolence, and self-sacrifice that they did not put into practice (Jarvis 1991:139).

The respondents almost invariably thought that the strict behavioral codes of Mormonism was one of the institution's most attractive features. The self-denial implicit in giving up such things as sex outside of marriage, alcohol, tobacco, and even coffee and tea gave Mormonism enhanced integrity and authenticity. The male French leader of a congregation in Paris was openly critical of Catholicism, his former religion, for "adapting its traditions to please the nonpracticing." A French LDS mother in the Parisian region considered it the most positive attribute, "to live the gospel, that transforms our behavior." An African member in Lyon saw a metaphysical dimension in the rigorous behavioral requirements of Mormonism: "To give things up is an indication of true spirituality" (Jarvis 1991:139).

CONCLUSIONS

A growing number of scholars in recent times have begun to reconsider religion as what Robertson (1992:1) described as "a site of expression of issues, the issues of modernity." That has been my purpose here. Earlier in this chapter, I characterized Mormonism as being among the more clearly structured and most enduring expressions of nineteenth-century American religious and material utopianism. However, unlike the Shakers, the Amish, or other religious utopian movements that have been unable to move beyond their American past, the Mormons are successfully adapting to modern conditions. And they are doing so through a broad appeal that transcends national, racial, ethnic, and tribal borders in a highly effective manner.

Mormonism may be best described today as a religion for troubled times. History is partially responsible for this circumstance. The LDS Church was born amid the difficulties, social upheavals, and rootlessness of the American frontier over a century and a half ago. The organization's ability to adapt and prosper in such an environment prepared it well for success in the world today. Recent reports by the United Nations have revealed that more people are living in refugee camps around the world than at any other time in human history. Floundering economies, failed political systems, and civil wars in both the first and third worlds are encouraging millions of immigrants each year to leave their homelands in hopes of finding better lives elsewhere.

Yet, even those people who stay home, amid the relative security of good jobs and stable social systems, do not escape the uncertainties brought on by profound changes in the world. The French have suffered a nationwide cultural shock in recent years as Islam has replaced Protestantism as their nation's second largest religion. Like the French, people everywhere are concerned about changing religious and social values, the loss of community, and the decline of the family. Indeed, times are changing. As national borders come down in the face of international trade and banking, as international travel becomes a common feature of life, as global communication networks link areas of the world as never before, and as new political alliances are formed in Europe, North America, and Southeast Asia, all people are finding themselves increasingly in unfamiliar surroundings.

In the face of these significant transformations, Beyer (1994) argued convincingly that using economics, politics, or science as a conceptual base for analyzing the dynamics of change overlooks important dimensions of the world. I contend that although economic, political, and scientific frameworks may be helpful for studying the directions that larger forces are taking on the global level, a religious framework is essential for making sense of how most human beings choose to respond to these forces on the individual level.

On the basis of my analysis of developments in France, Mormonism is one religion that is currently offering concerned individuals ways they find useful and meaningful to cope with the uncertainties of the world around them. The unique genius of Mormonism is the organization's emphasis on a universal element that has the power to bring people together in relative harmony and productive interaction despite profound cultural differences. In the French case alone, the Church unites into a working community a fixed local population with a migrant-immigrant population representing over twenty different racial and ethnic groups from around the world. The use of the family as a transcendent value *and* a key organizational unit provides common ground for such a globally diverse population. By making the family the core of its belief system and the cornerstone of the complex organization that has been developed to support these beliefs, the LDS Church has fashioned a message and an organization that promises to do well in the years ahead. In the words of Stark and Iannacone (1994), the Church has effectively "specialized" in France's pluralistic religious economy with a compelling appeal to the "special needs and tastes" of people there.

Other religious movements, political and social groups, and globalizing businesses have much to learn from the French Mormon model about building a common ground among peoples with radically different cultural backgrounds. By refashioning traditional beliefs and values to emphasize a powerful and universally appealing element—the family—Mormonism has become much more than a quaint utopian movement born on the American frontier and limited in appeal to people there. The Mormon Church is a dynamic young institution that competes extremely well on the global stage. With its family-centered worldview and its message of collective salvation, it embodies a core culture that is likely to continue to provide meaning and fulfillment to a great variety of people throughout the world who look to the family as a place of refuge in troubled times.

Notes

Field research for this chapter was generously supported by a grant from the Society for the Scientific Study of Religion. I also acknowledge the conceptual support, advice, and warm encouragement provided by Dr. Armand Mauss of the Department of Sociology, Washington State University.

1. One congregation had lost its congregational clerk shortly before my research, and thus I could not get all the data I wanted for this congregation. This problem is reflected in the reduced *N* for Table 9.6.
2. Although 1,300 persons were in my overall study, data from the membership roster were not available for all the questions because of the absence of the congregational clerk of one congregation. The clerk is the person who keeps track of attendance and membership information. Full information was obtained on 1,178 members.

References

Arrington, Leonard J. 1958. *Great Basin Kingdom: An Economic History of the Latter-Day Saints, 1830–1900.* Cambridge, MA: Harvard University Press.

Arrington, Leonard J., and Davis Bitton. 1979. *The Mormon Experience, a History of the Latter-Day Saints.* New York: Alfred A. Knopf.

Baubérot, Jean. 1988. *Le Protestantisme, doit-il mourir?* Paris: Seuil.

Beyer, Peter. 1994. *Religion and Globalization.* London: Sage.

Bush, Lester E., Jr. 1979. "Mormon Medical Ethical Guidelines." *Dialogue: A Journal of Mormon Thought,* 12(3): 97–106.

———. 1981. "The Word of Wisdom in Early Nineteenth-Century Perspective." *Dialogue: A Journal of Mormon Thought* 14 (3):46–65.

Bushman, Richard L. 1984. *Joseph Smith and the Beginnings of Mormonism.* Urbana: University of Illinois Press.

Center for Applied Research in the Apostolate. 1982a. *Supplementary Tables: Value Comparisons in Nine Countries.* Washington D.C.: Author.

———. 1982b. *Values Study of the U.S.* Washington D.C.: Author.

Cross, Whitney R. 1950. *The Burned Over District; The Social and Intellectual History of Enthusiastic Religion in Western New York, 1800–1850.* New York: Harper & Row.

Davis, David Brion. 1953. "New England Origins of Mormonism." *New England Quarterly* 26:147–68.

Deseret News 1989–1990 Church Almanac, The Church of Jesus Christ of Latter-Day Saints. 1989. Salt Lake City, UT: Deseret News.

Deseret News 1993–94 Church Almanac, The Church of Jesus Christ of Latter-Day Saints. 1994. Salt Lake City, UT: Deseret News.

Eglise de Jésus Christ des Saints des Derniers Jours. 1986. *Méthode uniforme pour l enseignement de l évangile.* Torcy, France: Author.

Evron, Vera, Mark Keller, and Carol Gurioli. 1974. *Statistics on Consumption of Alcohol and on Alcoholism.* New Brunswick, NJ: Rutgers Center of Alcohol Studies.

George, Pierre. 1986. *L'immigration en France, faits et problèmes.* Paris: Armand Colin.

Hansen, Klaus J. 1967. *Quest for Empire.* East Lansing: Michigan State University.

———. 1981. *Mormonism and the American Experience.* Chicago: University of Chicago Press.

Hervieu-Léger, Danièle. 1990. "Situation du Christianisme dans le nouveau contexte socio-culturel en France." *DOCUMENTS EPISCOPAT; bulletin du secrétariat de la conférence des évêques de France* No. 4 (March).

Hinckley, Gordon B. 1987. "Reverence and Morality." *Ensign* 17 (5):45–48.

Jarvis, John. 1991. "Mormonism in France: A Study of Cultural Exchange and Institutional Adaptation." Unpublished doctoral dissertation. Ann Arbor, MI: University Microfilms International, Dissertation Services.

Kanter, Rosabeth Moss. 1972. *Community and Commitment.* Cambridge, MA: Harvard University Press.

Leone, Mark. 1979. *The Roots of Modern Mormonism.* Cambridge, MA: Harvard University Press.

McConkie, Bruce R. 1966. *Mormon Doctrine.* Salt Lake City, UT: Bookcraft.

Monneron, Jean-Louis, and Anthony Rowley. 1986. *Histoire du peuple français: Les 25 ans qui ont transformé la France.* Paris: Nouvelles Librairies de France.

Roberts, B. H., ed. 1902. *History of the Church of Jesus Christ of Latter-Day Saints, Period I.* Salt Lake City, UT: LDS Church.

Robertson, Roland. 1992. *Globalization: Social Theory and Global Culture.* London: Sage.

Shipps, Jan. 1985. *Mormonism: The Story of a New Religious Tradition.* Urbana: University of Illinois Press.

Smith, N. Lee. 1979. "Herbal Remedies: God's Medicine?" *Dialogue: A Journal of Mormon Thought* 12(3):37–60.

Stark, Rodney. 1984. "The Rise of a New World Faith." *Review of Religious Research* 26(1):18–27.

Stark, Rodney, and Laurence R. Iannaccone. 1994. "A Supply-Side Reinterpretation of the 'Secularization' of Europe." *Journal for the Scientific Study of Religion* 33(3):230–52.

Starr, Paul. 1982. *The Social Transformation of American Medicine.* New York: Basic Books.

Stoetzel, Jean. 1983. *Les valeurs du temps présent: une enquête européenne.* Paris: Presses Universitaires de France.

Verdié, Minelle. 1989. *L'état de la France et de ses habitants.* Paris: Editions la Découverte.

Zeldin, Theodore. 1979. *Histoire des passions françaises: Gout et corruption.* Paris: Recherches.

———. 1982. *The French.* New York: Pantheon Books.

CHAPTER 10

The Rebirth of Judaism in Kiev After Babi Yar and Communism: The Interplay of Family and Religion

M. HERBERT DANZGER

This chapter examines the paradoxes involved in the "return" to traditional religion in a family-centered religious community in the midst of massive societal change. The specific case is that of Jews in the Ukrainian city of Kiev.

Although Kiev was once a thriving center of Jewish religion and culture, the 1941–43 wartime massacre of almost 100,000 Jews and the suppression of Jews and Judaism under communism combined to destroy Jewish life and institutions. Throughout the period of communist domination, Jews in the Ukraine were cut off from contact with Jews of the West and elsewhere. However, by 1989, with the impending collapse of the Soviet communist regime,[1] Kiev could once again communicate with other Jewish communities.

By the time I visited the Jewish community of Kiev in 1996, it had reopened two of its synagogues; built a matzo bakery, a ritual bath, soup kitchens, and day schools attended by more than 700 children; developed a program of aid to the aged; and was maintaining a variety of other programs. The central goal of these efforts was to create a model of Jewish life so that youngsters could see how this life was lived and learn to be part of it. In effect, this ongoing project sought to reestablish a religious tradition whose chain of transmission had been broken. This task was all the more difficult because the primary practices and rituals of Judaism, particularly Orthodox Judaism, are rooted in family, rather than in the synagogue.

THE SOCIOLOGICAL PROBLEM

The focus of the study presented in this chapter is how some Jews in Kiev have become newly traditional. At issue is the interplay among familial and religious forces associated with the conversion process of young secular Jews to traditional Judaism. Particular emphasis is placed on cases in which children led the move toward traditional religion and parents followed.

Although to the casual observer the process of "return to tradition" (Danzger 1989) appears to involve only individuals, in reality entire families come to be involved. This point is often missed by sociologists who tend to interview only the "converts." Religious "conversion" or Jewish "return" strains longstanding relationships among family members as the returnees attempt to live life in accordance with the new set of norms (Danzger 1987). In the conversion from one Protestant denomination to another in the United States, this process is rarely seen because the religious rules of different Protestant denominations are relatively easy to accommodate. This is not the case for conversions to fringe religious groups, commonly called cults, which typically require converts to adopt radically new behaviors that result in what some have called an "implosion" of social relationships (Snow and Machalek 1984).

Such stress sometimes develops in the return to traditional Judaism because of its emphasis on ritual behaviors that tend to set the observant apart from the nonobservant. For example, the laws of *kashrut* (which require that only kosher food be eaten) make it difficult for an adult who becomes Orthodox to live with parents who do not observe these rules. What should sons and daughters who have become newly Orthodox do in this situation? Should they continue to take meals with their parents as if they have not changed, when doing so would betray their new religious commitment? Should they reject their parents or friends or even husbands or wives, when these are people they love? And this is only the beginning of the dilemma. What about the rules of Sabbath observance that forbid one to turn lights on or off, answer a phone, or drive a car? What does one do when one celebrates a family occasion, such as a wedding, a bar mitzva, or even a Passover seder that, by the newly Orthodox person's standards, is not kosher? I have discussed these issues as they relate to the newly Orthodox in the United States elsewhere (Danzger 1989). In the situation of the former Soviet Union (FSU), the circumstances that shape the answers to these questions are different. In this chapter, I focus not on the relationship between parents and adult converts, but on the relationship between parents and minor children. The youth of the children, combined with the extensive authority of the parents, adds an additional dimension to these issues.

Family is powerfully affected by religious conversion and has a powerful effect on the enabling or retarding of this process, which has been practically entirely overlooked in the sociological study of conversion. Over the past thirty years, scholars have studied conversion processes in many different societies and have examined various sects, cults, and mainstream religions, but they have paid little attention to the involvement of the family. For example, Lofland and Stark (1965) and Lofland (1977) discussed conversion in terms of the mechanisms utilized by the recruiting group and the situation of the recruits, as well as the conditions for conversion and the stages and steps of the process. Their model includes a consideration of both the social psychological state of the recruit and the techniques by which the recruiting organization attempts to manage this recruitment. But their model does not consider how other members of the convert's family relate to this process.

Snow and Machalek (1984) provided the most extensive and detailed overview of theories and concepts on conversion. They discussed conversion as radical social change, as role change and as alternation, as a change in one's universe of discourse, and as a paradigm shift. They considered empirical indicators of conversion, including rhetorical indicators, biographical reconstruction, and the embracement of the convert role. They explored the analytical status of the convert's account, its socially constructed character, temporal variability, and retrospective character. They inventoried the causes of conversion, listing responses to coercion and induced stress, predisposing personality traits and cognitive orientations, social attributes, and the structural availability of converts. Among the social influences they mentioned were social networks and role learning. They also discussed causal process models of conversion. But what they omitted is the fact that members of a family may impel others along the path of conversion or actively retard such conversion.

Kilbourne and Richardson (1989) discussed a variety of theories of conversion. However, in their conclusions regarding the processes of socialization and conversion, they did not explicitly take the family context of conversion into account. And the many studies that have explored intermarriage or the impact of marriage on religious switching (see, for example, Musick and Wilson 1995) have all been demographic studies of factors that affect denominational choices. Such studies have not dealt with conversion processes. Nor have studies of the dynamics (rather than demographics) of conversion taken family into account. By addressing this dearth of attention to the family, this chapter contributes to the sociological literature on conversion.

ETHNOGRAPHIC APPROACH

Besides materials gathered directly in Kiev, the data drawn on in this chapter were from two interview projects: (1) an earlier study of Israeli and American Jewish returnees and (2) a study that is under way of Soviet émigré returnees to traditional Judaism in the United States and Israel. Both studies involved in-depth interviews that typically lasted from forty-five minutes to two hours, with an average of about an hour and a quarter. A few individuals, usually the administrators or teachers in outreach organizations, were interviewed several times, some for as much a six hours.

In the first study, data on American and Israeli "returnees" were gathered between 1975 and 1987 (see Danzger 1989:8–10 for details of the methodology). A total of 204 interviews were conducted, 41 with women. Among the interviewees, 54 were rabbis, administrators, or religious outreach workers, and almost half the 54 were also "returnees" who had been reared in non-Orthodox homes. The large number of such outreach workers was not accidental. It reflects an attempt to find a number of different strategic entry points to the population of returnees so as not to bias the findings with the results of a single "snowball." Material on Israel was gathered during two trips, the first during the year I spent as a Fulbright professor (1975–76) and the second during the summer of 1982.

The study of Soviet émigrés was begun in 1990 and, in addition to interviews and observations conducted in the United States, has included three research trips to Israel (in 1992, 1995, and 1996), as well as a 1996 trip to three cities in the FSU (Kiev, Moscow, and St. Petersburg). For this study, 141 interviews have been conducted thus far, 39 with women and 102 with men. Of the 141 interviewees, 62 were administrators, rabbis, or teachers in outreach programs, more than half of whom were returnees. Of the 62 administrators and teachers, 21 were women. (No rabbis were women because Orthodox Judaism does not permit women to be ordained, and Reform and Conservative Judaism have had only a tiny presence in the movement of return.)

Specifically for Kiev, information was derived from in-depth interviews with leaders and members of the Jewish community and from observations and site visits. Direct observation of Jewish life was carried out during a short visit in May and June 1996, when my wife and I immersed ourselves in the life of the community for five days. We lived in an apartment in the Podol suburb of Kiev that was owned by the synagogue and was located one block from it and half a block from the apartment where Rabbi Jacob Bleich and his wife lived. We had close contact with the rabbi, having been invited to take the three Sabbath meals with him and his wife in their home. At other times, we ate in the synagogue soup kitchen and in the Kiev community's kosher restaurant that was under the supervision of Rabbi Bleich. The rabbi and other members of the community helped us by serving as translators and guides. We participated in morning and evening synagogue services, visited the schools and attended classes, and interviewed leaders of communal agencies. Rabbi Bleich even invited me to accompany him to the private birthday party of one of the leading Yiddish writers of the Ukraine. As the rabbi's guest, I was received with great honor, presented with one of the author's books, and had my photograph taken with the author at his request.

Through contacts I had made in my earlier studies of Jewish return to tradition, I had learned of Yad Yisrael, the organization that sponsored Rabbi Bleich's nomination as Chief Rabbi of Kiev. Yad Yisrael, in turn, put me in touch with Rabbi Bleich. I called Rabbi Bleich from New York City some weeks before I traveled to Kiev, and he graciously offered to provide the synagogue apartment as housing and to arrange for a driver and translator. It was at this time that he also invited my wife and me to take the Sabbath meals with him and his family.

My background and that of my wife made entry into this community easy. We both speak Hebrew and Yiddish fluently, and my wife also speaks Hungarian fluently and some French. We are both fully familiar with Orthodox Jewish life in the United States since we were raised in Orthodox families. Furthermore, we spent two years in Israel, where I had academic appointments, first, as a senior lecturer at Bar Ilan University and second, as a Fulbright professor at Hebrew University. My earlier work on returning to tradition was well received in the Orthodox community. In sum, my credentials in the Orthodox Jewish community facilitated this research, and my experience in this area suggested which observations would be the most fruitful. But perhaps most important was the assistance we received from Rabbi Bleich and, through him, the community.

HISTORICAL BACKGROUND

Kiev, the capital of Ukraine, had Jewish residents at the time it was founded in the eighth century. Most of the Jewish residents were merchants, attracted by Kiev's strategic commercial location on the Dnieper River. In 1320, when Kiev was annexed by Lithuania, Jews were granted rights ensuring their lives and property. But like the rest of the Jews in Lithuania, the Jews of Kiev were expelled in 1495. They were permitted to return in 1503 and were expelled again in 1619. Of the few who remained, some were killed during the Chmielnicki massacres of 1648. In 1667, Kiev was annexed by Russia, and Jews were once again driven from the town (Slutsky 1972).

The Jewish community was reestablished in Kiev in 1793, but it faced continued religious hostility. Jews were banned from Kiev several times during the nineteenth century. In 1861, Jews who were entitled to reside in Kiev were assigned to two suburbs, Lyebed and Podol. A large synagogue was constructed by wealthy Jewish families. Persecutions continued, including a pogrom in 1881, but the Jewish population continued to grow. In 1913, Jews constituted 13 percent of the population and numbered over 81,000. By 1939, despite continued persecutions, the Jewish population had reached 175,000, and Jews constituted 10 percent of the population of Kiev. From 1919 to 1939, the early years of the communist regime, Jewish culture flourished in Kiev (Slutsky 1972).

Kiev fell to the Germans on September 21, 1941. One week later, the Germans began the massacres at Babi Yar in Kiev, killing 33,771 in two days. During World War II, about 200,000 people were slaughtered in Kiev, of whom probably 100,000 were Jews (West 1972).

Following the war, the Soviet authorities permitted only the synagogue in the Podol suburb of Kiev to open. The largest synagogue in Kiev (Brodsky) was turned into a puppet theater. From the 1950s through the 1980s, the Podol synagogue attracted an overflow crowd of several thousand for Yom Kippur and the Memorial Day of the Babi Yar massacre. However, attempts to acknowledge the Babi Yar massacre publicly were repeatedly quashed, and when a monument was finally erected in early 1976, no mention was made of the slaughter of Jews. In general, Jewish religious and memorial activities outside the synagogue were forbidden. Religious services that were held in private homes were severely punished when discovered. And Jews were imprisoned for baking Passover matzot in their homes, for performing ritual circumcision (*brit*) and for other religious observances (Ofer 1972).

PERESTROIKA AND REBIRTH IN A CEMETERY

By 1989, little organized Jewish life was left in Kiev. Nonetheless, informal estimates by Jewish religious and charitable organizations serving the community suggested that there were probably 100,000 Jews in Kiev. The Podol synagogue had not had a rabbi since 1960. Its facilities for baking matzo, for ritual baths, and for the ritual slaughter of poultry were outmoded, in disrepair, and hardly used.

In the late 1980s, with the opening of the Ukraine and other parts of the Soviet Union to foreign travelers for the first time in seventy years, the Karlin-Stolin Chassidim in Brooklyn decided to visit the graves of their great Chassidic founders in the Ukraine. Forty Chassidim arranged to fly to Kiev in 1989 for the Sabbath between Rosh Hashana and Yom Kippur, the holy Days of Awe, when it is traditional to visit the graves of deceased parents, great rabbis, and *tzaddikim* (the especially holy and righteous). Arriving in Kiev, they found that although their visas were in order, additional official documents were required for them to travel the roughly 100 miles from Kiev to the graves of their holy leaders. Hoping to get permission, they submitted an appeal to the police and stayed in Kiev for the Sabbath awaiting the outcome of the appeal. The police turned down their request. Rather than leave, they decided to visit the graves of other holy persons in the Kiev area.

Arriving at the cemetery, they found that many local Jews had come, as well, to visit the graves of their parents. Rabbi Bleich, one of these Chassidim, described the scene to me:

> We didn't expect to find anyone at the cemeteries. When we arrived, there were people visiting gravesites because this is the holy season for visiting graves of parents and others. When they saw us, they must have thought they were seeing ghosts of the past. We were wearing our usual black coats and hats. We had beards and *peyot* (earlocks). They ran to us and asked to touch our garments, to kiss our *siddurim* (prayer books). We couldn't believe it.
>
> When we got back to the United States, later on I saw an advertisment asking for a rabbi to serve in Kiev for the summer (1990). Because of what happened in the cemetery, I said to myself, these people are still attached to Judaism. There is still a spark there. I'll go back and give it a try. I went back for the summer of 1990 with my wife, and we have been here ever since.

Rabbi Bleich was appointed Chief Rabbi of Kiev in 1990.

THE KIEV JEWISH COMMUNITY: MAY–JUNE 1996

The Podol synagogue, the main synagogue of Kiev, was built in 1892. It was renovated once, about eighty years ago, to close off the front entrance and reinforce the doors and windows with iron gates to protect against mob violence. The entrance no longer faces the street but is now situated on what was the side, in the courtyard surrounding the synagogue. The synagogue can accommodate about 1,000 worshippers in the main area and in the traditional women's balcony above. When one enters the synagogue, one faces the Holy Ark of the Torah. The Ark is a commanding presence and is reached by climbing two sets of steps, an unusual arrangement.

On the second floor, at the rear of the synagogue building, are the offices of the rabbi, the Jewish community leader, the caretakers, and the secretaries. All the offices are equipped with telephones, fax machines (which sometimes work), and computers. Except for the rabbi's office, which is well furnished, the other offices are furnished in communist East European style. From these offices, all kinds of community matters are attended to. When I was there, one of the teachers at the local Jewish day school spent a good part of two days on the phones in these offices trying to raise the $200 needed to bury a pauper with no relatives whose body was at that moment in a large refrigerator in a synagogue outbuilding (a severe breach of Jewish custom).

The synagogue also houses a yeshiva and a *kolel*. Traditionally, these are a seminary and an advanced school for the study of Talmud, respectively. However, in Kiev, the people in these schools appear to have no more than basic skills in reading Hebrew. Adjacent dormitories to house these students appear to be primitive and in disrepair. Nonetheless, the attempt to make housing comfortable includes a small game room and other facilities. Twenty to thirty students are enrolled in this yeshiva, and we observed seven to nine students in the *kolel*. Enrollment varies by season. The yeshiva students are in their teens, and the *kolel* students are older.

In the synagogue compound, there is a newly refurbished ritual bath (*mikveh*).[2] The old ritualarium stands in a dark basement of the synagogue, is badly lit, and somewhat primitive. It is now available for other ritual uses. Two brand-new ritual baths have been built that include modern showers and baths and a modern system for heating water. They are well lit and newly tiled. They meet the standards one might find in a middle-class neighborhood in New York City.

The synagogue courtyard contains a newly equipped matzo factory that is capable of producing 1.5 tons of matzo a day. This matzo is strictly kosher and is used in the celebration of Passover. (This huge capacity is necessary because all the matzo for Passover is produced in the two months preceding the holiday and is distributed for holiday use throughout the Ukraine.) The courtyard also houses a small slaughterhouse for chickens and other fowl. The birds are cleaned, koshered, refrigerated, and offered for sale to those who are interested in kosher meat. Occasionally the *shochet* (ritual slaughterer) travels to a nearby abattoir to slaughter a cow, whose meat is then sold at the same facility.

In the synagogue courtyard, too, are a dining room and large kitchen for preparing food. The dining room, which is accessible by a steep outdoor metal staircase, is furnished with long wooden tables and benches. During the week, it serves as a soup kitchen, offering free breakfasts to about a dozen old men who come to morning prayer services at the synagogue. The breakfasts consist of a large portion of gefilte fish, a krupnik soup, and thick slices of fresh kosher bread, washed down with hot, sweet tea. The men's presence guarantees that there is a *minyan*, the requisite quorum for the prayer service.

REBUILDING A COMMUNITY THROUGH CHILDREN

By 1989, when Rabbi Bleich first came to Kiev, the Ukraine permitted Jews to visit the grave of Rabbi Nachman of Bratzlav in Uman. Visiting this grave had long been a practice of some Chassidim, known as the Chassidim of the Dead Rebbe. The visit was not part of an organizational strategy of outreach but, rather, a spontaneous activity by a group of Chassidim (and some of those new to Chassidism) to visit holy gravesites. Apparently, this practice paralleled the attitudes of Christian Ukrainians regarding veneration of the dead. Rabbi Bleich described the cemetery they visited the first time as "packed with people" who swarmed around them. It was this ritual activity that gave Bleich and others the hope that it might be possible to revive Judaism in the Ukraine.

As was noted earlier, the organization that sent Bleich back to Kiev the next year was Yad Yisrael, a charitable organization of Karlin-Stolin Chassidim in the Boro Park section of Brooklyn, New York. Its work had heretofore been primarily restricted to local charitable efforts in Brooklyn and in Israel. But when the members of Rabbi Bleich's group returned from their trip and other reports further confirmed the strength of Jewry in the area and the opportunities for outreach, Yad Yisrael mobilized to send Rabbi Bleich back. By this time, the rabbi's wife had become infected with his enthusiasm and joined him on his return, despite her awareness of the hardships and loneliness that would await them.

When they returned in the summer of 1990, Rabbi Bleich and his wife organized a Sunday school. The first week, after distributing flyers and advertising, they had 27 students. Within a few weeks, 250 boys and girls were participating without further advertising. It was clear that this effort was tapping into an existing community need that had not been met.

In September, the rabbi and his wife decided to open a religious day school that would offer a full day of studies, secular as well as religious. However, at that time, the government did not permit religious schools. To get around that problem, the rabbi and his wife arranged to rent a ferryboat (with funds provided by Yad Yisrael) on which classes would be held. (The ferry was used for tourist rides on the Dnieper during the summer season and, generally, was out of service until the late spring because of the lack of tourists.) Given the depressed state of the Ukrainian economy at that time, the ferry could be rented for a nominal fee.

This school opened with thirty-seven children attending full time. During the 1990 fall semester, the rabbi explored the possibility of moving the school to land. The city of Kiev had a number of school buildings that were not used because of the decline in the population. The city transferred a school to Rabbi Bleich's administrative care to be operated as a Jewish "ethnic" school, rather than as a religious school per se. There was no bar to teaching religious subjects as long as any Jewish child could attend, whether or not the child was religious.

Starting with Grades 1–8,[3] the school expanded quickly. A second school building was provided two years later as the school enrollment grew. In 1996, 700 children were attending at the two locations. One building was used for the boys and another for the girls—following the traditional religious orientation of Chassidim (and consistent with the existence of some other separate-sex schools in Kiev and elsewhere in the region).

The religious day schools provide a sense of the value of reidentifying with the Jewish community. About half the students in the school come from families in which one parent (usually the father) is not Jewish. Although, since 1983, the American Jewish Reform Movement has accepted as Jews children whose fathers are Jewish, even if the mothers were not, the historic Jewish position has been matrilinearity. Thus, if a child's mother is Jewish, the child is Jewish, regardless of whether the father is Jewish. But if the child's father is Jewish and the mother is not Jewish, the child is considered non-Jewish. The parents pattern of exogamy seems to suggest that the parents have broken their ties to the Jewish community. Nonetheless, children whose parents seemed willing to leave the Jewish community are now enrolled and identified as Jews.

The Curriculum and the Extra-Curriculum

The Jewish schools in Kiev are required by the government to provide the full course of study in language, literature, mathematics, geography, national and world history, and other subjects studied in the general school system. These subjects are supplemented in the Jewish schools with the study of Hebrew, Jewish history and customs, the Bible, and Jewish thought, adding one to two hours to the school day, depending on a student's schedule of classes. Secular studies are enhanced by equipment and donations from abroad, as well as by the contributions of time, energy, and expertise from the parents. Thus, the school has an excellent computer facility provided through a donation by a Canadian Jewish philanthropist. It also has a large room furnished as a fine, although small, gym, that was built almost single-handedly by one of the parents who was a nationally known gymnastics instructor. This man now serves as the gym instructor for the school.

An important part of the curriculum is devoted to religious studies. Yet parents who are not religious and who are not interested in maintaining their Jewish identity send their children to the schools for their superior education; the possibility of receiving training with state-of-the-art computers, excellent classes in science and physical education; and, not the least, because the children are fed three times a day at the school (albeit kosher meals).

A substantial portion of the parents are interested in having their children attend the schools in preparation for immigrating to Israel. They believe that if their children attend these schools, the children will be better prepared to integrate into Israeli society. Moreover, whether or not it is true, the parents often believe that they will have a better chance of immigrating to Israel if their children attend Jewish schools. In essence, then, the influence of the hope of going to Israel shapes the actions in Kiev and involves the parents in what Merton (1968) called "anticipatory socialization" into the society they wish to enter: Israel. This goal, in turn, provides the basis for renewed ethnic and religious identification.

In addition to the immigration objective, there is a more immediate way in which the schoolchildren influence their parents. To provide kosher bread for students who are learning about Jewish religious laws of kosher food, the school has a bakery, where bread is made free of nonkosher ingredients, such as lard. This bakery is a large operation and also provides bread to what is the only kosher restaurant in Kiev. The restaurant, an elegant establishment, is an important facility for religious Jews from abroad—particularly delegations from philanthropic agencies—and serves the Kiev community as well. In addition, bread baked at the school is available for purchase. Most important, children take home kosher bread from the school's bakery so they can continue to eat kosher food at home. For the Sabbath, the children are sent home with challah, the special braided bread that is traditionally eaten at the Sabbath dinner. Other foods, such as kosher meat or special Passover holiday foods, are also provided.

These practices introduce the religious pattern of kosher diet into the home and enable the children to maintain the religious behaviors they are taught at school. Certainly, the parents can object and the children may eat nonkosher foods. But the parents do not object and, at times, share the food that is made available. In Kiev, where food is relatively expensive, the schools' contribution to the upkeep of the children, and, thus, indirectly to the household budgets, is not insignificant. All this means that the parents learn something about kosher food practices through their children.

The three meals offered daily by the schools are not intended merely to provide kosher food; during the meals, the children also learn the customs and prayers surrounding the meals. Before each meal, all the children wash their hands in a ritual manner, pouring water from a large cup twice, first on their right hand and then on their left hand, and pronounce the blessing, "Thank Thee Lord, King of the Universe, who has commanded us to wash our hands." This blessing is followed by a blessing over bread thanking God "who gives forth bread from the earth." At the end of the meal, all the children sing Grace After Meals in Hebrew. This extended blessing takes about five minutes and is sung with joy and verve; it does not take long before the children have memorized it.

For the younger children, the school day typically opens with breakfast and is followed by Daily Morning Prayers. These prayers include the recitation of *Shema*, the affirmation of God's unity and the command to love Him. In the higher grades, prayers precede breakfast, because daily prayer is required before eating. The main meal of the day is served at lunchtime and may include meat, sausage, or chicken, as well as potatoes, apple sauce, bread, a fruit drink, and some cookies. A smaller meal or snack is served later in the day. At each of the meals, the order of washing and blessings is maintained. The advanced students also say afternoon prayers, which may take fifteen minutes.

Sabbath and Holidays: Synagogue as Surrogate Home

The in-school religious practices still leave the students without a sense of how to turn the home into a Jewish home, that is, how to celebrate the Sabbath or holidays. Yet the core of the Jewish religion is practiced in the home. It is in the home that holidays are celebrated through festive meals, that one has a seder on Passover, and that the family builds a *succah*, a hut roofed by vegetation to celebrate the harvest festival. The schools instruct the children on what is to be done. But socialization is ideally a process of mimesis rather than book learning; one needs to see how the blessings over the Sabbath candles are actually made, to experience how and in what matter the hymns are sung at the Sabbath table. In this regard, the rabbi and his wife are the instruments of socialization.

Rabbi Bleich invites a group of boys to the synagogue each week. Because the synagogue also serves as a school and dormitory for advanced students, some sleeping facilities are always available. In addition, the soup kitchen and dining room are open for these students to take their Sabbath meals, and a teacher usually joins the students and leads the meal. I observed a late Saturday afternoon light meal of challah and salads led by Rabbi Bleich. Fifteen or so of the students aged 12 to 15 were there, together with a few of their fathers. The rabbi offered a Torah lesson, and the boys sang some hymns. This occasion provided an opportunity to ask the rabbi questions on a variety of topics. Because this was a long summer day, when the sun did not go down until 10:30 P.M., the meal started at 8:00 P.M. On winter days, it is a much shorter affair; the students gather after an early Friday evening meal for a similar experience.

While the boys were in the synagogue, the girls gathered in the rabbi's home under the direction of his wife, the *rebbetzin* (her title as the rabbi's wife). A somewhat similar format of Torah lesson, song, and prayer occured. In this case, however, the girls were called upon to give a Torah lesson.

The girls and boys who attend these functions are the most highly motivated students, and they do so by invitation. Their behavior toward each other and toward the rabbi and his wife indicates deep sincerity.

FAMILY INVOLVEMENT IN THE PROCESS OF "RETURN"

As was indicated, the conversion of one member of a family to a new religion may place immense stress on family relationships, but it seems to be more disruptive when the new religious recruit is an adult. It also seems clear that the younger the child, the more the power in the relationship is tilted toward the parents and the less stress the family will endure; the parents can simply override the child's choice. By and large, this is true for parents in the FSU. But children in the FSU who are converting have a special role in Jewish families compared to that found in either the United States or Israel.

In the American and Israeli contexts, new recruits to Orthodoxy are under enormous pressure not to become involved in the new religion. The new faith suggests to family members that these persons have chosen to cut themselves off from them. The families may seek to persuade the new recruits to leave their newfound commitment, sometimes with gentle persuasion and sometimes with arguments and hostility. Although families have not attempted to "snatch" returnees and "deprogram" them, the experience can be painful for all who are involved (Danzger 1987, 1989). Occasionally, family members follow the new recruits into the new faith as a way of maintaining family ties. In contrast, in Kiev and in the FSU in general, I have found that the parents of children who have become newly traditional tend to follow their children into the new practices.

A series of interviews I conducted with members of one family illustrate this point. In the summer of 1992, I interviewed Sophie, 46-year-old woman who was then employed as secretary and administrative assistant for a religious outreach organization in Jerusalem. Sophie had come to Israel from Russia with her two daughters and her husband in 1990.

Sophie had grown up in a nonreligious Jewish family in Moscow. She graduated college with a degree in engineering, took a job with a government agency, and soon after met and married her husband. Her husband, Victor, who was a physicist, also came from a secular Jewish family. The couple had two girls four years apart. When the elder girl, Tamara, was 12, she joined a Jewish youth group. It was 1982, and a number of Jewish underground groups had been formed in Moscow to study and teach Judaism. Although teaching Judaism per se was not illegal, the study of Hebrew—which was necessary for the study of Judaism and for prayer—was forbidden as a sign of dual loyalty. Hebrew was the language of Israel, and the Soviet Union was hostile to Israel. Nor was it possible to be openly religious. Those who were identified as religious could not hold jobs as teachers or researchers or work in the government.

Sophie encouraged Tamara to join the group, but she did not consider the outcome. Tamara became increasingly interested in religion and in learning about Israel. Over the next four years, Tamara's interest more and more involved the family. Sophie began to light the Sabbath candles on Friday evening and prepared a festive dinner on Friday night. Victor objected to the whole idea, fearful that if they were discovered, he and Sophie would lose their jobs. But Tamara pressed on. She became increasingly involved in these activities, learning Israeli dances and songs and geography and Hebrew and becoming more engaged in religious practices. Sophie followed hesitantly. Tamara's younger sister followed her into the groups and also became involved in Israeli-related activities and the practice of Judaism.

With the disintegration of the Soviet regime, it became possible to be more open about religion and to identify openly with Israel. And, when it became possible to emigrate to Israel in January 1990, the family decided to leave. Although Victor was hesitant about leaving, and his views as husband and father should have outweighed Tamara's, the family left for Israel.

In Israel, Tamara took a teacher's training course. Soon after she graduated, she got a job in a religious seminary, where she taught a variety of Jewish religious subjects in Russian to high school and college-level girls. Sophie found work as a secretary and administrator, as mentioned. The younger sister finished high school and started college. Victor could not find a position and remained unemployed. At the time of the interviews, in the summer of 1992, he was studying Hebrew and Judaism and had taken to wearing a *kipa*, a skullcap signifying religious commitment. Tamara married a religious Israeli in early 1992. Both she and Sophie wore their hair covered in the manner of the strictly Orthodox. Tamara and her husband lived in Kiryat Arba, a town within walking distance of Hebron, a hotbed of Arab-Jewish conflict. Commuting from Kiryat Arba to work in Jerusalem every day meant risking stoning and occasional firebombs. Tamara was fully aware of the danger, but, nonetheless, chose to live there.

By the time of my 1992 interviews, all the family members had become strictly practicing Orthodox Jews, although Victor was still visibly behind the others. In the summer of 1995, I interviewed Sophie again. It was clear that the family was deeply entrenched in Orthodoxy, and there was little likelihood of them backsliding.

Another aspect of children-led "return", is that the mothers and children tend to become involved in religion, but the fathers tend to be unmoved. In Kiev, Esther, the mother of a teenage boy and a daughter aged 7, had been befriended by Rabbi and Rebbetzin Bleich. A tall, attractive woman of 37, Esther worked as a medical technician in a hospital. Her husband was an engineer in a governmental agency. Her son, Boris, had attended the Kiev Jewish High School directed by Rabbi Bleich since 1991 and, over the five-year period, had become a committed Orthodox Jew. In addition to his observance of the laws of *kashrut*, he prayed regularly at Rabbi Bleich's synagogue on the Sabbath. His mother and sister were often guests of Rabbi and Rebbetzin Bleich for the Sabbath and, when they were, Boris would eat with other young boys at the synagogue. We met Esther and her daughter at the rabbi's home and interviewed Boris and Esther, both of whom were eager to go to Israel. However, the husband remained a committed communist and indicated that he would not join them if they left for Israel. It became clear in the course of the interviews that this family would split as a result of these religious differences.

Since 1990, I have met and interviewed several other newly Orthodox young people in Israel whose mothers had come with them and whose fathers had remained in the FSU. I did not meet a single person who had come with his or her father while the mother remained in the FSU.[4]

Another instance of a family split caused by a child's return to tradition was revealed in my interview with Ina, an immigrant from Kiev, who came to the United States in 1978 with her father, mother and grandmother. As a new immigrant from the Soviet Union, she was welcomed by American Jews and enrolled in Yeshiva University High School for Girls with a full-tuition scholarship, a substantial monetary benefit. The school had a kosher cafeteria, where Ina could take all her meals. On weekends and holidays, Ina often was invited to the homes of her classmates. Her mother and grandmother made some attempts to become involved in traditional Judaism, even though they were inconsistent. However, her father wanted to have nothing to do with it. Within a year of their arriving in the United States, Ina's father and mother were divorced. Ina completed college in New York and went to a university on the West Coast to receive a law degree. She married a young Russian immigrant who had become a dentist. Their religious practices were not Orthodox, but they became affiliated with a synagogue, and, when their son was born, he had a *brit* (Jewish ritual circumcision).

The tendency for fathers to leave the family if the religious issue is pressed on them appears to be widespread. There was general agreement among my informants that the Soviet and post-Soviet family bond is relatively weak and that husbands and wives are quick to break up, primarily because they view marriage as little more than a convenience. High divorce rates (Turgeon 1993) and social science research (Bodrova 1995; Shlapentokh 1984) support this assessment.

MEN AS LEADERS IN THE "RETURN" PROCESS IN KIEV

Despite the pattern of children leading and fathers resisting, when husbands do lead, wives tend to follow, or, more accurately, when men lead, women tend to follow. This was the case for Rabbi Eliyau Essas, an early Moscow dissident, whom I interviewed for some earlier unpublished research. Rabbi Essas became religious after he and his wife were married. Interviews with both of them indicated that she was following his lead. Herman Branover and his wife described a similar transition, as did several other interviewees. The same pattern held for American men and women, and the causes are rooted clearly in Orthodox Jewish practices (Danzger 1989). Yet in the United States, there were also a number of cases in which a woman's return led her husband or fiancé to return. That I have not found a single case in Russia or Ukraine where women lead and men follow probably has more to do with the culture of the FSU than with Judaism or typical patterns of recruitment and conversion to religion.

CONCLUSIONS

Family is powerfully affected by religious conversion and has a powerful effect on this process. This dynamic has, for the most part, been overlooked in the sociological study of conversion. This omission is due partly to sociologists' tendency to interview individuals, rather than the entire families of the newly religious.

When a family-oriented research strategy is used, it becomes clear that although parents often lead young children into religion, once children have reached adolescence, they may be the leaders in this process. This latter pattern seems to occur more often among Jews in the FSU than in the United States. Furthermore, men in the FSU tend to leave their families if they are pressed to become religious more frequently than men in the United States. Finally, it also seems that in the FSU, men lead women into religion; women do not lead men. This pattern of the return to Orthodoxy is common in the United States as well, but in the United States, women are sometimes the leaders in this respect.

NOTES

I am grateful for the support provided for this research by the Research Foundation of the City University of New York, the Memorial Foundation for Jewish Culture, and the Lucius N. Littaur Foundation.

1. The government of the Soviet Union formally ended in late 1991, but the collapse was preceded by the gradual liberalization in the era of perestroika under Mikail Gorbachev. In the religious sphere, new freedoms were granted in 1988, and by 1989, de facto religious freedom was apparent for most groups. The passage of new legislation on religion in 1990 concretely marked the new stage of openness in religion for the Soviet Union and then for its successor societies (Pankhurst and Welch 1993).
2. A *mikveh* is a pool of water for the purpose of ritual purification, constructed in accordance with Jewish religious requirements. It is used primarily by married women a week after their menstrual periods, after which they may resume marital relations with their husbands.
3. In the course of the development of the Ukrainian school system, there was a change in school structure. Previously, students in the first to fourth grades went to one school and students from the fifth grade up went to another. When the schools were restructured, the first three grades were grouped together, and mid-

dle school began at the fifth grade. Thus, there is no fourth grade in the Ukrainian schools.

4. No doubt such cases exist as evidenced by the soldier who was killed in battle in Lebanon and whose body was returned to Russia at his mother's request. She lived there although the son and father had gone to Israel (Schmemann 1998).

References

Bodrova, Valentina. 1995. "The Russian Family in Flux." *Transition* 1(16):10–11.

Danzger, M. Herbert. 1987. "Towards a Redefinition of 'Sect' and 'Cult': Orthodox Judaism in the United States and Israel." *Comparative Social Research* 10:113–123.

———. 1989. *Returning to Tradition: The Contemporary Revival of Orthodox Judaism*. New Haven, CT: Yale University Press.

Kilbourne, Brock, and James T. Richardson. 1989. "Paradigm Conflict, Types of Conversion, and Conversion Theories." *Sociological Analysis* 50:1–22.

Lofland, John. 1977. "Becoming a World Saver Revisited." *American Behavioral Scientist* 20:805–18.

Lofland, John, and Rodney Stark. 1965. "Becoming a World Saver: A Theory of Conversion to Deviant Perspective." *American Sociological Review* 30:862–74.

Merton, Robert. 1968 *Social Theory and Social Structure* Enlarged Edition. New York: Free Press.

Musick, Marc, and John Wilson. 1995. "Religious Switching for Marriage Reasons." *Sociology of Religion* 56:257–70.

Ofer, Zvi. 1972. "Kiev: After World War II." Pp. 996–98 in *Encyclopedia Judaica*. Jerusalem: Keter.

Pankhurst, Jerry G., and Carolyn Welch. 1993. "Religion Under Gorbachev." Pp. 322–36 in *The Gorbachev Encyclopedia* edited by J. L. Wieczynski. Salt Lake City, UT: Charles Schlacks, Jr.

Schmemann, Serge. 1998. "A Soldier Dies, and a Forlorn Family Shames Israel." *New York Times*, February 11, p. A4.

Shlapentokh, Vladimir. 1984. *Love, Marriage and Friendship in the Soviet Union: Ideals and Practices*. New York: Praeger.

Slutsky, Yehuda. 1972. "Kiev: The Jewish Community Before 1667; From 1793." Pp. 991–95 in *Encyclopedia Judaica*. Jerusalem: Keter.

Snow, D. A., and R. Machalek. 1984. "The Sociology of Conversion." *Annual Review of Sociology* 10:167–90.

Turgeon, Lynn. 1993. "Afterword." Pp. 353–57 in *Democratic Reform and the Position of Women in Transitional Economies*, edited by Valentine M. Moghadam. Oxford, England: Clarendon Press.

West, Benjamin. 1972. "Kiev: Holocaust Period." Pp. 995–96 in *Encyclopedia Judaica*. Jerusalem: Keter.

CHAPTER ELEVEN

"We Don't Celebrate Christmas, We Just Give Gifts": Adaptations to Migration and Social Change Among Hindu, Muslim, and Sikh Children in England

HEIDI LARSON

THE CONTEXT

Several places in England have large populations from India, Pakistan, and Bangladesh. One such place is Southall, on the western edge of London, one of England's most densely populated urban areas, which has an old and large community of "Asians"—the British term for people from the Indian subcontinent. The majority of the Asians in Southall came from the Punjab areas of northern India and Pakistan. They share a common language, music, dance, dress, and food that distinguishes the Punjab from other regions of India, as well as the experience of migration and adjustment to life in England. What they do not all share is a common religion—a difference that, in 1947, divided the original Punjab area of India into the Muslim state of Pakistan and the Sikh-dominated state of Punjab, India, where violence between Sikhs and Hindus still persists.

In Southall, these historically hostile religious groups live side by side, buying from each other's shops, taking their children to the same schools, and often lining up at the same job centers and welfare offices. Although the religious differences in Southall are not divisive, they are articulated throughout children's daily lives. After-school religious classes at the Muslim mosque, Hindu temple, and Sikh Gurdwara reinforce social networks that evolve among extended families and neighbors who share the same religion. At government-supported schools, children socialize regularly with others of different faiths, but separate language classes (English is the language of instruction, but other language classes are taught as electives) for Punjabi and Urdu writing, for instance, distinguish the Sikh students from the Muslims.[1] In Southall, the schools are virtually 100 percent Asian, and the children have little contact with English children, so their ethnic identities are not challenged in day-to-day interactions. The children are aware of being "Asian" in the society at large through television, their English schoolteachers and lessons, and older siblings or parents who work or attend college outside Southall, but inside Southall, the differences that the children find among themselves are religious, and the children identify and distinguish themselves mainly as Muslim, Hindu, or Sikh.

Most of the research on Asians in Britain has been specific to one religious group, such as Gujarati Hindus, Punjabi Sikhs, or Pakistani Muslims (Burghart 1987; Dahya 1972, 1973, 1974; James 1974; Saifullah-Kahn 1974; Shaw 1988; Werbner 1979), and focused primarily on the impact of the alien cultural environment on the maintenance of traditions. Little attention has been given to the dynamics among different religious groups within Asian communities.

This chapter examines how Southall children learn about and reconcile their religious differences in this ethnically homogenous, religiously plural, "Little Punjab." It argues that children do not confuse or lose their sense of religious identity in the face of other religions. Instead, their interactions and play with children of other faiths helps them define and strengthen their own notions of identity and belonging. The distinct religious identities established among children aged 7 to 10 are not divisive, though, since there is an overarching common Punjabi identity and the experience of being Asian in a predominantly English nation state.

CULTURAL SYNTHESIS OR CULTURE SHOCK?

Early studies of Asians in Britain tended to characterize the first generation of Pakistani and Indian children born in England as "caught between two cultures" (Anwar 1976; Hiro 1971; James 1974; Taylor 1976; Thompson 1974; Watson 1977). These studies often described this phenomenon as culture shock and suggested a cultural impasse. More recent research has recognized that cultural synthesis is more prevalent than culture shock among Asian children who grow up in England (Agnihotra 1980; Ballard 1979; Rashid 1981; Yates 1988). Ballard (1979:128) describes this situation poignantly:

> The notion that young Asians are likely to suffer from "culture conflict" is a gross oversimplification of a wide range of complex personal experiences. It assumes a straightforward clash, a tug-of- war, between East and West, traditional and modern, rural and urban, repression and freedom, resulting in an unbridgeable gulf between the generations. In reality, young Asians are not faced with an either/or situation. They have difficult dilemmas to resolve and in resolving them they work towards their own synthesis of Asian and British values.

As Ballard noted, Asian children in England confront a wide range of conflicts. These children are not in what Van Gennep (1960) and Turner (1969) called a "liminal" stage that is "betwixt and between" cultures—a state more familiar to their parents. Rather than being a tabula rasa on which the old culture has been erased and the new host culture has yet to be etched, these children are active scribes—communicating the new culture to the old and the old culture to the new. Furthermore, it is in this passage across different ethnic and religious boundaries that the children determine the parameters of their own identities. The children have a unique access to these boundaries. Taboos are often relaxed for them, and they are more readily excused from the social rules of adulthood. The often-unspoken sanction for children to cross into areas that border but may not interact with their more bounded adult lives is vital to the development of their unique religious and social identities.

Kureishi (1986:160) described well the social and cultural innovation—rather than trauma—that is inherent in being a second-generation immigrant:

> When I was in my teens, in the mid-sixties, there was much talk of the "problems" that kids of my color faced in Britain because of our racial mix or because our parents were immigrants. We didn't know where we belonged. It was said we were neither fish nor fowl. I remember reading that kind of thing in the newspaper. We were frequently referred to as "second-generation immigrants" just so there was no mistake about our not really belonging in Britain. We were "Britain's children without a home." The phrase "caught between two cultures" was a favorite. It was a little too triumphant for me. Anyway, this view was wrong. It has been easier for us than for our parents. For them, Britain really had been a strange land and it must have been hard to feel part of a society if you had spent a good deal of your time elsewhere and intended to return. Most immigrants from the Indian subcontinent came to Britain to make money and then go home . . . and many, once here, stayed for good; it was not possible to go back. Yet, when they got older the immigrants found they hadn't really made a place for themselves in Britain. . . . But for me and the others of my generation born here, Britain was always where we belonged, even when we were told—often in terms of racial abuse—that this was not so. Far from being a conflict of cultures, our lives seemed to synthesize disparate elements: the mosque, two or three different languages, rock'n' roll, Indian films. Our extended family and our individuality co-mingled.

The between-two-cultures challenge has been regarded almost exclusively as a problem, and sometimes as even painful or traumatic. Although some children experience stresses and difficult aspects of growing up between cultures (some of the problems are due, in part, to the process of growing up, in general, and are not specific to the experience of being children of immigrants), little attention has been paid to the creative, playful aspects of negotiating new cultural terms. Abramson (1979:8), one of the few to point to this more dynamic aspect of migration, wrote: "It is only in contact between cultures, as in the classic role of migration, that ethnicity and religion assume a dynamic and social reality of their own." Fischer (1986: 196) suggested a similar dynamic among Chinese Americans:

> Ethnicity is something reinvented and reinterpreted each generation and by each individual . . . ethnicity is not something that is simply passed on from generation to generation, taught and learned; it is something dynamic. . . . To be Chinese-American is not the same thing as being Chinese in America. In this sense there is no role model for becoming Chinese-American. It is a matter of finding a voice or style that does not violate one's several components of identity.

Three levels of identity are at play among Southall children: religious identity within an all-Asian context, Asian identity within the larger British population, and being British Asian within the context of a global network of Asians overseas and against those who remained on the Indian subcontinent. Several Southall children commented about their visits to India or Pakistan, where they were called the "English" cousins. Similarly, their relatives who settled in Uganda or Kenya were known as the "African" cousins.

Although there are some tensions inherent in negotiating these different identities, the research presented in this chapter found that children aged 7 to 10 were more likely to be resourceful and innovative than to have problems with their emerging senses of self.

THE APPROACH

Children, aged 7 to 10, who lived in Southall, were the key informants in my study. I observed and interviewed them and recorded conversations among peers at school, at home, and in their places of worship. I chose the children of three Muslim families as the core group of children through whom I met extended family members, friends, classmates, and neighbors because Muslims are the most recent arrivals to Southall, and I was particularly interested in learning about children whose parents were first-generation immigrants. Since many of the Sikh and Hindu children's parents were born in England, their grandparents having been the first-generation immigrants, I also had the opportunity to study the different dynamics among first- and second-generation immigrant children.

Although the overall research included interviews with and observations of Muslim, Hindu, and Sikh children and their families in the local school and neighborhood where the three families lived, I conducted more in-depth interviews and visits with the three core families—including their extended families in Pakistan.

I first met the children at a Koran class where I interviewed twenty-five children about themselves and their families. The children of the three families I identified all went to the same school and lived in the same neighborhood, although two of the families came from rural villages in the Punjab area of Pakistan and one family came from the city of Lahore. Of the two rural families, one father had saved money working in a local factory and was about to start his own business, while the other had been unemployed for several years. I selected these children so I could observe how their interactions varied from the religiously plural school context to the different households.

Few anthropologists use children as their primary source of information; for the most part, they have looked at children, rather than listened to them (Hardman 1973; Lancy and Tindall 1975; Schwartzman 1978; Skinner 1988). "In general," La Fontaine (1986:10) noted, "anthropology has retained an outdated view of children as raw material, unfinished specimens of the (adult) social beings whose ideas and behavior are the proper subject matter for a social science." Anthropological studies of children have usually focused on formalized rites of passages, stages of development, and play as a direct imitation of adult life. As Hardman (1973:86) stated, "None of the main approaches to children revealed the beginnings of an anthropology of children concerned with beliefs, values or interpretation of their viewpoint, their meaning of the world." Some of the best field-method models for an anthropology of children are outside anthropology. For instance, the child psychiatrist Coles (1967, 1986a, 1986b) distinguished his work by bringing his psychiatry out of the clinic into the field, where he observes and listens to children in their own context. The following sections draw extensively from the children's interpretations of the world around them—through their conversations, drawings, and play.

In addition to recording the content of the children's conversations, I examined where and how the children learned and exchanged their information and views. I frequently asked the children where they learned some of the things they told me and listened for exchanges between parents and children and teachers and children, as well as among the children themselves to identify the sources of their views and perceptions. I also discussed the views the children raised with their teachers, religious instructors, parents, and older siblings. In the course of my two years of research in London, I also made two two-month trips to Pakistan and India to visit the home villages and relatives of several of the children in Southall. These visits were valuable for establishing rapport with the families and giving me an insights into a significant other part of their lives.

Photography as a Research Method

Photography played a critical role throughout my work. Drawing from Collier's (1967) classic text, I used photography not only as a means to illustrate situations and interactions that supported my research, but to document people and events that I wanted to learn more about. Photographs became, for me, questions as well as answers or confirmations of known information. I printed my photographs weekly to show to the children and families who were pictured and to ask them about the events or occasions that were depicted. The discussions around the photographs helped me identify kin relations, as well as various people's feelings about and attitudes toward the occasions and the people in the pictures. These casual interviews also helped guide my research because they often directed me to related events and people with whom I visited and often photographed in my ongoing attempt to piece together the cultural puzzle I faced.

In addition to the many photographs I took because of my own questions and interests, I often asked the people I photographed to tell me how *they* wanted me to photograph them and what they thought was important for me to shoot in their community. I explained that unless there was a particular request for personal photographs, I intended to use the photographs in my research and teaching about the experience of Pakistani children and their families in England. I encouraged people to ask me if they needed photographs, since I considered their requests for photographs to be significant markers of the events and people they valued. In both Southall and Pakistan, taking and giving pictures was also a valuable means of gaining rapport with families. And as a photographer, I was invited to several events—particularly family ones—that I might not have otherwise been invited to. I cannot emphasize too much the valuable role of taking—and giving—photographs in my fieldwork.

PLAY AND RELIGIOUS IDENTITY

> The universe comes into existence through God's creative power (Maya) and it ceases to exist at his will. According to Guru Gobind Singh, it is "a play" and exists only until He brings "the play" to an end.
>
> —G. S. Sidhu, *A Brief Introduction to Sikhism*

Southall children learn about and participate in each other's religions in different contexts. School trips bring Muslim, Hindu, and Sikh children into each other's places of worship. And on two occasions—the Muslim festival of *Eid* and the Sikh celebration of the Guru Nanak's birthday—the local mosque and temple send blessed sweet rice to all the classrooms.

One of the more frequent arenas for culture exchange is the school assembly in which plays about religious festivals are staged. In this context, Muslim children are sometimes cast in dramas about Sikhism or Hinduism, and Hindu children are sometimes cast in roles in Christmas pageants. Although the neighborhood and school in Southall where I conducted my research was virtually 100 percent Asian—few of whom were Christian—television, magazines, newspapers, and the English schoolteachers brought Christmas into the schools. Although the children regularly played different roles in the various religious dramas, they were keenly aware that, as one child put it, "this is play; this is not what *we* believe."

The children enjoyed being in plays about each other's religions and, when asked, felt no conflict in doing so. They recognized their participation as play.

HL: Tell me the story of the play you were in this morning.

MUNEZA: I was in the crowd when Guru Gobind Singh comes out and he says, "I need 6 Sikhs."—Shall I say it in Punjabi?

HL: Yes.

MUNEZA: *"Meenee chaiya 6 Sikh . . . kan apnee jan dee sakta?"* That means "Who will give their life to me?" and one boy says, *"Mee dunga!"* "I'll give it!" And he says, "Come here" and then Sarvot [a Muslim classmate] opens the tent and goes in, and someone stamps on the ground and pretends he chopped his head off. He has two swords. One is pink, and he gets the pink one and says, "Blood!" *"Khun!"* And everyone goes "Oh!!" [gasping]. Then they get so shocked. And he says, "I need four Sikhs, four Singhs. Who will give their life to me?" And Harry [a Sikh classmate] says, "I will." *"Mee dungi."* And his servant opens his tent and then goes in and bashes again like he killed him.

RIZWANA: Tell her the next part! When you come in. . . .

MUNEZA: Then he says what he has to say again, "Who will give their life?

HL: Why does he want people to give their lives?

MUNEZA: He wants to check out who is the bravest of all the Sikhs. At the end when I come in and another boy comes in. . . .

RIZWANA: Say your part! Say your part!

MUNEZA: Then he goes, "I need two Sikhs. Who wants to give their lives?" And this boy says, "I will!" And I go, "I want to give it!" and I stand up and come in. I haven't said things like that before! And guess what they did! They pulled my shirt and he opened the tent and then we all came out. Our heads were chopped off, but we were alive!! You saw that part.

HL: What is the point of the story?

MUNEZA: Guru Gobind Singh wanted to check out all the Sikhs—five beloved ones—five bravest people. Who will be brave like me?? He tries to see of the people out of the crowd—who's so brave out of all these people?? And he asked everyone!

HL: What happened to the people in the real story.

MUNEZA: Everybody else—they thought that we were dead.

HL: But what happened to the bravest people?

IMUNEZA: They got a lamb—you know, Guru Gobind Singh—he got a sheep and then cut his head off. Then he got blood—real blood—and then they thought that they killed people on the sword, *but* it was a sheep.

Muneza's detailed account of the school play reveals her attention to and interest in the story of the Sikh leader, despite her own faith as a Muslim. Though she did not draw parallels to it in her account of the Sikh drama, the Muslim festival of Bakr Eid, celebrates a similar story. Bakr Eid remembers Abraham's sacrificing a lamb instead of his own son, a tale that, for Muneza, may have lent credibility to the story of Guru Gobind Singh.

Another aspect of the Guru Gobind Singh drama that has parallels in other religious stories is the play-within-the play. The play is about Guru Gobind Singh's pretending—or "playing" at—killing devotees. Another play within a play came up at the Christmas pageant about Father Christmas when Muneza talked about Father Christmas being a pretend character.

MUNEZA: On Christmas Day, they have Father Christmas come to people's houses. Sometimes, WHEN THEY'RE CHRISTIANS, they get stockings from shops and they put them near the bedroom. The children, they put them up and they PRETEND that Father Christmas is going to come. And their own father, HE puts the costume on and HE comes through the bedroom window. He buys things for them and puts them in their stocking, and afterwards, when the children wake up in the morning, they see things in their stocking and they THINK Father Christmas was there. . . .
RIZWANA: Miss, but how come Father Christmas . . . this girl, she told me and SHE PROMISED THAT IT WAS TRUE. She goes [said] that she stayed awake. She just put her head on her pillow and she just looked and she heard her Mum and Dad sleeping and someone came down the chimney. She heard it and it came in her room. And then he put something in her sock.
MUNEZA: ONLY CHRISTIANS! IT ONLY HAPPENS TO CHRISTIANS! I think that it only happens to Christians. CHRISTIANS BELIEVE IN THAT.

Muneza's final comment that "it only happens to Christians" suggests that the pretend aspect of Father Christmas is only in the eyes of nonbelievers. Furthermore, her comment suggests that for those who do believe in something, even "pretend" actions can have meaning. The implications of this belief are particularly significant in the immigrant context, where, as the children pointed out, the "real" thing is back in India or Pakistan or Mecca. Removed from the source of their religious traditions and having to re-create or "pretend" at the ways things are done in India or Pakistan, belief becomes particularly important in empowering rituals in England.

The role of belief in distinguishing what is play and what is "real" is critical to the Southall children's evolving sense of religious identity. The children regularly cross boundaries to participate in each other's religious traditions, though they maintain a clear sense of their own religious traditions. Muslim children, for instance, occasionally go with a Sikh or Hindu friend into their temple, where they make an offering and receive some *prasad*—the blessed food—and Hindu, Sikh, and Muslim children often exchange cards or gifts at Christmas and even eggs at Easter. This playing out of others' traditions has a less defined pretend frame than staged performances at school, although the children still maintain a clear distinction between their own traditions and beliefs and those of others. Muslim children are quick to send Christmas gifts and cards because "Jesus is our prophet." "BUT," as one 9-year-old Pakistani girl explained, "we do not believe he is the son of God." Another girl, on her way out the door to go "Christmas shopping" told me that "we don't CELEBRATE Christmas, we JUST give gifts."

The children's ways of reconciling the "shoulds" of their faith and their sometimes contradictory actions came up on several occasions. In one instance, a girl came running up to her sister's lunch table at school to tell her that she thought she had eaten ham by mistake. Sitting across from the older sister and overhearing the exchange, I was quickly told by the older girl, "Oh my God! My sister ate that," pointing to another girl's plate of cafeteria casserole. "She's Muslim and she thought that it was fish, but it's ham!" Another Muslim girl, Uzma, who was sitting at the same table, interrupted to remind the concerned older sister, "If she prays to God, 'sorry I ate it,' it will be better."

Seven-year-old Uzma felt compelled to tell me on different occasions about the ways in which she maintained her faith, despite the dominantly non-Muslim environment that surrounded her. I asked her one day about the school trip to the local Sikh temple, about which she remarked, "I have been with the school, and I didn't look at anything. I just closed my eyes." When I asked her why she did not look at anything, her friend interrupted to explain, "Miss, we [Muslims] are not really supposed to go there." Uzma then told me, "I closed my eyes and . . . I was holding on to the front person." I again asked why, to which her eager friend again interrupted to say, "We're supposed to go into *masjids* [Muslim mosques], not *gurdwaras* [Sikh temples]." "We're not allowed to see the *gurdwara*," Uzma continued, "so I just closed my eyes and said, 'No, thank you' and I walked away."

The children's ability to maintain their own belief system, despite the religious pluralism around them, was different from the attitude of many of their parents who feared that their children were being "brainwashed" by alien, particularly Christian, holidays. The parents' fears were epitomized in a scathing article called "A White Christmas" (Alibhai 1987), which bitterly argued that school Christmas pageants are a means for the dominant white culture to sway Asian children from their own religious traditions. The children, on the other hand, revealed a different level of religious conviction than their parents seemed to be aware of and were not easily swayed from their faiths. Instead, they tried to understand other religions in terms of their own.

The children often talked about Christmas, since it is the major English holiday with which they can compare their own festivals. The Muslim children frequently described the major Muslim holiday of Eid at the end of the Ramadan fasting month, as "our Christmas," and the Hindu and Sikh children did the same about their major holiday Diwali.

Burghart (1987:242) discussed this process of interpreting other cultures in terms of one's own:

> One might say that in an alien cultural milieu a people may see themselves through foreign eyes, and find meanings in their own culture which are roughly equivalent to those of the other culture. Such meanings are not "exchanged" between cultures, but functionally equivalent meanings are established.
>
> This process of finding "roughly equivalent" meanings is frequent among children in Southall. In addition to interpreting others' rituals such as Christmas to accommodate their own notions of faith, Southall children also adapt their own traditions to fit into the cultural context which surrounds them.

On Halloween, for instance, a few Hindu children were talking about going trick-or-treating. I asked if they ever did tricks when they did not receive treats. They told me that they sometimes threw eggs, but that they always asked first if the person was a vegetarian because then they would throw a tomato instead.

On another occasion, close to the Muslim festival of Eid, three young Muslim girls were explaining the festival to me when one of them decided to tell me she really wanted to give me a present for Eid. She paused to think for a minute, and then her friend excitedly suggested that she give me an "Eid egg—like they do at Easter." Everyone thought this was a great idea. Her friend then added, "Father Eid! Father Spring!" borrowing the notion of a Father Christmas figure delivering my Eid egg. I asked them what they bought with their Eid money (called *Eidi,* which is given to children at Eid), and one child brought out a small electronic piano that included the tunes for four songs: "Hark the Herald Angels Sing," "Joy to the World," "Jingle Bells," and "We Wish You a Merry Christmas."

The children in Southall regularly transformed manifestations of the dominant Christian culture to accommodate their own faith. On another occasion, a Muslim girl named Mumtaz walked into a birthday party wearing a medallion around her neck that was embossed with Jesus's praying hands. On the back it read:

> Oh God
> Give us serenity to accept
> what cannot be changed
> courage to change
> What should be changed
> and wisdom to distinguish
> the one from the other.
> AMEN

I asked where she bought the medallion, and she responded, "It was a Christmas bazaar! You can find really nice things. It was only 2p, and it's really nice! I didn't see anything about Jesus," she added, somehow justifying the praying hands, "so it was all right. A person of any religion can wear it." Although I did not ask about the praying hands, Mumtaz felt compelled to acknowledge that it was all right for her—a Muslim—to wear the medallion.

In the face of this cultural interplay, and despite the seeming cultural confusion, the children maintain a strong sense of their own religious identities. This distinction between action and meaning was made particularly clear in a conversation with two Muslim girls—Waheeda and Rizwana—who told me about a Jewish play they were performing in at their school.

RIZWANA: Would you like to come see our Jewish play? We're gonna do a play about Jerusalem with Moses, and it's got Jewish dancers. It's gonna be about when Moses went up to God and said "go to . . ." what's the king's name? . . . and the king said, "I want all the baby boys killed." So he sent a plague of frogs and he made Moses stick a stick into a snake and he made fresh water into blood.

HL: Do you believe that?

RIZWANA: Yeah, because Moses is our prophet. BUT, we don't believe Moses is God's son. We just think he's our prophet. [She continued talking about the Ten Commandments, and I asked if Muslims believe in them.]

WAHEEDA: We believe in EVERYTHING. Judaism, Christianity, even more. The more is our stuff.

HL: And Jesus?

RIZWANA: We believe in him, but not as God's son.

WAHEEDA: We treat him the same as other prophets. Christians stopped at Jesus, but, if they would have carried on believing in prophets, they would all be Muslim. This is what I think. No one told me this.

Here Waheeda went beyond reaffirming already established Islamic beliefs she had been taught; she projected her own notions about Islam and its relation on to other religions. One aspect of Islam that came up frequently as setting the Muslim children apart from their peers at school is its taboo on plays and imagery.

Whereas the Sikh, Hindu, and Christian faiths all abound with stories that can be dramatized in school plays and each has prophets or gods and goddesses who can be represented in drawings, Islam prohibits any images or representations of the Prophet. Rather than performing plays that enact stories in the Koran, Muslim children are allowed only to read passages from the Islamic holy book. At the most, they imitate their visiting relatives and preparing meals for the Muslim holidays. The stories about the reasons for the holidays, though, are never staged. The teachers were often frustrated in their efforts to give the Muslim children equal attention in the school assembly because there was so little they could draw on to dramatize.

The Muslim children often felt left out because they did not have a realm of images to draw from in their own faith—particularly when they sat next to Hindu children who were drawing elaborate images of gods and goddesses. Although the taboo on images limited the Muslim children in some ways, it also provoked them to use their imagination. "People say that God is a He, mostly," one 8-year-old Muslim girl told me. "But, God is neither of them. He's just a twinkle of a star who helps everybody. We can't draw God; He's just a twinkle of a star." "We can draw camels! He liked camels!" her classmate suggested. "We can draw his house (The Ka'aba, Mecca)," a third classmate remarked.

One Muslim girl started to draw an amorphous shape with several eyes, mouths, and arms (see Figure 11.1). "God has so many eyes!" she exclaimed. The number of eyes and appendages were not, as I had thought, a metaphor to suggest God's all-seeing power. They were, I soon learned, copied from the Hindu classmate's picture of a Hindu goddess with many arms. Throughout their drawing sessions, the children would frequently correct each other's drawings in light of their own traditions.

ASMA (*MUSLIM*): Miss! God's got five hands!
HL: Five?
RITA (*HINDU*): Miss, this is what WE have. We have a shelf in our temple. That's where photographs are. . . . Four eyes and two mouths and three mouths and five arms. . . . My God!
ASMA: She can hold everything in the world!
RITA: She made all the Gods.
HL: She did?

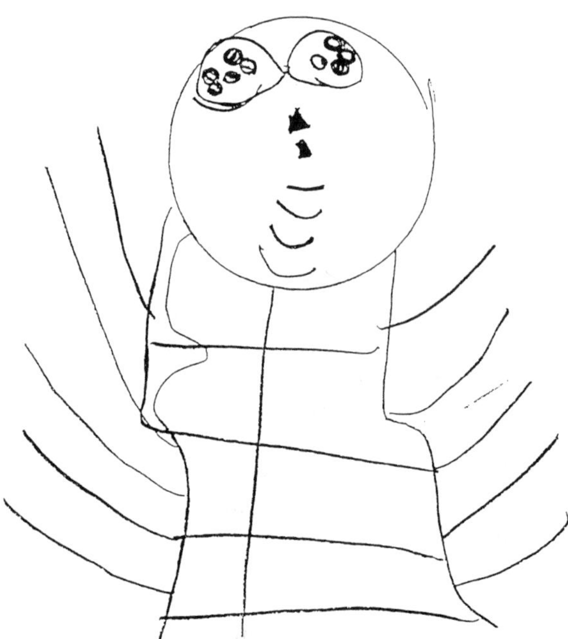

Figure 11.1. "God has so many eyes." Asma Ali. March 7, 1987.

AFSHA (*MUSLIM*): She made all the children and all the dead.
HL: Really? Where do you see her?
RITA: We don't see HER, BUT we have the poster. . . . "Shri Lanka" is her name.
AFSHA: Miss, that's God's woman.
ASMA: God doesn't got a woman!
RITA: That's the one with five hands . . . Hindu god. God doesn't have that many eyes. She's just making that up.
ASMA: He has! He has!
RITA: She's making fun of God! She's making fun of God!
ASMA: No! No!
RITA: It might be . . . I think it might be her Allah.

On another occasion when a Hindu girl was drawing pictures of her temple and its gods and goddesses, her Muslim classmates, Shazia and Muneza, talked about not being able to draw their god.

SHAZIA: We're not allowed to have pictures of our god.
HL: Do you know why?
SHAZIA: I don't know why.
HL: Who told you that you re not allowed?
SHAZIA: My mom told me.
MUNEZA: Our god? We can't because if we do we get punished. We can't say that we can 'cause we only can see light. When we go to the Natural Museums, I think people say that they only see light, sort of light shining out and can't see the real picture. NOBODY CAN DRAW THE PICTURE. You know the other? The Sikh's god? They just make models.

In both conversations, the children were keen to point out what is real and what is representation. Muneza justified the lack of imagery in Islam by remarking that the Sikh and Hindu images are only "models." Rita, a Hindu, said about her own faith that despite the abundance of imagery that fills their temple, "We cannot see HER [the goddess], BUT we have the poster."

Theories about children's ability to distinguish between play and real are valuable in understanding the Southall children's explorations of each other's rituals. Although the children in Southall readily played out each other's rituals, they knew the extent to which an action did or did not have meaning to them.

JAMILA: TRANSFORMATIONS

In one of the three key families in my study, I met 17-year-old Jamila. Jamila's 10-year-old sister, Muneza, had been one of the first children I had met in Southall, and Muneza was eager to introduce me to her older sister, Jamila.

Muneza had told me about Jamila and her baby sister, Nabila, who was born in England. Her family story touched on many of the issues that confront children who grow up between cultures, and I welcomed her invitation to meet her family. Muneza, Jamila, and Nabila lived with their parents in a small row house. I never expected Jamila to be as articulate and open with me as she turned out to be, and I ended up spending a considerable amount of my two years in Southall sitting in her small kitchen listening to her stories and feelings about life in England. Having been raised in Pakistan until she was 14, Jamila was conscious of the differences between those who grow up "back home" and those who were brought up in England. It was particularly surprising to Jamila to find out that there are different kinds of Islam. In Pakistan, Jamila thought that there was only one kind—the kind she grew up with. It was not until she came to England that she discovered that there is not only more than one sect of Islam, but that there are different extremes of faith.[2]

Two incidents especially impressed on Jamila that there were other ways of being Muslim. At a college where Jamila took English classes, an Iranian girl in her class introduced herself as a Shi'a Muslim. Jamila had never heard of a Shi'a Muslim and asked the girl, "Then what are we [in Pakistan]?" Jamila learned from her Iranian classmate that she was probably a Sunni Muslim.[3] "I never knew that in Pakistan," Jamila told me. "I thought we are all [the same] Muslims. I didn't know there was a difference." On another occasion, when Jamila and I were watching the evening news on television, a news broadcast came on about a demonstration in Tehran. A crowd of banner-waving, slogan-shouting Muslims swung their fists in the air cheering the Ayatollah's "Down-with-Reagan" speech. Jamila turned to me with a sad face and remarked that she never knew that there were these kinds of Muslims when she lived in Pakistan.

Jamila's notions of faith had changed considerably since she lived in England. The most significant change was her awareness that there are different ways of being devout. In addition to her new knowledge about different kinds of Islam at a formal level, Jamila had seen how, in England, Muslims have adapted their religious holidays and even evolved new ways of praying. Jamila herself had new convictions about prayer:

> If you're reading the Koran, you should cover your head. But, if you don't have the book in front of you and you are just praying, IT DOESN'T MATTER WHAT YOU WEAR OR WHERE YOU ARE.
>
> I think that everyone should have their OWN WAY of defining Islam and not be told what Islam is. You should have your own feelings about what Islam is in your life and why we should do certain things. Everyone has personal views.
>
> If someone forces you to believe in something, but you don't really believe in it, for that time—an hour or two hours—IN FRONT OF THEM—you WILL say that you believe in it. But, afterwards, when you're not in front of them, you don't believe.

> I would NEVER force anyone to do anything they don't want to. You can't. You CAN force somebody to do something once, twice, maybe even ten times, but YOU CAN'T FORCE THEM ALL THEIR LIVES.

Jamila conviction about choosing her own way of praying was one expression of her growing awareness of the choices she had in England. In our conversations, Jamila frequently talked about the possibilities she realized in England that she never knew in Pakistan. Her new awareness of options changed her attitude about her own life in England and gave her a different outlook on her village in Pakistan. In England, she became critical about the resistance to change in her village—a resistance that was not apparent to her until she left Pakistan.

> I know some ladies think that you're always supposed to be in the kitchen. Well, there ARE some ladies going out, and they feel they have some choice in England. It could be the man that stays in the house and the lady who goes out in England. But, in our society—in our village—it's different. Like my dad, he's not working. But, my mom is not going to work. I know she can't get a job and she doesn't want to go out to work. But, I'm just saying, if she COULD find a job, my dad wouldn't accept it EVER to stay in the house and look after the baby and take care of the housework. Never! He'd say, "I'd rather go out and earn." If he's educated and more realistic, then he can accept the wife going out working part time. But, if he's not working—especially OUR dad—if he's not working, he won't EVER accept that he can stay in the house and the woman goes out for a job.

Freedom of choice is the most significant change that Jamila has felt since she came to England. Jamila did not aspire to become English in her dress, eating habits, or even interactions with people. What she wanted most was the freedom to choose—to be who she wanted to be even if it meant being her Pakistani Muslim self in England. Jamila's aspirations to be who she wanted to be were epitomized in her admiration for her friend who cut her hair despite the Islamic taboo against it:

> My friend who got married. She went back to Pakistan, and she had a haircut. She didn't care. She said, "If they want to talk, let them talk. I'm not going to hide. I'm not going to sit quietly behind people's backs. I wanna be like I am. I wanna be like I feel."
>
> She cut her hair. Everything she did! She used to put makeup on and she wore jeans. But people living in the past, people living in our village, they always take her and say, "She's not under her parent's control anymore. She shouldn't be like that."
>
> I want to cut my hair in front, but I'm not allowed. I don't want to ask because my father would be ashamed of me. You should not cut your hair. Whenever I say to my aunt, "I'm gonna cut my hair," she always says, "No, because these hairs are the only thing that goes with you when you die." Because, when you die, there's nothing. Even that white cotton that they

put you in. But, that hair is the only thing which goes with you wherever you are. It doesn't matter. You should keep your hair long.

I don't know. IF WE'RE NOT GOING TO LIVE IN PAKISTAN, WHY SHOULD WE FEAR WHAT THEY THINK, WHAT THEY WANT?

CONCLUSION

Q. And what nationality are you then Anthony?
A. Welsh 'coz my Dad's Welsh . . . or British, I think . . . except. . . .
Q. Yes?
A. Well, we live here don't we?
Q. Where's that?
A. In London, so I suppose we're Londoners.
Q. And what about your friend who was in here before? Where's he from?
A. Oh, he's from Uganda or one of them places.
Q. Yes, but he's living here too, isn't he?
A. He is, but his dad's in India.
Q. So what is Thakar then?
A. Oh, I don't know. I suppose it depends what he thinks of himself. Isn't it? (Dove 1974: 255)

A key change between first- and second-generation Asians in England is the sense of where they feel they belong. This changed sense of belonging extends beyond an attachment to a particular country or a new feeling of belonging—or not—in the various social situations encountered in daily life. Cohen (1982:4) discussed the importance of understanding culture "by trying to capture its experiential sense—to discover 'what it feels like' to BELONG to a culture."

For Pakistani Muslims in England, there is a difference between their ethnic center—such as India or Pakistan—and their religious center—Mecca. Unlike the Hindus and Sikhs whose religious centers are historically and geographically bound to their cultural homeland, Muslim identity transcends nationality and ethnicity. Saima, a girl whose parents are from Pakistan confessed that if she had her choice of places to live, she would live in neither England nor Pakistan; she would move to Saudi Arabia. "That's where God's house is," Saima explained. "Most of the Muslims live there, and everyone leaves their shops open. I'd really love to live down there because no one steals and no one touches you there. If anyone touches you, they chop their hands off. No stealing down there, no burning."

Saima's urge to move to Saudi Arabia was not inspired merely by her religious classes at the mosque. She had close relatives living in Jeddah whom she had visited twice—once to attend her uncle's wedding and once to visit her grandparents who lived there while her grandfather worked for Pakistan Airlines. Her concern about feeling safe also reflects her parents' anxiety about the crime and discrimination they face in England.

Saima and other classmates from Pakistan and India talk about moving and traveling regularly. Their travels are not limited to the Indian subcontinent; they attend weddings and visit relatives in the United States, Canada, Kenya, France, Holland, and Dubai. These trips—particularly for weddings—are often planned at the last minute. Children in school seem to disappear, and their classmates shrug their shoulders and say, "Guess they went back to India."

Most of the families in Southall already have a legacy of migration. Some came to Southall from East Africa, where their families migrated from India to build the British railways three generations ago. Many of those who came straight from the Indian subcontinent were part of the mass migration across the Punjab at the time of the partition of Pakistan and India in 1947. Some Muslims remembered their ancestors' forced migration from the Bukhara area of the Soviet Union into northern India years earlier. Others traveled extensively while in the service of the British army. "We are like international gypsies," one father remarked.

Even though they felt "like gypsies," people in these immigrant and diaspora communities developed a strong sense of belonging. It was a sense of belonging not to a particular place, but to a shared system of beliefs that transcend place. Jamila often spoke of the difference between real faith and attachments to routine traditions. Being an immigrant challenged her notions of faith and her perceptions of her religion. In England, Jamila and her younger sisters and their schoolmates developed an inner notion of faith that was not dependent on an all-Muslim environment, such as that in Pakistan where their parents were raised. For many first-generation immigrants, leaving Pakistan meant leaving behind the religious traditions that went with it—its mosques, the daily calls to prayers, and a virtually 100 percent Muslim population, most of whom observed the same religious holidays and had the same eating habits. As Jamila pointed out, the real changes emerge when people on the move look inward rather than outward to establish their sense of religious and cultural identity:

> Twenty years ago, when people came here, they came for jobs because they needed money. They didn't come to build mosques. They didn't have any idea that they would build a mosque. One day they woke up. They didn't start building a mosque, they just rented a room, a hall, and prayed there. Like on Townsend Road, it doesn't have a minaret. IT'S INSIDE WHAT YOU BELIEVE IN.
>
> Sometimes my mum and dad say "You don't pray." I say "it doesn't matter." I pray on my own time. You don't have to sit by the mosque. You can pray on the bus. IT'S MORE IMPORTANT TO BE BELIEVING IN IT THAN BEING IN A PARTICULAR PLACE OR PRAYING IN A PARTICULAR WAY.

The children in Southall reiterated this sentiment in their daily exchanges at home, at school, and in the community as they explored and played out each other's religions while they maintained a clear sense of the boundaries of their own faiths. As evidenced in the play episodes and passages presented here, the children used play as a medium through which they learned the parameters of their own and others' religions. Many of the children in Southall may never have had this opportunity in Muslim-dominated Pakistan or in the Sikh-dominated state of India. The opportunity to play out each other's religions seems to have diffused the hostility that often grows from not knowing how the other side lives, plays, and prays. This opportunity, combined with the common experience of being Punjabi Asians in England, allowed the children to use their religious differences creatively as they negotiated their new identities in England.

Notes

1. Hindi is not taught in the elementary schools because the majority of the students are either Sikh or Muslim. Hindi is taught at the high school level, and courses are available through Hindu temples and organizations.
2. Jamila lives in a small village in Azad Kashmir, Pakistan, remote from any urban area. People in the urban areas of Pakistan—particularly those with television sets—are more likely to be aware of different sects of Islam.
3. There are both Sunni and Shi'a Muslims in Pakistan, although Sunni Muslims are, by far, the majority.

References

Abramson, H. J. 1979. "Migrants and Cultural Diversity: On Ethnicity and Religion." *Social Compass* 26(1):5–29.

Agnihotra, Rama Kant. 1980. "Processes of Assimilation: A Sociolinguistic Study of Sikh Children in Leeds." Ph.D. dissertation, University of York, York, England.

Alibhai, Yasmin. 1987. "A White Christmas." *New Society*, December 18, pp. 15–17.

Anwar, Muhammed. 1976. *Between Two Cultures: A Study of Relationships Between Generations in the Asian Community in Britain*. London: Community Relations Council.

Ballard, Catherine. 1979. "Conflict, Continuity and Change: Second Generation South Asian Migrants." Pp. 109–29 in *Minority Families in Britain*, edited by V. Saifullah-Kahn. London: Macmillan.

Bateson Gregory. 1972. "A Theory of Play and Fantasy." Pp. 177–93 in *Steps to an Ecology of Mind*. New York: Ballantine Books.

Burghart, Richard, ed. 1987. *Hinduism in Great Britain: The Perception of Religion in an Alien Cultural Milieu*. London: Tavistock.

Cohen, Anthony P. 1982. *Belonging: Identity and Social Organisation in British Rural Cultures*. Manchester, England: Manchester University Press.

Coles, Robert. 1967. *Children of Crisis: A Study of Courage and Fear*. Boston: Atlantic-Little, Brown.

———. 1986a. *The Moral Life of Children*. Boston: Atlantic Monthly Press.

———. 1986b. *The Political Life of Children*. Boston: Atlantic Monthly Press.

Collier, John. 1967. *Visual Anthropology: Photography as Research Method*. New York: Holt, Rhinehart & Winston.

Dahya, B. 1972. "Pakistanis in Britain." *New Community* 2:25–34.

———. 1973. "Pakistanis in Britain: Transients or Settlers?" *Race* 14:241–77.

———. 1974. "The Nature of Pakistani Ethnicity in Industrial Cities in England." Pp. 77–118 in *Urban Ethnicity*, edited by A. Cohen. London: Tavistock.

Dove, L. A. 1974. "Racial Awareness Among Adolescents in London Comprehensive Schools." *New Community* 3:255–61.

Fischer, Michael. 1986. "Ethnicity and the Post-Modern Arts of Memory." Pp. 194–233 in *Writing Culture*, edited by James Clifford and George Marcus. Berkeley: University of California Press.

Hardman, Charlotte. 1973. "Can There Be an Anthropology of Children?" *Journal of the Anthropological Society of Oxford* 4(2):85–89.

Hiro, Dilip. 1971. *Black Britain, White Britain*. New York: Monthly Review Press.

James, A. G. 1974. *Sikh Children in Britain*. London: Oxford University Press.

Kureishi, Hanif. 1986. "Bradford." Pp. 147–70 in *Trouble Again*: *GRANTA* 20. London: Penguin.

La Fontaine, Jean. 1986. "An Anthropological Perspective on Children in Social Worlds." Pp. 10–30 in *Children of Social Worlds: Development in a Social Context*, edited by Martin Richards and Paul Lights. Cambridge, MA: Harvard University Press.

Lancy, David and B. Allan Tindall, eds. 1975. *The Anthropological Study of Play: Problems and Prospects: Proceedings of the First Annual Meeting of the Association of the Anthropological Study of Play*. Cornwall, NY: Leisure Press.

Rashid, Syra. 1981. "Socialization and Education of Pakistani Teenage Girls in London." M.Phil. Thesis, School of Oriental and African Studies, University of London.

Saifullah-Kahn, V. 1974. "Pakistani Villagers in a British City." Ph.D. dissertation, Bradford University, Bradford, England.

Schwartzman, Helen. 1978. *Transformations: The Anthropology of Children's Play*. New York: Plenum Press.

Shaw, Alison. 1988. *A Pakistani Community in Britain*. Oxford, England: Basil Blackwell.

Skinner, Debra. 1988. "Negotiations of Identity Through Cultural Devices: Nepali Children's Understanding of Self and Others." Paper presented in the panel, "Through Children's Eyes and in Children's Voices," at the Annual Meeting of the American Anthropological Association, Phoenix, AZ.

Taylor, J. H. 1976. *The Half-Way Generation*. Slough, England: National Foundation for Educational Research.

Thompson, M. A. 1974. "The Second Generation—Punjabi or English?" *New Community* 3:242–48.

Turner, Victor. 1969. *The Ritual Process: Structure and Anti-Structure*. London: Routledge and Kegan Paul.

Van Gennep, Arnold. 1960. *Rites of Passage*. Translated by Monika Vizedon. Chicago: University of Chicago Press.

Watson, James. 1977. *Between Two Cultures: Migrants and Minorities in Britain*. Oxford, England: Basil Blackwell.

Werbner, Pnina. 1979. "Ritual and Social Networks: A Study of Pakistani Immigrants in Manchester." Ph.D. dissertation, University of Manchester, Manchester, England.

Yates, Paul. 1988. "Negotiating Life Texts: Youth, Ethnicity and Cultural Production." Paper presented at "The Social Construction of Youth, Maturation and Aging" Conference, School of Oriental and African Studies, London.

PART IV

Economic Factors as a Force for Change

CHAPTER TWELVE

Land of the Rising Son? Domestic Organization, Ancestor Worship, and Economic Change in Japan

STEPHEN R. SMITH

INTRODUCTION

There is a strong and clear relationship between family and religion in Japan. Earhart (1982:9) identified "the religious character of the family" as one of the "persistent themes in Japanese religious history," and Hori (1968:57) noted that ancestor worship is "basic to the social structure in Japan." Painting with broad brush strokes on a large canvas, this chapter elaborates on the relationship between Japanese family and religion, arguing that domestic organization influences religious doctrine, ritual, and organization and that the content of ancestor worship is transformed in response to changes in domestic organization and macroeconomic forces. More specifically, it is contended that the traditional Buddhist emphasis on unilineal ancestor memorialization practices was consistent with the stem extended family *cum* unit of production in a feudal, agricultural economy. In modern Japan, however, urbanization and the creation of an industrial, and now a postindustrial, economy have produced a preponderance of nuclear families (Kumagai 1986) with concomitant shifts in Buddhist philosophy and practice, including the change to bilateral kindred memorialization (R. J. Smith 1974) that is based increasingly on affect (Morioka 1984).

CONCEPTUAL FRAMEWORK

Although numerous threads of the complex Japanese religious tradition are mentioned, the focus of this chapter is on Buddhism. The theoretical perspective underlying this work is loosely that of cultural materialism. As articulated by Harris (1993:114–15), this theory consists of three elements: infrastructure, structure, and superstructure. Infrastructure is made up of the conditions of subsistence production (e.g., available resources, technology) and the circumstances that influence the reproduction of the population (e.g., mortality, contraception). Social structure is institutionalized groups and their rules of organization, divided into domestic life (e.g., age and gender roles, kin relationships) and political economy (e.g., political organization, castes). Superstructure is ideological systems, including such areas as art, law, values and "common sense," philosophies, and religions. A premise of this approach is that infrastructural conditions may determine social structural conditions, and these two sets of conditions, in turn, determine superstructure. In short, systems of ideas develop and survive or wane as epiphenomenal responses to economic and social systems. Without denying the possibility of ideological influence,

> the resolution of any deep incompatibility between an adaptive infrastructural innovation and the structural and superstructural components will usually consist of substantial changes in the other [noninfrastructural] components. In contrast, innovations that arise in the structural or superstructural sectors (for example, new religions) are likely to be selected against if there is any deep incompatibility between them and the infrastructure (if they substantially impede the system's ability to satisfy basic human needs and drives) (Harris 1993:115–16).

This theory clearly is derived from the writings of Marx and the rejection of Hegelian dialectical idealism. As Marx ([1858] 1970:21, quoted in Harris 1991:403–04) stated, "The mode of production in material life determines the general character of the social, political, and spiritual processes of life. It is not the conciousness of men that determines their existence, but, on the contrary, their social existence that determines their conciousness." Cultural materialism deviates from Marxian dialectical materialism, however, by rejecting the dialectic as a mode of analysis and by denying any assumptions of historical determinism. The materialist perspective does not contradict a sociological analysis, but does presuppose material constraints and assumes that dominant ideological systems tend to reflect the vested interests of those in power.

JAPANESE DOMESTIC ORGANIZATION

Ie: The "Traditional Household"

The use of the word, *family* with reference to Japanese social history is misleading. In English usage, the first meaning of the word is "nuclear family," that is, parents and their children. Even in its more generalized applications, the word connotes biological relatedness, despite the reality of adoption. Although the Japanese word, *kazoku*, means something close to the Western idea of a nuclear family, it was invented in the nineteenth century to deal with the introduction of an alien concept. The traditional Japanese term for the indigenous conception of the domestic unit is *ie* (pronounced "ee-eh").

Even though the *ie* was articulated in the familiar terminology of descent and marriage, membership was defined by coresidence and participation in the *ie* economy, rather than necessarily by ties of kinship. Furthermore, unlike the nuclear family, which ends with the birth or death of each generation, the *ie*, once established, was expected to continue through succeeding generations. Although rules of succession, inheritance, postmarital residence, and the like varied with reference to such factors as class, gender, locale, and historical period, the overriding conception of the *ie* was that of an ongoing corporate group, with the survival of the *ie* overshadowing the rights or desires of any individual member. The term, *ie*, therefore, sometimes is translated as "house," as in the royal houses of Europe, or, what is a common translation, and the one used here, as "household." A household, with its connotation of coresidence, may include members who are unrelated by socially recognized ties of blood, marriage, or adoption and thus stands in contrast to the kinship-based term, *family*.

The household was often the same as the family, but not always. And it was the *ie*, or household, that was the minimal and most important unit of society. "The organization of a community in rural Japan is built only on the basis of the household, not on the individual of the family, or on the descent group" (Nakane 1967:2). Since the *ie*, not the individual, was the key unit of society (Fairbank, Reischauer, and Craig 1989), one's place in society was determined by the status of one's household and one's role in that household. One's personal fortunes were linked to the collective. Civic responsibilities were allocated to the *ie* and fulfilled by one member as the representative of the household. The successes of one member brought rewards to all members, and the misdeeds of one member would lead to collective sanctions, such as ostracism from the community (R. J. Smith 1961), for all the members.

The members of the premodern *ie* included not only the living members, but the dead ancestors and unborn descendants. The ancestors of that household were "all the household heads together with their wives since its founding" (Morioka 1984:202). Living members of the *ie* had a moral obligation of gratitude to the ancestors and a responsibility to manage household resources for the descendants. They initially had to perform appropriate funerary and memorialization ceremonies for the dead and then honor the ancestors for their benevolence, keep them informed of the important occurances in the household, and behave in such a way as not to bring shame upon the *ie*.

The ie as an Economic Corporation

The primary injunction of the household was that it should survive in perpetuity. The justification for this imperative was often made in terms of a Confucian need to produce sons who would perform ancestor rites, such as was found in China and Korea. Yet, whereas patrilineal descent was of the utmost importance for the Chinese family (*chia*) and the Korean family (*chip*), membership in the Japanese *ie* did not require blood ties. Indeed, Nakane (1970) argued that an essential characteristic of Japanese society is that a "frame," or locality of shared, purposive, group interactions, takes precedence over such universalizing "attributes" as class and kinship. It is useful, therefore, to see the *ie* not as a kin group, but as an economic corporate body, a unit of production, that was articulated in a biological mode.

Conceptually, the *ie* included not only the members, but the *ie* economy (e.g., farming, retail sales, crafts production, and acting) plus resources (e.g., land, goods for sale, tools, and scripts) (Fukutake 1982). Although recruitment into the household was primarily by birth and marriage, membership in the household was defined, not by blood, but by coresidence and participation in the *ie* work. Thus, along with those born and married into the household, faithful servants and respected employees could also become household members and, ultimately, ancestors. Furthermore, unlike the Chinese and Korean Confucian imperative that there must be sons (direct male descendants) to take over the headship of the household and perform ancestor rituals, the Japanese placed greater emphasis on qualified stewardship. A son-in-law who took on the family name was as good as a son. Japanese routinely adopted men of proved competence to become the successors to the heads of households, even, on occasion, skipping over direct biological heirs if they were of equivocal ability.

The structural core of the *ie* was not the household head and his wife. Nor was it the narrowly defined Confucian dyad of father and son. Rather, the defining relationship of the *ie* was that between the head and the successor apparent, reiterated over the generations. Because the perpetuation of the household was independent of biological continuity, unrelated people would occasionally take on a household name and "revive" a defunct *ie* (Plath 1964).

When the *ie* is viewed as an economic corporation, then rules governing succession to household authority and the inheritance of goods become central to its continuity. In the Classical Period (710–1185), at least among the elite, there was partible inheritance. The *ie* estate was divided among all the children, including the daughters. The rise of the samurai (warrior) class and the steady militarization of Japanese society during the Medieval Period (1185–1600) saw an accompanying decline in the social position of women (Bingham and Gross 1987), leading ultimately to their exclusion from inheritance and public authority. Equal male inheritance, in the Chinese fashion, was fostered by the political leadership during the Kamakura Period (1185–1336) to prevent potentially competing families from building an economic power base. Since each son had an equal, legitimate claim to inherit, the patrimony was divided and dispersed with each new generation. This pattern of inheritance would be replaced during the Muromachi Period (1336–1573) by nonpartible inheritance through male primogeniture (Frederic 1972). Even among peasants, inheritance of the intact patrimony by only one child became the standard, although inheritance by the firstborn female or by the last-born child (ultimogeniture) existed as regional variations (Befu 1971:41).

The practice of dividing family goods equally among children meant that authority and resources were inevitably splintered with the passing of each generation, usually destroying the economy that made the household a unit of production. On the other hand, nonpartible inheritance meant that resources could be maintained. The Japanese pattern of "kinship" (really domestic organization) thus evolved into the "stem extended family," a pattern that prevented the dispersal of accumulated patrimony. The first principle of succession is that a single, competent heir inherits all. Most often, the firstborn son was the ideal successor to the household head, inheriting authority over the members, economy, and resources. In that case, the younger brothers would be expected to leave the household upon marriage and to establish new unilineal, stem households of their own. Daughters would marry out of their natal *ie* and into those of their husbands. In any generation in the *ie* stem household, then, there should be no more than one married couple (no coresident, married collaterals). For example, in a three-generational stem household, there might be grandfather and grandmother, their first son and his wife (his siblings having moved out at the time of marriage), plus the successor in the third generation (with or without a spouse) and any unmarried siblings.

One possible mechanism did exist for keeping nonsuccessor children within the fold of their natal *ie*. It was possible to develop a system of hierarchically related households, known as a *dōzoku*, based on economic dependence. For example, if a farmer had enough land to support more than one household, he might supply a nonsuccessor son with land and permit that son to use tools and other *ie* resources. A highly successful economic enterprise, such as an *ie* pharmaceutical company, could generate multiple branch houses off the main house and off the branch houses, with many collateral generations, each being set up with a retail drugstore. The houses of origin, or main houses (*honke*), would be acknowledged as the economic, political, and ritual superordinates of the branch houses (*bunke*). Like the *ie*, the *dōzoku* was based on a kinship model but was basically an economic entity and could incorporate nonkin houses (Befu 1971).

The *ie* is central to traditional Japanese social organization. To this day, the *ie* system is widely held as the cultural ideal for domestic organization. More important, Japanese tend to organize social behavior around the small group, recapitulating the household (Nakane 1970). Hierarchical relations, resembling those of parent-child (*oya-ko*) and older sibling-younger sibling (*senpai-kohai*), are the building blocks of other contemporary institutions, from business (Abegglen 1958; Kondo 1990; Rohlen 1974) to organized crime (Lebra 1976) to not only the relationship between Buddhist abbot and priest (Morioka 1975), but also between priest and parishioner (Reader, 1993). (For further information on the Japanese domestic organization, see Goode 1963; Levy 1955; S. R. Smith 1992; Vogel 1965.)

The ie and Ancestor Rites

The ideological justification for this system of domestic organization (*ie seido*) was articulated in terms of the filial responsibilities of the young to the old and the living to the dead. Such ideas derive, in part, from indigenous folk-Shinto beliefs in the dead becoming "spirits" (*kami*), as well as from Confucian notions of filial piety. More important, for the purposes of this chapter, there developed the Buddhist belief that the dead must be assisted out of this world and into the next by numerous rituals, so they might achieve their otherworldly rewards. From their extraterrestrial vantage point, the ancestors might then be able to intercede in this-worldly affairs for the benefit of their descendants or, at the least, would not be left as dissatisfied spirits who might cling to the living and disrupt their affairs.

Ceremonies for the dead show a great deal of local variation, yet "conform to a general pattern that reflects (with rare exceptions) a commonality of attitude and belief throughout the country" (R. J. Smith 1974:70). Some practices were—and still are—intended to transform the newly departed individuals (*shirei*) into ancestoral spirits (*sorei*), while others were intended to honor the ancestors collectively. Many funerary rites were led by priests, although the postfeudal trend has been a weakening of the influence of institutionalized Buddhism (R. J. Smith 1974). It was the household, however, that was responsible for most ancestor rites. The household head played a central role in such formal services and was considered responsible for the care of the memorial tablets (*ihai*) for the dead (R. J. Smith 1974). Following the funeral of the former household head or spouse, there were ceremonies every seventh day until the forty-ninth day and again on the hundredth day after death. At ceremonial stages, the memorial tablet, bearing the name of the deceased, was advanced by the household head to a higher level within the domestic altar (*butsudan*), indicating a purification of the spirit. There were other death anniversary memorials over the next fifty years. (In the case of the *dōzoku*, or hierarchically related households, it was only the main house that had the altar and tablets, and the subordinate houses would participate in ceremonies there (R. J. Smith 1974.) *Ie* members often made daily offerings of food and drink at the *butsudan*, sometimes stopping to speak to the dead, informing them of the activities of the living. The members would also gather at the household grave on New Years' Day, at the spring and autumn equinoxes, and at the Festival of the Dead (*bon*) in mid-August to wash the gravestones and honor the dead.

The relationship between "family" (*ie*) and religion in premodern Japan is found in the performance of rituals of ancestor worship. Ancestor worship reflects several overlapping traditions in Japanese religious thought—as is elaborated in the next section—and, as such, may be understood as having supplied the spiritual, emotional, or psychological comfort attributed to religions. But within the materialist perspective, ancestor worship can also be understood as epiphenomenal to social structural and infrastructural conditions, consistent with domestic organization (the stem household with male primogeniture and nonpartible inheritance) and productive circumstances (domestic production). Memorializing ancestors legitimates the social status of those who are destined to succeed to ancestorship, usually the firstborn sons. Likewise, rituals that symbolically underscore the importance of filial piety produce acceptance of superordinate (older generational) authority. Furthermore, services that periodically remind members of the benevolence of the ancestors cultivate appreciation of the benefits received from the *ie* and stimulate a commitment to continuity (Morioka 1984). Such stimulation of sentiment is important when most individuals ultimately are excluded from significant largess of the *ie*, which is to say that all siblings except the successor will leave empty-handed. Yet, although unitary succession and nonpartible inheritance are not egalitarian or even meritocratic, they are part of a system that prevents the disruption of economic production. The ancestors-to-be can be seen as direct beneficiaries of the system. Unike the Chinese family, in which partition of *chia* materiel might leave the patriarch with insuffient resources to survive, the leadership of the *ie* always stayed empowered to the limits of the house.

The necessary rites and rituals for the dead should be performed on some occasions by the head of the household in the home or in semipublic ceremonies, while on others, they are to be performed by priests as professional ritualists. A prescribed series of funerary and memorial rites, over the course of fifty years, cleanses the soul of worldly contamination and transforms it into an ancestor in paradise. Historically, in Japan, such ministrations were ultimately assigned primarily to Buddhism, but they were consistent with the beliefs and practices of several elements of the Japanese religious tradition.

JAPANESE RELIGIOUS TRADITIONS

Although the focus of this chapter is on the relationship of the household and Buddhism, it is worthwhile to note briefly the larger context of religion in Japan. The Japanese religious tradition in general, with a few notable exceptions (e.g., Nichiren Buddhism), shows not only tolerance for philosophical diversity, but the active syncretism of belief and practice. For the sake of clarity, this section discusses religious life to distinguish a few of the dominant influences. The most significant of these traditions are Shinto, Japanese folk religion, Taoism, Confucianism, and Buddhism. A number of these separate ideologies reiterate common themes, including the centrality of the family and the importance of venerating ancestors.

Shinto, or "the way of the spirits" (*kami*), is an indigenous and distinctive Japanese religion. Often identified as animistic, early Shinto held that awe-inspiring natural phenomena (e.g., fertility and thunder) and objects (e.g., mountains) have a sentience and spiritual existence. Similarly, members of the imperial family; famous historical figures; and, for that matter, all Japanese people, have a spiritual essence that survives beyond death to become benevolent ancestors or numerous kinds of problematic wandering specters. The line between the living and the dead (*kami*) is permeable. The living will become *kami*, and the *kami* often behave in ways that are all too human.

Shinto has had three historical manifestations: Sect, State, and Shrine. "Sect Shinto" is organized around deities (*kami*) of some renown. There may be one or many shrines dedicated to the worship of a particular spirit, with an organized clergy and formalized doctrine. The priesthood performs religious ceremonies, such as the blessing of the newborn and consecrating marriages. "State Shinto" was conciously developed out of the desires of the late Tokugawa period (1603–1868) to cultivate nationalism based on the divinity of the emperor. This ideology was promoted, and the organization supported, by successive governments, but, following World War II, State Shinto was outlawed as a source of militarism and imperialism.

"Shrine Shinto," the third manifestation of Shinto, is inextricably part of Japanese folk religion. Folk religion is made up of indigenous beliefs, popular understanding of formalized religions, and local customs (Earhart 1982). Indigenous religious beliefs may be said to have been formalized into the orthodoxies of sect Shinto while continuing in folk religion. Conversely, orthodox tenets of institutionalized religions (e.g., Taoism and Buddhism) are naively transformed by popular understanding. Distinctive local customs can add to this vital—though less sophisticated—religious tradition.

Within Shrine Shinto, elements of folk religion appear in rules concerning the avoidance of spiritual pollution and rituals for purification following contact with contaminants, such as death, blood, skin diseases, or sexual fluids (Norbeck 1952). Another extremely important Shinto element in folk religion is communication with ancestors. People pay respect to the deceased through offerings and prayer and request intercession by the *kami* in worldly difficulties. The communication may take place at a shrine, a grave site, or at home where small shelves (*kamidan*) are hung as a residence for the *kami* and where offerings and prayers are directed.

Taoism came to Japan from China at least as early as the sixth century. Religious Taoism was absorbed into Japanese culture and has left few direct manifestations, with the exception of the Koshin cult (Blacker 1975; Earhart 1982; Ohnuki-Tierney 1984). On the other hand, many Taoist artifacts, like the concept of yin-yang (*onmyo*), complex calendars filled with days both auspicious and dangerous, and techniques for prognostication (e.g., *omikuji*) and spiritual protection (e.g., *omamori*) pervade Shinto, Buddhism, and Japanese popular thinking.

Confucianism also came to Japan from China. Strictly speaking, Confucianism is not a religion but a set of ethical guidelines for right living and political organization devised by Master K'ung in the fifth century B.C. Be that as it may, the Confucian emphasis on filial piety and honoring one's ancestors reinforces the importance of family that is found so often in other Japanese philosophical and religious traditions. "Confucianist ideas have been expressed in religious terms largely through the medium of Buddhism, which itself had absorbed Confucian elements in its movement across Asia from India into China and beyond" (Reader 1991:30).

Buddhism is based on the teachings of Siddhartha Gautama, the Buddha or "Enlightened One," who was born in what is now Nepal in the fifth century B.C. After an early life of privilege and luxury, Gautama set upon a spiritual quest to discover how best to escape the cruel cycle of reincarnation. Rebirth, in that context, does not assume the passing on of a soul or eternal personality, but, rather,—like the touch of a dying flame to a new candle—continuation of a process. The quality of one's life is the product of *karma*, or the actions one took in preceding lives. Earnest spiritual struggle in one life produces advancement on the ladder of existence in the next, but contrary behavior may send one spiraling down the spiritual chutes to return as a lower form of life. The goal of the spiritual quest is to attain *Nirvana*, a condition of nonbeing in which one is freed from the ignorance and anguish of rebirth. In Gautama's world, ascetics who mortified the flesh were believed to be on the fast track to Nirvana. After years of yoga and austerities, Gautama came to recognize the benefits of moderation, or the "Middle Way." Eventually, following extended meditation, Gautama attained enlightenment, or buddhahood, meaning that he understood the illusory nature of temporal reality and would not be subjected to another life. For the next forty-five years, he taught the Four Noble Truths and ways of the Eight-Fold Path by which it is possible to overcome spiritual ignorance and achieve Nirvana.

In the centuries following the death of the Buddha, his ideas were transformed into two main schools of belief. Theravada, or the "teachings of the elders," spread to Sri Lanka and Southeast Asia. Relatively close to the original teachings of Gautama, this school holds that each individual must attain his or her own enlightenment to be set free. The individual who attains enlightenment, and therefore will enter Nirvana after death, is known as an *arhat*.

Theravada is also called Hinayana Buddhism to contrast it with the Mahayana school. The fundamental theological difference between these schools concerns those who achieve enlightenment. Whereas the arhats of Hinayana pass on to Nirvana, the *bodhisattvas*, or buddhas, of Mahayana are moved by compassion for the suffering living, delay their escape, and remain to dedicate themselves to aiding the spiritually less advanced. Like saints, the bodhisattvas are available to help the devout, both with their travails in this life and in attaining salvation after death. With the assistance of a bodhisattva, one can be assured of achieving Nirvana or some form of heavenly reward immediately following this life. It is this Mahayana form of Buddhism that entered Japan.

THE INFLUENCE OF DOMESTIC ORGANIZATION ON BUDDHISM

Premodern Influences

The Indigenization of Buddhism in Premodern Japan. Indigenization occurs wherever religions have moved, but Mahayana Buddhism's exceptional tolerance for lesser "relative truths" has led to remarkable syncretisms and transformations. Buddhism came to Japan from China via Korea. For approximately 500 years following its arrival in China, Buddhism was believed to be a variant of Taoism that introduced a new concept, the eternal soul. Yet the concept of an eternal soul is antithetical to all Gautama taught. How could such a radical transformation of original Buddhist tenets take place?

The most basic East Asian ethical principle—formally articulated in Confucianism—is filial piety. Children leaving their homes, withdrawing from the world, and not procreating—the monastic practices of Theravadan Buddhism—are contrary to core East Asian cultural values. These values, it should be noted, are the product of agricultural subsistence, in which children are necessary to provide care in old age and even a young child can be a productive participant in a family economy.

As early Buddhists in China tried to make sense of the teachings from India, accommodations were made in line with native understanding and values. Interpreting a third-century text from Central Asia, the Chinese first held that offerings made to the Buddha and priests on behalf of unenlightened spirits—or more exactly, "hungry ghosts"—would speed the restless dead to their higher goal. In time, the third party was removed from the ritual and the offerings were made directly to the dead. By the sixth or seventh century, there was Confucianized Buddhist ancestor worship in China. This was the same period in which the Japanese were receiving the teachings of Buddhism and avidly seeking other continental ideas. Filial piety, also an indigenous value, thus became a core tenet of Buddhism in Japan (R. J. Smith 1974). Proper treatment of the dead would come to require not just the ministrations of the household head, but rituals performed by Buddhist clergy.

By legend, Buddhism entered Japan in 552, when scriptures (*sutras*) and images of Buddhas were sent from the pre-Korean state of Paekche to the Yamato court. The Japanese had little understanding of the artifacts, but appreciated them as a superior form of continental magic. Buddhism was embraced by political forces competing within the dominant Yamato clan (*uji*), whose political rule was theocratic, legitimatized by their control of Shinto ritual. Buddhism, as alternative, esoteric, ritual knowledge, removed the exclusive control of the source of theocratic legitimacy from one political faction. The ultimate political success of the opposition Soga clan confirmed the superiority of the new rituals, and Buddhism's place at court was secured (Fairbank, Reischauer, and Craig 1989). In 685 all royal families were ordered by imperial decree to have a private family altar (*butsudan*) at which they prayed for the dead (Reader 1991). Buddhism began as a religion of the elite but, by the thirteenth century, had entered the religious life of the masses as well.

The twelfth-century popularization of Buddhism in Japan was led by Honen (1133–1212) and his disciple Shinran (1173–1262), founders of the Pure Land sect and the True Pure Land sect, respectively. Honen said that salvation is achieved through the practice of reciting the name of the Amida

Buddha, rather than by having priests perform rituals. Shinran carried the teaching another step, arguing that a single utterance of Amida's name, spoken in true faith, would be sufficient to guarantee salvation. Shinran went even another step further in promoting the universal compassion of the Buddha and rejecting the spiritually privileged position of priests. He repudiated monastic Buddhism, calling on priests to marry and live normal lives among their parishioners (Fairbank, Reischauer, and Craig 1989).

Although doctrines of simple ritual and faith might be expected to diminish the authority of Buddhism by obviating the need for temples and priests with esoteric knowledge, the result was to attract adherents by taking doctrine further away from karma, the cycle of rebirth, and multitudinous lives spent in arduous spiritual advancement. Any individual, with the assistance of a bodhisattva, can now become a buddha immediately following this life: You will, I will, and all the ancestors have.

The teachings of Honen and Shinran fell on fertile soil. True Pure Land and Pure Land, in that order, are now the largest sects of Japanese Buddhism. The True Pure Land practice of clergy marrying has become the standard practice of all Japanese Buddhist sects. Today, approximately 80 percent of Buddhist priests are married (Reader 1991:89, 251 note 16).

Why would a doctrine so radically alien to continental Buddhism as the marriage of priests take effect in Japan? What are the consequences for institutional Buddhism? I would argue, again, that the celibacy and monasticism of Buddhism are in conflict with the structure of *ie* and other units of production with *ie*-like organization. The driving forces behind *ie* values (superstructure) are the structural imperatives of the household. Above all else, the *ie* household must continue as a corporate unit of production. This goal is achieved through nonpartible inheritance and unitary succession, usually male primogeniture. It is reinforced ideologically within the household by the household head's obligations to perform memorial rituals. The *ie* became the standard pattern for social relations—including institutional Buddhism—and ideologies that ran counter to that system were not likely to dominate.

Premodern Institutional Buddhism and the Household. In materialist terms, ideology (ancestor worship) may be seen as epiphenomenal to economics and social structure (the household as the unit of production). Local Buddhist doctrine began to look epiphenomenal, too, but not just to the household. Rather, Buddhist institutions were also economic corporations seeking their own survival. To justify its indigenizing transformation, theologians of Japanese institutional Buddhism revised ideology. One need not necessarily be cynical about the motives of actors, such as the founders; arguably, they acted out of sincere commitment to their faith. Personalities arise every day with new or alternative ideas, rather like mutations. Depending upon the environment, most new ideas fail, but sometimes one is a good fit with changing material and social conditions. Whatever the initial motivation for the Pure Land and True Pure Land reforms, their universal (Japanese) acceptance and functional success are evidence of their fit with material and social conditions.

What one finds, then, is that, in the institutionalization of marriage for Japanese Buddhist priests, the priests, their families, and their temples, took on characteristics of the *ie* household or unit of production. The priesthood in Japan became a profession, rather than a calling. Men became temple priests because it was the family occupation. An estimated 80 percent of today's Soto Zen temples have been inherited by sons from their fathers (Reader 1991:251, note 16).

And whereas individual temples may be seen as taking on *ie*-like characteristics, larger sectarian organization began to look like the *dōzoku* organization of related *ie*. In traditional Japan, the candidate for priesthood (usually the son of a priest) was, at age 15, initiated into the order in a ceremony paralleling the coming-of-age rite (*genbuku*) for young men. As in the *genbuku* ritual, the boy's head was shaved and the boy was given new clothes, indicating his transformation. More significantly, the ritual would establish fictive kinship relations and, in the Buddhist case, the abbot became the father to the new priest (Morioka 1975). Like the creation of the *dōzoku*, Buddhist sects are organized pyramidally, with hierachical chains of allegiance culminating in the founding temple as *honke* (main house). The collective organization remains an economic entity in which advancement is determined by achievements in "study, scholarship, leadership in sect administration, length of priestly service, and *the amount of money remitted to the head temple*" [emphasis added] (Norbeck 1970:66).

As Buddhism became increasingly identified with the household through the funerary and memorial rituals, a political link between the family and temples was established by governmental fiat. In the early seventeenth century, fearing foreign threats to the regime, the Tokugawa government (1603–1868) set about tightening its control over the populace. The national borders were closed (*sakoku*). Christianity was outlawed, and thousands were martyred. To ensure that the citizenry did not have loyalties to the Vatican and to keep a census, in 1640 the government required all households to be affiliated with a local Buddhist temple. This arrangement was known as the *danka seido*, the parishoner system or temple-house system, and household participation was mandatory, sometimes on pain of death (Reader 1993).

The political transformation of Buddhist temples into governmental census offices would have consequences for the religious content of Japanese Buddhism. Pre-Tokugawa records indicate that not all family members were necessarily members of the same Buddhist congregation (R. J. Smith 1974). With the creation of the temple-house system personal choice no longer was possible. As individual inclination went out of temple affiliation, doctrinal differences were no longer of any consequence. Spiritual guidance ceased to be a priestly function. The temples did not need to attract parishioners, and "the fees received from funerals and the series of rites that were required to transform the dead soul into a full ancestor formed the basis of the Buddhist temple's economy, a function they still have to this day" (Reader 1993:142). In time, all temples served the government as registration offices and the people as funeral homes. Institutional Buddhism became spiritually moribund.

To this day, the overwhelming majority of temple affiliations are a product of the Tokugawa registration. Contemporary affiliation is seen as a family tradition, called into action only upon the death of a member, for funeral and memorial services. For the majority of Japanese, personal belief and inclination have nothing to do with the choice of sect or temple that officiates.

Early Industrialization, Nationalism, and State Manipulation of Religion

The end of the Tokugawa Period, officially over in 1868, saw the creation of a new Japan. Feudalism and military (samurai) dominance were legally abolished, and the temple-house system was abandoned. In the period prior to World War II, the Meiji (1868–1912), Taisho (1912–25), and Showa (1925–89) governments suppressed Buddhism and encouraged State Shinto in order to build nationalism. The imperial line was declared ancestral to all Japanese households, hence linking the people to the body politic and obliging them to observe filial piety (R. J. Smith 1974). When it became clear that Buddhism could not be simply eradicated and State Shinto rituals put in its place, Buddhism was once again tolerated, but only within specific guidelines that reflected nationalist militarist ideology (R. J. Smith 1974). All religious expression was constrained, and many organizations were forced to disband. Numerous sectarian expressions of Buddhism were forced to consolidate into a limited number of state-approved sects.

At the same time as the state sponsored Shinto and suppressed other religious institutions, the government was passing into law judicial supports for the *ie* household system. Samurai patterns of patriarchy, patrilineality, and male primogeniture, as well as general authoritarianism and social hierachy, were required of the entire population by legislative fiat in the Civil Code of 1898. Legal support for the *ie* household system continued until 1947, when it was renounced by the new, postwar Japanese Constitution. In the new Constitution, marriage, for example, was declared to be a union of individuals, not of households. The union is based on the consent of adult partners, not the consent of household heads. Household heads no longer had absolute authority over family members. The legal requirement of unitary, nonpartible inheritance was abandoned.

It is one of the ironies of Japanese history, although perhaps it should come as no surprise, that the Meiji government was attempting to legislate the traditional, samurai household organization for every domestic unit at the very time that social and economic changes were rapidly undoing the functional logic of the *ie*. Unilineal descent and unitary inheritance made economic sense when the household was a unit of production and there were resources to be preserved. But beginning with industrialization in the late nineteenth century, and at a much accelerated rate during the national reconstruction following World War II, people left rural, *ie* farms and moved to cities to be wage laborers. An ever-growing number of Japanese lived not in multigenerational *ie* households, but in nuclear families. Production took place in factories and offices, so families did not have *ie* resources and economies to keep intact and then pass on.

Postwar Influences

Postwar Buddhism: Domestic Practices. Morioka (1984:207) found that in 1966, 92 percent of the households in an agricultural community (farm owners), 69 percent of the households in a business district (family enterprises), but only 45 percent of the households of white-collar employees (salaried, office workers) had domestic altars (*butsudan*). Furthermore, Morioka (1984:207) reported that in a 1967 study that distinguished local residents from new arrivals and multigenerational families from nuclear in three areas, almost every multigenerational household had a *butsudan*, but fewer local nuclear families (73 percent) and half as many (38 percent) newcomer nuclear families had them. For the new urbanites and suburbanites, the material raison d'être for the *ie* household had ended. And with its passing, the religious practices lost much of their urgency.

As the rural population decreases and the urban population expands, fewer people live in large farmhouses and more live in the infamous "rabbit hutch" apartments. The urban press exacerbates the difficulties of home ancestor worship by squeezing out the *butsudan*. A farmhouse had space to devote to an altar, but urban apartment dwellers are increasingly inclined to get a small *butsudan* and put it in a closet. Alternatively, they put up a small shelf or some other space-saving substitute. Many delay getting a *butsudan* or simply do without one.

But the diminishing number of *butsudan* does not mean that ancestor rituals have been forsaken completely. In fact, a 1981 survey by the Japan Broadcasting Corporation (Nippon Hōsō Kyōkai) (cited in Swyngedouw 1993:54) found that 61 percent of thóe houses have *butsudan*. More interesting yet are changes in the objects of memorialization and the performer of the rituals. First, despite the facts that there are more Buddhist altars in households in farm communities than in business districts and that ownership is the lowest in white-collar residential areas, the highest levels of regular offerings and ritual observances among *butsudan* owners are not in "traditional" rural areas, but in the suburbs (Morioka 1984:209). Second, today, it is housewives, not household heads, who are performing the rituals (Reader 1991:95). The explanation for both these surprising facts is that members of farm households—men and women—are busy at work outside the home all day. But while male white-collar workers are typically in the office from 9 to 5 or longer, their wives are more likely to be housewives, staying home to take care of their houses and children. These suburban wives thus have the time to perform the rituals. Third, and equally unanticipated, is the fact that a growing number of memorial tablets for nonlineals (e.g., wives' parents) are appearing in *butsudan* (R. J. Smith 1974:174).

The Japanese also prove to be active in family-based, semipublic rituals of ancestor worship. Prescribed annual rituals include visiting and cleaning grave sites (*haka mairi*) at the spring and autumn equinoxes (*higan*) and at the late-summer Festival of the Dead (*obon*). Such ceremonies are not somber but prove to be family reunions that bring together dispersed members. The Japan Broadcasting Corporation Survey (cited in Swynggedouw 1993:55) found that 89 percent (69 percent regularly and 20 percent occasionally) visit ancestral tombs on these occasions.

It is time, then, to consider that the meaning of ancestor rituals is changing. In the *ie* household, the rituals were performed by the head of the household and served such latent functions as the regular reaffirmation of the unity of the male descent group and the validation of the succession of the head.

> The immobile social classes and rules of descent and inheritance of the [Tokugawa period] made lines of descent of the utmost importance, thereby incorporating the deceased ancestors into the living social organization. Funerals, later commemorative rites, and fixed annual rites of Buddhism that honor ancestors were preeminently familial rites serving to promote family solidarity which, in turn, was vital to the maintenance of the individual as well as reinforcing the status quo. (Norbeck 1970:111)

But today the descent group ordinarily is inconsequential. Men have little to reaffirm through memorializing a lineage. Instead, it is the mother, the nurturer of the nuclear family, who makes offerings to people, both her husband's kindred and her own, who are emotionally important. Rituals no longer serve the jural function of validating an economic corporate group, but increasingly serve the personal, affective functions of consoling the grieving and keeping alive warm feelings for loved ones.

Likewise, the almost universal custom of annually visiting ancestral tombs is not an affirmation of a single descent line by coresident participants in the productive *ie* household. Rather, it has become a reunion of immediate kin (siblings and their families) who have moved apart. Adult siblings of the traditional *ie* would be relatively unsupportive—emotionally and financially (Nakane 1970:6)—because they were members of separate, lineal descent groups; that is, upon marriage, all but one entered a new *ie*. One might reasonably expect that blood ties have become far more important today, providing an "attribute" (Nakane 1970:1) network that connects people in the contemporary Japanese society of mobile, nuclear families.

Postwar Buddhism: Institutional Adaptations. The processes of industrialization and urbanization that altered the family likewise affected Buddhist sects and temples. Sect members left the countryside for the city, but the urban temples had no mechanisms for integrating new arrivals. For centuries, affiliation had been determined by households, following the law.

World War II took its toll on Buddhist temples, too. Temples invested in large land holdings before the war; land reform during the U.S. occupation resulted in the seizure and redistribution of those holdings. Urban temples were destroyed in fire bombings, further diminishing the supply for a population that, in truth, had little demand for Buddhism except when death created the need for funerary rites.

Recognizing that parishioners have little or no personal interest in their temples or sects, contemporary Buddhist organizations have sought ways to form connections with the laity. Increasingly, Buddhist theologians have idealized the nuclear family and, thus, have tried to link the individual and family to the sect and temple. According to Reader (1993), numerous techniques are used to draw family and temple together. Pastoral counsel holds that a good mother is one who instills Buddhist values in her children, for they will then be healthy, successful, and happy. Buddhist literature and sermons emphasize that the priest's family is a role model for the families of the congregation. The Buddha and founders of the sects are to be worshipped in the same manner as ancestors.

Postwar Buddhism: Institutional Alternatives. The Japanese recognize not only long-existing or established religious institutions, but a number of more recent sects known as "New Religions." (The sects founded since World War II are sometimes distinguished as the "New New Religions.") These new religions are overwhelmingly syncretic adaptations of traditional religious groups in Japan, predominantly Buddhism and Shintoism. A common trait among the New Religions is the emphasis on family and ancestor; yet, while their doctrine is dominated by discussion of the importance of the household (*ie*), religious practice often supports the bilateral kindred of the nuclear family.

For example, Reiyukai, a Buddhist-based New Religion, makes ancestor worship a central practice, emphasizes "traditional" values, and calls for a return to the old family system (*ie seido*). Under that old system, unitary inheritance was reinforced by having the firstborn son receive the *ie* altar (*butsudan*) and the funerary tablets (*ihai*) of each *ie* member or installing the tablets in a temple. But, in Reiyukai, individual tablets are not used. If you are single, when you die your name is written on a tablet with those of your parents, and if you are married, your name is combined with your spouse's. Both these arrangements are bilateral. The tablet is burned after both spouses die. "Thus, the cult is based upon the conjugal pair and is not perpetuated beyond the demise of the nuclear family formed by their marriage" (Hardacre 1984:106).

CONCLUSIONS

The thesis of this chapter has been that family and religion are closely linked in Japan. The nature of that linkage is that religious behavior—both domestic and institutional—is a reflection of domestic organization, which is dominated by economic interests. The traditional Japanese household, or *ie*, was the standard unit of production in premodern times. From the fourteenth century on, the ideal pattern of domestic organization was the stem extended family. The most notable element of this domestic pattern was nonpartible inheritance. Originating in the dominant military class, in which stipends for samurai were passed on intact to the firstborn sons, the pattern spread to the households of other classes for which nonpartition made sense in maintaining a unified domestic economy. Under these economic and domestic conditions, religious behavior centered on household and institutional rituals, predominantly Buddhist, that reinforced unilineal descent and validated the position of the family head. Institutional Buddhism, under these circumstances, was modified in ways that reflected the dominant pattern of domestic organization—a unit of production with nonpartible inheritance. Temple priesthood was transformed from a calling to an occupation. Once a celibate and monastic order, Japanese Buddhist priests were allowed to marry; the role of priest and the family temple were passed from father to son, like house resources. Established Buddhist sects took on a pyramidal hierarchal structure, recapitulating the interrelated household structure of the *dōzoku*, and priestly rank was determined, in part, by money remitted to the head temple. When all Japanese were required by the Tokugawa government to become registered members of a Buddhist temple and the incomes of temples were guaranteed, established Buddhism became spiritually moribund.

Industrialization and urbanization have transformed the Japanese family, and ancestor worship has followed suit. The traditional *ie* system was outlawed by the postwar Constitution, and urban housing is too cramped for large families, but the most important reason why the old unilineal household structure with nonpartible inheritance has died out is that there is no longer a patrimony to keep intact. Most Japanese are not self-employed and have no family business to pass down to the next generation. The worship of a line of household heads is no longer necessary for the validation of an existing head and unitary inheritance. Domestic ancestor worship has been transformed increasingly to acknowlege not a unilineal ideal, but the emotional reality of parents on both sides—parents who are of equal importance (or lack of importance) to the nuclear family. Institutional religion, too, has been transformed in ways that make it consistent with changes in domestic organization. Established Buddhist sects have sought to recast their image and function in response to family-centered (not household-centered) domestic life. Alternative institutionalized religions—the New Religions and New New Religions—have found widespread support by reflecting the realities of nuclear families, even when articulating doctrine in terms of the importance of the traditional household.

The ceremonies focusing on the domestic unit are central to Japanese religious life. Although this chapter has focused on Buddhism as but one facet of Japanese religion, it is arguable that "the family" is the religion of Japan.

As domestic organization is altered by economic changes, so, too, will Japanese religion be transformed.

REFERENCES

Abegglen, James C. 1958. *The Japanese Factory: Aspects of Its Social Organization*. Glencoe, IL: Free Press.

Befu, Harumi. 1971. *Japan: An Anthropological Introduction*. New York: Harper & Row.

Bingham, Marjorie W., and Susan Hill Gross. 1987. *Women in Japan from Ancient Times to the Present*. Women in the World Area Series. St. Louis Park, MN: Glenhurst.

Blacker, Carmen. 1975. *The Catalpa Bow*. London: Allen & Unwin.

Earhart, H. Byron. 1982. *Japanese Religion: Unity and Diversity* (3rd ed.). Belmont, CA.: Wadsworth.

Fairbank, John K., Edwin O. Reischauer, and Albert M. Craig. 1989. *East Asia, Tradition and Transformation* (rev. ed.). Boston: Houghton Mifflin.

Frederic, Louis. 1972. *Daily Life in Japan at the Time of the Samurai 1185–1603*. Translated by E. M. Lowe. New York: Praeger.

Fukutake, Tadashi. 1982. *The Japanese Social Structure*. Tokyo: University of Tokyo Press.

Goode, William. 1963. *World Revolution and Family Patterns*. New York: Free Press of Glencoe.

Hardacre, Helen. 1982. *Lay Buddhism in Contemporary Japan: Reiyu kai Kyodan*. Princeton, NJ: Princeton University Press.

Harris, Marvin. 1991. *Cultural Anthropology* (3rd ed.). New York: HarperCollins.

———. 1993. *Culture, People, Nature*. New York: HarperCollins.

Hori Ichiro. 1968. *Folk Religion in Japan: Continuity and Change*. Chicago: University of Chicago Press.

Kondo, Dorinne K. 1990. *Crafting Selves: Power, Gender, and Discourses of Identity in a Japanese Workplace*. Chicago: University of Chicago Press.

Kumagai, Fumie. 1986. "Modernization and the Family in Japan." *Journal of Family History* 11:371–82.

Lebra, Takie Sugiyama. 1976. *Japanese Patterns of Behavior*. Honolulu: University of Hawaii Press.

Levy, Marion J. 1955. "Contrasting Factors in the Modernization of China and Japan." Pp. 496–536 in *Economic Growth in Brazil, India, and Japan*, edited by Simon S. Kuznets, William E. Moore, and Joseph J. Spengler. Durham, NC: Duke University Press.

Marx, Karl. [1859] 1970. *A Contribution to the Critique of Political Economy*. New York: International Publishers.

Morioka, Kiyomi. 1975. *Religion in Changing Japanese Society*. Tokyo: University of Tokyo Press.

———. 1984. "Ancestor Worship in Contemporary Japan: Continuity and Change." Pp. 201–13 in *Religion and the Family in East Asia*, edited by George A. De Vos and Takao Sofue. Berkeley: University of California Press.

Nakane, Chie. 1967. *Kinship and Economic Organization in Rural Japan*. London: Athlone Press.

———. 1970. *Japanese Society*. Berkeley: University of California Press.

Norbeck, Edward. 1952. "Pollution and Taboo in Contemporary Japan." *Southwest Journal of Anthropology* 8:269–85.

———. 1970. *Religion and Society in Modern Japan: Continuity of Change*. Houston, TX: Tourmaline Press.

Ohnuki-Tierney, Emiko. 1984. *Illness and Culture in Contemporary Japan*. Cambridge, England: Cambridge University Press.

Plath, David. 1964. "Where the Family of God Is the Family: The Role of the Dead in Japanese Households." *American Anthropologist* 66:300–17.

Reader, Ian. 1991. *Religion in Contemporary Japan*. Honolulu: University of Hawaii Press.

———. 1993. "Buddhism as a Religion of the Family: Contemporary Images in Soto Zen." Pp. 139–56 in *Religion and Society in Modern Japan*, edited by Mark R. Mullins, Shimazon Susumu, and Paul L. Swanson. Berkeley, CA: Asian Humanities Press.

Rohlen, Thomas P. 1974. *For Harmony and Strength: Japanese White-Collar Organization in Anthropological Perspective*. Berkeley: University of California Press.

Smith, Robert J. 1961. "The Japanese Rural Community: Norms, Sanctions, and Ostracism." *American Anthropologist* 63:522–33.

———. 1974. *Ancestor Worship in Contemporary Japan*. Stanford: Stanford University Press.

Smith, Stephen R. 1992. "The Family in Japan." Pp. 154–67 in *Asia, Case Studies in the Social Sciences: A Guide for Teaching*, edited by Myron Cohen. Armonk, NY: M. E. Sharpe.

Swyngedouw, Jan. 1993. "Religion in Contemporary Japanese Society." Pp. 49–72 in *Religion and Society in Modern Japan*, edited by Mark R. Mullins, Shimazon Susumu, and Paul L. Swanson. Berkeley, CA: Asian Humanities Press.

Vogel, Ezra F. 1965. "The Japanese Family." Pp. 287–300 in *Comparative Family Systems*, edited by M. F. Nimkoff. Boston: Houghton Mifflin.

CHAPTER THIRTEEN

A Woman's Pillow and the Political Economy of Kedjom Family Life in Cameroon

SUSAN DIDUK
KENT MAYNARD

When a Kedjom women dies, there are often two funeral observances. First, there is a funeral in the husband's compound. Then, representatives from the woman's compound of birth seek the wooden pillow, *kǒnbǒnta*, on which she slept and return it to her father's compound, the compound of her own patrilineage. Only then can the woman's extended family "cry her die" a second time at her father's compound. Patrilineages, often referred to in the literature as "agnatic descent groups," are made up of male and female kin who can trace their common descent by "birth," through the male line, to a single real or fictive male ancestor.

In this chapter, we examine why many Kedjom women have two funerals in two different compounds and with two different sets of kin. The work is based on extensive ethnographic research carried out from 1981 to 1983 and 1989 to 1990 in Kedjom Keku and Kedjom Ketinguh, in the Republic of Cameroon, and on interview and archival research in Germany, Switzerland, and the United Kingdom.

We focus on the ritual return of a woman's pillow at her death, as well as on her two funerals. By looking at the symbolic parity given to a woman's death by two households, her husband's and father's, one can begin to unravel what Kedjom indigenous religious ritual implies about kinship and other socioeconomic ties. When one investigates the passage of the pillow—if, when, and why it travels between the compounds of birth and marriage—one sees the sacralization of ongoing links between extended families and other groups beyond any spiritual import given to lineal descent alone. Spirituality may root a society in its past, but it also justifies the flexibility of strategic and affective alliances with a wide variety of affines (in-laws) and nonrelatives. Indeed, this dynamism is always part of a society's past.

KEDJOM HISTORY AND THE PLASTICITY OF "TRADITION"

To understand the importance of a woman's funerals and the journey of the *kǒnbǒnta,* one needs to place them in a wider historical context. They reflect a plasticity in Kedjom society that is not simply attributable to the succession of the colonial, trusteeship, and postindependence eras of the past 100 years. The Kedjom, as well as the entire highlands region of Cameroon (cf. Nyamndi n.d.; Rowlands 1979), were clearly undergoing significant social change well before the Germans arrived in 1889.

Cameroon remained a German colony until 1916. After World War I, it became a mandated trust territory of the League of Nations, administratively divided between Great Britain and France, with British territory including the Bamenda highlands. Cameroon was united as an independent country following a plebiscite in 1961. In addition to these European political and economic forces, the Kedjom have been influenced, particularly since the 1930s, by the Swiss (Presbyterian) Basel Mission; North American Baptists; and Irish, Dutch, and Tyrolean Catholic priests and nuns.

Although most Kedjom under age 50 are either Protestant or Catholic, virtually all continue to participate in indigenous religious rituals as well. These rituals include the calendrical rites tied to the agricultural year; rites of passage over the life course, such as birth, marriage, and death; medicinal rites to prevent or intervene in untoward events that affect individuals, compounds, lineages, or the entire "fondom" (chiefdom); as well as other religious and divinatory practices. Funerary rituals, in particular, remain inextricably bound to precolonial beliefs and practices, though the influence of Christianity and the colonial state, as we note later, is readily apparent.

In this lineage-based society, ancestors continue to be involved heavily in the affairs of the living, but figures like twins (referred to as "God's children") (Diduk 1993) and human witches also exert a strong influence for good, evil, or simply mischief in community life. Although the names and functions of many Gods have faded and some ritual activities (such as the use of poison ordeals and human sacrifice) are but a memory, indigenous Kedjom spirituality is an ongoing and dynamic reality. Indeed, as is true of twin rituals, which were banned by Protestant missions, there has been a reemergence of several aspects of precolonial religious activity.

The Kedjom (referred to as the "Babanki" by the Germans) occupy the independent, but contiguous, chiefdoms of Kedjom Keku and Kedjom Ketinguh (a.k.a. Big Babanki and Babanki Tungoh) in the Bamenda highlands in the Northwest Province of the Republic of Cameroon. The Kedjom are a patrilineal, horticultural society of between 20,000 to 30,000 people, who share much in common with other groups in what is known as the Grassfields region (Diduk 1988, 1993). The Grassfields region has an average elevation of 4,500 feet and an equatorial year divided between a rainy season and a dry season. The Kedjom indigenous language is Ga Kedjom, but people also frequently use Pidgin English as a common means of communication.

Most Grassfields ethnic groups have a dualistic political system with a hereditary chief (*fon*, in Ga Kedjom) and a male secret society (*kwifon*), which share the responsibilities of governance (cf. Chilver and Kaberry 1967:47). Kedjom Keku and Kedjom Ketinguh have a common cultural history; they split politically in the 1870s over a dispute about succession to the "fonship." Separated by some thirty miles as the crow flies, they share the same language, rituals, political organization, and subsistence practices and continue to be connected through intermarriage. As horticulturalists, they practice the hand-hoe cultivation of farm plots. Their crops include corn, cassava, cocoyams, beans, melons, and a variety of leafy-green vegetables and favor European vegetables like potatoes, tomatoes, onions, and carrots (and, until recently, coffee) as cash crops. Although women cultivate most crops for household consumption, among other things, men grow cash crops; sell petty commodities; and work as tailors, bricklayers, carpenters, bar owners, taxi cab drivers, and so on.

Land is inherited through the male line and is "owned" nominally by the patrilineage or extended family. Male "successors" inherit the right to allocate and even give away their fathers' lands, while women have use rights to land through their fathers, their husbands, and sometimes their brothers. Only within the past twenty years have individuals begun to buy and sell land (Diduk 1988). No more than a handful of women, however, are included among those who have a legal title to farm plots. Women's lack of control over sufficient cash and a cultural ideology and history that associate land with men both account for the paucity of female land owners.

A WOMAN'S DEATH AND MORTUARY RITUALS

Kedjom mortuary rituals begin, but do not end, with the funeral, or "bad die," which occurs shortly after a death. Funerals commemorate the passing of a member from the community. But, a later death celebration, or "good die," moves the deceased into the ancestral world beneath the Earth. The good die is imperative as much for the living as for the dead. The longer the ancestor's death goes uncelebrated, the more likely it is that he or she will prove troublesome, bringing illness and other misfortune to the living. The good die ideally should occur shortly after the funeral, but is more likely to be celebrated several years after the death, partly because amassing the large financial and food resources from children of the deceased takes time and effort. Indeed, the death celebration may not occur until illness or some other misfortune in the compound leads a diviner to recommend that "the die" be celebrated.

In the past, just as today, the funeral and death celebrations brought together nuclear and extended family members, as well as friends and neighbors, to mourn and honor a person in death. In the patrilineal society of the

Kedjom, men's funerals take place only in one compound, either in their fathers' or in their own if they have established them. Married women are buried in their husbands' compounds, but the funeral ritual, which includes the same three-day period of mourning, may be observed both there and in the compounds of their own patrilineal descent groups.

Funerals: One for Men, Two for Women

With any death, the daily rhythm of life halts, and the community, family members, and friends take time to grieve. News of a death in the village carries quickly. If it is not heard by word of mouth, it soon becomes obvious from the firing of guns and/or ringing of church bells. Within hours, mourners arrive at the respective compounds. Funerals are almost always accompanied by a consultation with a diviner who offers explanations for the death and remedial ritual actions. Only male lineage members may participate in such consultations; women do not attend, regardless of their status or lineage membership. As we note later, women should avoid contact with death and dying because they threaten their ability to reproduce.

In the event of a woman's death, close lineage members of the husband attend her funeral in his compound, while members of the deceased woman's own lineage go to the second funeral in her father's compound. In the husband's compound, female friends of the deceased harvest food from any of the plots on which the dead woman farmed and present it to the husband's lineage. Women also bring cooked food to be shared with the visiting mourners, while men bring raffia wine, corn beer, or European beers and soft drinks.

Forty to fifty years ago, before the period of more direct scrutiny by the missions and colonial state, high-ranking men, such as lineage heads, were given special burials. In some families, graves were dug six-feet deep inside a compound head's sleeping house; in other cases, men were buried just outside their houses. The choice of burial location seems to have been correlated less with specific statuses than with different family customs. In either case, the dead were buried in a seated position, and care was taken to place several strong sticks beneath their chins because the skulls were exhumed once the bodies decomposed. The sticks prevented the skulls from falling into the bottom of the graves, which was considered to be inauspicious[1] (Kaberry 1952).

The jaws of lineage elders (and, in some cases, women, such as princesses who married out from the royal household), were placed in a compound ancestral shrine (*fam*). In the precolonial period, these jaws were removed on important ritual occasions and touched to the forehead of each lineage member as a sign of group unity. Since the 1930s, when exhumation waned under the prohibitions imposed by European missions and the British government, drinking horns have been substituted for the jaw bones. Now, solidarity is invoked annually as family members collectively drink beer from the carved horn of the lineage or family head.

At all funerals, whether for men or women, people sit quietly and converse in low tones, at least initially. Especially in the event of an untoward death or the death of a young person, conversation may focus on the circumstances that led to the death and on the explanation and ritual remedies offered by a diviner. For people who have led a long life, with a large family to mourn their death, funerals are far less desultory, with wide-ranging and even spirited conversations and laughter.

The actual burial occurs as quickly as a coffin can be made and is delayed only by the need to notify members of the immediate family by radio if they live outside the village. Announcements of death are routinely delivered to regional radio stations, since few houses have telephones. Close lineal relatives remain in the compound for three days following the burial. Only more distant relatives and friends leave the compound to return to their own homes so they can cook meals for family members or look after young children.

Each child of the deceased is charged with providing one piece of white cotton cloth that will be used to wrap the corpse and money to make the coffin. Each also contributes a fowl to feed the many visitors to the compound. Guests are always served a hot meal and something to drink while they visit, but the food is not prepared by members of the household. From the moment of a death in any compound, the members neither cook nor bathe, nor is the compound swept until the rite of passage is complete. On the third day, the end of mourning is marked symbolically by shaving the hair of each close male and female relative of the deceased. Until every person is shaved and bathed, daily life does not resume.

These events follow the same pattern at each of the married woman's bad dies—first, in her husband's compound and, then, in her father's. Although mourners attend funerals along lineage lines—close members of the woman's patrilineage go to her father's compound and those of her husband's lineage go to his compound—the descent principle alone is insufficient for predicting who participates and where. A large number of people outside these two patrilineal groups also attend because of friendship, neighborliness, age, or common membership in voluntary associations. It is especially at funerals that one can see how nonagnatic ties intersect with lineage solidarity. Neighbors, for example, frequently do not go to the farms during the three-day mourning period; instead, they cook for the many visitors and contribute food, drink, and labor. If the person was a member of a church choir, the choir may attend and sing at the funeral. Comembers of a savings association (*njangi*) or of male secret societies may also contribute food, drink, and sometimes cash.

Good Die Celebrations

As with funerals, the later-occurring death celebrations also draw a wide variety of community members. For example, in two village savings associations that we know well, individual members always made small cash contributions that were pooled and then donated to members celebrating the deaths of one or both their parents. In addition to comembers, friends, neighbors, and age-mates may attend. Masquerading societies may dance, or *nzowain* (a female fertility society) may "come out" to sing and dance.

We have noted that good dies refer to the celebrations that usher the deceased into the realm of the ancestors. Kedjom ancestors who have not had their deaths celebrated are said to remain "on the road"—not fully incorporated into the village of ancestors under the Earth. They "vex" easily and shape daily social life by causing disease, miscarriage, injury, death, or other inauspicious events; hence, the diviners frequently prescribe that a death celebration must be transacted to restore personal health and social harmony. After the good die is held, plentiful births, good harvests, and fine health should prevail. As one friend put it:

> [O]nce you do a good die for your mother and father, they will no longer bring bad to your compound. There is now no need to hear them . . . because you have fulfilled their law. Father and mother, when they die, they will say, "cry my die very well. Do not make me be annoyed with you. Look out for the family for always and rest well." They will put great strength for your hand . . . [and] will say, "may you live fine." Like Mr. Mbegoh [a neighbor], as he is a carpenter, if he climbs on top of a house, he may no longer be injured by his mother and father. . . . It is as if he washed all germs. The germs are washed away so they cannot wound the skin.

Good dies are hosted by both the sons and daughters of deceased parents. Intricate food and drink exchanges occur, which may be carefully accounted for in a primary school notebook, to be repaid in the future. Payments are given to a variety of mortuary and dance societies to sing and dance at the death celebration. Men act as mediators between the living members and ancestors of the patrilineage and extended family. Invitations to the groups performing at the good die are usually made by sons on behalf of their parents, and by husbands on behalf of their wives, as representatives of the women's patrilineal groups or families. Men also compensate dancers for their performance. It is considered culturally inappropriate for women to act on their own behalf in such ritual contexts, as we noted, because direct contact with death rituals is said to threaten the fertility of women.

Transacting this movement of the deceased to the "die world" is equally essential for female and male ancestors because both influence their relatives. It is important to note, however, that male and female ancestors do not just affect people in their own lineage; they can also influence family members who are in a different lineage and who are related only by marriage. For example, a mother who died can annoy and bring ill will to her daughter's nuclear family, including her daughter's husband and his relatives. Or she may instruct her son in the art of becoming a "traditional" doctor—coming to him in a dream with the knowledge of where to find herbs and how to make medicines—even though he belongs to his father's patrilineage, not to hers. In short, the relationship between ancestors and the extended family and other individuals, not just the patrilineage, is a reciprocal one.

DESCENT AND ALLIANCE THEORY AND KEDJOM SOCIAL RELATIONS

The relationship between family and lineage becomes clearer if one recalls our earlier reference to Kedjom history. We want to avoid any reification that may mask the diversity and dynamism in either Kedjom ethnicity or descent. Neither the term *Kedjom* nor the names of other highlands groups, for example, refer to primordially distinct ethnic polities. From at least the eighteenth century, the entire Grassfields area has been in flux because of the expansion of the Hausa and Fulani empires to the north and the advent of slave raiding, population growth, and warfare over the control of trade routes. Both large-scale migration and ethnic intermixing have been routine. The Kedjom, for example, variously report past links with both the Bafut and Kom peoples.[2] And as with many Grassfields groups, the Kedjom have absorbed "stranger" groups, refugees from either war or political disputes, as well as smaller neighboring groups who recognize the Kedjom's superiority with annual tributes (e.g., the Futoh clan, originally from Metá, and the Mujung peoples, respectively). Even the Kedjom themselves split over a dispute about which prince would ascend to the fonship (circa 1870) and moved to their present politically autonomous fondoms.

Patrilineality is the other potential source of confusion. Although the Kedjom have a principle of patrilineal descent, we do not wish to overemphasize the singularity of its cultural importance or the degree to which it reflects actual practice. In the course of this chapter, we hope to show that the Kedjom do not rely exclusively on patrilineages to organize either the political economy of household production or their religious activities.

Now, if descent cannot be said to dictate the social affairs of unilineal societies, the classic alternative in anthropology was to argue that it must be marriage ties that cement ongoing social life. This dichotomy was the basis of the now-famous dispute between descent and alliance theorists during much of the 1960s and 1970s (cf. Kuper 1982). Descent theory suggested that political, social, and economic life in Africa was best understood through principles of descent in which blood was the bond that joined people into discretely bounded, corporate groups. Descent became the principle of order and group reproduction. In contrast, alliance theory argued that social relations were established primarily through ongoing links between lineages or clans that were expressed through the exchange of marriage partners. This argument was best illustrated in cross-cousin marriage in which lineages reproduce themselves by repeatedly exchanging classificatory sisters over time.

This theoretical debate deserves its notoriety because, to a large degree, both camps shared an erroneous assumption that societies with lineage models are in structural balance; the two schools of thought simply attributed equilibrium to different sources, either descent or marriage exchange. Over the past decade, anthropologists have come to view both descent or lineality and marriage as *principles* that are inherently dynamic and enormously elastic (cf. Karp and Maynard 1983). These principles can facilitate diverse and flexible social relations that accommodate all manner of interests and potential contradictions. As Hutchinson (1990:393) said of marriage, for example, it can be "less a state of being than an extended process subject to competing interpretations and manipulation."

Our research found that most Kedjom do not give great depth and import to patrilineages and clans,[3] primarily because of historical circumstances. In the nineteenth century, the Kedjom were a small political polity, whose survival amid large and powerful neighbors, like the fondoms of Bafut and Kom, depended on defensive political strategies and the easy incorporation of foreign populations within Kedjom boundaries. The Kedjom also settled high on the escarpment, which, as a smaller group, gave them a tactical advantage in warfare.

Given that political instability and widespread population movements, rather than the stately order envisioned by both descent and alliance theorists, have been a way of life in the Grassfields for at least two or three centuries, it makes sense that the Kedjom would emphasize porous clan and lineage boundaries to facilitate the swift incorporation of strangers into the Kedjom settlement. Today, as was probably true in the past, the royal clan and large "stranger" clans like the Futoh give greater emphasis to their genealogical depth and corporate nature than do most other extended families. The Kedjom royal clan, for example, includes eighteen chiefs whose reigns date back to the fifteenth century. In contrast, though commoners may refer metaphorically to their *ngwa* (literally "seed"), they much more frequently invoke a far shallower organization, the *nsan* (lineal "branch"). Many Kedjom can name a common clan ancestor, but few have detailed memories of the genealogical links by which they are connected. When we gathered family histories, it was typical for commoners to recount a lineage, or extended family, depth of no more than three generations.

Likewise, not all Kedjom families stress marriage alliances in the same way. For example, not all patrilineal compounds in the precolonial era sent a pillow with a woman into marriage to be returned on her death. And similar variations in the patterns of descent and marriage alliance, as well as in the ritual of the pillow, continue today.

THE POLITICAL ECONOMY OF FAMILY AND DESCENT

The Kedjom family-and-descent structure must also be understood in light of the nuclear family as a unit of production and consumption. The patrilineally based system of land tenure means that land has been distributed by male lineage heads. Women and their children cultivate farm plots for their own household consumption and to feed husbands. In the event of a polygynous marriage, each wife is responsible for providing food for herself, her own children, and her husband. Each wife also makes additional food contributions to her husband for hosting lineage rituals and death celebrations and for the secret societies of which he is a member.

Women hold usufruct or use rights in land. In patrilineal societies, land is typically vested in male descent groups; women have rights over the use of land but cannot buy or sell it. Historically, for example, women in many patrilineal Grassfields groups had the right to keep using the plots they farmed as adolescents on their fathers' lands, as well as to beg farms from their mothers' fathers' lands, in other words, from two different patrilineal groups—one by blood, the other by marriage (Kaberry 1952). Land pressure, as we will see, has exacerbated this need for flexible sources of land. Indeed, as Kaberry (1952:41) noted for the Nso, a Grassfields fondom to the northeast of Kedjom Keku and Kedjom Ketinguh, with the increase in population in the 1940s, women were begging farm plots from a variety of lineages and friends.

Until the 1970s, many Kedjom families were polygynous, so wives either prepared food for their husbands and older sons on alternate days or in smaller quantities daily. In periods of food scarcity between agricultural production cycles, a husband often supplemented the maize and, in the nineteenth century, "guinea corn" or sorghum supplies of his wives from plots he kept in reserve. These farms were planted by husbands and harvested with the help of wives and children. The crops were stored in the men's houses and were used for payments to the men's voluntary associations, as well as at fondom, lineage, and compound rituals. As a rule, such distribution of food was controlled by male heads of compounds.

Nuclear family units, however, also had fluid boundaries, given the frequency of migration, warfare, trading, and slavery. Although "export" slavery ceased in the nineteenth century, "domestic" slavery continued in the Bamenda highlands, and elsewhere in Cameroon and Nigeria until at least the 1920s (a fact that the British administration and League of Nations knew well; see, for example, Moorhouse 1923:3–4). Slaves were captured from other ethnic groups and were quickly incorporated into nuclear families as wives of compound heads or as dependent men. Their own children had the full rights of any Kedjom inhabitant and received allotments of land from the heads of their adoptive lineages on which they could farm and establish their own compounds.[4] One older Kedjom man, with whom we had many conversations, recounted that his father was an important dealer in slaves who had taken a slave woman as an additional wife in his large polygynous household. Thus, it is clear that domestic slavery had a significant impact on the shape of nuclear and extended Kedjom families.

Such arrangements stem, in part, from the fact that, in sub-Saharan Africa in general, power was not drawn from control over land as much as control over labor, which accounted, at the compound level, for attempts to attract a large number of dependents. For the Kedjom, efforts to add dependents also included the usual practice of patrilocality in which wives moved to new houses built by husbands in the husbands' fathers' compounds. Large compounds were made up of compound heads, their many wives and children, slaves, and dependent men seeking alliances with wealthy "big men." For example, a man might give his son to live in a blacksmith's compound for an extended period of apprenticeship.[5]

During our ethnographic work in the Kedjom communities, we were reminded daily of this porous family structure, both as we collected family histories and by the widespread custom of fostering. Siblings and close friends sometimes give one or more of their own children to one another for rearing. They become the children's fictive parents and may raise them to adulthood, at which time the children marry and establish their own compounds. Likewise, children who are orphaned and are the last members of a lineage are quickly incorporated into other families. In the precolonial period, such children were taken to live in the *fon's* palace and were automatically drawn into the royal clan. Given these ready solutions, the very concept of an orphan seems a misnomer.

As a result, most Grassfields groups have a long record of the elaborate and creative use of *both* descent and marriage ties, as well as the establishment of links with several different lineages and, we should add, even "friendship" within and between ethnic groups (cf. Brain 1969; Kaberry 1952). If ties by blood, marriage, and ethnicity are creative and diverse, one might expect religion to recognize and bless them as well.

PATRILINEAGES, AFFINES, AND A WOMAN'S PILLOW

To illustrate the premium on flexibility in Kedjom life, we again look to rituals involving descent and marriage. As we said earlier, at the time of marriage, a Kedjom woman left her father's compound to reside with her husband in the larger compound of the husband's father or neolocally in a new compound. The move to a new compound often occurred after the couple had spent several years in the husband's father's house amassing the wherewithall to build their own compound. Along with other personal belongings, the new wife brought her wooden pillow, the *kǒnbǒnta,* usually an undecorated block of wood, some six inches in diameter and fifteen inches in length.

This pillow is only understandable within the context of Kedjom marriage and the bride wealth (or "dowry" in Pidgin English) given by a husband to his in-laws.[6] In the past, bride wealth consisted of some money—whether cowries (small shells used for coins), copper rods, or shillings—and especially an ongoing series of gifts, such as firewood, meat, salt, palm oil, or iron blades for hoes. Bride service, with an extended period of labor in the compound of one's father-in-law, was also crucial. Since World War II, the Kedjom and other Grassfields groups have been incorporated increasingly into a market economy with salaried labor. As a result, the cash payments of bride wealth have come to overshadow bride service and gift giving, although both still occur. Since many young married couples, for example, leave the fondom in search of employment, sons-in-law are much less likely to do farm labor or build houses for their in-laws.

The amount of bride wealth was fixed by the male lineage head and paid in installments, up to the time of a woman's menopause, by the groom and his close kin to the bride's family in the person of her father. And a large portion of the bride wealth had to be paid before a new wife left her parents' compound. The Kedjom continue to view bride wealth, in part, as compensation to the bride's kin group for the loss of her labor and as assistance to a new patrilineage. This practice is in line with Keesing's (1981) argument that in societies in which labor and surplus production are "crucial elements" for establishing political alliances, special importance is placed on the labor power of young men and women and on female fertility. Yet, today, the Kedjom also consider bride wealth to be a "reimbursement" for the expense of raising the young woman to adulthood, particularly if she has been sent to secondary school.

In this patrilineal society, people say that a husband initially only "buys the lass" (that is, the body from the neck down) of his wife at marriage, rather than her "head." This is a metaphor for compensating her own lineage for the loss of her labor and control over her reproductive abilities. But if bride wealth is not paid, her children jurally remain identified with her own patrilineage. Only when the husband has fully paid his wife's bride wealth and, in former times, completed all his bride service to his father-in-law (also usually completed at a woman's menopause or if a woman bore no children, at her death) is he said to have bought both the "lass" and the "head" of his wife. "Buying the head" is also a patrilineal phrase—as is "buying the lass"—to the extent that the new wife's identity and the identities of her children become even more tied to the husband's lineage.

But Kedjom are also adamant that women continue to be affiliated with their natal compounds and their fathers' patrilineal groups. One male friend put it this way:

> Even if someone buys the head of a woman, she still belongs to her father's compound. Blood is still there. You cannot drop her father's compound. She stays with the *ngwa* [clan] of the father and the husband.

Kedjom, like all people, acquire a sense of who they are in the midst of more than one group. When a Kedjom is born, he or she is born to a woman who is usually living in her husband's compound. Biologically, the fetus is considered to be the husband's child, an amalgam of sperm "carried" in the mother's uterus, a part of the husband's lineage, with the proviso that the proper bride wealth be paid. For women, much more than men, lineal ties become complicated over the course of the life cycle and even after death.

In life, a woman calls on both her own biological kin and her in-laws to help her gain access to and cultivate her various farm plots, to assist in child care, and to support her in gaining entry into voluntary associations. As an ancestor, she again keeps her ties to both her parents' and her husband's compound and lineages. She continues to influence the health of her husband and children, and her children are obligated to celebrate her death in her husband's (their father's) compound. It is no wonder that at a woman's death, many people, in so many different statuses, come to mourn her passing, not once, but twice in two different compounds.

A husband, in contrast, has shorter-term ties to his wife's compound of birth. After he has made his final bride-wealth payment to his father-in-law, he can say, as did one man in our study, "When I pass my in-laws on the road, they are nothing to me." Of course, this is a statement about the end of jural obligations, not necessarily of affective ties. But for his *children*, these jural duties continue after the death of their mother, and, usually, there is an abiding affection as well. For Kedjom generally agree that the good die for your mother (a woman not in your own lineage) is far more important and celebrated at greater length than even a good die for your own father.

When social relations are strained between consanguineal kin and affines, as they sometimes are in Kedjom life, women still retain undisputed ties to both their natal compounds and those of their marriage. Until recently, for example, a woman was known to the community, even after marriage, by her father's and mother's lineal names. And she continues to have important economic and moral obligations at the funeral and later death celebrations of her parents.

Given this situation, it makes sense that many Kedjom families insist that their daughters' pillows be returned on their daughters' deaths and that the daughters receive two funerals, one in the compound of their husbands where they are actually buried, and the other in their fathers' compounds. Today, most people no longer literally use wooden pillows—they sleep on foam mattresses with foam pillows—but they continue to bring the metaphor of the wooden block with them to the marriage. And on a woman's death, the wooden block is still returned metaphorically to her natal compound. Either a spirit being, in the form of a masquerader (*mukum* in Ga Kedjom; *juju* in Pidgin), or members of a compound ritual association or dance society (*nzan*), are sent to the widower's compound to claim the pillow so the second "die" can commence.

That a woman receives two funerals, we think, has everything to do with the cross-cutting importance of both descent and marriage, lineage and family, along with other ties, and the advantages conferred on women by maintaining economic and other social rights in both their own and their husbands' compounds. Lineages and extended families were complicated by both their association with specific nuclear families and their links to the wider institutions of Kedjom society, principally other lineages and the prerogatives and prestige of the royal household. Although individuals, and even nuclear families, were firmly embedded in the political and economic identity of the patrilocal compound, the compound itself remained interconnected with broader lineage, clan, and ethnic loyalties. These ties were visibly expressed in the rituals surrounding death and the birth of children, particularly twins (cf. Diduk 1993). They also were played out in ongoing economic and labor contributions, given by husbands to their in-laws in the natal compounds of their various wives. By following the ritual path of a woman's pillow, both in life and after death, we have tried to trace these complex links between kin groups.

As we argued, historical evidence suggests that shallow lineage and clan genealogies were common for all but the royal and stranger clans in the Kedjom fondoms. That few commoners can recall intricate genealogies stands to reason, given the dynamic population movements of nineteenth-century Grassfields fondoms in general. These loosely organized polities were of different sizes and consolidated political power through their incorporation of foreign populations and monopolization of trade networks. The viability of small fondoms like the Kedjom, especially, depended on the fondoms' ability to incorporate stranger groups. The diffuse clan and lineage histories so typical of contemporary Kedjom are a commentary on the necessity of increasing group membership by all sorts of "fictive" and other strategies.

A WOMAN'S DUAL FUNERALS IN THE CONTEMPORARY ERA

The growing tide of individualism and wider economic shifts clearly have had an influence on these kinship ties, as well as on Kedjom ritual life. Yet more often than not, the pillow returns, along with a reassertion of the identity of the dead wife in her ancestral lineage. When we asked individual Kedjom why they continue to return the woman's pillow to her father's house and have two funerals, they generally replied, "because that is the way we in this family do things." This practice acts as a standard of etiquette by which they mark their prestige and set themselves off from others. But it also, we think, ritually marks the importance of a woman's multiple ties to family and lineage.

A woman's death represents a loss both to her own lineage and to the lineage of her husband. But a woman's funerals are not just cried by members of these two groups. They are cried in the context of two compounds with members of all the nuclear and extended family represented. One goes to one or the other funeral, not solely based on one's lineage membership but also based on ties of residence, friendship, neighborliness, and marriage. Again, one's choice of which funeral to attend is not strictly prescribed—there is an element of individual choice, and some people may decide to attend both dies.

The Decline in Marriage and the Loss of a Woman's Resources

Although the journey of the *kǒnbǒnta* and a woman's dual funerals are still much in evidence for the Kedjom, they are being challenged by the increasing number of young women who are neither marrying nor joining affinal compounds before they bear children. Within the past ten years, all over the Grassfields, a growing number of elementary, secondary, and college-age women have become pregnant while still at school (cf. Goheen 1991). Few such women marry, and if they do, only as second wives, because they are believed to be "second-hand" and inappropriate partners for a first marriage. Their best chance for marriage, as a second or third wife into a polygynous compound, comes at a time when polygyny is declining for economic reasons, including the rising cost of bride wealth. There are also scant well-paid labor opportunities for unmarried mothers, unless they migrate to the provincial capital of Bamenda or other urban areas. But few women do so, perhaps because even if they have urban-based relatives to provide housing and help them find employment, people are reluctant to aid women with dependent children. As a result, most single mothers and their children become permanent residents in their natal compounds.

In 1990, in Mbuase, the largest quarter[7] of Kedjom Keku, we counted twenty-four single women with children, all of whom were in their mid- to late teens and resided in twenty-four of the approximately fifty-nine compounds in the quarter. In contrast, in 1980, we did not count a single unwed young mother in the entire quarter. Although this latter point is true from the Kedjom perspective, we should note a technical exception. In 1981, there were at least two compounds in Mbuase in which a father had "kept" an unmarried daughter in the compound because he and his wife had no male heir. To ensure that the lineal group continued, the daughter was designated his temporary "successor" and allowed to take a lover until she could bear a son. She remained unmarried intentionally so her son could be incorporated into her own and her father's lineage as his proper successor.

Widespread and frequent bemoaning of nonmarital births by members of the community also suggests that there are many unwed mothers in other quarters of the fondom. Certainly, the phenomenon is present throughout the Grassfields area as a whole. In 1989–90, newspaper articles in Bamenda and radio broadcasts referred to illegitimacy as a worrisome trend. Hospital and health-center personnel also mentioned it as a significant and pervasive social problem.

These facts have important consequences for the sacred domain, kin relationships, and political economy of everyday life. Unmarried mothers learn to support themselves by farming with their biological mothers or by cultivating their own farms on land in which they have been given use rights by their fathers. Patrilineal family groups are adapting to these emerging family units by incorporating the new dependents. Since no bride wealth has been paid, the woman's children simply become members of her own lineage. This kind of adaptation had already taken place elsewhere in the Grassfields by the 1940s. Kaberry (1952:12) noted that for Nso, although unwed parenthood was rare, the children of unwed mothers were incorporated into their fathers' lineages.

Yet the prospects for continuing incorporation seem increasingly problematic because of the growing population density and scarcity of land, factors that affect all women adversely, whether single or married. The Northwest Province is one of the most densely populated regions in Cameroon, with an average of fifty-three inhabitants per square kilometer (Scott and Mahaffey 1980:2).[8] In 1980, it was already common for farmlands to be fallowed for shorter periods and cultivated for more seasons than in the past. Significant land scarcity and declining soil fertility are contemporary realities that shape the future of women. Many women are forced to depend on their own economic activity and to form alliances with as many sources as possible (for example, borrowing land from friends). Hence, a woman's dual funerals remain important because they reassert her ties with her own (and her father's) lineage, keeping the network for potential alliances as large as possible.

Furthermore, married women are increasingly less able to rely on their husbands' lineage. As land becomes commodified, it is not unusual to find husbands who have sold farm plots that have been regularly cultivated by their wives. One woman in our study, for example, returned to a plot in the new agricultural cycle only to find a stranger already hoeing it; her husband had sold it without informing her. (On other occasions, she had to "beg" plots from her female friends). Much of the available farmland near the village center, even plots around personal compounds, has been sold off to a few landholders. Several of our neighbors sold such land to Kedjom employed outside the village. One can barely see the original mud-block houses for the cement block Western-style houses immediately in front of them. As a result, women are having to make longer daily treks or to build overnight shelters to farm plots up on the escarpment. It is also common for some husbands not to contribute to the purchase of palm oil, salt, fish, meat, soap, kerosene, and other petty commodities for their wives and children. The curtailment of such contributions is related to growing economic hardship for rural farmers in general and to an erosion of cultural expectations about duties toward families.

Despite these socioeconomic problems that are becoming more and more common for married women, the socioeconomic circumstances of single women are even more difficult. Although married women may have to fight hard for the assistance of their husbands and their husbands' lineages, they still have a wider circle of agnatic and consanguineal relatives on which to call for economic assistance. Affines will still help a married woman to host celebrations like the birth of children, annual agricultural rituals, ceremonies that mark a growing family, or occasions when appeals are made to ancestors to secure family well-being and auspicious futures. In contrast, single women are forced to depend much more heavily on their own descent ties, precisely at a time when their fathers are increasingly hard pressed economically to take care of their other unmarried children, especially in terms of bride-wealth payments and school fees. This economic squeeze is reflected in many other groups, such as the Bamileke who live to the south of the Kedjom. Ouden (1987:20) pointed out that Bamileke "men increasingly refuse [to extend] cultivation rights to their married sisters, daughters and other female members of their lineage, although this is not to say that women have *completely* [emphasis in the original] lost the battle for their customary rights."

The economic viability of brothers is compromised, too, by the increase in unmarried mothers living in their fathers' compounds. First, brothers who are designated "successors" to their fathers must continue to provide land and other commodities (such as meat, oil, and salt) to such sisters. Second, and more important, brothers can no longer use the bride-wealth payments from such sisters to pay for their own future wives. This is a significant problem, given that such payments had risen for the Kedjom to an average of 250,000 Cameroonian francs (or cfa) by 1990—a substantial sum compared to the average annual per capita income of approximately 15,000–20,000 cfa in the Northwest Province (Scott and Mahaffey 1980:3). Unless young men can use the bride-wealth payments received from the fathers-in-law of their newly married sisters or money saved from well-paying urban employment, they find it increasingly difficult to establish their own families. And, of course, this difficulty, in turn, leads to a further increase in the number of young women who enter relationships with men and bear children before marriage.

Despite the growth of a cash-market economy and increasing individualism, many rituals rooted in the extended family or at the lineage or palace (that is, the wider community) level, continue to occur. But changes are evident even here. On the whole, the economic importance of a woman's father has declined relative to her husband's, particularly for husbands with salaried positions. When women are married to salaried husbands, they generally continue to farm but do less of it and hire other village women to cultivate their farms; instead, they engage in activities that are revenue producing, for example, selling petty commodities or beer. Nevertheless, a woman's independence per se, as we have noted, has grown in relation to both her husband and father. In the precolonial era, larger structures at the lineage or palace levels complicated and blurred the margins of the extended family and compound unit; now, it is the emerging nuclear family and individual autonomy that encroach on the compound's centrality to economic production and social life.

Because affinal alliances for single mothers are not a possibility and the responsibilities of descent groups are more difficult to fulfill, both men and (especially) women have become economically vulnerable. The precarious position of women is underlined by the fact that land—the resource that guarantees men and women a livelihood—is still controlled by men. As we said earlier, Kedjom women do not have an independent claim to the land that they cultivate; they appeal to their husbands or fathers (and others) for its allotment. This continues to be the norm today. By the 1980s, some men began to register their land with the national government and to receive individual land titles. With few exceptions, women have not been able to follow suit because they have neither traditional rights in land nor the capital or credit to pay the expense of traveling to governmental offices in Bamenda or to pay for the land title itself. Although most women are now involved in some form of petty trade like selling palm oil, prepared foods, or farm produce, such activities do not generate sizable sums of money. As Goheen (1991:28) showed for the Nso:

> [f]or the majority of women . . . entrepreneurial activities allow for sheer maintenance rather than growth and accumulation. Most women have neither the time nor the access to credit which would allow them to pursue capital-producing endeavors.

Since women's access to land is also threatened by population growth and land is being sold off, it will become more and more difficult to obtain use rights to farm plots. This problem is exacerbated by the growing presence of Fulani pastoralists and their cattle herds throughout the Northwest. Already in 1947, Kaberry (1952:2) noted that there were at least 1,500 Fulani men (not counting their families and dependents) in the old Bamenda Province, along with 156,870 cattle that grazed on the unfenced pastures of the highlands. Unmarried mothers, as well as lineages that have never had sizable land holdings, are particularly vulnerable in this situation. Indeed, in most Grassfields societies, and certainly in the two Kedjom communities, there simply is no more unclaimed "bush" where one could stake out new farm plots. And the number of such families who have little or no land is increasing, given that land is unevenly distributed in the two Kedjom communities and the Northwest Province in general (Scott and Mahaffey 1980).

The same economic tenuousness is felt by sons who are not successors. It is male successors who inherit the compounds and farmlands of their fathers, and while other brothers may receive use rights to plots of land, they may well have to look beyond the Kedjom fondom to thrive economically. The fall of world cocoa and coffee prices in the mid-1980s and the subsequent waning fortunes of the Cameroonian economy make such expectations problematic. Since 1989, the state bureaucracy has curtailed many civil service jobs in response to structural-adjustment restrictions imposed by the World Bank, and urban unemployment, in general, has increased for primary and secondary school leavers. And because cash-crop farmers have lost their outlets on the international market and have not been paid regularly since 1986, the commercial cultivation of coffee and cocoa has declined dramatically, along with paid labor opportunities. Men are shifting significantly to growing cash vegetable crops, such as beans, onions, and potatoes, but these crops do not yield the kind of cash that coffee farmers earned in the late 1970s and early 1980s.

Given the economic and kinship-related consequences of the increase in unwed mothers, what are the religious implications? The most immediate and obvious impact is that these will have only one funeral; since the *kǒnbǒnta* will not have gone with the woman to a husband's compound in the first place, it cannot return. The woman's burial and funeral will be joined and will occur solely in the woman's father's compound. The woman's death celebration likewise will occur only in her natal compound, again a shift from that of a married woman for whom it takes place in the compound of her widower. Whereas married women can draw on multiple lineage ties, unmarried women are reduced in the social relationships on which they can draw, even in death. And as one can see, the complex and socially legitimated ties of married women receive conspicuous symbolic and ritual recognition, but the truncated social ties of unmarried mothers receive far less religious emphasis.

CONCLUSIONS

We have argued that Kedjom social organization cannot be understood, either historically or at present, simply through structurally differentiated descent groups that are self-perpetuating. The ritual return of the *kǒnbǒnta* and the fact that deceased married women have two funerals illustrate not only the elasticity of Kedjom ties to patrilineal groups, but the range of individuals and extra-kin groups who contribute to organizing the economic, social, and ritual activities of daily life.

At the same time, we argue that the rights and obligations of kinspeople are being modified and sometimes terminated by contemporary economic changes that are shaped by national and international conditions. When farmers lose markets for their cash crops and per capita income declines dramatically, as it has since the mid-1980s, the ability to carry out mutual economic responsibilities is also called into question. In these contexts, the well-being of single mothers is especially at risk. During more auspicious economic periods, single mothers could save money in savings societies and become small-scale entrepreneurs. But such activities are difficult today because teachers, nurses, agricultural-extension workers, and coffee farmers are not being paid. If women manage to sell food crops in the market, they face competition from other women, and increasingly men, as they all try to unload more produce on a shrinking monied elite.

Historically, the well-being of the Kedjom has been absolutely dependent on their ability to adapt rapidly to unstable economic and social conditions. Indeed, they, as well as other Grassfields groups, have been successful in doing so for at least two centuries. This "traditional" flexibility is reflected, as we have shown, in their indigenous religious rituals. Kedjom individuals—whether the unmarried woman who is paying for her child's school fees or the young man who is responsible for his own bride wealth—*are* more self-reliant than in the past. The new and harsher conditions of today, however, will demand more of the Kedjom's ability to draw on a wide circle of alliances. No doubt, these alliances may also become grist for new symbolic rites and ties.

NOTES

We gratefully acknowledge several agencies and institutions whose sponsorship and financial support have made possible our continuing ethnographic research in Cameroon and archival work in the United Kingdom and Switzerland. Susan Diduk has received a Fulbright-Hays Doctoral Dissertation Research Grant, a National Institute of Mental Health Research Doctoral Fellowship, and postdoctoral grants from the Wenner-Gren Foundation for Anthopological Research and the Social Science Research Council. In addition, Denison University has generously given several Faculty Development and Research Foundation Grants-in-Aid and research leaves of absence for the completion of this work. Kent Maynard has received two postdoctoral grants from the Wenner-Gren Foundation for Anthropological Research (one with Susan Diduk, principal investigator), as well as Faculty Development and Research Foundation Grants, and a Robert C. Good Fellowship from Denison University. Our work in Cameroon has been sponsored by the Delegation Generale à la Recherche Scientifique et Technique. We wish to thank especially its former deputy director, Dr. Paul Nkwi, Fon Simon Vugah II of Kedjom Keku, and retired Police Commissioner Michael Ntuni of Kedjom Ketinguh, for their gracious support of this research. Finally, we thank the people of both Kedjom Keku and Kedjom Ketinguh whose patience and immense insight have made this research possible; any errors of fact or interpretation are most assuredly our own.

1. High-status men are no longer buried in this fashion, but their children sometimes purchase elaborate coffins and wrap the corpses in expensive cloth or lace.
2. Chilver and Kaberry (1967) reported similar discrepancies in the Kedjom origin story. One has the "Kijem" related to Bafut; the other places them as a lineage that split off (*circa* 1845) from a patrilineal group still resident in the Belo Valley and part of the matrilineal Kom peoples. Ritzenthaler and Ritzenthaler (1962:15) also reported the former story and cited Hawkesworth's 1926 Assessment Report on Bafut, which argues that

   > Bafut and Babanki [Kedjom Keku] both claim the headship of this clan, but Bafut appears to have the stronger claim in that all records of other tribes mention Bafut only, while Bafut has seventeen ancestors to Babanki's thirteen.

   Although both Kom and Bafut origins were recounted to us by the Kedjom (who always claimed that the first Bafut *fon* was from the Kedjom royal clan), the dominant story confers a Kom link.
3. In contrast, clan and lineage membership in larger Grassfield fondoms, like Bali and Bafut, is regularly affirmed on ritual and political occasions.
4. Indeed, this swift incorporation into kin groups led scholars (see, for example, Miers and Kopytoff 1977) to argue that African slavery was markedly different in form and content from that of Europe and the New World.
5. The Kedjom are well known historically for their blacksmithing and carving traditions. Their iron implements, including hoe blades, spears, cutlasses, and other tools and weapons, as well as wood carvings, were traded to fondoms, such as Kom, Nkwen, Bambili, and Bafut.

6. The Pidgin use of *dowry* is less accurate than the terms, *bride wealth* or *bride price.*
7. Quarters probably originated during the colonial period when the Germans and later the British divided fondoms into smaller administrative units for tax purposes. Kedjom men appointed as "quarter heads," were responsible for collecting a "head" tax from every man. Today, quarter heads continue to collect taxes and administer community labor (such as clearing village paths), and quarters are often a basis for membership in voluntary associations, such as savings societies and cornmill cooperatives.
8. This figure seems conservative, given Kaberry's (1952:3) estimate from the 1947 census of sixty people per square mile for the Bafut Native Authority area. At the time, Kedjom Keku was part of the Bafut Native Authority.

References

Brain, Robert. 1969. "Friends and Twins in Bangwa." Pp. 213–27 in *Man in Africa,* edited by M. Douglas and P. Kaberry. London: Tavistock.

Chilver, Elizabeth, and Phyllis Kaberry. 1967. *Traditional Bamenda, The Pre-Colonial History and Ethnography of the Bamenda Grassfields* (Vol. 1). Buea: Ministry of Primary Education and Social Welfare and West Cameroon Antiquities Commission.

Diduk, Susan. 1988. "The Paradox of Secrets: Power and Ideology in Kedjom Society." Unpublished Ph.D. dissertation, Indiana University, Bloomington.

———. 1993. "Twins, Ancestors and Socio-economic Change in Kedjom Society." *MAN* 28:551–71.

Goheen, Miriam. 1995. "Gender and Accumulation in Nso." *Paideuma* 41:73–81.

Hutchinson, Sharon. 1990. "Rising Divorce Among the Nuer." *MAN* 25:393–411.

Kaberry, Phyllis. 1952. *Women of the Grassfields.* London: Her Majesty's Stationery Office.

Karp, Ivan, and Kent Maynard. 1983. "Reading *the Nuer.*" *Current Anthropology* 24:481–503.

Keesing, Roger. 1981. *Cultural Anthropology.* New York: Holt, Rinehart & Winston.

Kuper, Adam. 1982. "Lineage Theory: A Critical Retrospect." *Annual Review of Anthropology* 11:71–95.

Miers, Suzanne, and Igor Kopytoff, eds. 1977. *Slavery in Africa.* Madison: University of Wisconsin Press.

Moorhouse, H. 1923. *Report on the Cameroons Province* (Cameroons, Dispatches, Foreign Office, Miscellaneous Offices, Individuals, 1923; Document CO649/27, Public Records Office, Kew, England). Lagos, Nigeria: Government Printer.

Nyamndi, Ndifontah B. n.d. *The Bali Chamba of Cameroon: A Political History.* Paris: CAPE.

Ouden, den Jan H. B. 1987. "In Search of Personal Mobility: Changing Interpersonal Relations in Two Bamileke Chiefdoms, Cameroon." *Africa* 57:3–27.

Ritzenthaler, Robert, and Pat Ritzenthaler. 1962. *Cameroons Village: An Ethnography of the Bafut* (Milwaukee Public Museum Publications in Anthropology 8). Milwaukee, WI: Milwaukee Public Museum.

Rowlands, Michael. 1979. "Local and Long Distance Trade and Incipient State Formation on the Bamenda Plateau in the Late 19th Century." *Paideuma* 25:1–19.

Scott, William, and Miriam Mahaffey. 1980. *Agricultural Marketing in the Northwest Province, United Republic of Cameroon.* Yaoundé: U.S.A.I.D, Office of Agricultural and Rural Development.

PART V

Gender and Social Change

CHAPTER FOURTEEN

Women, Family, and Catholicism in Brazil: The Issue of Power

MARIA JOSÉ FONTELAS ROSADO NUNES

INTRODUCTION

This chapter takes a sociohistorical approach to Catholicism in Brazil during the period of its introduction and development, from the sixteenth through the nineteenth centuries. From the sixteenth to the eighteenth centuries, Catholicism in Brazil was a lay, male, and white phenomenon. Only in the nineteenth century were women included, and then it was in connection with the Church's plans for institutional reorganization and recovery of social, political, and economic power. Women's inclusion took different forms, depending on whether the women were poor or rich, black or white.

At this time, Brazilian Catholicism was undergoing a process of "feminization" that went hand-in-hand with "clericalization." This feminization occurred at a time when the creation of the restricted family began to confine women to the home. The submission of women and their social conversion into wives and mothers took place as obedience became a rule and virtue in the eyes of clergymen.

This chapter examines the role of women in the historical dynamics of the Brazilian Catholic Church and assesses the impact that women's changing patterns of religious participation had on the ideology and structure of the Brazilian family as it entered the twentieth century. The manipulation and subordination of women in the Church has relevance for women today.

WOMEN'S ROLE IN THE INTRODUCTION OF CATHOLICISM IN BRAZIL

Women have been considered by some authors to be the most important instruments for transmitting and disseminating Catholic doctrine and moral precepts in Brazil. Consecutive generations of female slaves were deemed "the axis of the Gospel's transmission." Hoornaert, Azzi, Van Der Grijp, and

Brod (1979) described a "feminine tradition," a kind of hereditary line of women that went from black mother to daughter and extended to the Afro-Brazilian religious and even "unofficial Catholic worship, which is almost always delegated to women" especially mothers, who "have always been the best catechists in Brazil" (p. 372). White women of the ruling class were thought to be opposed to poorer women, specifically, to black women. Hoornaert et al. (1979:371) noted that while poor and black women communicated the genuine evangelical values of popular Brazilian Catholicism, white rich women disseminated "a mere repetitive, mechanical religious formalism."

These claims are questionable in that they idealize black and poor women, stigmatize white women of the ruling class, and relegate all women to motherhood. Actually, neither black slaves nor poor white women were in a position to be part of the Church's project to introduce and disseminate Catholicism. This project required stable families to introduce the model of indissoluble, monogamous, Christian marriage in Brazilian society. However, a large portion of the female population appeared to be "transgressors" of the Church's official dictates and distant from its moral teaching, not compliant women who faithfully transmitted its doctrine. The most widespread form of union among the majority of the population (poor whites, Indians, and enslaved and free blacks) was concubinage (Marcílio 1993; Rosado Nunes 1991). The stable monogamous family pattern created by indissoluble Christian marriage was followed by only a small number of white families. Furthermore, women's "disgraceful behavior" and way of dressing were the subjects of countless sermons, and the many attempts to control women's "sensuality" led to the assumption that women's transgressions were customary. In short, women's family situations varied a great deal. The question remains, though, "What role did women play in the implementation of Catholicism in Brazil?" To answer this question, we focus first on indigenous women, then on white women, and finally on black women.

Role of Indigenous Women

Indian women came to the forefront in a colonization characterized by systematic violence against the indigenous populations. According to Burkett (1978:105):

> An intrinsic part of conquest— . . . overcoming or gaining possession and control of a people and the territory that they inhabit—is violence. It is in this light that rape of indigenous women must be seen, as a type of violent behavior intended to subjugate and oppress. The act of rape implicitly says: I am your master; you must submit to me, or I will force my will upon you. In that, it is symbolic of the very conquest itself . . . [V]iewed collectively, the rape of Indian women was an integral part of the drive for submission that characterizes all conquest.

Because of the scarcity of white women, indigenous women were incorporated into the colonial-proslavery scenario. The first ships to arrive at the new continent brought only men. The first white women did not arrive until the mid-sixteenth century, and they were orphans, reported to have been sent by the king of Portugal at the behest of Jesuit Manoel da Nóbrega. From the time of the arrival of the first ships, colonization was concerned with the settlement of the country to secure and occupy lands, patrol the borderlands, and bring riches to the cities by exploiting natural resources and developing agriculture. So, torn from their tribal roots and reduced to slavery, Indian women were destined to provide the foundations for the settlement of the colony. For them, colonization meant widespread physical appropriation by their large landholders, both in the work and carnal senses. Hence, their situation was intrinsically different from that of Indian men.

Colonial exploitation and domination turned Indian and, later, black slavery into a premise for reproduction. The Jesuits defended the Indians (but not the blacks) against slavery—a stance that was deeply etched into contemporary Catholic doctrine and ecclesiastical expansionism. But it was not the system of slavery that was on trial; it was the effects of it. For the religious, it was a question of fighting moral decay and unseemly couplings. At issue was a new moral order in which the reform of customs would be brought under the umbrella of monogamous Christian marriage. Christianity, through the work of the first missionaries, played a fundamental role in establishing the family model—stable monogamous families. This family form was seen as the basis for the promulgation of the Catholic faith and Christian morality. As Gallager (1978:150) wrote about Mexico:

> Almost from the beginning of the Spanish occupation of Mexico, the church manifested concern for the welfare of native women, particularly in seeing to their preparation for the role of Christian wife and mother. . . . Within a decade of the conquest, Spanish female teachers were on the scene, partly in hopes of alleviating the work of the friars and partly in the belief that they could better instill some of the principles of Christian womanhood in the indigenous women.

To indigenous Brazilian women, the imposition of the monogamous model was especially violent. The notion of being "mother and wife" was as extraneous to them as that of the "female role." Even though the role attributed to women in Brazilian tribal societies is not widely known, it seems that children belonged primarily to the tribe, which was responsible for their education. And the demand for monogamous marriage encroached on Indian womanhood in yet another sense. From the moment a white or native man was forced by missionaries to "choose" which of his women would be his "wife," the others were left to their own devices, together with their offspring. Beozzo (1984) and Burkett (1978) thought that women and men became the victims of religious and moral patterns extraneous to their customs, cultural traditions, and the moral rules pertaining to their own groups.

In addition, the Portuguese, despised the Indians and, because of their racist preconceptions, deemed it a disgrace to marry Indian women. "Many of them, who were linked with Indian women and who had children by them, judged the very idea of marrying them to be great dishonor," wrote Nobrega (quoted in Beozzo 1984:86) in 1551.

The solution proposed by the missionaries was to build "shelters"—a type of convent—to group unmarried concubines together (contemporary documents make no mention of their children). Such cases are supposed to be the origin of female religious life in Brazil (Azzi 1979; Beozzo 1984). If one accepts the assumption that Brazilian female religious life originated with unmarried indigenous mothers who were forced to become nuns, one must conclude that female religious life came under the auspices of a threefold domination: sexual, religious, and colonial. The indigenous women from these shelters were incorporated into the work of evangelism. They became indoctrinators—instruments for the implementation of the new religion, its ethics and moral laws. Their knowledge of the Indian tongue was essential for bringing Indians into the Christian fold.

Christianity thus came to Latin America and South America as part of the patriarchal colonial-proslavery regime, the latter setting the guidelines for religious practices. The "Christianization" of indigenous people can be understood only in the context of the process of integration that was forced on them by the colonizing process. Religion played an important role in legitimating colonization by expanding the Christian faith and asserting the monopoly of the Christian ideology. Colonizing was Christianizing, and vice versa. The concept of mission carried with it the notion of conquest, of "converting to Christ," the creation of a Christian nation, even if by force.

Role of White Women

The situation of white women was clearly different from that of Indian women. The Jesuits' task of establishing Christian moral principles by setting up Christian marriage-oriented monogamous families needed the cooperation of white women. In Brazil, however, there was no family-based settlement as in the United States and other countries. In Spanish-speaking America, as opposed to Brazil, high-ranking officials came with their families.

Russel-Wood (1977:33) attributed women's situation in colonial Brazil partially to the Portuguese mode of migration:

> The position of the white woman in Portuguese America differed from that of her counterparts in Spanish and English America. This was partly the result of different patterns of migration. Although there was a numerical predominance of males migrating from Spain to the New World, even during the first decade of the 16th century, approximately 10 percent of all licenses granted were to women and wives accompanying their husbands. Although

> extensive miscegenation did occur, Spanish America possessed a larger proportion of white women than did Portuguese America for much of the colonial period. In the case of the English colonies in North America, and once allowances have been made for differing migration patterns between New England and Virginia or the Carolinas, the customary form of colonization was the family unit.

Although colonization began in 1500, white Portuguese women were not sent to the colony until 1549, thus originating the new settlement policy on the one hand, and the Catholic strategy of enforcing the nuclear family as a fulcrum for implementing Christian morals and doctrine, on the other hand. According to Soeiro (1978:175):

> The policies of the Iberian monarchs were formulated in reaction to a complex interplay of social, economic and demographic forces. After an initial period of neglect, the primary concern of the Portuguese sovereign became the settlement and population of the Brazilian colony. From the first half century of its discovery when the Portuguese attention was riveted upon the profitable Asian trade, Brazil was of only secondary interest to the metropolis. Organized efforts to settle the colony date from the arrival in 1549 of the first captain-general, Tome de Souzam, whose company included a spectrum of settlers, among which were farmers, artisans, bureaucrats, churchmen, slaves and some women.

Contemporary missionary documents point to a colonial and religious policy by which women were used as elements of social equilibrium through marriage-induced control of their sexuality. When Norbrega asked the King of Portugal to send women to the colony, he meant those who had difficulty marrying—the poor, orphans, and even prostitutes—*ancorchè siano meretrici* (Beozzo 1984:81). He explained that because there was a dearth of white women and the Portuguese had no wish to marry the Indian women to whom they were linked, there were enough men for all women who might come. Thus, it would be possible to alleviate the problem of cohabitation. Social order would be guaranteed by implementing a rigid moral discipline. There would be "good families" made up of "good rich men" and orphans. Resorting to prostitutes would complete this picture of social order. As Beozzo (1984) suggested in his analysis of Norbrega, the "other men" would have access to the "other women." The Christian family would thus be preserved, thanks to the concurrence of the "best ones."

Therefore, while remaining fundamental elements in the formation of family, white women were inducted into the establishment of Catholicism within the Christian framework. However, although they fulfilled a function as religious teachers and could have become nuns, they were restricted in power. The Church assigned the task of transmitting Christian values and behavior and safeguarding religious worship and practice in these white families not to women, but to slave owners. The master's house, or *casa grande*, was the center of social, economic, and political life and in rural areas, the center of Catholic religious practice. Catechisms, novenas, baptisms, marriages, burials, and the feasts of the patron saints were celebrated in and near the master's house.

The lay nature of colonial Catholicism also centered on the action of men through brotherhoods (*confrarias*). Given that there were not enough priests and the system of *Padroado*—under which the Portuguese sovereignty acquired ecclesiastical jurisdiction in exchange for financing missionary activities—was in force, the development of religious life focused on the *confrarias*. Centered on the cult of given saints, these *confrarias* acquired great social and religious weight in Brazil. In urban areas, they were founded by laymen, and their internal regulations were approved by the king. The *confriarias* took responsibility for promoting piety; organizing religious services; and building churches that they then administered. They also built hospitals, called *Santas Casas de Misericórdia*. Some of them became powerful economically as well as politically. They can be seen as the expression of lay religious power as they gained control over religion through their work.

Confrarias were founded, headed, and managed by men. The only one that is reported to have had both male and female members is the Confraria do Rosario, which consisted of slaves. The Brotherhood of the Holy Sacrament (*Santissimo*) had only male members, since women were not allowed to approach the Holy Sacrament. There were "noble" brotherhoods, such as the Confraria do Carmo, whose members were white farmers, others, like the Confraria de São Francisco, that were made up of mulattos. Hence, the class, gender, and racial composition of these brotherhoods was the expression of social relationships that crossed, limited, and guided religious practice.

The exclusion of women from the Brotherhood of the Holy Sacrament, because of its link to the Eucharist, recalls the image of woman as sullying sacred space. The social effects of this image were the exclusion of women from religious power structures, no matter the color of their skin or social class. The *confrarias* either attributed a secondary role to women or excluded them from membership. They reproduced and legitimatized the inferior social status to which women had been regulated.

Role of Black Women

The formation of a black slave family never entered the Portuguese colonial system. The motherland was interested only in white families who could secure a hegemonic culture and the furthering of Iberian traditions. Referring to female African slaves in the United States, Dill (1987:103) asserted:

> Black women were brought to this country for two economic reasons: to work and to produce workers. Although they were valued for their reproductive function, as were white women settlers, it was only of equal importance with their labor.

The impossibility of forming black families may be ascribed to the very structure of colonial society, which was based on white masters owning extensive property and slaves. Economic requirements led slave owners to hinder or even bar marriages between blacks, thereby guaranteeing their continued ownership of slaves and their "broods" and keeping slaves as assets that could be converted into cash at any time. The family organization would have set limits on the use of slave labor by hindering the separation of family members.

The church deemed that black family units were not instrumental in the implementation of Catholicism throughout the colony. Even so, slave families were carefully kept under the auspices of the Christian family pattern. The Opening Statutes of the Archbishop of Bahia, in 1707, are clear (Venancio 1986:109–110): "According to Divine Right and human right slaves may marry other slaves or freemen, and their master shall neither prohibit marriage nor its use in the expedient time and place." Nevertheless, even religious slave owners did not follow these statutes, which conflicted with their financial interests. Thus, a canon issued by the Franciscan chapter in Imaculada province on March 5, 1859, stated: "Slaves from our convents are prohibited from marrying female slaves owned by laymen or members of another religious brotherhood, as well as freewomen" (quoted in Beozzo 1980:268). Furthermore, marriage fees presented a major barrier to such unions.

The possibility of separating integral "parts," as well as other issues arising from interslave marriages, posed problems for landowners. The question was asked: If a free Negro marries a female slave, does she become free? Or if two "parts" pertaining to different owners marry, to whom do they belong? It was only in 1871 that a law was passed that prohibited the separation of families: "In connection with transmission of slaves, whatever the case may be, separation of spouses or children under the age of twelve (12) years from either of their parents is prohibited, under penalty of annulment" (quoted in Beozzo 1980:267).

Another factor that restricted interslave marriages was the limited number of women compared to men. In the 1720s, for example, Giacomini (1988:25) noted that male slaves outnumbered female slaves by about 4 to 1. Nevertheless, even in regions with similar proportions of women and men, such as the North, the rates of interslave marriages were low. Figures from 1888 (cited in Beozzo 1980:268) show the following rates of married slaves by region: North (Pará and Maranhão), 3.4 percent; Northeast, 8.0 percent; West and South 3.7 percent; and Central South, 15.5 percent.

The slave owners' constant fear of mutiny by the black slaves also seems to have been a factor in their barring marriage by slaves and an encouragement to marriage among whites. Slave owners did everything in their power to avoid the possibility of solidarity among blacks. Since the family unit, as well as the religious rites of African groups, could foster solidarity, slave families and African religious practices were both restricted.

An indicator of the dearth of legally organized families is the rate of "illegitimate" or "natural" offspring. Venâncio (1986:113) observed that in spite of the "clergy's reform, whereby the loyal were indoctrinated and wrong-doers punished, the church in the 18th century failed in stamping out illegitimacy and managed to promote marriage within the free world and to a little extent in the slave world." Because of nonmarital births, it was impossible for slaves to be considered "instruments of evangelism" by the Catholic Church. The spread of Christian faith in the colony left the African population untouched.

As Boxer (1977) saw it, the Inquisition's relative complacency regarding the blacks' sexual transgressions suggested that the slaves' spiritual salvation was deemed difficult and unimportant. Black women especially were excluded from the Catholic framework of "Christian families" wherein they would be depicted as disseminators of moral values and ecclesiastically inspired behaviors. The exploitation of slave women as wet nurses ruled them out from the "noble mission of wives and mothers." The only function that could "save" them from the "sin" of womanhood—motherhood—was denied them. The slave women's babies were born slaves and belonged to the slave owners. They could be sold to other slave owners, which meant they would be separated from their mothers. The slave children were treated as things, as the property of the slave owners, and their relationships with their mothers depended on whether they remained with the same slave owners as their mothers. According to Davis (1983:15–16):

> The cult of motherhood, so popular in the 19th century, did not apply here [to Negro women]. Indeed, in the eyes of slave owners, Negro women were not mothers but, rather, only tools for workforce reproduction. They were only wombs, animals, whose only value lay in their capacity to multiply.

Black women were thought to be only "reproducers" of slaves; they were expected to act as mothers for the children of their *sinhás* (mistresses). Deprived of their own children, their "salvation" depended on their ability to become the "black mothers" of white children. Their incorporation as wet nurses into white families' reproductive cycles assured "the impossibility of a captive population constituting a reproductive entity of its own" (Magalhães and Giacomini 1983:81).

The social exclusion of black women was thus reinforced by their exclusion from Catholicism. That is, in addition to the barriers against their fulfilling the role of motherhood within the framework of a stable monogamous family, black women and half-caste women were forbidden to become nuns or to form racially mixed convents; they entered convents merely as slaves of the religious hierarchy (Azzi and Rezende 1983; Soeiro 1978). Neither as wife-mothers nor religious virgins were black women brought into the fold of Catholicism, but through a particularly contradictory and ambiguous integration.

In conclusion, this argument does not deny the importance of the part played by indigenous, white, and the black women in implementing Catholicism. Rather, it shows that women's social and religious actions were limited and oriented by their subordinated status. On the other hand, their resistance to oppression allowed social relations to be altered in ways that were often favorable to women.

WOMEN'S ROLE IN STRENGTHENING THE CATHOLIC CHURCH IN BRAZIL

Crisis and "Reform" of Catholicism in Brazil

According to church historians, the nineteenth century was a crucial period in the history of Catholicism in Brazil. As was mentioned earlier, the process of Christianization was influenced by the formation of Brazilian society within the framework of proslavery colonialism. The type of Catholicism that the Portuguese introduced combined with a peculiar blend of beliefs from, and religions practiced by, Indians and blacks. To be sure, 300 years of "evangelism" had forged a "Catholic nation." However, early in the nineteenth century, the Catholic Church in Brazil was a debilitated organization; it was disorganized internally, fragile, and losing its political and social power. As a result of three centuries of Padroado, and, in spite of the fact that Catholicism was openly declared to be "the religion of the empire" in the country's first constitution (1824), the church was in profound crisis. Its ties with Rome were thin. In addition, the bureaucratic ecclesiastical apparatus, consisting of bishops and clerics, did not suffice to meet the needs of the Catholic population, which at that time encompassed the entire country.

From the middle of the century on, some bishops made isolated efforts to "put some order" into the Church. But it was not until the republic was proclaimed in 1889, followed by the constitutional separation of church and state, that institutional renewal took place. The reform movement should be understood in the broader framework of the crisis of Catholicism in the nineteenth century, for it was a response to it. It should also be seen as part of the dynamics of change in Brazilian society, including the profound transformations that women were undergoing.

Starting in the eighteenth century, but even more so during the nineteenth century, the Roman Catholic Church engaged in powerful defensive activities to oppose the slow but steady destruction of Christendom; the rise of capitalism; the political emancipation of the modern state; and the implications of these developments, such as the reduction of religion to a private matter. This rejection of the "modern world," which took the form of an "intractable Catholicism" based on the 1864 Syllabus by Pope Pius IX, was more than a passive condemnation. The attempt by liberals to reduce Catholicism to "just another cult," a merely "spiritual" entity, and to limit the Church to purely ecclesiastical functions, led the Church to mobilize its followers, especially women, to serve the "grand design for the restoration of humanity upon a Christian basis, the performance of which is detailed and guided by the pontifical encyclicals" (Poulat 1980: 290). In Brazil, the conflict between state and church, at this time, (1872–75) was known as *the religious affair*. Culminating in the imprisonment of two bishops, this extremely bitter conflict demonstrated the antagonism between the liberal state, which was attempting to free itself from the Church, and the Church, which was bent on maintaining its domination over the state.

Late in the nineteenth century, the Catholic Church reversed the process of institutional degeneration, and by 1930, it had remarkable political and social power. The education of youths was in the hands of the Church through a large network of confessional schools. Hospitals (the *Santas Casas de Misericordia*), orphanages, and other "charitable institutions" allowed the Church to reinsert itself into society to such an extent that it was able to confront the state, asserting that the real nation is the Catholic people. Only a state that is "faithful to the church" can legitimately represent this Catholic nation (Mainwaring 1986).

For institutional reform and affirmation to be successful, the "clericalization" process was fundamental. The colonial age had been characterized by derth of clergymen and religious action dominated by lay whites via brotherhoods. To rectify this situation, the Church began to emphasize the training of clergymen, thus broadening their scope of influence and reducing the power of lay brotherhoods. In this regard, greater emphasis was placed on sacramental rituals for which priests were indispensable; popular creeds were discouraged and most contemporary religious practices were dismissed as superstitious.

The "Feminization" of Brazilian Catholicism

During the nineteenth century and the beginning of the twentieth century, huge transformations occurred in all spheres in Brazil. On the political front, Brazil became the center of the Portuguese Empire in 1808, gained its independence in 1822, and became a republic in 1889. In 1888, by decree Princess Isabel abolished slavery. Socioeconomically, slavery gave way to free labor. Along with increasing industrialization, urbanization expanded. Women were differentially affected by these changes, depending on their race and class. Black women began to be compensated for their labor. Black and poor white women became workers in the fledgling textile industry. Upper-class white women were allowed to receive a formal education, participated in the abolitionist struggles, won the right to vote; started a feminist movement that promoted the emancipation of women, and developed an important female press. Indian women were marginalized in the process of these changes. The changes that Brazilian society experienced throughout this period, supported by new laws, affected the family unit in particular, as well as the institutions that were responsible for social improvement, especially education and health care.

In the midst of the social turmoil in women's lives during this period, the conservative ecclesiastical project that was designed to include women in the reform of the Catholic Church became comparatively successful. From the Church's viewpoint, this success was rooted in a certain social process that had powerful consequences for women, namely, the establishment of urban nuclear families and the ideology of the "housebound dedicated mother" and "loyal wife" (Costa 1979). The extended family, the self-sufficient *casa grande* of colonial times, became more restricted, and the house became smaller, bringing family members into the "intimacy" of the home. Family relationships with the outside world began to change as people gained the ability to acquire products and services, hitherto provided within the confines of the home, in the marketplace. According to Costa (1979:141), "From a large socioeconomic body, the family [turned] into a cell within society." He also noted that family submission to medical hygiene precepts was an important mechanism in the setting up of urban nuclear families and the recognition of women, wives and mothers in Brazil. By using medical precepts, the state established the "hygienic" nuclear family." In the nuclear family a woman was confined to the home because of her love for her children and her dedication to her family, and the colonial patriarch became the new "father." Marriage was no longer the result of a parental agreement, but, rather, a "choice" to be made by passionate youths. The education of girls to be housewives and mothers and the regulations governing it were part of this process. And through Catholic schools, the Church played a key role in this process.

From a review of labor legislation and legal discourse on the family in Brazil during this period one can identify the sociohistorical path the state took to ratify the nuclear family and the place of women in the society. Under pretext that their chief function was to bear and raise children, upper-class women were "protected" from entering the labor force.

In this social and ecclesiastical context, women were mobilized to sustain institutional reform. For the first time in its history, the Brazilian Church developed an activity directly aimed at its female constituency; it incorporated women into the reform project. One of the main features of this project was the organization of clergy and laity according to the disciplinary recommendations of the Council of Trent. The clergy's compliance with the demand for celibacy and the laity's strict obedience to the hierarchy were parts of the "new mode of living faith." Thus, the Church included women in its reform project in an attempt to decrease or eliminate the power of male lay brotherhoods by clericalizing the institution. The "feminization" of Brazilian Catholicism was not intended to allow women to exercise sacred power; rather, it was a reinforcement of their subordinate status. "The church does not transform the female decree but, rather, supports it based on qualities traditionally recognized as pertaining to womanhood, as well as the functions ascribed to it" (Segalen 1980:53).

Three aspects of this reform are worth emphasizing because of their effect on the situation of women in the Catholic Church. First, to reduce the power of the lay brotherhoods and Third Orders (which were influenced by Freemasonry), the bishops founded associations of women for pious activities that were controlled by the hierarchy. In these religious movements, the emphasis was on receiving the sacraments, performing "intimate and sentimental" devotional practices, and engaging in "individual sanctification" (cf. Fayet-Scribe 1990; Segalen 1980).

Second, nighttime liturgical services, held during nonworking hours, were gradually eliminated and daytime services were substituted, making it more difficult for men to attend them and increasing the presence of women. For the most part, these women were housewives from the middle and upper classes, since during the daytime women from the lower class worked in textile mills, as street peddlers, or in housebound activities. Women became the majority in Catholic religious services and devotional practices at this time.

Finally, the Church invested in women's education by establishing a large network of Catholic girls' schools. One of the main goals of the reform was to promote Catholic influence through the educational system. Of all of the Church's initiatives at that time, this one had the greatest effect on women. In a country where the state was unable to serve the population's primary needs, the Church's educational work was fundamental in the development of women's access to formal education. For this purpose, another group was mobilized—foreign nuns. Many women, as well as men, came to Brazil to carry out the "mission" in schools and hospitals and to engage in other worthwhile activities.

Women's support of the Church's reforms was ironic. Azzi (1984:101) concluded that "*In spite of* [emphasis added] the fact that the reform had been established for the benefit of women, the church's attitude towards the female gender continued to be very restrictive." Indeed, this "restrictive" attitude toward women was the very reason why the Church managed to get them to join its efforts at institutional reform. In this regard, the mobilization of women was a sign not of a change in women's status in the Church but, rather, of women's subordination.

Any evaluation of the effects of the reform process on women must stress that until the beginning of the twentieth century, the Catholic Church was strongly against sudden social changes arising from the increasingly fast urbanization process and the gradual rise of the middle class. At the heart of its ecclesiastical stance lay an uncompromising defense of the need to preserve the family and women's status. The Church was fiercely against divorce and insisted on the observation of sexual moral rules, particularly by women. According to Azzi (1987:94–95), the ecclesiastical hierarchy, insisting on family ethics and sexual tradition,

> actually wished to build a dike to oppose sociocultural changes within the country, changes that clergymen thought would bring with them social disorder and anarchy. . . . Hence the keeping of the family within a conservative framework must comprise part of the church's overall efforts in preventing any changes whatsoever from happening in Brazil's contemporary social order.

In sum, three particularly significant initiatives that the Church undertook—the elimination of evening services, the creation of female religious associations, and the establishment of girls' schools—were designed to apply directly to its followers. All these initiatives were highly ambiguous. On the one hand, they promulgated female social cliques and women's access to formal education, but on the other hand, they left no room for free expression outside the confines of the ecclesiastical institution or the family. The "pious woman" was valued because she had become an important tool in institutional reform. Her household role as helper and her social recognition as mother and "home" keeper were reinforced by the education she received in religious schools and by speeches and practices developed in female associations. Ecclesiastical control over these sectors limited, to a great extent, the possibility that they would promote the development of female autonomy.

In connection with religious worship at that time, and of which women were the main promoters, the figure of the Virgin Mary played a central part. Both virgin and mother, Mary portrayed an extreme ambiguity that produced intense effects on women. By raising virginity to a cult status, the Church sought to control female sexuality, and by imposing restrictions on women, it intended to moralize their sexual behavior.

Nevertheless, to a certain extent, the Catholic Church's new practices were to women's advantage. First, religious schools were nearly the only means by which upper- and middle-class girls could have access to education, both in the cities and rural areas. The expansion of the Church's vast scholastic network ensured the elevation of the cultural levels of a large portion of the Brazilian female population. Second, access to a formal education played an important role in the move toward female social emancipation. Third, the Catholic Church created "spaces of female sociability" that were especially important in Brazil at that time, since it was difficult for women to gain access to other social arenas—the professions, politics, and the arts. And finally, the founding of charitable institutions for the sick, children, and the elderly provided many women with opportunities to broaden the scope of their activities.

CONCLUSIONS

The establishment of Roman Catholicism in Brazil in the colonial period and the institutional growth of the Church, from the nineteenth century onward, had the family as their main foundation. Both in its discourse and in its ministry, the Catholic Church always manifested a particular concern with maintaining the structure of the family. The "Christian home" was considered to be the first realm in which the Catholic faith should be kept and spread, as well as where the strict norms of sexual ethics should be preserved. Defending a family model according to Catholic precepts, the Church aimed its discourse and ministry mainly at women.

Catholic women, however, were not passive in this sociohistorical process. They responded to the Church's actions by accepting or refusing them, reformulating them and changing their meaning. As is known, the effects of social practices often escape the control of those who promote them, so the consequences of these practices are sometimes contrary to what their contrivers expected them to be. The responses by women to the Church's doctrinal principles and moral precepts varied widely—from full acceptance to total rejection, including covert and overt transgression, seeming acquiescence, and "disgraceful" behavior. Therefore, the Church's actions toward women were not those of an all-powerful and homogeneous institution affecting passive, inert subjects. Some women have always struggled and rebelled against the abusive power that the Church exercised over them, their bodies, their children, and their lives.

Women's history in Catholicism is one of struggles, power relationships, domination and insubordination, expropriation and reappropriation, prohibition and transgression, imposition and subversion. This does not mean that the Church completely failed to establish order and control over its followers, especially women. But the rearrangement of Church affairs was a contradictory and complex process, whereby social players fought one another and challenged each other's power. Women's mobilization in the twentieth century demonstrated this fact once again.

In two mobilizations in Brazil in the past thirty-five years, women were exhorted to take specific actions on certain social and ecclesiastical projects. In 1964, the right wing of the Catholic Church invited Catholic women to participate in the movement, to support the military coup; to march for God, nation, and family; and to fulfill their moral and divine obligations to the nation as mothers (Simões 1985). In the 1970s during the establishment of the "Church of the poor" and Ecclesiastical Base Communities (CEBs), the Church mobilized a large number of nuns and poor laywomen to form religious communities in poor urban and rural areas (Rosado Nunes 1991). These two mobilizations were different not only in the groups of women who were engaged in them, but in their politico-ideological motives and the ecclesiastical projects that inspired them. Nevertheless, they shared one thing in common: a powerful ideological appeal that engaged women in a process whose purpose escaped them. The women were "invited" to make the projects their own, and they did.

The ideological appeal is not limited to the Church's manipulation of women; social relationships are at stake. Women contribute a great deal of themselves—their work, their thinking, their feelings, their time, their lives—to these projects that are devised by others. But they also change the projects through their participation. Their investments in these movements, in which they were invited to participate, give rise to unexpected effects, displacements, and rearrangements in the relationships among the social players. And, what is surprising to those who promote women's action, women establish new objectives and promote discussions of their own problems as women to fight for their own freedom. Such is the case with the CEBs, for example.

Certain practices developed by the CEBs and the reinterpretations of the traditional theological discourse are leading women to seek self-sufficiency in both action and thinking, goals the Church must restrict because its continued existence depends on its ability to maintain control over its followers. These contradictions are catalysts for women's awareness that their subordination is both religious and social.

Current dynamics deserve much more critical attention than can be given here. Nevertheless, it is evident that the pattern of ironic contradictions that was described for the pre-twentieth-century Brazilian Church continues to be evident in Brazilian society today.

References

Azzi, Riolando. 1979. "A Instituição Eclesiástica Duranti a Primeira Época Colonial." Pp. 155–242 in *História Geral da Igreja na América Latina. Tomo II: História da Igreja no Brasil, Primeira Época*, edited by E. Hoornaert, R. Azzi, K. Van Der Grijp, and B. Brod. Petrópolis, Brazil: Vozes.

———. 1984. "A participação da Mulher na Vida da Igreja do Brasil (1870–1920)." Pp. 94–123 in *A Mulher Pobre na História da Igreja Latino-Americana*, edited by Maria Luiza Marcílio. Sao Paulo, Brazil: Loyola.

———. 1987. "Família e Valores no Pensamento Brasileiro (1870–1950): Um Enfoque Histórico." Pp. 85–120 in *Sociedade Brasileira Contemporânea: Família e Valores*, edited by I. Ribeiro. Sao Paulo, Brazil: Loyola.

Azzi, R., and M. Valéria V. Rezende. 1983. "A Vida Religiosa Feminina no Brasil Colonial." Pp. 24–60 in *A Vida Religiosa no Brasil: Enfoques Históricos*, edited by Riolando Azzi. Sao Paulo, Brazil: Paulinas/CEHILA.

Beozzo, José Oscar. 1980. "A Igreja e a Escravidão (1875–1888)." Pp. 257–95 in *História Geral da Igreja na América Latina. Tomo II: História da Igreja no Brasil, Segunda Época*, edited by J. F. Hauck, H. Fragoso, J. O. Beozzo, K. Van Der Grijp, and B. Brod. Petrópolis, Brazil: Vozes.

———. 1984. "A Mulher Indígena e a Igreja na Situação Escravista do Brasil Colonial." Pp. 70–93 in *A Mulher pobre na História da Igreja Latino-Americana*, edited by Maria Luiza Marcílio. Sao Paulo, Brazil: Loyola.

Boxer, C. R. 1977. *A Mulher na Expansão Ultramarina Ibérica (1415–1815): Alguns Factos, Idéias e Personalidades*. Lisbon: Horizonte.

Burkett, Elinor C. 1978. "Indian Women and White Society: The Case of Sixteenth-Century Peru." Pp. 101–28 in *Latin American Women Historical Perspectives*, edited by A. Lavrin. Westport, CT: Greenwood Press.

Costa, Jurandir Freire. 1979. *Ordem Médica e Norma Familiar*. Rio de Janeiro: Graal.

Davis, Angela. 1983. *Femmes, Race et Classe* [Women, Race, and Class]. Translated by Dominique Taffin et le Collectif Des Femmes. Paris: Des Femmes.

Dill, B. T. 1987. "The Dialectics of Black Womanhood." Pp. 97–108 in *Social Science Issues*, edited by S. Harding. Bloomington: Indiana University Press.

Fayet-Scribe, Sylvie. 1990. *Associations Féminines et Catholicisme—De la Charité à L'Action Sociale—XIXe-XXe siécle*. Paris: Les Editions Ouvrières.

Gallager, Ann Miriam. 1978. "The Indian Nuns of Mexico City's Monaterio of Corpus Christi, 1724–1821." Pp. 150–72 in *Latin American Women Historical Perspectives*, edited by A. Lavrin. Westport, CT: Greenwood Press.

Giacomini, Sonia Maria. 1988. *Mulher e Escrava: Uma Introdução Histórica ao Estudo da Mulher Negra no Brasil*. Petrópolis, Brazil: Vozes.

Hoornaert, E., R. Azzi, K. Van Der Grijp, and B. Brod, eds. 1979. *História Geral da Igreja na América Latina. Tomo II: História da Igreja no Brasil, Primeira Época*. Petrópolis, Brazil: Vozes.

Magalhães, Elisabeth K. C., and Sônia Maria Giacomini. 1983. "A Escrava Ama-de-Leite: Anjo ou Demônio?" Pp. 73–78 in *Mulher Mulheres*, edited by C. Barroso and A. O. Costa. Sao Paulo, Brazil: Cortez/Fund. Carlos Chagos.

Mainwaring, Scott. 1986. *The Catholic Church and Politics in Brazil* (1916–1985). Stanford, CA: Stanford University Press.

Marcílio, Maria Luiza, ed. 1984. *A Mulher Pobre na História da Igreja Latino-americana*. Sao Paulo, Brazil: Paulinas.

———. 1993. *Família, Mulher, Sexualidade e Igreja na História do Brasil*. Sao Paulo, Brazil: Loyola.

Poulat, Emile. 1980. *Une Eglise Ebranlée: Changement, Conflit et Continuité de Pie XII à Jean Paul II*. Paris: Casterman.

Rosado Nunes, Maria José Fontelas. 1991. "Eglise, Sexe et Pouvoir, Les Femmes Dans le Catholicisme au Brésil: Le Cas des Communautes Ecclésiales de Base." Ph.D. dissertation, Ecole des Hautes Etudes en Sciences Sociales, Paris.

Russel-Wood, A. J. R. 1977. "Women and Society in Colonial Brazil". *Journal of Latin American Studies* 9:1–34.

Segalen, Martine. 1980. "Sociabilité Feminine Villageoise et Attitude, de l'Eglise—Associations de Jeunes Filles au XIXe Siècle." Pp. 46–62 in *Oppression des Femmes et Religion*, edited by D. Hervieu-Leger (Colloque de l'Association Française de Sociologie Religieuse. Paris: CNRS, Ronéo.

Simões, Solange de Deus. 1985. *Deus, Pátria e Família—As Mulheres no Golpe de 1964*. Petrópolis, Brazil: Vozes.

Soeiro, Susan. 1978. "The Feminine Orders in Colonial Bahia, Brazil: Economics, Social and Demographic Implications, 1677–1800." Pp. 173–97 in *Latin American Women Historical Perspectives*, edited by A. Lavrin. Westport, CT: Greenwood Press.

Venâncio, R. P. 1986. "Nos Limites da Sagrada Família: Ilegitimidade e Casamento no Brasil Colônia." Pp. 107–23 in *História e Sexualidade no Brasil*, edited by Ronaldo Vainfas. Rio de Janeiro: Graal.

CHAPTER FIFTEEN

Converted Women Redefining Their Family Roles in Mexico

PATRICIA FORTUNY LORET DE MOLA

INTRODUCTION

There is a competition for members between Protestants and Catholics in Latin America. Protestantism is gaining more and more converts, primarily because of its relatively greater emphasis on rules than Catholicism. These rules structure a pattern of ascetism that involves the prohibition of activities related to the flesh as opposed to the spirit. What is forbidden varies from one church to another, but all Protestant churches in Latin America call for the abandonment of drinking, smoking, and extramarital sex. Pentecostal churches extend the asceticism to prohibit such activities as dancing and attending movies and plays and impose dress restrictions on women. Asceticism is the common element in the Protestant churches discussed in this chapter, but it is not limited to Protestantism; Mexican Spiritualists (Finkler 1983) have similar ascetic rules, as do people in Catholic Christian Base Communities (CCBCs) and the charismatic movement. The fact that traditional and official Catholicism both lack these types of restrictions is, in the eyes of Protestants, their major failure.

In Spanish-speaking Latin America, the term *Protestantism* has a specific meaning that differs somewhat from its use among English-speaking people. In particular, it includes Mormons and Jehovah's Witnesses, as well as less ascetic groups, such as Episcopalians, Lutherans, Methodists, and Presbyterians, that are usually called Protestants by English speakers (Martin 1990).[1] The latter groups, known as "historic" churches, have not experienced large-scale conversions comparable to the other Protestant groups. The Spanish term, *evangelico*, which roughly parallels the English term, Evangelical, excludes Mormons (members of the Church of Jesus Christ of Latter-Day Saints, or LDS), and Jehovah's Witnesses. For convenience, the term *Protestant* is used in this chapter to refer to Evangelical Protestants plus Mormons and Jehovah's Witnesses. The assertion that Protestantism is ascetic should be understood as applying to this special category of believers.

The predominant form of religion in the two Mexican cities included in the study presented here, Guadalajara and Mérida, is popular Catholicism, rather than official or institutional Catholicism, which is controlled by the clergy. Popular Catholicism refers to certain practices and beliefs, as well as to the social class that reproduces them (Isambert, cited in Kselman 1986:25). The form that prevails in the two cities that were studied consists of collective rituals, such as processions, novenas, rosaries, festivals of patron saints, and beliefs in miracles by the saints and virgins. Popular Catholics do not need the clergy for many of their activities; for example, laypeople organize novenas in their own homes and need only the images of the virgins or saints for which the novenas are being performed (Fortuny 1989).

Popular Catholicism has never forbidden smoking or drinking and has overlooked infidelity, all of which are widespread in Mexico, although, theoretically, infidelity is not allowed. Among Catholic men, it is very common to gather after work with friends, neighbors, relatives or co-godparents for drinking sessions. These drinking sessions have a serious effect on the standard of living of low-income families. Popular Catholicism is very flexible concerning such behavior and control over the everyday lives of Catholics, both believers and priests. It imposes only vague rules on the laity to orient them toward "living in the right way" (Rodrigues Brandao 1989:75–76). In fact, the sacrament of confession permits Catholics to break most of the Ten Commandments—except murder, which is a cardinal sin—and later receive pardon, as long as they repent for their sins. The institutionalized Catholic Church differs markedly from popular Catholicism in that it takes a hard-line stance against such practices as nonprocreative sex, abortion, homosexuality, and divorce.

The ascetic aspect of Protestantism has important implications for family life. Asceticism by the head of the family brings about not only material advantages but higher-quality relationships in the family. Protestant women appreciate that there is an organization other than Alcoholics Anonymous that can help them reform their husbands and recover income that would otherwise be invested in vices, such as drinking and extra-marital sex. They say they do not have to worry about their husbands because they know their husbands will return home after work and will not spend their salaries in bars or on other women.

This chapter compares the female members of three churches: Pentecostal, Jehovah's Witnesseses, and Mormon. In addition, since Mexico is a dominant Catholic culture, it contrasts Catholics with Protestants to illustrate the changes people experience when they convert from the dominant faith to Protestantism. In Mexico, most converts to the Pentecostal religion come from the lower classes, whereas among Mormons and Jehovah's Witnesses, there are converts from both the lower and the middle classes.[2] Several case studies are presented to indicate the consequences of conversion for family life. I show that, regardless of the denomination, Protestant churches—although they are not unique in this respect—offer middle- and lower-class women a privileged social space for developing personally and socially. As a result of the changes that female converts undergo, there is a redefinition of gender roles that affects their relationships with their husbands and children within, and sometimes even beyond, the domestic sphere.

Converted women feel stronger than they felt before conversion because they have the support of their congregations. Husbands, whether converted or not, try to comply with the norms of the churches because they know that the congregations will learn of their faults. To reinforce husbands' responsibilities to their wives and children, as well as mothers' role in raising their children, religious literature on the themes of parenthood is distributed to the members and those themes are frequently covered in Bible study meetings and sermons.

I analyze women and religion from two related perspectives. First, I focus on religious organizations, which at times apply contradictory policies with respect to women, permitting them to have some roles and discouraging them from taking on others. Second, I consider women's position in the family after they convert. It seems that converted women revalorize themselves through the positions, responsibilities or charismatic spiritual gifts they acquire from their participation in their congregations. The acquisition of a more positive identity permits them to relate to the men of their families in a more egalitarian way and to intervene more directly in the family decision-making process, including how the family's money is to be spent. The women also become more independent in making decisions about their own activities—for example, whether to attend services or Bible study meetings—as well as those of their children. It must be pointed out that this phenomenon is not unique to Protestant churches, since women in CCBCs[3] and the Renovación del Espíritu Santo, or charismatic Catholicism,[4] also have broad opportunities to develop themselves.

The results presented here are based on fieldwork carried out between 1988 and 1991 in Mérida and Guadalajara. In 1988, I studied two neighborhoods in Mérida; in neighborhood **A,** there were five Protestant churches and one church of popular Catholics; in neighborhood **B,** there were seven Protestant Churches and three types of Catholicism: popular, official, and syncretic, the latter incorporating Mayan elements. In 1989, I studied another neighborhood in Guadalajara, which had three Protestant churches, a community of Jesuits, CCBCs, and popular Catholicism. In 1990–91, I also investigated the Luz del Mundo Church—a Mexican Pentecostal Church that creates exclusive neighborhoods in which the members live, work, and pray—in its Guadalajara headquarters, the Hermosa Provincia *colonia* (neighborhood). I conducted in-depth interviews with several members of each church and with Catholics in each neighborhood, with the intent of constructing the informants' life histories and conversion process. I also conducted additional interviews, not all of them in-depth, with 18 Jehovah's Witnesses, 20 Pentecostals, 15 Mormons, and 18 Catholics. Finally, I attended some 40 religious services and other religious events to meet potential informants, to observe the rituals and believers, and to listen to the institutional discourse.

Although this chapter draws on the research just described, it is not simply a report of that research. Rather, I attempt to portray converted women's own interpretations of the adaptations they make in the religious sphere and the consequences of these adaptations for family life. Focusing on detailed portraits of four selected women informants to provide the authentic voice of female Protestant converts from Catholicism, I draw qualitative insights from the interviews and observations. My focal cases are married women aged 28 to 45 with children at home. Before their conversion to Protestantism, they were all Catholics; that is, they were born into Catholic families and practiced popular Catholicism. The important differences among them stem from their educational backgrounds and economic positions. Though not statistically representative of all converted women, these women's experiences exemplify the changes in everyday life that come from converting to a new religious faith in Mexico. The women's stories give a human face to the profound religious realignments that are occurring in Latin America today (cf. Martin 1990).

The remainder of this chapter is organized into four parts. In the first part, I discuss three studies, conducted in Colombia, Brazil, and Mexico, on the relationships among religion, family, and gender, that informed my research. In the second part, I describe the emergence of religious minorities in Mexico and point out the social and political position they occupy in society. In the third part, I analyze the four case studies, and in the fourth part, I discuss the patriarchal structures in Catholicism and Protestantism and their implications for women.

EARLIER STUDIES

Most studies of Protestantism in Latin America have found that these churches aid women's spiritual, psychological, and social development (Brusco 1986; Burdick 1990; Fortuny 1989; Fortuny and De la Torre 1991; Gill 1990; Kamsteeg 1990; Martin 1990; Rose 1987; Rostas 1993; Van den Hoogen 1990). The emphasis of some of the more recent studies (Brusco 1986; Burdick 1990; Rostas 1993) has been on changes that take place in women as a result of their participation in religious organizations and on the transformations which occur in gender relationships. These studies merit close attention, since they are important precursors to the present work.

Brusco (1986) focused on Evangelical churches in Colombia, including both Pentecostal and mainstream institutions like the Lutheran Church. Her main concern was to demonstrate that evangelicalism "has the power to change men to conform with female ideals and aspirations" (p. 130). She asserted that in a preeminently *machista* society like Colombia, evangelical religions fulfill the pragmatic function of "reforming gender roles"—changing conjugal relationships to improve the family's quality of life. Evangelical women reform male values, specifically machismo: "a public role [that] does not define how a man is to act as a husband or father. Machismo contributes to a man's lack of involvement in his roles as husband and father" (Brusco 1986:154). Machista behavior includes drinking, gambling, swearing, fighting, and womanizing, primarily outside the family. Evangelical women reorient male values, bringing them more in line with female values; that is, they make family values more important than the macho's individualist consumption. Protestantism does not attempt to reorder the public sphere (such as demanding equal wages for women and men); instead, it focuses on the private sphere as centered on the family. The changes stem from a reordering of male and female participation in household tasks. In an evangelical family, "The husband's aspirations change to coincide with those of his wife . . . the way he disposes of his income and his concerns regarding his family will probably be consistent with his wife's desires" (Brusco 1986:198). Thus, the Protestant family's quality of life improves not exactly because of higher income, but because of changes in consumption patterns; what the husband previously spent in the street, the bar, or the brothel is now invested in better education, food, and housing for all family members.

Burdick (1990) compared married women's experiences with three religious organizations in urban Brazil—the CCBCs, Pentecostalism, and Afro-Brazilian Umbanda. He found that the women of Sao Jorge (on the outskirts of Rio de Janeiro), all rural migrants, thought that their lives were better in the countryside. The new urban environment increased their domestic difficulties; they complained of "the threat to male authority represented by unemployment and the heightened competition for expenditure in the male prestige sphere on the one hand and children's education and the insecure urban household on the other" (p. 156). The loss of control over children was due to the conditions in the urban environment and the high frequency of household quarrels.

To resolve these domestic problems, the women preferred to consult a Pentecostal minister or a spirit medium, rather than go to a CCBC. According to various members of the CCBCs, these groups do not help resolve personal problems; they focus only on study of the Gospel. Members are generally neighbors and fear that confessing their personal problems will result in neighborhood gossip. Furthermore, couples believe that the priests are ignorant of everything relevant to married life and do not trust the priests' judgments in this regard. Pentecostalism and Umbanda cults manage and solve domestic problems more efficiently. Pentecostalism makes the devil responsible for all problems, whereas Umbanda cults blame various spirits. Hence, both options eliminate self-blame and offer a clear and simple way to address problems by eliminating evil spirits and attracting good ones. Burdick (1990) presented numerous accounts of how Pentecostalism and Umbanda helped women members of the three groups solve their domestic problems and improve their lives.

Rostas (1993) studied the Tzeltal Indian community of Tenejapa, Chiapas, Mexico. In most villages and towns in Chiapas, there are more than six small, mainly Protestant, congregations, as well as Jehovah's Witnesses and

Seventh Day Adventists. Rostas contended that Latin American societies, particularly indigenous societies, have experienced great ecological, economic, political, and cultural changes. Women are affected more by these changes, but are usually less able to respond because their activities have been restricted. For example, many more Tzeltal men than women speak Spanish, and the men get involved in new activities outside the community while the women do not. In the past, women shared a lot of agricultural work with their husbands, but today, with indigenous traditions breaking down, it is principally women who suffer from rural anomie. In this difficult new environment, women "find a source of empowerment in the new religions' social space" (p. 4) that enables them to validate their sense of self and to act.

In contrast to the works just reviewed, my study included Mormons and Jehovah's Witnesses. Scholarly work on Latin American countries has tended to pay little attention to these two religious groups, focusing mainly on Pentecostals and, to a lesser degree, other evangelicals. Assessing the gender-religion relationship among Mormons and Jehovah's Witnesses provided insights with which I could evaluate theoretical proposals concerning the potential of Anglo-Saxon Protestantism to remodel gender relations in Hispanic Latin America. In the next section, I describe the arrival of Protestant religions in Mexico, pointing to their political and social position within Mexican society, and discuss the dominant position of Catholicism as an important contextual factor in conversion to a Protestant group in Mexico.

RELIGIOUS MILIEU IN MEXICO

For more than four centuries, religions in Mexico were limited to Catholicism and pre-Hispanic traditions. The first Protestants came to Mexico at the end of the nineteenth century, but it was not until about 1950 that they began to gain importance. The political and social power of the Catholic Church, albeit diminished, continues to exercise considerable influence on Mexican society—a situation that has direct repercussions on other churches, which are labeled "second-class religions," and on their practitioners, who are labeled "second-class Mexicans" (Monsiváis 1991). Although Catholicism in Mexico includes all social classes, in return for economic support, the Church gives economic and political elites favorable treatment and overlooks their non-Christian lifestyles. This special treatment of the upper classes is one reason why the lower classes have embraced the new Protestant faiths.

In Mexico, Catholicism is not only the religion of the majority, but permeates cultural and even some national values. The relationship between the Mexican government and the Catholic Church is characterized by both natural understanding and rivalry, since both are trying to control civil society. This ambivalent relationship makes the political position of new religious movements unpredictable because their status is determined, to some degree, by the relationship between the Catholic Church and the government. In other words, religious pluralism in Mexico, although present in political rhetoric and in recent Constitutional law, is barely accepted in practice. The secularist weak state has been in constant confrontation with the strong Catholic Church, and that struggle is reflected in the entire society.

Pentecostalism arrived in Mexico in the 1920s and 1930s when U.S. and Canadian missionaries from the Fundamentalist movement first became active (Bastian 1983; Meyer 1989). At about the same time, among the poor Mexicans returning from the United States after the Mexican Revolution (1910–20) were converts to Pentecostalism who also started preaching the new gospel. Since the 1950s, these churches have grown in number in both rural and urban areas, although the increase has been greater in the large cities, since more and more rural people have moved to the cities to find jobs. The increase in Pentecostals has been such that, by the 1980s, they represented 70 percent of all Mexican Protestants. The majority of Pentecostal converts are working class, but some members have become middle- and upper-middle class since the 1970s. Particularly in large cities, such as Mexico City, Monterrey, and Guadalajara, predominantly middle-class Pentecostal Churches have emerged. For example, a survey of three northern Mexican cities (Casillas 1989:194) revealed that the Pentecostal Iglesia de Dios del Evangelio Completo (Church of the Full Gospel) had 45.5 percent low-income members, 54.5 percent middle-income members, and no high-income members. One way of explaining this upward social mobility among Pentecostals and most Protestants is the Protestant work ethic (Hollenweger 1991; Martin 1990).

Mormons arrived in Mexico in the nineteenth century, but it took them a long time to gain a foothold because of cultural clashes and political instability. They started to develop congregations in the 1930s, but it was difficult for them to proselytize at first because most missionaries were Americans and did not speak Spanish. However, since then, the LDS has been successful; in 1985, 25 percent of the total Latin American members were in Mexico (Tullis 1987:xiii). The relationship of the Mormon community with governmental officials is one of mutual understanding. According to a survey, (Casillas 1989), 22.7 percent of the Mormons in Mexico have high incomes, 36.4 percent have middle incomes, and 40.9 percent have low incomes. The work ethic is strong among Mormons, and they are frequently upwardly mobile. At present, men hold almost all principal administrative and religious posts in the Mexican LDS Church, which generally require university degrees.

The Jehovah's Witnesses arrived in Mexico in 1893 (Barret 1982:488 cited in Tullis 1987:44), but their number did not start to increase significantly until the 1950s. Mexico now has the second-highest number of Jehovah's Witnesses in Latin America, after Brazil. In 1993, Mexican Witnesses numbered around 300,000, or 8.5 percent of all Witnesses in the world. During the past two decades, they have expanded throughout the country, and many members are professionals. Unlike the LDS Church, the Watch Tower Society of Mexico endures a difficult relationship with the Mexican government and is sharply criticized by the society for its doctrinal attitude toward national symbols. Of the Jehovah's Witnesses in Mexico, 5.6 percent have high incomes, 47.9 percent have middle incomes, and 46.7 percent have low incomes (Casillas 1989).

The focus of this chapter is on the transformation of gender relations through women's conversion to Protestantism. As was noted earlier, all the women were Catholics before they converted. For this reason, it is relevant to explain briefly how Catholicism is practiced in Mexico.

Being Catholic in Mexico, as well as in other Latin American countries, means that individuals are believers and describe themselves as Catholics. However, identifying oneself as Catholic does not necessarily imply commitment to the Church, participation in ecclesiastical activities, or attendance at rituals, except on special occasions to celebrate rites of passage like weddings, baptisms, or first communions. Catholics who comply with all the precepts and are regularly involved in religious activities are a minority. If one takes Arizpe's (1989) findings for the state of Michoacán in western Mexico, which has the highest percentage of Catholics in the country (more than 94 percent) as an index for all Mexico, a third of the peasants interviewed stated that they never attended mass, not because they were not believers, but because of the lack of priests in rural areas. The study also revealed the predominance of women in religious activities in that 57 percent of the women but only 32 percent of the men attended mass every Sunday. Furthermore, 100 percent of the bourgeoisie, 56 percent of the petit-bourgeoisie, 61 percent of the workers, 37 percent of the temporary day workers, and 33 percent of the peasants attended mass regularly (Arizpe 1989:130). The degree of participation in the liturgy of the mass varied according to the classes' closeness with the ecclesiastical authorities. The upper classes (bourgeoisie and petit-bourgeoisie) link themselves with official Catholicism through the clergy, whereas other social classes, especially the lower classes, practice popular Catholicism, which is not necessarily mediated by the clergy. The lower classes participate less in institutional sacraments and more in private devotion to the saints and virgins.

CASE STUDIES

The following four accounts of conversion represent the complex interaction between belief and personal history. In the converts' stories, the new religious ideology contributes a different referential framework from the one that existed before conversion. Hence, in the narratives, the past is reinterpreted in light of the new doctrine.

Pentecostalism

The first two case studies are of Pentecostal women. In Pentecostalism, the "gifts of the Spirit" occupy a central place, but, practices vary in intensity, from controlled emotionality to apparently unlimited ecstasy (Droogers 1990:3). Hollenweger (1991:1) characterized Pentecostalism by its

> orality of liturgy, narrativity of theology and witness, maximum participation at the levels of reflection, prayer and decision-making and therefore a reconciliatory form of community; inclusion of dreams and visions into personal and public forms of worship; an understanding of the body-mind relationship which is informed by experiences of correspondence between body and mind.

Pentecostals produce their own theologies, liturgies, and ethics, which are usually expressed in songs, prayers, and collective biographies and rarely in documents. Pentecostal churches are able to incorporate local traditions and values, such as patriotism, into their religious interpretations, which makes them syncretic religious movements.

In Mexico, Pentecostal congregations in rural areas and marginal urban neighborhoods are usually small (20 to 60 members), and the members know each other and form a close-knit community. The social distance between the leader and the members is negligible, which allows believers to feel a high degree of closeness to and confidence in the leader. All members participate in the service through singing; praying; reading the Bible; giving testimonies; and recounting their dreams, visions, or revelations. Speaking in tongues (receiving the Holy Spirit) is a psychological, as well as a physical, comfort, that brings the converts social prestige in the eyes of the congregation. Healing through miracles helps solve health problems and reestablish personal and family balance.

The discourse of the Pentecostal churches has contradictory messages regarding women. On the one hand, the proscriptions on dress and conduct are rigid, and women's inferiority is justified biblically to make them more submissive to men. On the other hand, women are full members of the church with rights to most of the religious offices (Kamsteeg 1990). As Martin (1990:181) put it, "it is clear that women are among the 'voiceless' given a new tongue in the circle of Pentecostal communication."

Elisa: A Pentecostal in Mérida. Elisa's husband works as a construction laborer in Cancún and as a repairman of home electrical appliances. He earns the minimum wage (about US$4 per day in 1991). He and Elisa, their three children, and a relative live in a two-bedroom house made of perishable materials. They are in the lowest social and economic stratum. Elisa did not complete primary school.

At the time of the interview, Elisa had been attending services at a Protestant church for a year, but did not know which denomination it was. It was later determined that she attended a Pentecostal congregation called La Iglesia de Dios de la Profecía (Church of God of Prophecy) near her home. Some *hermanos* (brethren, members of the Church) had invited her to attend; although she did not want to go at first, they convinced her that it would help make her husband give up drinking. Elisa stated that before her conversion, she was unhappy because she and her husband argued all the time, and he hit her almost every day when he came home drunk. Now, he does not drink so often and occasionally attends services. The brethren have told Elisa that the Lord will help her with her problems, which is why she continues to attend services regularly even though her husband sometimes opposes it. Elisa does not consider herself to be a member of this Pentecostal church since she was not baptized. Nevertheless, she has begun to put the new religion's rules into practice and to deny herself popular entertainments like dancing and bullfights.[5] Elisa thinks that this denial is necessary for her husband to stop drinking. This case is similar to Burdick's (1990:161) cases of Pentecostal women in Rio de Janeiro because, through the brethren, the Protestant church has helped Elisa solve some of her domestic conflicts. She said that, although she used to be a Catholic, she almost never attended Mass.

Elisa's move to the new church has yielded a series of important advantages. Although she is still poor, her domestic conflicts have diminished. What she has learned from the Protestants has given her more authority in her relationship with her husband and has helped her to bear difficulties with greater tranquility and without blaming herself. Her connection with the denomination is as a sympathizer in the first phase of conversion. She did not even mention the salvation of her soul; rather, she expressed the meaning of the new religion as a viable alternative for improving her domestic life.

Elisa is a migrant from a little town in rural Yucatán and lives in a suburb of Mérida where she is isolated from her extended family and lacks the support that her relatives could give her. The brethren's support substitutes for her family's support and has given her self-confidence in her relationship with her husband. Now she is able to contradict her husband and attend religious services without his consent. Furthermore, the change in her husband has made it possible for Elisa to provide her three children with better food and clothes. It is evident that although Elisa is in an early phase of conversion, significant changes have already occurred in her life.

Gilda: A Pentecostal Minister in Mérida. Gilda is in charge of a small Pentecostal congregation—La Iglesia del Evangelio Completo (Church of the Full Gospel)—in a working-class neighborhood of Mérida. In her preaching, she alludes to the great suffering that has taken place in her life and how she finally overcame it with the help of the Lord.

Gilda belongs to the lower class and attended school only until the third grade. In addition to her domestic labors and religious tasks, she manages a small business in her home, acquiring merchandise wholesale from a large warehouse in the city and handling all the transactions herself. Gilda married for the first time at age 17 and has an adult daughter from that marriage. However, after a year she discovered her husband was being unfaithful and decided to leave him, seeking refuge for herself and her daughter in an aunt's house. The aunt put Gilda in contact with the Pentecostal church, but Gilda did not feel attracted to the new gospel. Years later, she married again, this time to a factory workmate, and had two children with him. Her second husband also was a womanizer and abused her physically. Gilda denounced him to the police and again began living alone with her children. Some months later, she met her third husband, with whom she had three more children, including twins. At one point, one of the twins nearly died but managed to survive. This event marked the moment when Gilda began to take Pentecostal religion seriously. Her child's cure had been "a sign from the Lord." From that point on, her life took on new meaning.

Gilda's current husband is not a believer, but she has not had difficulties with him on that account. She has defined this relationship such that he has to respect her religious work, and he does, as is evidenced by his knowledge that she gives money to the church without asking him. Gilda has warned him: "If you come between the Lord and me, I'll have to choose the Lord because He, not I, is the one who rules over me." In this way, she does not directly confront her husband, but interposes divine power, which her husband cannot oppose, between them. In Weber's (1981:172) terms, Gilda embodies charismatic authority combined with rational authority. Her spiritual role as an "exemplary person," together with the formal status that the religious institution grants her, have overcome her husband's traditional authority over her. The believers who constitute the religious community recognize Gilda as a charismatic authority figure. When the religious institution assigned her the position of congregational minister, it assigned her a position of rational authority and legitimated her in the eyes of the congregation and, to a certain extent, in the community.

Gilda's life history illustrates the problems and traumas that millions of oppressed women experience throughout the world. Having suffered humiliation, mistreatment, and disdain both from her husbands and from society, she defined herself as a "bad woman" because of her "remoteness from God." When she converted to the Full Gospel, she acquired a different self-image and became heroic—"another proof of the Lord." In Pentecostal discourse, the same past that the society would characterize as turbulent is redefined in positive terms as a sign of the presence of God. This redefinition permitted Gilda to overcome a path full of sin and, finally, to have a sanctified life. As a Catholic, Gilda had been unable to transform her identity in the way she did as a Pentecostal convert.

Gilda's case is not exceptional in Latin America. It is common to encounter lower-class women with little formal education or job training who are obliged to live with various men on whom they count for economic support, but with whom they must later break up because the men cause more harm than good (González de la Rocha 1986). The absence of either formal or informal organizations or alternatives beyond the extended family to counsel or protect women in difficult circumstances is a constant in these societies. In contrast, although they do not have formal organizations to fulfill these functions, some Protestant churches, like the Full Gospel, create informal groups to lend mutual aid and moral support through the frequent and tight contact they establish with women.

Jehovah's Witnesses

The Watch Tower Society has a hierarchical organization similar to that of the Catholic Church (Penton 1985). It is a millenarian religion and, despite its prophetic failures, has grown steadily during the past three decades, particularly in Third World countries. At the level of the congregation, it is not too difficult for a member to attain an administrative post. Concerning the Protestant work ethic, Witnesses are not oriented toward either economic progress or mystical activities. The most important activity for them is to proselytize by selling the literature. Witnesses devote most of their time to this activity, sometimes to the detriment of their own financial well-being. Unlike Mormons, Witnesses are forbidden many secular activities, such as belonging to political parties, trade unions, or civic associations; voting; serving in the military; boxing; gambling; and celebrating birthdays, Christmas, or New Year's Day.

Among Witnesses, women can "give speeches" in the Training Schools and in the District Assemblies. Generally, two women enact a sociodrama during the church service, but they do so off to one side, not in the center of the altar. When there are no men in the congregation, women can even preach.

Gabriela: A Jehovah's Witness in Guadalajara. Gabriela, a lower-class woman with few resources, attended school until the third grade and lives off her husband's work selling various articles in the markets of the city. The first time the Jehovah's Witnesses visited her home, Gabriela paid close attention to their message. During many of their visits, her husband Ricardo was invariably too tired, drunk, or hung over to listen to them, so Gabriela began to "study" before he did[6] (in this connection, the term *to study* means to converge gradually with the Church). Eventually, the Witnesses were able to influence Ricardo, and he began to listen to the message with interest; in fact, he was baptized before Gabriela was. Because of the conflicts she had with her family, who accused her of betraying the Catholic tradition, Gabriela postponed her baptism for three years. She explained her home circumstances before her husband's conversion:

> Before he "studied," my husband had other women and drank on the job. When he came home, he beat me and the children. All his pay went to his vices, and we never had enough to eat. The situation was so difficult and sad for me and for all the family that I was ready to get divorced.

Through their pragmatic doctrine, system of order, hierarchy, authority, and control, the Jehovah's Witnesses were attractive to Gabriela, who was in the middle of a crisis and had passed through a period of intense confusion, powerlessness, anxiety, and fear.

Jehovah's Witnesses share many features of bureaucratic organization with Catholicism. Penton (1985) stressed that Jehovah's Witnesses' organizational structure resembles that of the Catholic Church more than those of Protestant Churches: The authority and power of the ultimate head of the organization, the president, is similar to that of the pope for Catholics, and the Body of Governing Elders, in their headquarters in New York where all the literature is produced, resembles the Vatican in Rome. Nevertheless, Witnesses function differently from Catholics at the congregational level. A Jehovah's Witnesses group is usually small; the members know each other so well that the church becomes the main reference group for everyone who joins it, and the members apply the doctrine in daily life. In contrast, Catholicism is inconsistent in fulfilling its doctrine. As a Jehovah's Witness convert put it, "When I was into that religion [Catholicism], it was only enjoyment and banalities. They didn't prohibit anything. I carried on with my usual life, never worried about sinning. I did not even attend mass regularly." Furthermore, in a Protestant congregation, people usually feel close to and strongly identify with the spiritual leaders (such as ministers and deacons); in a traditional Catholic church, however, laypeople often feel alienated from the institution and its hierarchy. This sense of alienation is one of the main reasons informants give for their conversion to an alternative religion.

Unlike their Catholic counterparts, male converts spend most of their free time at home, and tend to give up such machismo activities as drinking, fighting, and womanizing—an obvious advantage for wives, mothers, sisters, and daughters. Gabriela preferred to have conflicts with her own family than to lose her husband when she decided to join the Witnesses. She evaluated the benefits she would obtain from joining. Themes like the integrity of the family and the care of children play central roles in the study and discussion sessions that are held during religious services, and there is specific literature on adolescence that all the faithful study together with their children.

The following brief description of an issue of *Awake!* (*¡Despertad!*), which the majority of active Witnesses throughout the world receive and share with other believers, illustrates the literature that Witnesses read. The July 1992 issue, whose general title was *La mujer merece respeto* (*Women Deserve Respect*), focused on cases in various countries where women are abused and humiliated. The authors condemned the mistreatment of women and their unfavorable position within the domestic group and in other spheres of society. The impact of this literature on family members' values and behavior merits future investigation.

For Ricardo, the Witnesses offered new order in his life. His conversion is interesting because in his youth he studied to become a priest for many years in a Catholic seminary but left because of the celibacy issue. Among the Witnesses, though, he discovered that he had a chance to study a spiritual profession and serve God and be married at the same time. Currently,

Ricardo is an auxiliary minister in his congregation, which obliges him to be honest, have only one woman, be active in spiritual matters, and be punctual in his duties. The use to which he puts his time has changed radically; he works only four days in secular activities and dedicates the rest of the week to his religious duties. He goes out to do missionary work several days a week, and in the afternoons directs studies for future converts. He attends Bible study groups and his congregation's regular services. Although his present income is less than before, he now invests it in domestic needs, rather than in drinking, partying, or women. This case resembles what Brusco (1986) found in Colombian Evangelical families: the change in consumption patterns after conversion and reorienting the available resources toward family needs.

Gabriela had been unable to change Ricardo's values and lifestyle before they joined the church, but, with the help of Witnesses' doctrine and practice, her desire for a better life was fulfilled. An atmosphere of unity and understanding, which had not existed before conversion, was created. Furthermore, the entire family found a solution to the crisis by joining the Witnesses. Gabriela and Ricardo's children (a married adult, two adolescents, and an 8 year old), all church members, spend their free time with other young Witnesses, which guarantees that they will use it "correctly" and not engage in drinking, taking drugs, or delinquency. Gabriela expressed the satisfactions obtained from her affiliation with the Jehovah's Witnesses congregation this way:

> My life has changed since I have studied, and my children have learned this and are very good young people. They come to the study meetings and attend parties with Witness friends. My life is very different since now we all sit and talk together. We ask our children what they hope for and we have a dialogue. Now he [Ricardo] doesn't have more than one or two drinks, never more; we have money for what we need; he doesn't beat me or the children; and is a man who worries about his family.

Mormonism

At the institutional level, the Mormon Church is well structured with six degrees of priesthood, from deacon to Great Prophet or the president of the Church. Women cannot reach the priesthood; it is exclusively male. Their fundamental mission is motherhood, and this duty relieves them of all other responsibilities. The doctrine is based on the teachings of the Book of Mormon and the Bible. The Protestant ethic, understood as an orientation toward material progress, is widely shared by the members. Traditional family values play a central part in teaching and practice, and all members are expected to tithe to the Church. In comparison with other Protestant churches, Mormons enjoy considerable freedom, since they can engage in secular activities like attending the theater and movies, playing sports, and even dancing. However, they may not smoke or drink alcohol, coffee, or tea.

During the Sacramental Sessions, or Sunday services, women are permitted and even encouraged to participate. They go to the front (but not to the altar) to give personal testimonies, direct the singing, and impart doctrinal teachings approved by the bishop. During the ceremonies, only men—the bishop, his two secretaries, two counselors, elders, teachers, deacons, presbyters, and so forth—are present on the altar. In spite of the visible presence of men, women fill the majority of active roles during the service, except for the central preaching, which is done by the bishop or a special guest.

Luisa: A Mormon in Mérida. Luisa attended college for one year and later had a brief business career. She now sells Tupperware, and her husband is a railroad worker. They own several houses that they rent out and are middle class. Luisa was baptized eighteen years ago, together with her sisters and a younger brother because they were told that the Mormons could help the brother stop drinking. The brother was 16 years old, and, on one occasion, someone put a pill in his beer that made him temporarily insane. Ultimately, the brother did not stay with the Mormons, but the sisters did. Luisa's husband did not accept Mormonism, since there were a priest and a nun in his family. However, their two children are both Mormons, and the older one was doing missionary work at the time of my interview. Luisa was immensely happy that her son was a missionary. The Church allocates scholarships for missionaries, so they can attend Mormon universities in Mexico or the United States, and such work raises their prestige in the congregation.

Luisa was a convert with many years of experience in the Church; she had made a sacred pact and had traced her ancestors back eight generations at the Mexican National Archives (Archivo General de la Nación), since it is obligatory for Mormons to identify their ancestors at least to the fourth generation. She stated:

> The Church teaches a lot of refinement. In the Aid Society they teach how to raise your children, how to set a table, correct table manners, painting, culture, great authors. They talk to us about authors of all nationalities. I am a leader, and I also teach. We have manuals for the classes, but they tell us that we have to research other books. When I give a class, it is very nice to teach what they don't know. The Church is very concerned with teaching us to be very well-educated people.

Luisa was soon going to receive the Seal (that is, be baptized) in the Mexico City Temple, since her husband had given her permission to go. At that time every married woman had to have her husband's permission, even to get baptized, although in 1990, this rule was changed so that a woman's pledge to obey her husband was replaced with a pledge to obey God (Sheler and Wagner 1992:77). Generally, the Church teaches women to obey their husbands because husbands will later have to answer for their wives before God. When I asked Luisa about women's position in the Mormon Church, she answered:

> We will be queens and priestesses in due time because, since before the creation of the world, the Lord instituted this and we know that God is never wrong. The Lord has promised it, and when it is suitable, we will rule and direct worlds together with our partners. Here on Earth, never.

Nevertheless, here on Earth, women also have opportunities to develop themselves and to progress significantly. Luisa was the president of the Aid Society's mission, which involved directing a group of 300–500 women. "It's a divine thing to have the souls of 500 women in your hands," she said. The women were from different districts of Mérida, Motul, Tizimín, Cancún, and Chetumal. Each weekend she went to a different place, where she taught what she described as "culture, spirituality, domestic arts and classes on refinement." The acquisition of knowledge is an important value among both the Mormons and the Witnesses. Luisa values this culture of education, which she has acquired through her work as a teacher and president of the Aid Society. The Mormon Church promotes reading among the believers. Although it gives preference to religious literature, middle-class Mexican Mormons have access to more information than do other Mexicans of the same class. González (1993:297) reported that only 3 percent of the Mexican population reads books and estimated that probably only 10 percent of researchers and teachers with university degrees are regular readers.

In Yucatán, the Mormon Church encourages women to study for professions, not as a means of making a living but to help their husbands, since responsibility rests on the men alone. Luisa said that if she had not joined this church, she would not have been able "to progress in all senses: emotionally, to have been able to make a stable home, immensely happy, all in all a stability I didn't have before." For Luisa, the Mormon Church has permitted her to achieve multiple personal satisfactions that center on family life.

When Mormons have a problem, they seek help from their bishop. As Luisa put it, "The bishop knows us as if we were his children. . . . When we have a problem, the first one to find out is the bishop. . . . I have absolute confidence in him. . . . He solves problems of every kind: economic, moral, social, spiritual. He is my spiritual father." This belief illustrates the reproduction of the patriarchal pattern of relationship between men and women.

IF CATHOLICISM AND PROTESTANTISM ARE BOTH PATRIARCHAL, WHAT IS THE DIFFERENCE FOR WOMEN?

To contextualize the case studies just presented, it is important to underscore some values in Mexican culture that stem from Catholicism and are relevant to gender relations.[7] These values will be contrasted with Protestant ideology.

Inconsistent Morality

Machismo is an important cultural value that influences all social and political relationships in Mexico. It appears in all social classes, and is one of the concrete ways in which patriarchy is manifested. Patriarchy is a system of social structures and practices through which men dominate, oppress, and exploit women (Walby 1992:19). Machismo, considered part of Mexican society's moral order, as well as of its immoral disorder, is expressed through the violence that men exercise over women in patriarchal relations, sexuality, and cultural institutions. The macho complex is

> formed by the possession, use and ostentation of [the formula] machos + broads + pistols + money + alcohol = power in competition with other men. . . . Mexican machos resolve their conflicts by measuring themselves against other men; they appropriate the other's power. Win or lose, the powerful and the subjugated always exercise their generic power over women, which permits them to mitigate their fear and their own feelings. (Lagarde 1993:419–20).

The cultural value of machismo is part of Roman Catholicism's sphere of influence. In an important ethnographic study in Zamora, Michoacán, on beliefs and other cultural patterns, Arizpe (1989:212) stated:

> In fact, machismo is one form of sexism profoundly rooted in the culture of western Mexico, perhaps even more obviously than in other regions of the country. It persists thanks to its hidden side, the cult of the feminine (*hembrismo*).

With respect to morality, Arizpe (1989:247) found that there are great contradictions between "the consistency in proclaimed beliefs and the inconsistency between beliefs and practices." One example of these contradictions is that despite the Catholic Church's moral prescriptions, men's transgressions are not occasional or circumstantial but are institutionalized in moral belief and manifested in the double standard; that is, married men generally have second families (called *casas chicas* in Mexico) and frequent bordellos, but married women must remain faithful. In Zamora, there is even a housing subdivision in which the *casas chicas* of the city are concentrated. In the moral field, the central element is sexual repression "of which the woman is the privileged custodian"; this field continues to be "the Catholic Church's exclusive social sphere of influence" (Arizpe, 1989:222), since neither the state nor the political parties have been able to influence it. Arizpe argued that with the economic changes and the influence of social liberalism in the Salinas period, machismo was changing because it was ever more useless in public life. However, it remains rooted in habitus (Bourdieu 1972:175) and is centered on the family, increasing men's violence against wives and children.

The central issue here is the opposite ways in which men and women practice moral laws derived from Catholic ideology with respect to marital fidelity and, more broadly, sexual conduct. As Marcos (1989:16) commented:

> In contemporary Mexico, the male is expected to have sexually aggressive conduct and an early sexual initiation. On the contrary, women must be chaste and preferably wait until marriage for their first sexual relationship. And with regard to religious activities, this is above all "a women's matter."

As Portugal (1989:43) noted, "The institutionalization of the double standard in territories colonized by Spain made the prohibitions and norms for men highly flexible, which signified at the same time rigidifying those of the women." These social practices are based on the extreme dichotomization of the sexes based on Catholic morality. The sharp separation between men's and women's behavior is reinforced in Latin American and other Roman Catholic countries by the antagonistic identification of women with Eve, the sinner, and Mary, the virgin mother. "Marianism is the cult of feminine spiritual superiority, which simultaneously embodies the ideals of nurture, maternity and chastity" (Bumster 1983, quoted in Portugal 1989:2). The Virgin of Guadalupe, the Mexican version of the Virgin Mary, is the feminine model for devoted Catholics to follow, but it is a schizophrenic model that is impossible to imitate because women cannot embody the ideal states of maternity and chastity at the same time.

Consistent Morality

Patriarchy, with its diverse structures including machismo, is also present in Protestant ideology. It is even legitimated and justified by means of biblical doctrine:

> Married women are subject to their own husbands as to the Lord; because the husband is the head of the woman, as Christ is the head of the Church. (Ephesians 5:22–23)[8]

In this sense, women converts do not undergo radical transformations with regard to their duty in society, since Protestant ideology also considers women to be inferior to men. However, in Protestantism, unlike Catholicism, there is no inconsistency between belief and practice or differential imposition of norms for men and women. Machismo is not practiced among Protestants in the same way as it is among Catholics *because ascetic norms are imposed in the same way on men and women*. For this reason, one speaks of the feminization or "domestication" of the macho (Brusco 1986) that results from conversion to a Protestant religion. In a study of poor Pentecostals in La Paz, Bolivia, Gill (1990:709) found that

> even though Pentecostalism legitimizes the power and authority of men, the puritanical teachings of the church modify aspects of male behavior that are harmful to women, such as wife beating and drunkenness, and this serves to enhance the emotional well-being and economic position of female converts.

Finkler (1983:293) discovered the same behavioral pattern in her study of Mexican Spiritualists:

> The change in drinking patterns imposed by Spiritualists provides an economic advantage to the household, and for the women there is the additional benefit that they are subject to less, if any, physical abuse at the hands of a drunken husband. In fact, unlike most rural Mexican males from comparable social strata, men who become Spiritualist adherents interact on a relatively egalitarian basis with their wives.

CONCLUSIONS

It is worth noting that in three of the four cases cited, alcoholism affected the men linked to the women converts. In her study, Rostas (1993) spoke of the implications of the tradition of Tzeltal ritual drinking for the domestic economy and the health of men. In Mexico, it is estimated that 76 percent of the deaths from cirrhosis of the liver are among men, especially those in the lower strata of society (Menéndez 1990:23, 25, 27). In this context, it is not accidental to find many cases in which women converts have been motivated to join a Protestant Church that prohibits drinking and is known to alleviate this problem.[9]

Upon joining a Protestant church, women find a privileged social space in which they can express discontent with their personal and social circumstances. Within the congregation, they discover that they are not alone in their material conditions and receive divine counsel and the hope of salvation that all Christian religions offer. In a Pentecostal church, any believer can carry out the "production, distribution and reproduction of symbolic goods" (Bourdieu 1971), and, in some cases, can attain a position of power and privilege in the congregation. In contrast, in traditional Catholicism, these activities are restricted to a few male clergy. Women acquire respect and recognition in Protestant and innovative Catholic movements because they have the chance to address others from a position of spiritual equality. Although they may be dependent on divine power, this respect and recognition liberate them from earthly oppression.

Lower-class women have few opportunities to gain personal satisfaction or to develop individual abilities away from the home. In this context, Protestant churches are an alternative for satisfying those needs. When a woman belongs to a Protestant church, she receives social approval for relating to her husband from a more egalitarian position. Furthermore, through her role in the congregation, she achieves a higher status that gives her more self-confidence and self-assurance that, in turn, allow her to rebuild her relationship with her husband's family and with her own. She gains some prestige in the eyes of the community, since her achievements in the individual sphere are socially esteemed. This does not mean that Protestant women achieve total emancipation through their religious participation, but they attain relative autonomy with respect to their husbands and broad social respect that they lacked before they converted.

At the same time, the churches analyzed in this chapter do not exist outside the regional societies in which they are found—in this case, Jalisco and Yucatán. The churches develop within a traditional society in which most civil authorities are male, it is unthinkable that the highest authority—the president—could be a woman, and the father continues to be the authority in the family. In this context, the restrictions these institutions impose on women are not much different from those imposed in the larger society and, especially, in traditional Catholic culture.

Aubert (1975, quoted in de Barbieri 1984:37) noted that the Catholic Church has been an obstacle to women's emancipation: "[O]n the institutional level and in its teaching, the Church continues to be misogynist and sexist, defying the Constitution." It requires women to be passive agents of ideological transmission and necessitates that their religiosity is directed toward the priest, *el padrecito*, upon whom they are dependent (Monteil 1985). Protestant churches make patriarchal principles more explicit and legitimate them by inscribing them with a biblical-theological basis. However, it seems that having a rigid system of norms helps marital relationships become more stable and peaceful. As Burdick (1990:163) found in his research among Brazilian women, "Pentecostalism helps women to achieve long-term resolution of domestic conflict."[10] As the case studies presented here illustrated, women do not complain about the strict rules that these churches impose on them because they value what they achieve in return more than they resent what they lose.

Although they impose restrictions on women, Protestant churches provide them with social spaces that they lack in the secular society and, to a lesser degree, in the traditional Catholic Church. It must be emphasized that urban working-class families in Mexico and other countries "are the scenes of physical, verbal and sexual violence which men exercise over women" (González de la Rocha 1988:223). These churches' often rigid, structured norms offer women and their families security and support and can minimize the manifestations of machismo. In addition, the religious communities have multiple aid and solidarity networks for their members, from the institutional ministries to informal relations.

Rostas (1993:5) found that in Tenejapa, Tzeltal women acquire empowerment through conversion: "They begin to be able to exercise a degree of freedom that they have not previously experienced, and it enables them to build up their self-esteem." It is significant that various researchers have arrived at such similar conclusions even though their universes of study are as different as an urban slum and an indigenous village. This consistency leads me to conclude that these new religious frameworks affect women's lives in a positive way. The new social space that the churches have created constitutes an important opportunity for women to commit themselves to a cause, an ideal—a career or calling in the Weberian sense—an activity that is taken seriously and exists apart from the duties assigned to the feminine gender.

Notes

1. Strictly speaking, Mormonism and Jehovah's Witnesses are not Protestants, but both groups emerged from U.S. Protestantism in the nineteenth century. According to Penton (1985), little of the doctrine of Jehovah's Witnesses is outside the Anglo-American Protestant tradition.
2. I would expect that throughout the 1990s, one would find more converts to Protestantism among the middle classes than among the lower classes than in the 1980s. The increasing process of secularization, which in Mexico means the break-up of the Catholic monopoly and the restriction of religious influence to the realm of culture, sets the stage for this class differential. As secularization proceeds, it will be possible for Evangelical and other Christian and non-Christian groups to flourish in the same society. Because the middle classes are more educated and experience the impact of globalization more directly—that is, they have greater access to information about the world—they are more open to alternative religions.
3. In one such case, Socorro, a member of a Guadalajara CCBC in the 1970s, became deeply involved in CCBC activities. She took Bible courses, attended meetings in which social and political problems were discussed, and learned how to apply Marxist terminology to everyday reality. She participated in demonstrations and organizations that aimed to acquire urban services, such as electricity, paved streets, and running water. In 1978, she decided to separate from her husband. She explained, "I did not want to accept any other will than God's. I felt that it was not true that my obligations were restricted to my family. The Gospel tells us that all persons need our help" (quoted in de la Peña 1990:90–91).
4. Under certain circumstances, charismatic Catholicism can create similar types of free social spaces for women. For example, if a woman has the gift of healing, she can exercise her talent and achieve prestige, which will make her almost equal to the priests. In some cases, these gifted and active women can even achieve positions superior to that of the priest (Juárez 1993).
5. In some areas of Yucatán, rituals for Catholic patron saints begin with bullfights. These rituals also are associated with pre-hispanic religion. When a round bullring is constructed, a ceiba (*ya'axche'*) branch is planted in the center. The ceiba is the sacred tree of the Yucatecan Mayans and represents the center of the world. Through its branches, souls ascend to heaven and descend to hell (Fernández & Quintal 1992).
6. As has been shown in other studies on Protestant religions (Brusco 1986; Fortuny 1989; Martin 1990; Rostas 1993), women are generally the first to convert. Wilson (1977:107) found that "seventy percent of Witnesses in Japan were women and . . . among the women about fifty percent were housewives. . . . It always proved easier to win the attention of women than men."

7. Pescatello (1976) traced the historic Iberian roots of family and gender values for Mexico and other Latin American cultures.
8. See also I Peter 3:1–6, Colossians 3:18, Titus 2:4–5, I Timothy 2:9–12, and I Corinthians 4:34–35.
9. Mariz (1990:43) analyzed the elements of Pentecostal spirituality that support sobriety.
10. Burdick (1990:163) demonstrated through his informants' statements that "in the context of male dominance . . . , many women find greater domestic tranquility by accepting a clearly subordinate role, rather than flirting with the progressive Catholic Church's call for greater equality between the sexes."

References

Arizpe, Lourdes. 1989. *Cultura y Desarrollo: Una Etnografía de las Creencias de una Comunidad Mexicana.* Mexico City: Universidad Autónoma de México, El Colegio de México, Porrúa.

Bastian, Jean Pierre. 1983. *Protestantismo y Sociedad en México.* Mexico City: Ediciones Casa Unida de Publicaciones.

Bourdieu, Pierre. 1971. "Une Interpretations de la Theorie de la Religion Selon Max Weber." *Archives Europeenes de Sociologie* 12:3–21.

Bourdieu, Pierre. 1972. "Estructuras, Hábitos y Prácticas." Pp. 179–189 in *Esquise d'une Theorie de la Practique: Précédé de Trois Études d'Ethnologie Kabyle.* Geneva: Librairie Droz.

Brusco, Elizabeth Ellen. 1986. "The Household Basis of Evangelical Religion and the Reformation of Machismo in Colombia." Ph.D. dissertation, City University of New York.

Burdick, John. 1990. "Gossip and Secrecy: Women's Articulation of Domestic Conflict in Three Religions of Urban Brazil." *Sociological Analysis* 50:153–70.

Casillas, Rodolfo. 1989. "Una Nueva Aurora Para las Utopías Religiosas: Líneas de Análisis de sus Contenidos Sociales." *Frontera Norte* 1:175–95.

de Barbieri, Teresita. 1984. *Mujeres y Vida Cotidiana.* Mexico City: Sepsetentas.

de la Peña, Guillermo. 1990. "La Cultura Política en los Sectores Populares de Guadalajara." *Nueva Antropologia* 11(38):83–107.

Droogers, André. 1990. "Visiones Paradójicas Sobre una Religion Paradójica: Modelos Explicativos del Creciniento Pentecostal en Brasil y Chile." Pp. 1–21 in *Algo más que opio: Una Lectura Antropologica del Pentecostalismo Latinoamericano y Caribeño*, edited by B. Boudenijnse, A. Droogers, and F. Kamsteeg. San Jose, Costa Rica: Dei.

Fernandez Repetto, F., and E. F. Quintal Avilez. 1992. "Fiestas y Fiestas," *Revista de la Universidad Autónoma de Yucatan,* 7:183, 39–48.

Finkler, Kaja. 1983. "Dissident Sectarian Movements, the Catholic Church, and Social Class in Mexico." *Comparative Studies in Society and History* 25:277–305.

Fortuny Loret de Mola, Patricia. 1989. *Religión y Sociedad en el Sureste de México.* Vol. 5, Cuaderno No. 165. Mexico City: Ciensas-Sep-Conafe.

Fortuny Loret de Mola, Patricia, and Renée de la Torre. 1991. "La mujer en La Luz del Mundo: Participación y Representación Simbólica." *Estudios Sobre las Culturas Contemporáneas* 4:125–50.

Gill, Lesley. 1990. "Like a Veil to Cover Them: Women and the Pentecostal Movement in La Paz," *American Ethnologist* 17:708–21.

González, Luis. 1993. El Libro en la Vida Cultural de México. Pp. 285–301 in *El Patrimonio Cultural de México*, compiled by Enrique Florescano. Mexico City: Fondo de Cultura Económica.

González de la Rocha, Mercedes. 1986. *Los Recursos de la Pobreza: Familias de Bajos Ingresos en Guadalajara, México*. Guadalajara: El Colegio de Jalisco/CIESAS/SPP.

———. 1988. "Las Mujeres y la Reproducción Social." Pp. 205–27 in *Mujeres y Sociedad: Salario, Hogar y Acción Social en el Occidente de México*, compiled by Luisa Gabayet, Patricia Garcia, Mercedes Gonzalez de la Rocha, Silvia Lailson, and Augustin Escobar. Guadalajara: El Colegio de Jalisco/CIESAS.

Hollenweger, W. J. 1991. "The Pentecostal Elites and the Pentecostal Poor: A Missed Dialogue?" Pp. 1–15 in *Pentecostal/Charismatic Movements Worldwide* (conference proceedings). Calgary, Alberta, Canada: University of Calgary.

Juarez Cerdi, Elizabeth. 1993. "Las Estructuras de Poder al Interior de un Grupo Religioso Católico: Estudio de Caso." Master's thesis, El Colegio de Michoacán, Zamora, México.

Kamsteeg, Frans. 1990. "Líderes y Laicos Entre los Grupos Pentecostales de Arequipa, Perú." *Cristianismo y Sociedad* 28(4):59–76.

Kselman, Thomas A. 1986. "Ambivalence and Assumption in the Concept of Popular." Pp. 24–41 in *Religion and Political Conflict in Latin America*, edited by Daniel H. Levine. Chapel Hill: University of North Carolina Press.

Lagarde, Marcela. 1993. *Los Cautiverios de las Mujeres: Madresposas, Monjas, Putas, Presas y Locas*. Mexico City: Universidad Autónoma de México.

Marcos, Sylvia. 1989. "Curas, Diosas y Erotismo: el Catolicismo Frente a los Indios." Pp. 9–33 in *Mujeres e Iglesia, Sexualidad y Aborto in América Latina*, edited by Ana Maria Portugal. Mexico City: Distribuciones Fontamara.

Mariz, Cecilia L. 1990. "Pentecostalismo y Alcoholismo entre los Pobres de Brasil." *Cristianismo y Sociedad* 28(3):39–44.

Martin, David. 1990. *Tongues of Fire: The Explosion of Protestantism in Latin America*. Oxford, England: Basil Blackwell.

Menéndez, Eduardo. 1990. *Morir de Alcohol. Saber y Hegemonía Médica*. Mexico City: Conaculta, Alianza Editorial.

Meyer, Jean. 1989. *Historia de los Cristianos en America Latina: Siglos XIX y XX*. Mexico City: Vuelta.

Monsiváis, Carlos. 1991. *Tolerancia y Persecusión Religiosas, Sobre la Libertad de Culto en México*. Mexico City: Casa Unida de Publicaciónes.

Monteil, Noelle. 1985. "Las Mujeres, Instrumento de la Iglesia Institucional para Mantener las Estructuras de Dominación." Pp. 159–76 in *Religion y Política en México*, compiled by Martín de al Rosa and Charles A. Reilly. Mexico City: Siglo XXI.

Penton, James. 1985. *Apocalypse Delayed: The Story of Jehovah's Witnesses*. Toronto: University of Toronto Press.

Pescatello, Ann M. 1976. *Power and Pawn: The Female in Iberian Families, Societies, and Cultures*. Westport, CT: Greenwood Press.

Portugal, Ana María. 1989. "Formación y Deformación: Educación para la Culpa." Pp. 35–48 in *Mujeres e Iglesia, Sexualidad y aborto en América Latina*, edited by Ana María Portugal. Mexico City: Distribuciones Fontamara.

Rodrigues Brandao, Carlos. 1989. "Creencia e Identidad, Campo Religioso y Campo Cultural." *Estudios sobre las Culturas Contemporáneas* 2(7):57–117.

Rose, Susan D. 1987. "Women's Warriors: The Negotiation of Gender in a Charismatic Community." *Sociological Analysis* 48:245–58.

Rostas, Susana D. 1993. "Conversion as Female Empowerment: Religious Change in an Indigenious Community in Mexico." Paper presented at the Congreso International de Ciencias Antropológicas y Etnológicas (CICAE), Mexico City.

Sheler, Jeffrey L., and Betsy Wagner. 1992. "Latter-Day Struggles: The Prosperous Mormon Church at a Theological Crossroad," *U.S. News & World Report*, September 28, pp. 73–78.

Tullis, F. LaMond. 1987. *Mormons in Mexico: The Dynamics of Faith and Culture*. Logan: Utah State University Press.

Van den Hoogen, Lisette. 1990. "The Romanization of the Brazilian Church: Women's Participation in a Religious Association in Prados, Minas Gerais." *Sociological Analysis* 50:171–88.

Walby, Sylvia. 1992. *Theorizing Patriarchy*. Oxford, England: Blackwell.

Weber, Max. 1981. *Economía y Sociedad*. Mexico City: Fondo de Cultura Económica.

Wilson, Brian. 1977. "Aspects of Kinship and the Rise of Jehovah's Witnesses in Japan." *Social Compass* 24:97–120.

Index